AF521683

The Great Workshop

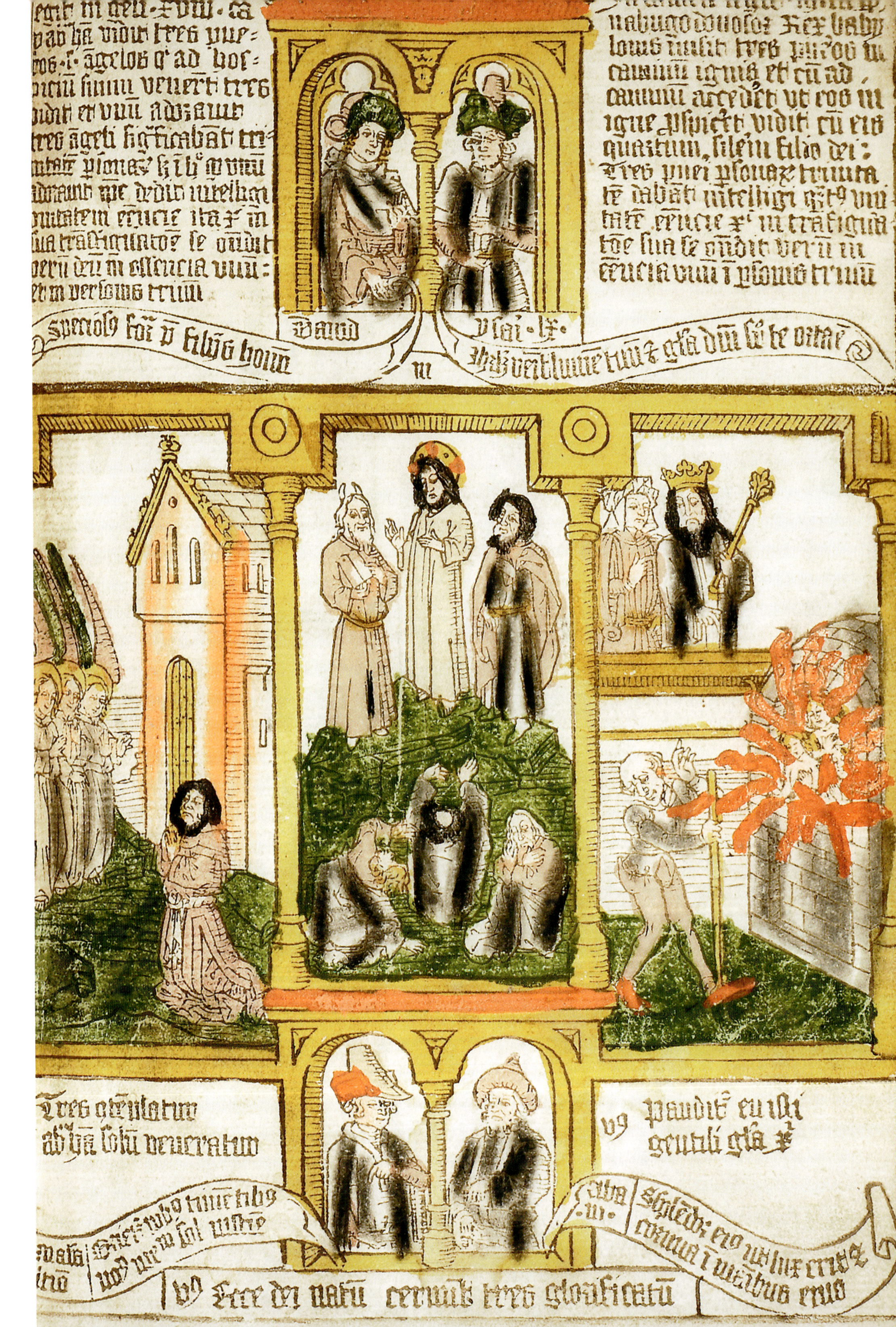
Dauid
Ysai · lx ·

The Great Workshop

Pathways of Art in Europe
(5th–18th CENTURIES)

UNDER THE DIRECTION OF ROLAND RECHT
IN COLLABORATION WITH
CATHELINE PÉRIER-D'IETEREN AND PASCAL GRIENER

AND WITH PETER BURKE,
ROGER CHARTIER AND KRZYSZTOV POMIAM

MERCATORFONDS

This book was first published on the occasion of the exhibition 'The Grand atelier Pathways of Art in Europe (5th-18th Centuries)' organized as part of the 2007 europalia.europa Festival in Brussels, Belgium

europalia.europa

AUTHORS
Roland Recht
Peter Burke
Roger Chartier
Pascal Griener
Catheline Périer-d'Ieteren
Krzysztof Pomian

PRODUCTION
Tijdsbeeld & Pièce Montée, Ghent

TRANSLATION AND EDITING
First Edition Translations, Cambridge

DESIGN
Pascal Van Hoorebeke

TYPESETTING
Karakters, Ghent

PRINTING AND BINDING
Die Keure, Bruges

ISBN 978 90 6153 801 [illegible]
D/2008/703/1

Distributed worldwide outside Belgium, The Netherlands and Luxembourg by Cornell University Press
ISBN 978 0 8014 4710 5

WITH SPECIAL THANKS TO

Bibliothèque royale de Belgique / Koninklijke Bibliotheek van België

KBR.be

and

Jean-Pierre Babelon, Helena Bussers, Laurent Busine, François de Callataÿ, Brigitte Chabard, Pierre Colman, Cécile Dupeux, Frank Grangé, Nicole d'Huart, Cecilia Hurley, Jean-Noël Jeanneney, Sophie Jugie, Marie-Pierre Laffitte, Sarah Laporte, Jean Leclant, Yves le Fur, Neil MacGregor, Raphaël Rosenberg, Arlette Rossi, Liselotte Saurma, Vit Vlnas, Raymonde Wicky, and anyone we may have forgotten to mention.

Frontispiece p.2
Biblia Pauperum, *c.* 1464 (Cat. X.1)

p.8-9
Hans Hammer's *Notebook*, *c.* or after 1500 (Cat. VII.11)

p.14-15
Johannes Lingelbach, *The Campo Vaccino in Rome* (Cat. XIII.24)

p.16
Jost Amman, *Allegory of Commerce*, 1585 (Cat. XIV.4)

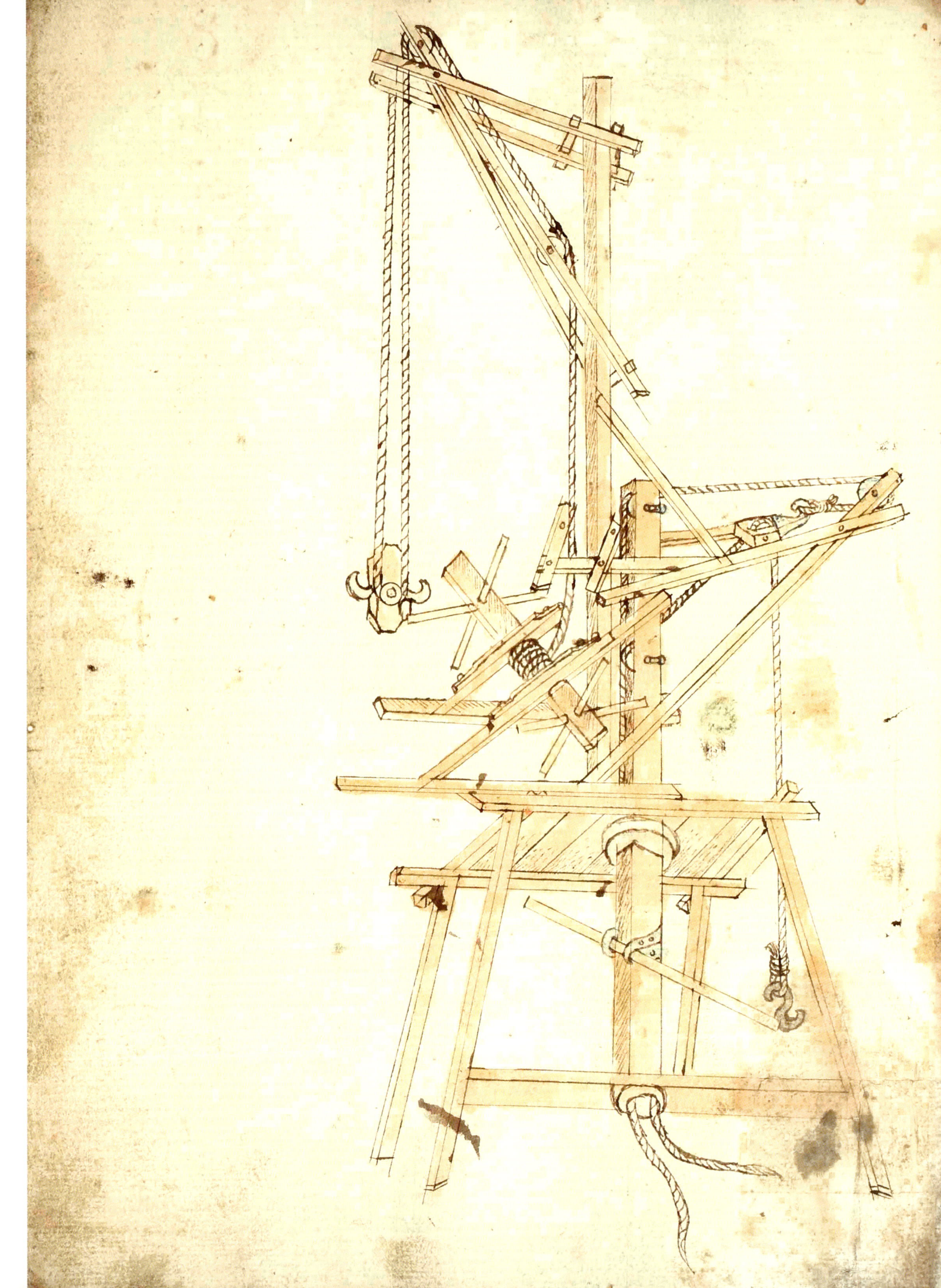

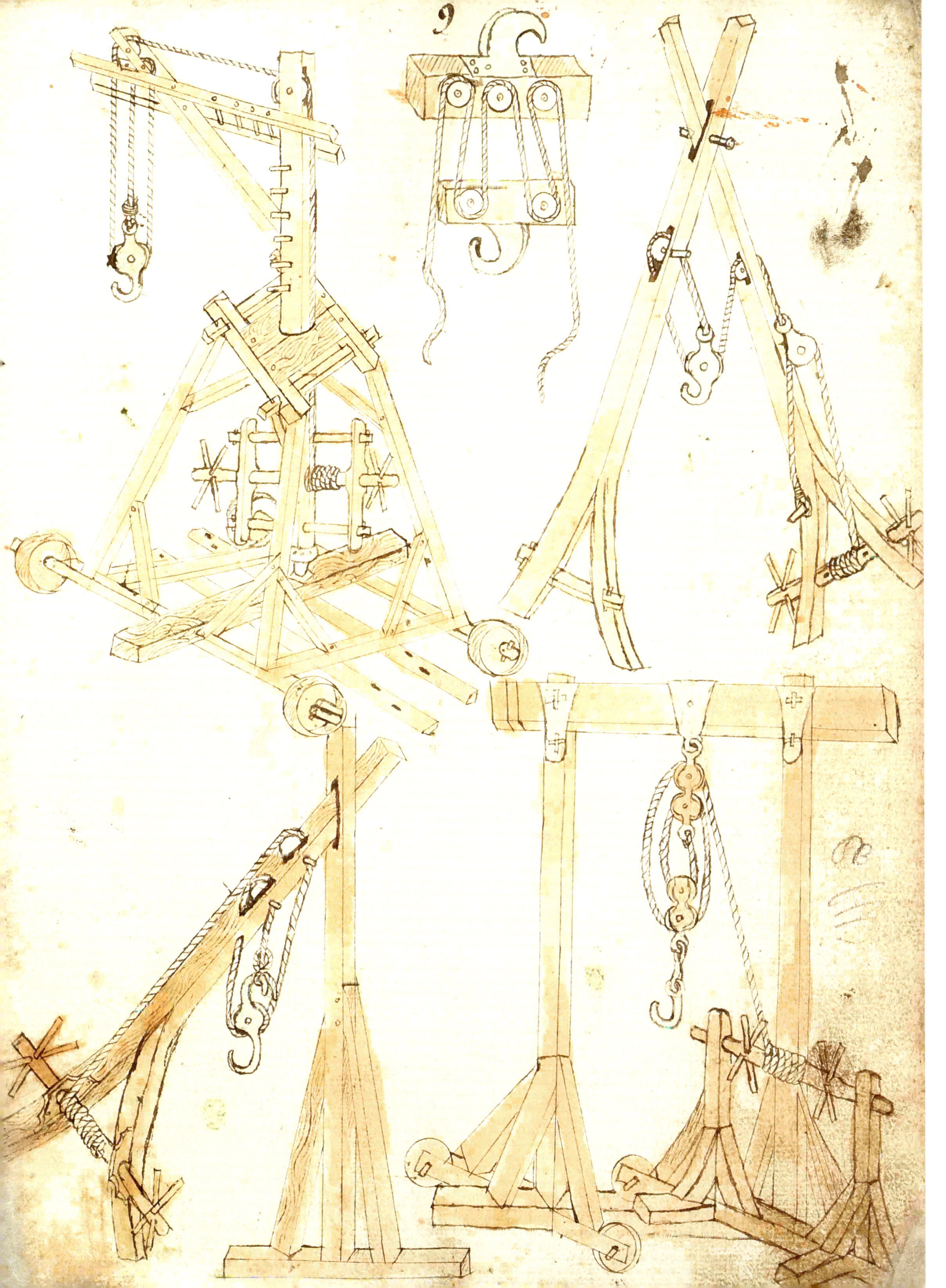

Welcome to the europalia.europa festival, the 21st in a highly successful series stretching back to 1969 that has marked itself out as one of Europe's premier cultural events. Unlike all previous Europalia festivals, which concentrated on the culture of individual states, this year we are pleased to present a first: an ambitious programme that incorporates all 27 Member States of the European Union and encompasses all artistic disciplines. The choice, of course, is not accidental. It marks and celebrates 2007 as the year of the 50th anniversary of the signing of the Treaty of Rome, with events continuing into early 2008. That Treaty and its successors have brought today's EU to the fullest realisation, east and west, of Robert Schuman's vision of creative reconciliation between European states and peoples. Yet our sense of Europe is both older and deeper than its contemporary political and institutional expression. It is the exploration of this feeling for Europe that is our festival's point of departure.

Our central event is *The Grand Atelier: Pathways of Art in Europe.* It traces in 14 steps, from the 5th to the 18th centuries, journeys in European art. Drawn from more than 120 museums, the 250 exhibits, masterpieces in many styles and forms, invite the visitor to contemplate the circulation of art, and artistic dialogue, in the emergence of the European cultural space. These works follow the routes of pilgrims and of traders. They reveal the tastes and preferences of patrons and of merchant princes. They are the legacy of artists and artisans from the celebrated to the anonymous. They range from the unique to the reproduced. They speak both of commonality and diversity in our European cultural heritage. With their Byzantine and Muslim roots they recall that our ancient continent's boundaries were always open to external influence. *The Grand Atelier* seeks to convey the pulse of European artistic streams from the collapse of the Roman Empire to the Age of the Enlightenment. We encourage each and every one of our visitors to feel that pulse themselves and to go with its flow.

The Film *27x27x27* brings us from the past to the present. It is the response to our invitation issued to 27 contemporary artists, in the widest sense of that term, from the 27 member states, to share with us their personal appreciation of a favourite work of European art.

Agorafolly offers a window on the future. It summons 27 young artists from each EU member state to produce a contemporary public work of art for outdoor display in each of 27 Brussels squares and marketplaces from 13 October to 9 December 2007. It offers another perspective on the theme of circulation and dialogue and the relationship between the marketplace and art.

It has been a privilege and a pleasure for me, as President of the International European Movement and past President of the European Parliament, to have been associated with this wonderful and inspiring exercise as Commissioner General. Europalia.europa encompasses many more exciting exhibitions and performances than those referred to above, incorporating all the arts from music to dance to film to literature. It reflects cultural Europe in all its rich diversity and is the result of painstaking preparation, hard work and dedication over many months. Enjoy it.

PAT COX
GENERAL COMMISSIONER OF EUROPALIA.EUROPA

I am extremely pleased to introduce this very special Catalogue of europalia.europa, 2007–2008 edition, particularly as this publication is dedicated, for the first time, to the artistic achievements of all 27 Member States of the European Union.

This year is really like no other, since Europalia takes place during a very important anniversary for us, the celebration of 50 years since the signing of the Treaty of Rome, with its motto 'Together since 1957', translated into all the Community languages and visible not only in Brussels, but equally across the EU's Member States.

I am also proud to say that this edition of Europalia has received both moral and financial support from the European Commission, emphasising our commitment to this successful and highly popular series of distinctive cultural events, highlighting European excellence in every aspect of cultural life.

But, let me take a look back at what happened not so long ago, on 1 January 2007. The latest enlargement of the European Union incorporated both Romania and Bulgaria, following the 2004 enlargement that allowed a large part of Central Europe to be reunited with Western Europe, after a long period of strife and aggression. This was a momentous change and a source of joy for us all. It was also a huge step by a continent that, more than ever before, is inching closer towards its aim of being united in diversity.

Each enlargement enriches the EU family, making it more comprehensive, but also more culturally diverse. The enlargement of 2007 has brought in two unique cultures, two new languages, a new alphabet and a set of valuable religious and spiritual traditions.

I am particularly delighted to see that a prominent place in the programme of the present europalia.europa is devoted to art and artists coming from those two new countries of the EU. The wider public, I am certain, will be attracted by these high quality events and discover a new and captivating face of Europe.

Respect for cultural diversity is not only a founding principle of the European Union. I am convinced that it is one of its most attractive features. The EU has a long-standing relationship with the world of culture in Europe and recognises more and more the crucial role that it plays in the European project.

Beyond the cultural dimension of many of our policies, our action in this sphere aims at supporting cooperation between cultural operators in Europe and paving the way for a common cultural space, where all of us would have their cultural expressions recognised and would be invited to discover those of others. The EU should be a commonality of mutual understanding, where Europeans treasure cultural diversity as part of the great wealth of our continent. In this spirit, europalia.europa anticipates that this EU priority will be highly visible next year, as 2008 has been declared European Year of Intercultural Dialogue.

This is a major challenge, not only within our increasingly multicultural society at European level but also in our relations with the rest of the world.

I trust that the rich and multifaceted programme of europalia. europa will stimulate and nurture our desire for diversity and dialogue.

JOSÉ MANUEL BARROSO
PRESIDENT OF THE EUROPEAN COMMISSION

What better way to celebrate Europe than by displaying the continent to itself? The exhibition marking the europalia.europa festival, *The Grand Atelier: Pathways of Art in Europa*, has the single aim of highlighting diversity within unity: the uniqueness of individual cultures, the artistic wealth belonging to each member nation yet in a sense shared by all.

It would be a dream come true if such an event could be reproduced in all the capitals of Europe, or even the world, as unfortunately not everyone will have the chance to visit the exhibition in Brussels.

To gather together twenty-seven countries under one roof and unite them in one enthusiasm is more than just a powerful political statement, though a necessary one in the present climate of accelerating globalization. It is also, and in a very fundamental way, a gesture of togetherness at the human level, collective as much as individual, by means of which everyone, peoples or individuals, nations or regions, is brought face to face with the others constituting this new community.

For this occasion, Europalia International has invited member countries to bring their works of art to the Centre for Fine Arts, not in a spirit of rivalry, but to showcase our European heritage: one that has, of course, many variations, but also from which, without eclipsing individual nuances, numerous common links will emerge.

Taking part means the contributors identify themselves, make themselves known, enter into a dialogue. In this case, as the exhibition covers thirteen centuries of art history, it involves laying bare the artistic, cultural and intellectual foundations of the cultures that to a great extent form modern Europe.

We wish this exhibition every success as it highlights, through the medium of art, the close links maintained by artists of all eras across most European nations, thus promoting the circulation of ideas favouring intellectual development. It underlines the fact that no single person or country has been responsible for Europe's image or its present status. All its achievements are the result of reciprocity between great creative figures.

Our warmest thanks to all those who have made it possible for this outstanding exhibition to become a reality. Our very special gratitude is owed to Baron Paul De Keersmakaer, President of Europalia, to the Commissioner-General Pat Cox, to the Exhibition's Curator, Prof. Roland Recht, and to Co-curators Prof. Catheline Périer-d'Ieteren and Prof. Pascal Griener; to the members of the scientific committee from the twenty-seven countries, the Europalia team under Kristine De Mulder and, finally, her counterparts at the Centre for Fine Arts.

PAUL DUJARDIN
DIRECTOR-GENERAL
CENTRE FOR FINE ARTS,
BRUSSELS

ÉTIENNE DAVIGNON
CHAIRMAN
CENTRE FOR FINE ARTS,
BRUSSELS

This year, the Europalia festival has chosen to honour the culture of the European Union, which is celebrating its fiftieth birthday. Europe is, of course, more than a political and economic entity. For centuries it has been a melting pot of peoples and ideas from which our present culture and civilization have emerged. The roots of modern Europe lie way back in its past. But, to quote Jorge Semprun, this European heritage will remain alive only if we can pass it on and draw from it the inspiration to build our future. It is precisely this legacy, in all its shapes and forms, that Europalia has brought to the public eye on the past twenty occasions.

It was therefore only natural that Europalia should represent the cultural side of this year's celebrations in Brussels. The twenty-seven member states, as well as the European institutions – in particular the European Commission and the European Parliament – have given our project enthusiastic support, backing us both financially and by loaning exhibits. Without them, without the sponsors and organizations that have funded us, without our cultural partners, the festival would never have seen the light of day. To them, then, must go our very special thanks.

The tireless efforts of Pat Cox, the festival's Commissioner-General, of Jan de Bock, Belgium's Permanent Representative throughout the preparatory stage, and of numerous co-workers and diplomats from the Ministry of Foreign Affairs, have played a key role in the development of this European festival. Our heartfelt thanks to them and the other European diplomats involved, as well as to the liaison committee, which oversaw links with the twenty-seven participating countries.

The europalia.europa festival highlights certain landmarks in our collective cultural memory as well as a selection of today's great artists and the young hopes of tomorrow. The themes of dialogue and of the circulation of people and ideas very quickly emerged as the threads running through the event, which has acquired a multidisciplinary, dual focus: what differentiates us culturally and what unites us .

The star attraction of europalia.europa, the exhibition *The Grand Atelier*, is the work of Prof. Roland Recht, in collaboration with Prof. Catheline Périer-d'Ieteren, Prof. Pascal Griener and an international scientific committee. For the last eighteen months they have cooperated with the whole Europalia team to assemble over three hundred masterpieces from some hundred and fifty museums – an exceptional achievement. We owe them an immense debt of gratitude, also to our longstanding partners, the President and Director-General of the Palais des Beaux-Arts – Étienne Davignon and Paul Dujardin – and their associates.

Europalia.europa is the result of the joint action of a large group of Europeans with a common passion for art and culture.

Europalia.europa exists, thanks to them, both for them and for all our fellow citizens.

KRISTINE DE MULDER
DIRECTOR-GENERAL
EUROPALIA INTERNATIONAL

PAUL DE KEERSMAEKER
PRESIDENT
EUROPALIA INTERNATIONAL

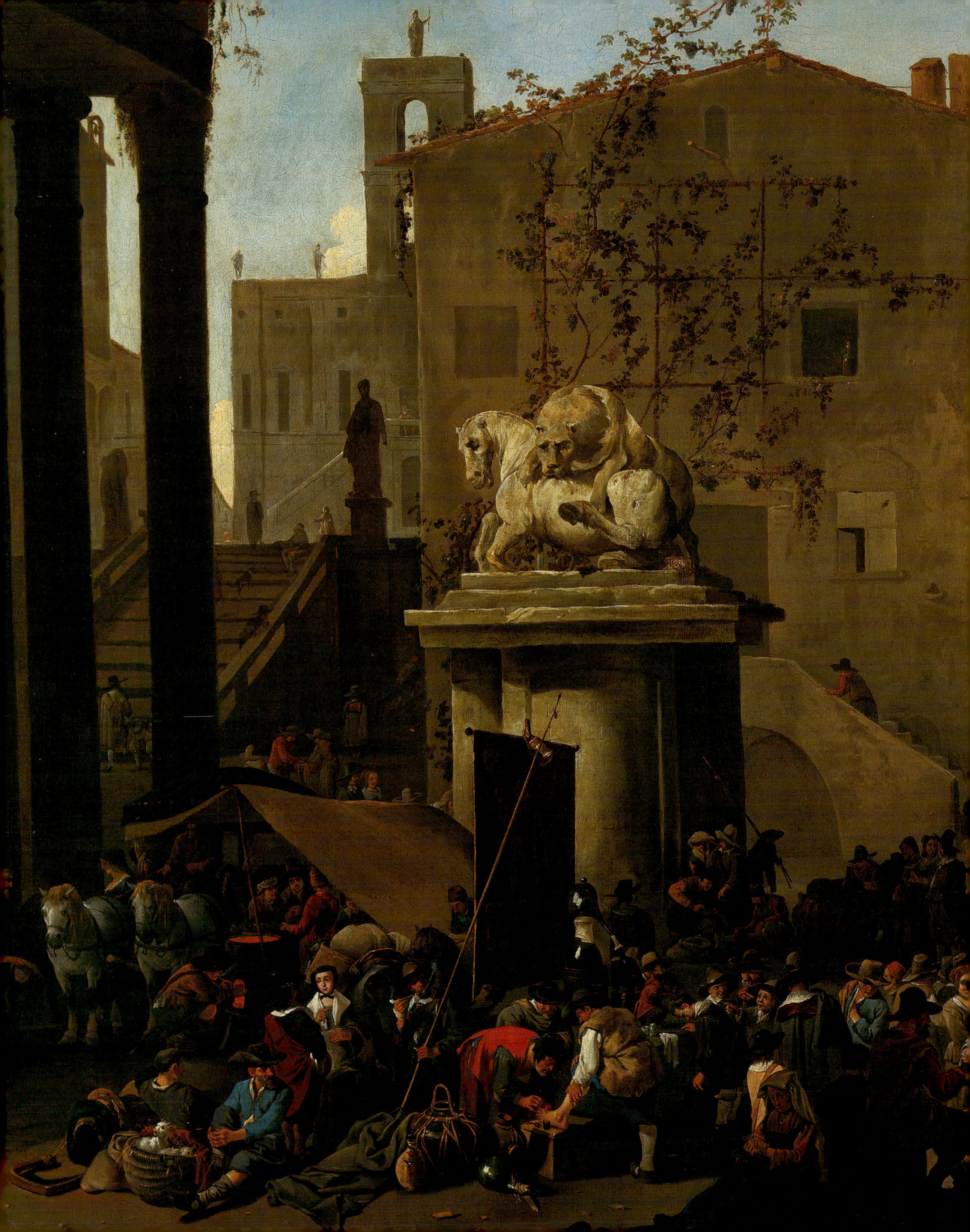

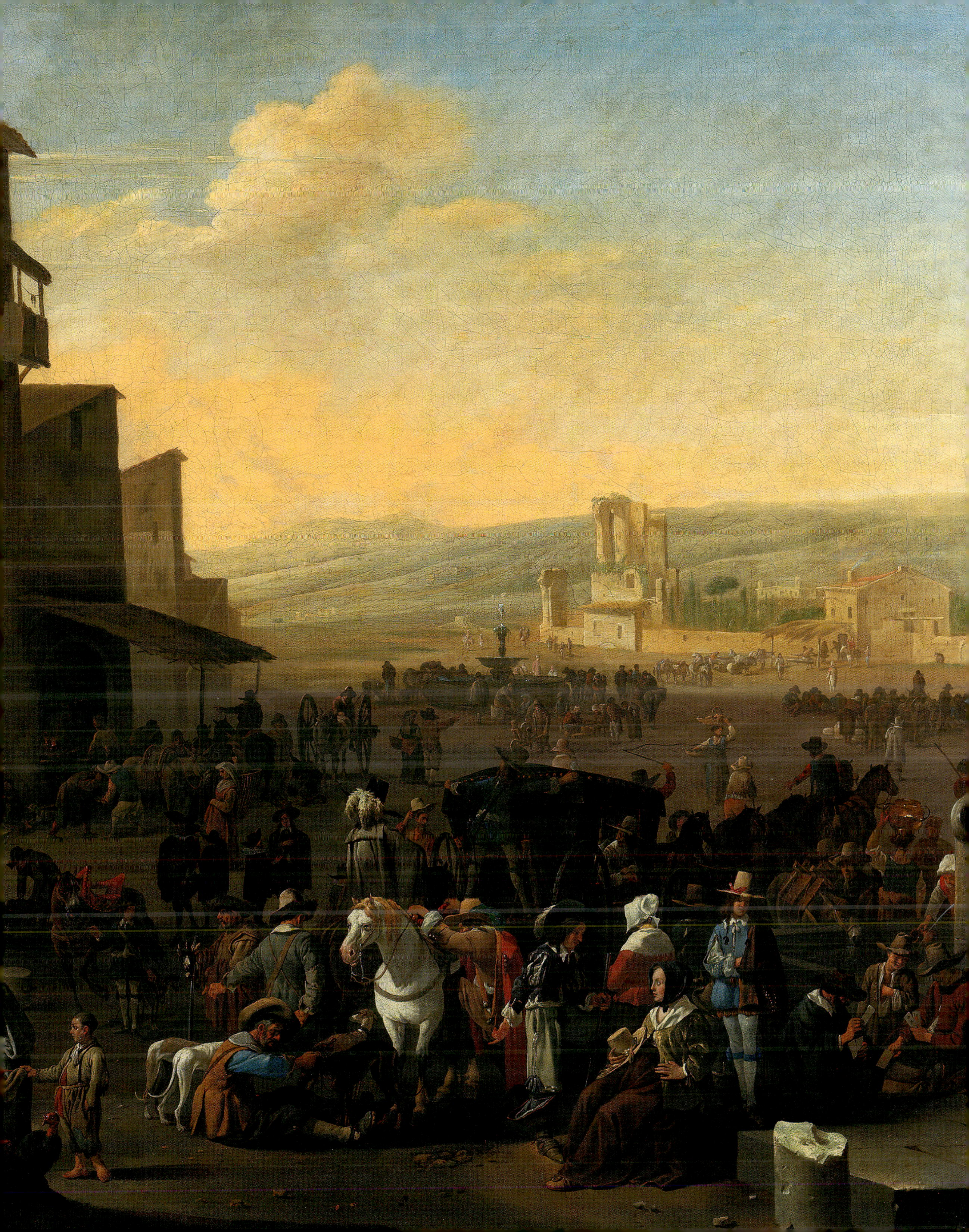

Eigentliche Abbildung deß ganzen Gewerbs der löblichen Kaufmannschafft/ samt etlich der nahmhafft- und fürnehmsten Handelstädt

Signatur und Wappen/ darinnen zum Theil fürnehmlich die Märckt und Messen begriffen seyn/ so deß Jahrs über in jedem Monath einfallen/ auch hin und wider in Europa zu unterschidlichen Zeiten gehalten/ und von fürnehmen und geringen Gewerbs- und Handelsleuthen/ aus allerley Nationen besucht und gebauet werden; wie durch derselben mancherley Schild und Wappen hie unten und zum Eingang bey dem *Mercurio* angezeigt ist. Samt der löblichen schönen uralten Kunst deß Buchhaltens/ dardurch alle Kaufmanns-Gewerb schleunig und richtig unterhalten werden; Neben andern wolgemeinten Erinnerungen/ welche den Handelsleuthen nothwendig zu wissen und zu beobachten sind.

Wend hieher dein Gesicht; Richt hieher deine Augen!
Soll zum Bericht und Lehr dir die Figur recht taugen.
Beschaue dise Wag/ die in der Mitte die
Ihr Zunge/ doch zugleich stellt im verborgen für.
Was kan doch dises wol bezeichnen und bedeuten?
Diß/ daß ein Richter sich nicht lassen soll verlaiten
Das Ansehn der Person/ Gunst/ Gaben/ und Geschenck/
Das Recht zu beugen/ und auf Unrecht sich nicht lenck.
Dann Er soll beiderley Partheyen so anhören/
Daß Er den frommen Theil deß Rechtens soll gewähren.
Gleich wie *Mercurius* auch eben diß mit Fleiß
In disem Bild anzeigt/ jedoch Geheimnus-weiß.
Der in der Rechten Hand die Wage hält und führet/
Auch wie Verstand und Witz dieselbige regieret.
Wardurch erkläret wird die richtige *Bilanz*,
Die man einrichten soll gerecht/ gleich/ billich/ gantz.

Wird solche Wage nicht/ wie bräuchlich/ innen stehen/
So kans ohn Irrthum nicht im Handlen leicht abgehen.
Hier merck es: Dise Kunst komt von den Alten her/
Eh Christus noch im Fleisch erschin/ die Mensch/ zur Ehr/
Dann *Sidon*, welche lag in der *Phœnicer* Lande/
Die Haupt-Statt in dem See/ und an deß Meeres Strande/
Hat solche Kunst geübt/ und in den Stand gebracht.
Und disen haben es die Griechen nach gemacht;
Italien hat sie den Welschen anbefohlen/
Bey welchen man noch heut hiervon Bericht kan hohlen;
Die der Buchhalterey berühmte Wissenschafft
Zu geben wissen/ Maß/ und guter Ordnung Krafft.
Aus Welschland aber ist auch auf die Teutschen kommen/
Wie man im Handel soll recht schaffen seinen Frommen;
Damit je mehr und mehr das Menschliche Gewerb
Mit GOTT befördert werd/ und nicht was Gut verderb.

DEBITOR. ANTVERPIA. CREDITOR.

Introduction

ROLAND RECHT

Having confidence in the Europe of tomorrow requires us, it would seem, to throw some light on its past. And, after all, its works of art are the most eloquent surviving witnesses of its history.

Today, however, a global approach embracing all the principal aspects of European art history is both irrational and impractical. Irrational because archaeological research and scientific studies of the continent's artistic heritage are multiplying exponentially. We have moved on from the days of the major synthesis to the micro-history of art, striving to abandon the old classifications – into static 'schools' and monolithic 'styles' – in favour of infinitely more subtle methods. Impractical, too, because the great masterpieces necessary to create such a broad and necessarily representative panorama cannot be assembled without endangering the conservation process, and the major museums with which they reside have other plans for them. The public may hanker more than ever for the 'big picture', but the time has never been so unfavourable. This is no small paradox of the times we live in.

And so we have chosen to proceed by other routes, sketching out a few broad lines of European art history. Opting for short 'dossiers' rather than a superficial panorama, we have developed a number of themes analysing the *circulation of art and the artistic community* – collectors, art-lovers, patrons, artists – over a substantial geographical area ranging from Dublin to Palermo, from Cordoba to Stockholm, Rouen to Sofia. In days gone by this intense circulation led men and artists in search of information or clients – not to mention the works commissioned from them – on arduous journeys not only by road, but often by river, and in areas far from their origins. We tend to underestimate these peregrinations, but they are revealed as crucial when we attempt to understand the migration of themes and formal motifs.

One result of Europe's conversion to Christianity during the lengthy period from Constantine to the 9th century was the role it played in federating disparate peoples. As far as the history of art is concerned, the Carolingian era is of capital importance because it allows us to witness a progressive mutation as forms borrowed from Antiquity were adapted to Christian iconographical programmes. This appropriation implies both a continuity and a rupture, and even if the Frankish imperial dynasty is no longer considered by a consensus of historians as the first manifestation of a collective Europe, it does represent a kind of beginning from the viewpoint of art. Here we are faced with a contradiction: just like the decorative art of the period of the invasions, the ancient figurative tradition found itself at the service of a religion that placed neither Nature – like the pagan migrants from Eastern Europe – nor Man – as in the Greco-Roman ideal – at the centre of its world vision, and therefore of its art. And it was this art that, over the course of a millennium, would shoulder the task of extolling faith in a single God and the promise of Salvation.

The Classical heritage did not simply disappear in the 9th or 10th century. It continued, in fact, into the 1800s, even up to the time of Picasso in different guises, of course. We wished to underline this continuity, with reference, for instance, to the 12th-century Mosan goldsmiths, medieval sketchbooks, the rediscovery of Vitruvius after 1400 and the art of the 18th century. In other words, we do not hold the opinion that the Renaissance should be exclusively credited with the rediscovery of the ancient world. The thread that links so many artists to the Classical Age is one that visitors to the Grand Atelier will have little difficulty following.

Another key thread in the exhibition is the book. In the first place, it was through books that Greek thought – recopied, transmitted via translations and elucidated with commentaries – became the cornerstone of European civilization. Sometimes, as with certain important philosophical treatises, this thought was spread throughout Europe by the intermediary of Arabic translations. Here again, Charlemagne played a major role: without the labours accomplished in the scriptoria of his Empire, all of this legacy would have come to a very different end.

Of Eastern origin, the religion that would come to dominate Europe and a large slice of the world relied on written tradition. The Bible and the books that composed it would be the object of innumerable commentaries, but at the same time they inspired images bringing the texts to life. The religious book was at the origin of a whole gamut of medieval art.

Of all the objects that we come across, books were the most mobile. The book travelled most easily, facilitating the transmission and exchange of knowledge. Books in their many forms are a recurring theme of the exhibition.

Nonetheless, the zone we know as Europe was never shuttered against the outside world. Byzantine art helped to fertilize that of Europe for century after century; the attraction of Beauty, of precious materials and complex techniques excited men's appetites for wealth. If the Orient was for so long an exotic place of myth, far out of reach of Westerners, it was partly because of the artifacts it unleashed on the Western shores of the Mediterranean. These items gave the appearance of a civilization – Islam – with a highly developed sense of refinement. Even if its religious practices were foreign to those of Christian Europe, even if its writing remained unreadable, there was an overwhelming temptation to acquire these objects, resulting in a prosperous trade all around the Mediterranean basin. Despite conflict – and there was plenty of that, when pillage took the place of peaceful exchange – any examination of the artistic scene reveals how the quest for Beauty and the enjoyment associated with it often caused men to forget that those with whom they were trading were their erstwhile enemies.

Thus the fourteen themes we have chosen tell, each in their own way, a tale of the movements of men, forms and techniques. This choice is arbitrary, but so are the alternatives. Our chosen time limits are also, we admit, open to debate... The 5th century we have adopted for the earliest limit as marking the beginning of the Christianization of culture and political structures in Western Europe as well as a massive migration of peoples from East and North, completing the disintegration mantling of the Roman Empire. Our latest limit is the 18th, century on the basis that it ushered in a new form of access to the arts.

The passion for collecting, already surfacing at the courts of the Valois princes in the late 1300s, lent the 17th and, especially, the 18th centuries a completely new aspect. The considerable development of the art market, the growing importance of art-lovers and 'antiquarians' – we would call them archaeologists – the demand for greater access to accumulated treasures resulting in the establishment of museums, the development of a critical spirit and skill in judging works, the birth of art history as a branch of historiography in its own right: these were the factors that profoundly modified the perception of art and its social function in the Age of Enlightenment.

When collections were opened up to the public the circuits followed by aficionados and artists alike underwent a change. The accumulation of treasures in a single location, which, like the Louvre at its inauguration in 1793, acquired a quasi-religious status, also corresponded with the opportunity now offered to artists to compare their own development with that of their illustrious forebears. Finally, Winckelmann's *History of the Art of Antiquity* was more than just the first work of its kind. It implied that the Ancients belonged to a vanished world that could be scrutinized and understood thanks to the artistic heritage of which we are henceforth the universal beneficiaries.

As for the choice of themes, we have been guided neither by chronology nor respect for major classifications. For example, Romanesque art – or *arts*, we should perhaps say – and Gothic have no place here as such. The art known as

'International' – in essence, 'European' – of around 1400 has also been omitted for the simple reason that recent years have seen a glut of exhibitions in its honour. And with the Renaissance we have concentrated on one particular aspect: the appearance of the book, as analysed by Roger Chartier in an introductory essay.

And so we end up with fourteen sections. The first is entitled *Europe on the Move*. It examines material evidence from early works of the great migratory movements that swept Europe from the 5th century, as well as the place of Irish art; in the first case we find that oriental decoration dominated the iconography of non-sedentary populations, while in the second ornamentation was placed at the service of Christian imagery. The latter imposed geometric forms on plant and animal motifs and would, in series of distinct mutations, haunt artists' choice of form up to the 12th century.

The second section deals with a vital chapter in European art history: *The Carolingian Empire and its Legacy*. It was only in the course of our preparations that we learned the Bibliothèque nationale de France was itself about to stage an exhibition devoted to its quite unique treasure of Carolingian manuscripts. All the same, we have been able to assemble a very handsome collection of books and ivories brilliantly illustrating both this period and its later echoes in Insular art at the dawn of Romanesque.

Europe and the Mediterranean brings together works reflecting Europe's connections with the area from which so much inspiration derived throughout its long history. The conquest of a large part of Spain by the Arabs, the role played by Sicily – susceptible to both Byzantine and Arabic influence – the place of Venice in exchanges with the Orient and as a sort of halfway-house for Byzantium: all these aspects are illustrated by a handful of representative items.

With *Goldsmiths' Workshops*, we have attempted a more detailed approach to a phenomenon that is frequently neglected: in addition to the large-scale vindications of Divine Providence on the Romanesque tympana of 12th-century churches, the goldsmith's art was employed to enrich the treasures of religious buildings with images based on learned theological commentaries and whose formal inspiration was, properly speaking, Byzantine or Classical. The existence in Liège of an archaizing work like the St Barthélémy font – formerly attributed to Renier de Huy but undoubtedly from another region of Europe – acted as an important stimulus for as universal an artist as Nicolas de Verdun, who occupied a singular place in the Europe of around 1200.

Contrary to received opinion, medieval works of art were frequently developed from prototypes upon which they were merely variations. In certain cases we can even speak of mass production. In the next section, *Art for Export: Enamels, Alabasters and Altarpieces*, we present a representative panorama of three artistic practices that involved such a process, though for very prestigious commissions. We could have included other techniques, such as stained glass in the late Middle Ages, or ivories; instead, we have made the decision to illustrate the expansion of the above export market from Portugal to Scandinavia.

Section 6 is designed along different lines: it takes in a wide historical field since the works illustrating it belong to different chronological eras. The most widespread image in the Christian world between the end of the 12th century and the beginning of the 15th was unequivocally that of the Virgin Mary. This development was contemporary with the idea of courtly love and a unique view of womanhood and corresponded to a trend that sought to humanize the sacred. For these reasons the section is entitled *The Image of the Virgin and the Courtly Ideal*, linking the two themes.

A medium that favoured the circulation of ideas in every period of European art was paper, and its predecessor, parchment. With *The Circulation of Drawings in Europe*, our interest refocuses on paper's long term and evolving status. If, until the 14th century, it merely recorded copies of existing works in apparently servile fashion, artists began to accord it a quite different significance in the late 1300s / early 1400s. The model sheet or book, in Italy, metamorphosed into the sketchbook, the medium for ideas and experiment, or for the development of universal knowledge, as with Leonardo da Vinci. This section recalls how drawings enabled architects of the Gothic period to record their plans and publicize them for possible projects.

With *The European Careers of Sculptors at the End of the Middle Ages* we concentrate on three cases. The first is a truly European atelier established by Emperor Sigismund in his castle at Buda. Next comes Nikolaus van Leyden, known only through writings and a handful of works – yet the latter rank among the finest in the history of sculpture. Finally, another master, Veit Stoss, who headed a large colony of sculptors and was in addition a painter and engraver, thanks to which skills he was able to pass on his prodigious technical inventions to other artists. His success even impacted on Renaissance Italy, reputedly hostile to the Late Gothic style.

We know of no other civilization in which there took place such a seismic upheaval in pictorial technique as that which affected the representation of space in 15th-century Europe. Almost simultaneously in Flanders and Florence there was a move from the two-dimensional composition that underpinned medieval religious imagery to a three-dimensional approach. And as a result of the resurgent interest in Aristotle, iconography began to borrow from the mineral, vegetable and animal world, presenting figures and scenes in an ever more naturalistic setting. This went so far as to create on the rectangular panel the illusion of a homogeneous space extending that of the viewer. In *Conquest of a New Pictorial Space* we examine the representational system that would continue unchallenged until the advent of Cubism.

In the age of the Internet, with its revolutionary means of communicating information and its innovative content, it seemed worthwhile reminding visitors to the Grand Atelier of the role played by the birth of printing. *Europe and the Printed Book* looks at an assortment of books that form part of Europe's patrimony with their themes of Reform and Humanism and their radically new scientific curiosity. This section accords a place of honour to the Roman architect Vitruvius and his *De Architectura*; the latter took Europe by storm from the 16th century onwards and was responsible for the bulk of the continent's Classical architecture.

Prints in the Service of Arts and Crafts examines the debt the decorative arts owe to ornamental engravings circulating from the 1500s to an extent that is virtually impossible to quantify. The motifs transmitted by this medium formed a repertoire that every artistic profession could draw upon. Under the circumstances, this section has necessarily to be restricted to a handful of examples and could never attempt to embrace all the relevant fields.

This is equally true of the subsequent section, *Perceptions of Other Worlds*. This brief overview hardly claims to give a complete account of the attention Europeans have lavished on other continents since the Age of Discovery. But this interest, the relative degrees of which we are only just beginning to understand, underwent an evolution from a distinct sense of the superiority of Europeans over 'savages' to a semi-scientific curiosity characterized by the voyages of Captain Cook. Coming to terms with oneself and one's own cultural identity necessarily involves contact with alien civilizations.

From the 15th century, imitation of the classical world became a kind of common currency in the whole of Europe. Greco-Roman art was the ideal that was to guide every artist's training; an original personality, it was thought, could only emerge through contact with the Ancients. This is why, from the 17th to the 19th century, Rome was the goal for pilgrimages by artists and art-lovers alike. But they discovered more than just Antiquity on the peninsula: they were able to meet Italian artists, the first in Europe to enjoy recognised status and public prestige, so that men like Leonardo da Vinci or Michelangelo were honoured like princes.

And so, from the 1500s, we can distinguish the emergence of a 'Republic of the Arts' that would finally blossom into the Age of Enlightenment. It consisted of painters, who acted as courtiers as well as creators and artistic counsellors to the nobility; antiquarians, scattered across Europe, who helped study aspects of the continent's heritage that were not necessarily derived from Antiquity; and finally the art-lovers and collectors who exchanged information, works of art or recommendations about a particular artist.

The Europe of Masters and Collectors will provide a few glimpses of the intensity of these exchanges. In particular, a strong nucleus grew up around Bartholomaeus Spranger, born in Antwerp and active in Rome, Vienna and Prague – an eminent representative of Mannerism, familiar with every artistic current, the archetypal European painter, just as his patron, Rudolph II, was the model of the art-loving prince.

The final section – *The World in a Room: Collectors and Art Dealers* – is the opportunity to unite a quite exceptional group of paintings representing the 'Cabinet of Curiosity', a room set aside for the contemplation and study of paintings and objets d'art, and which helped mould the tastes and judgment of a large proportion of the aristocracy and the urban bourgeoisie. They were worlds in miniature, and we hope that visitors will come to realize the role they played, long before the invention of museums, in defining modern disciplines and promoting a type of social interaction.

* * *

Europalia has been kind enough to entrust me with the curatorship of this exhibition commemorating the 50th anniversary of the Treaty of Rome. I could not have succeeded without the assistance of my colleagues, Professors Catheline Périer-d'Ieteren of the Université Libre (Brussels) and Pascal Griener of the University of Neufchâtel. For us it meant the chance to indulge in rewarding and stimulating intellectual debate. We worked side by side throughout the 18 months of preparation, as well as with the Europalia team. We hope the public will enjoy visiting the exhibition as much as we did devising and preparing it.

To introduce the catalogue accompanying it we have called on the help of three eminent colleagues: Peter Burke, a specialist in the Renaissance, Roger Chartier, whose research into the history of the book is well known, and Krzysztof Pomian, who studies the history of collecting. Their contributions, with those of Catheline Périer-d'Ieteren and Pascal Griener, will provide visitors with an amalgam of views casting a fascinating sidelight on the contents of the exhibition.

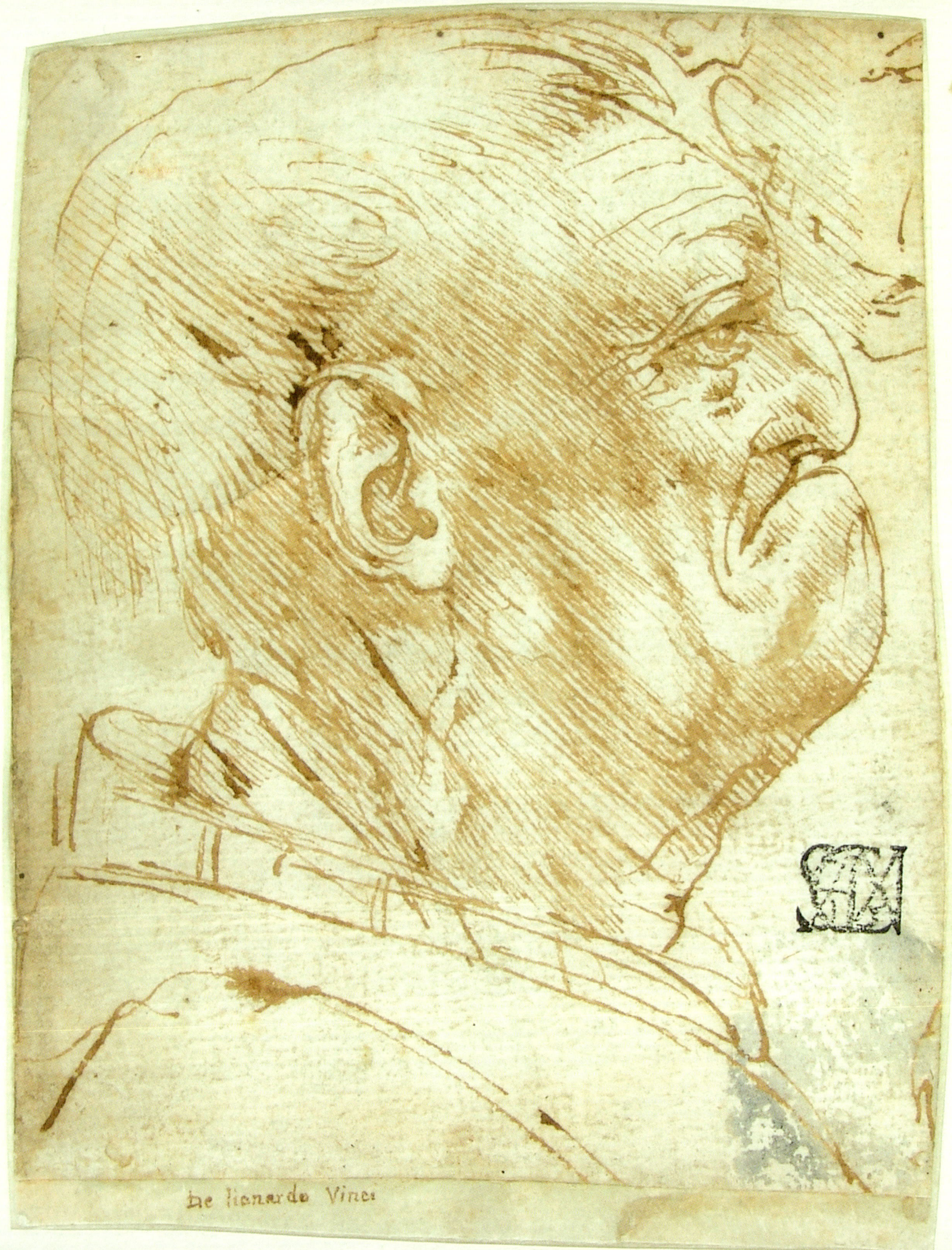
De lionardo Vinci

Artists, circulation and encounters

PETER BURKE

In the current cultural and economic changes that we describe as 'globalization', it is difficult to deny the importance of the circulation of people as well as commodities, information and ideas. Exchanges were less intense in the early modern period (more or less 1500–1800), sometimes described as the age of 'archaic globalization'. All the same, the circulation of people already played an important role in the process of cultural exchange and the diffusion of innovation, a topic that is – or at any rate should be – of interest to historians of art as well as to geographers and historians of science and technology.

The term 'circulation' may suggest a simple diffusion or flow from one part of Europe to another. To avoid this misleading implication, it may be better to speak of 'encounters', including encounters with objects such as ancient statues, medals, modern paintings, sculptures, engravings, manuscripts and printed books. Thanks to such encounters, some Europeans were already taking an interest in works of art produced outside Europe, while examples of Renaissance art were known to some individuals in the Ottoman, Persian, Mughal and Chinese empires.

However, it has been persuasively argued by economic historians and historians of science that 'Through the ages, the main channel for the diffusion of innovation has been the migration of people', and that 'The transfer of really valuable knowledge from country to country or from institution to institution cannot be easily achieved by the transport of letters, journals and books [or works of art]: it necessitates the physical movement of human beings'. In short, 'ideas move around inside people'.[1]

In 1752 the head of the French Bureau de Commerce, Trudaine de Montigny, had already made a similar point: 'The arts never pass by writing from one country to another.' Why should this be the case? Trudaine's ally in a plan to bring skilled English craftsmen to France, the textile manufacturer John Holker, explained that 'Good information would make little impression on a workman.' What was needed in order 'to transfer skills from one country to another' was practical example.

In the case of 'know-how', knowledge that has become part of the body's habitus, as the late Pierre Bourdieu would say, words and even images are less valuable than demonstration by a skilled practitioner.[2] This point about learning by doing, by imitating, is surely as valid for painting or sculpting as for weaving or watch-making.

It follows from this argument that anyone who is concerned to explain major cultural changes should pay special attention to diasporas. For example, the revocation of the Edict of Nantes by Louis XIV led some 200,000 French Protestants to emigrate to England, the Dutch Republic, Prussia and elsewhere. This emigration not only spread techniques of glass-making and silk-weaving but also encouraged the rise of professional journalism, as in the famous case of the *Nouvelles de la République de Lettres*, edited from Rotterdam by the exiled pastor Pierre Bayle.

In the case of the Renaissance, particularly well known is the contribution made by Greek scholars who took refuge from the Turks in Italy and elsewhere (before as well as after the fall of Constantinople in 1453). Another was made by

< LEONARDO DA VINCI, *Head of an old man in right profile, c.* 1485–90 (Cat. VII.8)

The diaspora of artists from the Netherlands was also important in spreading new styles, particularly in the age of the Renaissance and Mannerism. As in the case of the Italians, they sometimes worked and even emigrated in groups, like the team that Antonis Obberghen took with him to Kronborg in 1577, and included several generations or dynasties of artists. Leaving aside a few visits to Italy – by Justus of Ghent, for example, – in the 15th century, the movements of the Netherlanders began in the 1540s, when Hans Eworth and Willem Scrots came to England, and ended in the 1690s (Louis XIV's sculptor Martin van den Bogaert, better known as Desjardins, died in 1694). Their collective trajectory was therefore shorter than that of the Italians, but important nonetheless.

The Netherlanders were especially active in central Europe, in England and in the Baltic. In central Europe, the artists in the service of Rudolf II included a number of Netherlanders, among them the sculptor Adriaan de Vries, the painter Roland Savery, the engravers Joris Hoefnagel and Aegidius Sadeler II, and the goldsmith Paulus van Vianen.[9]

In England, between the ages of the Germans Hans Holbein and Godfrey Kneller, it is scarcely an exaggeration to say that the arts were dominated by Netherlanders. The leading portrait painters were Netherlanders: Hans Eworth, Willem Scrots, Marcus Gheeraerts (from Bruges), John de Critz (from Antwerp) and another Antwerper, Anthony van Dyck. Cornelius Cure, who came from Amsterdam, made funerary monuments in London, including the tomb for Edward VI (1573). Gerard Janssen, another Amsterdammer, together with his sons, executed about fifty English monuments, while Maximilian Colt, a Huguenot from Arras, made the tombs of Queen Elizabeth at Westminster and Robert Cecil at Hatfield.

Artists from the Netherlands also travelled to the Baltic. In Denmark, they included the architects Antonis Obberghen and Hans van Steenwinckel and the portrait painters Karel van Mander III and Abraham Wuchters. In Sweden, a leading figure was the sculptor Willem Boy of Mechelen, who made King Gustav Vasa's tomb at Uppsala.[10] Artists from the Netherlands who settled in Gdansk, more or less an independent city at this time, included Obberghen and the sculptor Willem van den Blocke.

A route map of travelling artists would show a significant contrast between the Italians, rarely to be found in the Baltic area, and the Netherlanders, a reminder that art, like heresy, often follows trade routes. In similar fashion, Fernand Braudel once noted that the spread of Italian merchants, first to western and then to eastern Europe, was accompanied by the spread of artists.[11]

Political networks were also important. The Italians who went to Spain in the age of Philip II were generally his subjects; Jacopo da Trezzo, Girolamo Miseroni, Pellegrino Tibaldi and the Leonis from Milan, Sofonisba Anguisciola from Cremona.

What was the attraction of these foreign countries for these artists? On the 'push' side, religious conflicts in the Netherlands probably encouraged emigration. We know, for example, that Karel van Mander and his family were Mennonites, while Marcus Gheeraerts and Lucas de Heere were Calvinists, and they all left in the late 1560s, a time of religious persecution.

On the positive side, the attraction exercised by courts was important for this 'talent drain'. The service of rulers offered high status. Indeed, the roles these artists played were not confined to art. Sofonisba Anguisciola was a lady-in-waiting at the court of Philip II, while Arcimboldo was master of ceremonies to the Emperor Rudolf.

A final question, but a central one, concerns the cultural effects of the circulation of artists, the extent to which foreigners were able to create or at least contribute to the formation of traditions or 'schools'. In the case of Spain, for instance, the arrival of an Italian artist, Paolo de San Leocadio, in 1472 is said to have 'changed Valencian painting almost overnight'.[12]

In the cases of the 'School of Fontainebleau' and the 'School of Prague', the contribution of expatriates is obvious enough. The French artists Pierre Bontemps, Antoine Caron and Charles Dorigny were all trained by working under the direction of Primaticcio at Fontainebleau, while the term 'School of Prague' refers to a style produced by the interaction of an Italo-Netherlandish group.[13]

In Russia, Italian émigrés trained Russians to be their successors, as Trezzini trained the architect Mikhail Zemtsov. In Japan, the Jesuit Niccolò established an art school in Nagasaki. In Mexico and Peru, Peter of Ghent and Bernardo Bitti trained indigenous artists.

Returning to the problem posed at the beginning of this essay, I should like to suggest that the circulation of people affects culture in different ways from the circulation of artifacts and that in certain respects it is more effective. Foreign objects are more easily absorbed or resisted, allowing both misunderstandings and deliberate adaptations. Emigrés, on the other hand, are able to explain to the host culture the meanings of new artifacts and styles as well as the techniques of producing them. Without the circulation of artists, the styles that we call Renaissance, Mannerism, Baroque and Classicism might still have spread across Europe and beyond – but in a much less coherent manner.

1 Cipolla 1972, p. 48; Ziman 1974, p. 259.
2 Harris 1998.
3 Burke 1995.
4 Lo Gatto 1934; Białostocki 1976; Karpowicz 1987; Kaufmann 2004.
5 Warnke 1985.
6 Knecht 1994.
7 Checa 1992.
8 Evans 1973, pp. 162–195; Kaufmann 1995, pp. 185–203; Kaufmann 2004, pp. 154–216.
9 Evans 1973, pp. 162–195; Kaufmann 1995, pp. 185–203.
10 Hahr 1907–1910; Christensen 1988.
11 Braudel 1989, p. 17.
12 Brown 1991, p. 20.
13 Kaufmann 1985.

BIBLIOGRAPHY

Białostocki, Jan, *The Art of the Renaissance in Eastern Europe*, London, 1976.

Braudel, Fernand, 'L'Italia fuori Italia', *Storia d'Italia*, vol. 2, Turin, 1974, pp. 2092–148, French trans. *Le Modèle Italien*, Paris, 1989.

Brown, Jonathan, *The Golden Age of Painting in Spain*, New Haven, London, 1991.

Burke, Peter, 'Hosts and Guests: A General View of Minorities in the Cultural Life of Europe', in Hugo Soly, Alfons K. L. Thijs (eds), *Minorities in Western European Cities*, Brussels, Rome, 1995, pp. 43–54.

Checa, Fernando, *Felipe II: mecenas de las artes*, Madrid, 1992.

Christensen, Charlotte, 'Christian IVs renæssance', in Svend Ellehøj (ed.), *Christian* IVs Verden, Copenhagen, 1988, pp. 302–35.

Cipolla, Carlo, 'The Diffusion of Innovations in Early Modern Europe', *Comparative Studies in Society and History*, 14, 1972, pp. 46–52.

Evans, Robert, *Rudolf II and his World*, Oxford, 1973.

Hahr, August, *Studier i Johan III's Renässans*, 2 vols, Uppsala, Leipzig, 1907–10.

Harris, John R., *Industrial Espionage and Technology Transfer*, Aldershot, 1998.

Karpowicz, Mariusz, *Artisti Ticinesi in Polonia nel '500*, Lugano, 1987.

Kaufmann, Thomas Da Kosta, *L'école de Prague: la peinture à la cour de Rudolphe II*, Paris, 1985.

Kaufmann, Thomas Da Kosta, *Court, Cloister and City: The Art and Culture of Central* Europe, 1450–1800, London, 1995.

Kaufmann, Thomas Da Costa, *Toward a Geography of Art*, Chicago, 2004.

Knecht, Robert, *Renaissance Warrior and Patron*, 2nd edn, Cambridge, 1994.

Lo Gatto, Ettore, *Gli artisti italiani in Russia*, Rome, 1934.

Warnke, Martin, *Hofkünstler*, 1985, English trans. *The Court Artist*, Cambridge, 1993.

Ziman, John M., 'Ideas Move Around Inside People', *Puzzles, Problems and Enigmas*, 1974, reprint, Cambridge, 1981, pp. 259–72.

The appearance of the printed book

ROGER CHARTIER

In 1455, in Mainz, Johann Gensfleich – known as Gutenberg – lost the suit that had been brought against him by Johann Fust, a local bourgeois. Fust demanded that Gutenberg reimburse money that had been advanced for 'Werk der Bucher', i.e. the publication of the first book, the forty-two line Bible, which had been printed the previous year using a new technology.

The credit for this invention had been fought over very early by Gutenberg, and was variously attributed to Laurens Janszoon Coster of Harlem, to Procopius Waldfoghel – a Czech living in Avignon who taught '*ars scribendi artificialiter*' – and even to Fust himself (later confused with Doctor Faust). The association of a series of 15th-century innovations had made printing possible; these included advances in metallurgy, in particular the ability to separate different metals, mass production of woodblock prints, where images were often accompanied by captions and phylacteries (banderoles), and the appearance of copperplate engraving, which brought together engraved plates and the use of a press. The technique perfected by Gutenberg thus placed lead and copper type and the machinery of the printing press at the service of text reproduction. Finally, there was the spread of paper, which had been introduced in Muslim Spain in the 12th century. One hundred years later, thanks to the use of water-power and the mechanical pulping of rags, paper manufacturing was perfected in Fabriano, Italy. This new medium – far less expensive than parchment – made mass production of books conceivable.

The frequent comparison with the invention of moveable characters in China and Korea in the 12th and 13th centuries (and perhaps earlier), obliges us not to be too hasty in identifying printing with the Western technique invented in the 15th century – seemingly without any knowledge of its Asian predecessor. On the one hand, the use of moveable type (in clay, wood or metal) does not imply an Oriental use of a press but only of rubbing. On the other hand, xylography is itself also a printing technique. Although impressions made from moveable type were no doubt less common in China than has long been thought, the engraving of texts and images on wood remained the most widely used technique. It would therefore be an error to presume the absolute superiority of typography over woodblock printing, which is to say of West over East. The technique that allowed for the printing of texts from engraved blocks brought a printing culture to China that was very close in its commercial organization and its productions to those of the West. Conversely, woodblock printing played an ongoing role in the West, as attested to by the coexistence, until 1475, of block-books such as the *Biblia pauperum* with the first typographical editions. Woodblocks continued to be used for illustrations and initial capitals, and their predominance was only surpassed at the end of the 17th century by copper engraving[X.1].

Was it the invention of the printing press that constituted this admirable revolution, celebrated as of the 17th century and recognized by historians to the point of considering it as marking the real 'appearance' of the book? One thing is certain: with Gutenberg's invention, more texts entered into circulation and each reader could read a greater number of them. By ensuring the reproduction and distribution of texts on a scale unknown at the time of hand copying, the printing press met demands that had begun to emerge in Italy in the 13th century and somewhat later in Germany. These demands were not confined to universities and ecclesiastical settings: they were fuelled by the search for manuscripts, the increased number of copies and the creation of libraries. As

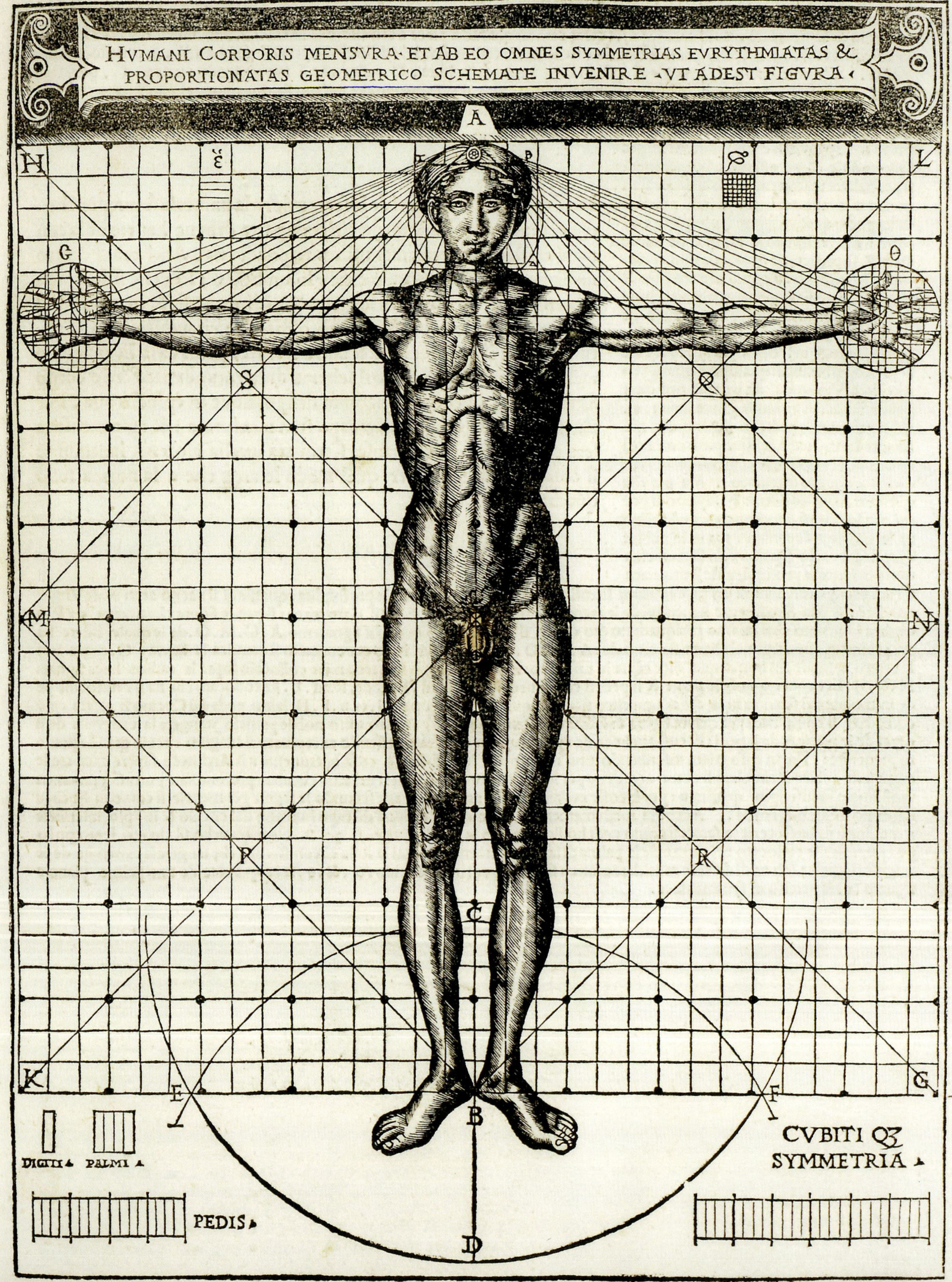
HVMANI CORPORIS MENSVRA· ET AB EO OMNES SYMMETRIAS EVRYTHMIATAS & PROPORTIONATAS GEOMETRICO SCHEMATE INVENIRE ·VT ADEST FIGVRA·
A
H
L
G
Θ
S
Q
M
N
P
R
C
K
G
E
F
B
D
DIGITI·
PALMI·
PEDIS·
CVBITI QZ SYMMETRIA·

proof, witness the rapid growth of this new technique, which was spread in Europe by travelling German typographers such as Johann Neumeister, who worked in Mainz, in the Subiaco monastery near Rome, in Basle and in Toulouse before becoming a printer in Lyon – one example among many others. Printing, which in 1500 was already present in more than 250 towns, was dominated by German and Italian workshops that published, respectively, 30–40 per cent of the 30,000 editions of the incunabula period.

CONTINUITIES

Nevertheless, it would be an error to downplay the continuities within which the typographical workshops took their place. The first of these were the technical continuities. The printed book inherited the fundamental structures of manuscript books, i.e. the distribution of texts between signatures, folios and pages, which is the distinctive feature of the *codex*, whatever techniques were used to produce or reproduce it. This new form of book, which emerged in the first centuries of the Christian era, allowed for usage that was completely impossible with the scrolls read by Greek and Roman readers. It became possible to leaf through a book, easily locate a passage, compile and use tables of contents and indices, and to write while reading. We should therefore take care not to attribute to the printing press and moveable type these textual inventions (indices, tables of contents, concordances, the numbering of folios, pagination), which for more than ten centuries had already accompanied the book's most recent incarnation. Within the long existence of the *codex*, one must also situate the hierarchy of formats that printing inherited – large formats, those of reference books that had to be placed on a table or lectern in order to be read, and little books that one could take along on a voyage (and thus texts that were published for the common reader), but also editions of the Greek and Roman classics by the Venetian printer Aldus Manutius.

Then there is the question of graphic continuities. All or nearly all printed characters are derived from the handwritten scripts that preceded them. Thus it was with fonts that imitated Gothic lettering, which survived the longest in England – as 'Black Letter' or 'English Letter' characters – and in the German-speaking world, as fonts copied from handwriting used by chancery scribes. But the same was true for scripts that broke with medieval forms; these were invented by 15th-century Italian humanists, including Poggio Bracciolini and Niccolo Niccolini's Roman type or 'littera antiqua' and Bartolomeo Sanvito's italic or 'italica'. Furthermore, at least until the first third of the 17th century, printed works reproduced manuscript books: they had a colophon instead of a title page; the text was laid out in two columns and was surrounded by glosses in the margin in the manner of scholastic works; and they were adorned with initial letters and miniatures painted by the same illuminators who decorated the pages of manuscripts. Finally, they were not considered finished until a corrector or rubricator had added – in ink – running titles, margin headings and punctuation signs. The *Missale Lugdunense*, printed in Lyon in 1482 by Johann Neumeister – already mentioned above – is a perfect illustration of the extent to which incunabula depended on manuscripts, whose form they reproduced as accurately as possible [X.3].

And finally there were textual continuities. The inventory of printed titles in the incunabula period shows the conservative role of a technical revolution that was not, in the same way, a cultural or textual revolution. The lion's share of the first published works – most of them in Latin, the language of three-quarters of incunabula – consisted of scholastic manuals, books of law and theology, ancient authors, calendars and almanacs. As Henri-Jean Martin wrote in *The Coming of the Book*: 'Thus, the printing workshop no doubt facilitated the work of scholars in certain domains. But on the whole, one can consider that it in no way accelerated the adoption of theories or new knowledge. On the contrary, by popularizing certain long-held ideas, and by firmly rooting

< *Di Lucio Vitruvio Pollione de Architectura libri decem traducti de Latino in Vulgare affigurati, commentati* [...], Edition illustrated by Cesare Cesariano, Como, Gottardus da Ponte, 1521 (Cat X.24)

old prejudices – or attractive errors – it seems to have put up a force of inertia against a number of new ideas.'

A NEW WRITTEN CULTURE

We should not, however, advance this argument too far. Gutenberg's invention brought about profound changes in written culture. The printing of books often played only a small part in the activity of typographical workshops. It should be emphasized that Gutenberg's first printings, perhaps *c.* 1452, were letters of indulgence printed in thousands of copies. Over the long term, the production of these workshops consisted, for the most part, of bills, pamphlets, petitions, posters, forms, tickets, receipts, certificates and many other ephemera, or 'town works', which brought in most of the revenue for these firms. The printer's shop thus made familiar items out of objects that were unknown or rare in the age of manuscripts and, at least in urban settings, writing took over walls, was read in public places, and transformed both administrative and commercial practices.

Further, the printer's shop created new usages for handwriting, as we can see from objects that encouraged their owners to fill, in their own hand, spaces that printing had left blank. This was true of empty pages left in almanacs, spaces for handwriting in forms, printed headings in commonplaces, and the wide margins and line spacing in school editions for accommodating the comments of students. The interconnectedness of handwritten pages and printed texts was not limited solely to those objects that explicitly organized such relations. Readers in the past, learned readers in particular, put their stamp on newly printed books in various ways. These included correcting with pen and ink the errors that they found, drawing up useful indices or handwritten errata, annotating the margins, and even creating original books by gluing together fragments of printed editions that they had cut up.

Gutenberg's invention also transformed the relationship between the text, the book and the page. The printed book meant that works by the same author could be assembled in a single volume, a practice that was less common with manuscripts. This was not, of course, a completely new idea. Starting in the 13th century, certain authors who wrote in Vulgar Latin – first among them Petrarch – established the practice of assembling in one volume only those texts of which they were the authors. This broke with the dominant tradition of the manuscript era, i.e. miscellanea that brought together texts of different genres from various dates written by very different authors. But this practice gained momentum with the printed book. The 1616 Folio of the works of Ben Jonson, published by Jonson himself, and the 1623 Folio of Shakespeare's plays, printed at the initiative of two fellow actors and a consortium of four London bookshops, are two illustrations of the link that existed between the materiality of the printed book and the idea of an *oeuvre.*

As soon as it was freed from imitating the layout of manuscripts, the printed book offered a new way of placing texts on the page. The revolution of blanks, which introduced paragraphs and indented lines into the typographic composition, had its origins in two innovations from the mid-16th century. These were the separation of the Bible into verses in the editions printed by Robert Estienne, and the division of the Latin classics into numbered chapters. Using these examples as models, publishers broke with the prevailing convention of blocks of text without line breaks.

There are two critical issues associated with this new way of presenting texts. First, it shows that decisions concerning the setting of books were the domain of the master printers, correctors and above all the typesetters, rather than the authors themselves. This is a reminder that authors did not write books, because a book was an object whose form was the result of multiple skills and techniques. Second, it gave a new readability to texts. This resulted in the rapid incorporation of the new typographical arrangements in works destined for readers who were not scholars. It also brought about a profound shift in the concept of the written word. The written discourse, whether in manuscript or printed form, was long regarded as a simple recording or substitute for speech. Starting in early modern Europe, however, it was perceived as possessing its own logic – and its layout contributed to the reader's understanding of that logic. Thus, in France in the first half of the 17th century, oratorical-type texts (legal pleas, sermons and speeches) continued to be printed without indented lines, as if the printed text were merely the transcription of the continuous flow of a human voice. Blanks became the rule, however, in spiritual works, books of philosophy and novels.

MANUSCRIPT PUBLICATION AND CONTEMPT FOR THE PRINTED WORD

We must strongly emphasize, however, that Gutenberg's invention, at least during the first four centuries of its existence, did not bring about the disappearance of manuscript publication. This should be understood as the long-term effect of the disparagement of the printed text. There was no shortage of texts stating that the proliferation of books was more a source of confusion than of wisdom, and denouncing the greed and dishonesty of printers and booksellers – always ready to deceive authors who published their own works, and to infringe on the privileges obtained by their colleagues. They attributed the decline in texts to the ignorance of typographers and to readers who were unable to understand the works to which the printing press had given them access. This is why the Catholic Church, without banning it outright, severely limited access by the faithful to the Vulgate Bible. This is also why Luther himself, having translated first the New and then the Old Testament into German, was frightened by the uses that could be made of the words of the Bible, and emphasized those mediations whose exact meaning could be explained: preaching and the catechism[x 17].

Publication of manuscripts represented an alternative to errors introduced at the printer's: it separated literary exchange from economic interests (except when it took on a commercial form, as in the case of *nouvelles à la main*) and it protected texts from alterations introduced by clumsy typesetters. But there were also more positive reasons for the continued presence of manuscript copies, although the mechanical reproduction of texts made possible by Gutenberg's invention appeared to signal their disappearance. Manuscripts allowed for a controlled and limited distribution of texts that could be circulated more discreetly than printed works, and thus ran less risk of falling into the hands of uncomprehending readers. Hence, manuscripts constituted a crucial vehicle for the distribution of heretical, dissident and licentious texts. In addition, the very form of the manuscript, open to corrections, changes of opinion, and additions at every step in its creation – from composition to copying to binding – allowed for writing at various times (as was the case for 'mirrors for princes', to which new texts were added in each generation) and in various hands (such as for collections of poems of which readers often became authors).

A EUROPE OF THE BOOK

Copied by hand, and pulled from the presses in ever-increasing numbers, the circulation of books and the works they contained played an essential role in the creation of a European space of reading and readers. Let us take one of the most famous examples: *Don Quixote.* In chapter three, Don Quixote asks the bachelor Samson Carrasco, who has just returned from Salamanca, 'So, then, it is true that there is a history of me, and that it was a Moor and a sage who wrote it?' To this, Carrasco replies, 'So true is it, senor, that my belief is there are more than twelve thousand volumes of the said history in print this very day. Only ask Portugal, Barcelona, and Valencia, where they have been printed, and moreover there is a report that it is being printed at Antwerp.' In fact, a figure of twelve thousand volumes in print between 1605 and 1615 is entirely plausible since, by that time, nine editions of the novel had been published in the various kingdoms and territories of the Catholic Monarchy: Castile, Aragon, Portugal and the Netherlands. These included three editions in Madrid (two in 1605, and one in 1608), two in Lisbon (both in 1605), one in Valencia in 1605, one in Milan and two in Brussels (not Antwerp) in 1607 and 1611. If we accept that the average press run for an edition was 1500 copies, this would make 13,500 copies of *Don Quixote* in Castilian in the decade following the publication of the edition produced by Juan de la Cuesta's workshop in 1605. The book thus encountered many readers who could read Castilian, both in Spain and beyond its borders – in Europe and even in the New World. For the year 1605 alone, the Archivo Géneral de Indias lists the arrival of several hundred copies of *Don Quixote* in the Americas, shipped to bookshops in Mexico and Peru by their Castilian suppliers, or brought by travellers who had made the transatlantic crossing. Very quickly, however, Cervantes's story became accessible to other readers: in 1612, it was translated into English by Thomas Shelton, and in 1614 César Oudin produced a French version. Translations into German (1621) and Tuscan (1622) followed shortly thereafter.

Editions and translations were not the only vehicles for the circulation of *Don Quixote*, whose characters existed even outside the pages of the story. The presence of the knight errant and his squire in court jousting matches and popular processions is attested to very early, in Spain, Peru and Mexico. In addition, the apocryphal continuation by Avellaneda, which appeared in 1614, a year before that of Cervantes, was another means by which the text circulated outside of the text. And, as we know, starting in chapter fifty-nine of Part Two, Cervantes continuously makes ironic and comical allusions to the book by the mysterious Avellaneda, thus transforming it into material for his own story.

Don Quixote is only one of the many spectacular examples of books that, through their physical form and textual identity, crossed space and were the object of multiple appropriations. Over time, they were read in various ways, but they nevertheless formed the basis of a common culture. Other works include legal corpuses and their glosses, both before and after Gutenberg; Vesale's *De humani corporis fabrica*, which authorized and legitimized the dissection of corpses; and Vitruvius's *Ten Books of Architecture*, which were republished in Latin, translated into living languages, abbreviated, adapted and imitated. All of the above are magnificent examples of a sharing that knows no boundaries.

BIBLIOGRAPHY

Bouza, F., *Del escribano a la biblioteca. La civilización escrita europea en alta Edad Moderna (siglos xv xvii)*, Madrid, 1992.

Braida, L., *Stampa e cultura in Europa tra xv e xvi secolo*, Rome, 2000.

Eisenstein, E., *The Printing Revolution in Early Modern Europe*, Cambridge, 1983.

Febvre, L., H.-J. Martin, *L'Apparition du livre*, Paris, 1958, reprinted, 1999.

Füssel, S., *Gutenberg und seine Wirkung*, Frankfurt, 1999.

Hirsch, R., *Printing, Selling and Reading 1450–1550, Wiesbaden, 1967.*

Johns, A., *The Nature of the Book. Print and Knowledge in the Making*, Chicago, 1998.

McKitterick, D., *Print, Manuscript, and the Search for Order 1450–1830*, Cambridge, 2003.

Martin, H.-J., *Histoire et pouvoirs de l'écrit*, Paris, 1988, republ., 1996.

Petrucci, A. (ed.), *Libri, scrittura e pubblico nel Renascimento*, Rome-Bari, 1979.

Princely collections and art museums north of the Alps

(16–18th centuries)

KRZYSZTOF POMIAN

The museum was, until the 17th century, an Italian institution. This remained true even longer for the art museum, which only made its appearance north of the Alps in the first decades of the 18th century, and with a different orientation than its southern counterpart. Indeed, the passion for collecting – sparked by the discovery of engraved gems and ancient coins – split into two distinct camps starting in the 15th century. One of these, more Italian and scholarly, favoured antiquities, while the other, more Nordic and princely, preferred paintings. Nevertheless, the two trends influenced each other, similar to Italian and Northern painting.[1] In Italy, the Medici and the Farnese balanced the two, although various generations and individuals displayed quite different tastes. However, the Gonzaga family of Mantua and the House of Este of Ferrara and later Modena, both of whom collected a great many antiquities, became well known as collectors, particularly due to their galleries of paintings.[2]

THE CIRCULATION OF WORKS: ANTIQUITIES AND PAINTINGS

In the transalpine countries, where paintings took pride of place, antiquities were also objects of desire. Frances I, king of France (1515), had 125 ancient sculptures brought to Fontainebleau, as well as casts of a great many more, including several statues from the Belvedere, in order to make copies in bronze – and this was just the initial delivery.[3] Albert V, the Duke of Bavaria as of 1550, amassed a sizeable collection of antiquities that had been purchased in Augsburg from Johann Jakob Fugger as well as in Italy, particularly in Venice. He displayed it in the Residence in Munich in a specially built room that was dubbed the Antiquarium.[4] Among his contemporaries, Maximilian II, who became emperor in 1564, was particularly interested in antiquities. The antique dealer Jacopo Strada worked on the emperor's behalf, as well as for Albert V. Maximilian's successor, Rudolf II (1576–1612), was a compulsive collector whose chateau in Prague contained quite a large number of ancient sculptures, both originals and copies.[5]

Later, Thomas Howard, Earl of Arundel, had a series of ancient marbles brought to England from Italy, Greece and Asia Minor. These became famous because they included the Parian Chronicle.[6] Arundel appeared to have inspired Richelieu as well as Mazarin, who served as an apprentice in Rome.[7] And this brings to a close the list of great collectors of ancient statuary north of the Alps prior to the 1720s, a period in which antiquities came to the forefront.

Until this date, princes and other eminent figures were far more interested in paintings than antiquities. The example was set from above. Charles V of Spain, though not a collector, expressed his preferences for paintings,[8] and his son Philip II assembled an extraordinary collection that he displayed particularly in the Escorial.[9] In Prague, Charles's cousin, Rudolf II, amassed a collection that was similarly impressive in terms of size, but whose artistic orientation was different.[10] Rudolf's collection was extremely influential, as it launched the fashion of collecting paintings, both in Prague itself[11] and elsewhere, both within the Empire and in other central European countries.[12]

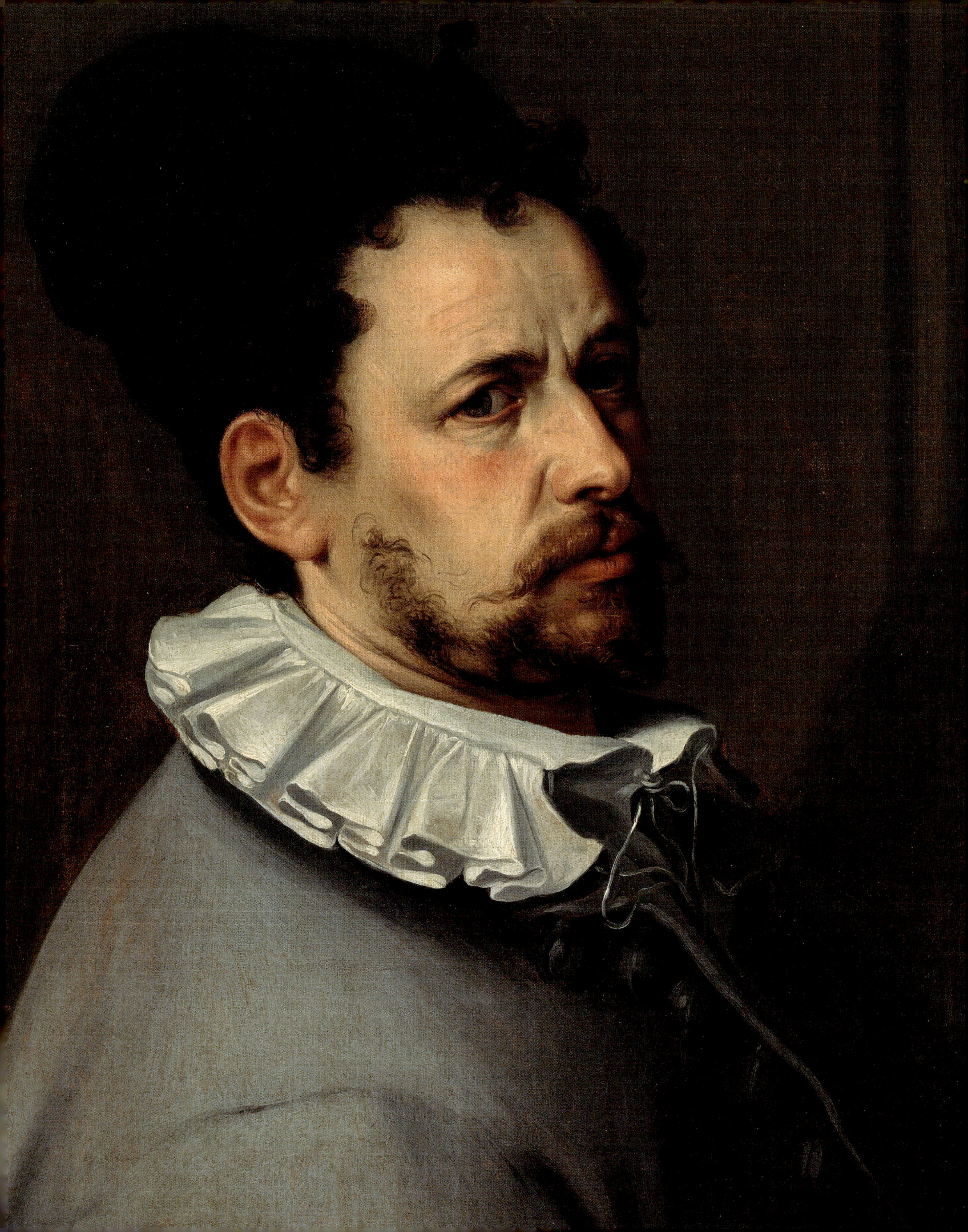

The sack of Prague in 1648 by Swedish troops resulted in the arrival of a great number of paintings in Stockholm; this was the origin of the collection of Queen Christina. She took possession of Italian paintings, and after she abdicated the throne in 1654, she brought them with her to Rome when she moved there in the following year. Once there, she added paintings and drawings to her collection. After her death, the paintings were sold almost in their entirety to Philippe II, Regent of France (1715–23); they ended up in England and a number of other countries. The drawings were also dispersed.[13]

Under Philip IV, whose reign began in 1621, the size of the Spanish royal court's collection went from 1500 to 4500 paintings. This inspired desires for collecting both within the Spanish aristocracy and among other European princes.[14] It was on a visit to Madrid in 1623 that Charles I, the Stuart king of England, Scotland and Ireland, who ascended to the throne in 1625, perfected his training as a collector that had begun under the tutelage of the Earl of Arundel and the Duke of Buckingham. Driven by a passion for paintings, the king managed, in the space of fourteen years (1624–38), to assemble a collection that would become legendary. In particular, he did so by purchasing several paintings from the collection of the Gonzaga family of Mantua.[15]

The English Civil War in the mid-17th century resulted in the partial or complete dispersion of several aristocratic collections on the international market. Thus it was that Archduke Leopold Wilhelm, governor of the Spanish Netherlands (1647–56), was able to purchase the collections of the Dukes of Buckingham and Hamilton: in all, more than 400 works, including several masterpieces (Section XIII).[16] After Charles I had been tried and sentenced to death, his art collection, which had been confiscated along with his entire estate, was put up for auction in October 1649 by parliamentary decree. The sale, which lasted until January 1654, has been recounted in detail by Jonathan Brown, in a book from which we have taken all of our information on the topic. Suffice it to say here that this 'sale of the century' (Brown's expression) was, as he amply demonstrates, one of the most significant events in the history of the circulation of works of art in Europe. The great foreign collectors, in particular the Spanish and the French, did not attend the sale itself. In an effort to remain behind the scenes, they purchased works acquired by English buyers and acted through intermediaries. It was in this way that Luis de Haro, the King of Spain's chief minister from 1643 onwards, Cardinal Mazarin and the Parisian banker Everhard Jabach took possession of prize pieces from Charles I's collection, the sale of which redistributed a total of 1410 paintings amongst several European capitals, where many of them still remain. In particular, the Louvre and the Prado house many of the collection's *membra disjecta*.[17]

In the rivalry to take possession of these paintings, which was so fierce that it caused those involved to carry on regardless of hatred for the rebels and compassion for the king who had been expropriated and beheaded, the French monarchy was for a long time conspicuous by its absence.[18] None of François I's successors had a collector's temperament. It must be admitted that they had had other, more pressing concerns: the Wars of Religion, which had begun in 1562 and would not end until 1598. In all, Henri IV would know only a dozen years of peace. Louis XIII, although the son of a Medici, had not inherited his ancestors' interest in collections, and his entourage, with a few rare exceptions, were incapable of taking this path. But although the King was not drawn to either paintings or antiquities, his chief minister Cardinal Richelieu collected both, as well as various objects of curiosity. His 272 paintings did not give him a very high ranking on a European scale, but he was France's principal collector, and he set an example.[19]

His successor, Cardinal Mazarin, amassed one Europe's greatest collections: sculpture, paintings, furniture, tapestries, *objets d'art* – he collected everything, and by the hundreds. In Italy, the cardinal purchased antiquities, modern sculptures, gemstones, gold and silver plate, and paintings.

< BARTHOLOMAEUS SPRANGER, *Self-portrait*, 1580s (Cat. XIII.26)

In Brussels and England he bought tapestries; he received donations and enriched his collection from the spoils of war. In January 1649, during the Fronde, Mazarin was sentenced to banishment by the Parlement of Paris. Shortly thereafter, a second decree ordered the sale of his collections. The furniture was first to go. Three years later, his library and antiquities went under the gavel. The losses were heavy, but most of the paintings were saved, as well as the statuary. Starting in 1653, Mazarin acquired paintings from Charles I's collection that had been purchased by English buyers, and others from private collections. In this way, he took possession of several masterpieces and enlarged his collection of tapestries. When he died, he left only a fraction of what he had assembled to the King. Colbert, who had been Mazarin's right-hand man before becoming Controller-General of Finances (1661) and Superintendent of Buildings (1664), purchased a dozen tapestries, seventeen paintings and some thirty busts, figures and vases for the King. Later, more objects from the same source would rejoin the royal collections.[20]

ART COLLECTIONS: FROM PRINCELY PLEASURES TO AFFAIRS OF STATE

Although he was nominally king of France starting in 1643, Louis XIV's personal reign only began after the death of Mazarin. When the king's uncle, Gaston, Duke of Orleans, died a year later in February 1660, he left Louis his collection of drawings on vellum of birds and plants, as well as his collections of medallions, engraved gemstones and other antiquities. This was, as Antoine Schnapper has shown, the act that re-established the royal collections after more than a century of decline.[21] Enriched by both gifts and purchases after the death of Mazarin, they expanded rapidly under Colbert. Although, when Louis XIV ascended to the throne 'nearly all of his meagre collection of paintings were to be found at Fontainebleau', assembled for the most part by François I, 'by the time the court moved to Versailles, the king possessed nearly 400 paintings, i.e. a tenfold increase in twenty years' time ...'. Acquisitions of paintings and antiquities continued at an even faster pace until 1685, and came to a halt in 1695.[22] Was this because the King was getting older, or because the country had entered a period of major financial difficulties caused by the cost of the war, or both? Let us leave this question unanswered.

It is of secondary importance to understand the extent to which Louis XIV was a true lover of paintings and antiquities, or in what measure the acquisition of such treasures, aside from their decorative value, were part of a policy of prestige that required, for reasons of state, that the King be first in everything.[23] The crucial change that took place during his reign was something quite different. Under Louis XIV, the acquisition of paintings and antiquities was elevated to the rank of an accepted component of state policy. Starting with Colbert, such purchases were made in the name of the King, and were part of the remit of the Superintendent of Buildings; this was not the case when works of art were purchased by Richelieu or Mazarin, no matter how great their power was.[24] 'In the name of the king' specifically meant 'in the name of the State'. Louis XIV, perhaps more than any other monarch of his time, was aware that he was not only a physical being, but also something much greater: the personification of France.

In practice, this meant that painting and antiquities – like the books in the Royal Library and the natural history collections tended by the Academy of Sciences – were overseen by a specialized government office. Le Brun's 1683 inventory is the earliest inventory of the royal painting collection to have survived, and probably the first ever to have been created. It was drawn up for purely fortuitous reasons: the death of Colbert and the transfer of the Superintendency of Buildings to Louvois. Other inventories would soon follow, starting with that of Nicolas Bailly (1709–10), which listed more than 1500 paintings, three times as many as in Le Brun's time.[25] This is proof that the royal collections were expanded, even though Louis XIV, as we have seen, lost interest after 1695. In particular, they were enriched via commissioning of living painters, and also, but more rarely, by purchases at auction. Henceforth, officials were entrusted to make sure that masterpieces of the arts were represented in the King's collections. Such purchases were limited by budgetary constraints, and the acquisition of old paintings was not a priority. As a result, many works left the country during the 18th century. The fact remains, however, that from the time of Louis XIV onwards, a royal collection of paintings and antiquities existed in France, not as an expression of the king's pleasure but as a stable institution, and one that was becoming separate from his person. Barely thirty years after the death of Louis XIV, La Font de Saint-Yenne asked his successor to publicly exhibit the royal painting collection in a gallery of the Louvre. In other words, he asked that this collection be made into an art museum.

This request would be granted. A total of ninety-nine paintings and twenty drawings from the royal collection were installed in the east wing of the Palais du Luxembourg, whose west wing contained the Marie de Medici gallery, created by Peter Paul Rubens. Starting in October 1750, both wings were open to the public on Wednesdays and Saturdays for three hours: in the morning in the winter, and in the afternoon in the summer. A printed guide was available.[26] Until it was closed in 1779, the Palais du Luxembourg was thus a painting museum in the strict sense of the term. It is all the more strange that the word 'museum' seemed never to have been used in reference to it. The fact remains that, along with the Galerie d'Orléans, which had served as a museum in Paris since the 1720s (there was a printed description and the Galerie seems to have been easily accessible[27]) the Palais du Luxembourg represented a third type of art museum. The other two types were the museum of antiquities (Venice, Verona) and the gallery that displayed both a collection of antiquities and art works that were created after the 'renaissance of the arts', i.e. after Raphael. The Uffizi is the best example of such a museum, and the Capitol was another, after a gallery of paintings was installed in it in 1749.

The concomitant evolution in the status of art and the model of what was a gentleman was a European phenomenon: it began in Italy in the 16th century, was extended in Spain, and developed in France. In the 18th century, it resulted in the creation of a relatively large public that was interested in painting, sculpture and antiquities. Before this, however, it had stimulated the assembly of art collections in all of the princely courts. This had begun in several countries in the mid-16th century, before being interrupted by civil and foreign conflicts: thus in Spain, as we have seen, whose nobility served as a model for the French nobility, just as the artistic policy of its kings had influenced that of Louis XIV. In England, the roots of the royal collection went back to Henry VIII, but it was under Charles I that a new attitude towards art found its first converts among the aristocracy. The propagation of this new view, which was interrupted by the English Civil War (1642–60), returned under the Restoration in a cultural climate that was marked by French influence. Charles II, who ascended to the throne in 1660, began to rebuild the royal painting collection. It was expanded considerably in the 18th century, thanks to several exceptional acquisitions, in particular the purchase in 1762 of some 500 paintings from Joseph Smith, the British consul in Venice.[28]

The rapid increase in England's wealth following the Glorious Revolution of 1688 meant a great many more English visitors to the Continent, especially in Italy, and a corresponding increase in the number of collections of antiquities in country houses[29], while paintings became an indispensable component in the lifestyle of the well-to-do: Venetian painters prospered through a great number of commissions[30], and paintings were imported in ever-increasing numbers. In the second half of the 18th century, an English school of painting became established, and the Royal Academy was founded in 1768.[31]

By the end of the 18th century, England had become the centre of the European art market. Large quantities of paintings flowed in, primarily from France – the Orléans collection was being sold in London – as well as from Italy and Spain, both of which had been torn apart by revolution and the Napoleonic wars.[32]

Sweden, which for a century had been one of the leading European powers, was also a player on the art scene, except that the Swedish kings added to their collections through war. Gustav Vasa created the royal painting collection, which was enlarged during the Thirty Years' War. After the fall of

Munich in 1632, Gustavus Adolphus brought back to Sweden whatever books and paintings that Maximilian I, Duke and Elector of Bavaria, had not been able to hide away. In 1648, after the Swedish army had taken Prague, the collections of Rudolf II also made their way to Stockholm. Even if Christina had taken the collection's Italian paintings when she left Sweden for Rome, what remained was a quite rich collection, which was further augmented by conquests in Denmark and Poland. Other collectors could be found in the King's entourage: his generals knew how to make the best of their victories.

Sweden ceased to be a European power after its defeat at the hands of Russia at the Battle of Poltava (1709). After this point, the royal collection was expanded via acquisitions. Specialists in artistic matters emerged, who had been so lacking during the reign of Christina, who had been obliged to appoint her tailor to the position of keeper of the royal collections. The royal painting collection reflected current tastes thanks to purchases in Paris and Italy. Gustav III returned from Rome with a collection of antiquities and the desire to create a museum, which opened its doors in June 1792, shortly before his death.[33]

In the late 17th century, under Peter the Great, collections in line with the rest of Europe also appeared at the court in Moscow. Peter, however, was mainly interested in natural history; it was Catherine II, who reigned from 1762 onwards, who developed the court's collections via a wide-ranging acquisitions policy. Boatloads of paintings, sculptures, antiquities, drawings and engravings arrived in Russia, not to mention the engraved gemstones of which she was so fond. It is Catherine II who may be called the real founder of the Hermitage, but this building did not become a museum in the full sense of the term until the mid-19th century.[34] Stanislas August Poniatowski (king of Poland from 1764–95) had assembled a gallery of paintings, with the idea of giving them to the nation in the form of a museum. However, the third partition of Poland and his death put an end to this project, and the works of art that he had assembled were dispersed.[35] In the lands of the Holy Roman Empire, the collections of the emperor himself and those of several princes were sometimes founded on treasures from the Middle Ages, and sometimes on 16th-century *Kunst-* and *Wunderkammern* (art and curiosity collections). During this period, some also collected paintings and antiquities (Section XIV). We have already spoken of the Antiquarium in the Residenz of the Dukes of Bavaria in Munich; a 1598 inventory of the Wittelsbach collection listed 3407 objects of all sorts, including 778 paintings, most of them portraits. Among these were works by German painters of the first half of the 16th century: Dürer, Altdorfer, Cranach and Holbein, among others, although the inventory does not list their names, assembled under Albert V. These became part of the gallery of Maximilian I, a passionate collector of paintings, and many of them are still part of the Bavarian collections.[36]

The Thirty Years' War was a time of devastation and losses, and it put a stop to the expansion of the German princely collections for a long time. There was, however, an exception to this: the Habsburg collection. Although it experienced severe losses in 1648, it was expanded through the acquisitions of Archduke Leopold Wilhelm, who, when he returned to Vienna from Brussels in 1656, brought his painting collection with him **XIII.39-43**. He installed it on the first floor of the royal stables – the Stallburg. It should be pointed out to the modern reader that this was an excellent location for the collection: it was heavily protected against fire and theft, and the temperature was more or less constant thanks to the building's thick walls.

With the exception of the Habsburgs, it was only in the final decades of the 17th century that the German princes began once again to expand their collections. The successive wars after 1688 did not always spare German lands, but they rarely attained the level of horror of the first half of the century. Conditions were thus more favourable to commissions and acquisitions. After the Treaty of Utrecht and the Seven Years' War (1756–63), these reached their first peak, and the trend continued in the 1770s. It was driven by powerful psychological motivations, in which the love of art, sometimes quite genuine, interfered with issues of prestige and political motives.

TOWARDS PUBLIC ACCESSIBILITY

A number of German princes travelled to Italy and visited Versailles, and they dreamed of recreating their own Versailles in order to play the part of Louis XIV. They were aware that the protection afforded to the arts was an instrument that allowed them to establish themselves on the international scene, and to enjoy a European renown that could be useful, if the circumstances were right. Thus, they brought Italian and French painters and architects to their courts to serve as artistic advisers. They maintained envoys and agents in both France and Italy. Finally, they simultaneously extended and modernized their collections, which, in the late 17th century, had kept their character of *Wunderkammern*. This modernization consisted of separating out various classes of objects and, above all, in developing two areas that hitherto had not been central to the collection – paintings and antiquities.[37]

For example, Frederick Augustus I, elector of Saxony from 1694 and king of Poland (under the name Augustus II the Strong) from 1697, took a personal interest in his collection. In 1718, he began to divide his encyclopaedic collection into groups of similar objects: paintings, ancient and modern sculptures, porcelain, precious objects, natural artifacts, etc. Inventories of the collection began four years later.[38] At the same time, he instituted an acquisitions policy that was unmatched in Europe, and that was carried out unceasingly until the Seven Years' War. In 1699, the king purchased his first painting; in 1722, the inventory of his paintings had 3500 entries. Beginning in 1717, Augustus also became interested in antiquities; eleven years later, in Rome, he succeeded in purchasing the Chigi collection, as well as that of Cardinal Albani. Under his successor, Frederick Augustus II, elector of Saxony from 1733 and king of Poland (under the name Augustus III), antiquities were relegated to secondary importance, while the acquisition of paintings was carried out on an unprecedented scale, culminating in the 1746 purchase of one hundred masterpieces from the Duke of Modena's gallery for the incredible sum of 100,000 sequins (Venetian gold coins).[39]

Saxony's artistic policy was particularly flamboyant thanks to revenues from the kingdom of Poland; the Saxon princes possessed means not found elsewhere. Elsewhere in Germany, it was not exceptional, but collections of paintings were assembled in several principalities. The pioneer in this effort seems to have been Anton Ulrich, who was governor of the duchy of Brunswick-Wolffenbüttel from 1666, and its duke from 1704. His collection of some ninety paintings was first displayed in the inhabited section of the chateau of Salzdahlum, which he had built between 1688 and 1694. After 1701, they were installed in a specially built gallery adjacent to the main building; this was the first structure of its kind in Germany. Anton Ulrich was evidently concerned that his merits as an art connoisseur and collector be known: during his lifetime, at least four publications were dedicated to his coin collection, his paintings, and his chateau with its furnishings.[40]

Johann Wilhelm von der Pfalz, one of Anton Ulrich's contemporaries, reigned as elector palatine from 1690 to 1716, while maintaining close relations with Italy – he had married Anne Marie Louise de Medici. He purchased paintings in Antwerp as well; his collection totalled some 340 works, and in 1711 he had them displayed in a gallery built to house them.[41] At Schleissheim, Maximilian II Emanuel, elector of Bavaria from 1679 until his death in 1726, had a new chateau built adjacent to the old one, where he placed the paintings that he had purchased when he was governor of the Spanish Netherlands.[42] In Hesse-Kassel, Charles I, landgrave from 1677 to 1730, became interested in paintings, but it was his son, Wilhelm VIII, who was a true collector, and on a large scale. Once in power in Hesse after 1720, he purchased paintings on behalf of his brother Frederick, who had married the queen of Sweden, and who had served in the military for the Swedish Estates-General. In particular, Wilhelm bought paintings in the United Provinces, but also in Paris. Around 1750, he had more than 500, not including portraits, and the collection was of very high quality. A gallery was completed in 1751 that allowed him to display them.[43]

Prussia was the last of the German states to take its place on the artistic scene, but Frederick the Great, who reigned from 1740 to 1786, rapidly proved to be a very active participant. In 1742, he purchased the famous collection of Cardinal de Polignac, which brought about the reorganization of the old *Kunstkammer*.[44] He continued, on a much larger scale, the acquisitions that he had begun in the mid-1730s, when still heir to the throne. His agents were present on the Paris market, where they first began collecting contemporary French painting; starting in 1750, Frederick became interested in Italian painting of the 16th and 17th centuries. In 1755, he began the construction of a gallery; the project was interrupted by the Seven Years' War, and was only completed in 1763. At that time, the Sans-Souci gallery contained 146 paintings; ten years later they numbered 172, and the various palaces held more than 600. For all that, Frederick did not neglect antiquities: in 1761, he purchased the Baron de Stosch's collection of engraved gemstones, which was as celebrated a collection in its field as that of the Cardinal de Polignac in that of ancient sculpture.

Leaving aside the King's personal convictions, what matters to us is that Frederick the Great understood very well the new phenomenon of public opinion, particularly French public opinion. As a consequence, he strove to make sure that he was seen as a philosopher-king, and a lover of literature, the sciences and the arts. The fact that such an image corresponded in large part to reality does not render it less efficient as a political instrument. Frederick surrounded himself with great men; for three years, Voltaire was a guest of the court. He also received Algarotti, Maupertuis and a number of figures of lesser stature. For the same reasons, his acquisitions were widely publicized and his collections were described in 1764, a year before those in Dresden. This was certainly not the first time that a German prince had published a description of his gallery of paintings. However, Frederick's appeared after a twenty-year interruption in such publications, and it would be followed by others.

Saxony, the Italian models, Paris's Palais du Luxembourg, and the British Museum, which was well known in Germany – in the last third of the 18th century, all of these examples began to be emulated. An antiquities gallery was opened in Mannheim in 1769; those unable to see the originals in Italy could admire casts of the most famous ancient statues, which had hitherto been known only through engravings. It functioned like a real ancient art museum, and its importance is attested to by the visits paid by the greatest names in German culture of the time: Goethe, Lessing and Schiller. Ten years later, an event of equal stature took place in Kassel with the opening of the Museum Fridericianum. This specially constructed building was the very first of its kind – in Italy, interior spaces were only adapted for the purpose of displaying art. The Kassel museum, which was primarily a museum of antiquities, shared the building with a library and a natural history collection; in this, it was similar to the example of the Institute of Bologna. Its originality was no less great: it was built in a central square in the city, and was opened to the public. During the same period in Kassel, the painting gallery was given a visitors' book in 1775, which meant that they were henceforth welcome. The 1783 publication of a catalogue indicates that this part of the collections had become accessible to a much wider circle.

As it turned out, paintings were enjoying a heyday just about everywhere. Starting in 1780 in Vienna, the public could visit the newly installed gallery in the Belvedere, to which the Habsburg paintings were moved from the Stallburg, as had been ordered by Empress Maria Theresa (1717–80) four years earlier. This collection, which was already one of the richest in Europe, had recently (1775) been still further enriched; following the suppression of the Society of Jesus (1773), a number of paintings, including several large canvases by Rubens and Van Dyck, made their way to Vienna from Belgium, where they had been removed from former Jesuit churches and colleges. Joseph II (1741–90), Holy Roman Emperor as of 1765, had entrusted the arrangement of this new gallery to Christian von Mechel (1735–1817), an engraver and merchant from Basle, who published a catalogue of the collection in 1783.[45]

Also in 1780, in Munich this time, the public was able to view some 700 paintings in the newly erected Hofgartengalerie; some of these works of art came from Mannheim in 1778 with Karl Theodor von der Pfalz, who had become elector of Bavaria the previous year. The rest of the collection came from the chateau of Schleissheim and other residences of the royal family. The catalogue was published in 1787.[46] It was Bavaria, along with Saxony and Hesse, which offered the best example of progressive change in the status of princely German collections, including those of paintings. In effect, while remaining private in the legal sense, they were slowly transformed into museums, and were symbolically appropriated by the public long before this shift was sanctioned by law.

As for art museums that existed outside Italy and the Holy Roman Empire during the final decades of the 18th century, the list is a short one. In The Hague, William v, prince of Orange, opened his gallery of paintings to the public in 1774. It consisted of some 200 paintings, mainly by Dutch artists. No prior introduction was needed to visit it, and it was open several hours a day.[47] And let us not forget the art museums in several French cities,[48] which were hard to clearly distinguish from local history museums. At Besançon, the remains of the collection of the Perrenot de Granvelle family, which had been famous in the 16th century, was gathered up by the scholar Jean-Baptiste Boisot. At his death, Boisot left them to the Benedictine monks of the Saint Vincent monastery, where he had been *abbé commendataire.*[49] In Arles, where interest in antiquities had been a subject of interest since the late 17th century, a collection of Gallo-Roman vestiges in the courtyard of the Minimes convent was opened to the public in 1784.[50] In Nimes, Jean-François Séguier, a well-known scholar, left his collection (which included antiquities) to the city on the condition that it be opened to the public three days a week. In 1785, a plaque placed on his private residence, where the collection was located, presented the site as the 'Séguier House and Nimes Museum'.[51]

The situation was much clearer in Toulouse. In 1751, the city's art school had been awarded the privilege of calling itself the Royal Academy of Painting, Sculpture and Architecture. From this year on, and for forty years, the Academy organized annual exhibitions of paintings from its own collection and from the city's private collections, whose owners were exhorted to fulfil, 'in loaning their treasures, the duties of a patriot and those of the true lover of art'.[52] This was, as we would call it today, a prefiguration of a museum; several American museums got their start in such a manner. Another indisputable art museum was born in Dijon, in the wake of a drawing school that had been set up in 1766 by the Estates of Burgundy, on the initiative of François Desvoge. The school built its collection through purchases and donations, as well as with the prize-winning work of its pupils. In 1775, again at the initiative of Desvoge, the Estates of Burgundy instituted two Rome Prizes, one for sculpture and one for painting. The winners were obliged to make copies of famous paintings and masterpieces of ancient sculpture. The school's museum, which was created by order of the Estates in 1787, was thus mainly filled with copies.[53]

Our survey of the situation has led us to an unexpected conclusion: on the eve of the French Revolution, with the single exception of Vienna, the art museum was absent from the capital cities of the great powers who would decide the destiny of Europe. It was absent from Madrid, which had, it must be admitted, ceased to be the capital of a great power. It was not to be found in London, Berlin or St Petersburg. And it was no longer in evidence in Paris, where the Luxembourg museum closed its doors in 1778, and where the works required to open the Louvre museum, though well advanced, were far from reaching completion.

This geography of the European art museum in the closing years of the 18th century is all the more interesting when compared with that of the natural history museum. This institution was present in all of the major capitals with the exception of Berlin, where, up until 1805, the Kunst- und Naturalienkammer was not a museum in the same sense as the British Museum or the Cabinet du Jardin des Plantes. Though not easy to explain, such a distribution of art museums nevertheless forces us to abandon the idea that draws a direct causal link between 'museum' and 'Enlightenment'. Although the European capitals of the Enlightenment – Paris and London were the first to endow themselves with natural history museums, when it came to art museums, they were outstripped by much more conservative cities, such as Vienna.

Of course, there was the case of the Luxembourg museum in Paris, which was in operation for twenty-eight years, and which probably served as a model for other establishments created at the same time, albeit only after it had closed. The fact remains that it was a false start, and that the French monarchy did not manage to create an art museum that lasted. It is also a fact that in Great Britain this was not even attempted. Finally, there is the fact that, with the exception of Vienna, the cities that hosted art museums at the end of the 18th century were capitals of small states (small compared to Prussia, let alone France) or provincial capitals like Toulouse and Dijon. And many of these also boasted natural history collections that were open to the public.

1 See Bernard Aikema, Beverly Louise Brown (eds), *il Rinascimento a Venezia e la pittura del Nord ai tempi di Bellini, Dürer, Tiziano*, Palazzzo Grassi, Venice (exhib. cat.), 1999, with discussions of the artistic and intellectual exchanges between North and South.

2 For the Gonzaga, see David Chambers, Jane Martineau (eds), *Splendours of the Gonzaga*, Victoria and Albert Museum, London (exhib. cat.), Milan, 1981. For the House of Este, recently published, Jadranka Bentini (ed.), *Sovrane Passioni. Le raccolte d'arte della Ducale Galleria Estense*, Galleri a Estense, Modena (exhib. cat.), Milan, 1998.

3 Vasari, VII, 407 Milanesi. See also André Chastel, 'Fontainebleau formes et symboles', in *L'Ecole de Fontainebleau*, Grand Palais, Musées Nationaux (exhib. cat.), Paris, 1972, pp. XIII–XXVIII; here, pp. XVII–XVIII.

4 See Heike Frosien-Leinz, 'Das Antiquarium der Residenz: erstes Antikenmuseum Münchens', in Klaus Vierneisel, Gottlieb Leinz (eds), *Glyptothek München 1830–1980*, Glyptothek, Munich (exhib. cat.), 1980, pp. 310–21. Friedrich Wilhelm Hamdorf, 'Du "theatrum mundi" à la glorification des ducs de Bavière', in Annie-France Laurens, K. Pomian (eds), *L'Anticomanie. La collection d'antiquités aux 18e et 19e siècle*, Paris, 1992, pp. 39–48.

5 See *Festschrift des Kunsthistorischen Museums zur Feier des fünfzigjährigen Bestandes*, vol. 2, Alphons Lossky, *Die Gechichte der Sammlungen*, Vienna, 1941–1945, pp. 158 et seq., 242 et seq., 277, 290

6 See Adolf Michaelis, *Ancient Marbles in Great Britain*, Cambridge, 1882.

7 See Patrick Michel, *Mazarin, prince des collectionneurs*, Paris, 1999, pp. 22 et seq., 56-7, and on the arrival of antiquities: Luigi Beschi, 'Collezioni dell'arte greca in Italia', Il Veltro, 27, 1983, pp. 253–66, and Irena Favaretto, *Arte antica e cultura antiquaria nelle collezioni venete al tempo della Serenissima*, Rome, 1990, pp. 158 et seq.

8 See Fernando Checa, *Tiziano y la monarquia hispanica. Usos y funciones de la pintura veneciana en España (siglos XVI y XVII)*, Madrid, 1994, p. 197 et seq.

9 See F. Checa, *Felipe II mecenas de las artes*, Madrid, 1992, pp. 97 et seq., 406 et seq.

10 See Robert John Weston Evans, *Rudolf II and his World: A Study in Intellectual History, 1576–1612*, Oxford, 1973. Thomas DaCosta Kaufman, *Variations on the Imperial Theme in the Age of Maximilian II and Rudolf II*, New York, London, 1978.

11 See Lubomír Slavíček (ed), *Artis pictoriae amatores. Evropa v zrcadle pražkého barokního sběratelství*, Národní Galerie, Prague (exhib. cat.), 1993.

12 See Thomas DaCosta Kaufmann, *Court, Cloister and City. The Art and Culture of Central Europe 1450–1800*, London, 1995. It is likely

that the example of Rudolf II played a role in the formation of the collection of Sigismund III Vasa (1566–1632), king of Poland (1587), and of his two sons and successors to the Polish throne, Ladislas IV (1595–1648) and Jean-Casimir (1609–1672). Under Jean-Casimir, the collection included 150 paintings and 25 portraits. It was sold at auction in Paris in 1673. See Ryszard Szmydki (ed.), *Vente du mobilier de Jean-Casimir en 1673*, Warsaw, 1995, p. 36 in particular.

13 See *Christina Queen of Sweden, a Personality in European Civilization* (exhib. cat.), Stockholm, 1966. S. Åkerman, *Queen Christina of Sweden and her Circle*, Leyden, 1991. J. Q. van Regteren Altena, *Les dessins italiens de la reine Christine de Suède*, Nationalmusei skriftserie 13, Stockholm, 1966.

14 See J. Brown, *Kings and Connoisseurs. Collecting Art in Seventeenth-Century Europe*, Princeton, 1995, pp. 97 et seq., 145. On the sale of Mantua Luzio and new publication.

15 Ibid., pp. 10 et seq. (Arundel, Buckingham, Hamilton, Charles I).

16 Ibid., pp. 160 et seq.

17 Ibid., 59 et seq.

18 On the history of the French royal collections see Arnauld Brejon de Lavergnée, *L'inventaire Le Brun de 1683. La collection des tableaux de Louis* XIV, Paris, 1987, preface by Antoine Schnapper and introduction by A. Brejon, pp. 40 et seq., and A. Schnapper, *Curieux du Grand Siècle. Collections et collectionneurs dans la France du XVIIe siècle*, Paris, pp. 285 et seq.

19 See Lizzie Boubli, 'Les collections parisiennes de peintures de Richelieu' and John Schloder, 'Richelieu mécène au château de Richelieu', in *Richelieu et le monde de l'esprit*, Sorbonne (exhib. cat.), Paris, 1985, pp. 103 et seq., 115 et seq., and on Richelieu's collection of antiquities: Marie Montembault, John Schloder, *L'album Canini du Louvre et la collection d'antiques de Richelieu*, Paris, 1988. Overall view: A. Schnapper, *Curieux du Grand Siècle*, pp. 125 et seq., 136 et seq.

20 See Patrick Michel, *Mazarin, prince des collectionneurs*, passim, and on objects placed in the royal collections pp. 314 et seq.

21 Cf. A Schnapper, *Curieux du Grand Siècle*, pp. 286, 296 et seq.

22 Ibid., pp. 289, 317, 327 et seq

23 This is the thesis of J. Brown, *Kings and Connoisseurs*, p. 225. The position of A. Schnapper is more nuanced. See *Curieux du Grand Siècle*, pp. 326 et seq., 346 ('collectionneur intermittent'). Also see A. Brejon, *L'inventaire Le Brun de 1683*, pp. 79 et seq.

24 See *Colbert 1619–1683* (exhib. cat.), Paris, 1983, ch. III, pp. 221 et seq., especially pp. 373 et seq.

25 See A. Brejon, *L'inventaire Le Brun de 1683*, pp. 30–33.

26 See Andrew MacClellan, *Inventing the Louvre. Art, Politics, and the Origins of the Modern Museum in Eighteenth-Century Paris*, Cambridge, 1994, pp. 13 et seq.

27 See Dubois de Saint-Gelais, *Description des tableaux du Palais Royal avec la vie des Peintres à la tête de leurs ouvrages*, Paris, 1727. On the conditions for admission, see La Font de Saint-Yenne, *L'Ombre du Grand Colbert...*, pp. 229 et seq.

28 See Christopher Lloyd, *The Queen's Pictures. Royal Collectors through the Centuries*, National Gallery, London, 1991 and Frances Vivian, *Il console Smith mercante e collezionista*, Vicenza, 1971, pp. 60 et seq. and the inventories of paintings pp. 173 et seq.

29 See Adolf Michaelis, *Ancient Marbles in Great Britain*, Cambridge, 1882, pp. 55 et seq.

30 See our 'Venise dans l'Europe artistique du XVIIIe siècle'.

31 See Iain Pears, *The Discovery of Painting. The Growth of Interest in the Arts in England, 1680–1768*, New Haven, London, 1988, particularly appendix 3, pp. 207 et seq. (importation of paintings between 1722 and 1774).

32 See William Buchanan, *Memoirs of Painting with a Chronological History of the Importation of Pictures by Great Masters into England since the French Revolution*, London, 1824, 2 vols. Hugh Brigstocke, *William Buchanan and the 19th Century Art Trade: 100 Letters to his Agents in London and Italy*, privately printed, 1982.

33 I offer here a broad outline of Per Bjurström's *Nationalmuseum 1792–1992*, Stockholm, 1992, pp. 8 et seq., 56 et seq.; see the English abstract.

34 See B. B. Piotrovski, *Istoria Ermitazha. Kratki otcherk. Materialy i dokumenty*, Moscow, 2000, especially p. 21 et seq., 127 et seq.

35 See K. Pomian, 'La collection de Stanislas Auguste et les origines du musée en Pologne', in Stéphane Loire et al. (eds), *Bernardo Bellotto. Un peintre vénitien à Varsovie*, Milan, 2004, p. 21–25.

36 See *Alte Pinakothek München. Erlaüterungen zu den ausgestellten Gemälden*, Munich, 1983, p. 583 Gisela Goldberg, 'Dürer Renaissance am Münchner Hof', in: Hubert Glaser (ed.), *Um Glauben und Reich. Kurfürst Maximilian I. Beiträge zur Bayerischen Geschichte 1573–1657*, Munich, 1980 (*Wittelsbach und Bayern*, II/1, pp. 318–22 and Peter Diemer, 'Die Gemäldesammlung in Maximilians Kammergalerie', *Ibid.*, II/2, pp. 500–01.

37 See Ruth and Max Seydewitz, *Die Dresdener Kunstschätze. Zur Geschichte des Grünen Gewölbes und der anderen Dresdener Kunstsammlungen*, Dresden, 1960, pp. 34–35. In Austria, the modernization of collections began under Charles VI (1685–1740, emperor in 1711). See Alphons Lhotsky, *Festschrift des kunsthistorischen Museums zur Feier des fünfzigjährigen Bestandes*, vol. 2, *Die Geschichte der Sammlungen*, Vienna, 1941–45, pp. 387 et seq.

38 See Werner Schmidt, 'Kolekcjonowanie dzieł sztuki w Dreźnie za panowania Augusta Mocnego i Augusta III', in *Pod jedną koroną. Królewskie zbiory sztuki w Dreźnie*, Muzeum Narodowe w Warszawie (exhib. cat.), Warsaw, 1997, pp. 25–34.

39 For antiquities see Martin Raumschüssel, 'Die Dresdener Sammlung antiker Skulpturen im 18. Jahrhundert', in Klaus Vierneisel, Gottlieb Lenze (eds), *Glyptothek München 1830–1980*, Glyptothek München (exhib. cat.), Munich, 1980, pp. 354–58, here, pp. 354–56. Heinz Protzmann, 'Zbiór antyków [The antiquities collection]', in *Pod jedną koroną*, pp. 37–38. For paintings, see the very complete article by Johannes Winkler, 'Storia di un acquisto straordinario', in: Johannes Winkler (ed.), *La vendita di Dresda*, Modena, 1989, pp. 27–57.

40 See A. Fink, *Geschichte des Herzog-Anton-Ulrich-Museums*, pp. 20 et seq., especially pp. 26, 30–1, 137 et seq.

41 See *Alte Pinakothek München*, pp. 581–2.

42 Ibid., p. 593.

43 See Georg Gronau, Erich Herzog, 'Geschichte der Galerie', in E. Herzog, *Die Gemäldegalerie der staatlichen Kunstsammlungen Kassel*, Cologne, 1969, pp. 12 et seq., 24, 40.

44 See Christian Theuerkauff, 'Zur Geschichte der Brandenburgisch-Preussische Kunstkammer bis gegen 1800', in Josephine Hildebrand, Ch. Theuerkauff, *Die Brandenburgisch-Preussische Kunstkammer. Eine Auswahl aus den alten Beständen*, Berlin, 1981, pp. 13–33; here, pp. 28 et seq.

45 See A. Lhotsky, *Die Geschichte der Sammlungen*, pp. 443 et seq.

46 See Hermann Bauer, 'Kunstanschauung und Kunstpflege in Bayern von Karl Theodor bis Ludwig I', in Hubert Glaser (ed.), *Krone und Verfassung. König Max I. Joseph und der neue Stadt. Beiträge zur bayerischen Geschichte und Kunst 1799–1825*, Munich, 1980 [Wittelsbach und Bayern, III/1], pp. 345–55; here p. 346 and note 9, p. 355. *Alte Pinakothek München, op. cit.*

47 See B. M. J. Brenninkmeyer-De Rooy, *Schilderijengalerij Prins Willem V. The Prince William V Gallery of Paintings*, The Hague, 1982, and for the history of the collection of the princes of Orange, H. R. Hoetink, *Mauritshuis. The Royal Cabinet of Paintings. Illustrated General Catalogue*, The Hague, 1977, pp. 7 et seq.

48 For everything concerning French provincial cities, see E. Pommier, 'La naissance des musées de province', in Pierre Nora (ed.), *Les Lieux de mémoire*, II *La Nation*, Paris, 1986, pp. 451–95. These references are to more recent publications.

49 Cf. *1694–1994: trois siècles de patrimoine public. Bibliothèques et musées de Besançon*, Musée des Beaux-Arts et d'Archéologie (exhib. cat.), Besançon, 1995, pp. 16–17 and E. Pommier, 'La place du "musée" Boisot dans la France et l'Europe du temps', in *Ibid.*, pp. 41–49.

50 See Dominique Serena-Allier (ed.), *Le goût de l'antique. Quatre siècles d'archéologie arlésienne*, Espace Van Gogh (exhib. cat.), Arles, 1990, pp. 39 et seq., especially 52 et seq.

51 See E. Pommier, 'La naissance des musées de province', p. 453.

52 Quoted from Pommier, 'La naissance des musées de province, p. 461.

53 See Emmanuel Starcky, Sophie Jugie (eds), *L'art des collections. Bicentenaire du Musée des Beaux-Arts de Dijon*, Musée des Beaux-Arts de Dijon (exhib. cat.), Dijon, 2000, especially pp. 91 et seq.

The Grand Tour

The European discovery of the work of art in Italy in the 17th and 18th centuries

PASCAL GRIENER

In the 17th and 18th centuries, the European Grand Tourist arriving at the Piazza del Popolo in Rome would breathe a sigh of relief. He would have evaded bandits in Romagna, and survived the bone-breaking mail coaches. The masterpieces of the Eternal City were within reach at last – the traveller knew them almost without ever having seen them, from handbooks pointing out what statues to admire, sketching a brief history of each, and finally deciphering their symbolic elements, duly referring to the history of the customs of antiquity. Contemplation of the artistic form was brief in those days. It was something done in society, and was food for polite conversation. Objects of antiquity were 'familiarized' by the evocation of a Latin verse, or by the recollection of an episode in ancient history – in short, such contemplation was reduced to book-derived culture, reinforced by convincing but unreliable facts.

Such practices continued to dominate at the end of the 17th century, but their implementation became problematic. Jacqueline Lichtenstein has shown brilliantly how the analysis of the picture as a process distinct from its literary description would only really come into its own with Roger de Piles. Before the 17th century, the difference between text and image was clearly characterized but this did not radically question the dogma of '*ut pictura poesis*' ('as is painting so is poetry'). The most elevated work of art was still expected to exhibit the structural equivalent of a text, even if this was through the qualities of the painting itself. Roger de Piles surmounted this obstacle. His impact was all the greater because he addressed himself mainly not to artists but to the connoisseur. From Roger de Piles and Lessing through to Giuseppe Guattani, various connoisseurs would succeed in envisaging the relationship between visual and literary culture in new terms. We should not forget, however, that most of their contemporaries would prefer to swear allegiance to a comfortable platitude, as Petity's *Manuel des artistes*, among others, proves.

The discovery of an artistic accomplishment that cannot be assigned to language is the symptom of a much wider and more complex phenomenon: the discovery of the experimental nature of observation made by a sensitive person, which writing must take into account in an organized manner. Appreciation of sculpture, particularly ancient sculpture, would have been a prime place for such a discovery in the 17th century.

In his *Geschichte der Kunst des Altertums* (1764), Johann Joachim Winckelmann teaches the art of understanding form. His lessons would be assimilated throughout Europe. Winckelmann suggested an approach involving organized observation, but enriched by, rather than being blinded by, erudition. For him, the observer must show himself capable of recognizing effects in order to derive pleasure from them, from a single detail to the work as a whole. He must know how to balance emotion and reason. At the end of the century, the Enlightenment traveller was keen to experience beauty for himself, in the very presence of the work. The result would be a real 'co-naissance', as Paul Claudel described it: the work is born in the very attention granted to it by a gaze. It enlightens, it moves, it transfigures the author of the gaze. Sculptures with an erotic dimension would then be favoured. Attraction towards a beautiful form distils more clearly the feelings of the onlooker – an attraction that is refined by dialogue with an analytical gaze armed with cultural references and formal criteria of judgment.

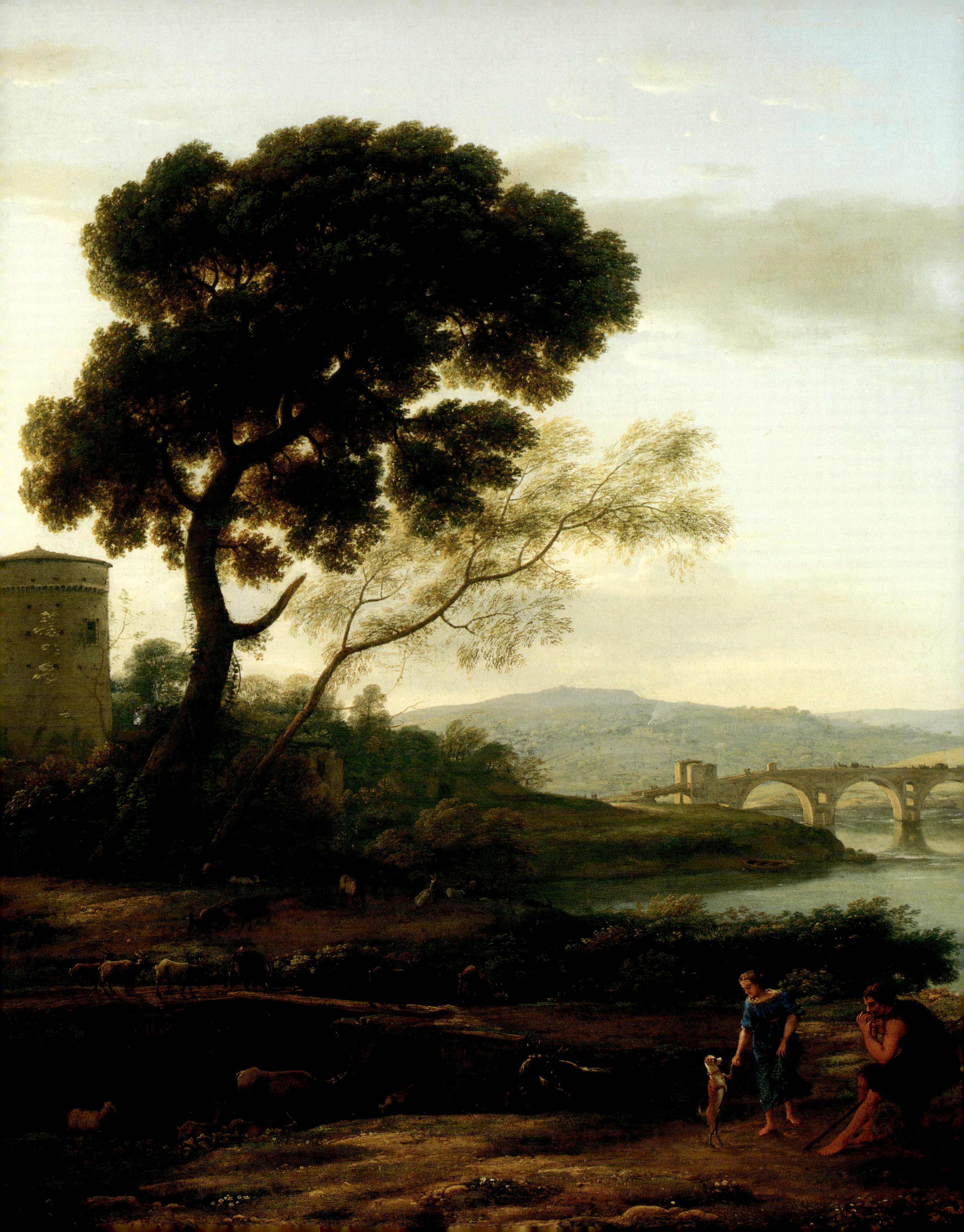

One of the major consequences of this new approach was the transformation of the literary exercise that should interpret it and record its results. Neither travels in Italy nor guides could provide the Grand Tourist with anything but a handy viewpoint indicator. When the observer encounters the work of art and stands in front of it, all the work is yet to be done. At the end of the 18th century, President (of the Bordeaux parliament) Dupaty was no longer content to refer to Richardson when he contemplated the Venus de'Medici at the Uffizi in Florence. He wanted to disclose how, and according to what laws, this work of art affected him. He conveys the build-up of emotion: 'I sat before her, pen in hand.' Dupaty admits the basic inequivalence between the work and any description that one might ever make of it: 'This is the fourth time that I have come to see her, and I still haven't seen her. I have been looking at her for two hours, and I can't stop looking at her. I wanted to be able to paint her and I can't even describe her. She still evades the brush, the chisel and the word. There is no language in the world that can model so many charms.' . This admission of powerlessness comes from a platitude – it had already been expressed at the end of the description of the Apollo of the Belvedere by Winckelmann, and was read throughout Europe: 'How to paint and describe him? Art itself should have helped me and led my hand to finish the lines I have just sketched. I place at his feet the image that I have made of this statue, like crowns from those who have not been able to reach the heads of the gods they wanted to crown.' This avowal has the same effect as the analogon in an epistemological manifesto. It signals the death of the 'ut pictura poesis', which had governed, since time immemorial, the relationship between the work of art and the literary description.

In a famous essay, Cesare Brandi reasserted that the work of art cannot be reduced to its message. This specific character of the work, he wrote, 'indicates a basic opposition between the constitution of presence that is the work of art as a simple reality and the transmission of information'. Brandi called the constitution of presence 'astanza' and the transmission of information 'semisosis'. 'If the perceived automatically refers to an object, it is no less true that the conscience possesses the object within. To detach the perceived from a direct representation of the object, the conscience only has to switch off the power uniting the perception to the object.' In the 18th century, this question would be treated as part of a debate on Allegory in art.

The encounter with the work is then that of a presence that throws the onlooker into a state of dumb-struck admiration. The visual work is constructed in artistic language that cannot be consigned to written words. Verbalization then becomes a truly infinite task. The presence of the work asserts itself all the more powerfully for the fact that it defies words to penetrate its secret. Here, too, the contemplation of a picture or of a statue arises out of a single moment in time – the here and now. Each person applies a particular gaze, an individual sensitivity. The task of the art writer then takes on quite a different dimension. It will be to model a sensitive approach able to inspire other future observers, without however substituting himself for their own responses. If possible, this approach should have a general educational quality, opening up the sensitivity of the readers to other discoveries. Practices will then be proposed to readers that demand to be tested and adopted. Even among antiquaries, obsessed by the historical uses of the object, the aesthetic subject will gradually take on due importance – they will gradually long, not only to know ancient history by its visual monuments, but also to feel all the beauty of a sculpted masterpiece. How can I check the accuracy of contemplation? And because it takes place almost always in a social context, how can I avoid the ridicule of a false sentiment, badly expressed, while preserving the originality of my observation? Will not I be mocked? A number of literary strategies testify to a realignment of the discourse regarding works of art. In 1691, one Maximilien Misson wrote his *Nouveau Voyage d'Italie*, which quickly became famous. After a second journey, Misson republished his

< CLAUDE LORRAIN, *Landscape with view of the Molle Bridge* (detail), 1645 (Cat XIII. 22)

guide and inserted numerous additions to the body of the text (these amendments are easy to spot because they are printed in italics). The reader has complete leisure to assess the accuracy of remarks that have been duly checked, weighed and corrected. The sensitive person will suddenly discover his body to be a perceptive piece of equipment, a producer of perceptions that can be amended by other perceptions. Thirty years later, President (of the Dijon parliament) Charles de Brosses wrote his *Lettres d'Italie*. The French parliamentarian offered a free account, supposedly authentic, of his feelings, for the benefit of his friends who remained in the country of his birth. This sophisticated report betrays the strong personality of its author. With the first letters, we notice that de Brosses frequently refers to the name Misson, even if he often criticises this author. The beginning of *Lettres* emphasizes their authentic character, grounded in real experience, and marking a permanent departure from previous dogma. When de Brosses arrived in Rome, the traveller was the victim of an *'acte manqué'* – a slip-up that turned out to be highly significant. De Brosses recounts that he had not hidden the second volume of the Misson guide very well in his luggage. He did know, however, that at the border with the Papal States, the government searched for any suspect printed matter. Sure enough, the customs men seized on the second volume of the *Voyage*, the one describing the city of Rome, and immediately confiscated the work. The author, a Protestant exile in England after the revocation of the Edict of Nantes, was on their blacklist. The president was now left to his own devices in the Eternal City, unable to follow in the footsteps of his great role model. This situation is a guarantee of freshness and authenticity. Sometimes, then, de Brosses looked for meaningful works of art for his own hesitant perceptions, even if he was to differ explicitly from them now and again; sometimes he tended to reject any piece in order to assert the fresh immediacy of his own relationship with it . The experience of the work of art would then often be exhibited as a triumph of direct perception as opposed to a perception mediated by artistic literature. This position is deceptive – it often conceals literary larcenies borrowed from all of European literature, even while seeming to forbid any borrowings from the eyes of others.

I will present here two cosmopolitan approaches, examples of sculpture, illustrating the uncomfortable discovery of this reality. The first documents the emergence of a new protocol for reading a work of art. It was the work of a British antiquarian, Joseph Spence. Born in a country where artistic literature was still underdeveloped, this scholar was forced to 'cobble together' his tools using materials drawn from European literature on art. The second example illustrates a very common practice in the 18th century: the critical presentation of the aesthetic perception of an object by contrast with models offered by artistic literature. Here, the author of the revolt is Franz Johann Lorenz Meyer.

JOSEPH SPENCE

The discovery of the subject of contemplation is a fascinating one among English writers of the 18th century. They were not as fond of art theory as the Italians and French. As I have said, British artistic literature developed slowly during the Enlightenment, but in particular, an empirical culture made the travelling Englishman a remarkable witness of transformations to works of art in the middle of the Enlightenment. Only a few convincing examples are necessary. In 1720, Edward Wright undertook a Grand Tour, with, in his luggage, a stack of books on art and Italy. Ten years later, he published *Some Observations made in Travelling through France, Italy &c.* Here he recounted the story of his visit to the Holy of Holies, the Stanze of the Vatican decorated by Raphael. What could be said of these works of art? Wright resorted lazily to those that preceded him: 'I shall not pretend to give any particular Description of these admirable Performances; 'twould be but actum agere; they have been so largely and fully describ'd by Bellori and others formerly, and by Mr Richardson of late.' Description: an absurd endeavour that would merely retell what had already been so perfectly formulated. In contemplating the Stanze, Wright could only verify the aptness of a guide that had become canonical. He was prepared to merge his own perceptions with those of the famous writer and connoisseur – the latter had said it all. The entire visit to the Stanze therefore amounts to a simple 'Been there, done that!, I have been on location to verify the correctness of a text.' Throughout the century, British travellers would slowly discover the capabilities of an independent person, able to appreciate art using two indispensable tools: their sensory apparatus and the capacity to look inward. Laurence Sterne's *Sentimental Journey* shows, in the manner of a caricature, the extreme point of such an appreciation: someone who is completely withdrawn into his own consciousness. Yorick, the traveller who is the hero of the book, remains obsessed by the tremors of his own heart, swept along willy nilly wherever his adventures take him, and does not offer us a single credible evocation of an outside landscape – the narrator is too preoccupied with ceaselessly examining his own soul. He wants to conquer the vast world, but cannot even step out of himself.

Joseph Spence was a gifted experiencer of the work of art. He was well-read, and a scholar and professor of poetry at Oxford University, before becoming Regius professor of history there. In his youth, this man without means became the ideal companion of young aristocrats wishing to complete their own Grand Tour. He was what was known as a 'bear-leader', a guide paid for his services. In particular, visits to the great Italian sites and the great collections of the peninsula were his speciality. This very shrewd man was able to identify the new difficulties associated with his mission. A connoisseur of ancient literature, he refused to be satisfied with a simple projection of the world of poetry onto that of the fine arts. Spence's great work, *Polymetis*, methodically explores this model of perfection. Indeed, he discovered its limitations. But Spence was no theoretician and was content to examine specific themes and works. The title of the work is clear: *Polymetis, or an inquiry concerning the agreement between the works of the Roman Poets and the Remains of ancient Artists. Being an Attempt to illustrate them mutually from one another.* The purpose of the book and its structure are perfectly well set out. It is clear that this work pays tribute to Spence's mentor, Alexander Pope. Spence's work notes have been preserved, he collected them carefully in a series of hand-written volumes.

Preparing for his first journey to Italy, he asked the most knowledgeable connoisseurs what should be admired there. In particular, he inquired of the Chevalier Ramsay what works of art were not to be missed. The Scotsman's responses demonstrate that he had read the usual works on the matter. Spence must have asked about Florence: his goal was none other than the Venus de'Medici, one of the most admired ancient statues on the Grand Tour. Here are some notes by Spence: 'The Venus of Medici in the Great Duke's study at Florence: Ramsay observed three different passions expressed in it, in three different postures. Before, she seems to invite you to her; move to the right and she seems in a more rapturous degree of pleasure; and on the left she seems to turn away from you, either in scorn or being tired: disdaining, inviting, and enjoying. The connoisseur said twenty men of taste had observed the same before.' Such fables filled the guides to Italy in those days. Their truth coefficient was generally negligible, but the travellers were only too happy to 'recognise' the different expressions of Venus. This induced recognition reassured them. This model, entirely composed of an aesthetic perception, offered as a simple subject of belief, satisfied almost all the visitors at the beginning of the 18th century. Through a fable fictititiously organizing the various expressions of Venus, the sculpture at the Uffizi became a moving statue. As one approached her, she seemed to unfold multiple meanings. Such a fable legitimizes an attitude of aesthetic 'consumerism' towards the work, on a principle that is totally based on trust. This experience, repeated by twenty connoisseurs, cannot be false. The multiplication of such acts of trust artificially attest to the certain nature of the experience. So many visitors having had similar experiences cannot deceive. Spence was not taken in by such arguments. He wanted to experience for himself. When he himself entered the Tribuna, the octagonal room housing the most superb treasures of the Uffizi, he approached the Venus de'Medici along the prescribed route. Then he gave his mentors the slip: 'The critics in statuary are perhaps as apt to find out imaginary beauties, in a favourite figure; as the critics in poetry are, in a favourite author. There are some that have practiced this in regard to the figure before you. You see, her face is turned away a little from you. This single article has given several people occasion to observe, that there are three different passions expressed in the hair of the head, of this Venus. At your first approaching her, as she stands in the fine appartment assigned to this figure in the Great Duke's gallery, you see aversion or denial in her look; move on but a step or two farther, and she has compliance in it: and one step more to the right, they tell you, turns it into a little insidious and insulting smile; such as any lady has, when she plainly tells you by her face, that she has made a sure conquest of you. The moral of all this may be very true and natural; but I think it is not justified by the statue itself: for though I have paid, perhaps, a hundred visits to the Venus of Medici in person; and have often considered her, in this very view; I could never find out the malicious sort of smile, which your antiquarians talk so much of.' The fable purveyed by Ramsay transformed the apprehension of the statue into a process of seduction. Venus was in turn disdainful, then welcoming, finally celebrating her triumph over the person contemplating her, whom she has conquered. However, this erotic vision of perception/seduction demands no effort on the part of the observer. Caught up as he is in a dance that is completely codified, the tourist can only fall into step with the rhythm of the appropriate pas-de-deux in the direction of the statue, and persuade himself that the latter has the power to seduce him. Nothing is easier – nobody likes to admit that he has not sensed what so many others have perceived. Spence sets against this process a radically different method. As a scholar of the antiquities, he easily recognized the iconography of the statue, i.e. its intrinsic meaning. However, he was very sensitive to meanings specific to poetry or sculpted art. Here he refers to the gaze of Venus. 'This must have given the poets an advantage, in describing the quick and uncertain motions of Venus' eyes; and occasions our meeting with some expressions in them, which cannot be explained either from statues, or paintings. Such is the epithet of Paeta, in particular, which the Roman writers give to Venus; and which refers, perhaps, to a certain turn of her eye, and her catching it again, the moment it is observed; as your favourite does, Philander, when she is kinder to you in her heart, than she would appear to be by her eyes.' Spence is therefore criticizing Ramsay: because the latter wanted to recognize in the sculpture the exact equivalent of the Paeta, he produced an erroneous interpretation of the sculpture. Then Spence began to divide the form into elementary and significant components. Each detail – nose, eye, brow etc. – is the subject of specific appreciation. Spence's model here is the famous text from the *Entretiens* by Félibien. Spence sets in context the scope of this 'disassembly', emphasizing the importance of the whole that was so precious to Roger de Piles. Three principles of articulation influence the perfection of a statue: its proportion, expression, and finally the grace residing in the movement of the body selected by the sculptor. Finally, Spence amends the method favoured by Roger de Piles, by suggesting the measurement of beauty. We know that Roger de Piles, at the end of his *Cours de peinture par principes*, proposes what he calls a 'balance des peintres', a weighing up of painters, assessing their relative qualities in the various parts of the picture: composition, drawing, colour and expression. Spence wanted to transfer this quantification into the specific evaluation of human beauty. Here it was no longer a question of measuring the value of an artist, but that of an individual form. This shift of attention, already applied by Jonathan Richardson in 1719, is of capital importance. It introduces quantitative assessment into the appreciation of all the qualities of a sculpture. But, above all, it involves a real work of evaluation on the part of the spectator. The projection of a fable onto the work of art, as we have seen, draws an immediate meaning from the work that is in a way exhaustive. Spence himself, in practice, discovered a new reality: the patient work necessary to construe the meaning of a work of art.

FRANZ MEYER

The second example is a young German, the son of a wine merchant who undertook his Grand Tour of Italy in 1783, after having received a sound education during studies at Göttingen, a bastion of critical thought. Having taken holy orders and been appointed a canon of Hamburg cathedral, he published his *Darstellungen aus Italien* in 1792. Like the other Grand Tourists, Meyer visited the cortile of the Belvedere at the Vatican. He paused for a long time before the famous statues of the Belvedere Apollo and Laocoon.

Meyer was a German Catholic. Nevertheless, he was astounded by the pride of Pope Pius VI. The latter, a renovator of the Vatican museums, had had his name marked in gold letters on the pedestal of all the antique statues acquired or restored under his pontificate. Such vanity shocked the young visitor and he said so. As if to neutralize this conspicuous appropriation of ancient art, Meyer had the idea of making a night-time visit to the museum, torch in hand. He invited to come with him, on the eve of his departure from Rome, all his fellow citizens whom he respected, many of them artists. The semi-darkness effaced the vain inscriptions of the reigning pope: they dissipated at the arrival of the visitors, as the white marbles began to shine. The statues had taken on life and were shimmering in the torchlight.

This is the scene chosen by Meyer as he confronted the history of the art of his time. He was familiar with, as he had read it, the *Geschichte der Kunst des Alterthums* by 1764. The German antiquarian interprets the expression of the Apollo of the Belvedere, who, he declared, 'had just killed the Python…his mighty foot found, then crushed it. From the heights of his divine restraint, his sublime gaze, as if carried to infinity, went far beyond his victory. Scorn dwells on his lips and the anger, still blazing within him, inflates his nostrils and rises to his magnificent forehead.' The ideal figure of the Apollo is serene, but it bears the marks, still visible, of a terrifying pathos. Meyer refused to insert the sculpted figure into this narrative. It is a sublime Apollo of the sun, that the sculptor wanted to magnify, as he skimmed the earth to 'make the day triumphant'. Meyer based his own interpretation, not on a historically founded hypothesis, but on his own contemplation, in the torchlight. He recognized the anachronistic nature of this modern experimentum, even if it permits the statute to confer its most convincing meaning: 'The Greek artist could not suspect, when he created his work, the effect it would have.' Moreover, 'The feeling that this statue gave me, which I will report here, although it is not in opposition to the ancient myths, is not based on any tradition.' It was based on reason because the hypothesis also satisfied 'sensitivity and reflection'. Meyer did not make any mystery of his presuppositions. 'Contemplating this marvellous and truly divine figure, I took pleasure in abandoning myself to this first impression.' Meyer then sought, in a significant afterthought, to base on knowledge an interpretation so liberal and so diametrically opposed to that of any renowned scholar. He found his material in the article 'Allegorie', from the *Allgemeine Theorie der Schönen Künste* by Johann Georg Sulzer, an aesthetic text and not an ancient history. Meyer, liberated from any scholarly constraints, justified his sentiment by citing the author who had experienced the same emotions.

Thus it was that the tales of Grand Tourists attempted to efface the traces of the European literary substrate that nevertheless underlie their attempts to gain access to the work of art with a new directness stripped of predefined notions. Stendhal, more than any other guide, would be seized by this dialectic. It would be another century before literary apparatus in the service of contemplation would be characterized as an aid to interpretation and accepted as such. When Paul Hertz made his journey to Italy in 1874, it would already be in place. The young German mentioned the works that were inextricably part of the experience he would have. This experience itself would enable him, he thought, to consider their utterances in context.

On imitating the creative masters

Some lessons learned from reading texts and works

CATHELINE PÉRIER-D'IETEREN

In the last two sections of Le Grand Atelier we have presented various works focused on a principal theme: the taste for collecting. In those sections, it was not our ambition to offer an 'anthology' of the great painters who have attracted collectors. Nevertheless, those artists considerably influenced one another and we know that exchanges of that kind also formed the tastes of art lovers. The mechanisms of taste, collecting and aesthetic choices therefore cannot be understood unless several general factors are borne in mind, particularly the knowledge of pictorial techniques. This section will be devoted to that subject.

Since Antiquity, thanks to the works of a few writers, painters and humanists, the memory of eminent artists has never been effaced. However, art enthusiasts must not be content with mere biographical facts. They also need to understand the work of those artists from the twin point of view of style and technique – art that is born in a perpetual movement of relationships, appropriations and personal creations that have emerged from a crucible of reinterpreted borrowings.

The exhibition invites us to follow certain guidelines. The influence of the ideas and forms of Antiquity that permeates the centuries, fertilizing the arts, is one of them. The dialogue of the masters is another, and we shall approach it here from the less familiar angle of 'picture making' and the lessons provided by artistic theories or the biographies of artists, which, sometimes explicitly and sometimes between the lines, beg to be decoded. They then throw new light on the pictures concerned that is not achieved by merely reading the pictorial surface, and give us a better understanding of the plastic choices and creative journeys made by the geniuses of European painting. From among those masters we shall select the names of a few painters who were exceptional ambassadors of the culture of their countries: Titian, Rubens, Van Dyck and Velázquez. Those painters were entrusted with both diplomatic and artistic missions, most of which consisted of producing portraits or historical paintings to order, but also of copying famous works or even finding them for royal collections. Rembrandt, Jordaens, Watteau and Boucher are other artists adored by art lovers who incessantly received commissions from their fellow citizens or European courts.

In the 16th century, Titian was doubtless the most famous European artist and the most esteemed by the courts of his day. He revolutionized painting techniques and had an enormous influence on his contemporaries and on the painters of the 17th century, including Rubens and Van Dyck in the southern Netherlands, Rembrandt in Holland and Velázquez in Spain. All of them saw some of their famous predecessor's paintings and some actually owned one or two. Fascinated by Titian, Rubens had six of his paintings in his private collection and made thirty-two copies of his works, including all the paintings produced for Philip II of Spain. Those painters expressed their admiration of the Venetian master and, under the sway of his compositions, changed the way they painted, not slavishly but by making the principle of *aemulatio* (emulation) an end in itself.

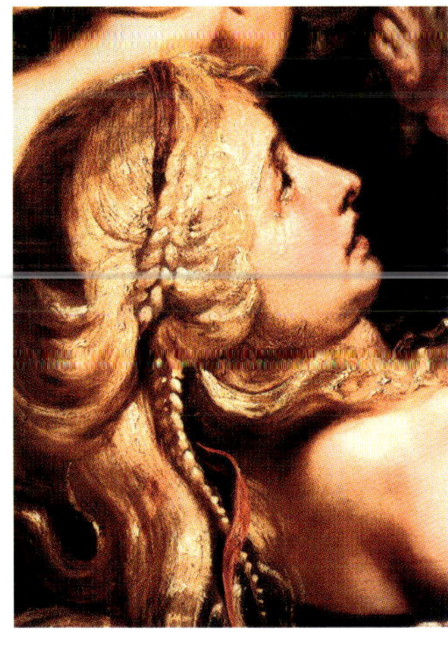

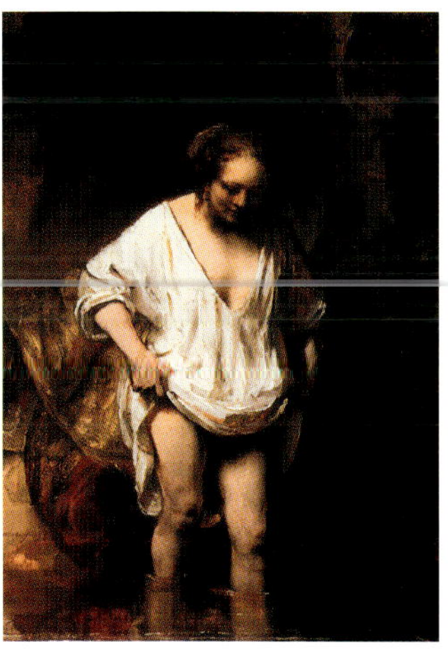

Fig. 1
THE RAISING OF THE CROSS
Peter Paul Rubens, 1611

Fig. 2
A WOMAN BATHING IN A STREAM
Rembrandt, 1658

From his earliest works Fig. 1, XIII.14, Rubens thus seized on Titian's vibrant use of colour and luminosity and reflected it in fulsome displays of paint in which the brushstrokes mark the material rather than dissolve it. Rembrandt adopted the symphony of yellow ochres, browns and reds with their sultry tonalities, a symphony so specific to the Venetian but, after the 1650s, shaded his figures like a sculptor in successive rough outlines: carving, crushing and scratching the material Fig. 2 where Titian had made it leap forth in a burst of juxtaposed colours Fig. 3. Velázquez abandoned the tenebrism of his Sevillian paintings, typified by sharp contrasts of light in the manner of Caravaggio and lightened his palette after his first visit to Italy. He visited that country at the suggestion of Rubens, whom he had met at the court of Philip IV in Madrid and with whom he formed a friendship.

The Spanish painter then transformed the pictorial surface of his works in an illusionist style, using rapid and fluid splashes of colour, which, in his last paintings, presaged the art of the Impressionists. His freedom of touch and the lightness of the layers of pastel shades, and simple chromatic allusions, in turn revolutionized the course taken by European painting. The subtle modulations of his blacks and his atmospheric compositions were again to influence Manet and Renoir in the 19th century and even Picasso in the 20th. Thus, the chain of successive influences, the source of pictorial renewal, continues from generation to generation.

Le vite de' più eccellenti architettori, pittori, e scultori (The Lives of the Most Illustrious Architects, Painters and Sculptors) by Giorgio Vasari (1550) and the *Schilder-Boeck* (Book of Painters) by Karel Van Mander (1604) give us much valuable information on the lives and works of famous painters. However, it is up to us to compare that information with the painted work in an effort to see how the masters conceived their compositions and transformed the material to express their own artistic sensitivity. In the *Vite*, Vasari recounts the biographies of the greatest Italian artists from Cimabue to Titian. He travelled throughout Italy and visited studios to gather evidence, as well as all the palaces to see the artists' works, and, in his *Libro dei Designi*, even assembled drawings by those he admired most.

Vasari devotes a whole chapter to the genesis of Titian's compositions and his pictorial technique, in the light of which we can apprehend the scope of the innovations Titian introduced to European painting. Those innovations include what is called painting in 'dabs', which, by breaking with the previously used smooth techniques, distinguishes his work from the standard practices of his contemporaries. From then on, the type of technique adopted was to become the source of passionate debate in studios and among the art theorists of the 17th century. Those two methods, that is, rough or smooth, were to be a matter of deliberate choice by each of the great painters and would be adapted by them according to their artistic individuality and their own stylistic development. We shall return to this subject.

Karel van Mander was mainly concerned with the Northern painters of the 15th and 16th centuries, and, as he himself confessed, drew his information from Vasari's writings for those of the South, whom he covers in his second volume. What is more, he discusses in depth Vasari's monumental work and vies with him in constructing an imposing work in turn, but in Flemish and concerning the Flemish, Dutch and German painters. The theoreticians of the 17th century drew much of their inspiration from him.

Thus, these *artistic biographies*, are part of a literary genre born in Roman times with Pliny's *Historia Naturalis*, one of the most often copied works of Antiquity. It was used throughout Europe as a volume of historical reference by humanists, following a route similar to that taken by painters,

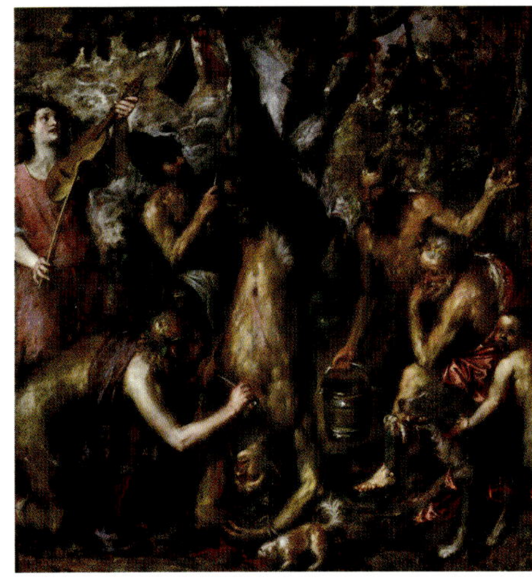

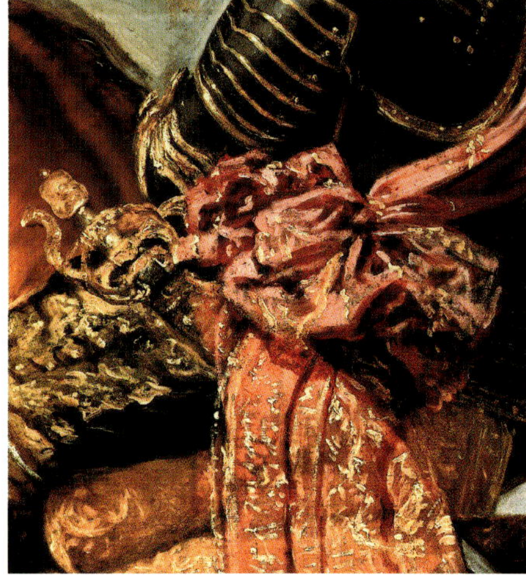

Fig. 3
THE FLAYING OF MARSYAS
Titian, *c.* 1570–76

Fig. 4
EQUESTRIAN PORTRAIT OF THE COUNT-DUKE OF OLIVARES
Diego Velázquez, 1634

who first imitated the artists of Antiquity and then sought to innovate and even to surpass them. In fact, with the simple copy, as Leonardo da Vinci wrote, 'painting declines from age to age and is lost if painters have no guides other than what was done before them'.

These 'biographers', themselves painters, captured the attention of cultivated people because they were interested not only in the masters who had preceded them but also in their contemporaries. Vasari was an example, particularly regarding Michelangelo, and Van Mander Goltzius – his new Michelangelo – or again Spranger, a writer who 'glorified the name of painters as a legitimate consequence of the brilliance of their merit'. Those two writers also examined the part played by the artists they studied in transmitting the art of painting and studied the pictures that inspired them, thus pointing out some celebrated connections.

Motivated by a lively curiosity, Karel van Mander drew information from every source to recount the lives of the painters as objectively as he could. As he lived surrounded by picture dealers and collectors, of whom his uncle and master, Luc de Heere, was one, he seized the opportunity to question the artists he met. He also studied and commented on the works exhibited in the galleries of art enthusiasts (Section XIV) and in royal or princely collections (Section XIII).

Unfortunately, unlike Vasari, and later Samuel van Hoogstraten, Van Mander delivers very little information on painters' techniques. In 16th-century painting, he considers that art is above all a natural gift. Therefore, although he recommends arduous work, Van Mander favours inspiration. The painter must draw this from nature, 'imitate it and follow it, so as to try to equal it'. When art reaches its point of perfection 'it surpasses nature'. Here again, he takes up that idea of Vasari's, who wrote: 'He who has scarcely studied or drawn in accordance with the most excellent ancient and modern works…cannot give the things he copies from nature that grace and perfection by means of which art surpasses nature.' Again, Van Mander says that a beautiful work is achieved only if *invention, arrangement and expression* are in accord within it, but these must be enhanced by impeccable technique. Thus, he praises the extraordinary realism of Flemish painting since Van Eyck and presents the Ghent Altarpiece as 'a model, a lesson for painters'. He naturally attributes the invention of oil painting to the Flemish master, as does Vasari, and believes that it revived the art of painting: 'Italy, land of the arts, was dazzled by it and felt constrained to send Painting to Flanders, its own infant, to suckle at other breasts.' Although it is now acknowledged that Van Eyck did not invent painting in oils, it is true that he transformed the principle of shading styles. They were achieved not by flat washes or mixtures of colour but by a subtle superimposition of layers of colour and translucent glazes. The whole was lit from within by the reflection of light on the white preparation or the light-toned background, as is so well illustrated by Van Eyck's *Virgin at the Fountain* **VI.13**. This type of shading was seen in Italian paintings as from the last quarter of the 15th century. A comparison between the portraits painted by Hans Memling and Antonello da Messina, for example, shows the extent to which Italian painters assimilated the Flemish technique. Glazing was used to perfection by Leonardo da Vinci and Raphael, and later by Titian in his smooth paintings and in his rendering of certain clothes, while Velázquez achieved the same effect by sometimes replacing the glazing with subtle mixtures of colour with chalk added, creating a delicate veil on the surface. The art of

Rubens was also born of the meeting between those two great European pictorial traditions. Rubens was inspired by Italian painting, with which he became familiar during the eight years he spent at the court of Mantua in the service of Vincent I of Gonzaga, copying the masters from Michelangelo to Caravaggio. However, he belongs to the technical tradition of the Flemish primitives and, like them, sought to achieve the maximum degree of luminosity in his shading. This he did in two ways [Fig. 1]: the traditional method, based on the transparent properties of paint, and the other using covering layers, developing the use of light and very dense impasto, as the Venetian school was already doing in the 16th century. To give depth to his shading, Rubens, like his predecessors, used the light preparation layer and the translucence of glazes, but then covered the preparation with a thin grey or brown paint layer (*imprimatura*), which was itself translucent. Using this new technique, Rubens drew not only on the optical effects generated by a warm, transparent tone applied to a light preparation, but also introduced an additional layer into the shading. In fact, a space develops behind the *imprimatura*, perceived as a translucent screen between the preparation, which remains visible, and the layers of colour themselves. These characteristics can be seen more clearly in his painted sketches [XIII.13].

The manuscript of Théodore Turquet de Mayerne, a physician and pharmacologist at the court of Charles I of England, is the richest source about the practice of painting in the 17th century. Passionate about art, Mayerne recorded in a notebook all the practical information he obtained from the many painters who stayed at the King's court. He thus describes the working methods of Rubens and Van Dyck, and reports their own words about recipes for colours, binding agents and varnishes.

Use of the resources of oil painting, which reached its first peak with Van Eyck, achieved its summit with Rubens. Through the variety in the density of the colours used, from fine, translucent glazes, whose thickness varied according to the intensity of the light sources, to thick impasto, Rubens created the most extensive range of opaque-transparent effects in the history of Northern painting.

If we compare the structure of a picture by Van Eyck [VI.13] with that of a picture by Rubens [XIII.14], we see that, although the principles remain the same, there are nevertheless marked differences in their execution. Rubens speeds up the process of oil painting from the moment he puts the composition in place by replacing the underlying drawing in the style of Van Eyck with a monochrome painted sketch (*doodverf*) and, when executing the picture, by *reversing the thicknesses*. Whereas in the shading of the Flemish primitives the layers of colour are thin in the light areas and thick in the shadows to obtain chromatic saturation, conversely in those of Rubens the light parts are thick while the shadows are painted with fine layers of glaze, allowing the *imprimitura* to show through.

Rubens transmitted his 'manner' to his pupil, Van Dyck. We see again the use of an oil impression, a binding agent

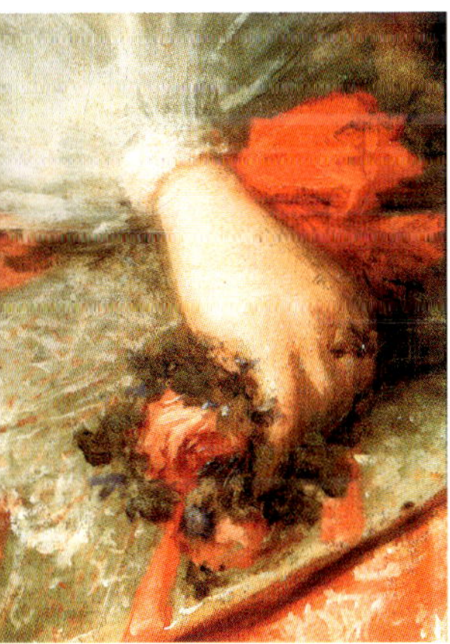

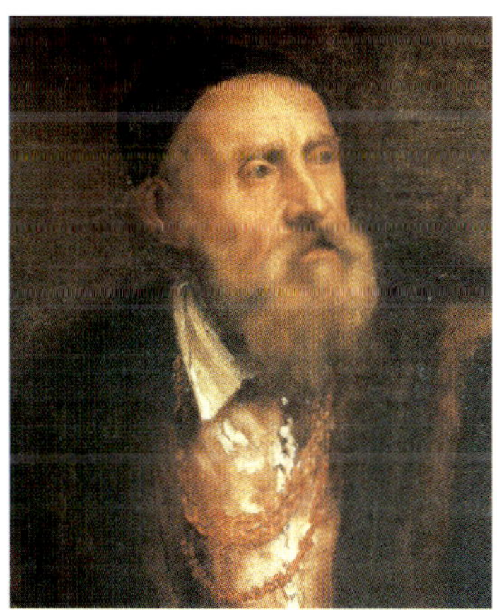

Fig. 5
THE INFANTA MARIA MARGUERITA
Diego Velázquez, *c.* 1651

Fig. 6
SELF-PORTRAIT
Titian, 1567–68

Fig. 7
PORTRAIT OF AN OLD MAN
Rembrandt, 1667

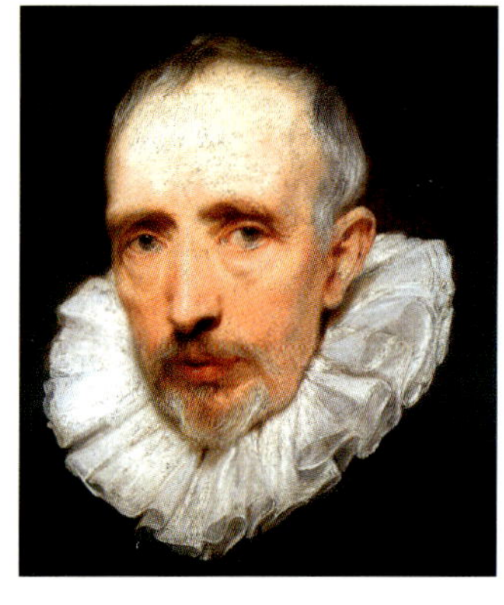

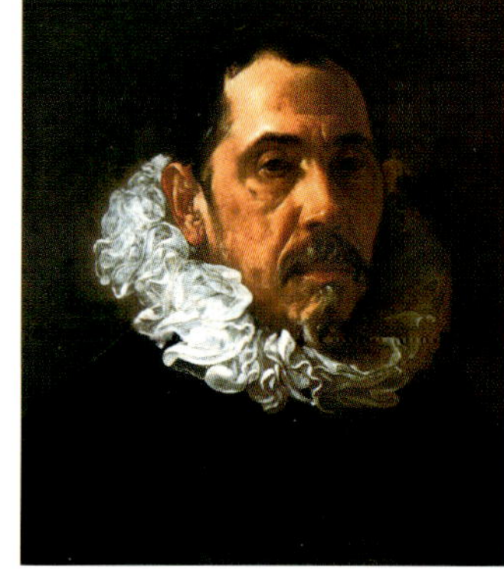

Fig. 8
PORTRAIT OF
CORNELIS VAN DER GEEST
Anthony Van Dyck, *c.* 1620

Fig. 9
PORTRAIT OF
FRANCISCO PACHECO
Diego Velázquez, 1619

based on linseed oil often diluted with turpentine, and pigments with resin added to them to make the binding agent more oily and increase the transparency of the colours [Fig. 8]. Rubens taught Van Dyck to master the art of colour based on the principle of the three primary colours (blue, red and yellow). As Van Dyck's art became more confident (Section XIII), he chose the most suitable colours from that range and associated them with half-tones of brown and grey, creating extremely subtle chromatic harmonies. His material is dryer than that of Rubens, but the different colours are blended with one another using skilful brushwork that distinguishes them from the more dynamic brushstrokes of Rubens, who constantly alternates fluid and thick areas.

Thus, Rubens profoundly influenced the painters of the various European schools of the 17th and 18th centuries, through both his style and the innovatory aspect of his painting technique, the source of an intense pictorial revival. Considering for a moment only the impression layer in translucent lightly coloured oil paint, we see it being used again in the paintings of Rembrandt and the Dutch landscape artists such as Van Goyen and Salomon Ruysdael, but also in Spanish painting, with Diego Velázquez.

Through the intermediary of Van Dyck, Rubens also strongly influenced the English school of painting in the 18th century, and Sir Joshua Reynolds in particular.

The first President of the Royal Academy, Sir Joshua promoted the status of the artist as an intellectual, abolishing all practical considerations concerning the manual labour involved in the creative process. However, he himself stubbornly tried to reproduce the pictorial effects of the old masters, but using a speedier technique. Thus, he experimented with pigments and binding agents, often with disastrous results.

Lastly, Rubens's influence also extended to French painters such as François Boucher [XIII.23] and Jean-Antoine Watteau. The latter tirelessly copied the Flemish master's drawings, engravings and paintings, demonstrating the fervent interest he took in his art. Moreover, as he worked for the Parisian decorator Claude Audran, the Concierge of the Luxembourg Palace, he had the opportunity of seeing the great *Cycle of the Life of Marie de Médicis* by Rubens in the picture gallery.

His pictorial technique demonstrates his fondness for Flemish methods. Thus, in many of his works, including the *Embarkation for Cythera*, he adopted a white preparation whose optical properties he used in his shading.

However, although Watteau owed much to Rubens, unlike him he appears to be the master of *free improvisation*. In fact, he always adapted his painting technique to the requirements of his creative and impatient temperament, often disregarding the established rules 'of the trade', which were the very foundation stone of Rubens's painting. Thus, many rethought details and compositional changes affect the relationship of the figures to one another and to the space they occupy. Dissatisfied with his work, while he was producing a painting Watteau constantly sought to improve or modify the picture to his liking. He painted the figures from studies drawn from life or drawings copied from other artists, including Rubens, seeking to find in painting the creative spontaneity of his drawn models without having to follow a prefigured plan in a preparatory phase. The picture dealer Gersaint wrote, 'I have often seen him getting annoyed with himself at what he could not render in paint, the spirit and truth he succeeded in achieving with his pencils.' Conversely, Rubens seldom made alterations during the production of a painting. If he did, they were aimed at correcting the balance of a composition that had been carefully studied through preparatory sketches on paper and *modelli* painted on prepared panels [XIII.13].

Watteau had no hesitation in repainting parts of a composition in oils, without worrying about the harmful effects that practice might have on the pictorial material: the premature cracking so often seen in his pictures. His attitude to his profession was therefore diametrically opposed to that of Rubens, who, in contrast, as he explains in his letters, took care over the siccative or drying qualities of the binding agent and the transparency of the colours, endeavouring not to tire the material so as to preserve its initial properties. Moreover, the technical perfection of Rubens's paintings explains their excellent state of conservation.

Although Watteau's work became spectacularly popular through his emulators or copyists, it never played such a preponderant part in the development of European painting as that of Rubens.

François Boucher, another successful and fashionable painter, adopted from Rubens his way of drawing the outline of forms with a very free red line, particularly faces and bodies. In contrast, in his endeavour to make his compositions more luminous, he loaded his colours with a great deal of white lead, contrasting light and opaque surfaces. He deviated from the tradition followed by Rubens of deeply orchestrating the shading obtained by using thin, warm-toned shadows and glazes.

Let us now return to Italy and Vasari's text. In the chapter in the second edition of the *Vite* of 1568 dedicated to the *Presentation of the work of Titian di Cadore*, Vasari explains what he means by painting in 'dabs', which radically changed the course of the history of European painting. Having started with a *smooth manner*, Titian then used the *rough manner*, that is, a style of painting in which the marks of the brush are very visible and the nuances of tone and colour take precedence over the shape Fig. 3. Vasari wrote, 'painted with broad brushstrokes in a dabbing style, so that one cannot view them from close to and must stand back to see their perfection'.

Behind the apparent ease of this style of painting in 'dabs' is a high level of knowledge and experience, to the point that Vasari wrote 'a young artist should not try this technique but should come to it late, after practising a fine and meticulous manner. Paintings produced in this way cannot be viewed from close to, but look perfect if seen from a distance'.

Vasari's words were to be reiterated almost literally by Van Mander in his *Schilder-Boeck*. They were to constitute one of the aspects discussed by the theoreticians of the 17th century and became part of the atelier culture that was transmitted orally. The circulation of these ideas was in turn facilitated by the circulation of artists.

Thus Rembrandt's teachers, above all Pieter Lastman, had spent time in Italy and it was through them and the *Vite* of Vasari that the young painter, who never visited Italy himself, learned to know Titian and became one of his closest spiritual heirs. Like Titian, during his long career Rembrandt changed his way of painting and eventually adopted the technique of painting in 'dabs' Fig. 7. Knowing that, from close to, all that could be seen were 'dabs' but that from a distance they blended to form a true image of reality, in 1639 Rembrandt wrote to Constantin Huygens about one of his canvases that it should be hung 'so that it can be viewed from a distance'.

Titian's influence on the practice of art in the 17th century is evident also in the use of 'rethinking' (*pentimento*), experienced as the affirmation of an artist's freedom concerning his creation and as the tangible proof of a painting reworked in the quest to achieve perfect form. According to Vasari, Titian thought that the best and most adequate way was to work directly on the painting without making preparatory drawings on paper. This step in the genesis of a composition was to lead to many modifications during production, which artists did not try to hide, since art theoreticians interpreted them as characteristic of *courageous* painters, to reiterate Van Mander's words.

Titian also constantly returned to his pictures. Vasari explains that he 're-covered them with paint so many times that the care taken in their execution became evident: an entirely considered manner, surprising and beautiful, which caused living paintings to come into being and reflected the artist's competence while concealing the huge amount of work that had been devoted to them'.

By favouring the free use of rethinking, Titian once again set the standard for 17th-century painters, including Rembrandt and Velázquez.

I

Europe on the move

ROLAND RECHT

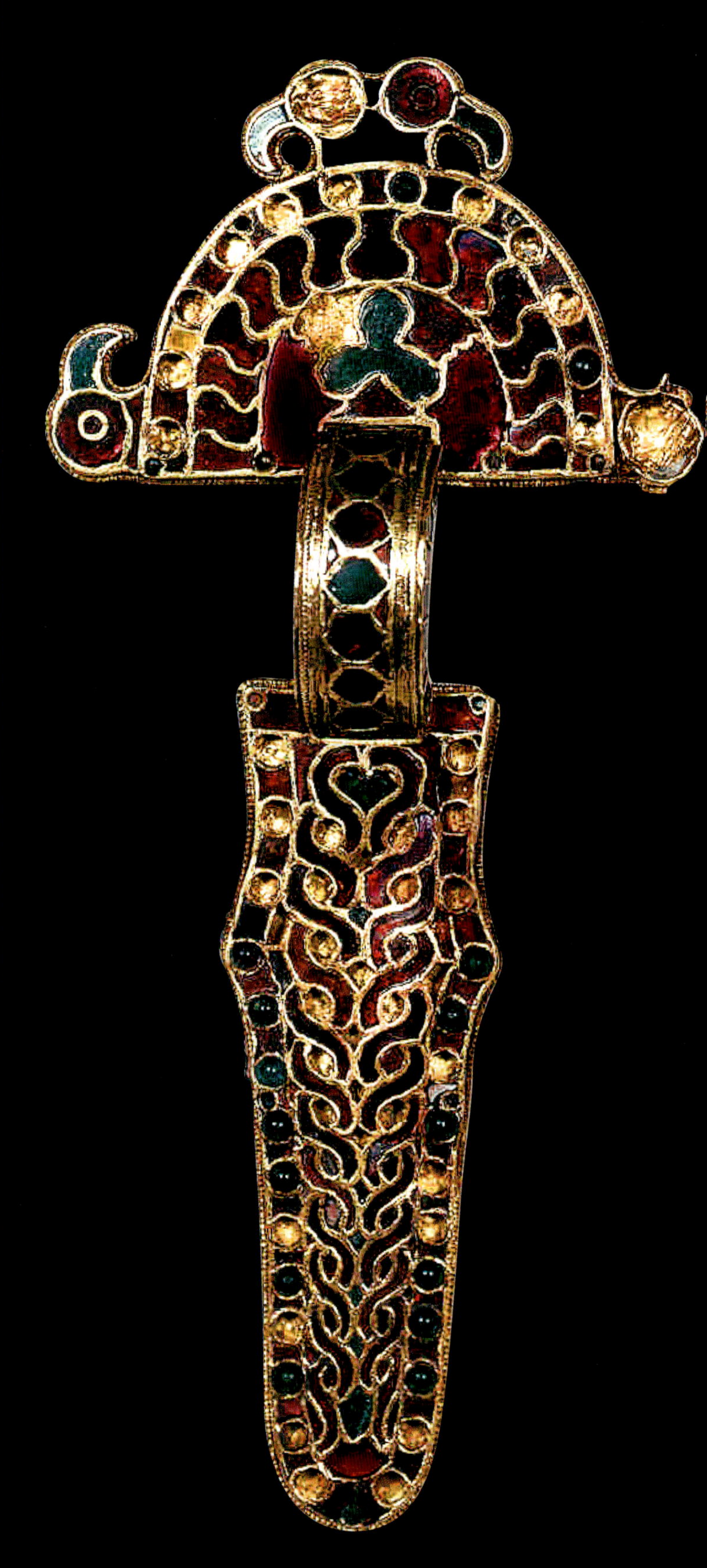

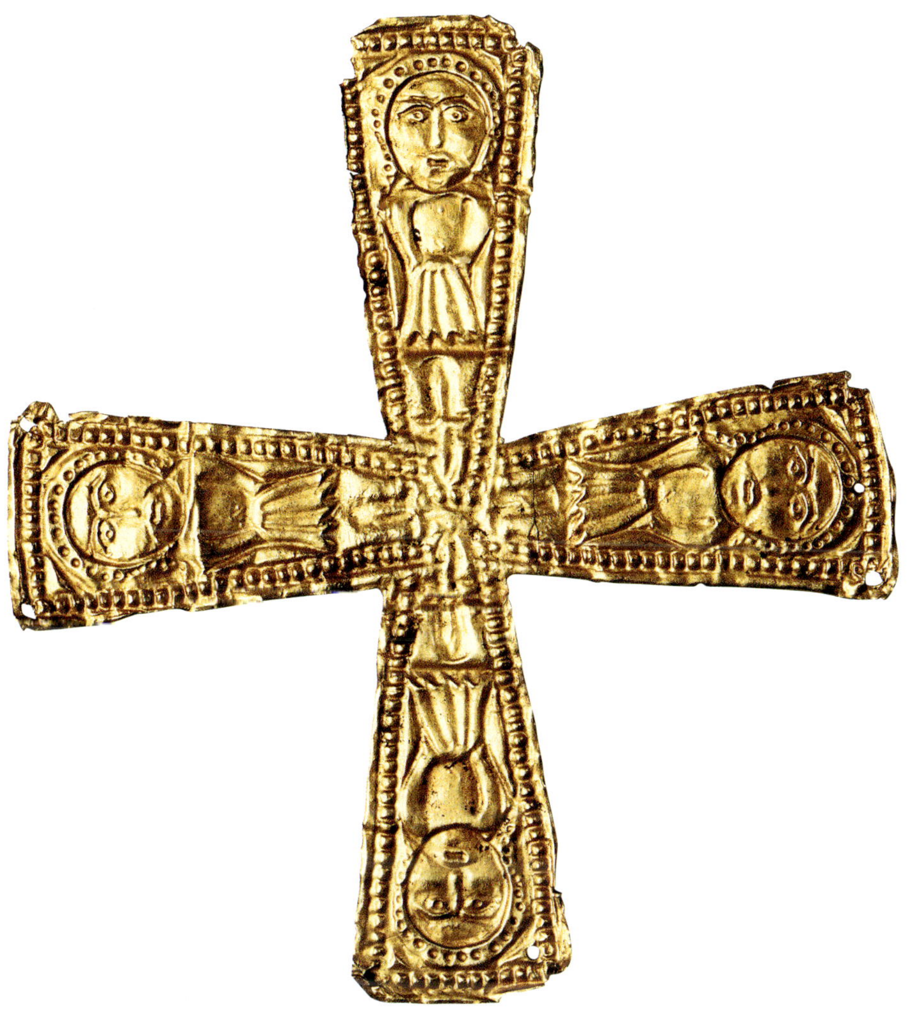

Cat 1.5
PECTORAL CROSS
Lombardy, 8th century

The migratory movements that occurred in the West during the first centuries of the Christian era would suggest that profound changes were taking place and would make the slow genesis of Europe intelligible if it were not for their great complexity. It was then that Europe first emerged, before Charlemagne made it function. Attaching the date of AD 476 to the end of the Roman Empire is nothing more than a convenience for history teachers. The houses, official monuments, lifestyles, clothes, language, work and habits of many centuries under the authority of Rome were not wiped out at a stroke, and yet, in the sphere of the plastic arts, a kind of exhaustion seems to have set in.

< Cat 1.8
ANSATE CLASP
Merovingian art (Ostrogothic interpretation), *c.* 500

Although it may look as if the Empire had planned its own demise via its progressive disintegration, conversely its survival could not have been planned. Its decline varied from one part of Europe to another. For long years and with differing degrees of success, the Empire withstood the thrusts to its very heart by the blades

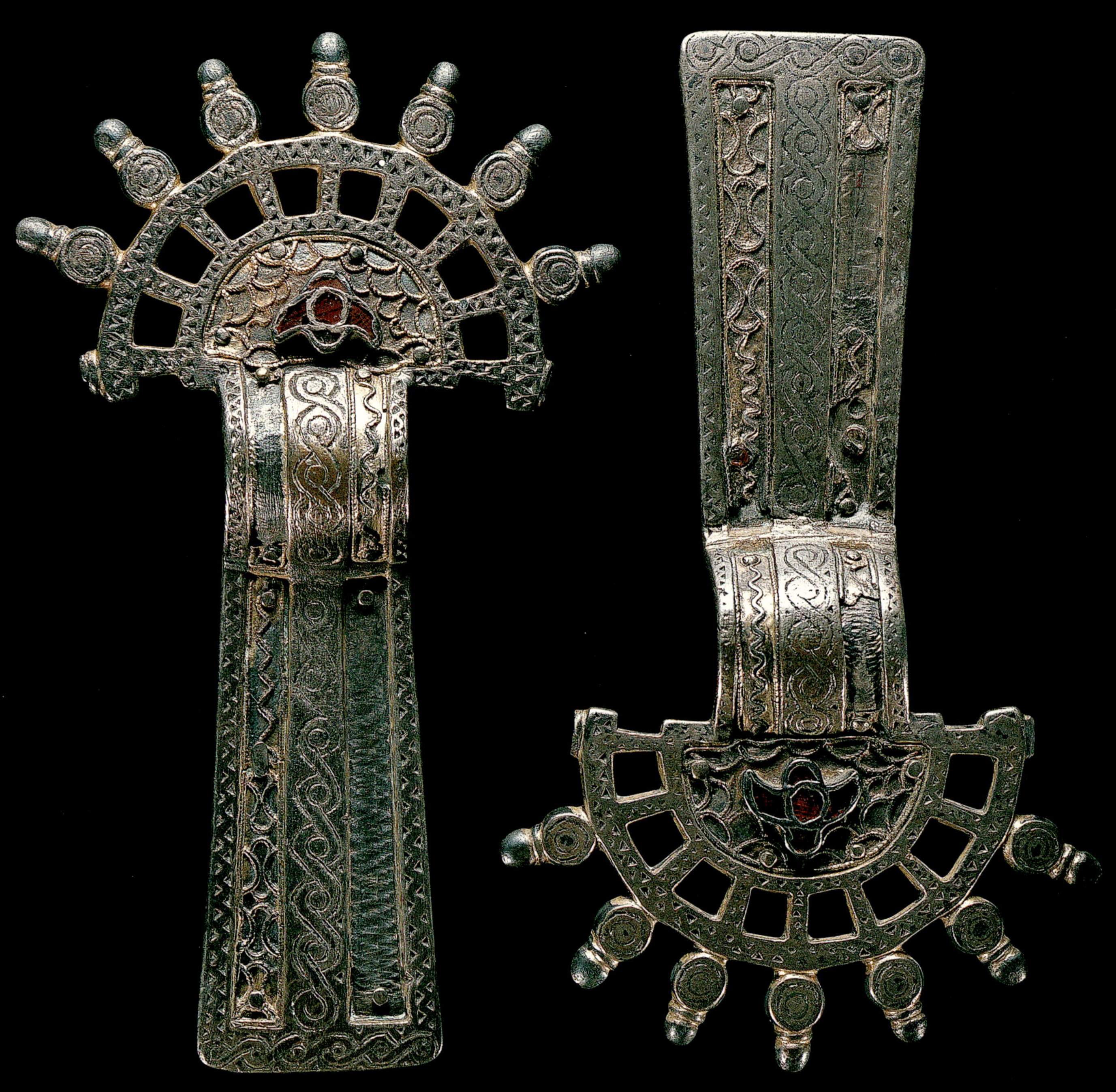

< Cat I.9
PAIR OF CURVED CLASPS
Northeastern France, late 6th or early 7th century

of those pejoratively known as 'barbarians'. The period of the great migrations in the 4th and 5th centuries started with the movement of a people of Asian origin, the Huns. They pushed ahead of them other peoples, who crossed the frontier of the Roman Empire, the famous *limes*. Their chiefs carved out territories for themselves in Western Europe. These waves of fast and fearless horsemen spread firstly into the lands of Eastern Europe and then moved steadily further west: the Saxons to Britannia (Britain), the Goths to Italy and even as far as Rome, the Vandals and Swabians to Spain. Gradually, they absorbed what they found worthy of interest in Roman civilization. But these invaders also succeeded in imposing their own ideas and particularly their forms of art. By the 5th century, 'barbarian' peoples had settled definitively in Western Europe.

Pope Gregory the Great's method of dealing with them was to prove a decisive factor: he aimed to unite them within the Church and that effort, at first only moderately successful, nevertheless constituted a yeast for the formation of Europe. The mission he sent to southern England was part of his strategy of spiritual conversion: Canterbury was to become a leading centre of learning for the whole Western world. The conversion of the Lombards, too – the evangelization of Germania – occurred a century later through the efforts of St Boniface, who had also reorganized the Frankish church. Pepin the Short, ruler of the Franks, became the first king by the Grace of God. Through his activity in Italy, the Languedoc and Aquitaine, he opened the way to the formation of the Empire later constituted by his son Charles.

The Christian religion is based on the Bible and through that book we see the first spiritual, intellectual and artistic constructions that man produced for the propagation of Christianity. This development is linked to monasticism, as it was in the workshops – or scriptoria – of the abbeys that its texts were prepared and, sometimes, enhanced with painted images. These 'illu-

Cat I.7
ANSATE CLASP
Pontic art (Germanic form), early 5th century

> Cat I.6
CLASP, WITH EAGLE'S HEAD
Pontic art
(Gothic form), c. 380

minated' books, the most outstanding of which included the four Gospels, circulated with their custodians, often covering long distances, and their arrival at a monastery or a cathedral must have been a highly memorable event. It should be remembered that these volumes were not designed for lovers of art. The text always took precedence. But their ornate initial letters or decorative representations added to the value of the texts. The care and, hence, the time a scribe devoted to copying the Gospels must have been increased by the addition of colours and ornamentation.

The 'barbarians' were not builders, at least not during their early incursions. They made objects related to clothing or arms and in doing so developed an acute decorative sense. This ornamentation did not incorporate the human figure – the first of the characteristics that distinguish it from the Greco-Roman tradition, in which not only human beings but also the human body were exalted. The 'barbarian' peoples used plant forms, which they stylized, i.e., they simplified their shapes so they were easy to assimilate. They also used animal forms, like their distant predecessors, whose traces we find in the cave paintings of Africa or the South of France. Lastly, whatever the object being decorated or the material of which it was made, they used simple, geometrical divisions. Within those geometrical shapes, the relationship between the background and the figure seems to be blurred, the two becoming interchangeable.

Using those devices, they opened up infinitely variable and renewable sequences of simple forms from which symbols were certainly not excluded – far from it. At first, this art of decoration was full of meaning. When practised by the peoples of the so-called 'Dark Ages' it was not merely an ornament to life, it was a reminder of values – the first of which was doubtless the courage of the warrior – to prevent them being forgotten. By its singularity, ornament may have meant membership of a particular people. It was a kind of vernacular language specific to the objects concerned. And then, through its unusual beauty, the decorated object may have provided a worthy reminder of the existence of the forces that animate Nature and could imperil the lives of men.

Decoration was one of the favourite activities of the peoples of the East. The Pontus Euxinus (Black Sea) constituted an outstandingly fertile route for Eastern art that the people migrating East–West were to exploit. The first phase in the massive importation of art from the Pontic or Black Sea region started, approximately, with first conquests of the Huns in about 375 and ended in 451 when their leader Attila was conquered by Aetius and the Visigoths. The most frequently found objects are clasps (fibulas) and belt buckles, in other words clothing accessories. The eagle-headed clasp from the Pietroasa treasure [I.6] is typical of the very first objects of Pontic art. The later, ansate (looped) clasp was found near Vienna [I.7]

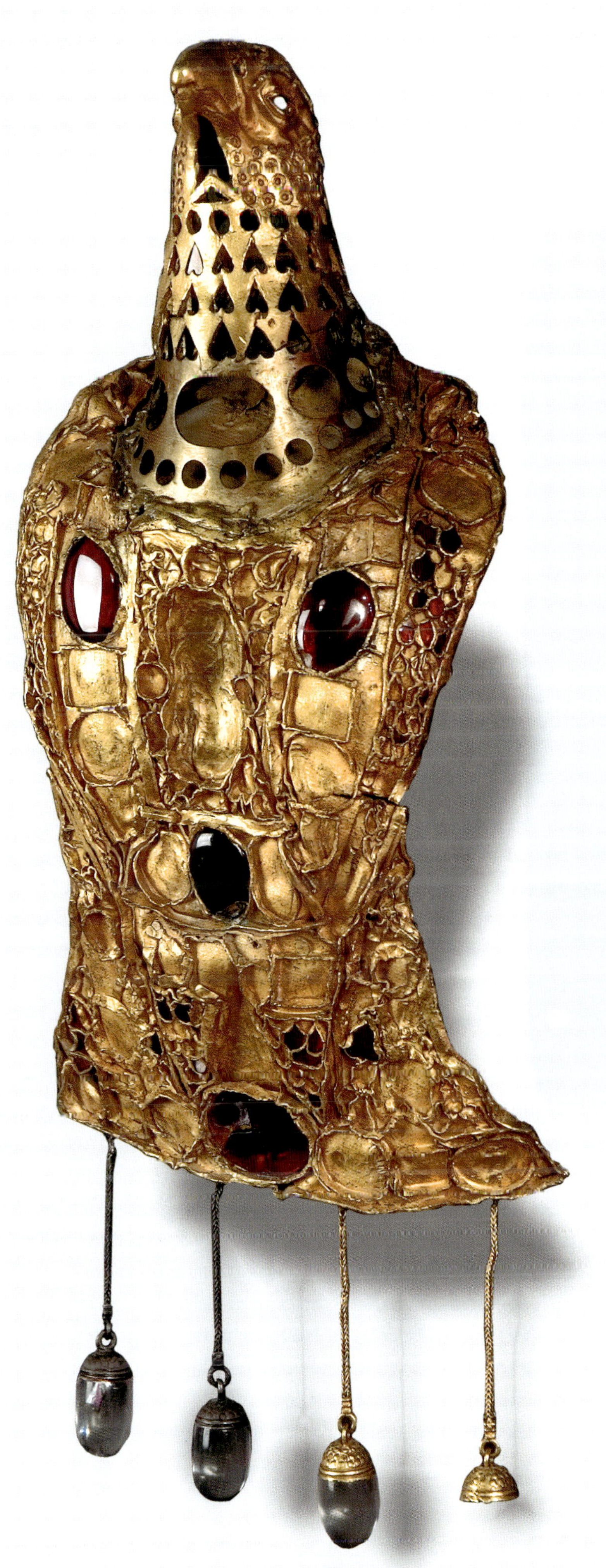

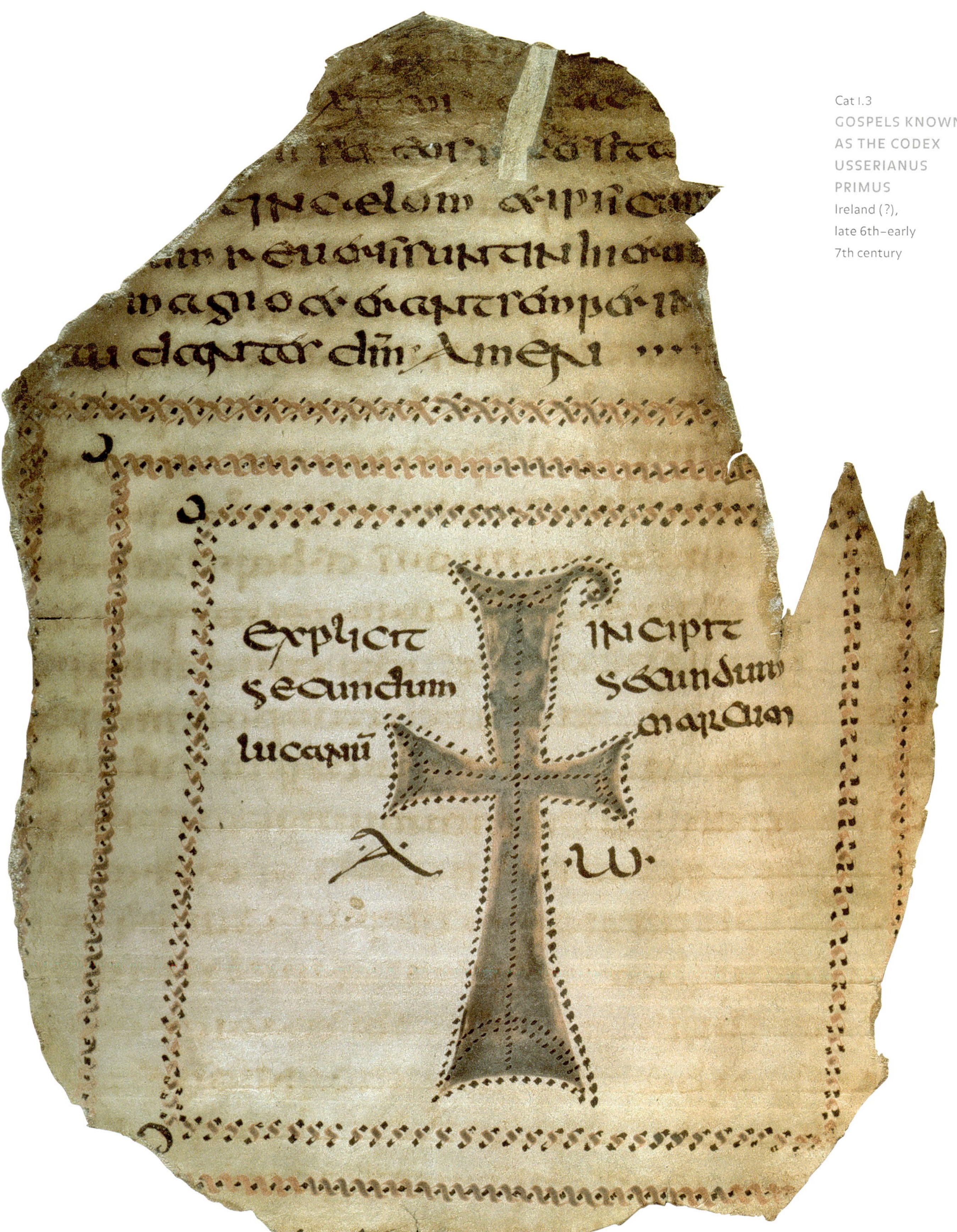

Cat I.3
GOSPELS KNOWN AS THE CODEX USSERIANUS PRIMUS
Ireland (?), late 6th–early 7th century

Perhaps he was referring to another Irish work? In any case, the Book of Kells combines all those superlatives and pursues them to the ultimate degree. To complicate them further would be sheer folly. More than any other, the Book of Kells deserved such enthusiasm. The greatest accolade of the acheiropoietic image – not made by the hand of man – is applied to a work seeming to have something superhuman about it. What is more, the writer refers to 'the sanctuary of art', enshrining the images as sacred in themselves. Lastly, this quotation, among many others, dismisses the notion that the period before the 15th century was an 'era before art'. On the contrary, it demonstrates a clear aesthetic sense.

Although the Book of Dimma is far from achieving the inventive genius of the Book of Kells, it nevertheless demonstrates the remarkable nature of Irish art. The portrait of St John is represented by his symbol, the eagle [I.15]. The front-facing figure of the bird spreads its wings inside a wide frame decorated with interlacing tendrils and lozenges. The points of its wings bend towards the four corners and its tail touches the lower edge. The design is completely dominated by curves intersecting in the centre to form two 'petals', a motif that occurs frequently, particularly in the Book of Dimma. The only features identifying the bird are its head and its claws: the other parts are subordinated to the taste for ornamental line that commands the painter's work. A whole web of interlacing lines covers the parchment page. It is easy to imagine the design of this page as an eagle-shaped cloisonné clasp.

The Irish monasteries produced many manuscripts that the monks took with them when they went to convert the Continent – for example, to Echternach, Saint-Gall (see Section II) or Luxeuil, but also to Bobbio [I.3]. In 612, the monks who had come from Ireland under St Columba to found a monastery at Bobbio in Emilia produced books there in the style they had used in Ireland, but their decoration owed much to the Italian tradition.

'Based on its simplest early forms', writes the historian Bernard Bischoff, 'throughout Christian art the Cross is the most widespread theme and the first sign of its symbolic language.' It first occurs in books dating back to the early Christian era. In an 8th century book of sermons (Heidelberg), in the four fields left empty by a cross covered in interlacing lines, an explicit text refers to the Cross itself, the strength it can procure and its symbolic value. The representation of the Cross was favoured in illustrated books in Italy, France and Germany during the pre-Carolingian and Carolingian eras. The painted cross in the Codex Usserianus Primus [I.3] is certainly inspired by similar crosses produced on the Continent. Linked to the monogram P, it is combined with the letters alpha and omega. Its position, not at the beginning of the Gospel but in the colophon, is a survival from the early Christian era.

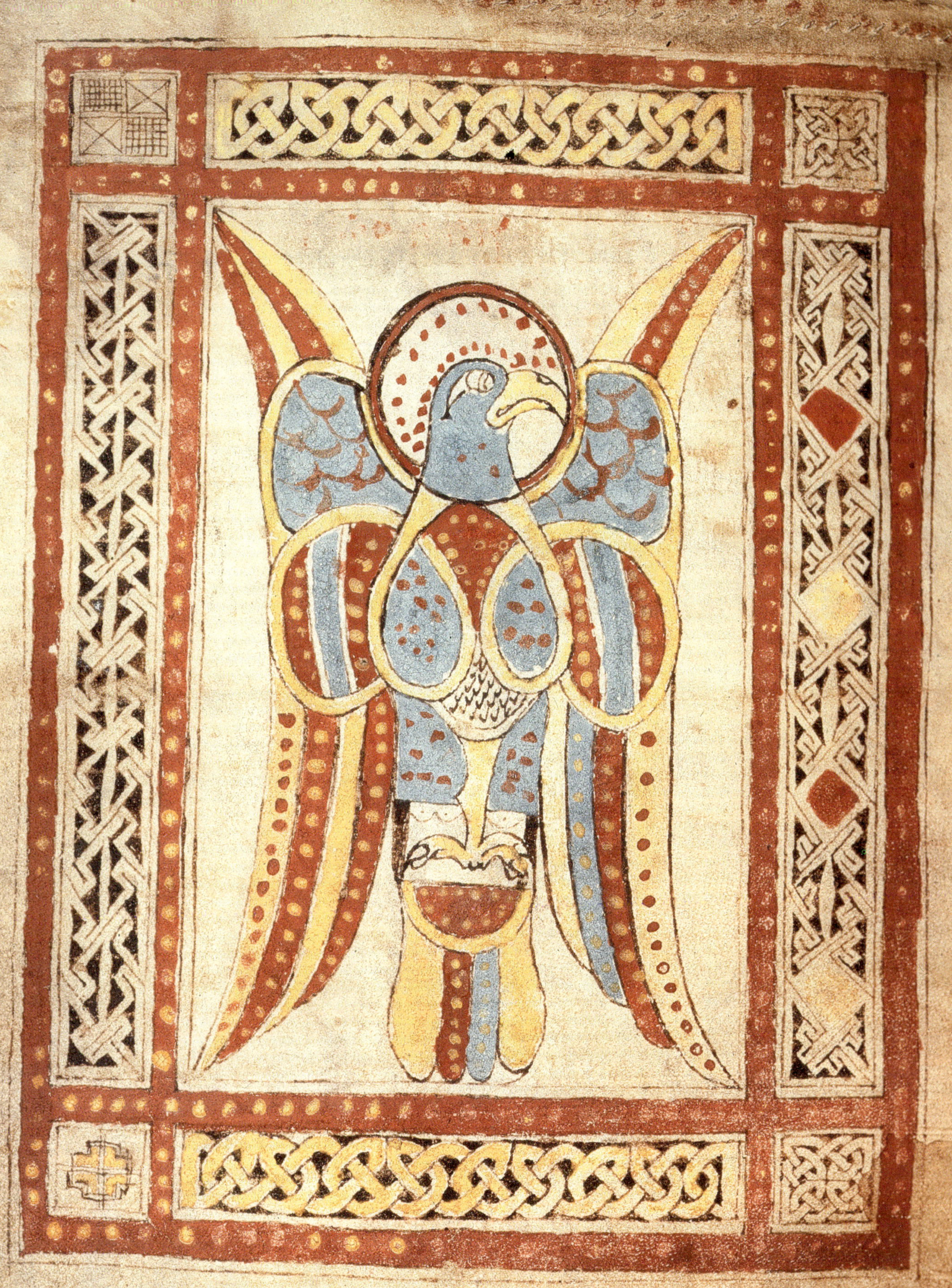
104

< Cat I.15
GOSPELS KNOWN AS THE BOOK OF DIMMA
Ireland, mid-8th century

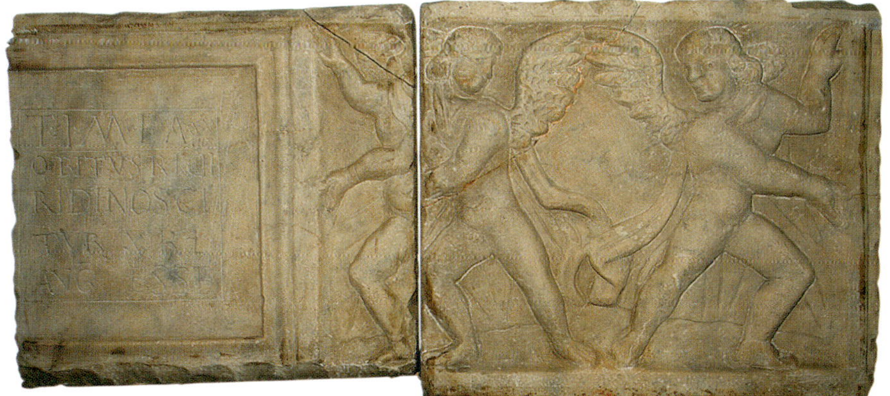

Cat I.2
FRAGMENTS FROM THE SARCOPHAGUS OF RICHAIRE
3rd–4th century

From that time on, we find the pectoral cross being worn in the West as well as the East. As an element of the liturgical vestments, it was not until the 12th century that it took its place as an amulet designed to avert evil and doubtless played that role. Some pectoral crosses may even have contained relics or been in contact with relics. The oldest examples of simple crosses cut out of a sheet of metal, or out of gold or silver leaf, and already bearing Christian symbols, date back to the 5th century. Lombardy and southern Germany produced many of them [I.4, 5].

The oldest representation of a cross with the head and shoulders of Christ appears in a Syrian gospel dated 634 and now at Wolfenbüttel, Germany. In the Echternach Gospel kept at Trier, the four Evangelist symbols appear, but the head and shoulders of Christ occupy the place of the Agnus Dei (Lamb of God). The arms of the cross and the frame of the composition are decorated with interlacing lines. On the page from the book of Orosius [I.16], it should be noted that this cross, although Latin in style, nevertheless looks somewhat Greek. As with the Syrian cross, its makers may have been thinking of the analogy it is supposed to offer with the axes of the sky. The Cross standing on Golgotha also has a cosmological meaning, as it has to occupy the centre of the world and its arms have to touch the north-south and east-west extremities of the celestial globe. Such analogies, developed in early Christian spiritual literature, must not be forgotten here. The design of the cross inscribed in an 'offset' square or rectangle to leave a square space in its centre, as seen in the work of Orosius, is often found in the Irish miniature. In the Gundohinus Gospels [I.17] the Tetramorph page's design

Cat I.4
PECTORAL CROSS
Lombardy (?), Southern Germany (?), second half of the 7th century

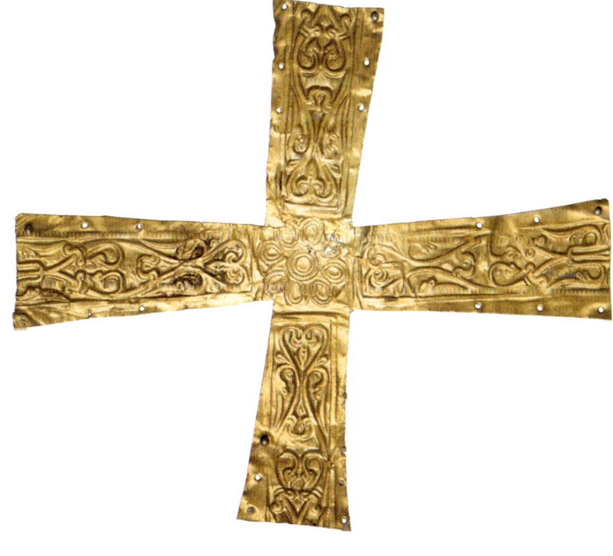

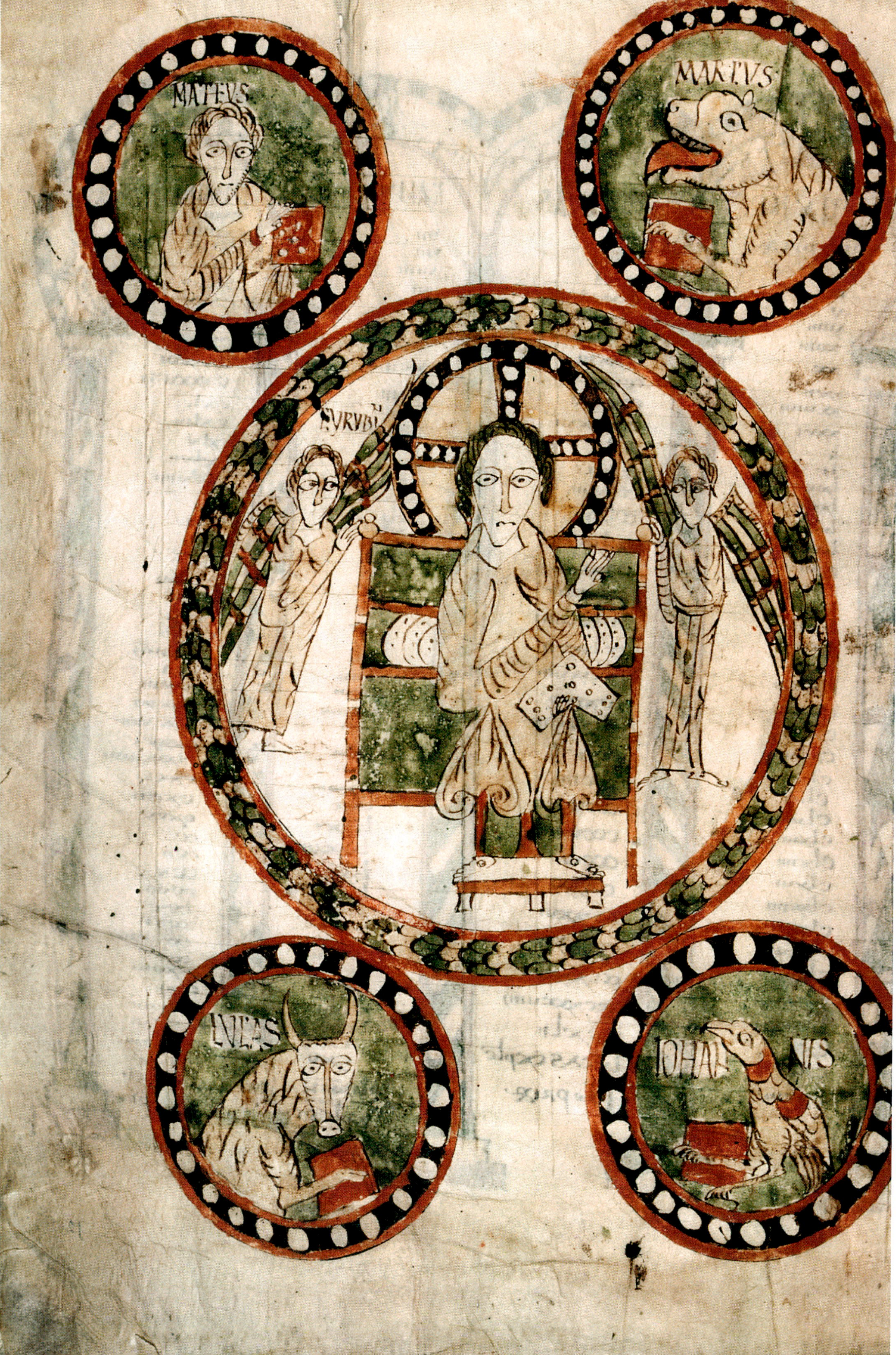
MATEVS
MARCVS
ÇVRVBI
LVCAS
IOHANNIS

< Cat I.17
GUNDOHINUS
GOSPELS
Burgundy, 754

still echoes the tradition of the Orosius manuscript [I.16] with its probable cosmological speculations. However, the fact that certain less elegant illuminations might refer to such models is indeed proof that the latter were not restricted to scriptoria where prestigious orders were being fulfilled. They were in fact intended for a wider readership.

The first section of this exhibition opens with a display of minimal artistic value, but one that eloquently demonstrates the transition from the pagan Greco-Roman civilization to the West that was gradually converting to Christianity. These are fragments of Roman marble sarcophagi [I.1, 2]. Countless similar cases occurred during the first millennium: Roman sarcophagi were not viewed with disdain as reflecting a pagan past but, rather, were valued for their venerable antiquity that brought them closer to the very source of Christianity.

BIBLIOGRAPHY: J. Hubert, J. Porcher, W. F. Volbach, *L'Europe des Invasions*, L'Univers des Formes, Paris, 1967; P. Harbison, *L'art médiéval en Irlande*, La Pierre-qui-Vive, 1998.

II

The Carolingian Empire and its legacy

ROLAND RECHT

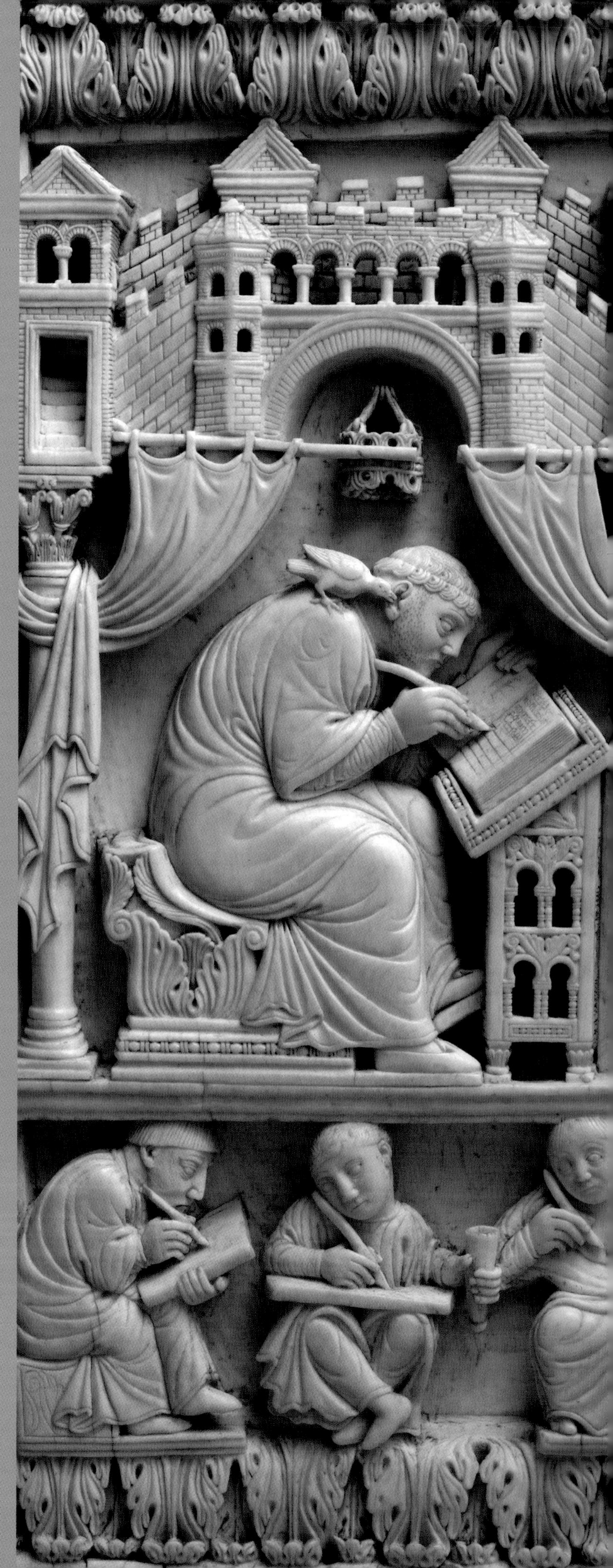

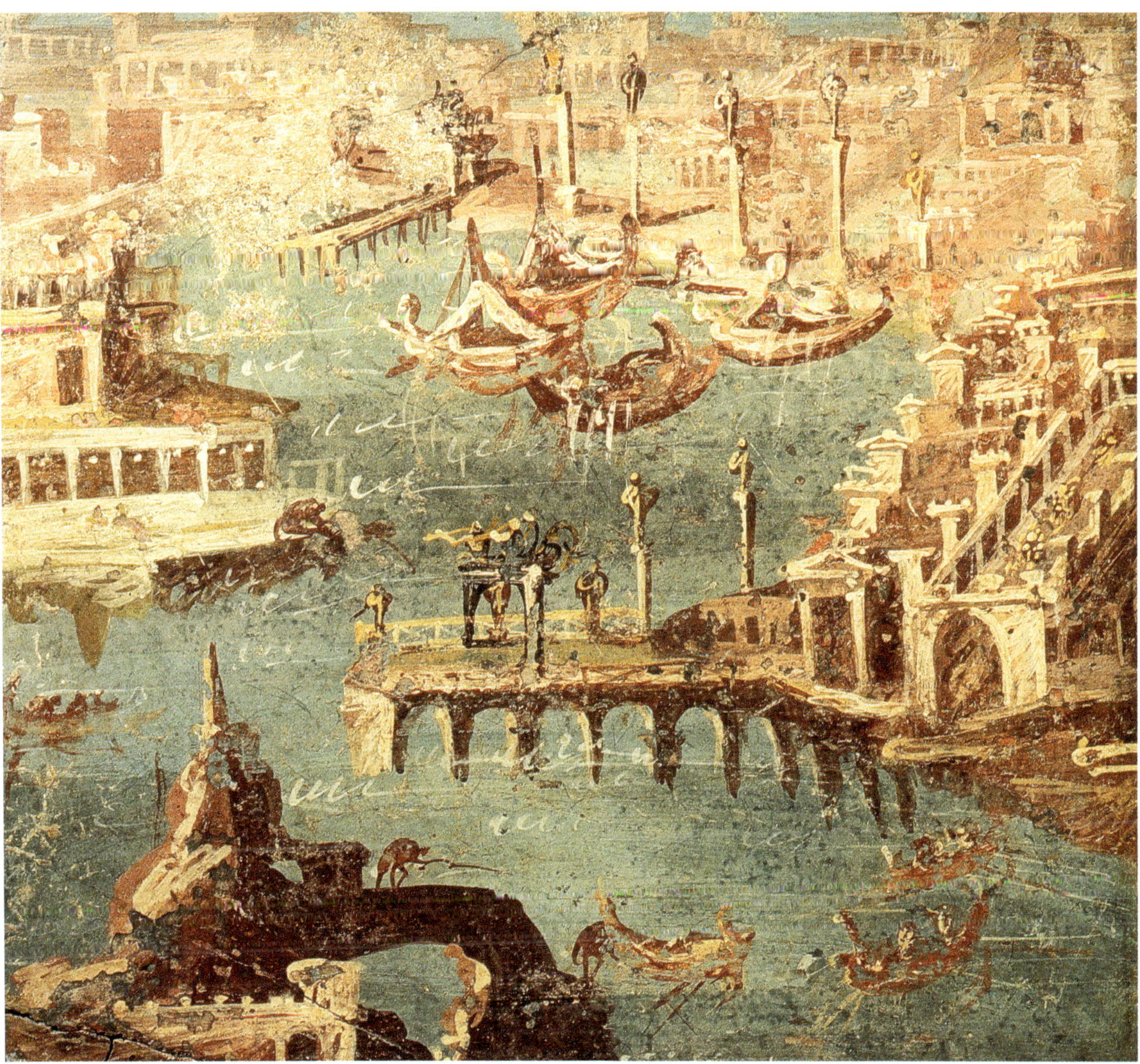

Cat II.6
LANDSCAPE
Naples, 1st century AD

The Carolingian Empire was born of a Frankish king's desire to bring the Roman Empire back to life. That ambition explains in itself the artistic leanings of most of the people close to Charlemagne, on whom he conferred the administration of dioceses or abbeys: they looked to Greco-Roman Antiquity or Byzantine art. An essential reporter of this era was Eginhard, who trained in the Court school and was the Emperor's biographer. He tells in the *Vita Caroli Magni* how Charlemagne had obtained from Pope Hadrian I the right to remove marble columns from the ancient monuments of Ravenna and Rome. But the inclination towards Greco-Roman art presented considerable problems – firstly, because the Christian iconography programmes that had to be fulfilled were rarely based on any previous figurative tradition and, secondly, because the models for the figures concerned were appropriate for antique mythology or literature but certainly not for the content of the Bible, or at least not without a considerable effort at transposition.

The Psalter conserved in Utrecht [II.5] is an admirable example of the capacity of the men of the 9th century to resolve those problems. It was probably composed and enriched with narrative scenes in the scriptorium of Hautvilliers near Rheims, which also produced the famous Ebbo Gospels. Its superbly executed pen drawings are not merely 'illustrations' of the Psalms but veritable decorated commentaries.

< Cat II.20
BOOK COVER, SHOWING ST GREGORY
Franco-Saxon (?), Metz school (?), third quarter of the 9th century

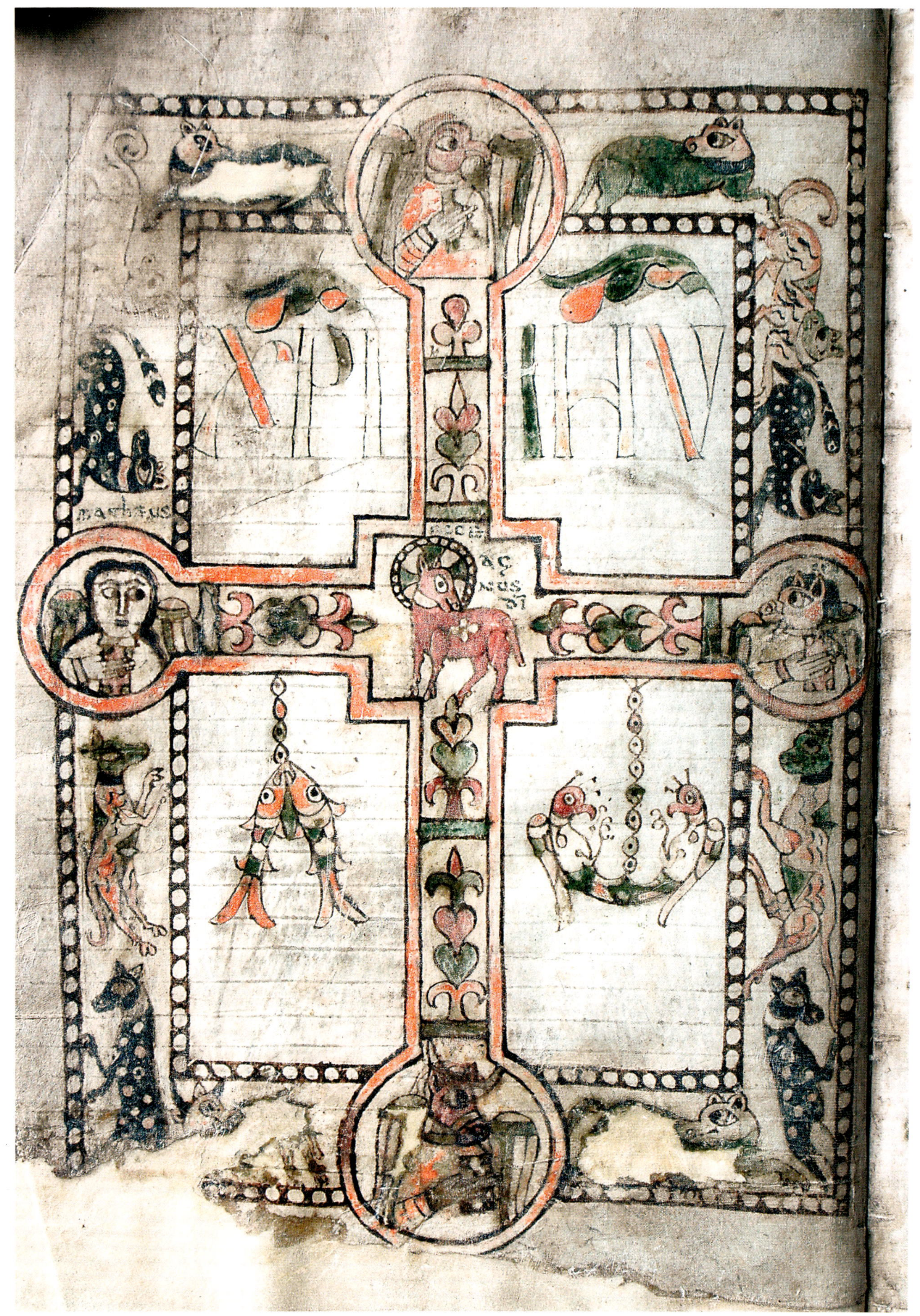
XPI IHV
ag nus dī

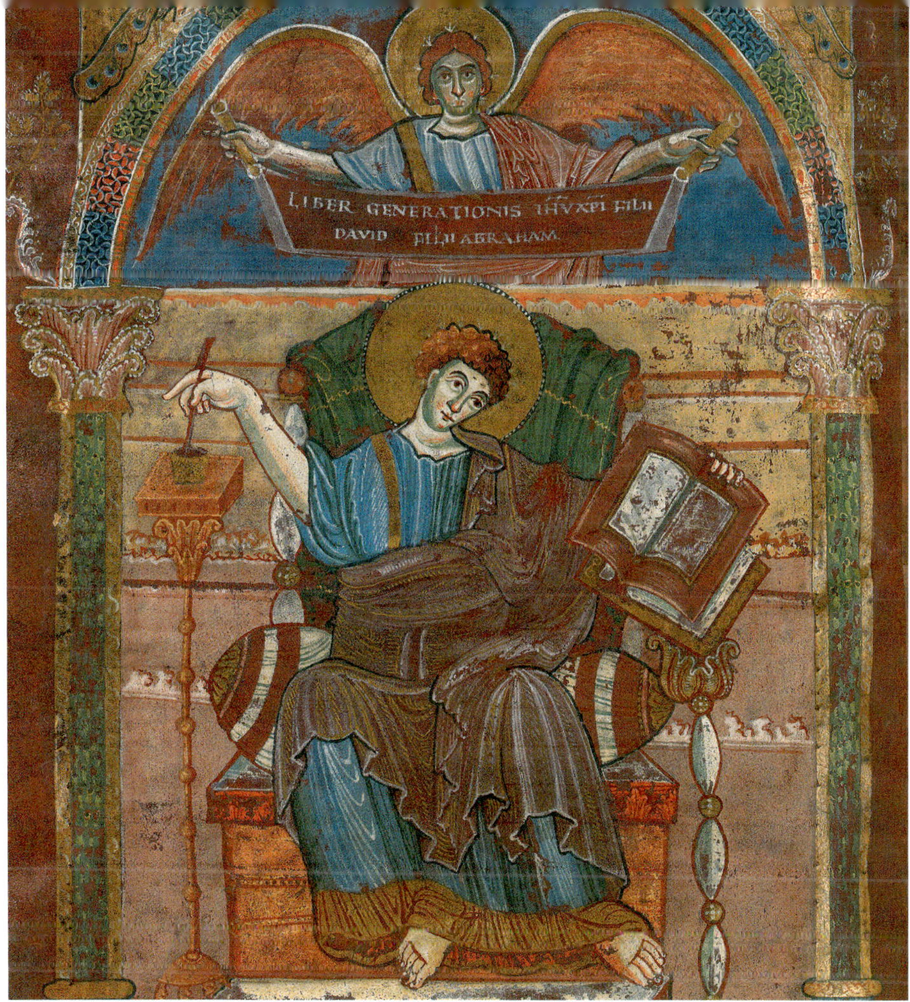

Cat II.2
CENTULA GOSPELS
(recto)
Palatine court,
late 8th century

Cat II.28
FIRST BIBLE OF SAINT-MARTIAL DE LIMOGES
Abbey of Saint-Martial de Limoges, second half of the10th century

The creators of those drawings were not only learned interpreters of the theologians with whom they collaborated, but were themselves familiar with Greco-Roman painting[II.6], whose motifs they succeeded in adapting motifs to Christian texts. They succeeded in conserving the fire and energy characteristic of those works of Antiquity.

But the Psalter also contributed to another of Charlemagne's ambitions – that of homogenizing religious practices and reorganizing the Church, a reform that had been started by Pepin the Short. The publication of liturgical books – such as sacramentaries[II.15] and gospels[II.2, 12] containing concordance tables supported the Empire's adoption of the Roman liturgy.

Books were therefore to play a central role in firmly establishing the imperial idea and anchoring it in Antiquity and in the vast programme for the reorganization of the Church. The scribes perfected a new form of writing that had been initiated under Pepin the Short, the Caroline form, which was to make texts easier to read, while the creation of scriptoria assisted the multiplication of copies intended for collegiate and ecclesiastical establishments, enabling them to compile prestigious libraries.

Charlemagne's personal participation in the development of art was considerable. When the second Council of Nicaea

< Cat I.16
OROSIUS, HISTORY AGAINST THE PAGANS
Laon (?),
mid-8th century

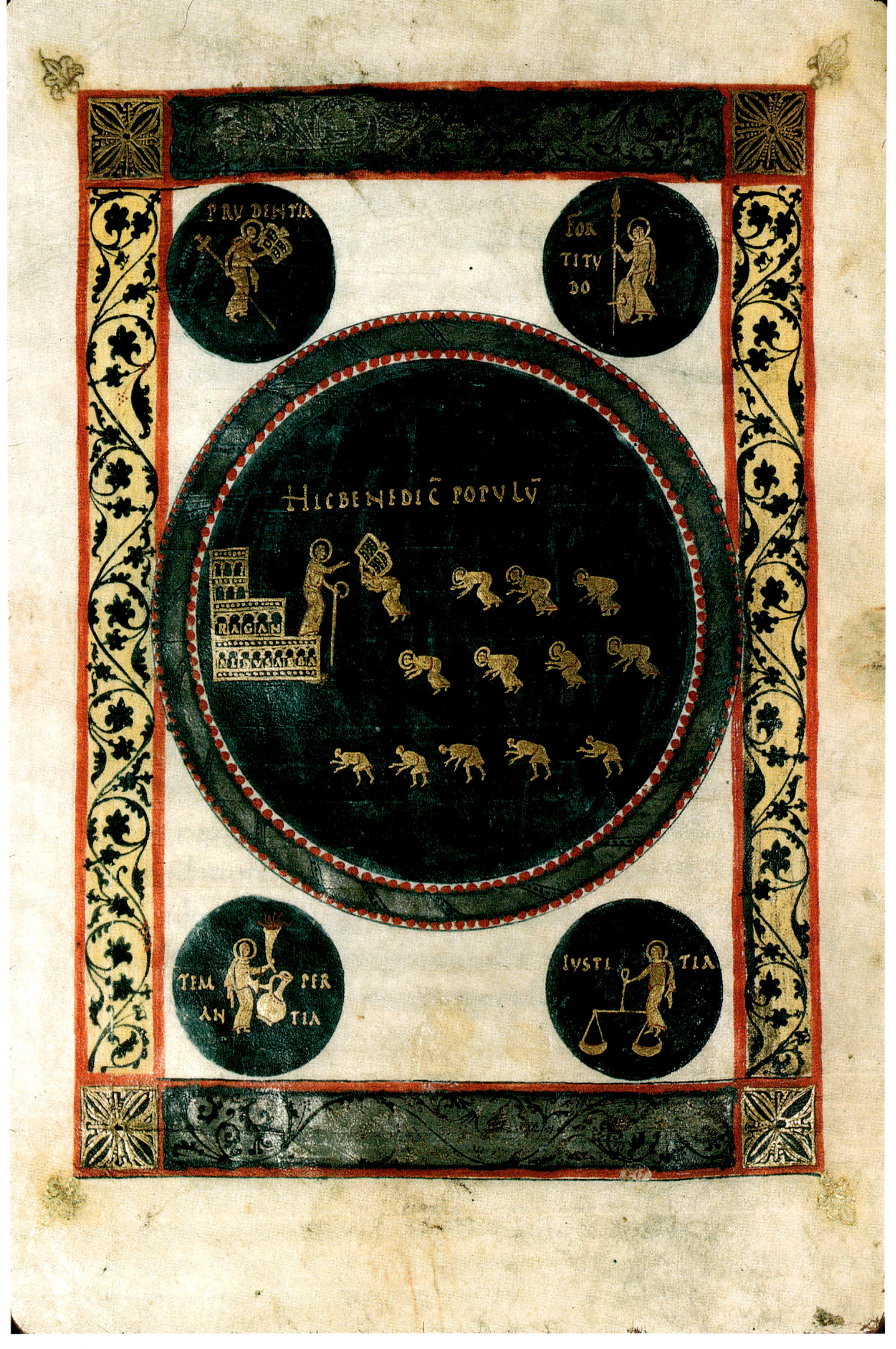
PRUDENTIA
FORTITUDO
HIC BENEDIC̄ POPULŪ
TEMPERANTIA
IUSTITIA

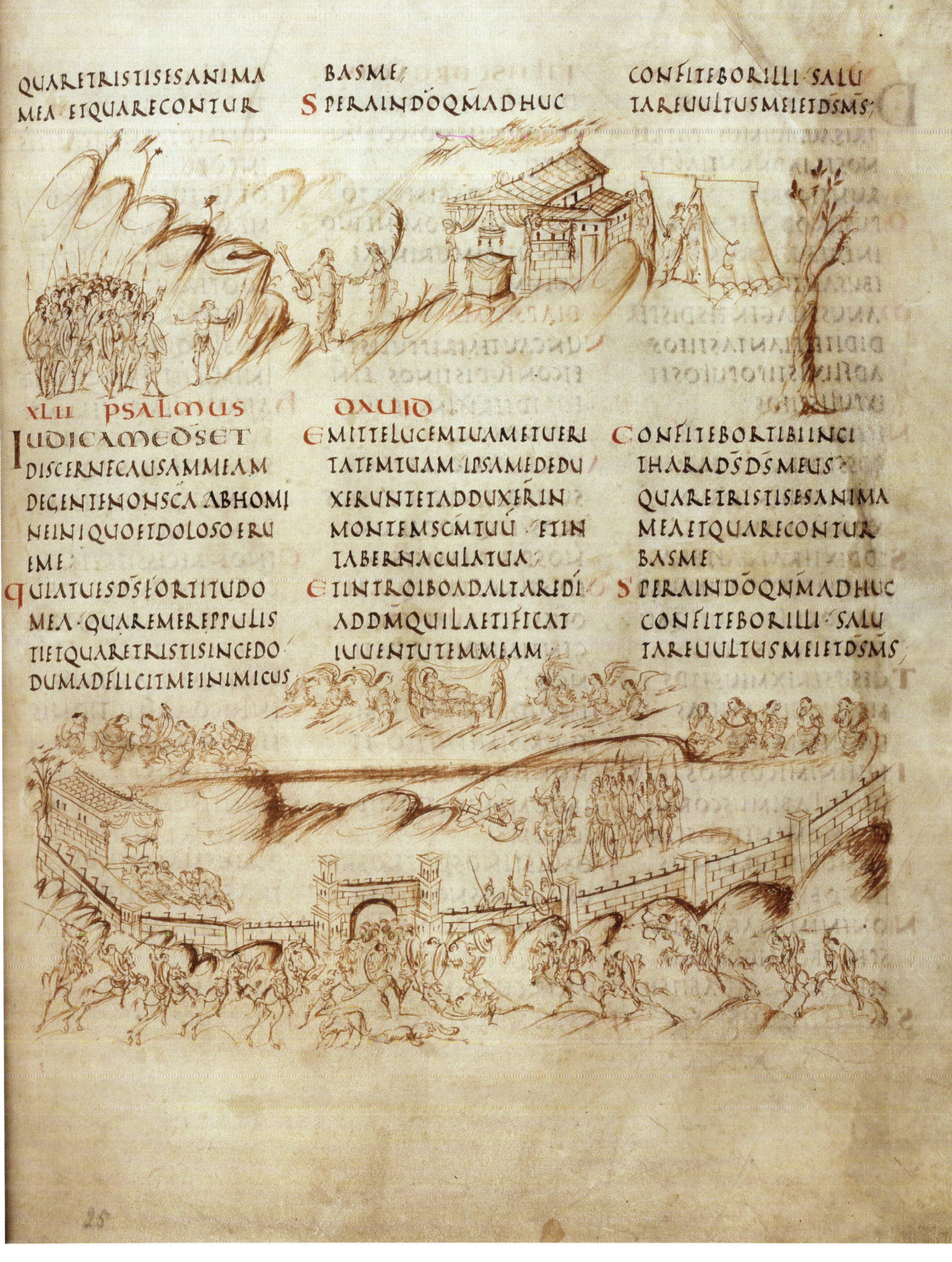

QUARETRISTISESANIMA
MEA ETQUARECONTUR
BASME
SPERAINDOQMADHUC
CONFITEBORILLI SALU
TAREUULTUSMEIETDSMS

XLII PSALMUS DAUID

IUDICAMEDSET
DISCERNECAUSAMMEAM
DEGENTENONSCA ABHOMI
NEINIQUOETDOLOSOERU
EME
QUIATUESDSFORTITUDO
MEA QUAREMEREPPULIS
TIETQUARETRISTISINCEDO
DUMADFLIGITMEINIMICUS

EMITTELUCEMTUAMETUERI
TATEMTUAM IPSAMEDEDU
XERUNTETADDUXERIN
MONTEMSCMTUU ETIN
TABERNACULATUA
ETINTROIBOADALTAREDI
ADDMQUILAETIFICAT
IUUENTUTEMMEAM

CONFITEBORTIBIINCI
THARADSDSMEUS
QUARETRISTISESANIMA
MEAETQUARECONTUR
BASME
SPERAINDOQMADHUC
CONFITEBORILLI SALU
TAREUULTUSMEIETDSMS

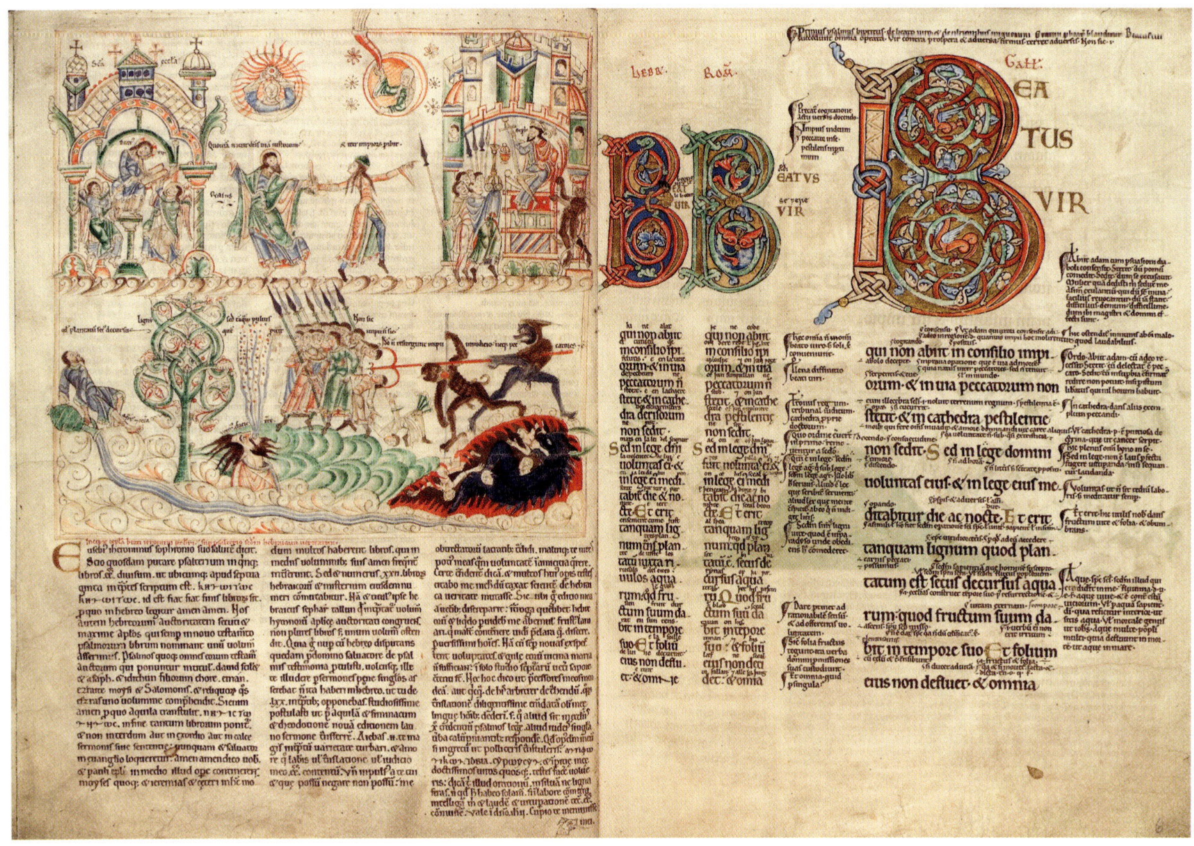

Cat II.8
EADWINE PSALTER
Christ Church, Canterbury, *c.* 1150–60 (with post-1160 additions)

(787) re-established the use of images in the Byzantine Empire and thus put an end to the iconoclastic crisis, Theodulf of Orleans, councillor to the Court, clearly refuted idolatry. However, Charlemagne himself favoured that form of worship and set an example by commissioning the production of highly prestigious images, as did Louis the Pious and then Charles the Bald, both of whom promoted active patronage.

Obviously, we do not know how the scriptoria were organized. There is every reason to assume that several scribes worked in each but that, except in unusual situations, they were not entrusted with illustrating manuscripts, illustration being reserved for the most prestigious commissions. It seems likely that, if a scribe took part in illustrating a book, he was content to draw and embellish the initial letters. The portrait in the Eadwine Psalter II.8 of its scribe (Eadwine), and the flattering words he uses to describe himself – 'Scribe: the prince of scribes am I: my praises and my glory will never be extinguished….' allow us to assume that he may have had a share in designing the illustrations of that exceptional work.

Many illuminators were probably itinerant – as were building foremen and craftsmen – and executed orders as they came in, travelling to one scriptorium or another. The case of the Lombard known as Nivardus, whom the royal abbey of

<< Cat II.15
MARMOUTIER SACRAMENTARY
Abbey of Saint-Martin, Marmoutier, Tours, 844–45

< Cat II.5
UTRECHT PSALTER
Hautvillers, near Rheims, *c.* 825–35

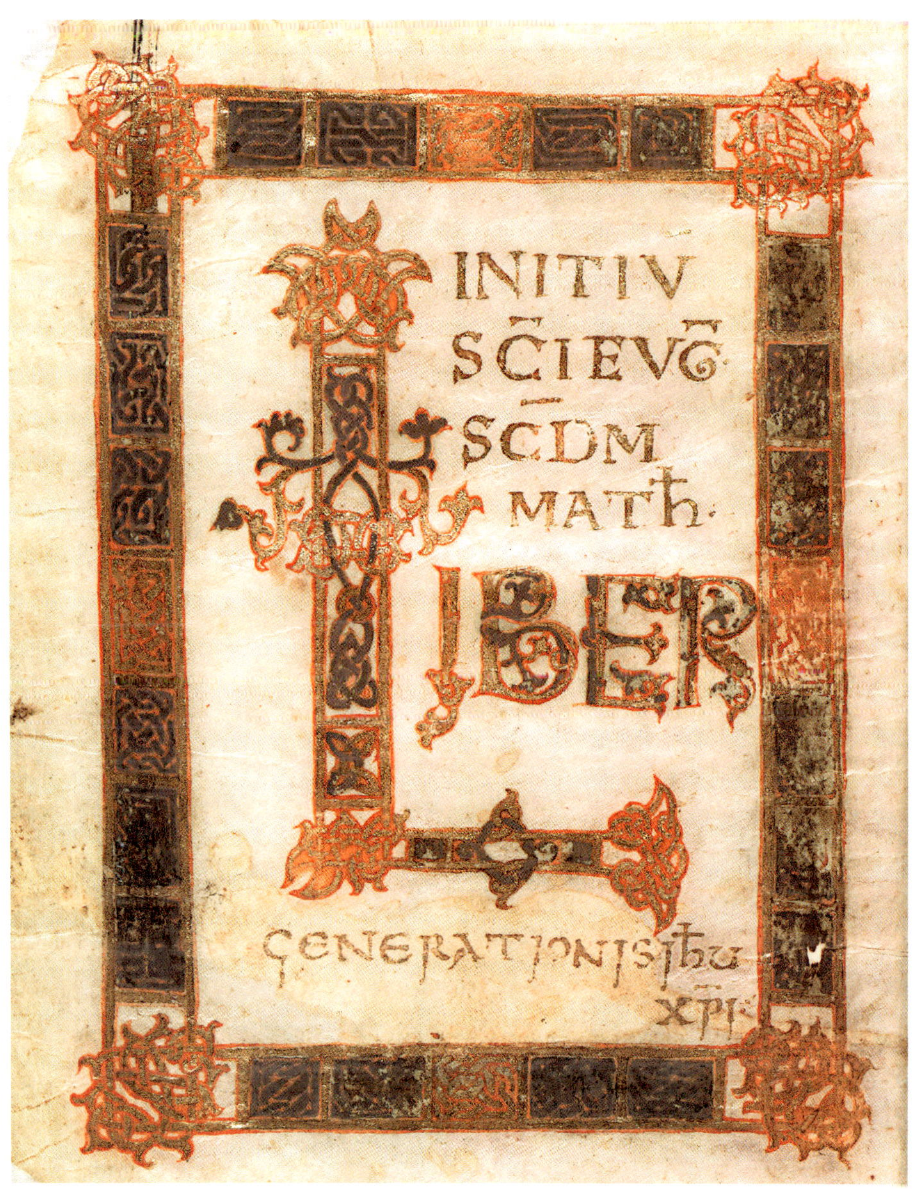

Cat II.29
GAIGNIÈRES GOSPELS
Fleury, early 11th century

Fleury commissioned to illustrate the Gaignières Gospels[II.29] at the request of Robert the Pious, cannot have been rare. We should also remember that many artists – often monks – were multitalented. The monk Tuotilo, who practised music, painting, sculpture and gold work, is mentioned at the abbey of Saint-Gall (in the period 895–912). He was probably responsible for the binding of the Evangelium Longum, which is still at Saint-Gall and may also have worked on the decoration of the Psalterium Aureum[II.21]. In the same scriptorium, Notker Balbulus, a poet, Ratpert, a chronicler, and Sintram, an illuminator, are likewise mentioned. Tuotilo was also called to Mainz and Metz to undertake commissions for an altar and a Virgin.

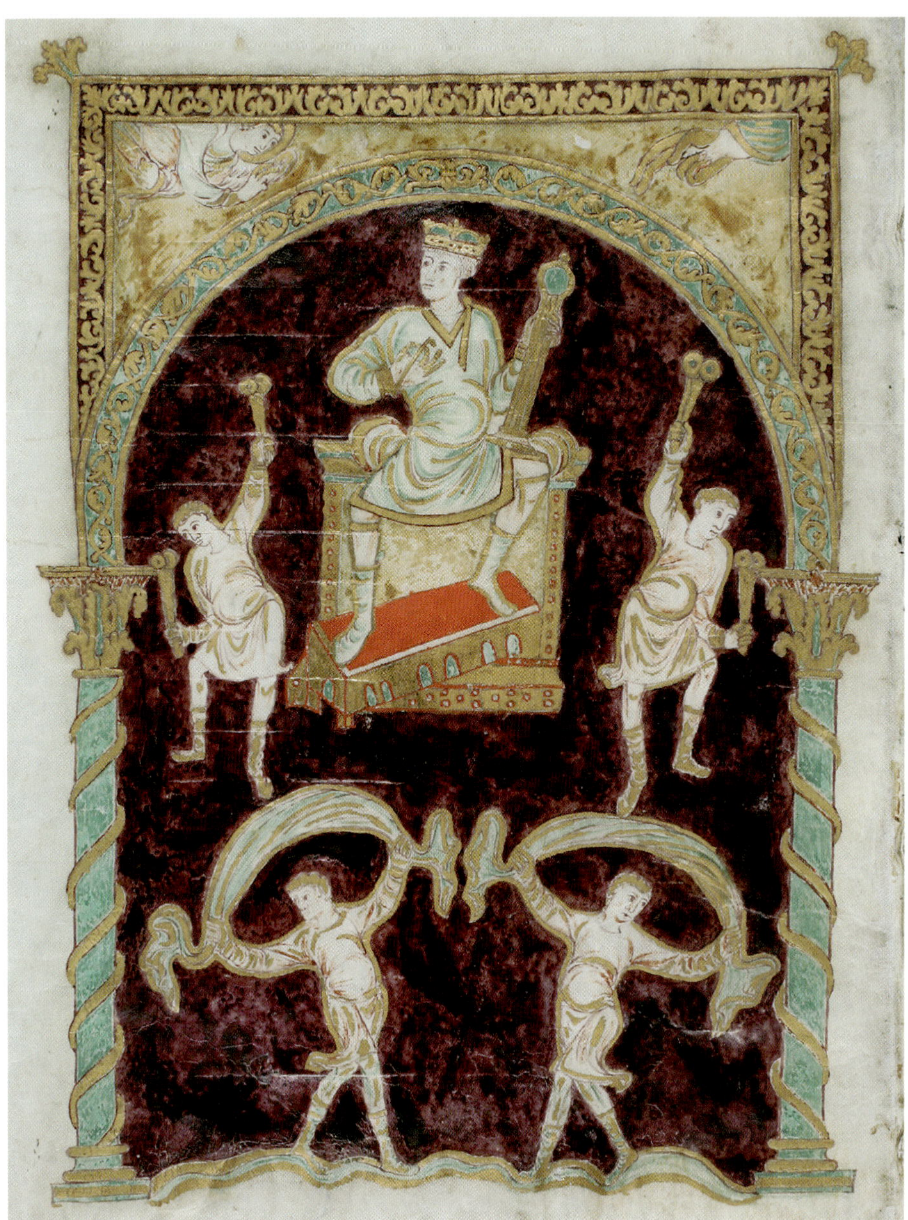

Cat II.21
PSALTERIUM AUREUM (GOLDEN PSALTER)
Saint-Gall, Switzerland
late 9th century

Thus, we should view with caution the concept of the classic historiography of 'schools' that produced both illustrated manuscripts and ivories. Metz was probably not the only place where productive scriptoria existed, and nor were Rheims, Tours or Fleury. Although itinerant artists predominated in terms of numbers, the notion that 'schools' of art existed is still a shaky one. However, we must acknowledge that it remains a convenient way of classifying such works.

The manuscripts and the ivories that have been grouped under the expression 'Palatine school' often owe much to Byzantine **II.2** or palaeochristian art **II.4**. The masterpieces of the style practised in Charlemagne's sphere of influence, the

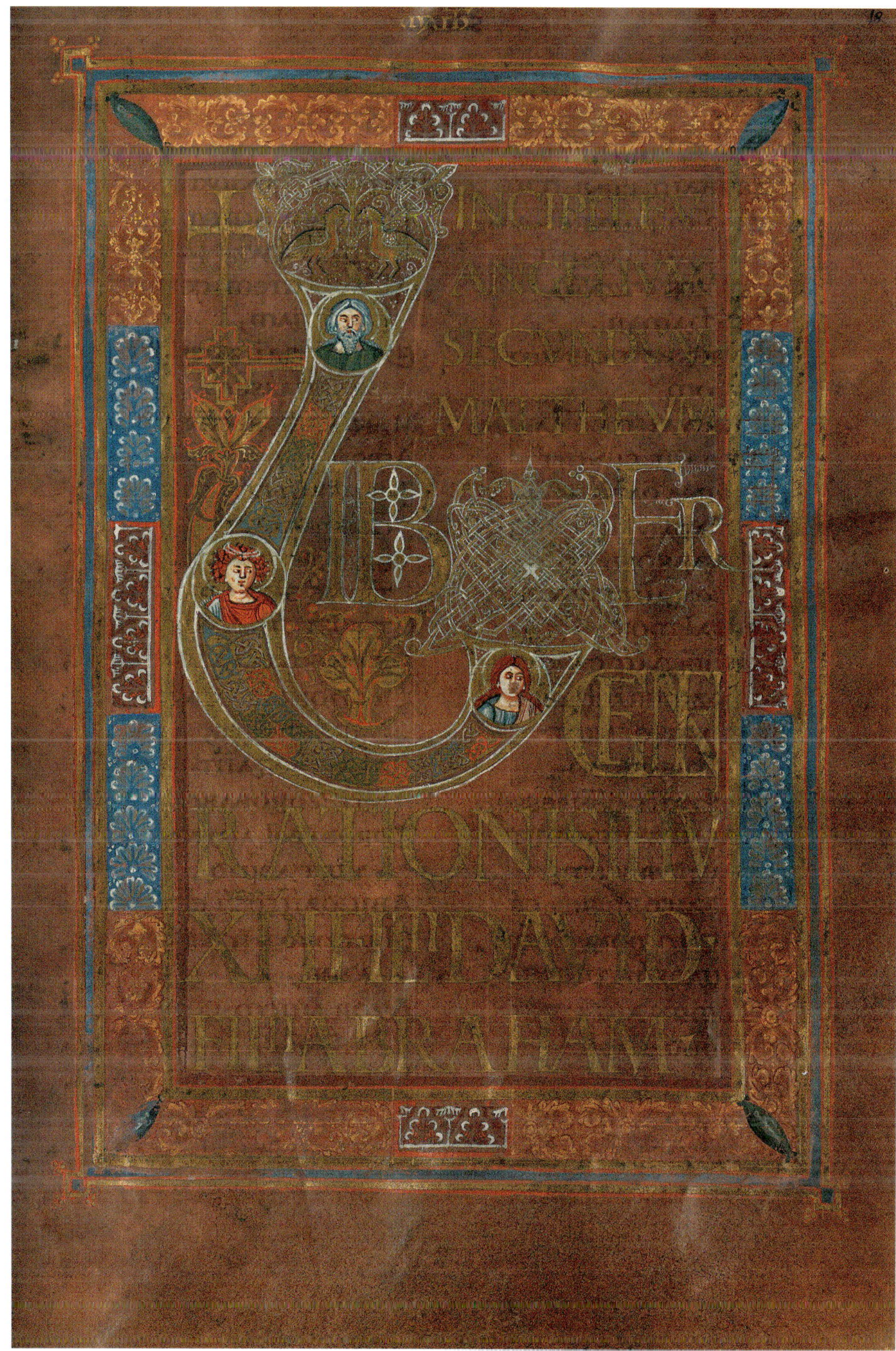

Cat II.2
CENTULA GOSPELS
(verso)
Palatine court,
late 8th century

Lorsch and Godescalc Gospels and the ivory diptique from the church of Saint-Martin in Genoels-Elderen (Musées royaux, Brussels) have also been classified as belonging to the 'Ada group'. The school of Rheims produced two outstanding works probably owed to the same 'workshop' or group of itinerant artists: the Ebbo Gospels (Bibliothèque municipale, Epernay) and the Utrecht Psalter [II.5]. Ebbo (775–851), the foster-brother and librarian of Louis the Pious, was archbishop of Rheims, where he was extremely active, particularly encouraging the production of books. The Ebbo Gospels are a luxurious manuscript whose painter was clearly one of the leading artists of the Middle Ages. The vigour of his brush and the

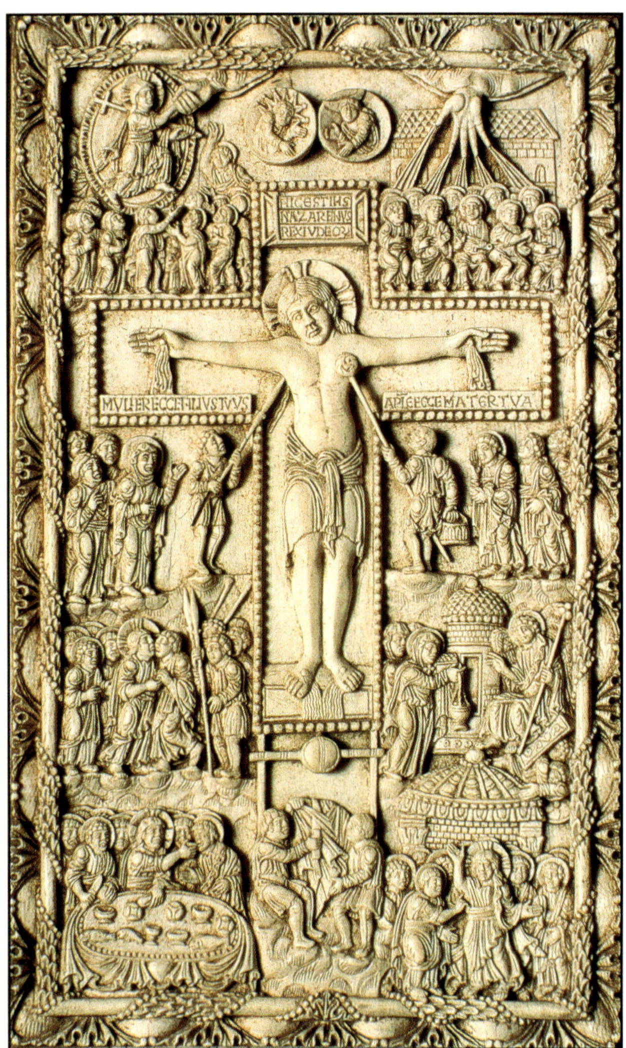

Cat II.4
BOOK COVER WITH CRUCIFIXION SCENE
Palatine court, early 9th century

resources of his palette give the Evangelists a kind of inner fire. Even the landscape is touched by that spark. It is the work of a visionary who allows himself complete freedom in the design of his pictures. This same expressive force is found in the Utrecht Psalter[II.5]. The singular genius of those two works is as enigmatic as that of the frescoes in the little church of Santa Maria foris Portas in Castelseprio near Milan. Here again, it is hard to grasp clearly the genealogy of a delightful creation that imposes its strength but that, in the case of Castelseprio, led nowhere. Thus, there are still many grey areas in our understanding of Carolingian art.

> Cat II.20
BOOK COVER, SHOWING ST GREGORY
Franco-Saxon (?), Metz school (?), third quarter of the 9th century

A set of ivories, attributed to the school of Rheims, is known as the 'Liuthard group'. It diverted the classicizing orientation of the ivory carvers who worked for the Palatine court, as did the Utrecht Psalter. The book covers that transpose the vigorous scenes of the Utrecht Psalter or the Ebbo Gospels to a material difficult to work constitute a high point in the art of carving in ivory[II.7, 13].

In about the year 1000, the Utrecht Psalter was taken to Christ Church abbey, Canterbury, in the context of the relations England was establishing with the Continent and the reform of the Benedictine monasteries. The monastic scriptoria of 12th-century England also called upon scribes and illuminators from outside the monastery. What we can infer from the time the Psalter spent across the Channel is the very particular way in which not an artist but a prestigious work would circulate. In the scriptorium of Saint-Martin de Tours in *c.* 800, Alcuin asked for English manuscripts to be sent to improve the writing of the scribes of Touraine which he considered mediocre.

We have assembled a set of manuscripts that offer different responses to the arrival of the Utrecht Psalter, a masterpiece from which the abbey seems to have derived great pride. Either it was a 'copy', like the Harley Psalter[II.9] or the Besançon Gospels[II.11], or a version that constitutes a solemn but highly exceptional amplification of it, like the Eadwine Psalter[II.8]. The painter of the Ramsey Psalter[II.10]

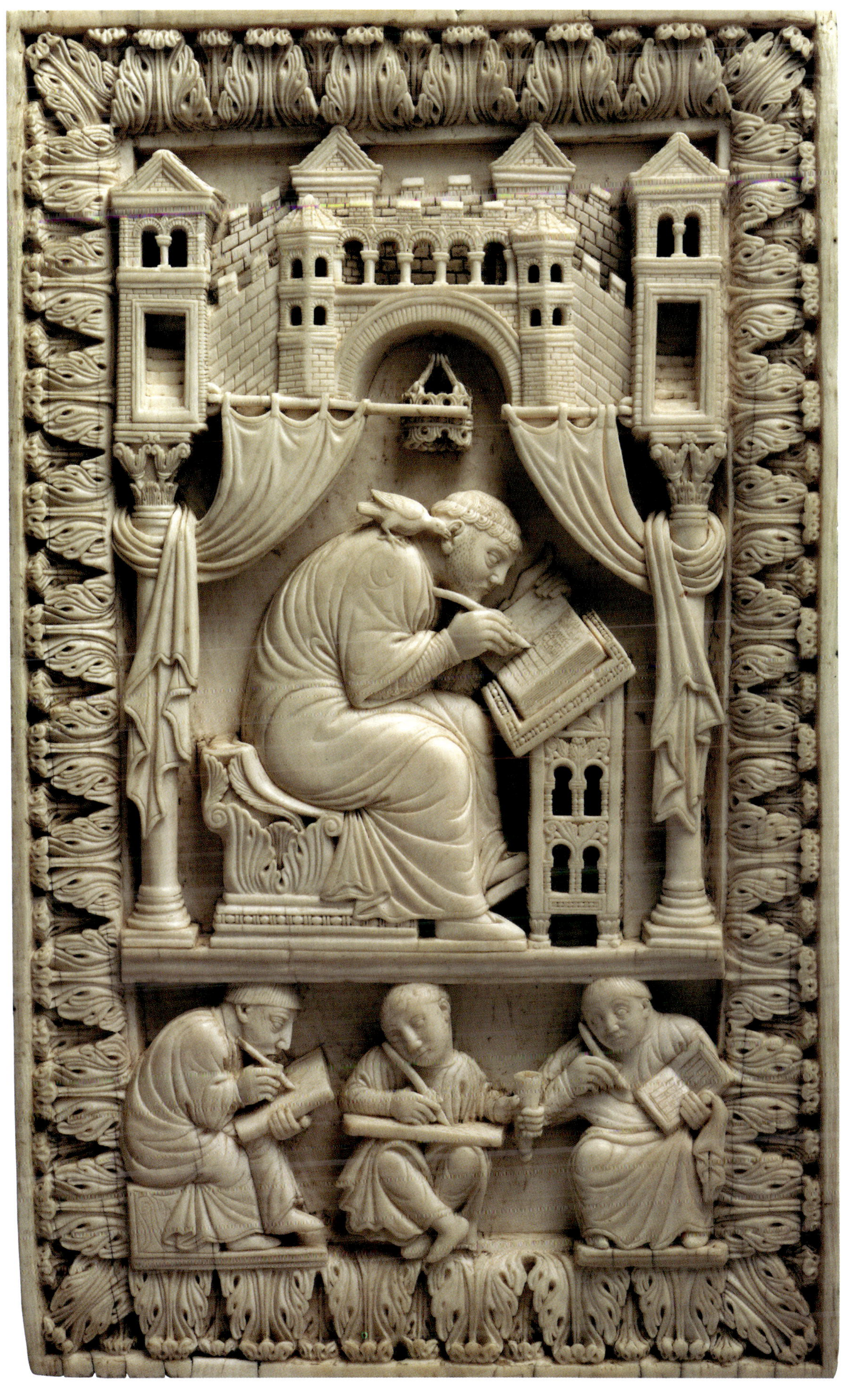

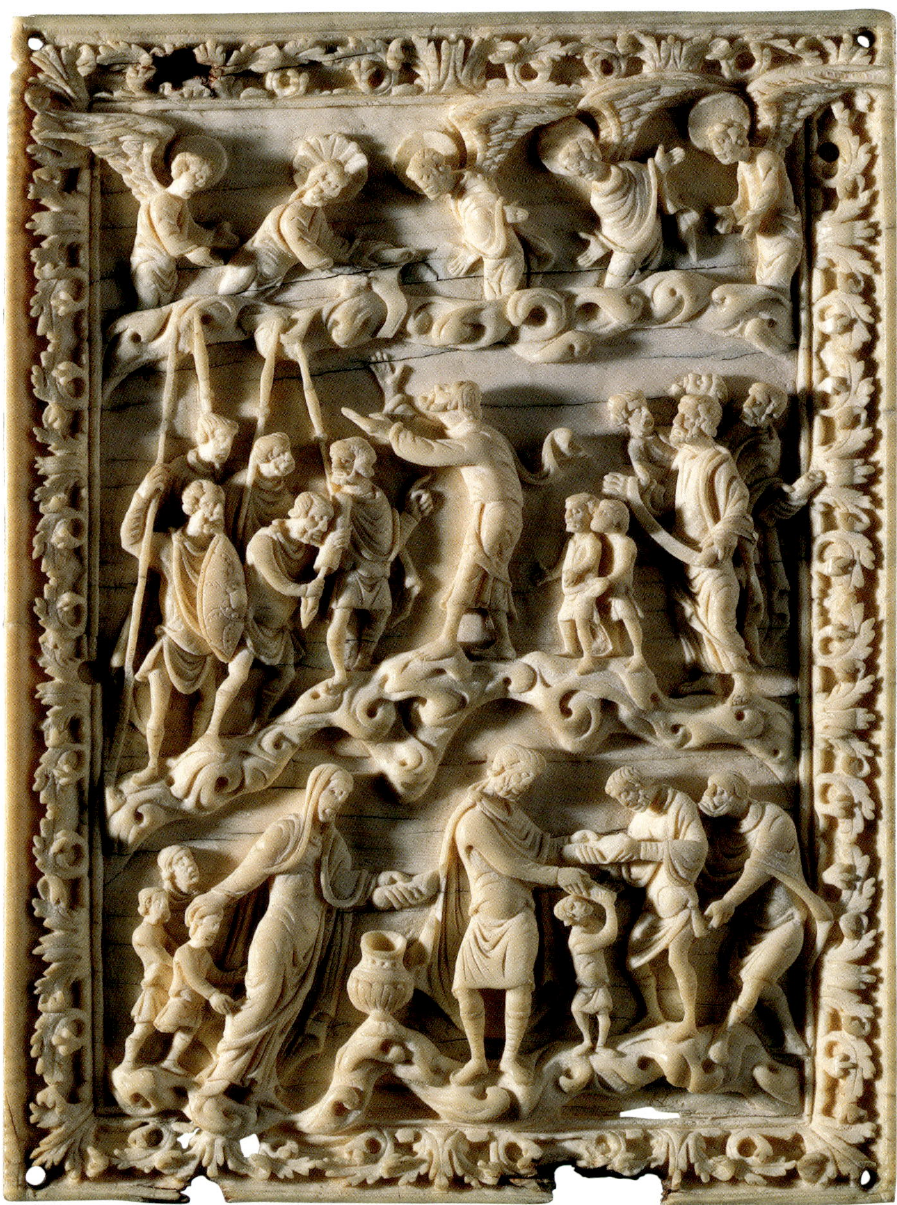

Cat II.13
COVER FROM THE BOOK KNOWN AS THE HOURS OF CHARLES THE BALD
School of the Palace of Charles the Bald, 846–69

attentively studied the illustrations of the Utrecht Psalter and, through him, that decorative style was to play an important part in the development of Anglo-Saxon art. That same painter illustrated the Boulogne Gospels at Saint-Bertin, a treatise on astronomy at Fleury and the Ramsey Psalter at Winchester or at Ramsey itself. He was a very great artist who went to Canterbury to study the Carolingian psalter there.

The Eadwine Gospels[II.8] constitute a very large and extremely costly book: gold and silver leaf were used for the first letter of each verse of each psalm. It must therefore have been a commissioned work for a high-ranking patron. Was it

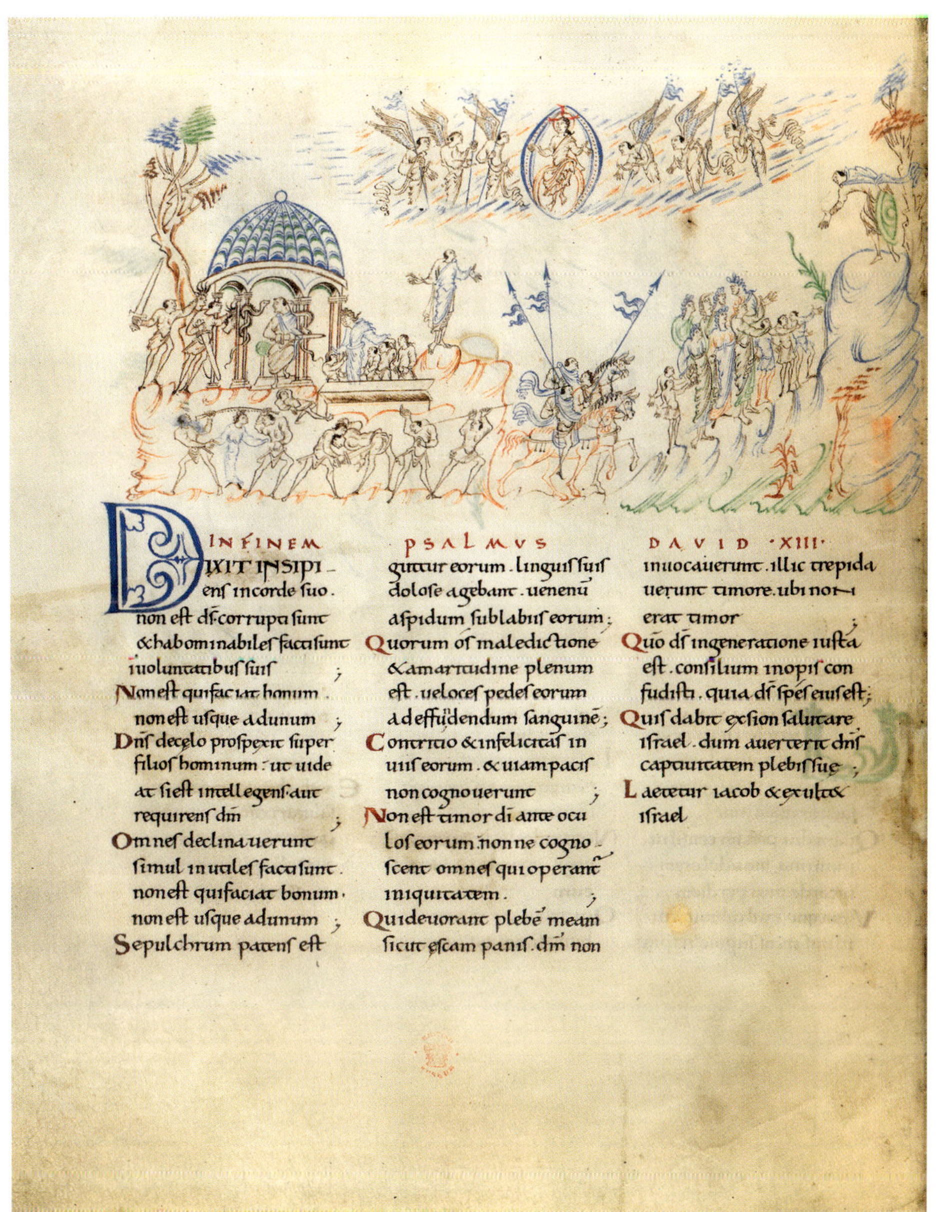

Cat II.9
HARLEY PSALTER
Christ Church, Canterbury, early 11th–early 12th century, unfinished

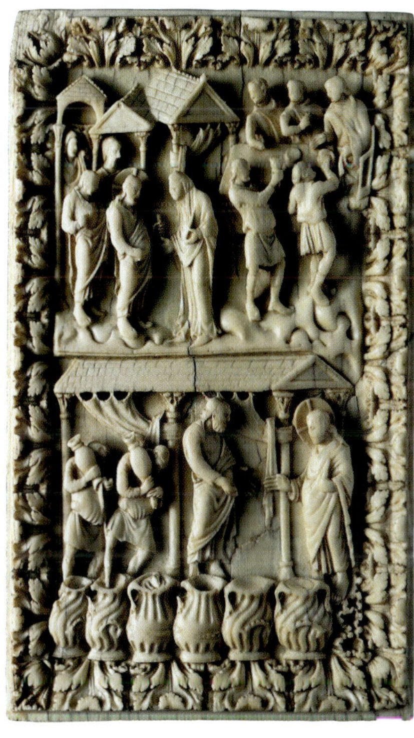

Cat II.7
BOOK COVER: THE WEDDING AT CANA
School of the Palace of Charles the Bald, Compiègne, 9th century

Eadwine, whose name appears in the book, who commissioned it? More probably, it was Prior Wibert, under whose leadership the psalter was produced and who would have been the scribe's hierarchical superior.

Other centres of learning linked to religious foundations are of significance. Thus, Bishop Drogo of the diocese of Metz, a son of Charlemagne born of an adulterous relationship, developed a large scriptorium that produced in particular a Sacramentary and two Gospels, all kept in Paris (BnF), and a collection of texts on astronomy and the computation of the calendar [II.16]. These works are among the most remarkable examples of Carolingian illumination.

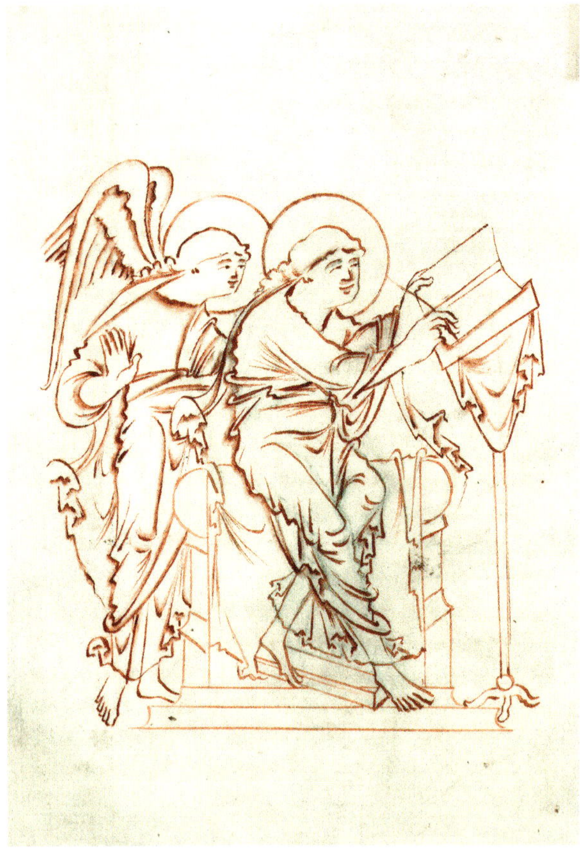

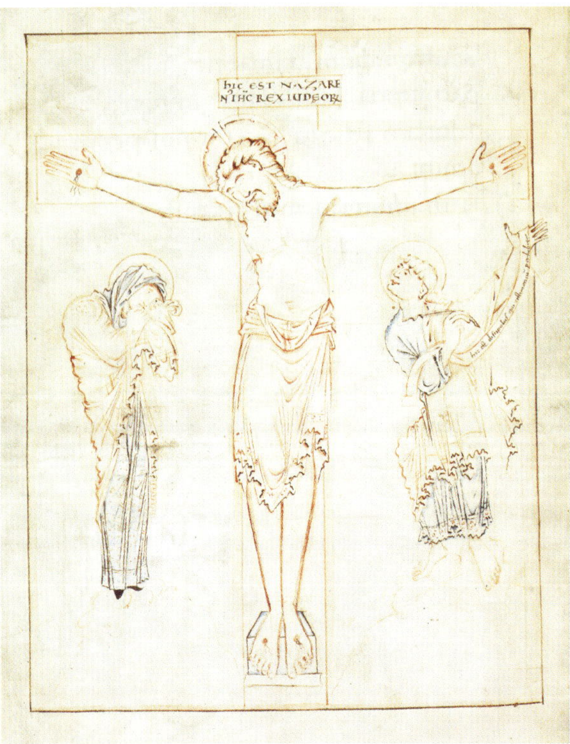

In the sphere of ivory, the school of Metz has left us eloquent evidence II.17, 18, 20. Here again, the notion of a 'school' should probably cover more extensive production centres located throughout Lotharingia (Lorraine), and even itinerant carvers. Moreover, some scholars have distinguished two schools of Metz, the first, owing to its chronological proximity, constituting the most direct route for the influences of the Palatine and Rheims schools, and the second, by far the most productive, which lasted until the end of the 10th century. It adopted the synthesizing approach of the first school, but often diluted its artistic value II.31.

The scriptorium of Saint-Martin de Tours II.15, of which Alcuin, the professorial adviser, was to become abbot in 796, also developed prodigiously, as did the abbey of Fleury II.14 under the abbacy of the Visigoth Theodulf, who became the archbishop of Orléans around 800, and was probably the author of the *Libri carolini* supporting the allegedly worship of idols in Byzantium.

It is known that Irish monks had brought to Saint-Gall manuscripts from their homeland ('*libri scottice scripti*') that were, of course, to play a part in the formation of the abbey's scriptorium (see Section I). Saint-Gall reached its apogee under the abbacy of Salomon III (in office 890 – 919) with the production of the famous *Psalterium Aureum* II.21.

If we want to assess the effect of Carolingian art on the centuries that followed we must turn to England. In the second half of the 10th century the Winchester style took shape under the direct influence of Carolingian art. The decoration of frames and certain formal idioms lent themselves to the Carolingian illumination of Tours. Winchester demonstrated an immoderate liking for decorative acanthus motifs and the strangest of combinations. In a certain way, it could be said that the power of the figures reiterates the works of the Palatine school but, equally the taste for ornamentation owes something to the Anglo-Saxon tradition too. The Benedictional of St Ethelwold II.22, who was abbot of Winchester between 963 and 984 and maintained contacts with the abbey of Fleury, was directly

Cat II.11
GOSPELS
Winchester (?),
c. 1015–30

Cat II.10
RAMSEY PSALTER
Ramsey (?),
before 988

Cat II.17
BOOK COVER WITH CRUCIFIXION SCENE
Metz or Lotharingia, third quarter of the 9th century

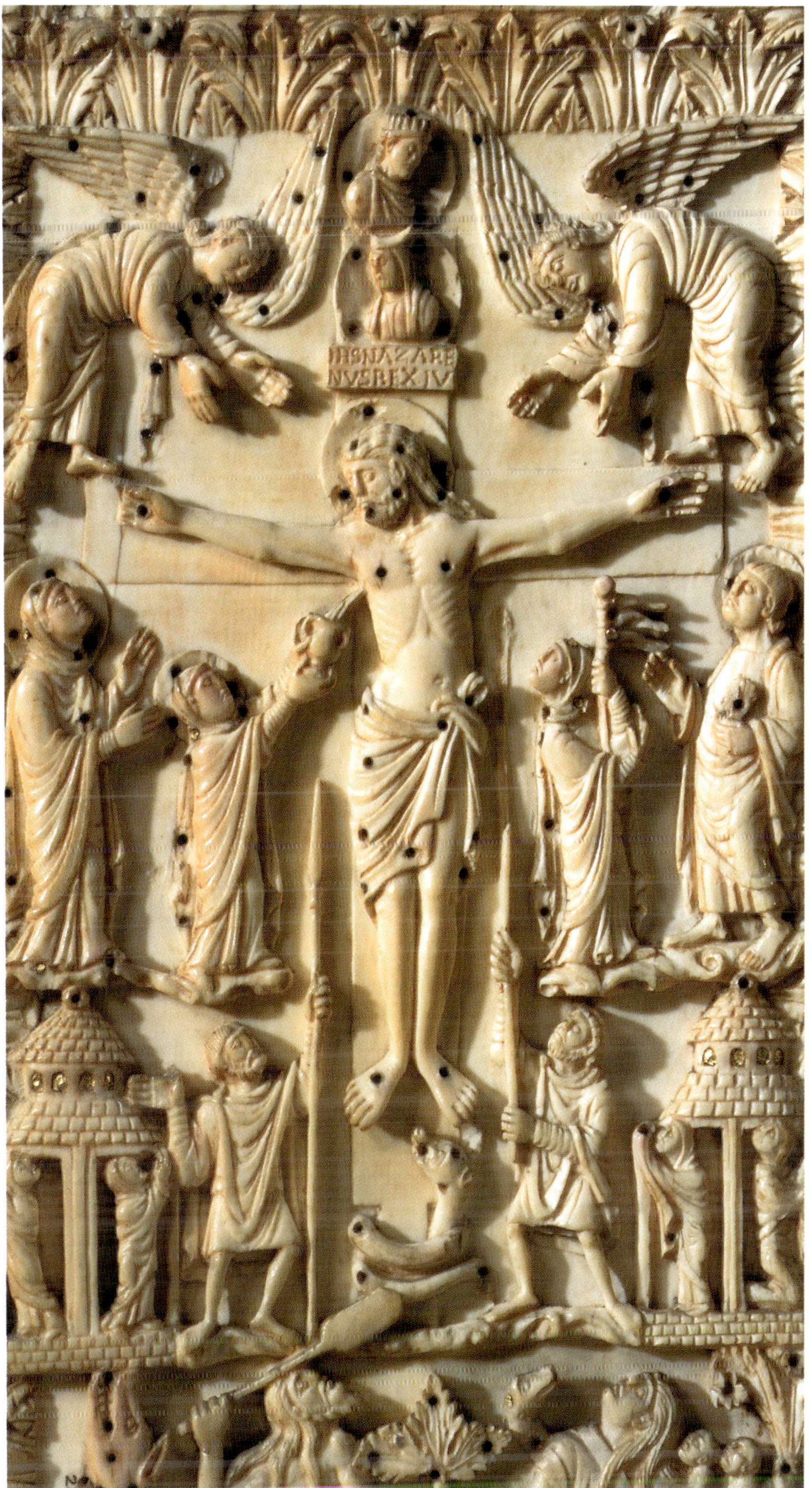

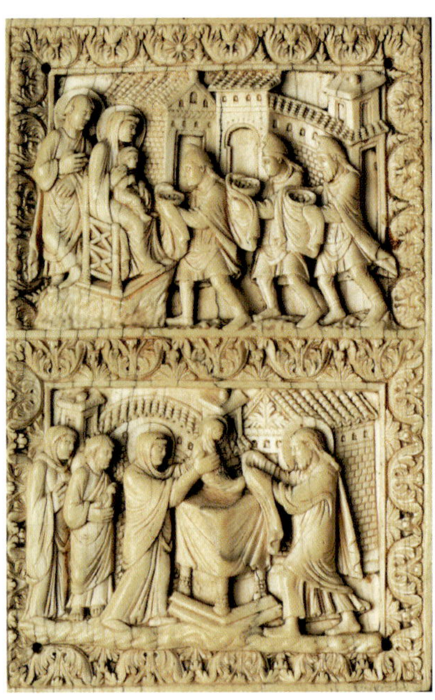

Cat II.18
BOOK COVER WITH THE ADORATION OF THE MAGI AND THE PRESENTATION IN THE TEMPLE
Metz, *c.* 900

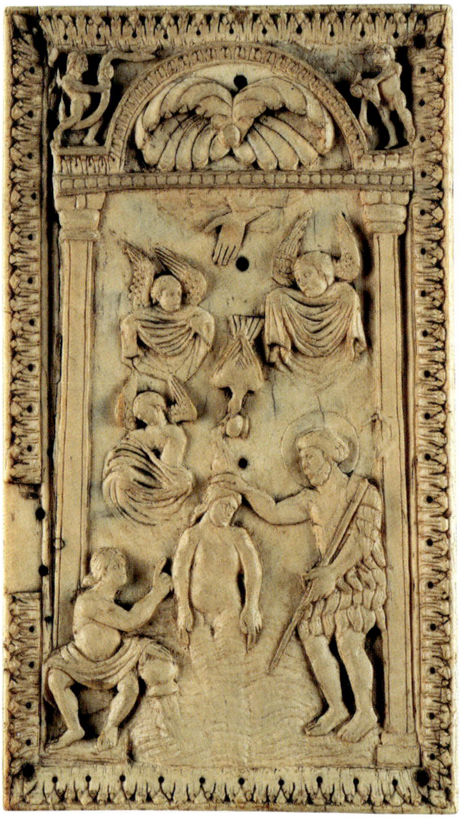

Cat II.31
BOOK COVER: BAPTISM OF CHRIST
Metz (?), 9th century

influenced by the Sacramentary ('Missal') of Robert de Jumièges **II.24**, which, moreover, drew on Carolingian sources that are more likely to have been derived from the Utrecht Psalter and the school of Rheims.

This Winchester style is also seen in some ivories **II.23**. A carver to whom a book cover's figure of St Paul **II.25** has been particularly attributed and who had worked in Trier betrays an indisputable similarity to this style.

The question of the Carolingian 'legacy' is highly complex. In the sphere of artistic production, it includes several appropriations and transformations, of varying rapidity, which led to the appearance of new forms and enabled Roman art to emerge from the shadows. The first heirs of the Empire built by Charlemagne were the Ottonian and Salian dynasts. Under the Ottonian rulers, there arose an art imbued with classicism that succeeded in deepening what Carolingian art had sometimes merely hinted at and that, above all, learned to innovate. One of its major contributions was the monumental crucifix (for instance the Cross of Gero in Cologne). That great bronze sculpture was the result of a new driving force and was to influence the goldsmiths of the 12th century (see Section IV) and also wood carvers. In the sphere of illumination, commissions emanated from the great prelates and courts.

> Cat II.14
COMMENTARIES OF ST JEROME
Fleury (?), 806

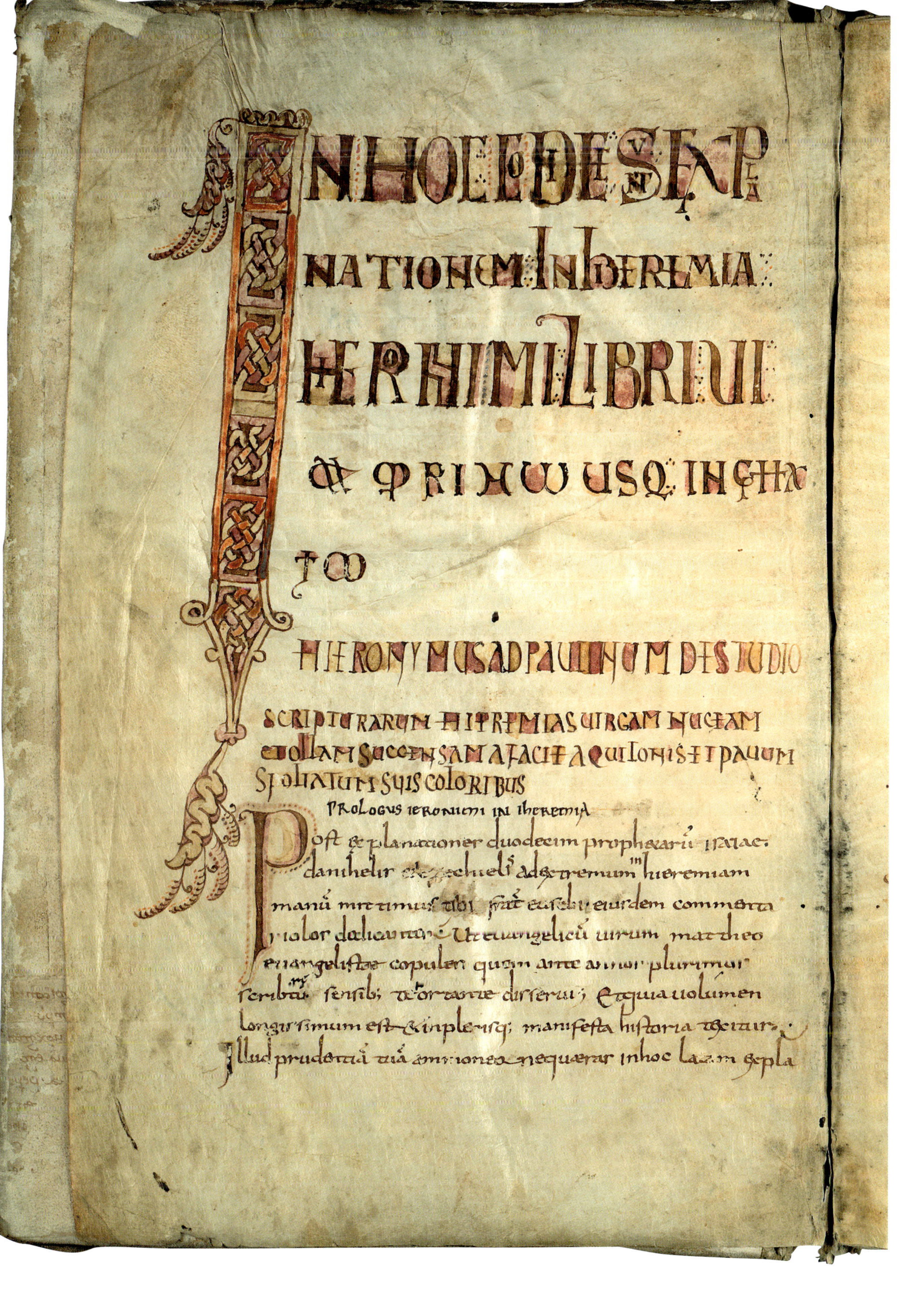

IN HOC EDE SUNT EXPLA
NATIONUM IN HIEREMIA
HIERONIMI LIBRI VI
A PRIMO USQ. IN CAPITULUM ...
... TO

HIERONYMUS AD PAULINUM DE STUDIO
SCRIPTURARUM HIEREMIAS UIRGAM NUCEAM
ET OLLAM SUCCENSAM A FACIE AQUILONIS ET PARDUM
SPOLIATUM SUIS COLORIBUS

PROLOGUS IERONIMI IN IHEREMIA

Post explanationem duodecim prophetarum isaiae
danihelis et ezechielis ad extremum in hieremiam
manum mittimus tibi frater eusebi eiusdem commenta
riolos dedicantes. Ut euangelicum uirum mattheo
euangelistae copulem quem ante annos plurimos
scribens sensibus eius ortatione disserui; Et quia uolumen
longissimum est et inpleuisq; manifesta historia texitur.
Illud prudentiam tuam ammoneo nequaerar inhoc laterm explanationem

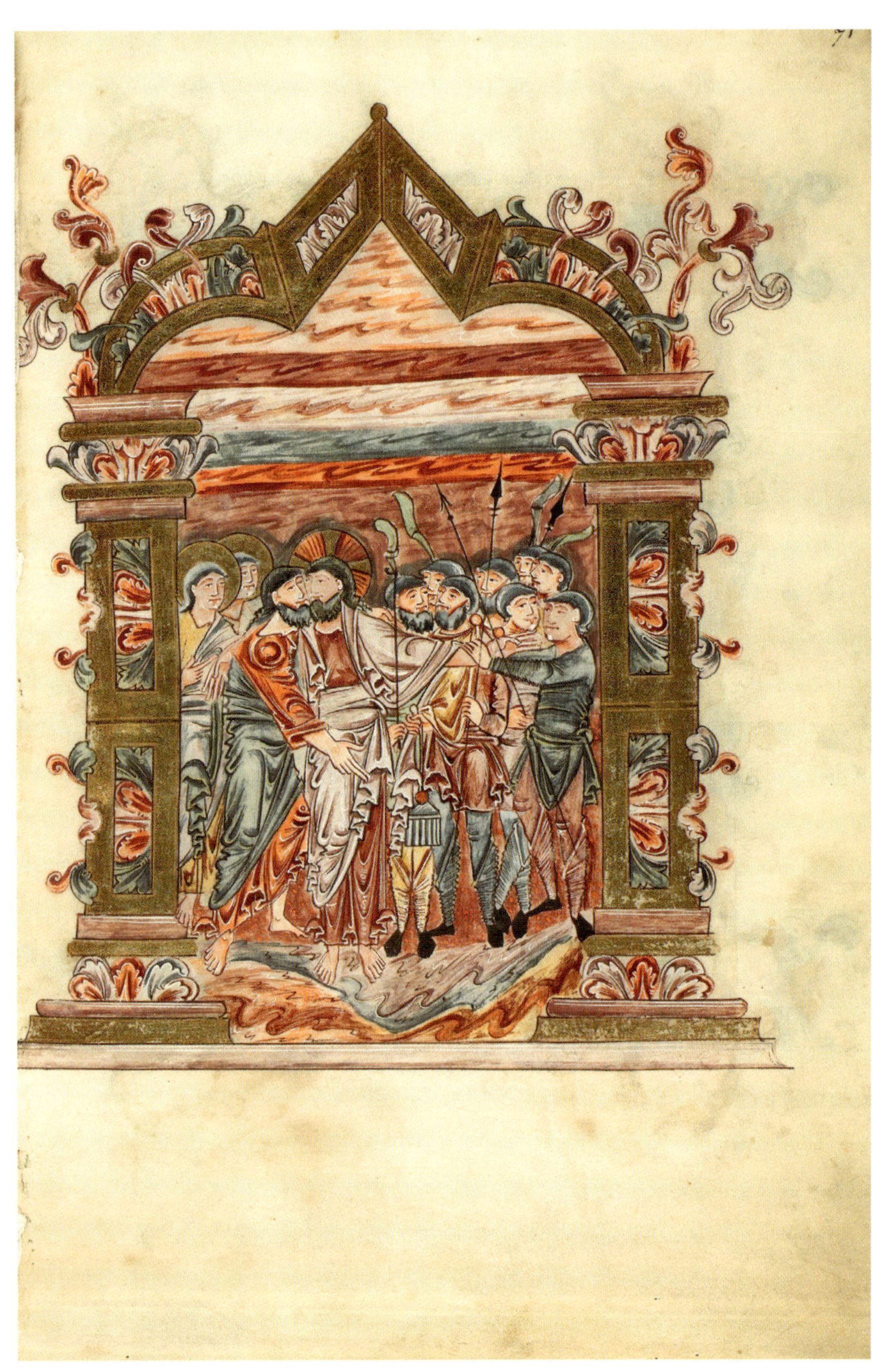

Cat II.24
SACRAMENTARY
('MISSAL')
OF ROBERT
DE JUMIÈGES
Ely (?), c. 1006–23

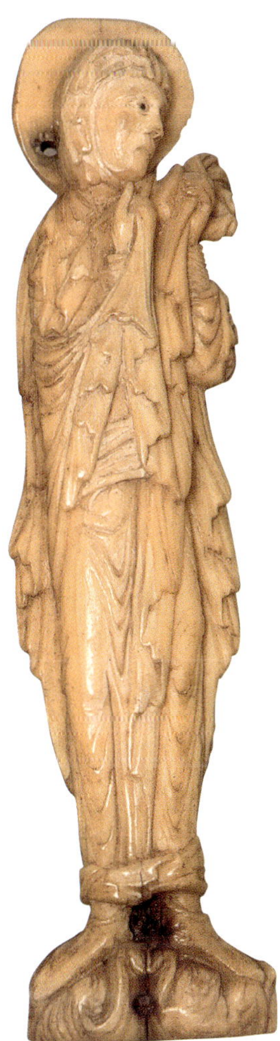
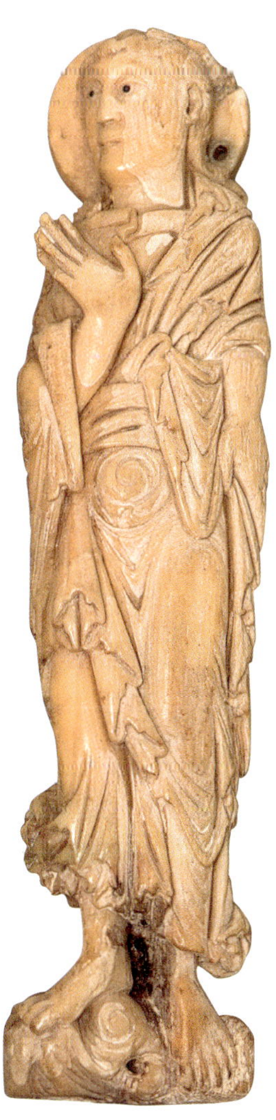

Cat II.23
APPLIQUÉ FIGURES: JOHN AND MARY
Winchester (?), Franco-Saxon (?), *c.* 1000

It was not unusual for Carolingian manuscripts to be explicitly referred to until the second half of the 11th century [II.27]. A particularly eloquent example shows the extent to which Carolingian art could be used as a reference for prestigious commissions in the reign of Otto the Great: the Gero Codex [II.33] kept at Darmstadt, illuminated at Reichenau and dedicated to the future archbishop of Cologne, takes as its model the Gospels of Lorsch, a masterpiece of the Palatine school dating from 815. The copying, at a suitably close date, according to the Ebbo Gospels, is certified in Mosan manuscripts [II.12].

In Liège [II.35] and elsewhere in the Mosan basin [II.36], painting absorbed the influence of Anglo-Saxon illumination but it is difficult to say what part was played by itinerant artists, particularly those from the scriptoria of Reichenau [II.33], who were also present in Cologne. The celebrated Gospels of Saint-Laurent-de-Liège [II.35] represent one of the high points of 11th-century illumination. Their exquisite pages could be attributed to a goldsmith who also practised the illuminator's art.

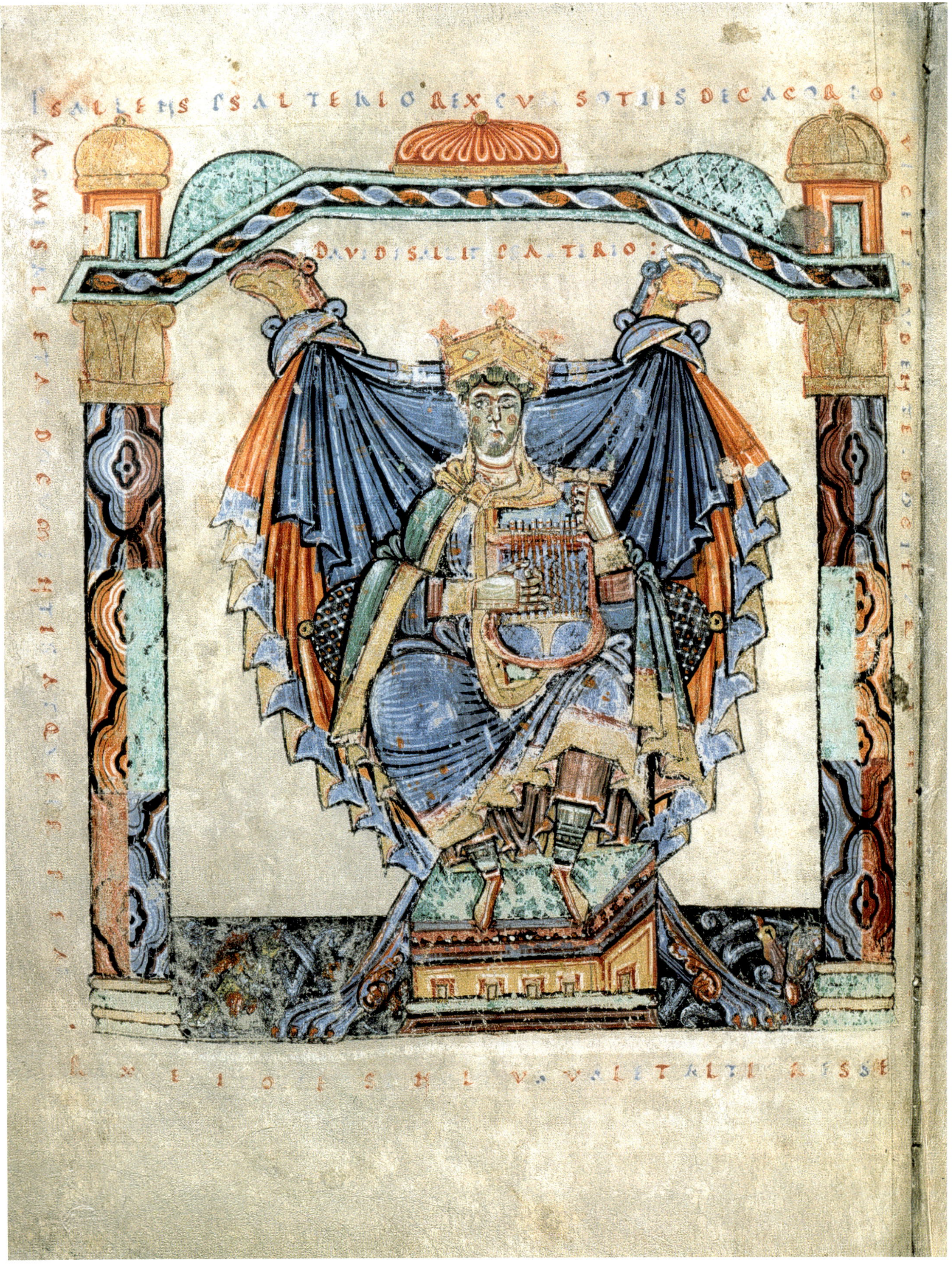
PSALLENS PSALTERIO REX CUM SOTIIS DECACORDO
DAVID PSALLIT PSALTERIO:

Cat II.25
BOOK COVER, SHOWING ST PAUL
Trier (the 'Deutscher Schnitzer'), late 10th century

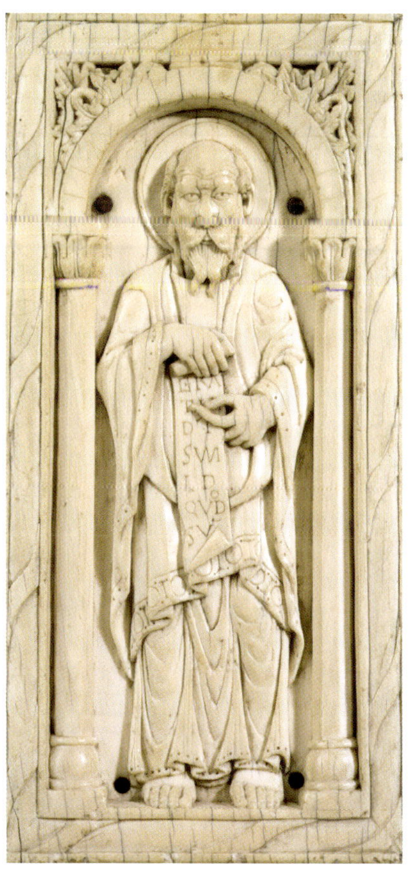

Cat II.33
GERO CODEX (BOOK OF PERICOPES)
Reichenau, 969–76

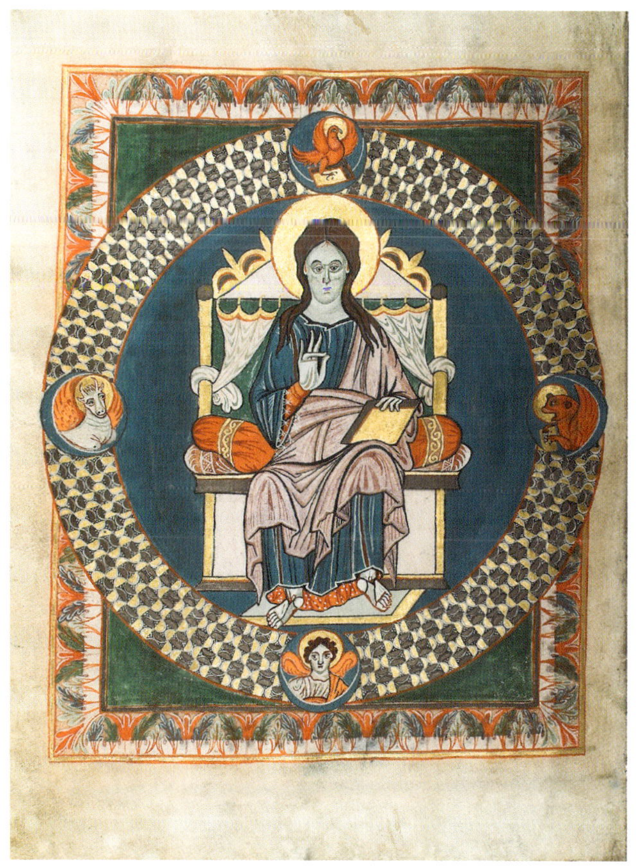

BIBLIOGRAPHY: W. Koehler & F. Mütherich (publisher), *Die Karolingischen Miniaturen*, Berlin, 1930 etc.; *Karl der Grosse* (exhib. cat.), Aachen, 1965; W. Braunfels (publisher), *Karl der Grosse. Lebenswerk und Nachleben*, Düsseldorf, 1965 etc.; J. Hubert, J. Porcher, W. F. Volbach, *L'art carolingien*, Paris, 1969; P. Lasko, *Ars Sacra 800–1200*, The Pelican History of Art, Harmondsworth, 1972; O. Mazal, *Buchkunst der Romanik*, Graz, 1978; *Mediaeval Mastery. Book Illumination from Charlemagne to Charles the Bold, 800–1474* (exhib. cat.), Louvain, 2002; F.O. Büttner (publisher), *The Illuminated Psalter. Studies in the Content, Purpose and Placement of its Images*, Turnhout, 2004; H. Mayr-Harting, *Ottonische Buchmalerei. Liturgische Kunst im Reich der Kaiser, Bischöfe und Äbte*, Stuttgart-Zurich, 1991; J.P. Caillet, *L'Art carolingien*, Paris, 2005; M.P. Laffitte, Charlotte Denoël, *Trésors carolingiens. Livres manuscrits de Charlemagne à Charles le Chauve* (exhib. cat.), Paris, 2007.

< Cat II.26
PSALTER
Angers, *c.* 1000

III

Europe and the Mediterranean

ROLAND RECHT

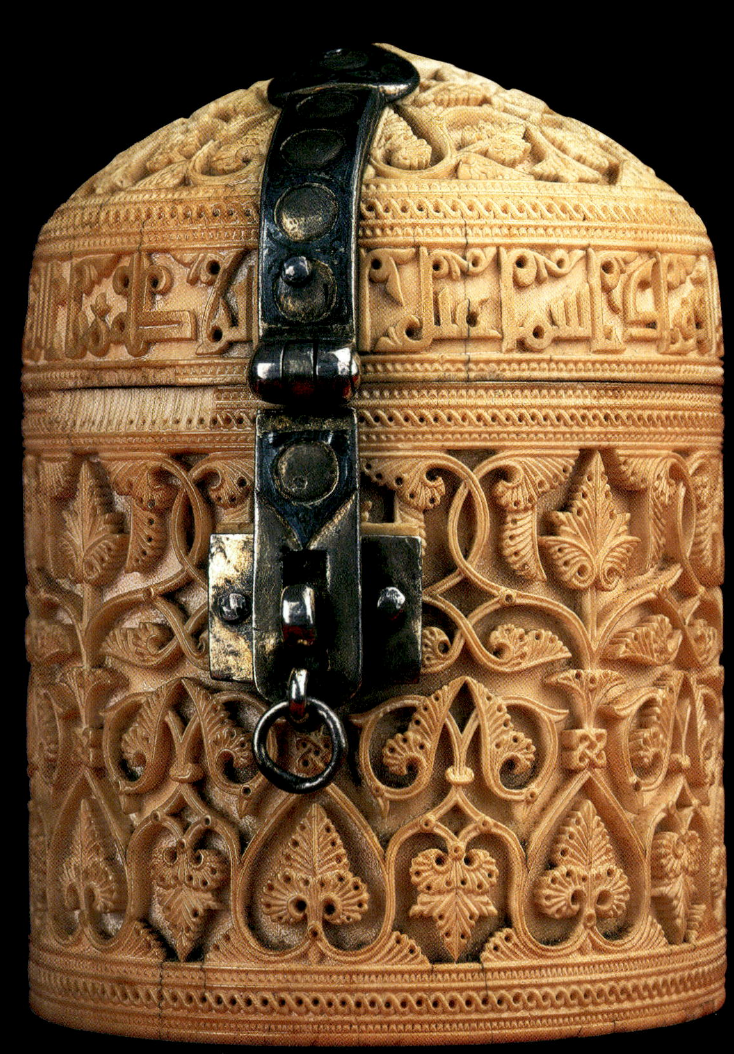

Cat III.16
IVORY BOX WITH COMBINATION LOCK
Arab (?), *c.* 1200 (?)

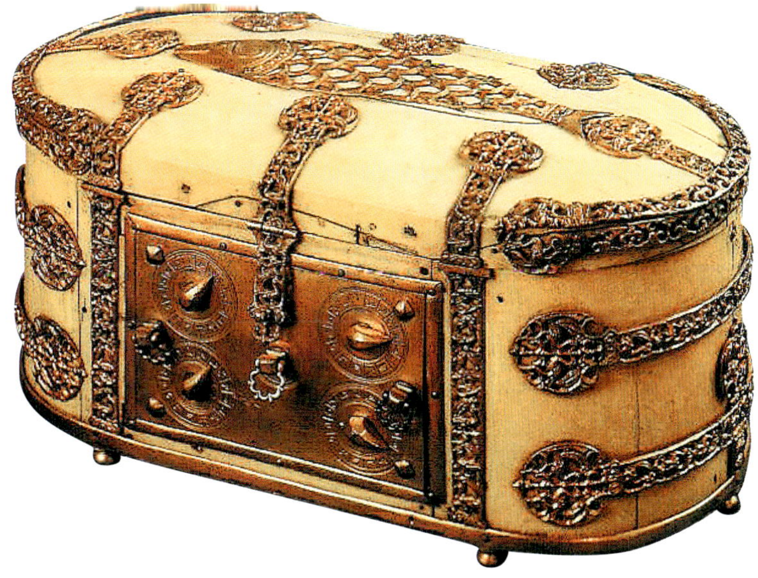

When Constantine decided to move the centre of power from Rome to the shores of the Bosphorus, he weakened the ability of the Roman Empire to resist invaders (see Section I). Its geographical position enabled Constantinople to escape invasions and, over the centuries, to develop and then maintain the artistic traditions that were to make its reputation throughout eastern and western Europe. Moreover, as the Byzantine state had retained strong support in the territories of the old Roman Empire – the Levant and the Italian provinces – and had extended its Empire to those countries of eastern Europe that had been evangelized by the Byzantine Church, the influence of its art travelled by many routes.

Byzantine art lasted a thousand years and enjoyed considerable success outside the Empire : architects, painters, creators of mosaics and ivory carvers worked outside its territory, in Serbia, Georgia, Sicily and Venice, but remained faithful to the traditions of late Antiquity. That heritage made the human figure central to the image and was adapted to the needs of the Imperial State and the Church. It was Constantinople, above all, with its workshops of goldsmiths, enamellers, painters and ivory carvers, that was to impose the artistic quality of its creations on the whole of Europe [III.2-6]. Many Byzantine works were imported to the West following the sack of Constantinople by the Crusaders (1204).

Byzantium developed certain artistic techniques that it definitively marked as its own, in particular those of cloisonné enamel [III.2] and mosaic [VI.7]. These two processes, which use small pieces of glass (for enamel) or cubes of hard material (for mosaic), require considerable dexterity. Small metal compartments are created and then encrusted with coloured glass, meaning that the process is less suitable for mass production than that of champlevé enamelling (see Section V). A mosaic icon takes longer to create than a painting of the same size. The success of these

< Cat III.9
CYLINDRICAL BOX
Hispano-Moorish (Cuenca), 10th century

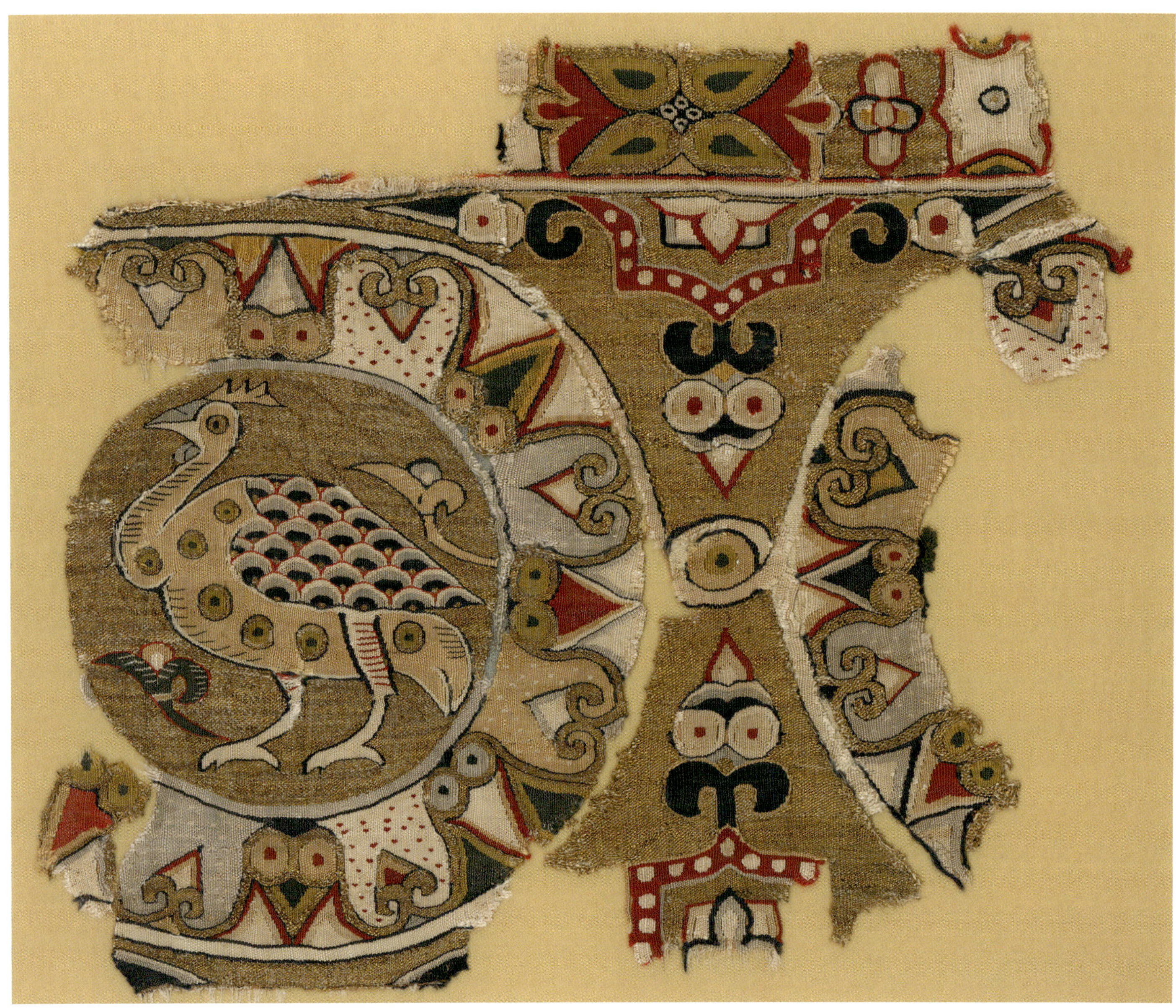

Cat III.15
THE 'PYRENEAN'S FRINGE'
Caliphate period, second half of the 10th century

two techniques alone demonstrates that, apart from the problem of the legitimacy of images raised by the iconoclast controversy, the production of works of art accounted for a huge share of the Byzantine Empire's economy.

Fidelity to types and methods of figural representation are characteristics of Byzantine art, and not only regarding icons. Adherence to the figurative tradition does not imply the fossilization of forms: very great artists created cycles of frescoes or works in gold whose style is unique. Thus, Byzantine art was perpetuated in certain regions well after 1453, when Constantinople was taken by the Turks.

Following the defeats suffered by the Byzantine Empire – the invasion of the Balkans by the Avars and the Slavs and then the Persian and Arab wars – the iconoclast crisis after 730 occurred in a climate of gloom and there was a tendency to believe that those misfortunes were partly attributable to the idolatry with which Christians surrounded their images. The 'iconodules' (those in favour of images) finally triumphed over their adversaries in 843, a time that also corresponds to the economic recovery of the Empire, by that time reduced to Asia Minor and a few European territories.

Throughout the Middle Ages, Sicily was a point of convergence for the art produced on the shores of the Mediterranean and in western Europe. The history of its successive political allegiances is eloquent in itself. It came under the domination of Byzantium in the 6th century, of Islam 827–1061 (which superimposed elements borrowed from Egypt and North Africa on the artistic tradition inherited from Antiquity) and of the Norman dynasty 1061–1194. This resulted in a form of synthesis between Byzantium, Islam and western Europe – prime examples are the Palatine chapel in Palermo and Monreale cathedral. Sicily was ruled by the Hohenstaufens 1194–1266, by the House of Anjou 1266–82 and then, by the House of Aragon. The style of the fragment of fine cloth from the Brussels Royal Museums of Art and History [III.12], with colours that are still completely fresh is reminiscent, given its gold background, of the surviving pieces known as the cloak of Roger II, King of Sicily 1133–44, created in the workshops of Palermo.

The West soon became fascinated by the beauty of objects made in the East: rock crystals carved by the Fatimids were brought back by pilgrims, Crusaders and merchants. Precious silks [III.12] were mainly used to wrap relics or to make liturgical vestments – some of these fabrics bore Kufic inscriptions praising Allah, but this did not trouble their users in Christian Europe. In the end, workshops were set up in Europe to fulfil the increasing demand for such products. So we see

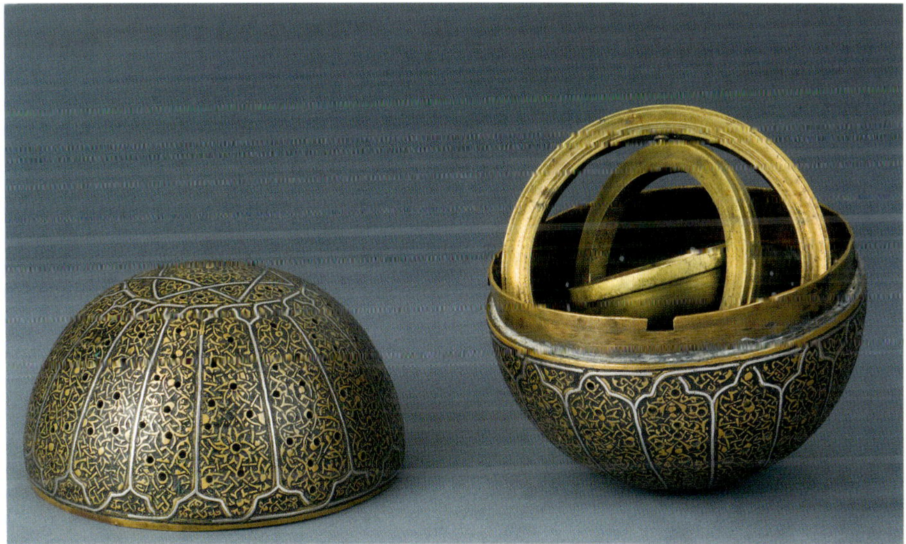

Cat III.8
SPHERICAL CENSER
Venice (?), 15th century

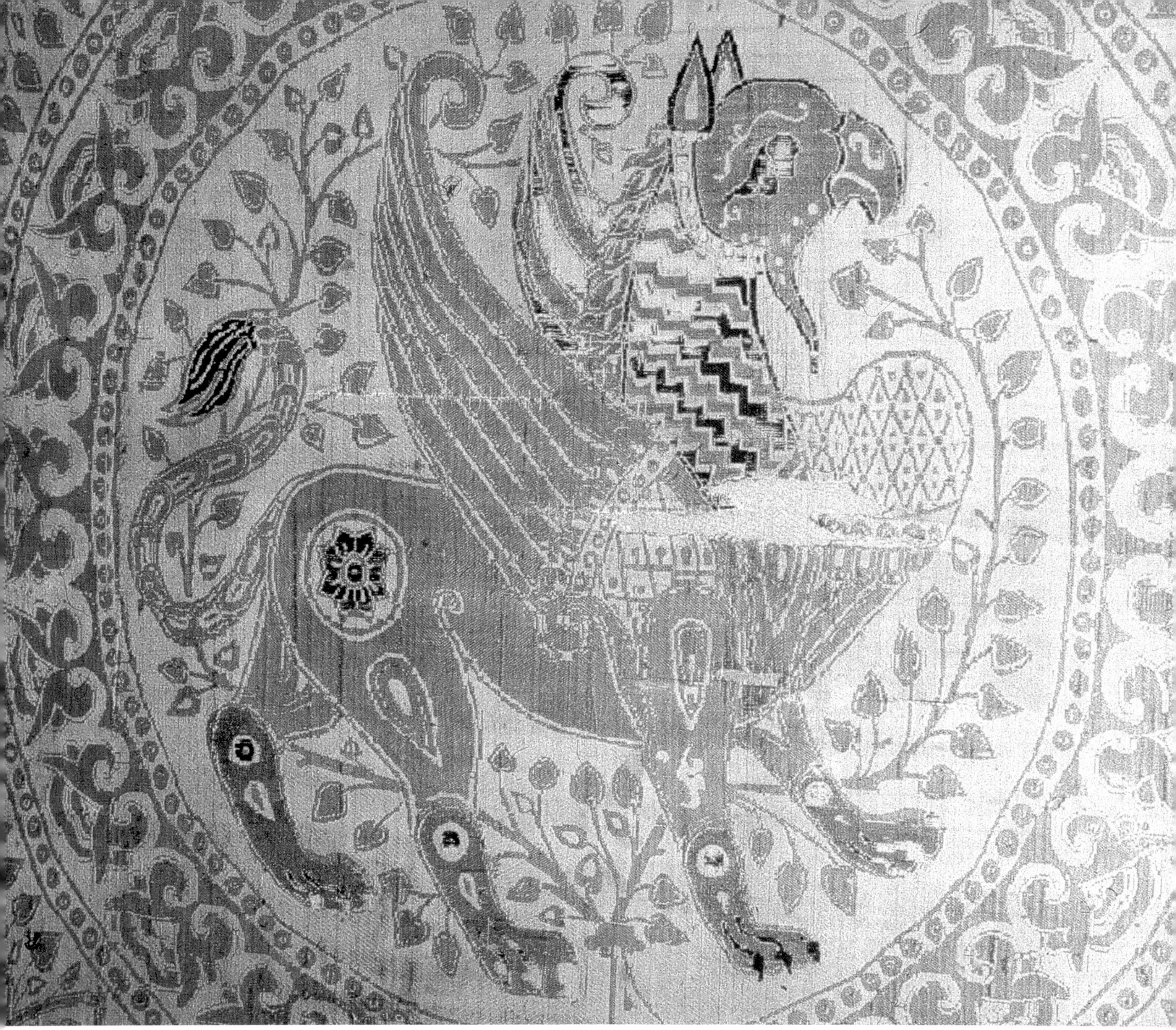

Cat III.3
SHROUD OF SAINT-SIVIARD
Byzantine art,
11–12th century

precious fabrics being made in Lucca, Tuscany, in imitation of those of Arab origin. Most of the ivory boxes or containers III.16 covered in Kufic inscriptions and ornamental motifs of oriental origin that are now found in churches or public collections originate from Sicily or southern Italy.

However, Arab civilization did extend its influence, sometimes by superimposing it on that of Byzantium (for example, in Sicily) but usually by instilling its culture and refinement over vast territories that then adopted them as their own. By the word 'Hispano-Moorish', historians refer to art that accompanied Islamic civilization extending over the Maghreb and the Iberian peninsula between 711 and 1492, the date when the last Islamic state, Granada, was reconquered by Ferdinand and Isabella.

The Abbasids [III.1] were a Muslim Arab dynasty that ruled most of the Islamic countries of the East 749–1258 – with their capital in Baghdad. In 750, they put an end to the Umayyad dynasty, which had exercised spiritual authority over Islam. However, Abd al-Rahman I, an Umayyad, fled to Spain and settled in Cordoba. In 785 he founded a great mosque there, which was to become the model for all the mosques the Berbers were to build from Spain to the Maghreb. Its influence over artistic expression extended to many spheres besides architecture and decoration.

During the 12th century, the *Reconquista* (Reconquest) pushed the Arabs back towards southern Spain. But, even after the conquest of Cordoba and Seville, in 1236 and 1248 respectively, the production of traditionally Arab ceramics continued. In Valencia, the manufacture of ceramics, which developed mainly from the 14th century, was still clearly Islamic in design but, at the beginning of the 15th century, Gothic motifs and even Latin inscriptions were added. The Hispano-Moorish dish [III.13] depicting two gazelles facing one another with good health formulated in Arabic, is a fine example of Valencia ceramics.

Cat III.1
CHALICE (?) WITH ROCK CRYSTAL
Base: Abbasid work (Iran or Iraq?), 9–10th century.
Chalice: Byzantine, 10–11th century

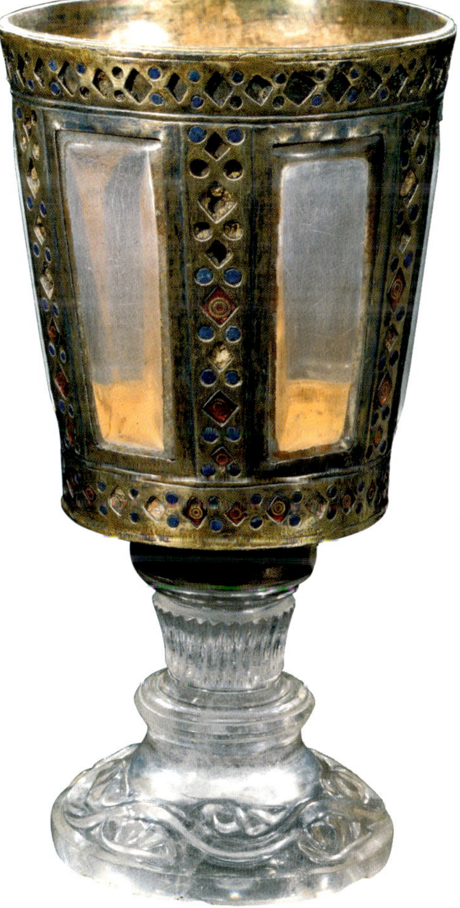

The piece of silk from Cordoba known as the 'Pyrenean's fringe' [III.15] bears a peacock motif that is also found on cloth from Sassanid Persia, sometimes transmitted via Byzantine fabrics. The peacock is found again in ivories produced in the Cordoban Caliphate as well as on ceramics. The choice of the peacock as an icon is probably linked here to courtly representations with a symbolic content (scenes of an Islamic paradise sometimes include birds and lions as symbols of royal power). In the late 10th century, Ibn Hawkal compared Cordoba to Baghdad and mentioned exports of cloth to Egypt and as far as the frontiers of the Khorasan province. The 'Pyrenean's fringe' [III.15] shows that in the 10th century the cathedral of Roda in northern Spain (whence this magnificent fabric originated) received religious objects from Count Ramon and his wife, including ecclesiastical garments of Hispano-Moorish or oriental origin (two panels used as shrouds, one in the Coptic and the other in the Persian tradition, are preserved among the cathedral's treasures).

Hispano-Moorish art came into being in Andalucia, then culminated in the 10th century in the workshops of Cordoba and Cuenca. Sassanid ornamentation endowed it with extensive subject-matter that is found everywhere from architecture to ceramics. Large quantities of secular objects were produced in

IV

Goldsmiths' workshops

ROLAND RECHT

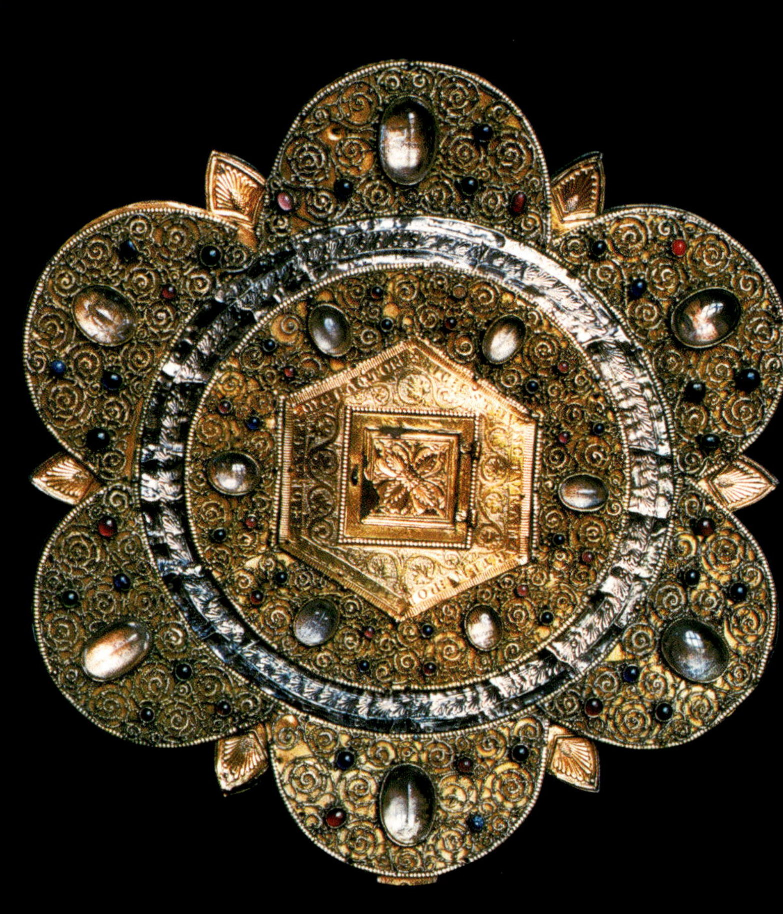

The beauty and price of the materials used by goldsmiths have earned these craftsmen an eminent place among the trades of the Middle Ages. The symbolic value of the materials also played a considerable part: several theologians developed a mystical theory of light through the use of gold and precious stones. Against the recommendations of his friend St Bernard, Abbot Suger, who was then devising his grand design for the abbey of Saint-Denis, was quick to justify the use of these materials because of their mystical value, i.e. the very fact that they reflected the Light of God (albeit surely much reduced).

It seems that, earlier than for other trades, the intention was to guarantee goldsmiths a professional status and good financial and legal conditions in the towns where they set up their workshops. The first mention of them is found in the Mosan basin. Some of them rivalled the nobility in establishing pious foundations. To assess their elevated status in the mid-12th century, we should remember the goldsmith Godefroid who worked for Abbot Wibald of Stavelot in Belgium. Wibald, a highly cultured man, had spent time in Byzantium and was the chancellor or adviser of three emperors. Like Suger, he decided to reform his abbey. He was the source of several large commissions entrusted to goldsmiths. In 1148 he addressed one of them, 'G' (= Godefroid), calling him friend and seeking to become the exclusive user of his services. Godefroid, a goldsmith and townsman of Huy, and working for Emperor Lothair and King Conrad, replied to him in Latin. He went on to live in Jerusalem for a time, returned to Huy in about 1173 and became a canon of Neufmoutier. He donated a belt buckle to its church that contained relics of St John the Baptist, which he had received from Bishop Almaris of Sidon (Lebanon) as a reward for the objects he had made for him. This same Godefroid seems to have visited numerous countries before reaching the age of thirty. The 13th-century manuscript source detailing Godefroid's career points out that he made countless reliquaries – containers for the relics of saints.

A record exists of the misadventures of another goldsmith, from Paris this time, who, on his way to Hungary, was taken prisoner by the Mongols and carried

< Cat IV.12
'PHYLACTERIUM' OF ST MARTIN
Hugo d'Oignies, c. 1230–35

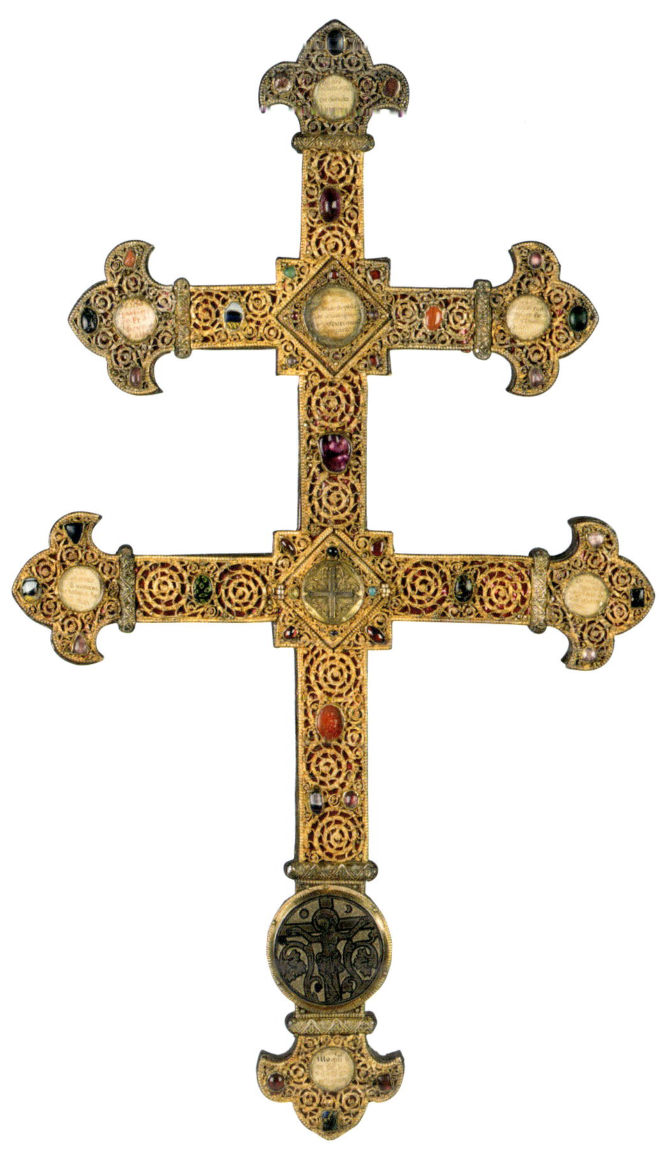

Cat IV.13
RELIQUARY IN FORM OF DOUBLE CROSS
Hugo d'Oignies, c. 1230–35

to the foot of the Himalayas. He lived as a goldsmith at the court of the Great Khan. The goldsmith's trade seems to have lent itself to business travel.

> Cat IV. 5
CHRIST CRUCIFIED
Meuse, *c.* 1150

We know that Nicolas de Verdun signed works in Klosterneuburg, near Vienna (an ambo – altar frontal) and Tournai. The Klosterneuburg ambo seems to have been made by a team of five goldsmiths under the direction of Nicolas, whose participation is also acknowledged in the creation of the Shrine of the Three Kings in Cologne. This seems to indicate that it was not only individual artists who travelled, but whole workshops. According to his own words, Abbot Suger invited goldsmiths to come to Saint-Denis from Lotharingia (Lorraine). At the end of the 12th century, the comte de Champagne granted a goldsmith called Arnoul the right to run a stall from which to sell his creations on market days.

The abbots, cathedral canons and even the bishops themselves probably understood in some detail this professional environment that played such an important part, alongside that of architects, in affirming the greatness of the Church by supplying an 'outward and visible' sign of their own prestige. The most outstanding of these commissioners of gold work are known to us: Abbot Hellin of Liège (d. 1118), Abbot Wibald of Stavelot (d. 1158), Abbot Suger of Saint-Denis and Abbot Wernher of Klosterneuburg, as well as the abbot of the Augustinian foundation of Malonne (Namur), one Gautier, who was to become bishop of Wroclaw, and his brother Alexander, bishop of Plock, two priests from the Mosan region who commissioned works of art in those Polish dioceses. The smelters and beaters of gold of Huy and Liège traded with England, Cologne and Lower Saxony. They also found buyers for their products in the fairs of Champagne or at Enns on the Danube.

We have tried to place the two goldsmiths we have chosen to discuss 'in their context': miniatures or other gold works should make it possible to situate them in their time and assess their importance. However, we should consider first the goldsmith whose reputation is exceptional because one of the indisputable masterpieces of the medieval goldsmith's art is attributed to him, the baptismal font of Liège. His name was Renier de Huy.

From the account of a contemporary canon we know that the baptismal font was put in place under the abbacy of Hellin and therefore between 1107 and 1118. Conversely, the oldest attribution of the font to Renier de Huy is in the *Chronique de 1402*, known only from a 16th-century copy. Like Pierre Colman, we are convinced that that attribution should be completely revised. We do not share all his views, but we agree that the Liège font is not of Mosan origin. Pierre Colman believes that its brass casting was made in *c.* 1000 by Roman and Byzantine artists for San Giovanni in Fonte, the baptistery of the church of St John Lateran in Rome, and that it is therefore probably a major product of the Macedonian Renaissance.

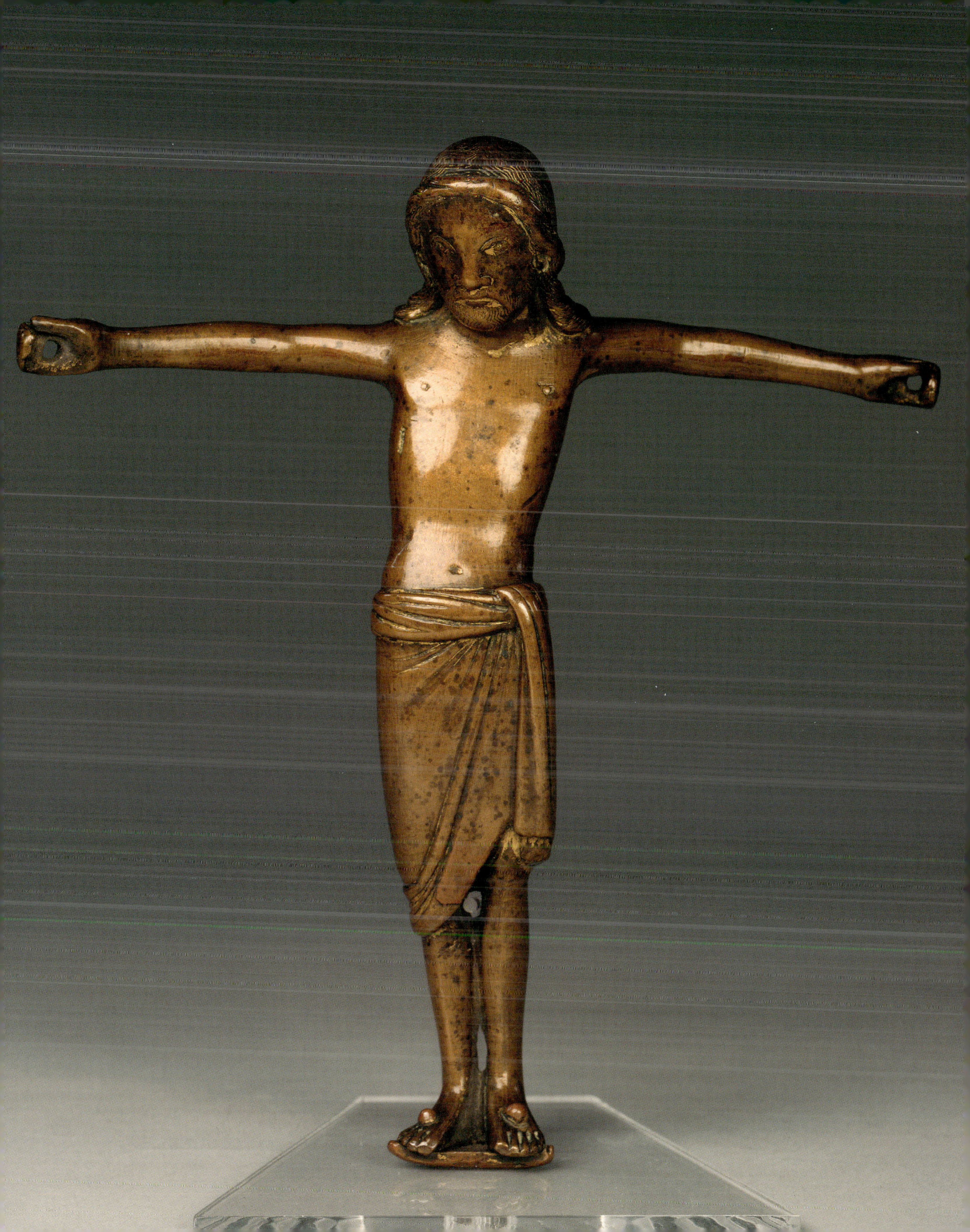

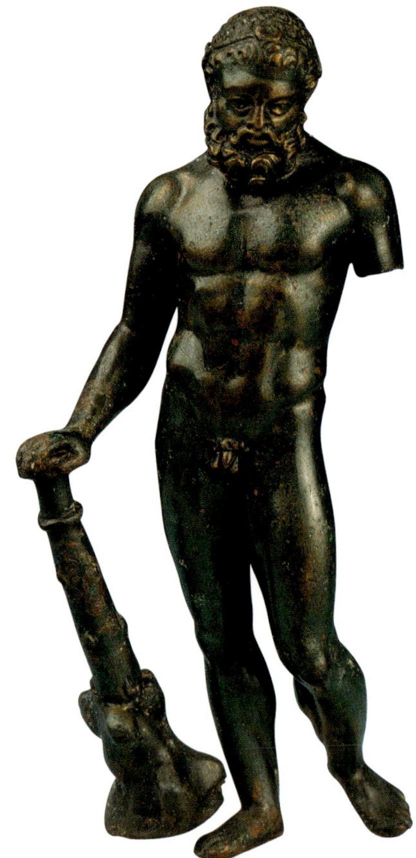

The font was stolen about a century later by Emperor Heinrich IV or Heinrich V – and then brought back from Rome by Abbot Hellin, where it long remained. This question deserves attention. In any case, it would help to solve one of the greatest enigmas in the history of medieval art: how could such a masterpiece have appeared in a region with no sign presaging its arrival?

What is more, none of the other works attributed to Renier de Huy are on a par with the font of Liège. Neither the two crucifixes [IV.4, 5] in the Musées royaux in Brussels nor the crucifix in Cologne's Schnütgen Museum present such a striking resemblance to the font of Liège that they might be attributed to the same hand. However, it would hardly be surprising if the extraordinary masterpiece that was present in Liège between the years 1115 and 1120 compelled the admiration of goldsmiths throughout the Mosan basin. The variants introduced by the Berlin collection of illustrations, possibly models for a psalter [VII.3], which copies certain scenes including fonts, should not surprise us: they are not photographic reproductions! All in all, once we cease attributing the font of Liège to Renier de Huy, all that remains of that goldsmith is his name, and no work can be attributed to him with certainty, at least according to the information available to us today.

Cat IV.2
STATUETTE OF HERCULES
Rome, 1st–2nd century

In our opinion, the Visé reliquary [IV.1] reveals the true characteristics of the art of the Mosan goldsmiths in the mid-12th century – the particularly imaginative skill of narration – and it is perhaps that quality that persuaded art historians to place the font of Liège in the Mosan basin too. Now, the difference between these

Cat IV.1
RELIQUARY OF SAINT-HADELIN
Mosan region, 11th century and *c.* 1130–50

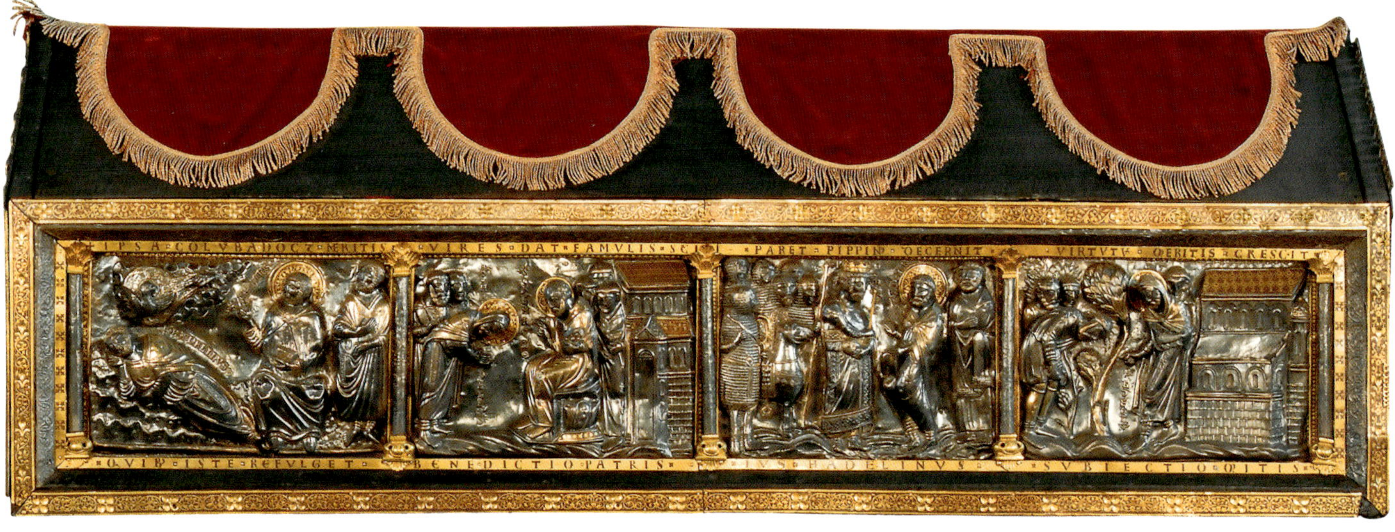

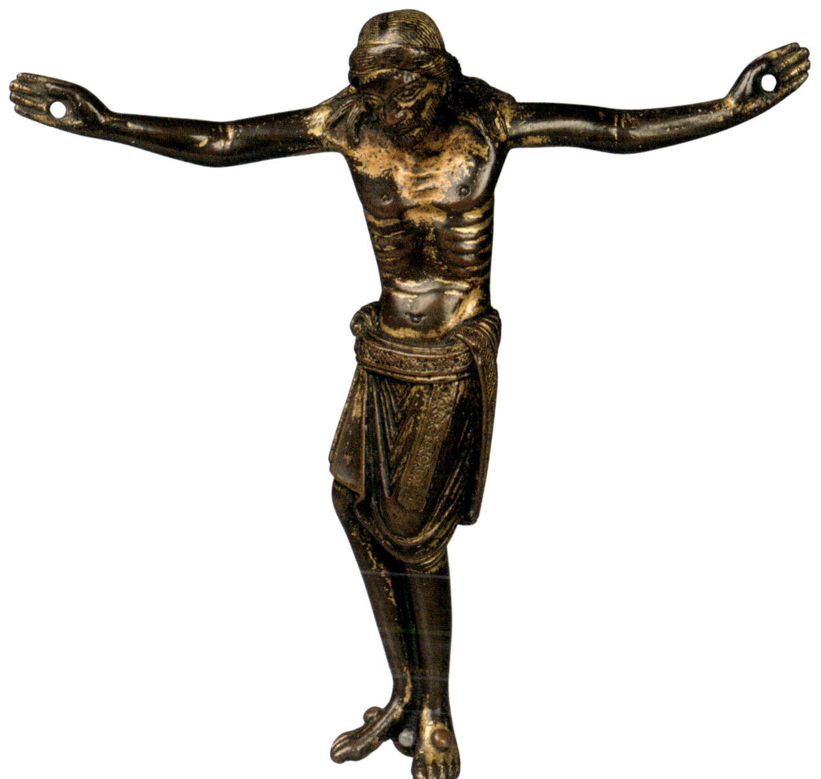

Cat IV 4
CHRIST CRUCIFIED
Meuse, second quarter of the 12th century

two types of narration is immediately striking: the Saint-Hadelin reliquary, by its division into registers, follows the structural design of the medieval image, while the font of Liège adopts narrative methods that are closer to Greco-Roman or early Christian models.

The statuette in the Rheinisches Landesmuseum in Bonn[IV.2] enables us to measure precisely the difference between this concept of form (close to that of baptismal fonts) and that of the crucifixes referred to above[IV.4, 5]. This small bronze statuette from the Roman provinces was probably well known to Mosan goldsmiths, but they left no direct interpretation of it.

The portable altar of Stavelot[IV.3] is a work of outstanding quality because of both its iconography (see catalogue) and the forms it adopts. It enables us to assess the level of perfection achieved by the Mosan goldsmiths in the mid-12th century. Two of the four Evangelists, of remarkably lifelike quality, have been compared with another, larger statuette, probably produced in the same workshop, from the former Oettingen-Wallenstein collection, which was put up for public auction in New York in November 1995. The scenes depicted on the portable altar are comparable to the narrative line of the Saint-Hadelin reliquary[IV.1]. An obvious stylistic proximity makes this altar similar to the Berlin collection of (psalter?) illustrations[VII.3]. What characterizes the style of the enamels is the use of coloured

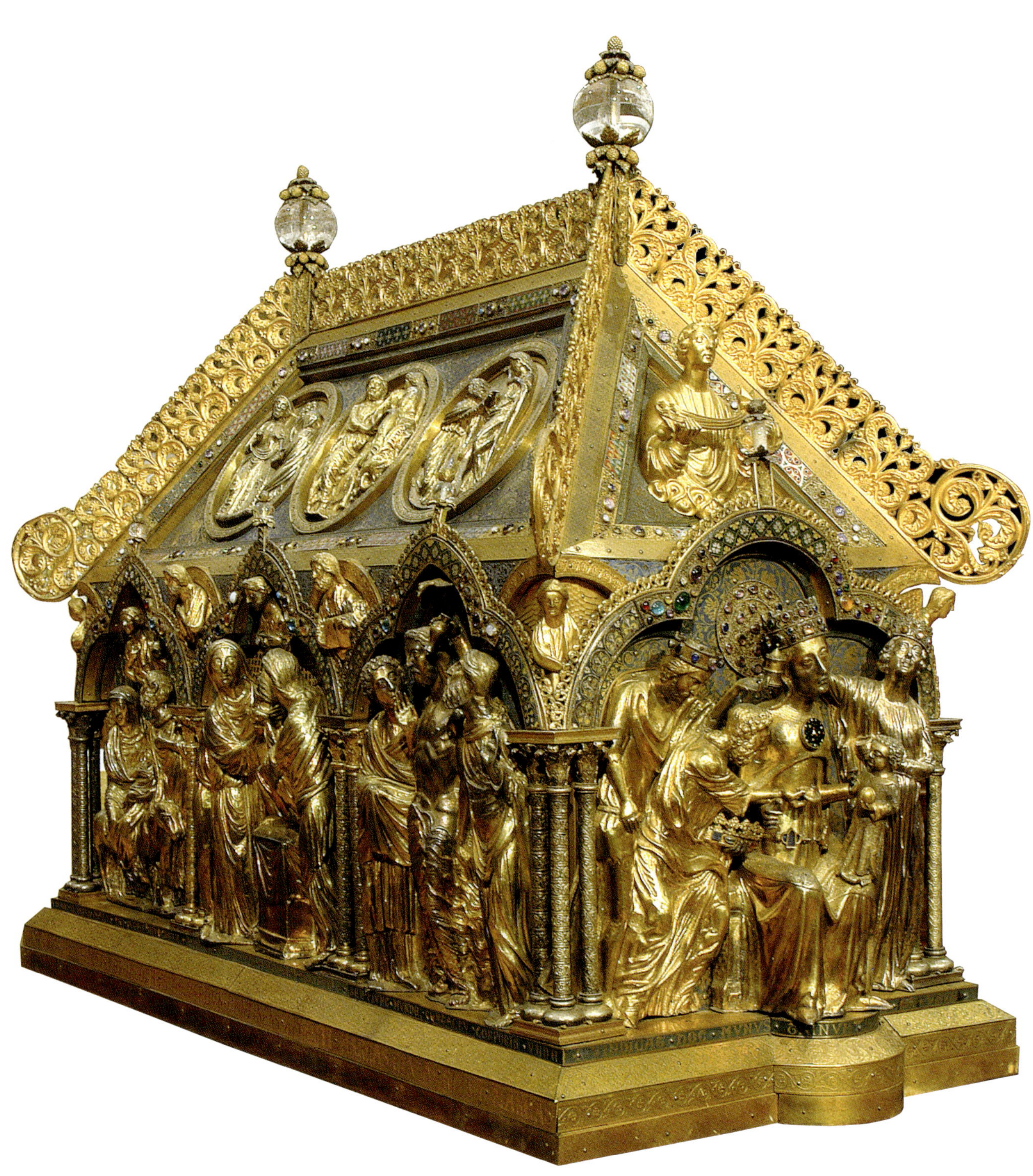

< Cat IV.6
RELIQUARY OF THE VIRGIN (SHRINE OF OUR LADY OF FLANDERS)
Nicolas de Verdun
Completed in 1205 (according to a modern, though faithful to the original, inscription on the base)

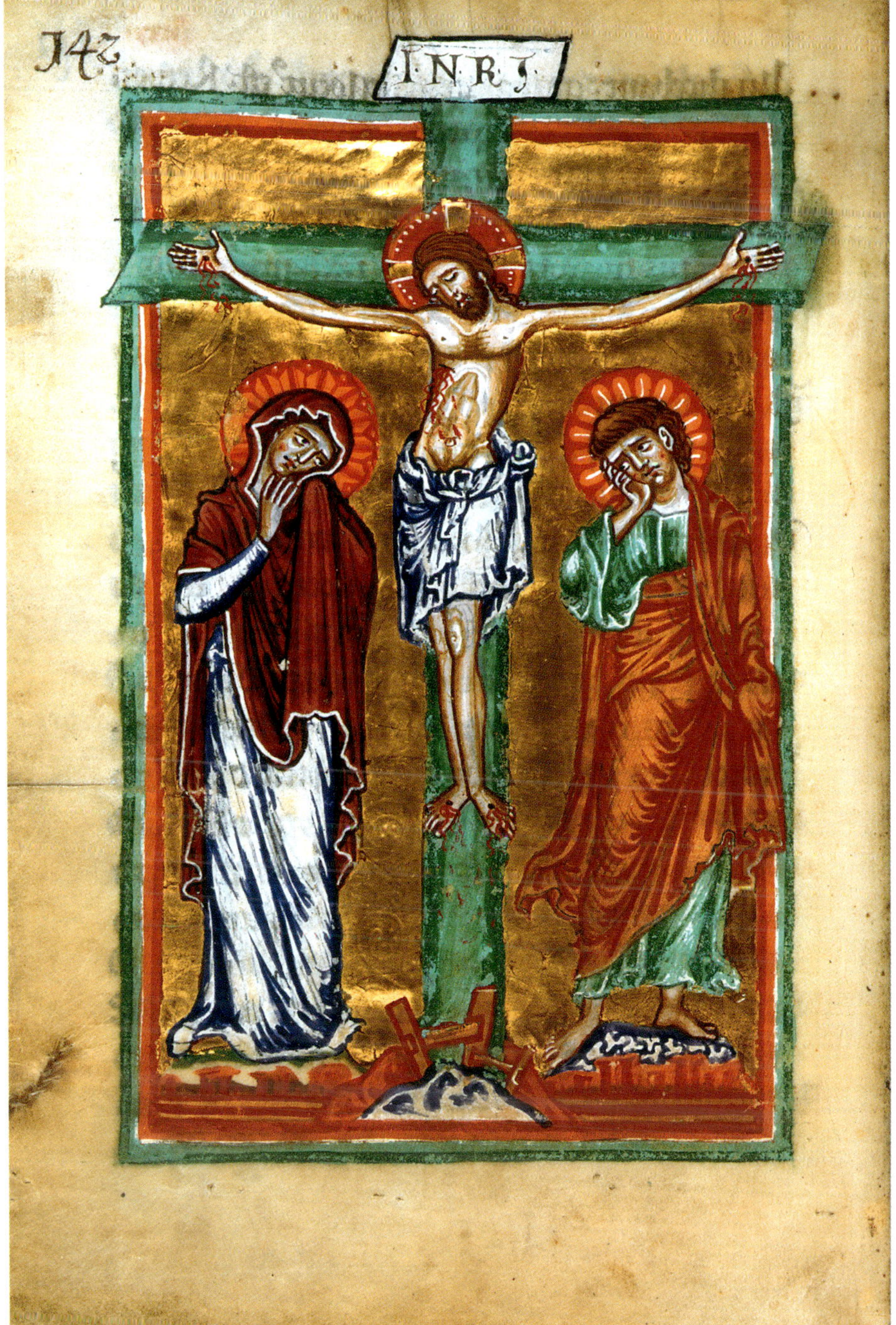

Cat IV.8
EVANGELISTARY OF GREAT ST MARTIN
Cologne, *c.* 1220–30

enamel for the ground but not for the heads, limbs and objects, which are completely devoid of enamel, contrary to the practice of enamellers in the Mosan region. This altar can be placed at the top of a long list of champlevé enamel works and small bronze statues (a portable altar in the Museo Nazionale, Florence; two bronze statuettes of Prudentia in Frankfurt and in the Louvre, Paris; the Lille censer; an altar cross in the Victoria and Albert Museum, London; and the Evangelist (?) from the Oettingen-Wallenstein collection.

From the end of the 12th century, we have better documentation about the personality of the most eminent of all the medieval goldsmiths, Nicolas de Verdun. Not only is his reputation justified, but we can be assured that he was the creator of most of the corpus of work attributed to him. His activity was certified in 1181 on the ambo of Klosterneuburg, signed and dated by the artist certainly done on the spot, and in 1205 on the reliquary of Notre-Dame de Tournai [IV.6]. The ambo is a masterpiece in champlevé enamel that Nicolas handled with outstanding mastery: he made each of the fifty-one plaques a striking and innovatory work of painting and drawing. The scenes are arranged according to what is known as a typological division, i.e. by juxtaposing the scenes from the Old Testament with those they prefigure from the New Testament. The design of this theological programme was probably the work of Honorius of Autun. Byzantine art was one of the chief sources from which Nicolas de Verdun drew his inspiration, particularly the mosaics of Sicily.

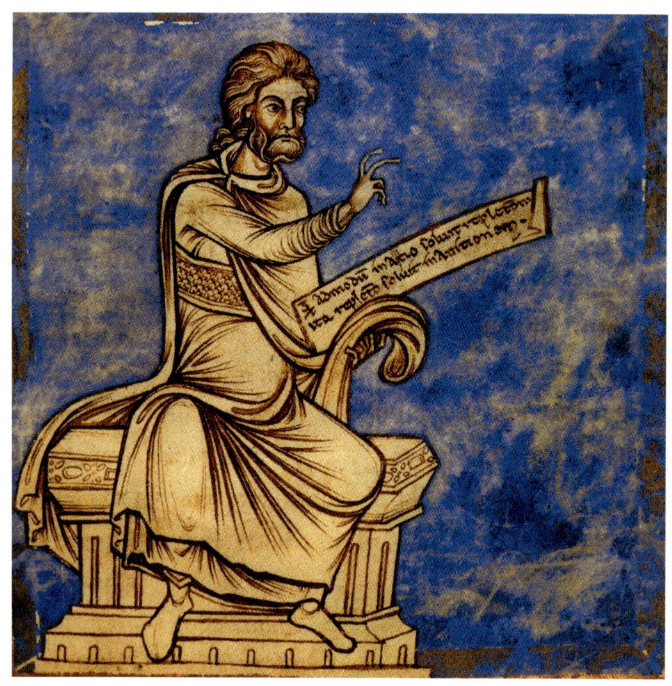

Cat IV.9
MEDICAL TREATISES
Mosan region (?), Champagne (?), *c.* 1175

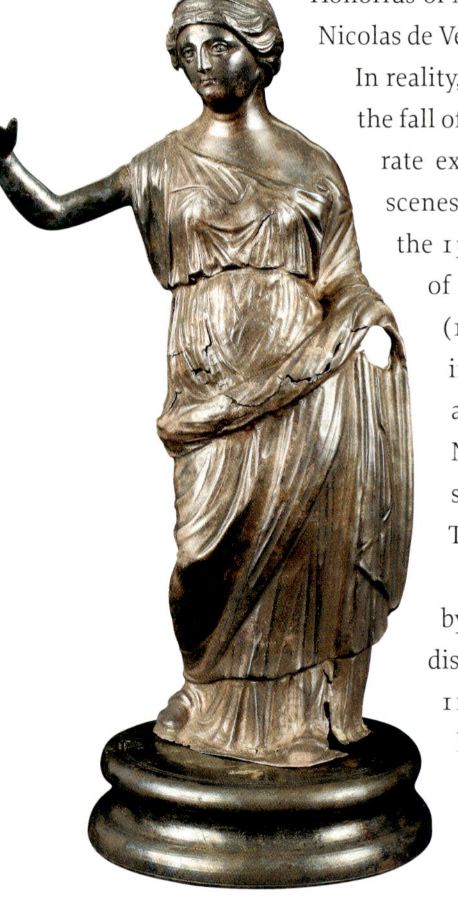

Cat IV.7
STATUETTE OF DRAPED WOMAN
2nd–3rd century

In reality, through the mastery with which he conveyed the bodies and the fall of the draped garments that intensifies their presence, the elaborate expressiveness of his faces and the dramatic intensity of the scenes, the art of Nicolas de Verdun presages the great creations of the 13th century. Although it probably belongs to a different type of art exemplified by the stained glass windows of Troyes (1190–1200), an illustration from a collection of medical treatises in the British Library [IV.9] nevertheless presents on parchment an equivalent of the supreme draughtsmanship practised by Nicolas. The Evangelistary of Great St Martin [IV.8] adopted a style close to that of the creator of the Cologne Shrine and the Tournai reliquary.

The Shrine of the Three Kings in Cologne was jointly produced by the workshop, but the high-relief figures of the Prophets are indisputably the work of Nicolas alone. Created between 1181 and 1191, they are one of the triumphs of that era's sculpture and herald the great monumental stone sculptures of the decade around 1200, in Laon cathedral, for example.

The Tournai reliquary must be viewed with caution. It was damaged in various places by successive restorations (mainly in the late 19th century), but its best preserved parts again show the final phase of the career of Nicolas de Verdun (see, for example, the relief of Christ in Limbo). In spite of the links between the work of Nicolas and the art of Byzantium, through the intermediary of Sicily, we must not forget the existence of the small bronze – or silver **IV.7** – statue from early Antiquity, many examples of which remain in the public collections of northern Europe. These works may also have played a part in the formation of that great goldsmith's art.

Just like the Psalter of Ingeborg, the missal kept at Douai **IV.10** was a transmission route for the art of Byzantium, whose strong influence on Nicolas de Verdun is clearly visible after 1181, particularly in the Klosterneuburg ambo. Hanns Swarzenski has said of the Ingeborg Psalter and what it represents that it demonstrates 'the international Byzantine style of western Europe'. In this case a strong anti-Roman current is apparent, indicating the route that the art we know as Gothic was going to follow.

Cat IV.10
MISSAL
Northern France (Anchin ?), early 13th century

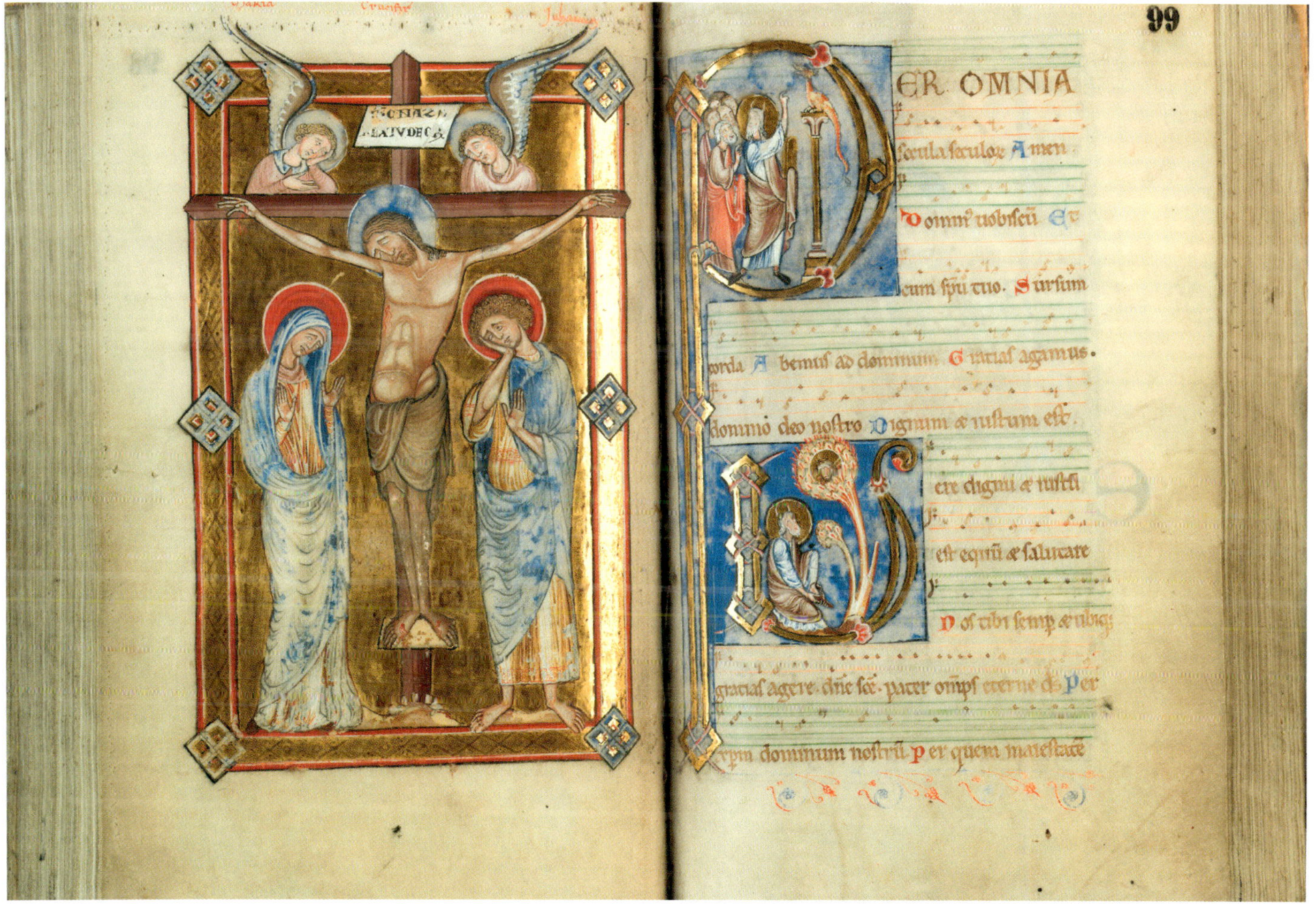

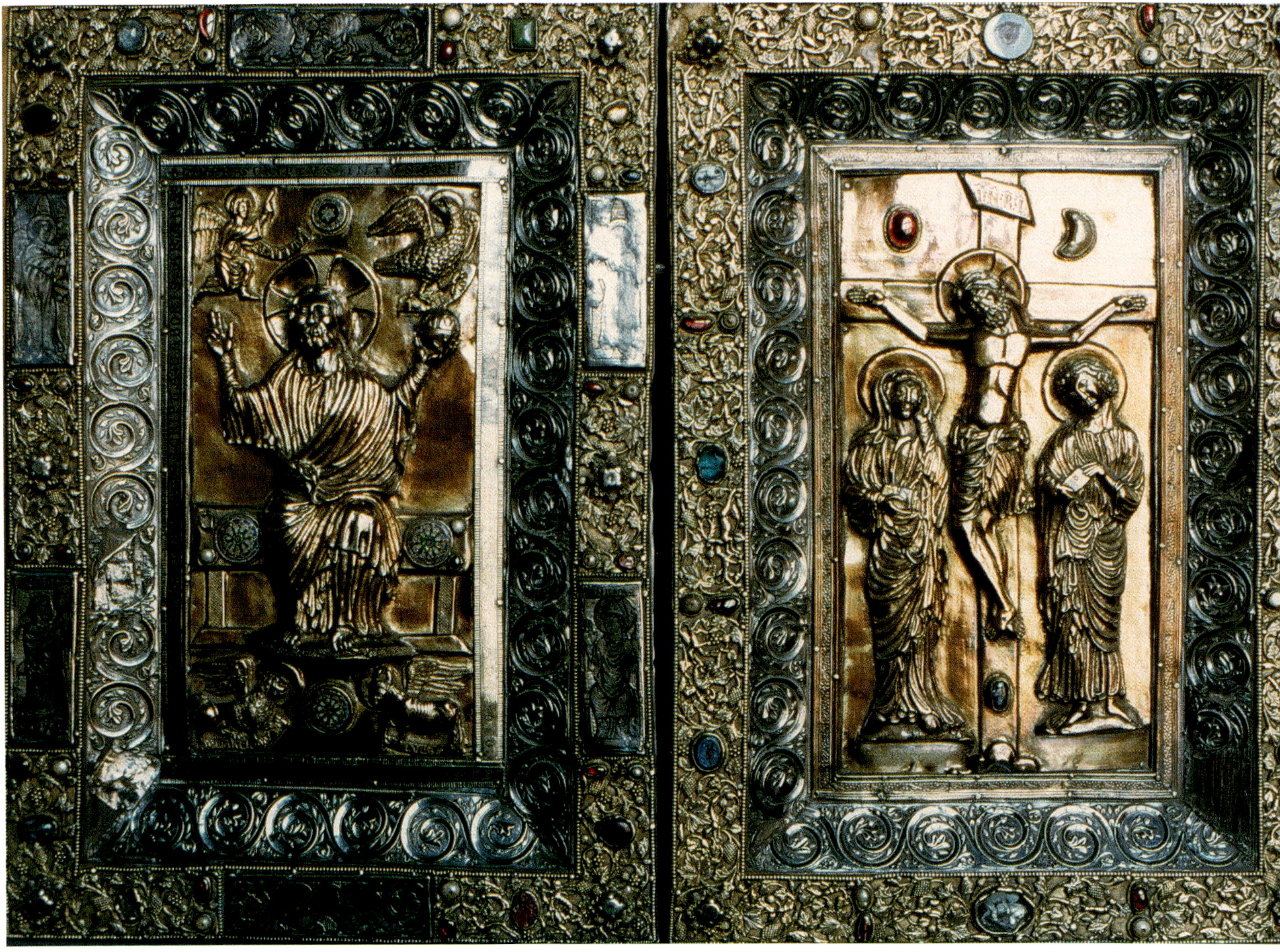

Cat IV.11
BOOK COVERS
Hugo d'Oignies, *c.* 1230

The contribution of Hugo d'Oignies is situated at the end of the development of gold work in the Mosan region and is a continuation of that of Nicolas de Verdun. Frater Hugo was born before 1187 in Walcourt, Belgium, and his three brothers seem to have founded a monastery in Oignies, Namur, of which one of them, Egidius, was apparently the abbot until 1233. Much of the great treasure of Saint-Nicolas d'Oignies passed to the sisters of Namur in 1818. Hugo d'Oignies followed the prestigious tradition of the great Mosan goldsmiths but at the same time his style is much more eclectic than that of Nicolas de Verdun. What is striking about his work is the juxtaposition of facial types that are still Roman and a plastic feeling that is far freer and more lively. The same matrix was used to emboss the ornamental parts of the double-cross reliquary and the 'phylacterium' of Oignies [IV.12]. The same process was used for the Shrine of the Three Kings in Cologne. In goldsmiths' workshops, the embossing of ductile metals was facilitated by these matrices, which could even be passed from one workshop to another.

The art of Hugo d'Oignies is interesting on several counts. It is tempting to grant him a greater talent as a 'designer' than as a sculptor. In book covers [IV.11] he reflects in soft and unstructured forms the fluent and supple design of the 'phylacterium' IV.12 in which elegance dominates.

Vast swathes of information about medieval art are still unknown to us: although texts allude to monks simultaneously practising several arts – such as Tuotilo in Saint-Gall (see Section II) and Fulco at the abbey of Saint-Hubert, sculpting in wood and stone and practising illumination – stylistic critics insist on distinguishing artists according to the techniques they used. Now, nothing is more likely than that a Nicolas de Verdun took part in the illumination of books or sculpting in stone. There is no reason why Hugo d'Oignies might not also have created illuminations or designs for stained-glass windows.

BIBLIOGRAPHY: A. Legner (ed.), *Rhein und Maas. Kunst und Kultur 800–1400*, 2 vols, Cologne, 1972; P. C. Claussen, 'Goldschmiede des Mittelalters', *Zeitschrift des deutschen Vereins für Kunstwissenschaft*, 1978, pp. 46–86; R. Hamann-Maclean, 'Byzantinisches und Spätantikes in der Werkstatt des Nikolaus von Verdun', *Kölner Domblatt*, 42, 1977, pp. 243 et seq.; P. C. Claussen, Über Antiken- und Naturstudium am Dreikönigsschrein', A. Legner (ed.), *Ornamenta Ecclesiae. Kunst und Künstler der Romanik in Koln*, Cologne, 1985, pp. 447–55; P. Colman, B. Lhoist-Colman, *Les fonts baptismaux de Saint-Barthélémy de Liège*, Académie Royale de Belgique, 2002; G. Xhayet, R. Halleux (eds), *Etudes sur les fonts baptismaux de Saint-Barthélémy de Liège*, Liège, 2006; F. Courtoy, *Le trésor du prieuré d'Oignies aux Sœurs de Notre-Dame à Namur et l'œuvre du frère Hugo*, Brussels, 1953.

V

Art for export: enamels, alabasters and altarpieces

CATHELINE PÉRIER-D'IETEREN
& ROLAND RECHT

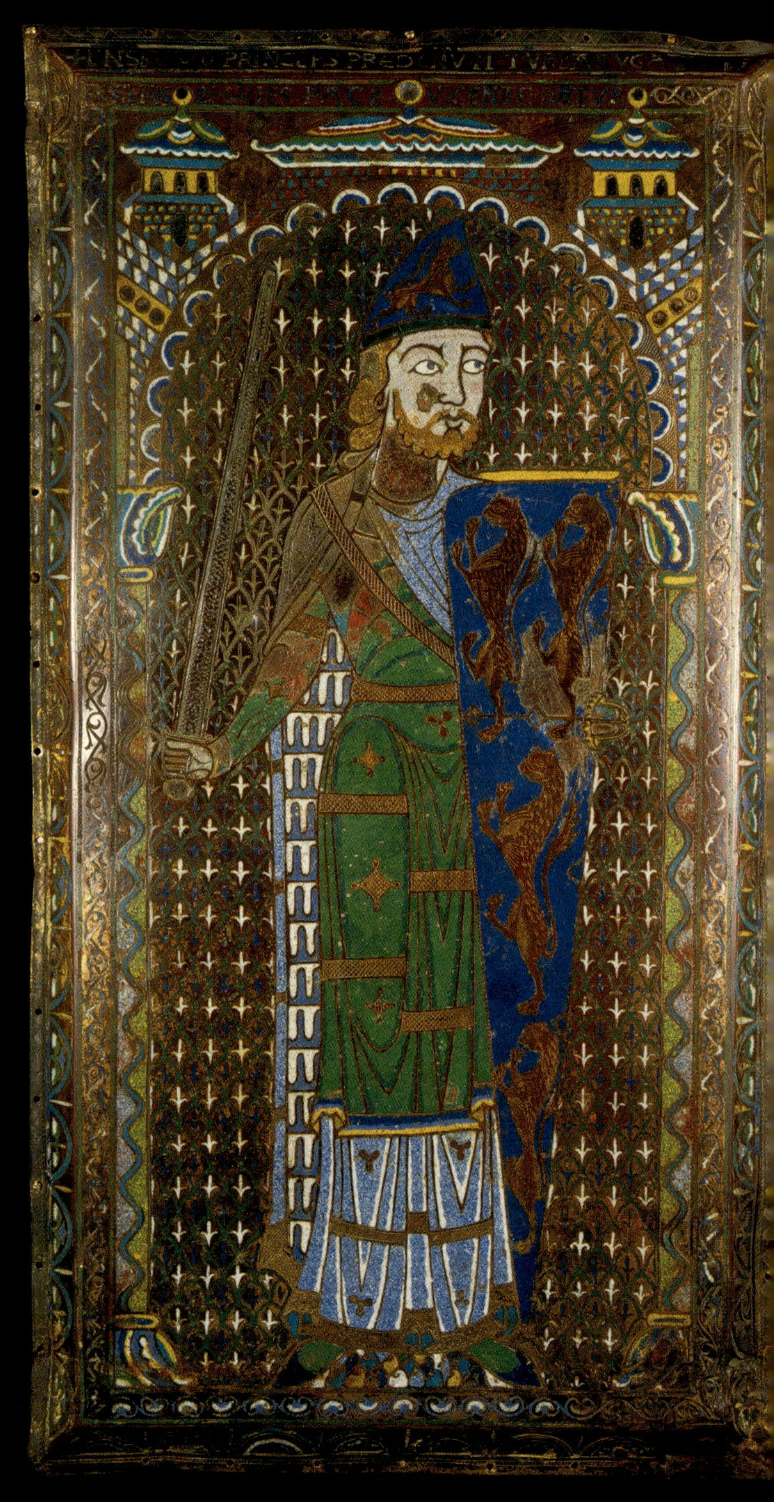

Contrary to what is usually believed, mass production was widespread throughout the Middle Ages. 'Copying' did not imply a slavish attitude. All medieval art demonstrates that the conception of artistic activity was similar to that of the *auctor* (author) of a book. The definition of mass production also included the reuse, with slight variants, of widely quoted exemplary texts or commentaries on them. Such activities were considered 'creative'. The mass-produced object was therefore a variant (rather than a mere reproduction) of a given model.

Mass production was a way of responding to a market economy and the desire for expansion. But 'mass does not mean multiple here: as a rule it meant creating technical conditions that would enable the same iconographical elements and themes to be reused while varying the way they were combined. The works of art that were mass-produced, usually objects related to worship or private prayer, also needed to be easy to transport as they were exported all over Europe following the trade routes. Particularly representative because of their success are three examples of mass production: Limoges enamel (12–13th centuries), English alabaster (14–16th centuries) and altarpieces, from Brabant in the southern Netherlands and, made of pipe-clay, from Utrecht (15–16th centuries).

LIMOGES ENAMELS

The Limoges enamelling technique practised by the enamellers of the 12th century consisted of carving into the copper backing plate the shapes that were then to be filled with vitrifiable powder – the champlevé method, as opposed to the cloisonné method favoured in Byzantine art (see Section III). The colour that dominated these glass surfaces was blue, often also found in the illuminated books and stained glass of that period. Enamellers quickly learned to make the most of the twin possibility offered by enamel: it could be applied to flat surfaces as well as curved ones, and to ornamentation as well as to figures. Countless devotional objects were made using this technique: altar fronts, bookbinding plates, chandeliers, reliquaries, censers, and so on. Enamels also had the advantage of being less expensive than gold or silver work. They were produced in Limoges, but also in the Mosan and Rhine basins (see Section IV). The enamels of Limoges, however were the most successful and widely distributed. The city

Cat V.2
MIRACLE OF THE CHILD FROM AMBAZAC
Limoges, *c.* 1250–70

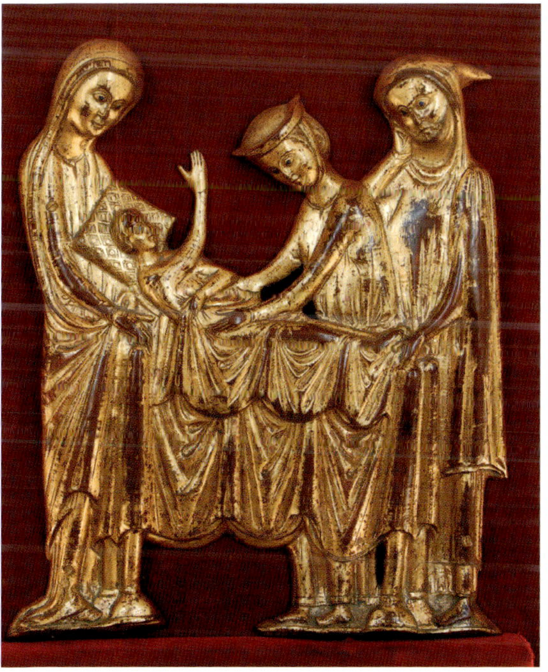

< Cat V.1
FUNERARY EFFIGY OF GEOFFROY PLANTAGENÊT
Le Mans (?), just after 1151

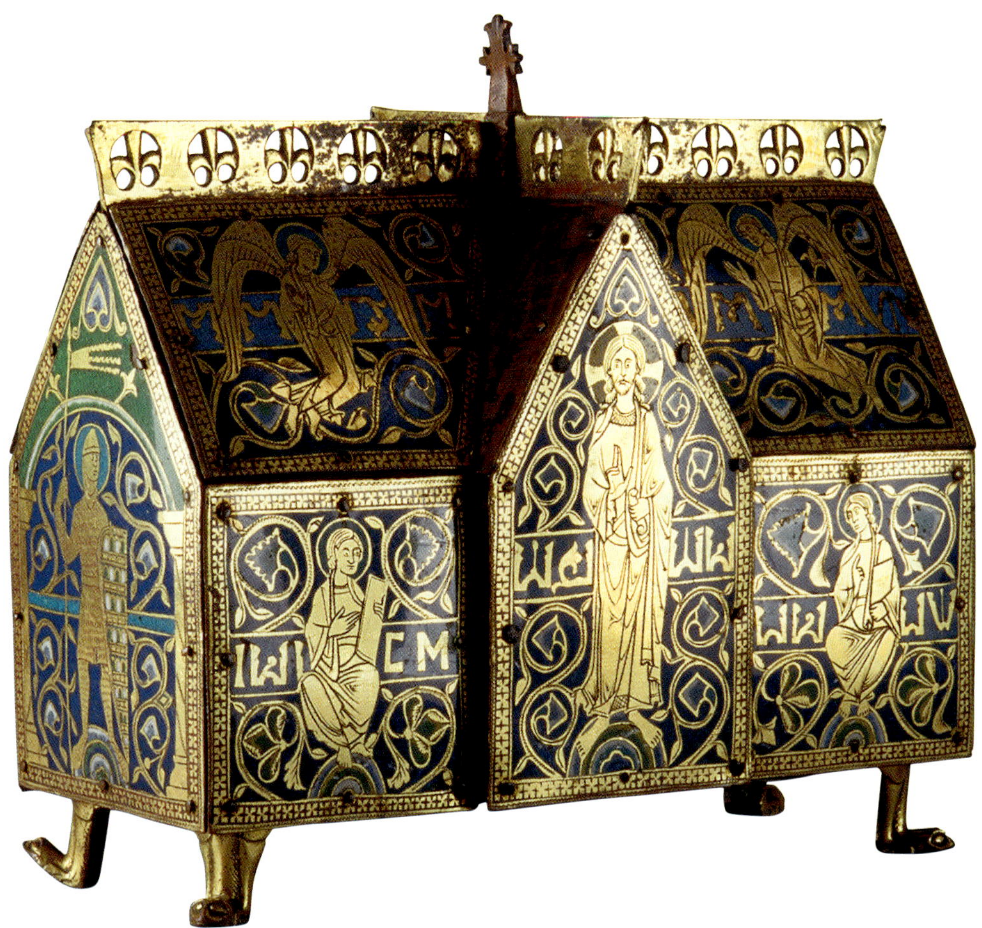

stands at the junction of several trade routes that were also used by pilgrims on their way to Rome and Santiago de Compostela – and did not St Eligius (Eloi), the patron saint of goldsmiths, come from Chaptelet near Limoges? A whole group of local monastic foundations used the services of enamellers and contributed to their prosperity. Itinerant monks thus assisted the dissemination of enamels. The patronage of the Plantagenets played an important part in the development of the *opus lemovicense* – Limoges enamel work[V.1], particularly because of the sponsorship that favoured the abbey of Grandmont[V.2], chosen at one stage to be the burial place of Henry II Plantagenet, and it could be argued that the monastic order of Grandmont was associated with the success of the enamels of Limoges.

Their dissemination of enamels in Italy, Spain, Scandinavia[V.3, 5] and the Holy Land is better explained by the artistic, economic and functional success of the objects. Moreover, enamel was equally prized by the clergy with modest resources as by the nobility: funerary plaques were commissioned in Brittany, Champagne and England.

The virtual monopoly held by Limoges was challenged towards the middle of the 13th century. The fashion for Limoges enamels led to the creation of workshops in other parts of Europe that often combined

Cat V.3
RELIQUARY
Northern Germany (?), early 13th century

Cat V.8
WILLELMUS CROSIER KNOWN AS RAGENFROI'S
England, c. 1175

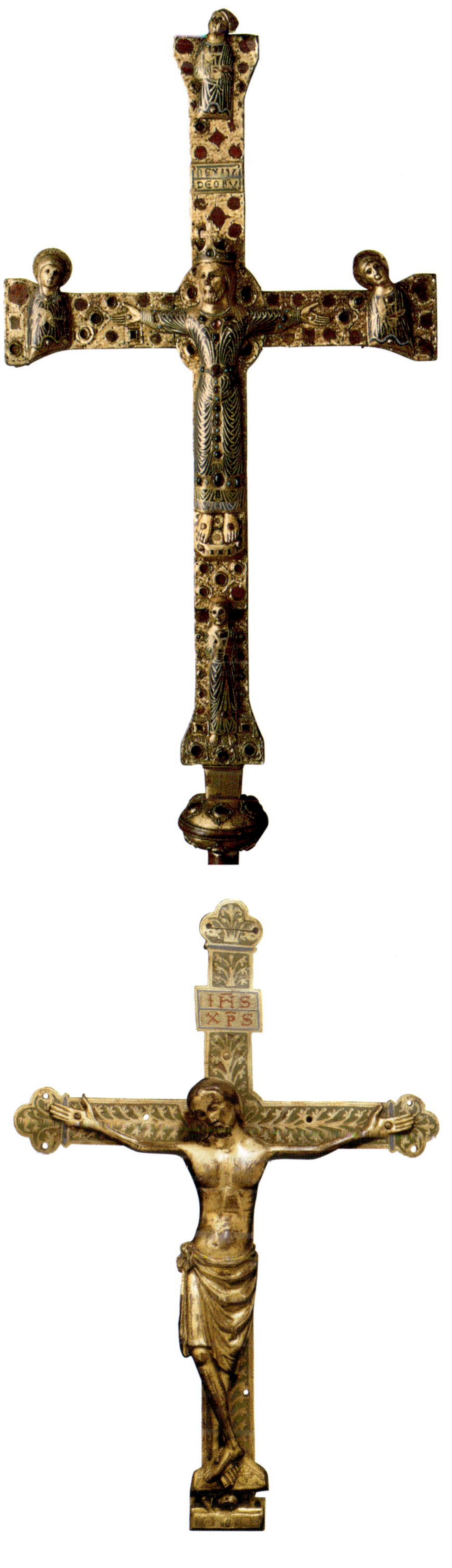

Cat V.5
PROCESSIONAL CROSS
Limoges, *c.* 1190–1200

Cat V.6
CHRIST ON THE CROSS
Limoges, *c.* 1240–50

the Limousin tradition with features specific to their own regions: this happened in the Île-de-France, Champagne, Sicily and northern Europe from Saxony to England. A very fine abbatial crosier, mixing formal idioms borrowed from the English miniature with indisputably Limousin and Mosan sources, is signed by Brother Willelmus [V.8].

Prestigious commissions multiplied in the 14th and 15th centuries. In the inventories of the riches they had accumulated, European princes of the 14th century revealed their unbounded taste for luxury and the huge sums they were capable of spending. As well as the papal inventories and those of Assisi, we should mention particularly those of Charles v, King of France, Jean, Duke of Berry and his brother, Louis of Anjou. They feature large numbers of enamels. An eloquent example of these sumptuous objects is the magnificent processional cross now in the Bargello [V.9].

ALABASTER

As from the mid-14th century, England specialized in producing alabaster panels and statues to enrich its own religious buildings but also for export to the Continent, as can be seen from the inventories of parish churches and monasteries as well as the archives of the English customs offices. Alabaster was used first to make tombs and later for the creation of altarpiece images. Two examples of exceptional quality, the origin of the use of this material for funerary sculpture, are still extant: the tombs of King Edward II of England in Gloucester cathedral (*c.* 1330) and of his son, Edward III, in Westminster abbey (1336).

Several alabaster deposits along the river Trent were exploited in the English midlands, at Tutbury in Nottinghamshire, particularly as from 1362, and at Chellaston in Derbyshire. Between 1470 and 1530 Burton-on-Trent and Nottingham were leading centres of alabaster sculpture. York also produced alabasters, but a little earlier, active alabaster sculptors being mentioned as early as 1450. These famous centres for alabastermen do not exclude other workplaces that are not yet known.

Alabaster, a soluble saline rock, is soft and easy to sculpt. It was therefore well suited to the mass production of religious objects, altarpieces or small panels (tabulae) and statuettes.

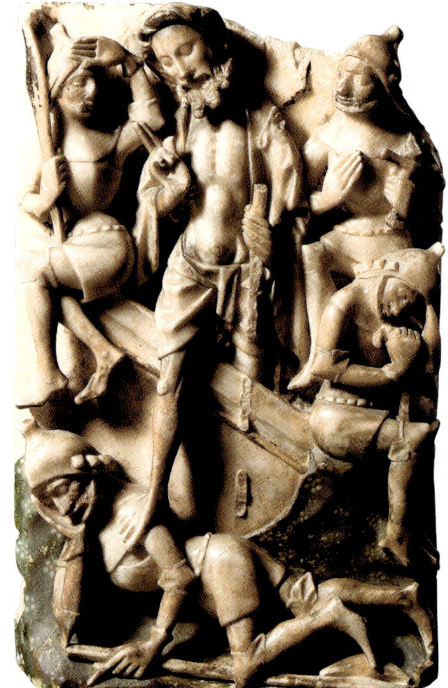

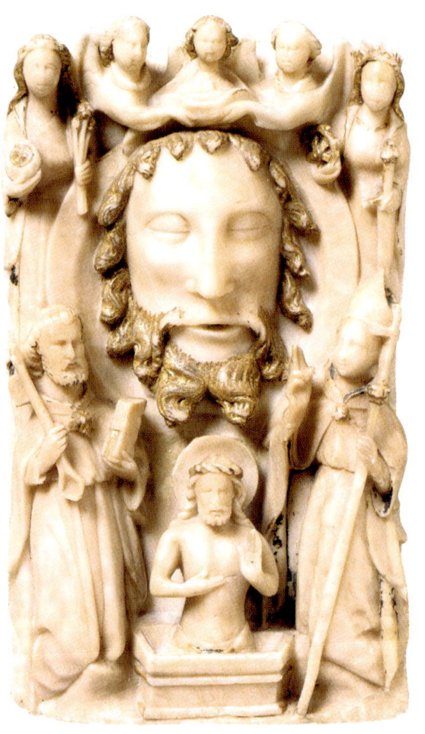

Cat v.13
RESURRECTION OF CHRIST
Nottingham (?), second half of the 15th century

Cat v.12
HEAD OF ST JOHN THE BAPTIST
Nottingham, end of the 15th century

Written records and accounts bear witness to orders and sales of this type of object as from 1367. At the end of the 14th century, the production and marketing of sculptures expanded considerably. It reached its peak in the mid-15th century and continued into the 1530s, when the Anglican Reformation halted the commissioning of religious images.

The most widespread iconographical themes for altarpieces were those of Christ's Passion and the Seven Joys of Mary (see, for example, the reliefs of the Resurrection kept in Rouen **V.13, 14** and the Annunciation in the Musée de Cluny in Paris **V.10**) and, for individual panels, statuettes of the Virgin and Child, the Apostles and saints, and heads of St John the Baptist **V.12**. Nottingham specialized in selling reliefs of this kind. They were mass-produced, sold throughout England and exported. Individuals displayed them in wooden alcoves in their homes so as to obtain assistance and blessing at the time of their death. The head of St John the Baptist now in Rouen with its dramatic expression is a fine example of these **V.12**.

In the second half of the 15th century, the elegance of the 14th gave way to an increasingly stereotyped style: elongated figures of people dressed in similar armour and linear garments, with bulging eyes, wide faces with fixed expressions and clumsy attitudes were recurrent characteristics. The use of many colours emphasized their facial expressions, while gilding enhanced the alabaster and completed the sculpted form. The distribution of these colours was governed by repetitive systems. Colour was applied to faces, beards, the details of clothing or decorative items, such as flowers with white petals and red hearts painted on the ground **V.15**. The use of a constant iconography, identical composition plans (compare scenes representing the Resurrection **V.13, 14**) and the persistence of a style looking back to earlier times make these objects difficult to date and attribute. The same is true of the mass-produced wooden altarpieces of Brabant. It is thus easier to identify a workshop than an individual craftsman and, in the absence of written texts, works can be catalogued chronologically only by referring to dated alabaster tombs, often decorated with relief panels at the bottom. Many such well-documented funerary monuments have been preserved.

Alabaster altarpieces appeared in about 1400. They were of two types, either fixed to one or two superimposed rectangular boards or forming a triptych. They usually consisted of five to seven compartments sculpted in relief and encased in a wooden frame based on recurrent models. Sculptures of standing saints at the ends of the altarpiece framed the principal reliefs. As from the last quarter of the 15th century, this customary type of altarpiece was sometimes replaced by a raised central panel.

The whole altarpiece was designed to be painted in many colours, the unpainted parts sometimes being polished. Often, however, the complete disappearance or poor conservation of their colours has transformed altarpieces into purely white objects, thus giving a false impression of their original appearance.

Similarly, most of the panels that have been conserved come from dismembered altarpieces, making them look like individual reliefs. They therefore need to be read as fragments of the whole composition of which they were once a part.

The widespread dissemination of these alabaster panels and sculptures, several hundred of which are still preserved in Europe – mainly in France and particularly

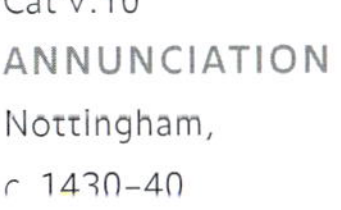

Cat V.10
ANNUNCIATION
Nottingham,
c. 1430–40

Cat V.14
RESURRECTION OF CHRIST
Nottingham (?),
second half of
the 15th century

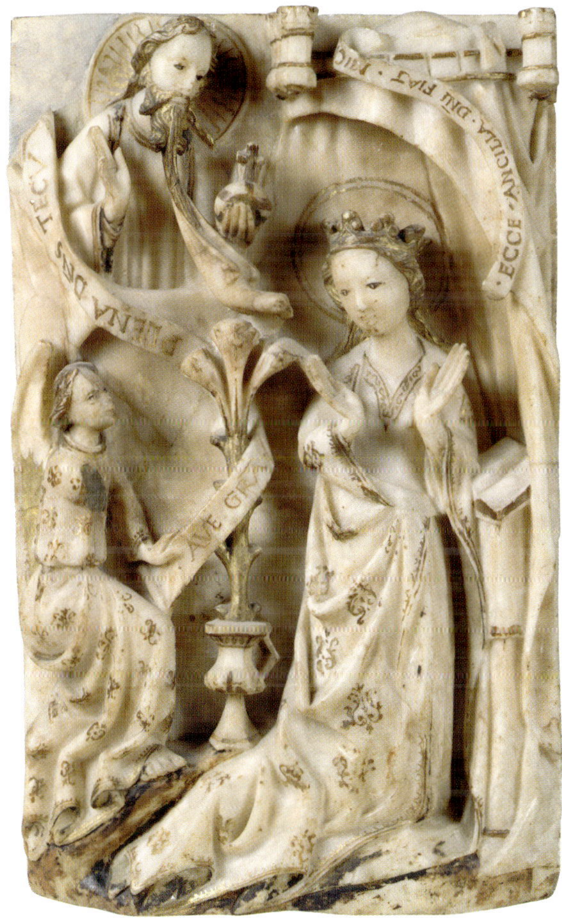

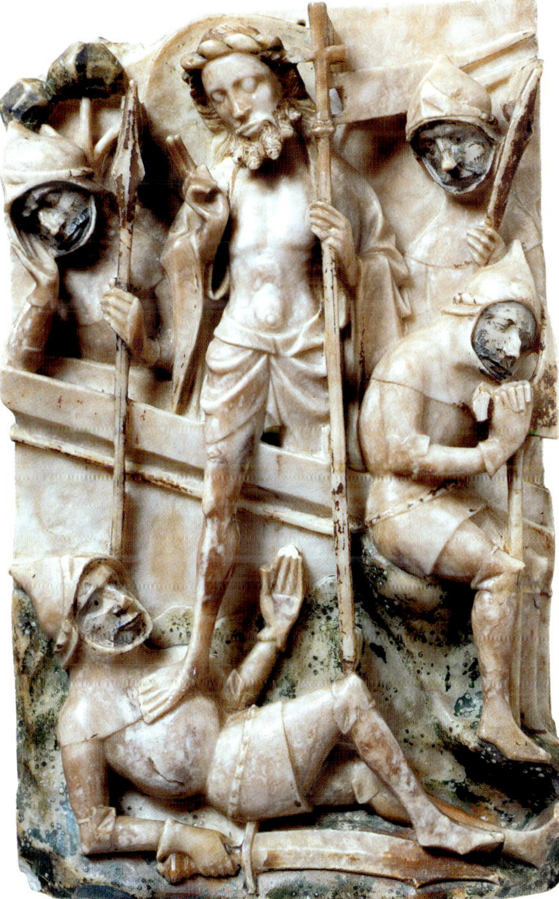

in Normandy and the Bordeaux region – demonstrate an enormous scale of production, which can be explained by the activity of merchants specializing in the sale of such devotional objects. Demand must have been great and partly motivated by the reasonable prices of the works, unlike the cost of statues and altarpieces of polychromed oak. The popularity of the pipe-clay statuettes from the Netherlands could have a similar economic explanation.

As always during the Middle Ages, the export of works of art followed the trade routes. Alabaster statuettes from England are first mentioned at the end of the 14th century **V.15** and references to them become more numerous in the 15th, while during the Reformation boats loaded with images 'rejected' by their country of origin arrived in France to be sold. Dispatched from the leading ports London and Bristol, the goods arrived in Normandy, Brittany and Paris. Leaving the ports of Dieppe, Caen and Cherbourg, they were then distributed in the interior of the country. Thus, the trade in wine with the Bordeaux region justified the generalized presence of alabasters in town churches. Apart from this mass production, intended for the free market, certain specific commissions were also issued by French churches, such as the order for the Life of Saint-Seurin for the church of the same name in Bordeaux. English alabasters were also exported to Spain, Portugal, Italy and even Iceland.

BRABANTINE SCULPTED ALTARPIECES WITH PAINTED WINGS

From the 13th century, there had been stone altarpieces placed on the altar, comprising a set of reliefs linked to the Passion. This formula developed during the 14th and 15th centuries, which first became possible through the use of wood instead of stone. The sculpted altarpiece soon became the subject of close collaboration between several trades – the 'sculptor' of images (in alabaster or wood), the painter, the polychromer, the gilder, the cabinet-maker entrusted with mounting the reliefs in detachable frames and the ironmonger who made the hinges. Although in the 15th century the carved and painted altarpiece with detachable wings reached an exceptional level of quality in many parts of Europe: the Kraków altarpiece by Veit Stoss, the Sterzing altarpiece (Italy) by Hans Multscher, the Constance altarpiece by Nikolaus van Leyden (which has disappeared but was famous in its day – see Section VIII), the St Wolfgang altarpiece (Austria) by Michael Pacher, etc. There follows a description of the altogether exceptional production of Brabantine altarpieces, which led to 'mass' production in large cities such as Brussels or Antwerp.

In the 15th and 16th centuries, the southern Netherlands was famous for producing sculpted altarpieces with painted wings. These works, distinguished by the high quality of their execution, found particular favour in princely courts, religious orders and among the middle classes. Some of them were the subject of

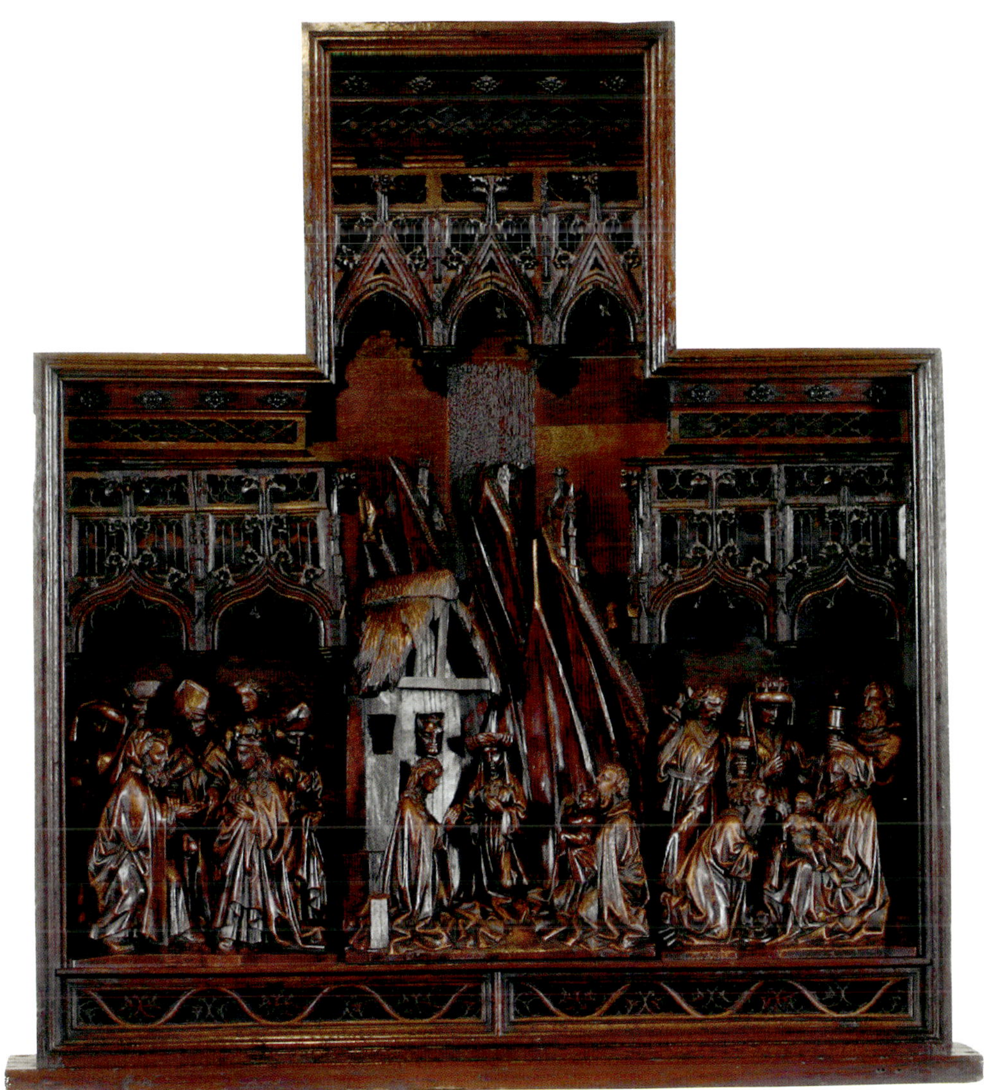

Cat V.21
ALTARPIECE OF THE NATIVITY OF FUNCHAL
Brussels atelier
c. 1440

commissions and contracts – as their iconography often fulfilled a specific request by a patron – while others were acquired on the art markets.

From the second quarter of the 15th century and particularly in the early 16th, the growing demand for altarpieces led to the development of an unprecedented market, implying that workshops had to be reorganized. Standards then appeared for the various parts of altarpieces and a complex division of labour arose among the various craftsmen working on them. As is clear from workshop inventories and people's wills, craftsmen collected stocks of finished or partly finished works to be submitted for buyers to select or sold on one of the art markets, the most famous being the Pand at the Cathedral of Our Lady in Antwerp, founded in 1460.

Although altarpieces were produced in other towns of the former Low Countries, most of them came from the workshops of Brussels, Antwerp and Mechelen. Those displayed in this section are from Brussels, those from Antwerp having been the subject of an important exhibition there in 1993. Much appreciated for their narrative character expressively illustrating the most common religious themes such as the Life of the Virgin Mary and the Life of Christ, particularly scenes from the Childhood and Passion of Christ, and the lives of the saints, they supplied the flourishing market for altarpieces for private use or export.

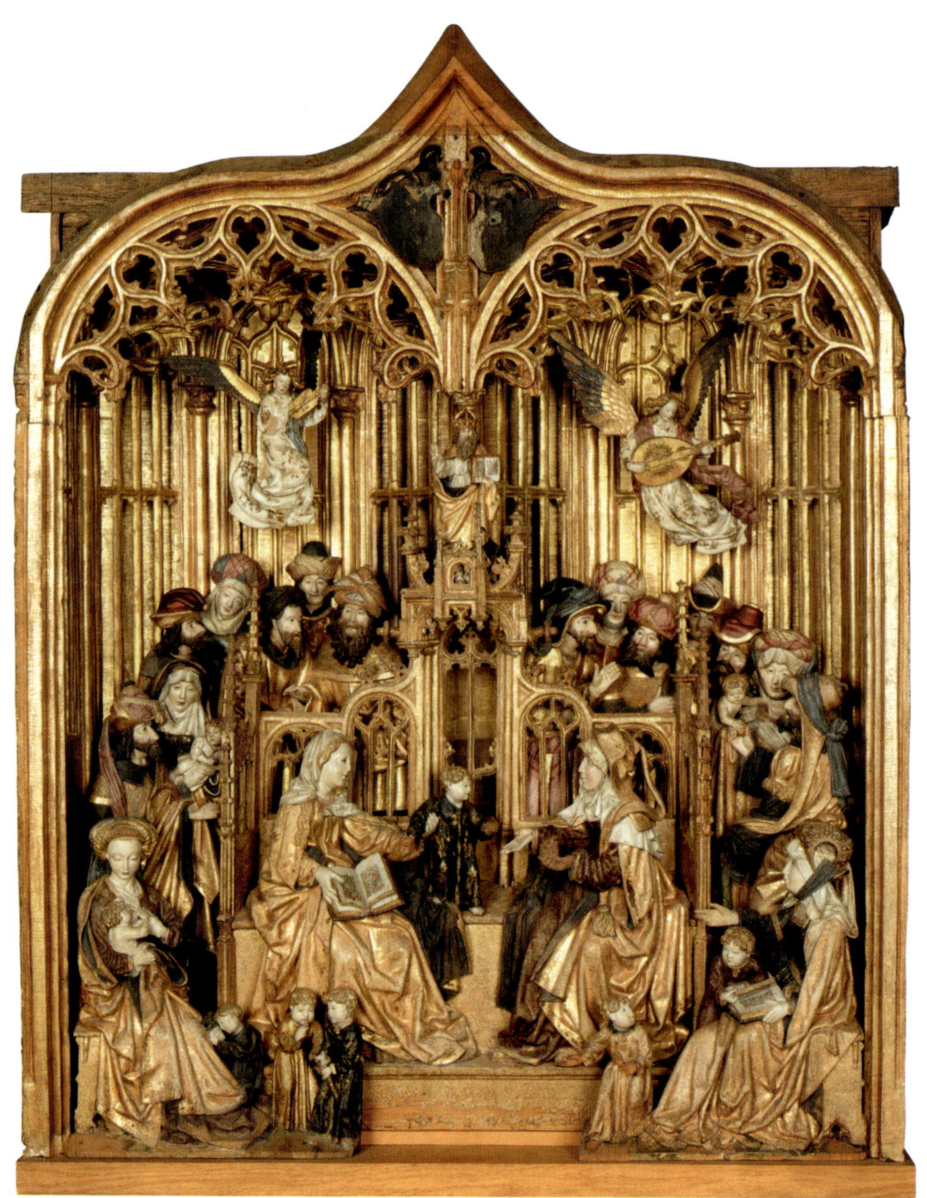

Cat V.18
FAMILY OF ST ANNE ALTARPIECE
Borman atelier, Brussels, *c.* 1500–10

sculpture the Borman dynasty dominated (Jean II, Pasquier and Jean III). These masters had an enormous stylistic influence on image carvers and wing painters.

Two altarpieces from the same gifted group of artists were included in the Antwerp exhibition: the altarpiece of the Family of St Anne **V.18** and the altarpiece of the Virgin of Strängnäs III **V.20**. The first is one of the jewels of the Brussels school. St Anne, the mother of the Virgin Mary, whose veneration was developing, especially at the end of the Middle Ages, is surrounded by her entire family.

This alcove, which was probably part of a larger set, comes from the chapel of St Anne in Val Duchesse in Auderghem (Brussels). It includes armorial bearings, albeit blank, indicating that it was a commissioned work. The superb quality of the carving and the wealth and refinement of the colours incline us to attribute this artwork to the workshop of the famous dynasty of Brussels sculptors, the Bormans. We recognize the fantastic hats, the structured, expressive faces and the interest in scenes from everyday life (children playing and musical instruments), as well as the features specific to the formal repertoire of that workshop

Of all the themes that Christianity helped to disseminate throughout eastern and western Europe in the Middle Ages, that concerning the Virgin Mary was certainly the most widespread in literature, music, painting and sculpture. The second Council of Nicaea (787), which put an end to the iconoclast crisis in the Byzantine Church, established two doctrines that formed the basis of the whole question of images and their role in the Church: God can be *worshipped* but saints can only be *honoured.* An icon is merely a reflection of a primitive image. Venerating it means that prayers are addressed to it only indirectly. This doctrine was to remain decisive for the various forms that images of the Virgin were to adopt in both the Orthodox and the Catholic Churches.

In the Europe of the 12th century, the representation of the Virgin was to undergo marked changes that can be attributed to two sets of circumstances. Firstly, the current of reform initiated by Bernard de Clairvaux in the monastic movement, which, while condemning the use of certain images in the Church, assigned an essential place to the veneration of Mary – a burning devotion, it could be said, typical of the mysticism of St Bernard. He barely distinguishes the Virgin's spiritual beauty from her physical beauty, and it is there that a contradiction arises that Bernard himself never entirely succeeded in removing. How could painters and sculptors present such spiritual beauty without transcribing it into physical features?

Alongside the part played by St Bernard's sensitivity in the cult of Mary, a second circumstance strongly affected it: the development of the courtly lyric and the image of the 'lady' it exalts. The art of love, ritualized by poets, places the idealization of woman at the heart of the spirit of chivalry. For a 12th-century knight, this meant achieving 'a cultural ideal blending with the ideal of love' (Huizinga). This aristocratic requirement enabled courtly love to retain that worldly character that it was never completely to lose.

It must be remembered that courtly love did not consider the beloved woman as unattainable, but believed that her love had to be deserved, and in the effort to overcome all the obstacles separating the lover from the object of his desire lay a virtue that is not entirely alien to a Christian one. In his *Miracles de Nostre Dame,* Gautier de Coinci (1177/78–1236) discusses all the human situations in which recourse to the mediating Virgin enables someone to return to God. Gautier borrows a repertoire from the discourse of love, which he places at the service of the veneration of Mary. In the first song in his collection, playing on words, Gautier defines the experience of venerating Mary as an 'enchantment':

'Sing of her, all you singers:
You will enchant the enchanter
Who often enchants us.

< Cat VI.1
ADORATION OF THE MAGI
Anglo-Saxon art, late 11th century

By singing to the Mother of God,
He who enchants will be enchanted.'

It should be remembered that this highly lyrical work is contemporary with the magnificent sculptures of the Virgin on the façades of cathedrals.

In the 13th century, poems dedicated to the Virgin were not confined to the shadow of the cloister. At that time, the mendicant orders (Franciscans and Dominicans) wanted to introduce them to a wider world, outside the liturgy, for example to accompany a sermon. Franciscan spirituality exalts the beauty of Creation and every living creature in a form of popular lyricism. Thanks to the Franciscans, the Virgin as mediator, praised by both Bernard de Clairvaux and Gautier de Coinci, became the model of the suffering Mother.

But devotion to the Virgin gave rise to a whole literature of its own, which shows the way it was practised. The same applies to the world of images. Some of them were designed to show the faithful the attitude they should adopt before the image of Christ, as in the Adoration of the Magi [VI.1]. The faithful were supposed to mimic the pious attitudes of the Wise Men. We should remember that well before she was represented on her own, the Virgin was included in the scene of the Adoration of the Magi in early Christian art.

The representation of the person praying at the interior of the image is a device comparable to that of the Magi, but instead of being incorporated into the heavenly space, the donor is excluded from it or is depicted at a lower level [VI.2]. It is only in Flemish primitive painting that the two levels correspond [VI.3]. Then the sacred realm to some extent invades the secular world in the form of a symbol. The idealization of woman and the humanization of the Virgin form that cultural background without which the multiplication of works of art glorifying the Virgin in the 12-15th centuries would be incomprehensible.

Among the first works in this section are two Sedes Sapientiae or thrones of wisdom [VI.4,5]. The Virgin is the throne of divine wisdom, as on her lap she holds the Child who unites

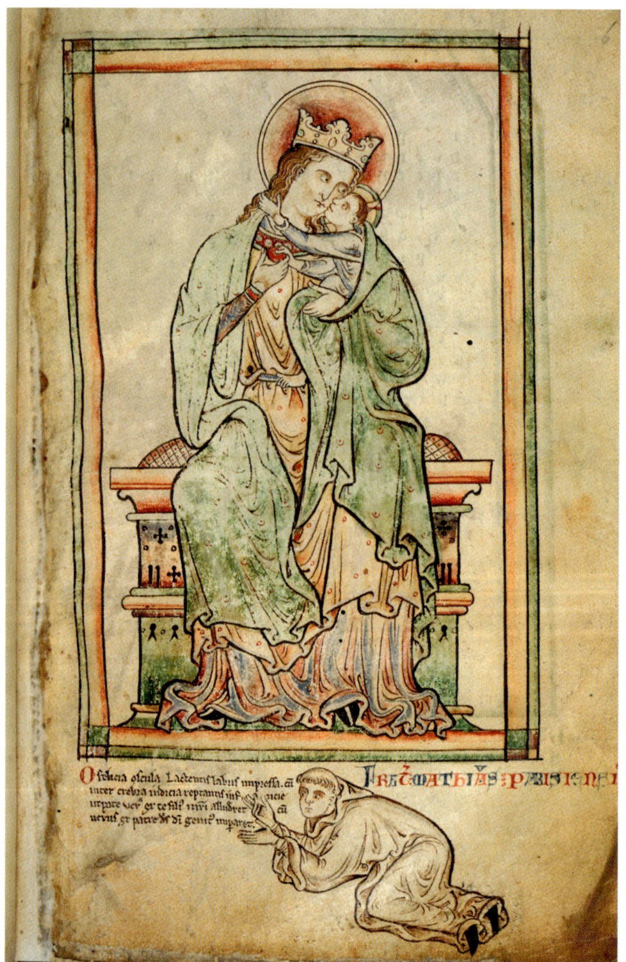

Cat VI.2
HISTORIA ANGLORUM ET CHRONICA MAIORA
Matthew Paris,
St Albans, 1250–59

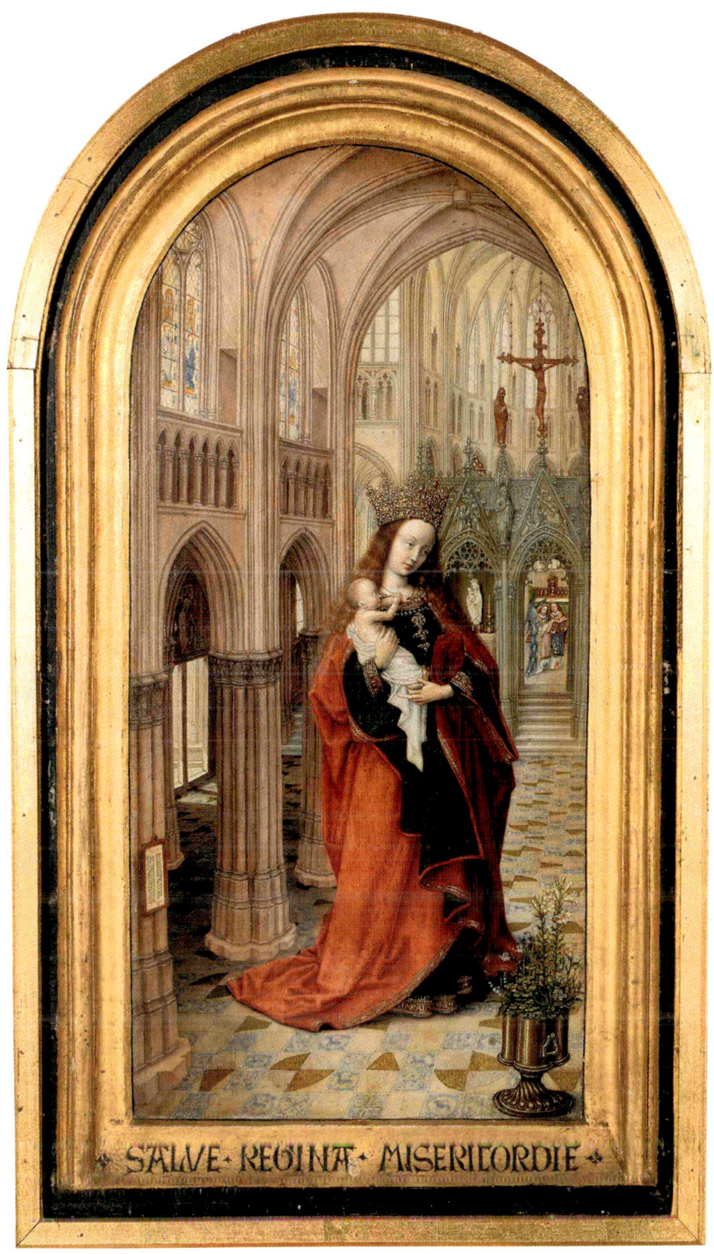

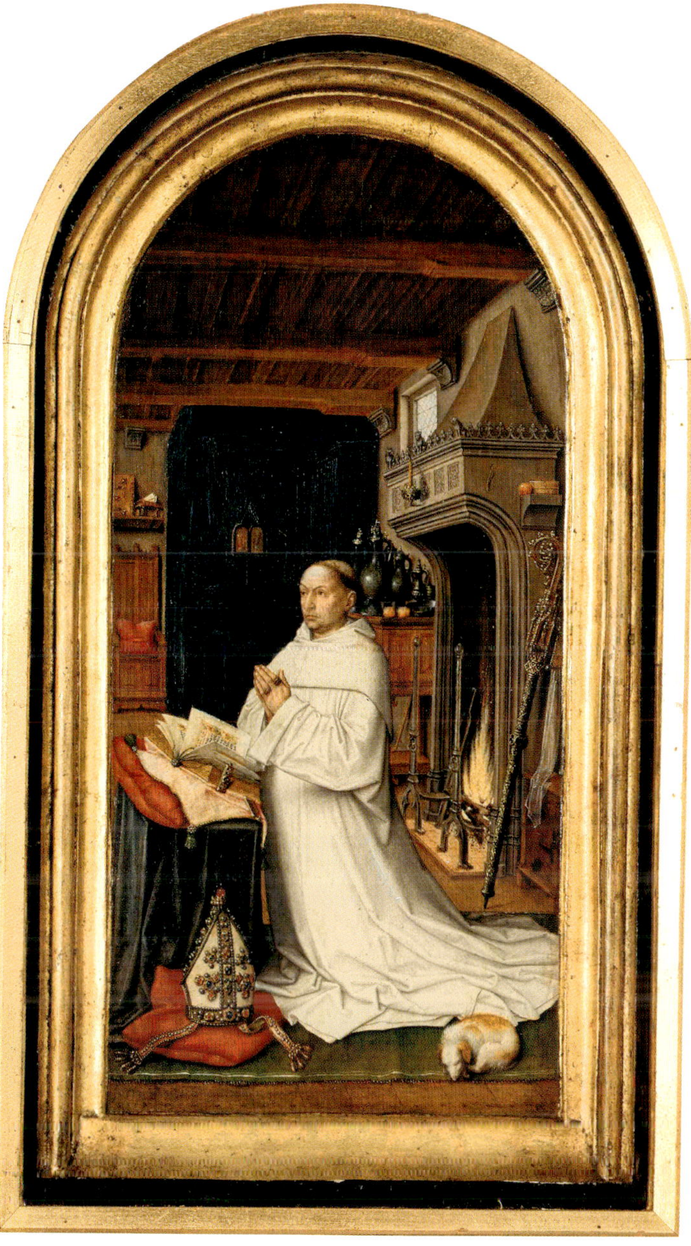

Cat VI.3
DEVOTIONAL DIPTYCH
Master of Bruges of 1499

within Him all wisdom and all knowledge. In its great beauty, the Sedes Sapientiae in Liège **VI.5** surely brings to mind that verse from the Song of Songs: 'you are entirely beautiful and full of charm ... like a dawn all shining with light ... fair as the moon, dazzling as the sun'. By the early 12th century, Rupert de Deutz had transposed the vocabulary and metaphors of the Song to the praise of the Virgin. In contrast to that aristocratic nobility, the Virgin kept in Stockholm **VI.4** was produced according to religious tradition and is comparable to the old Sedes – for example the 10th-century Sedes of Essen – that look more like pagan idols.

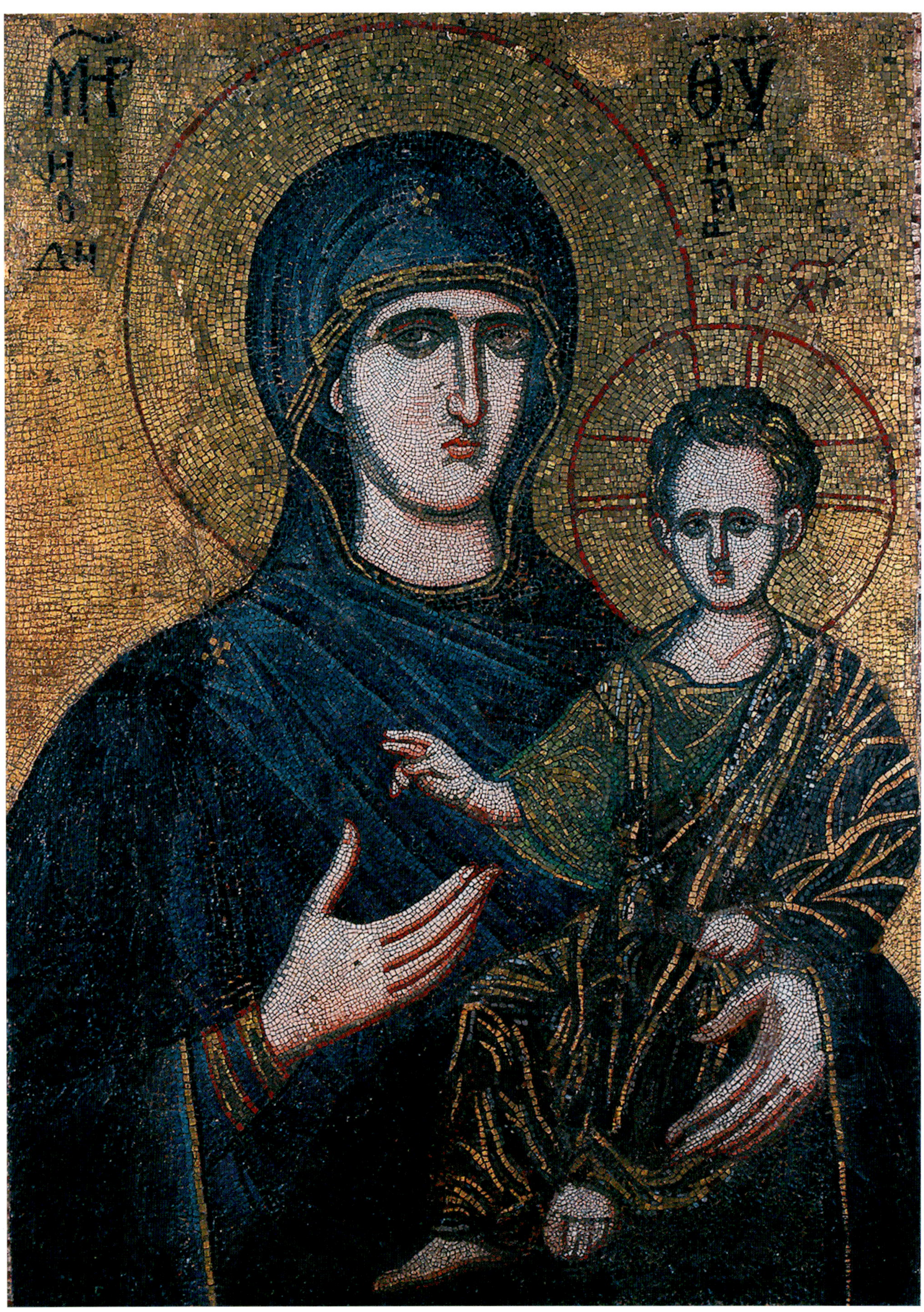
ΜΡ
ΘΥ

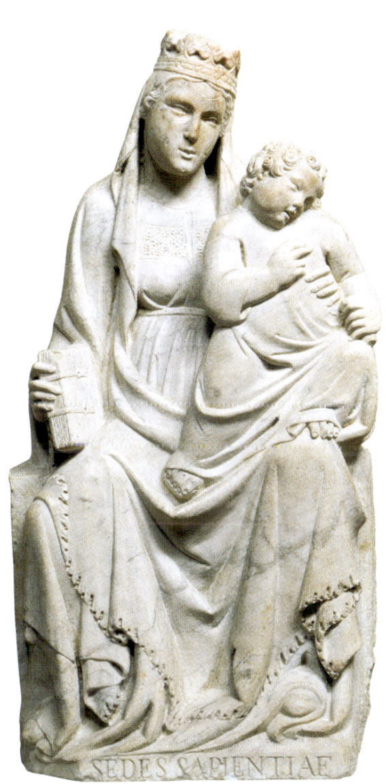

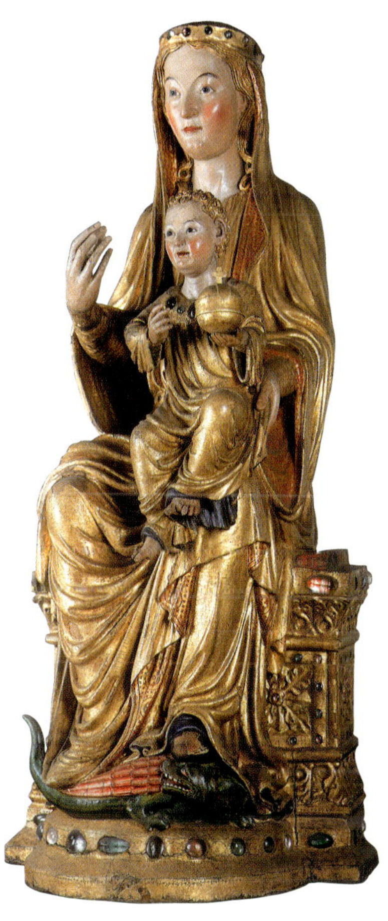

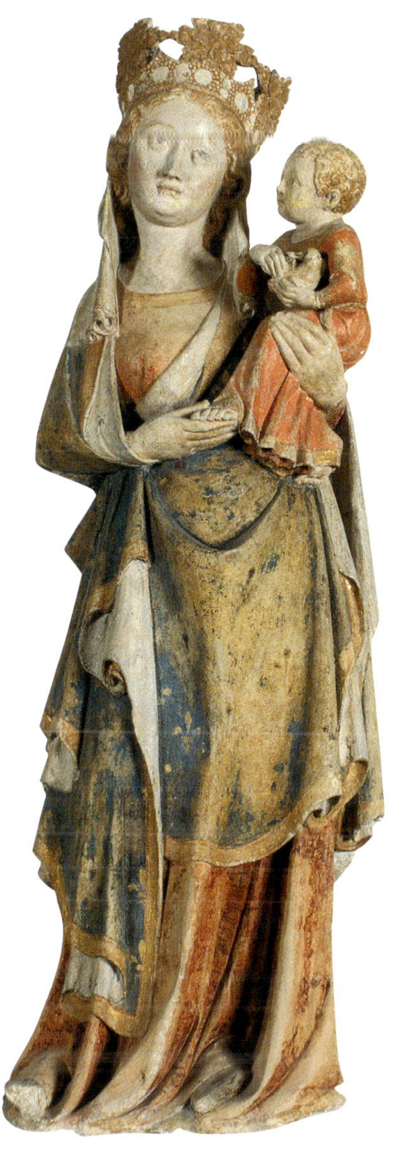

Cat VI.6
VIRGIN AND CHILD ENTHRONED
Tino da Camaino,
1318–19

Cat VI.5
SEDES SAPIENTIAE
Mosan region,
c. 1235–45

Cat VI.16
VIRGIN AND CHILD
Île-de-France,
c. 1320–40

The various attitudes adopted by representations of the Virgin throughout the centuries that concern us here, the relationship of the Mother to the Child and the gestures of both vary not according to the inspiration of the artists who created them but in response to well-defined devotional types. In all of them, a distinction must therefore be made between the *type* and the *style* of the works. The icons that emerged from the Byzantine tradition clearly illustrate that distinction [VI.7,11]. What we call Glykophilousa and Eleoussa Virgins correspond to theological definitions of the Virgin of tenderness and the Virgin of mercy. The painter was not free to alter these correspondences in any way within the commission entrusted to him, but could use his skill to make their attitudes more natural, for example.

With Western works, we are often tempted to confuse type and style, in that a work that is novel from the formal point of view seems to us, above all, the creation of an innovative artist, whereas it is innovative also because it incarnates a new theological equivalent. Depending on the position of the Child, 'Beautiful

< Cat VI.7
ICON OF THE HODEGETRIA VIRGIN
14th century

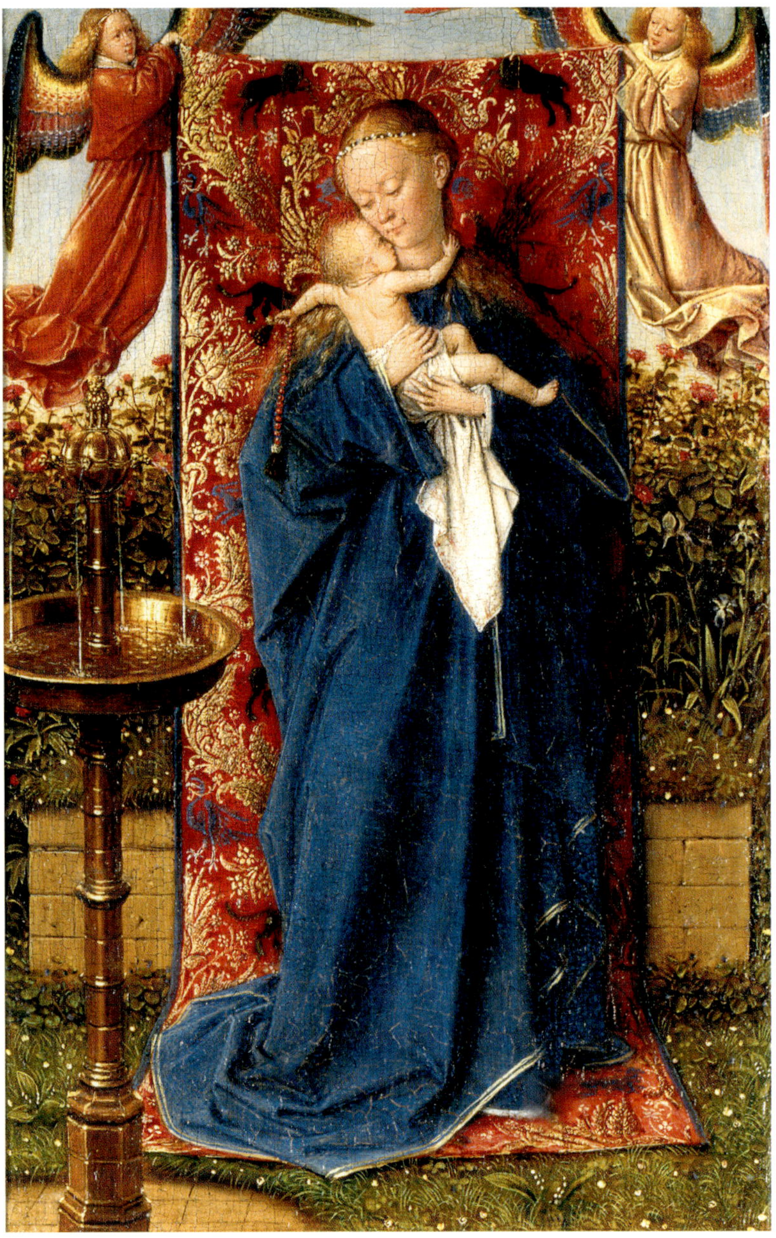

Cat VI.13
VIRGIN AND CHILD AT THE FOUNTAIN
Jan van Eyck, 1439

Madonnas' VI.9 can be divided into two main types that correspond to two distinct forms of worship. A work as surprising as the Virgin of Marcoussis VI.8 was designed to fulfil a particular intention of its donor, who wanted, as it were, to integrate his devotion to the Christ of the Passion into an image of Mary.

In his Virgin and Child at the Fountain VI.13, Jan van Eyck reinterpreted the Glykophilousa type by depicting the Child in a naturally affectionate attitude, and we see how a great artist can add symbols (such as the lion) or handle traditional iconographical themes by incorporating them into everyday life – here in a genteel and urbane environment. We can see the great distance that divides this concept of the glorification of Mary from that of Francesco Vannuccio VI.10, whose characters seem to be suspended in the abstract – heavenly – space of the golden background. In all these cases, we need to assess how much room was left to the artist's inventiveness compared with the regulatory constraints that so strongly determined it.

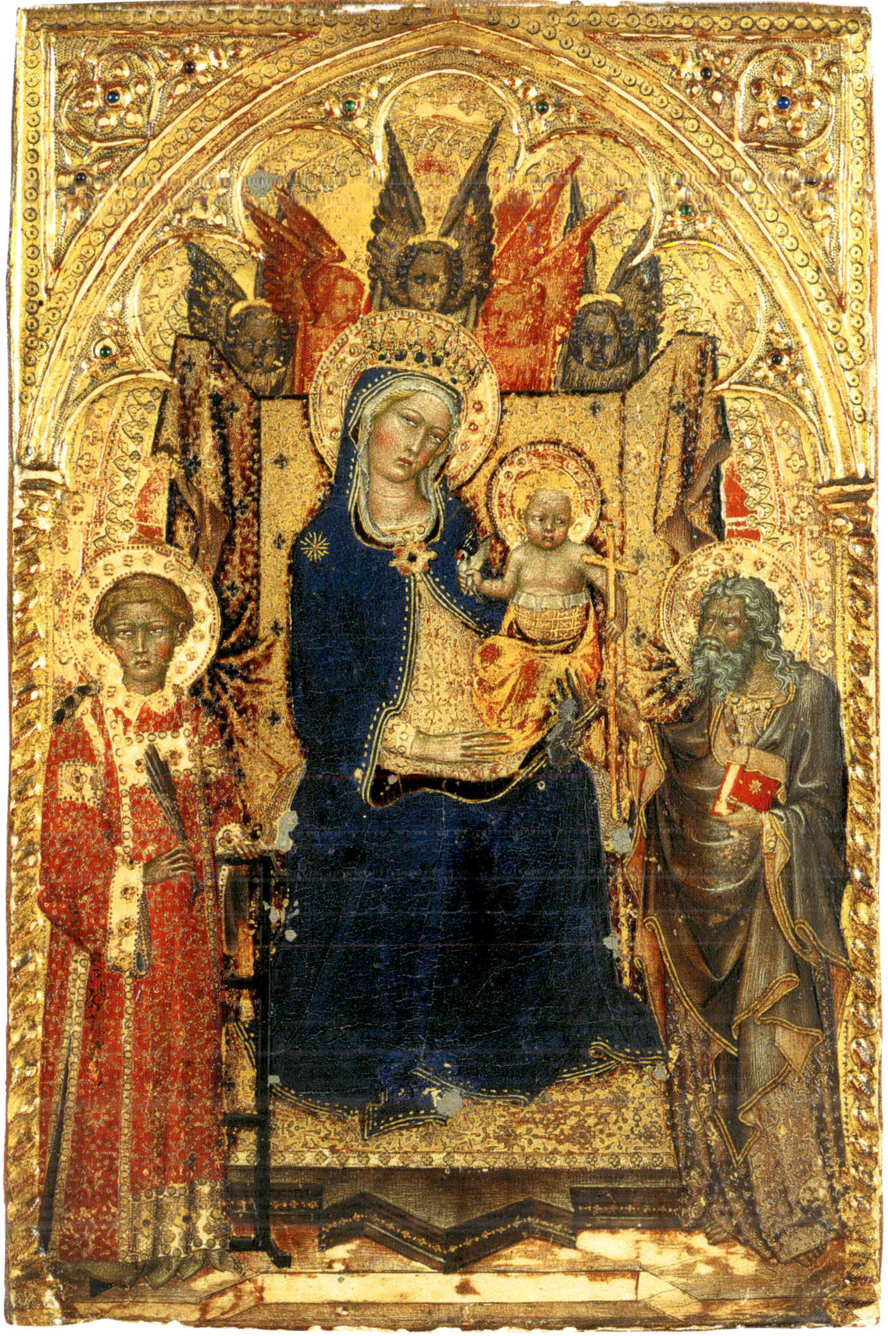

Cat VI.10
DIPTYCH OF THE VIRGIN ENTHRONED WITH THE CHILD, ST LAURENCE AND ST ANDREW
Francesco Vannuccio, c. 1380

Some Virgins certainly represented types determined at the devotional level. For example, an ivory Virgin and Child from Zwettl (Austria) can be identified as a prototype. The Virgin and Child from Picardy **VI.14**, now in the Louvre, reiterates that type, and was also inspired by its style, perhaps through the mediation of the Virgin in the treasury of the Sainte-Chapelle, Paris. Although it conforms to a type well established in the 14th century, a work such as the Virgin of Varennes-sur-Seine **VI.16** undoubtedly demonstrates great command. Consequently, it is clear that the richest patrons did not insist on typological innovation but did expect artistic quality.

A more detailed study of representations of the Virgin and Child in the 14th and, above all, the early 15th century, shows the extent to which sculptors combined

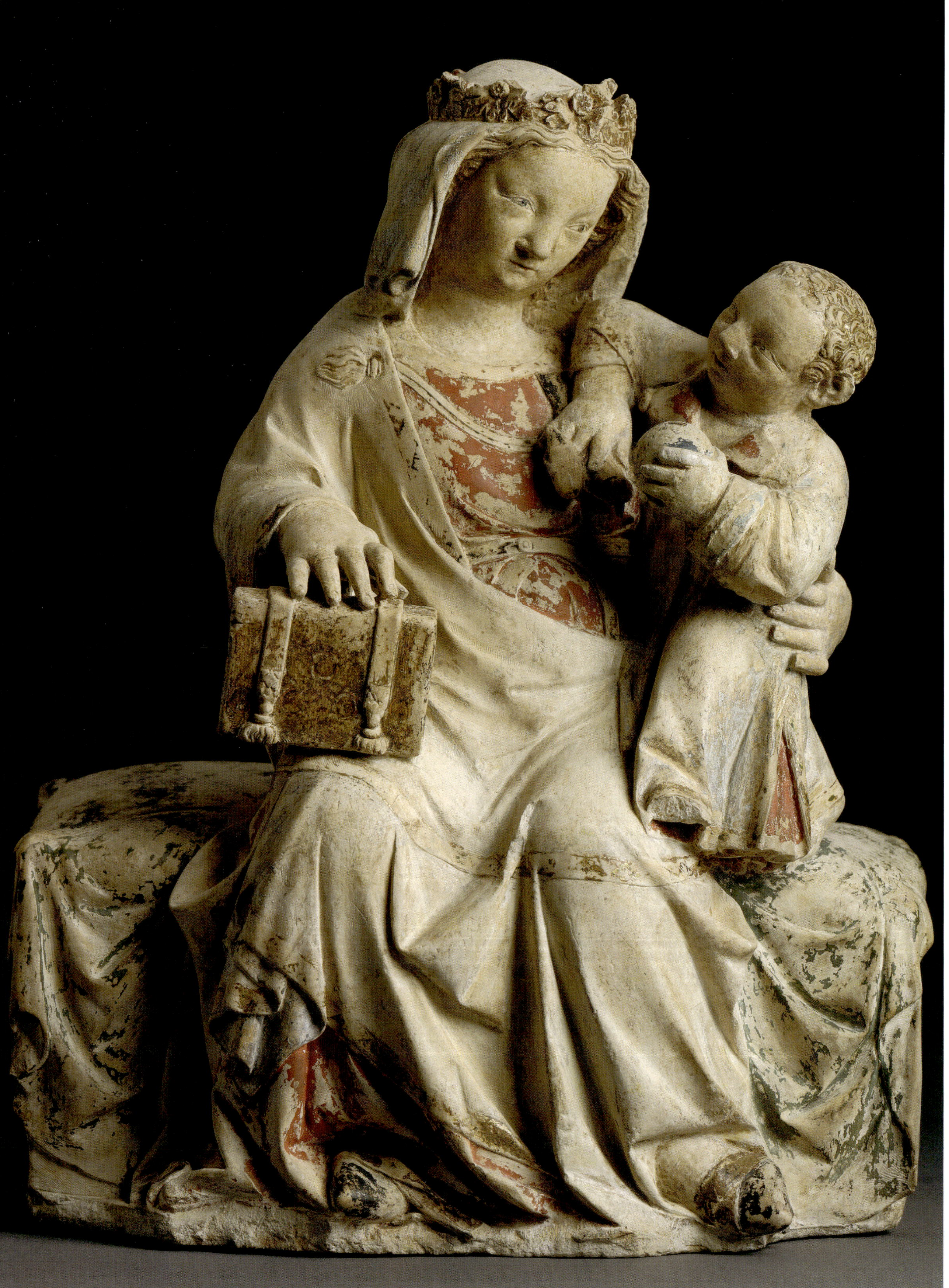

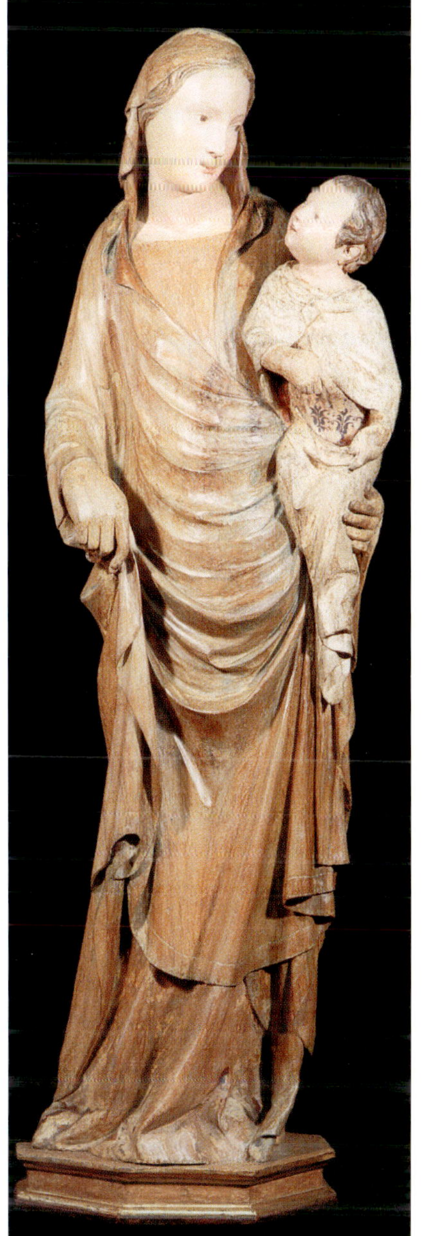

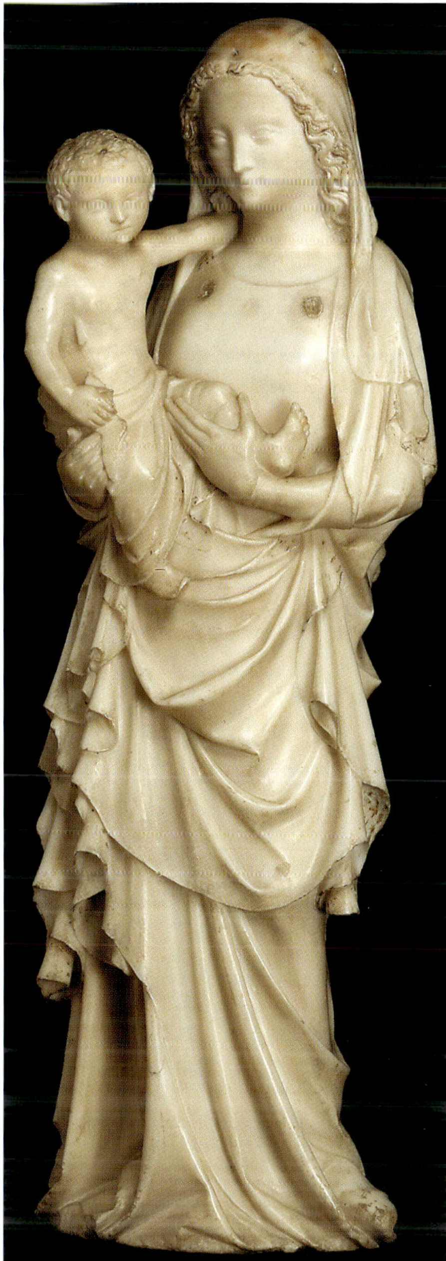

Cat VI.17
VIRGIN AND CHILD
Nino Pisano, 1360s

Cat VI.19
VIRGIN AND CHILD
Jean de Liège
(attributed), *c.* 1364

motifs. The Beautiful Madonna kept in Prague VI.9 illustrates this: if we deconstruct the statue, isolating the various motifs of the cloak, some can be compared to the prototype Beautiful Madonna of Krumlov (in Vienna), while others, such as the handling of the back, to works attributed to the the latter statue's creator, the Beautiful Madonna of Pilsen and the St Catherine of Iglau. This clearly means that the sculptor was free to combine elements derived from a relatively fixed repertoire so as to refresh the compositions. The identical observation could be made of the Lorraine Virgin VI.15, the Gosnay Virgin VI.18 and the Virgin attributed to Jean de Liège VI.19. Such observations help us clarify two aspects of medieval art: the meaning we should assign to the notion of 'artistic creation' as applied at that time and the way in which we should understand the operation of workshops.

We have selected a few objects to illustrate the courtly fashion mentioned earlier. Caskets produced for a couple VI.23,26 are part of a prosperous 14th and 15th century

< Cat VI.15
SEATED VIRGIN AND CHILD
Lorraine, first third of the 14th century

Cat VI.8
VIRGIN AND CHILD
Jean de Cambrai (?)

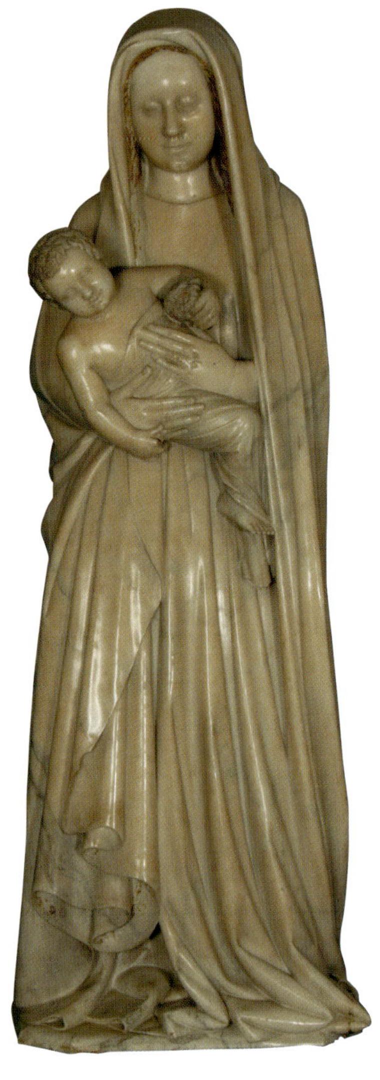

Cat VI.9
BEAUTIFUL MADONNA
Prague, after 1400

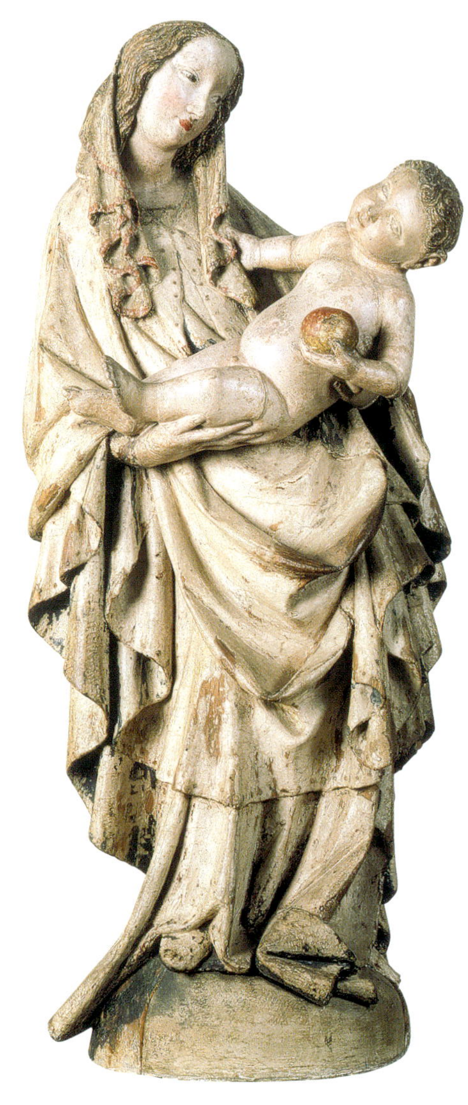

Cat VI.23
MARRIAGE CASKET
15th century

craft industry, enriched with a rarely renewed iconography also found in other media, such as tapestry, for example. We can see that these creations often combine a courtly iconography with a religious one.

The everyday objects a lady used included mirrors. Their cases were often of carved ivory **VI.24,25**. In his *Mirror of Marriage*, the medieval poet Eustache Deschamps reminds us of this:

'Comb, dressing-table to match
And mirror, to arrange one's looks,
Of ivory you must give me,
And the case must be noble, refined,
Hanging from silver chains.'

The iconography included in these mirror cases refers to scenes of chivalry or, sometimes, courtly literature. We should not always seek its origins in a specific literary episode. Above all, the people who bought

> Cat VI.27
THE REMEDY OF FORTUNE AND THE WORDS OF THE LION
Guillaume de Machaut, *c.* 1350–55

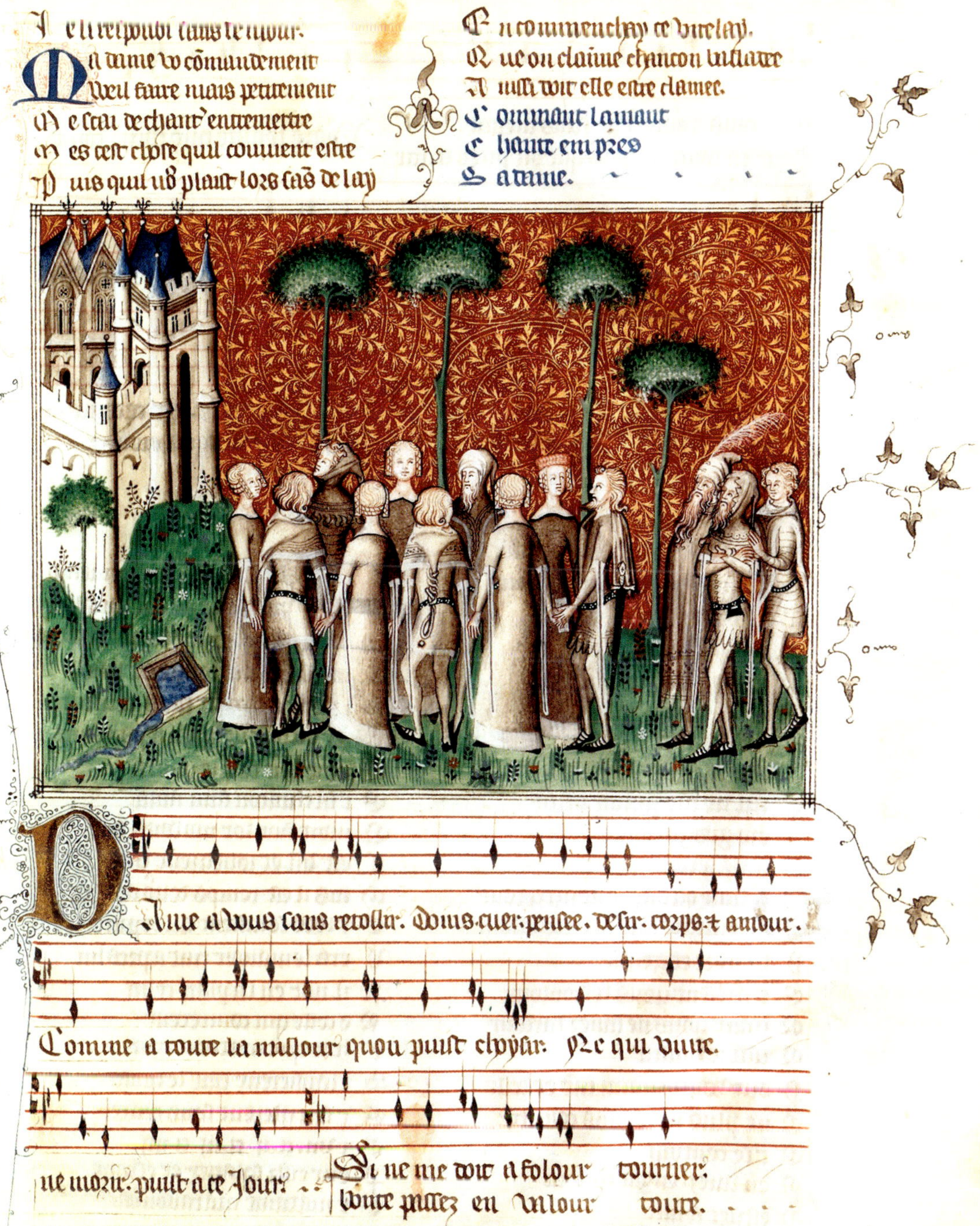
Je li respondi sans demour:
Ma dame vo commandement
Vueil faire mais petitement
Me scai de chant entremettre
Mes cest chose quil convient estre
Puis quil vous plaist. Lors sans delay
En commenchay ce virelay.
Que on claimme chancon baladee
Aussi doit elle estre clamee.
Comment lamant
Chante en pres
Sa dame.

Dame a vous sans retollir. Dong cuer. pensee. desir. corps et amour.
Comme a toute la millour quon puist choysir. Ne qui vivre
ne morir. puist a ce jour.
Si ne me doit a folour tourner.
Toute pitiez en valour toute.

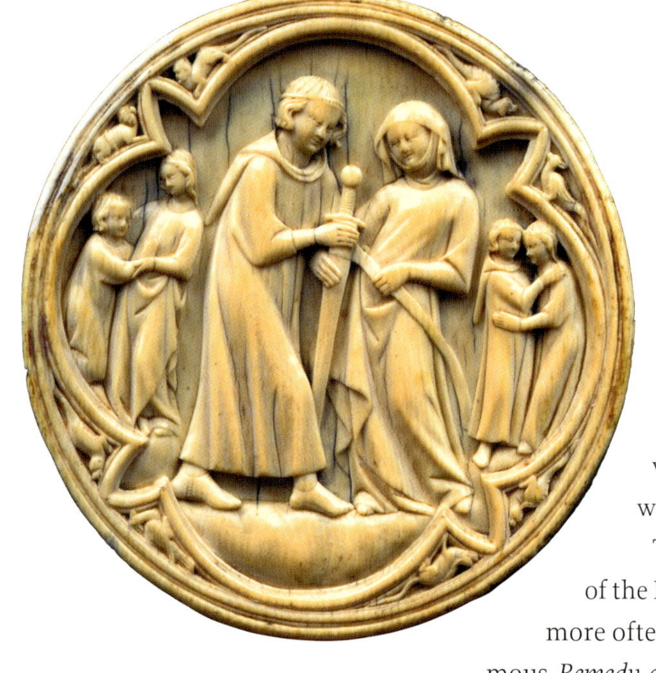

these objects wanted them to show couples in amorous conversation or 'clinging' to one another. In all the civilized courts of Europe, elegant people wanted to possess such objects (as well as combs or small writing desks), which, in the 14th and 15th centuries, were ordered from Paris where many ivory carvers were working.

Cat VI.25
MIRROR CASE
Paris, first half of the 14th century

This chivalry was no longer a reality at that late phase of the Middle Ages, but it nevertheless subsisted as an ideal or more often a form of nostalgia. In the mid-14th century, the famous *Remedy of Fortune* [VI.27], by the poet and musician Guillaume de Machaut, continued the tradition of the troubadours. His illustrations trace the life of the aristocratic, elegant and frivolous society in which the poet and the lady whose love he desires, exist. That lady is at the heart of the story. The amorous quest is not without analogy to the spiritual quest.

Cat VI.28
CHRISTINE DE PISAN, *COMPLETE WORKS*
Master of the Cité des Dames, Paris, 1410–11

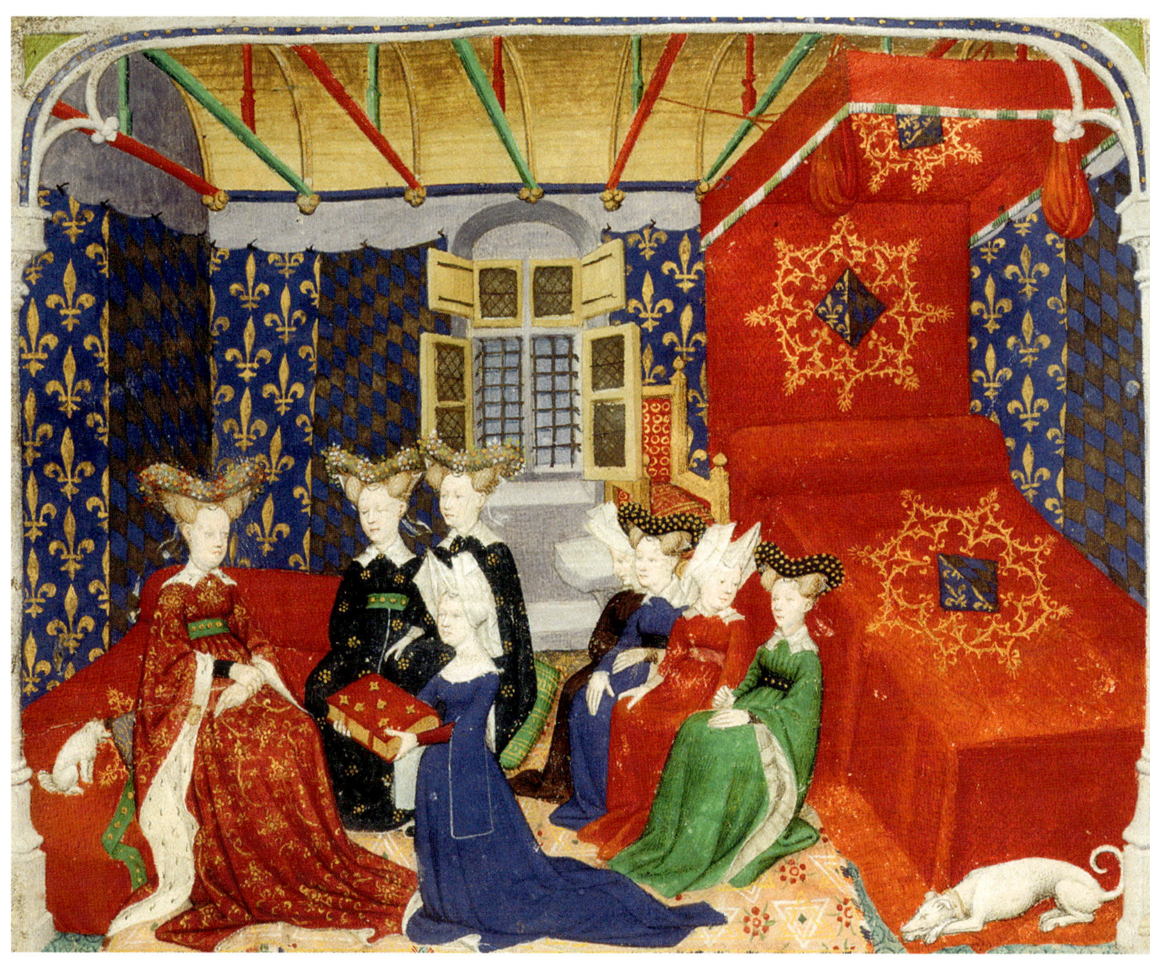

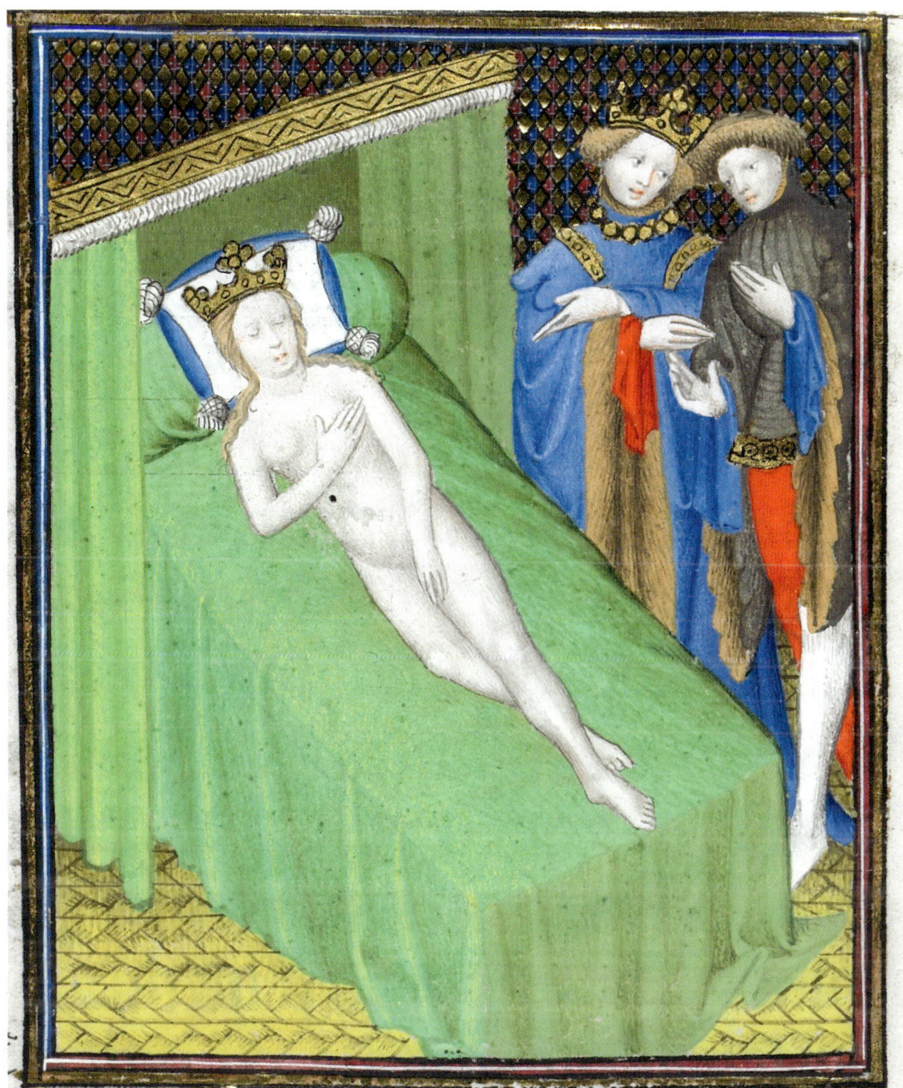

Cat VI.29
BOCCACCIO,
STORIES OF NOBLE MEN AND WOMEN
Paris, 1409–11

The existence of a feminine ideal (of which Mary incarnated the perfect image) must have had repercussions on social life. It is hard to imagine how a woman such as Christine de Pisan [VI.28] could have overcome the material difficulties that beset her and become a great and famous writer if the society of her time had denied her that possibility. Boccaccio had prepared a picture of the glories of the past, both masculine and feminine [VI.29]. In her highly original poetry on the theme of Mary, Christine de Pisan achieved a mixture of personal devotion and the courtly style. The Virgin's feminine traits were evoked to show that she represented the very image of a lady of the court and a loving mother.

The marvellous Jeanne de Toulouse [VI.30], a pure masterpiece of late 13th-century sculpture, perhaps offers, finally, the most evocative and moving illustration of the way artists sought to represent the beauty of woman in the secular world.

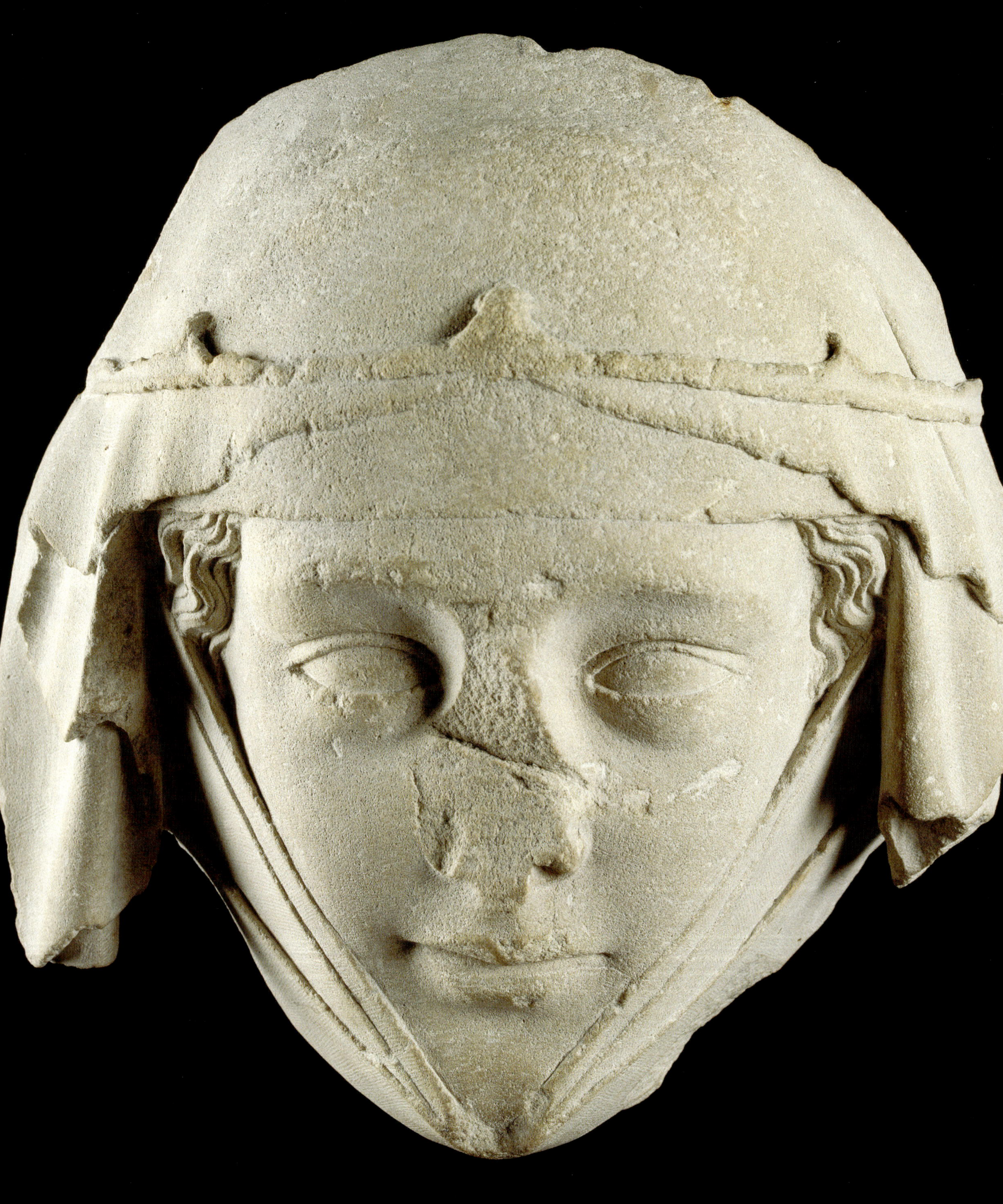

< Cat VI.30
MASK OF JEANNE DE TOULOUSE
Île-de-France, 1280s

Cat VI.31
ST AGNES
Adriaen van Wesel, *c.* 1480

BIBLIOGRAPHY: H. Belting, *Image et culte. Une histoire de l'image avant l'époque de l'art*, French trans., Paris, 1998; R. Recht, *Le croire et le voir. L'art des cathédrales (12e–15e siècle)*, Paris, 1999; N. M. Hauser, *The Standing Madonna Statue in the Île-de-France 1270–1350: Style and Iconography* (PhD. dissertation, University of Minnesota, 2003), Ann Arbor, 2005; B. Carqué, *Stil und Erinnerung. Französische Hofkunst im Jahrhundert Karls* v. *und im Zeitalter ihrer Deutung*, Göttingen, 2004; F. Lestringant, M. Zink (eds), *Histoire de la France littéraire. Volume 1: Naissances, renaissances, Moyen Âge–16e siècle*, Paris, 2006.

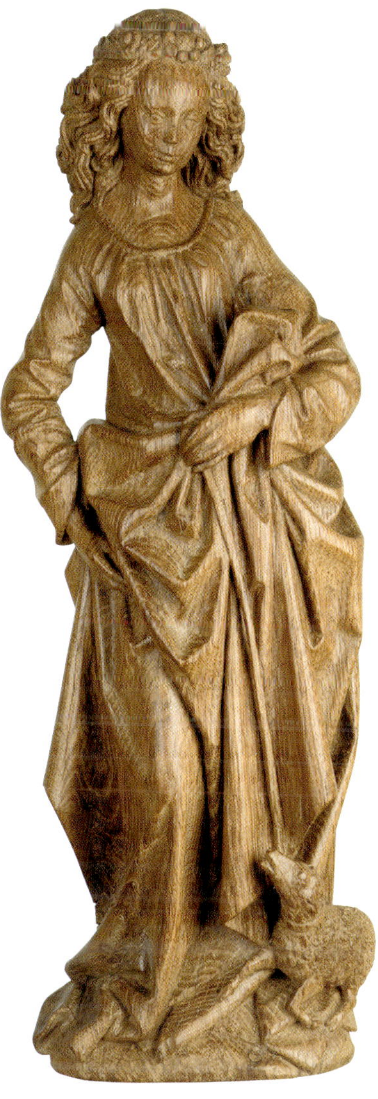

VII

The circulation of drawings in Europe

ROLAND RECHT

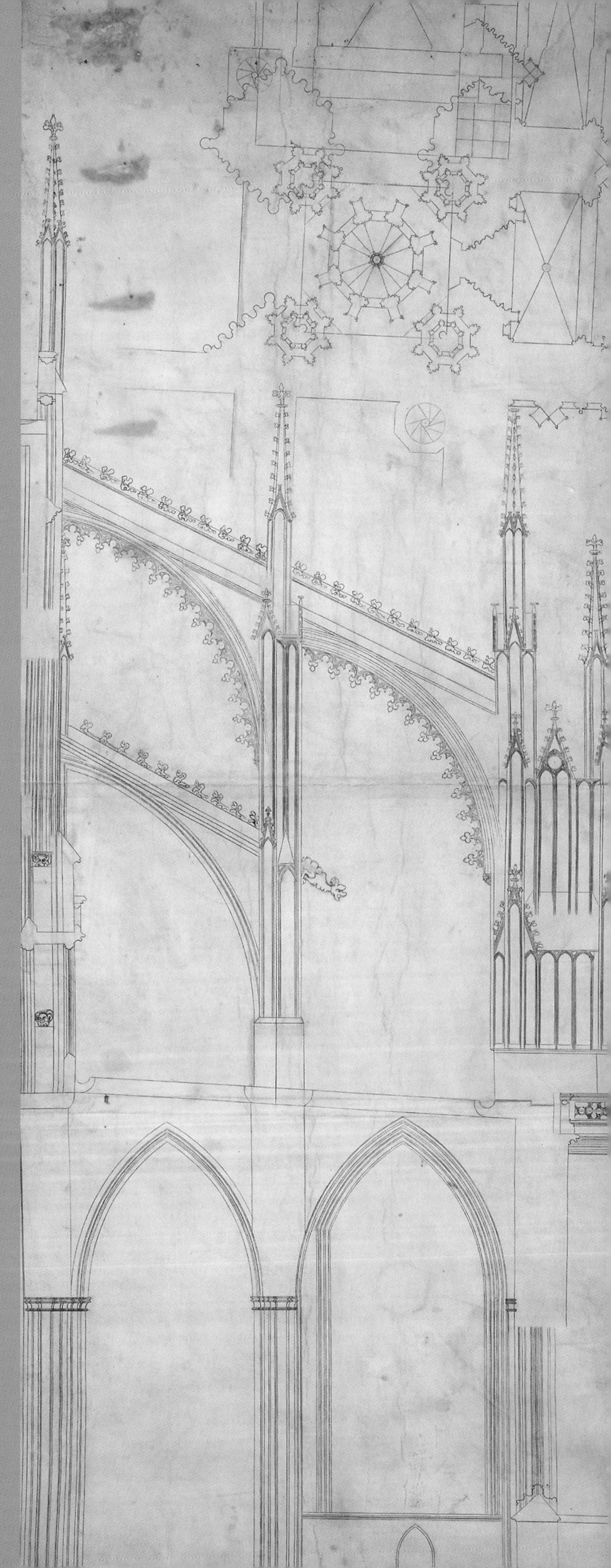

We have little knowledge of how artists in the Middle Ages copied, then imitated and often transmitted the 'models' (examples of creative work) that they encountered. What we do know about artistic practice, taking as our basis a hypothetical medieval aesthetic theory, is that the painter or sculptor took other work as his example rather than a living model or the actual scene. The creative process of a medieval artist involved a mental appropriation of what has already been seen, the 'déjà vu' of what had already appeared as 'art', and so a figurative tradition was perpetuated, feeding the visual culture of the time.

Because we have preserved certain examples of them, we assume that the main vehicle for transmitting such visual memories was parchment, then paper. But it is not impossible that the sculptors of Chartres or Rheims, Naumburg or Pisa, in addition to drawings, used earthenware or clay models, the extreme fragility of which would explain their almost total disappearance – there are some rare late examples. These *modelli* would not have survived frequent voyages and repeated handling.

On the other hand, there still reigns a certain confusion regarding the terminology used during the Middle Ages. In his celebrated album, in which he recorded all sorts of goldwork, sculpture and architecture that he saw either directly or through drawings, Villard de Honnecourt used the term *portraiture* to designate the art of the line, the drawing; the word *patron* (pattern or template), also employed, might refer to either a drawing or a model. One 14th-century painter, Jean Chatard de Lyon, called his drawings that were intended to serve as examples for paintings, *patrons*. *Exemplum* is a term widely applied in medieval times, particularly in the field of literature. It refers to an edifying short story that the writer or orator might easily recite. Nevertheless, its definition in this context is no better established than in the visual arts.

In all cases, collections of 'models' might have various functions. They might provide their user(s) with iconographical types intended to be used for any medium – frescoes, miniatures or sculpted reliefs. They could just as well serve to recall formulae, fulfilling a sort of mnemonic function. The existence of types, which is a central phenomenon in the production of devotional images (*Andachtsbilder*), obviously necessitates their memorization by the artists responsible for perpetuating them.

< Cat VII.15
CROSS-SECTION OF THE NORTH PART OF THE CHANCEL AT PRAGUE CATHEDRAL AND PLAN OF A TOWER
Last quarter of the 14th century

In all cases, although the medieval artist reused these figures or ornaments, this was nevertheless done in order to transform them. At that time, a copy was rarely servile. To copy was to interpret, as a musician interprets a work. We should also be careful not to endow the concepts of 'tradition' and 'innovation' with the sense that we give them today. There are no two identical interpretations of the same work/model. The status and function of these sheets or model books would change towards the end of the medieval period.

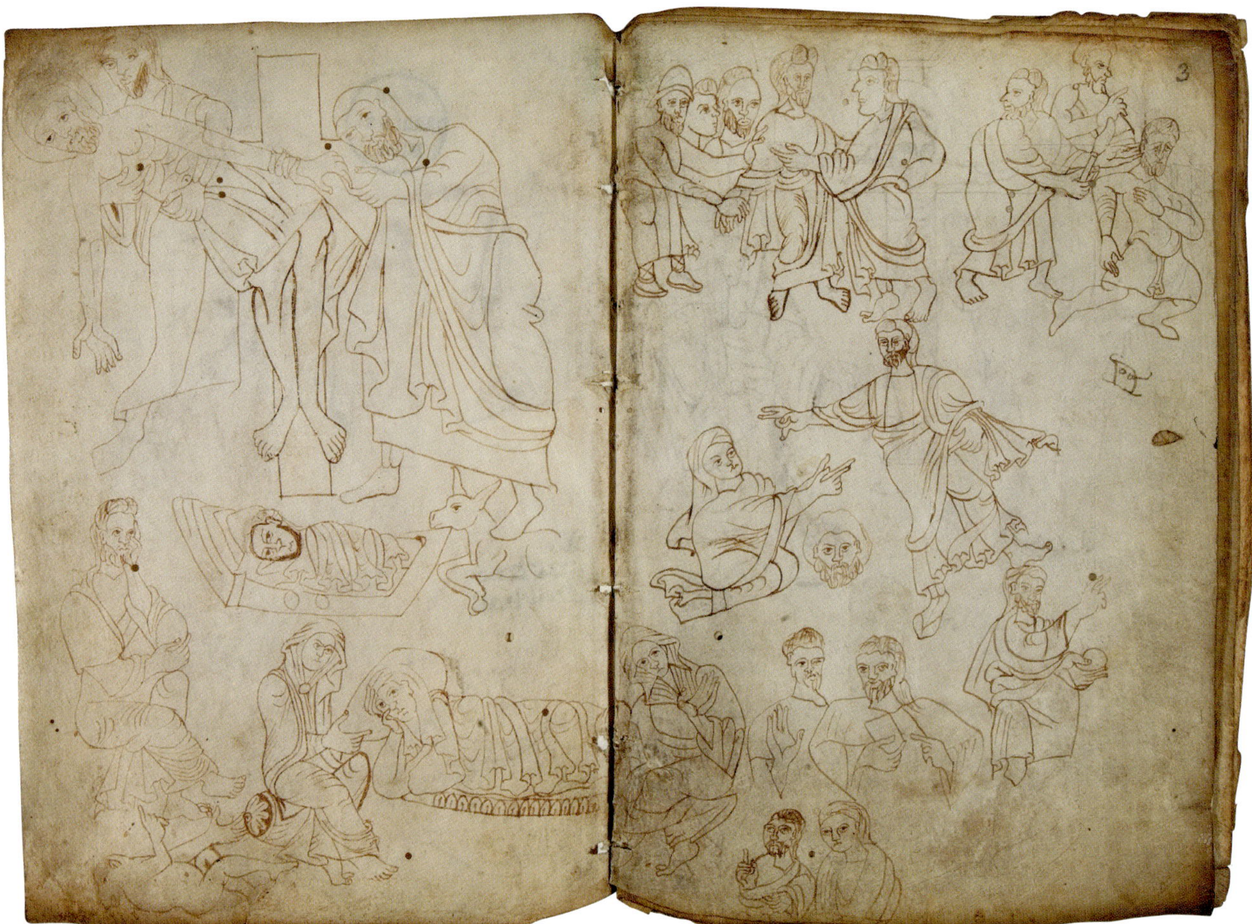

Cat VII.1
COLLECTION OF NOTES AND DRAWINGS
Adhémar de Chabannes, *c.* 1020

The collection compiled by Adhémar de Chabannes, born in 988 and a monk of Saint-Martial of Limoges, contains in particular illustrated texts. These are the *Psychomachia* of Prudence, the *Astronomicon* of Hygin and Aesop's *Fables*. It is interesting to try to find the models that the illustrator might have used for his drawings **VII.1**. They are perhaps merely second-hand heirs to a tradition of late Antiquity, especially in the narrative sense of scenes, that is, based on Carolingian objects, but they also imply knowledge of Byzantine and even Islamic models. The drawings were made first and the writing then adapted to the contours. They may date from between 1010 and 1028, at a time when Adhémar was in Saint-Cybard d'Angoulême.

The controversy even now dividing the academic world regarding sheets from the 'Musterbuch' (model book) of Wolfenbüttel **VII.2** equally takes into account the interest of the drawings, which may date to 1230-40. For some, they are a witness to the Byzantine influence on the Venetian ateliers; for others they are the work

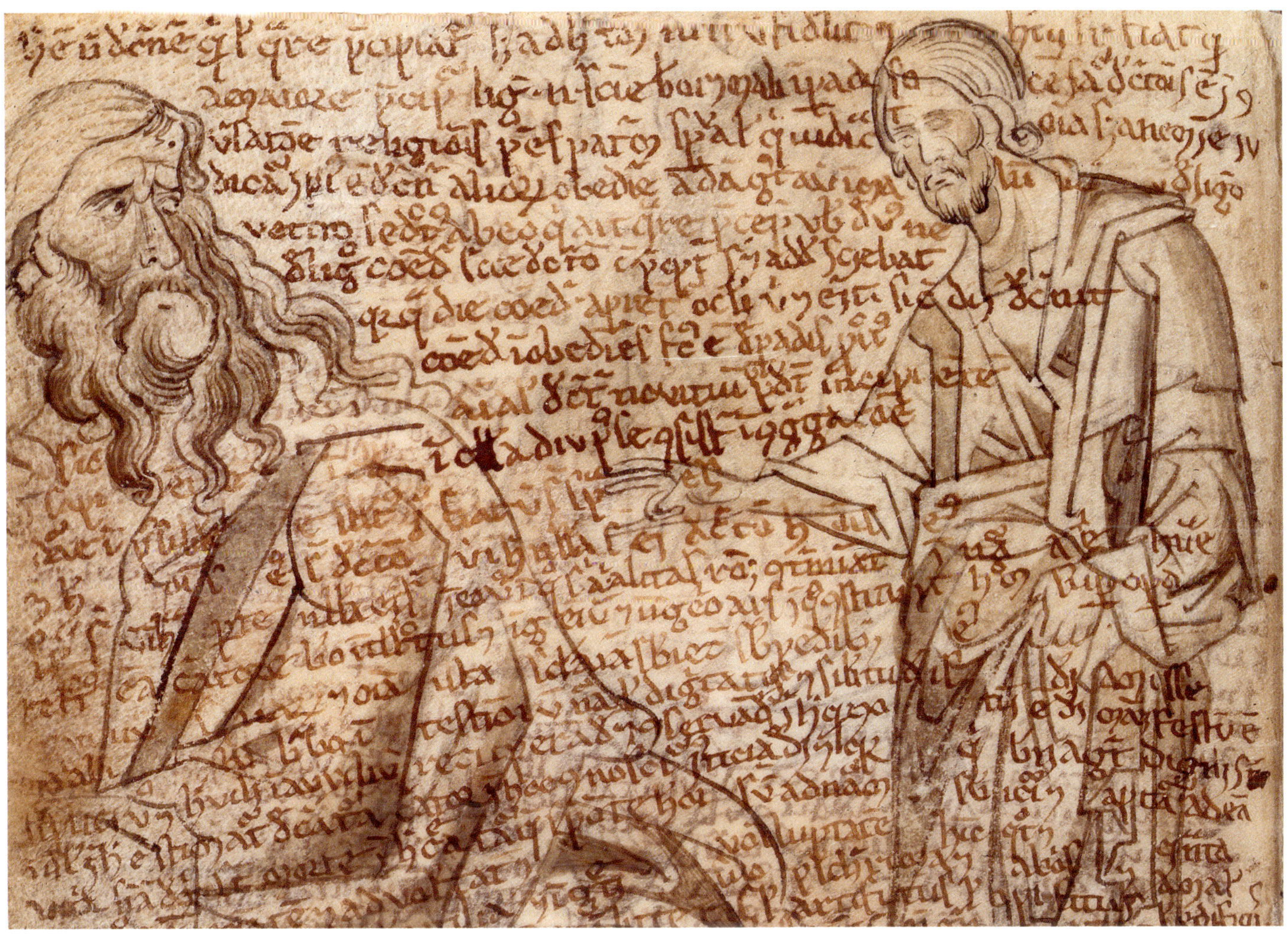

Cat VII.2
COLLECTION OF MODELS KNOWN AS THE MUSTERBUCH OF WOLFENBÜTTEL
(detail)
Venice (?), c. 1230–40

of Saxon painters, the Byzantine lineage of which is definite, however. The first hypothesis seems more probable today: the two very beautiful figures on f.93v reveal, by their difference in scale, a disparity of sources. The mosaics of San Marco in Venice would seem to contain the originals of several figures in the Wolfenbüttel collection (here, for example, that of Christ, which is almost identical to the same figure in San Marco, on the same Mount of Olives). The figure of the bearded old man with his accentuated pathos displays affinities with Byzantine works, though these do not necessarily predate the Musterbuch. This would lead us to believe that its – no doubt itinerant – author (or authors) compiled other sheets of Byzantine models that would form a common source.

The five double folios in the Staatliche Museen in Berlin [VII.3] are sometimes considered to be an incomplete and fragmentary psalter rather than a collection of models. They bear little resemblance, as a model book, to the two previous examples. A sort of harmony of iconographical schemes borrowed from

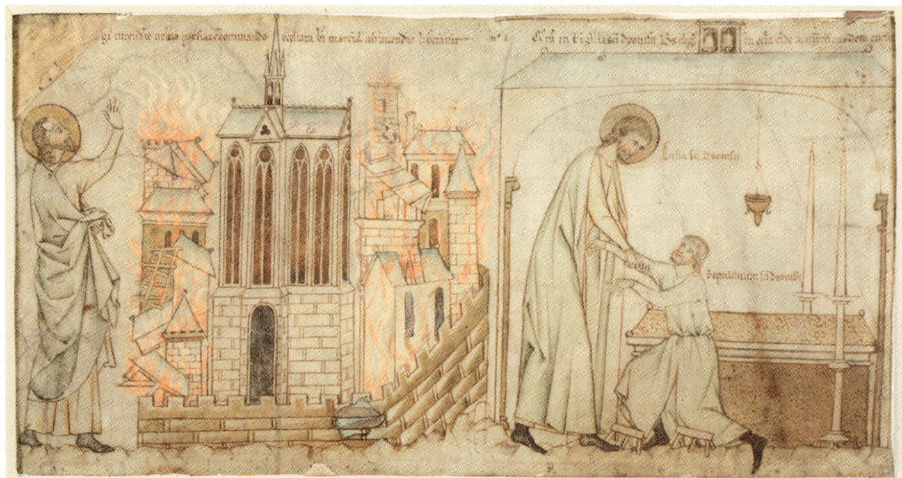

Cat VII.4
ST ELIGIUS SCROLL OF PARCHMENT (FRAGMENT)
Northern France, mid-13th century

various sources attests a concern with composition on the part of their author. The most interesting problem raised by this collection is that of its origin. Analogies with works produced in the Mosan region, e.g. the Stavelot altar [IV.3] and the baptismal font at Liège, are incontestable. But if we assume (with this author) that the attribution of the font to the goldsmith Reinier de Huy, and consequently its dating of 1118, will not stand up to close scrutiny but that it might well be a work completed in Rome during the 11th century then brought to Liège in the 12th century, some comparisons become disconcerting. The more-or-less true 'copy', by the painter of f.9v, of the Preaching of John the Baptist and the Baptism from corresponding scenes on the Liège font bears witness to the visual impact such a work was able to exert on painters in the second half of the 12th century.

St Eligius (Eloi) scroll at Noyon [VII.4] is a rarer example of a plan – here in the sense of a '*patron*' – for a monumental decoration only one fragment of which has been preserved: these drawings were certainly executed on a small scale for a wall decoration in the middle of the 13th century. The elegance of the figures is very characteristic of the Parisian style of the epoch of Louis IX, what Branner called the 'large fold style' derived from sculpture (the Sainte-Chapelle and the tympanum of the Last Judgment in Notre-Dame de Paris).

Collections of models definitely gathered on travels are rare. Ex-

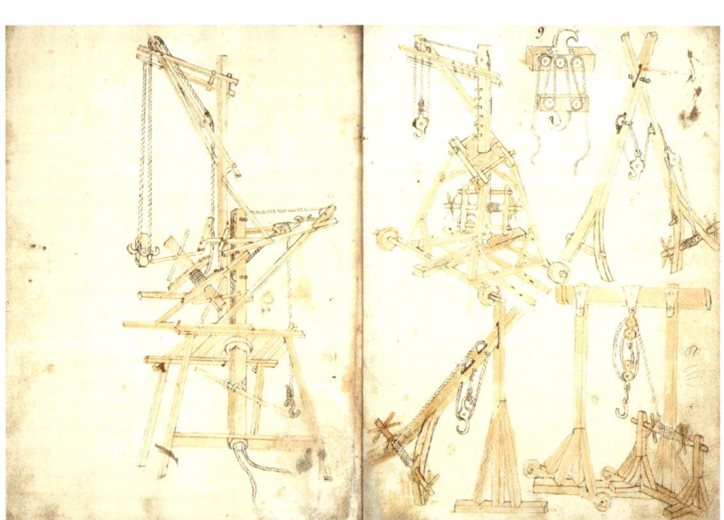

Cat VII.11
HANS HAMMER'S NOTEBOOK
c. or after 1500

> Cat VII.3
COLLECTION OF ILLUSTRATIONS FOR A PSALTER (?)
Mosan basin, mid–12th century

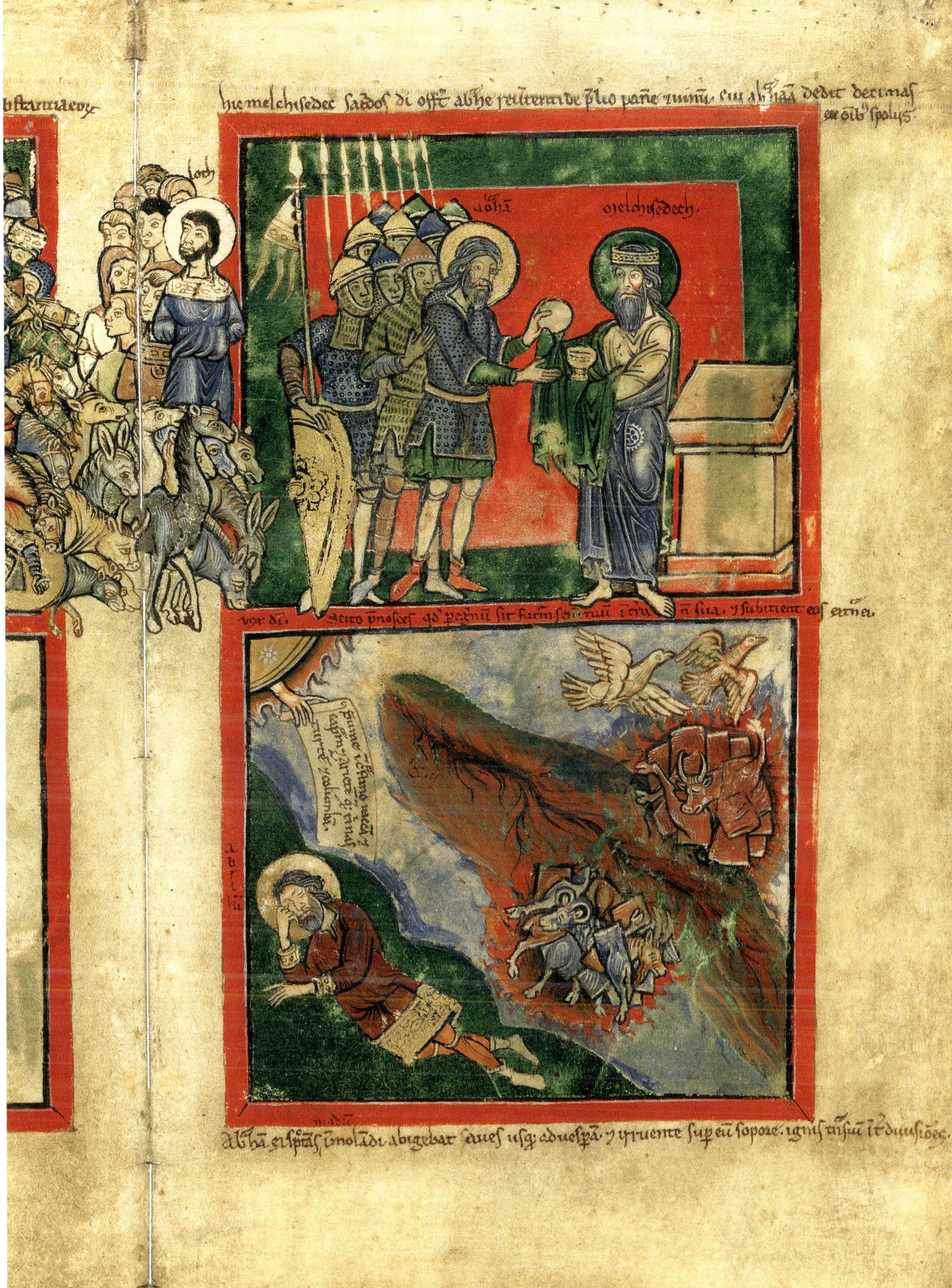
loth
melchisedech

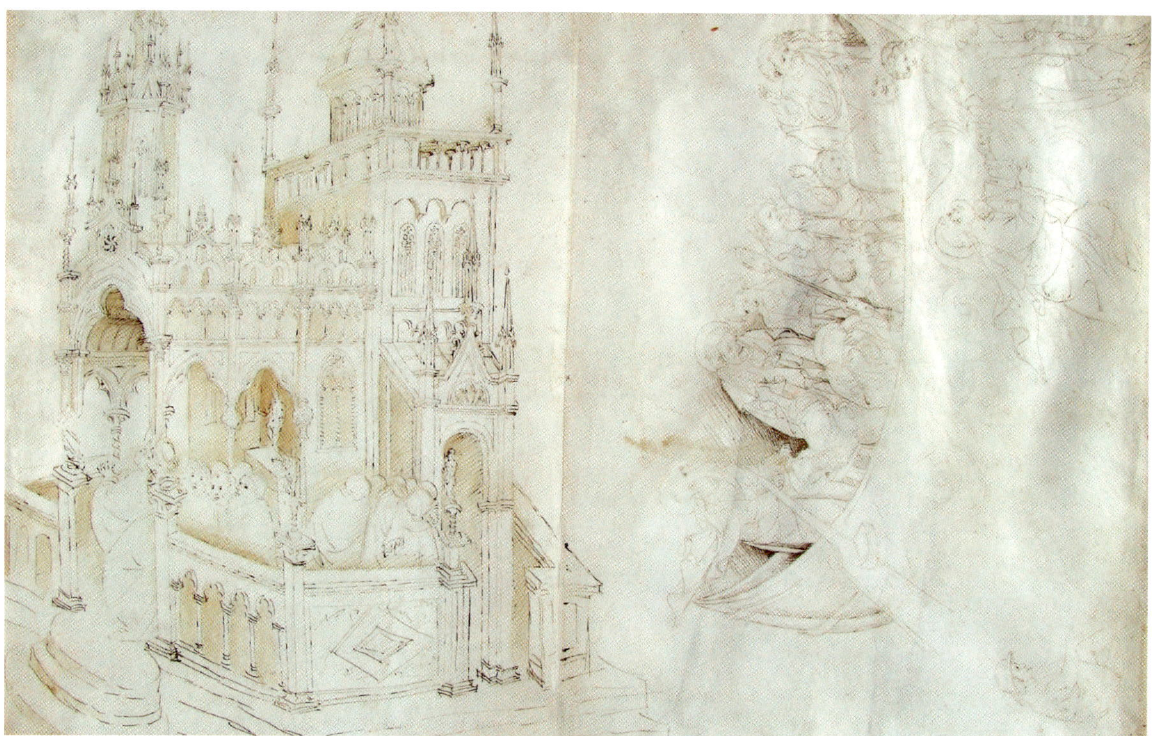

Cat VII. 5
'TACCUINO DI VIAGGI' (?)
Pisanello and atelier, Gentile da Fabriano, *c.* 1410–55

amples are the Hungarian travelogue drawn by Master Hans Hammer, architect of Strasbourg cathedral at the end of the 15th and beginning of the 16th century [VII.11]. The drawings illustrate two themes: planimetric projections of vaults and hoisting devices, representations that are especially useful for an architect. The hoisting devices provide remarkable documentation of the art of engineer/carpenters in the 15th century. Despite the poor quality of the drawings, set down in haste, it is easy to reconstruct these devices and then analyse their mechanisms.

Dated the first half of the 15th century, the 'Taccuino di Viaggi' (Travel Notebook), attributed to Gentile da Fabriano, Pisanello and his atelier [VII.5], is indeed an artificial collection of which we do not know the original function. The layout of the drawings and the disparity of sources they reproduce certainly indicate that they are medieval-type model sheets. On the bi-folio exhibited here, ornate Gothic architecture (as might be found in Venice) shelters characters next to a representation of the Miraculous Draught of Fishes.

As a result of the influence of Aristotelianism, which devoted increasing attention to direct observation, nature itself but also people in their daily activities caught the attention of artists. This change manifested itself in particular *c.* 1400. The oldest examples seem to be Italian. The sheet of paper is no longer intended just to be used to fix a memory. It permits greater creative freedom and is used for sketching forms. This function of drawing must be associated with the emergence of the modern figure of the artist demanding a certain freedom; it would not be long before these drawings began to take on a value of their own as works in their own right like paintings. The painter then began to 'invent' figures, developing studies of drapes, gestures or physiognomies. A sheet by Leonardo da Vinci [VII.8] from the Biblioteca Ambrosiana is small in size, corresponding to those books that the painter always carried round with him. Is the drawing a sketch hastily

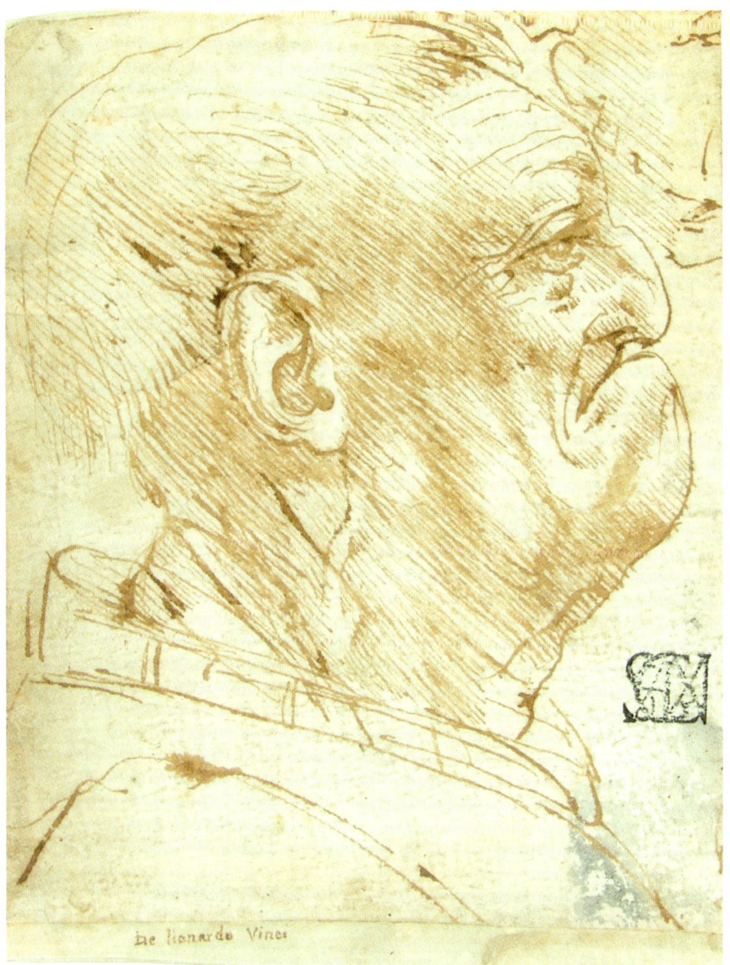

Cat VII.8
HEAD OF AN OLD MAN IN RIGHT PROFILE
Leonardo da Vinci, *c.* 1485–90

jotted down when he encountered an interesting face? Leonardo himself at one point noted down a '*viso fantasticho* noticed at the Sainte-Catherine hospital'! But such was his interest in physiognomy – he was contemplating a treatise on this subject – that it is very difficult, and even pointless in many cases, to affirm that a particular physiognomy was a caricature, a 'fantasy' or a simple portrait. Does this vagueness not touch on the central problem of artistic creativity? Another sheet bears witness to Leonardo's enormous scientific curiosity **VII.9**: his animal dissections (easier to undertake than on human bodies) were intended to deepen the knowledge of human anatomy. These two examples give us insight into another dimension of the artist's sketchbook, in which purely artistic study gives way to an encyclopaedic project. These sheets, in particular the first, which came from an easily portable sketchbook, were intended for the exclusive use of the artist.

The three crouching figures drawn by Filippino Lippi **VII.6** might almost represent the same character captured at three different moments. This is a sheet containing a masterly study that might be compared to preparatory works for the Roman frescoes (Carafa chapel), showing the ease with which the painter handles figures in space and succeeds in suggesting their psychology. Many study sheets from the Cinquecento are devoted to studies of drapes (see also Section IX). The feminine figure drawn by Fra Bartolommeo or an artist of his atelier **VII.7** on paper prepared using a technique widespread in Renaissance Italy, shows two variants in the position of the right leg: the artist is looking for the best formal solution, doubtless not using a living model but a 'manikin'. The drawing is on a grid, which means that it was intended to be scaled up.

Another type of document shows how intense was the exchange of artistic concepts and works of art in the Middle Ages. Architectural drawings were not

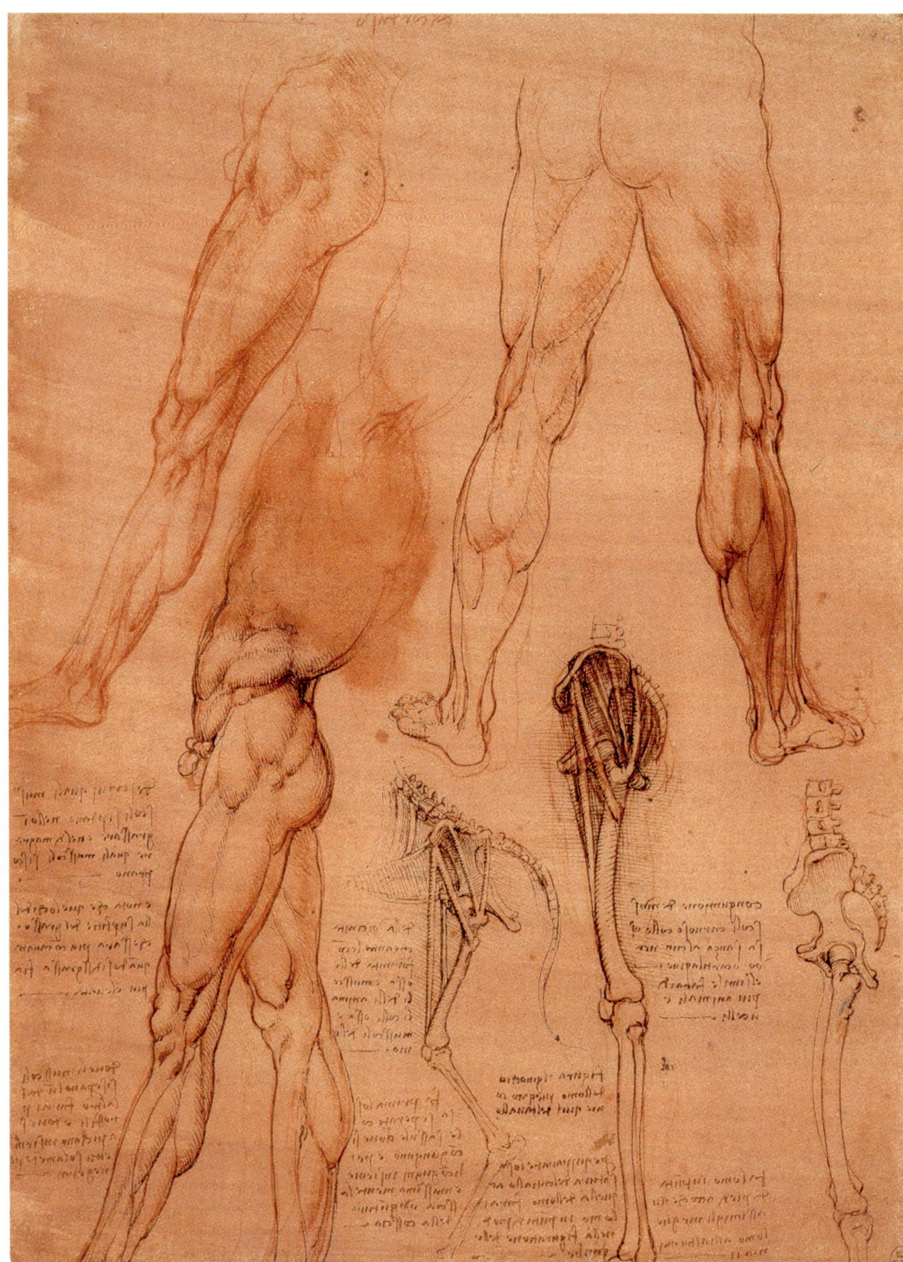

Cat VII.9
FOLIO OF COMPARATIVE STUDIES OF THE LEGS OF A MAN AND THE LEG OF A HORSE
Leonardo da Vinci, probably Milan, 1506–07

necessarily prepared prior to the opening of a building site. It is probable that before the 13th century, only ground measurements were taken, from which elevation was then easily deduced. The training of master builders, stonecutters and masons was such that such an approach to the construction process posed hardly any particular difficulty.

But when architecture became more complex, when the ground plan no longer took into account the structural complexities, and above all when the ambition of architectural projects became the subject of rivalry between bishops, increasing the status of the architect, he would devote much of his time not to surveying the site, but in drawing up designs. Often on a grand scale, these were intended to favourably impress prospective clients but also to serve as a contractual reference for the entire site. At the same time, construction drawings have also been found that seem to have circulated from site to site.

< Cat VII.16
DOUBLE-SIDED DRAWING. FRONT: ELEVATION OF THE SOUTH TOWER OF PRAGUE CATHEDRAL.
Second half of the 14th century, 15th century

Cat VII.19
ELEVATION OF THE STRASBOURG CATHEDRAL FAÇADE, NORTH PART
c. 1400

Cat VII.18
ELEVATION OF THE STRASBOURG CATHEDRAL FAÇADE (DRAWING B1)
Mid-14th century

BIBLIOGRAPHY: J. von Schlosser, 'Zur Kenntnis der künstlerischen Überlieferung im späten Mittelalter', *Jahrbuch der kunsthistorischen Sammlungen des Allerhöchsten Kaiserhauses*, XXIII (1902), pp. 279–86, 318–26; R. W. Scheller, *Exemplum. Model-Book Drawings and the Practice of Artistic Transmission in the Middle Ages (ca.900 – ca.1470)*, Amsterdam, 1995; F. Ames-Lewis, J. Wright, *Drawings in the Italian Renaissance Workshop*, London, 1983; B. Degenhart, A. Schmitt, *Corpus der italienischen Handzeichnungen 1300–1450*, 8 vols, Berlin 1968–90; A. J. Elen, *Italian Late-Medieval and Renaissance Drawing-Books from Giovanni de'Grassi to Palma Giovane*, Leyden, 1995; R. Recht (ed.), *Les bâtisseurs des cathédrales gothiques*, Strasbourg, 1989; R. Recht, *Le dessin d'architecture. Origine et fonctions*, Paris 1995; J. J. Böker, *Architektur der Gotik. Gothic Architecture. Bestandkatalog der weltgrössten Sammlung an gotischen Baurissen der Akademie der bildenden Künste*, Vienna-Salzburg-Munich, 2005.

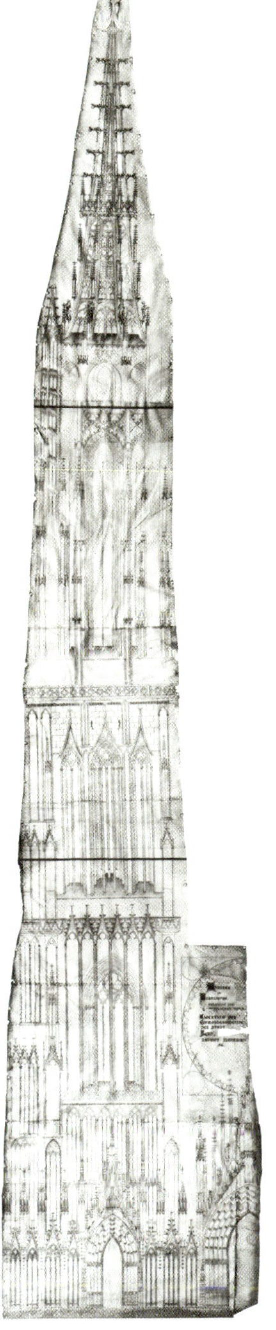

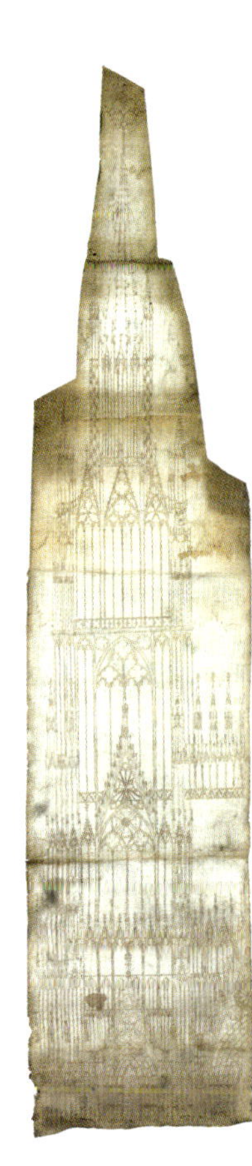

VIII

The European careers of sculptors at the end of the Middle Ages

ROLAND RECHT

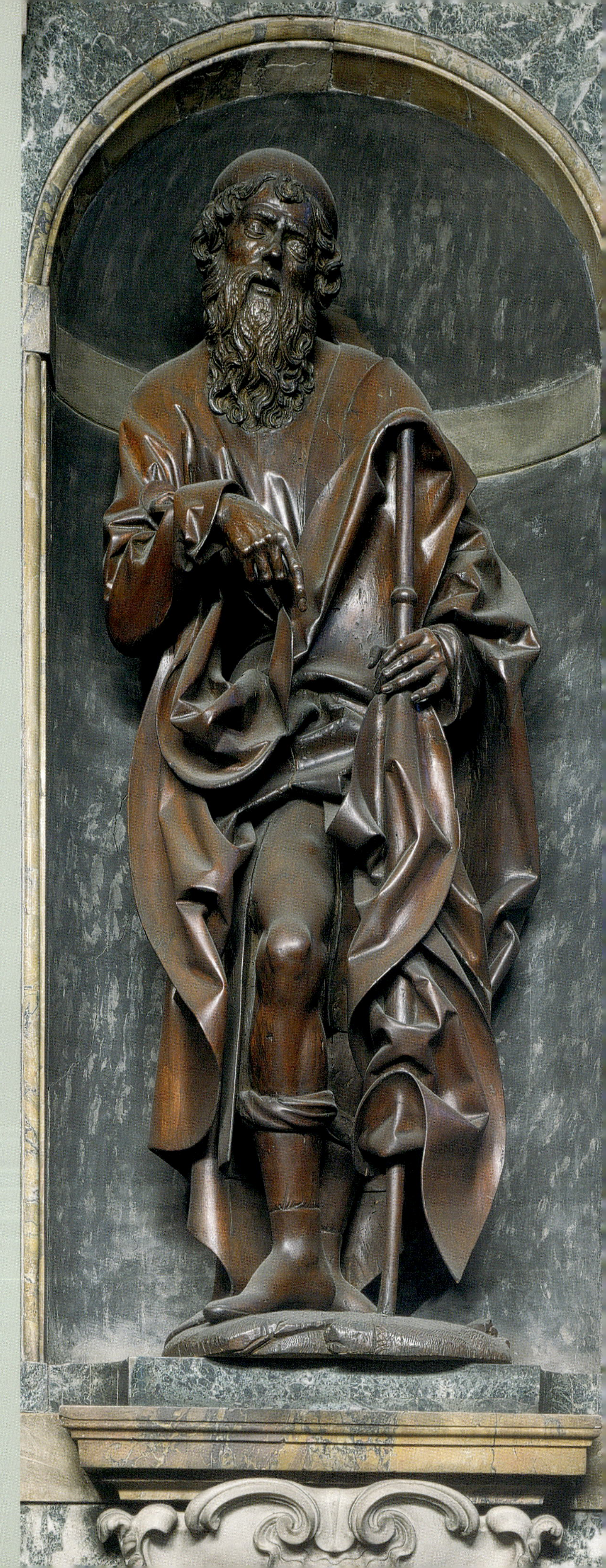

Towards the end of the 14th century, great royal or princely commissions from King Charles of France or his brothers Jean de Berry, Louis d'Orléans or Philip the Bold (duke of Burgundy), raised monumental sculpture into a position of special importance. Charles v had the perpetuity of the Valois dynasty portrayed in tombs for the abbey of Saint-Denis. He also commissioned major sculpture projects in Paris for the celebrated Vis (the monumental stairway) of the Louvre palace, for the Bastille, and for the church of the Celestins.

His brother Jean de Berry was represented in the immense mantelpiece of the château at Poitiers beside his wife, Charles vi and Queen Isabella; also in Poitiers, on the Maubergeon tower, there are statues of his counsellors; he himself kneels in the Holy Chapel of Bourges. Louis d'Orléans commissioned a magnificent tympanum for the doorway of the château of La Ferté-Milon; he also ordered the Nine Worthy Men at Pierrefonds and the Nine Worthy Women at La Ferté. The King's other brother, Philip the Bold, commissioned Jean de Marville then Claus Sluter to erect the portal and the Calvary group for the Carthusian monastery of Champmol, near Dijon. He had his tomb surrounded by a sculpted retinue of 'Pleurants' – mourners each expressing a form of grief (Section ix).

Apart from Sluter, about whom we are in possession of a few certainties, we are not really able to assemble satisfactory facts about the major sculptors – such as André Beauneveu, Jean de Liège and Jean de Cambrai. The first and last worked for the Duc de Berry (Section vi). However, the absence of information on the internal organization of workshops, the distribution of tasks and the degree of specialization practised renders the task of the sculpture historian particularly arduous. What does appear certain is that the royal commissions in Paris and the Holy Chapel of Vincennes set the tone, so to speak. The art of Jean de Marville, if he did indeed have a role in the design of the Champmol portal before Sluter, seems to draw its inspiration from the Parisian art of the last third of the 14th century. But royal example was not the only stimulus. On the orders of Philip the Bold, his painter Jean de Beaumetz and his sculptor Claus Sluter were sent to work on the building site of the château de Mehun-sur-Yèvre, designed for Jean de Berry, to take note of what was being done there.

Such exchanges were not restricted to the French princes. We know of the interest of Emperor Charles iv – father of Sigismund – in Parisian art, in the court of Avignon and in many other artistic centres. And the plan that he assigned to sculptors, both in Prague cathedral (busts in the triforium, the Premyslids' tomb) and in public buildings, show the lesson that he was able to draw from his visits to France: placing art in the service of dynastic continuity and representation of sovereignty. At St Stephen's cathedral in Vienna, Rudolph iv of Habsburg had the ducal family depicted in front of the portal.

Cat VIII.15
ST ROCH
Veit Stoss, 1515–20

The high level of refinement achieved by the creators of the celebrated 'Beautiful Madonnas', so widespread in central Europe *c.* 1400 (Section VI), demonstrates how much sculpture was, at that time, and throughout Europe, an art prized by both church and aristocracy. But this degree of sophistication encountered all over western Europe, in the context of courtly art, affirming art both as innovation and as model, had at the same time to introduce a sort of dichotomy between content (the pious image or the princely effigy) and form. The celebration of the work of art as such, the emphasis on the quality of its material – marble and polychromy with ample use of gold – the elegance of forms and poses, is one of the great novelties manifested first in France then in the rest of Europe in the final quarter of the 14th century. It was at this time that an aesthetic concept of art developed, a taste for precious objects and the accumulation of treasures quite apart from the value of their devotional use. All this eloquently demonstrates that the sovereign was able to evoke an entire mythical dimension, as well as dynastic continuity, exalting courtly life and the chivalric tradition in the form adopted by the great sculptures associated with the architecture of power.

The sculptural project – projects? – that Sigismund's ambition was to install in his castle at Buda, must be placed in this context. Sigismund (king of Hungary in 1387 and emperor in 1411) had contacts with the Berry court and that of Charles V. In Pisa's Duomo, the sarcophagus of Henry VII of Luxembourg, great-grandfather of Sigismund, is decorated with people close to the deceased. Here, the community of Pisa that financed the monument doubtlessly wanted to affirm that Henry VII owed his power to Pisan families and guilds. This idea must also have struck a note with Sigismund, whose monarchy was desirous of such support. It should be borne in mind that in Paris the great hall of the Palais de la Cité accommodated the succession of kings of France: such a model, dating back to *c.* 1300, might have played a part in Sigismund's ideas. The great hall of his palace was 70 metres long and 25 metres wide, and divided into two storeys, which gave plenty of space for such a project. Opposite the palace was the church of Our Lady, which Sigismund thought of as a royal chapel, the model for which can be seen in Notre-Dame, Paris. An envoy from Burgundy, Bertrandon de la Brocquière, who was staying at Buda in 1432, met out-of-work French stonecutters as well as a master loom setter from Arras in the service of Sigismund. The extension of the old royal palace of the Anjous by this sovereign transformed Buda into one of the most imposing strongholds in medieval Europe. But the work was interrupted as Sigismund transferred his imperial residence to Pressburg (now Bratislava).

The sculptures revealed by the excavations at the castle of Buda in 1974 are all thought to date from 1400–25. Sigismund combined a workshop employing sculptors from various European countries but this workshop was in operation only for a short time. The sculptures were certainly never installed and many of them remained unfinished. But, if we want to pinpoint the places of origin of the various sculptors who might have worked at Buda, our only recourse is stylistic analysis. The two groups into which these discoveries divide are the figures of Prophets and Apostles on the one hand and secular sculptures on the other. The first group [VIII.3] shows some affinity with western Europe – for example the Apostles of Bernay or the art at the court of Berry – but do not show great originality, despite their quality. The Brabant milieu – the Hakendover altarpiece, sculptures from Halle – as well as the Rhenish environment – the Saarwerden tomb in Cologne cathedral, the Apostles in the chancel at Aachen – might have served as a link with the work of artists such as André Beauneveu or Jean de Cambrai. The Master of Grosslobming (in Styria) may have trained sculptors who were sent to Buda. The second group displays a sense of form much more sophisticated, where the circle of Hans Multscher at Ulm might have played a part, but hardly a decisive one. Some examples from this group of works, however, have no equivalent.

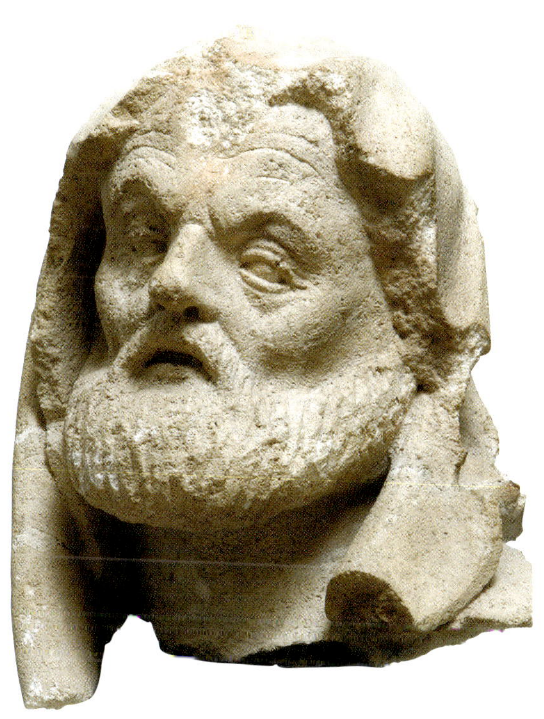

Cat VIII.3
HEAD OF A PROPHET
Buda, c. 1400–20

Sigismund's visit, during a long journey across western Europe, to the Council of Constance in 1417, might have facilitated the recruitment of artists and painters, goldsmiths and sculptors. We know that this Council, so important in the life of the church, and which attracted thousands of prelates from all over Europe, also provided artists with an opportunity to forge contacts and sign contracts. On the return journey, it is not impossible that Sigismund had the opportunity to take back with him artists from Stuttgart and Ulm [VIII.1,4].

The second topic to be discussed here is that of a well-identified sculptor, documented by archives. His oeuvre, though small, is of exceptional quality and shows his influence to be European in the truest sense. This is Nikolaus Gerhaert van Leyden, otherwise known as Nikolaus, son of Gerhaert of Leyden, a town where he may not have been born, but which was his last place of residence when the Strasbourg archives mention him for the first time. It seems that he may have been trained in Utrecht. As we travel up the Rhine, we encounter, at Trier, the tomb of Bishop Jakob von Sierck, which Nikolaus may have created since Strasbourg

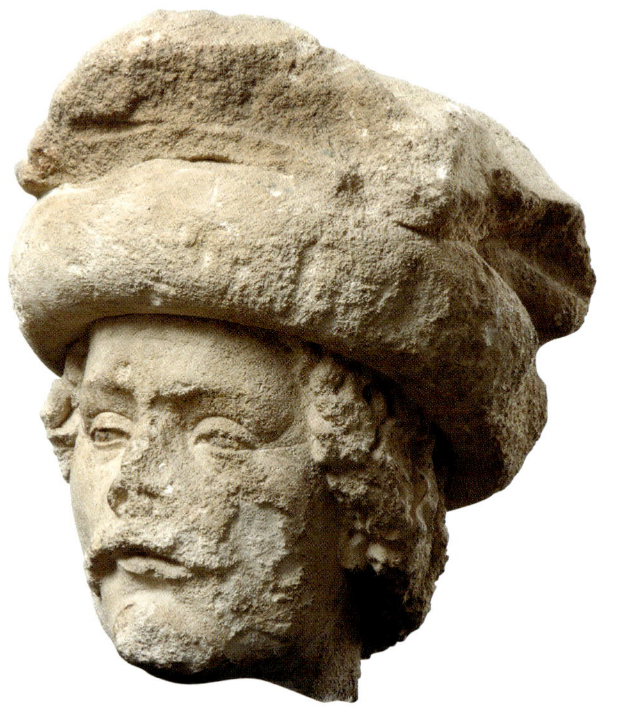

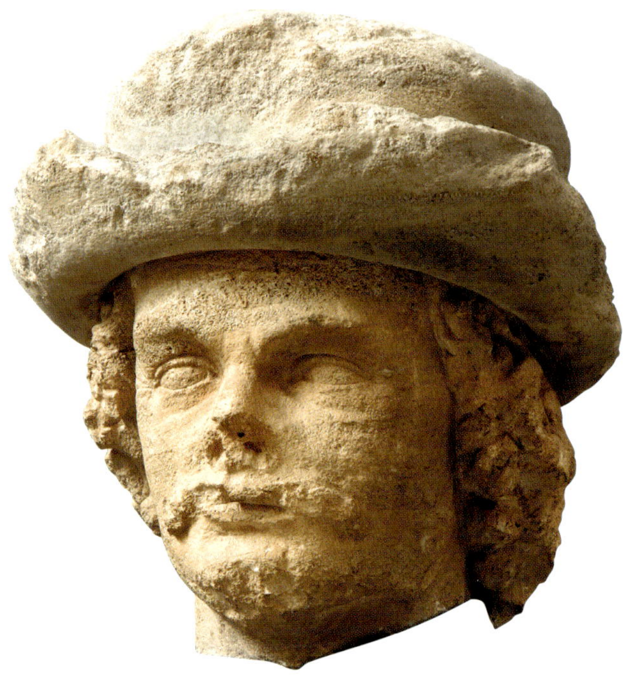

Cat VIII.1
HOODED MALE HEAD
Buda, *c.* 1400–20

Cat VIII.4
HOODED MALE HEAD
Buda, *c.* 1400–20

(dated by its inscription of 1462), then the imposing doorway of the Strasbourg Chancellery (1464), the memorial of a canon in the St John the Evangelist chapel of the cathedral (which translates into stone a composition similar to that of the Canon Van der Paele painting by Van Eyck), dated 1464; in 1466 he completed the altarpiece for the high altar in Constance cathedral and in 1467, the great stone crucifix for a surgeon to the margrave of Baden, for the cemetery of Baden-Baden. In the second half of the same year, he seems to have finally responded to the (second) request from Emperor Frederick III [VIII.12], who had commissioned him to create his tomb at Wiener-Neustadt. But then his trail goes cold: as the tomb seems to have been more a workshop project.

Each of Nikolaus' works is an iconographic innovation: the Constance altarpiece (now lost) seems to have introduced in particular the idea of busts, and the Baden-Baden crucifix develops with remarkable mastery a Christ with a serene countenance and stretched out limbs, which give an expressive poignancy to the Crown of Thorns and the perizonium.

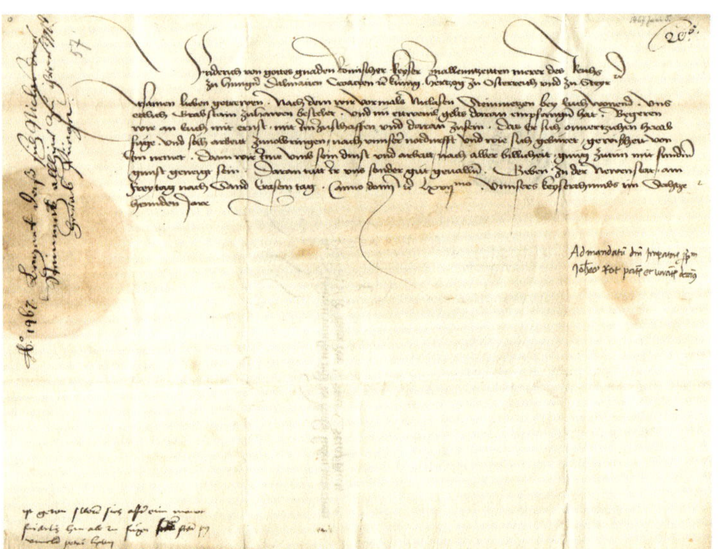

Cat VIII.12
LETTER FROM EMPEROR FREDERICK III
Strasbourg, 5 June 1467

With the busts of the leaning man [VIII.9] and of the turban-wearing man [VIII.10] Nikolaus van Leyden was not only innovative, but he introduced a psychological dimension never attained by his numerous

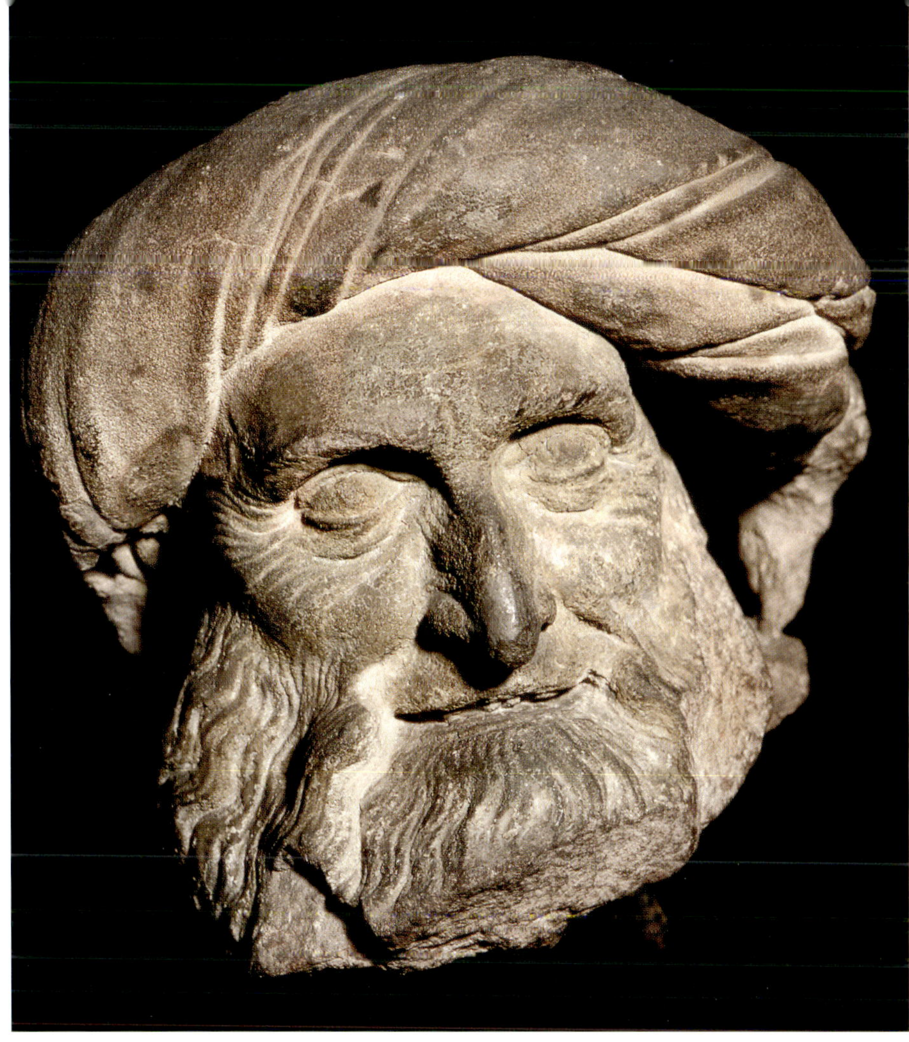

Cat VIII.10
MAN WEARING A TURBAN (EMPEROR AUGUSTUS ?)
Nikolaus van Leyden, 1464

imitators in southern Germany and central Europe. The monumental decor of the Strasbourg Chancellery, of which no more than two pieces have been preserved (one in VIII.10) but of which we do have a detailed description, was based on an iconographical plan that superimposed the three powers: municipal authority, imperial power and divine power. Above the entrance, the coat of arms of the city were surmounted by two busts representing Emperor Augustus and the Tiburtine Sibyl, pointing out to him the Virgin and Child in a glory of angels (scene of the Aracoeli), depicted on the third level. Such a project seems perfectly consistent with a building like the Chancellery.

But study of the sculptures of Nikolaus van Leyden is rendered problematic by the existence of two works that seem to have been created in Strasbourg during his stay there: these are the Nördlingen altarpiece, dated by its inscription of 1462, and the Dangolsheim Madonna, a surprising masterpiece that introduced a new type of 'Beautiful Madonna'. There are two opposing schools of thought: one attributing all these works to a single artist – Nikolaus van Leyden – and the others making the distinction. We think that Nikolaus van Leyden created the crucifix of the Nördlingen altarpiece at a time when, not yet having the right of citizenship, he had to work with an established master, whom we will call, for the sake of convenience, the Master of the Dangolsheim Madonna. This master, according to documentary sources, might well have been Hans Jouch, who is

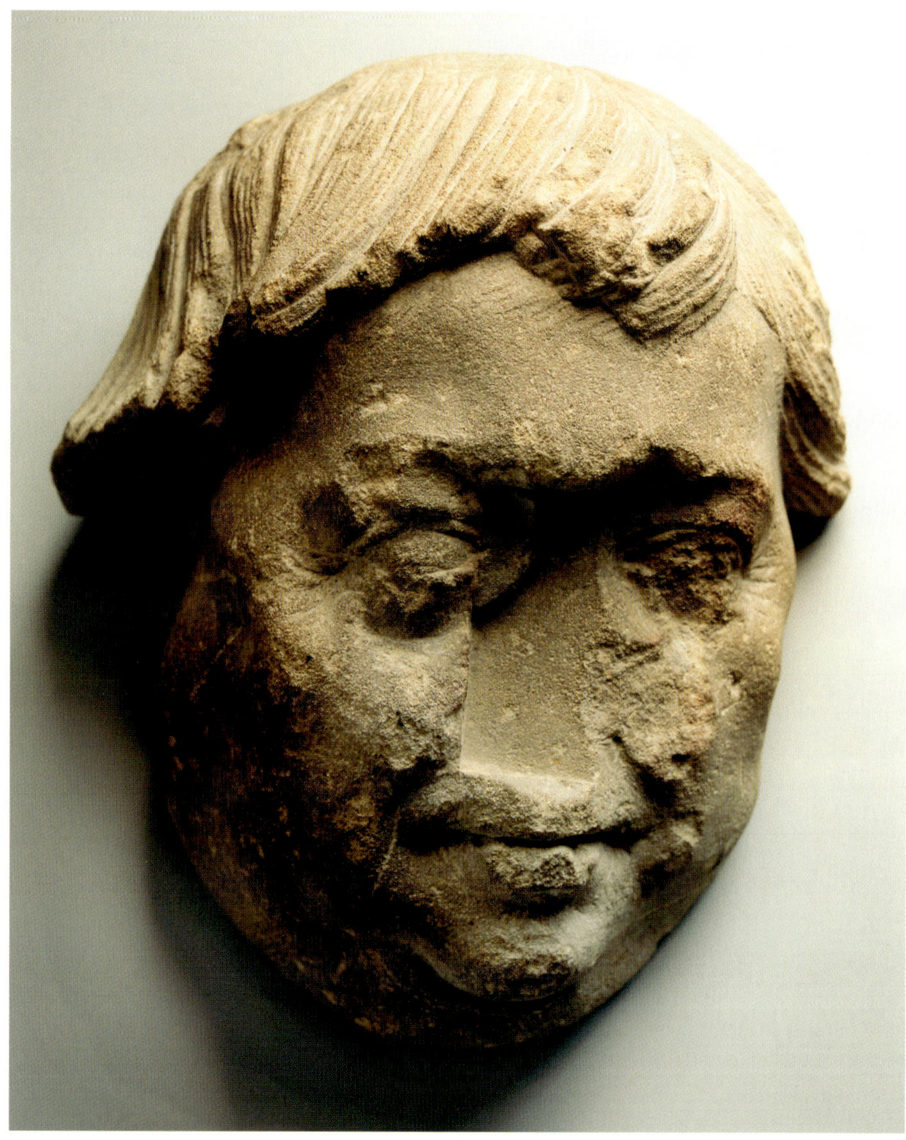

Cat VIII.11
HEAD OF A CANON (?)
Nikolaus van Leyden (atelier), before 1467

thought to have created, with his workshop, the other Nördlingen sculptures, of which the Dangolsheim Madonna and Child (no doubt originating in Strasbourg, either from the Carthusian monastery, or from the cathedral) is the masterpiece.

Nikolaus van Leyden not only introduced new iconographical concepts, which could only have been done with the agreement of theologians, but on each occasion had the ability to invent the appropriate expressive form, which he raised to an absolute degree of perfection. But what his profound originality and his inimitable grandeur do, is create an ability to suggest the life of the psyche [VIII.9,10,11]. He is, in one way, the first artist to anticipate humanism.

> Cat VIII.9
BUST OF MAN LEANING ON ELBOW
Nikolaus van Leyden, Strasbourg, 1465–67

Veit Stoss is a totally different personality. We know him as a sculptor, as a painter (even as a polychromist of the sculptures of other masters, like those of

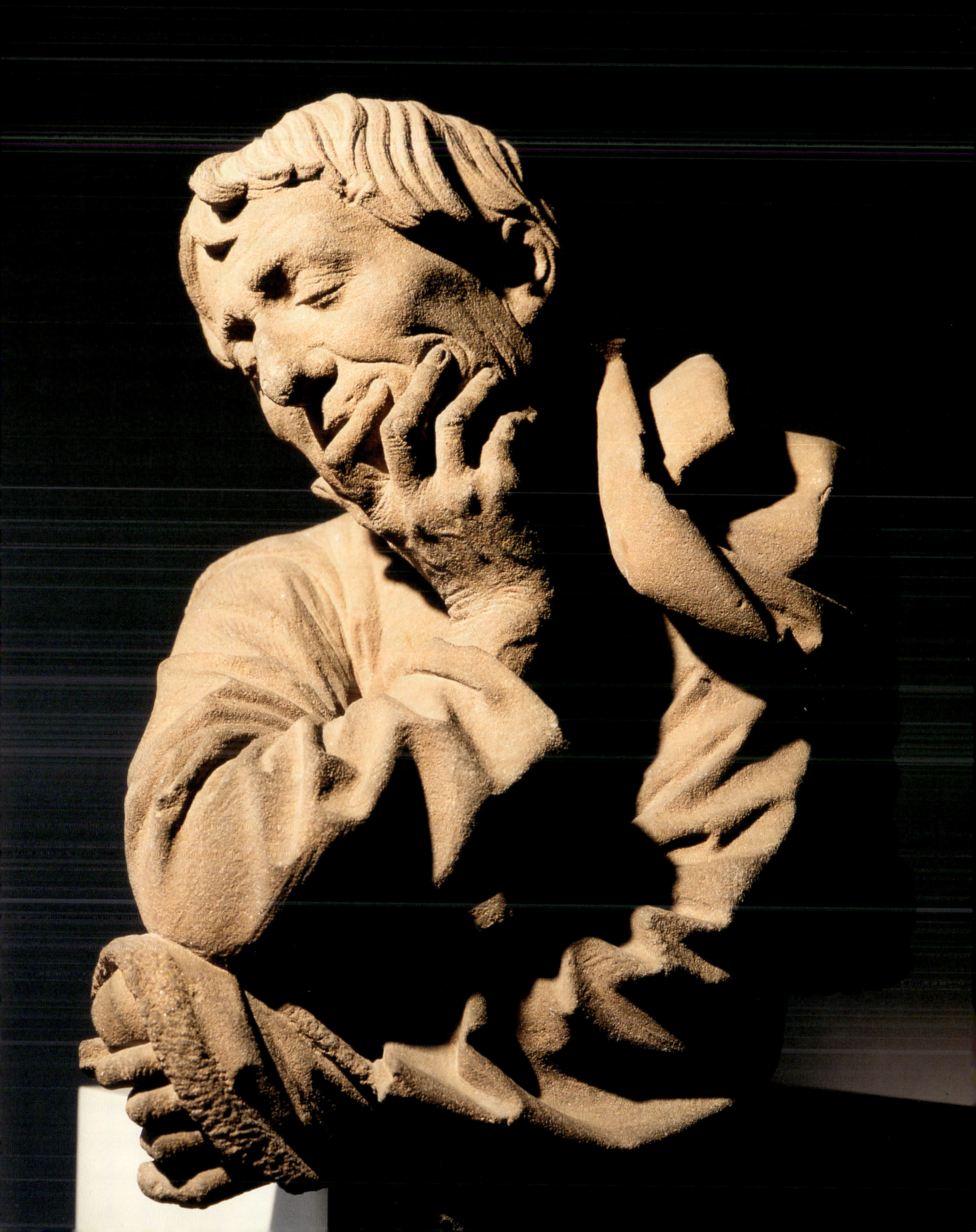

Riemenschneider at Münnerstadt) and as an engraver. His artistic temperament seems to have been much more impulsive than that of Nikolaus van Leyden. His art is dominated by a type of dramatic tension, giving his characters expressiveness and inimitable sculptural presence. After an educational journey along the Upper Rhine, where he became familiar with the works of Nikolaus van Leyden, he lived for a while in Nuremberg but renounced his right of citizenship in 1477 to go to Kraków. There he created the immense altarpiece devoted to the Assumption of the Virgin as well as the tomb of Casimir Jagellon (1492). Returning to Nuremberg in 1496, he completed many commissions including the Salutation of the Angel (1517–18) for the church of St Lawrence and the altarpiece for the church of the Carmelites (1520–23). The Florentine merchant Raphael Torregiani commissioned him to create a group representing Toby and the Angel for the church of the Dominicans in Nuremberg (1516), in which the sculptor seems to be seeking to translate this typically Italian iconographical theme into a type of choreography not to be found in his earlier work. It is without doubt again due to the initiative of Torregiani that we owe the completion of the St Roch preserved today in the Guadagni chapel of Santissima Annunziata in Florence [VIII.15]. This work very quickly acquired success in this city, which was recorded for us by the famous biographer Giorgio Vasari.

Cat VIII.14
ST JOHN THE BAPTIST
Veit Stoss (?), *c.* 1470

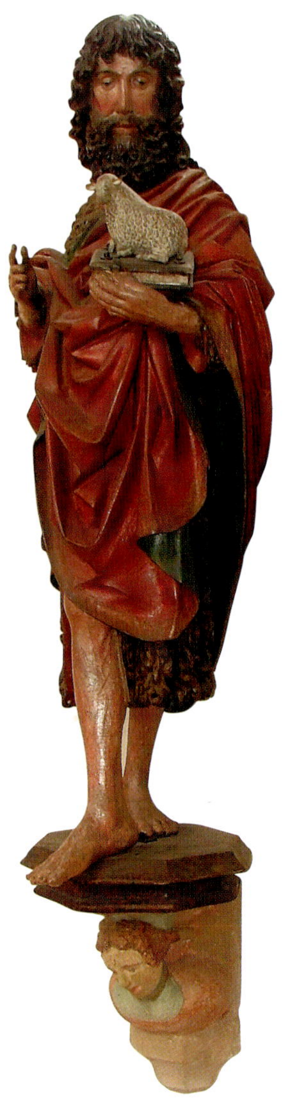

Taking some liberties with the historical facts, as was his wont, Vasari takes the creator of this sculpture to be one Maître Jean, of French origin, and states that he stayed for a long time in Florence, which does not seem to have been the case with Veit Stoss. Moreover, he credits the sculptor with having been able to adapt himself 'to the Italian style', which is evidently an aberration. But the passage in Vasari's *Vite* of 1550 (see Section x), deserves to be quoted:

'Even if strangers do not have such a developed sense of design as the Italians, they have been able to and can still create works of an astonishing finesse. One example of this can be seen in a work or rather a marvel in wood, by the hand of a Frenchman, Maître Jean. He established himself in Florence and made it his home; with his love of the plastic arts, he adapted himself perfectly to the Italian style. With much experience in wood, he carved a life-size statue of St Roch in lime, putting such delicacy into the execution of the drapes and giving them such suppleness and so much openwork with such a light appearance and such elegant folds that it

> Cat VIII.16
CHRIST ON THE CROSS WITH MARY AND JOHN
Master Paul de Levoča, 1520–30

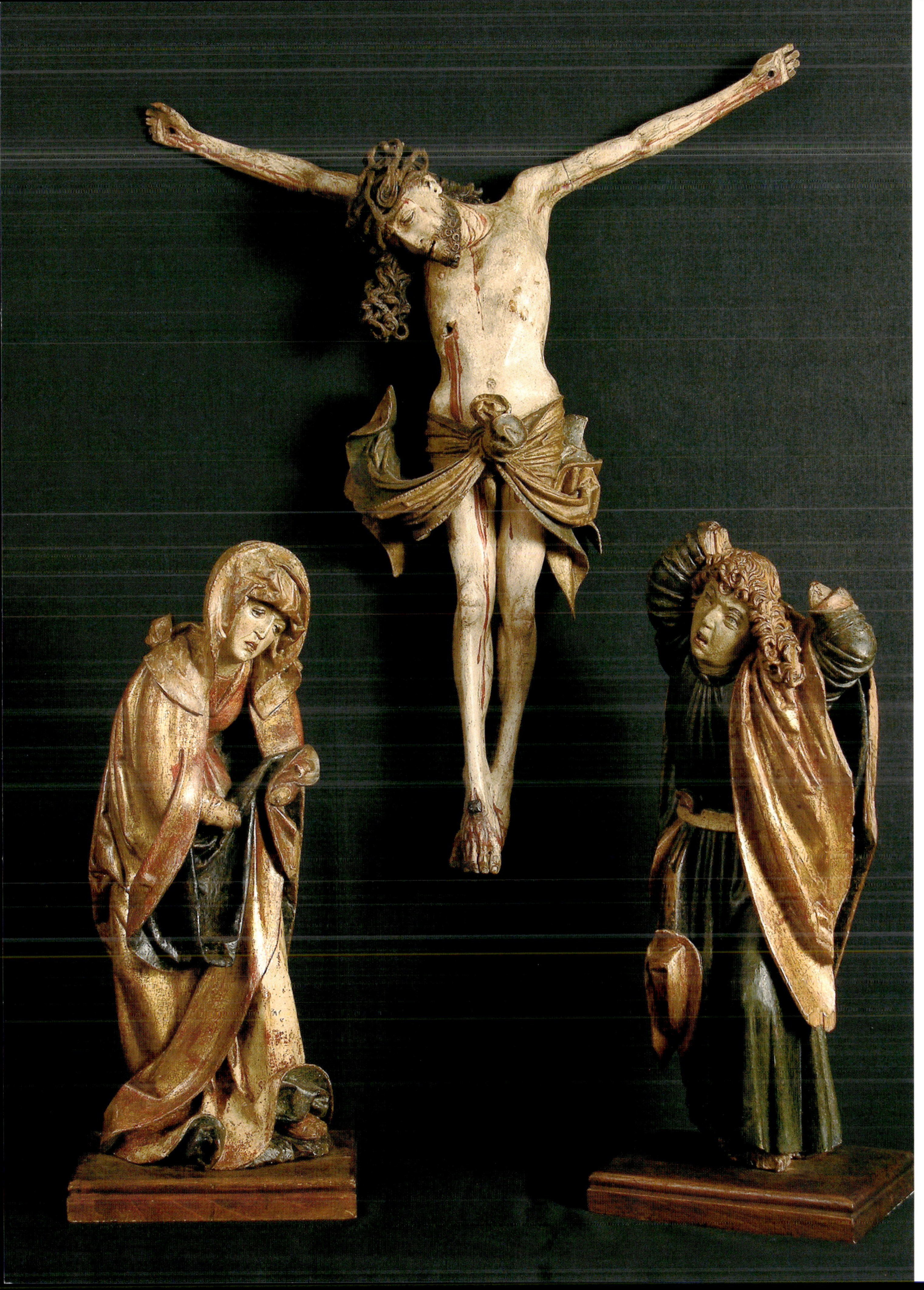

is difficult to imagine a more a dazzling work. The head, the beard, the hands and legs of the saint are so perfect that the chorus of praises excited by this statue will be eternal. So that everyone could admire it, it has been preserved at the Florence Annunciata under the pulpit, without any colouring coat, in the tone of the wood itself and with the perfect finish given to it by Maître Jean. It is the most beautiful sculpted piece to be seen.'

In contrast to the careers of most great sculptors towards the end of the Middle Ages, some of Stoss's paintings, drawings and engravings have survived. The drawings [VIII.17] provide us with information on the various approaches he used for his themes. The engravings [VIII.18,19] show his expertise. Doubtless familiar with the majority of the engravings of one Master E.S. and of Martin Schongauer, which were in abundant circulation in artistic workshops throughout the Empire in the last third of the 15th century, Stoss certainly had more direct knowledge of Netherlandish art, in particular that of Rogier van der Weyden. The engravings of Stoss, much less numerous and of a more nervous feel and impressive virtuosity, enabled the artist to spread his formal innovations more widely than his sculpted or painted works would have allowed. The works of Veit Stoss had a significant impact on the artistic production of the first decades of the 16th century in Franconia and central Europe. We have selected here an eloquent example, that of a sculptor who led a workshop that enjoyed a sort of monopoly, Master Paul de Levoča [VIII.16], active in Slovakia. Although this sculptor is duly credited with great talent, it is clear to see how much he owes to Stoss.

Cat VIII.17
TRINITARIAN ST ANNE
Veit Stoss, 1512

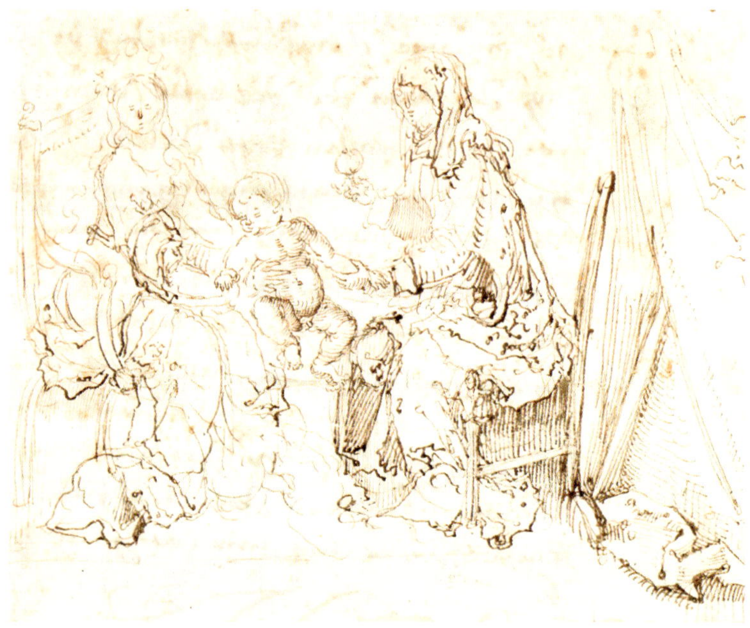

In the cases of Nikolaus van Leyden and of Stoss, we do not always know how the works reached their destinations. Was the St Roch created in Nuremberg, then simply 'delivered' to Florence? Or did Stoss spend some time in the Tuscan city? Similarly, did Nikolaus van Leyden create the Trier tomb while he was in Strasbourg? Deliveries over great distances were a common practice. The great altarpiece destined for the church of Sterzing/Vipiteno was created by Hans Multscher in his workshop at Ulm, then transported by carriage across the Alps and subsequently installed with the help of a cabinet-maker. Works of art, like people, frequently travelled.

BIBLIOGRAPHY: R. Recht, A. Châtelet, *Automne et Renouveau, 1380–1500*, L'Univers des Formes, Paris, 1988; M. V. Schwarz, *Höfische Skulptur im 14. Jahrhundert. Entwicklungsphasen und Vermittlungswege im Vorfeld des Weichen Stils*, Worms, 1986, pp. 457–68; G. Pochat, M. Wagner (eds), *Internationale Gotik in Mitteleuropa*, Graz, 1990; I. Takacs (ed.), *Sigismundus Rex et Imperator/Kunst und Kultur zur Zeit Sigismunds von Luxemburg 1387–1437* (exhib.cat.), Budapest-Luxembourg, 2006; A. Schädler, 'Studien zu Nicolaus Gerhaert von Leiden. Die Nördlinger Hochaltarfiguren und die Dangolsheimer Muttergottes in Berlin', *Jahrbuch der Berliner Museen*, NF16, 1975, pp. 99–106; R. Recht, *Nicolas de Leyde et la sculpture à Strasbourg (1460–1525)*, doctoral thesis dated 1978, Strasbourg, 1987; M. Baxandall, *The Limewood Sculptors of Renaissance Germany*, New Haven, London, 1980; P. Skubiszewski, 'Der Stil des Veit Stoss', *Zeitschrift für Kunstgeschichte*, 41, 1978, pp. 93–133; R. Kahsnitz (ed.), *Veit Stoss in Nürnberg. Werke des Meisters und seiner Schule in Nürnberg und Umgebung* (exhib. cat.), Munich, 1983.

IX

The conquest of a new pictorial space

ROLAND RECHT

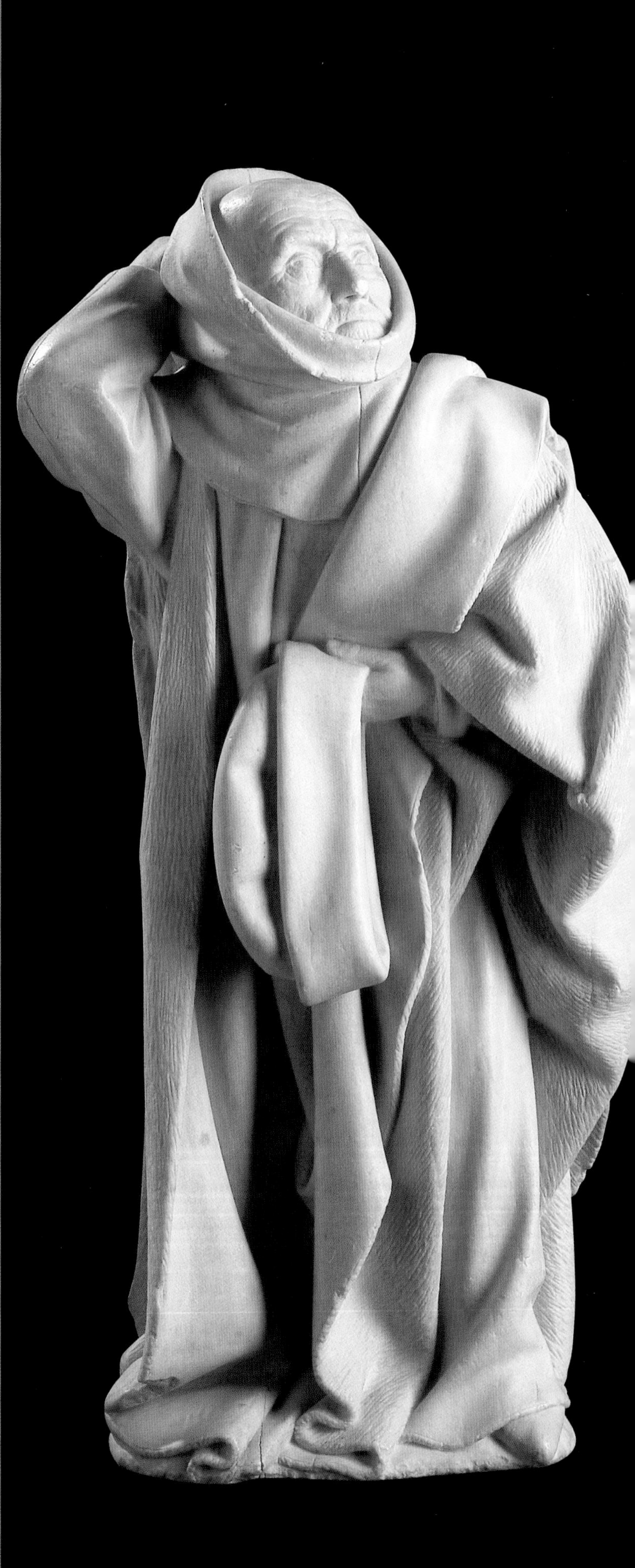

At the dawn of the 15th century, simultaneously in the southern Low Countries and in Florence, the third dimension was introduced into pictures to produce an illusion of space. No equivalent is known, in any of the world's civilizations, of such a radical change in the system of symbolic representation that is painting.

In ancient Greece and Rome, the concept of space had produced remarkable illusory effects (see Section II). The artists of those times could even be said to have handled indoor or outdoor architecture, as well as the landscape, with an acute sense of spatial suggestion. The flat surface of the wall did not present any obstacle to the illusion of space because painters used all sorts of devices to make flat things appear 'hollow'. The reduction of the size of figures or objects according to their distance from the viewer, as our eyes experience it in reality, was reproduced on the flat surface, and both colour and light assisted that artifice.

Section II has shown how that illusionist sense of space of late Antiquity was adopted by Carolingian painters and at the same time became fixed in conventions that then progressively renounced it. It would be a mistake to think that this renunciation can be attributed to the painters' ineptitude or ignorance. It was the result of a choice that was not imposed on their minds from one day to the next but occurred as a result of the rigour of the programmes they had to follow. An artist would turn to the models he needed in order to fulfil the demands imposed on him by his clients. In the Middle Ages, in both the West and the East, the Church prepared symbolic systems – with the 'portrait' of the Evangelist or the Virgin, Christ on the Cross, etc. – or narratives, which artists were to deploy in a 'closed' two-dimensional space, for the characters of the Old and New Testaments were not supposed to have moved within a space equivalent to our own. The use of a gold background or simply an ornamental carpet as scenery corresponds to a theologically established vision of the Christian image, and architecture that did not seek to represent real architecture in either its scale or its arrangement was not the disastrous result of a lack of skill. It did not occur to the artists of the Middle Ages to develop a system of spatial figuration based on flat geometry, as Piero della Francesca **IX.6** was to do, and yet they were familiar with geometry, just as we are today. For modern viewers, that also means that the painted medieval space is not a homogeneous one that extends our own, simply because it did not have to be. When, in his treatise *De Pictura*, Alberti wrote that 'painting applies itself to representing visible things', he defined a singularity of modern art that radically differentiates it from that of the Middle Ages, whose ambition was not to 'represent visible things' but rather to make the invisible visible.

The first disruption of that order of things dates back to Giotto and his quest for a homogeneity of the visible world, using shadows and the interaction of characters, and treating space as a cube in which the story being represented unfolds.

< Cat IX.10
'PLEURANT' (MOURNER) FROM THE TOMB OF PHILIP THE BOLD
Claus Sluter (?), 1404–06

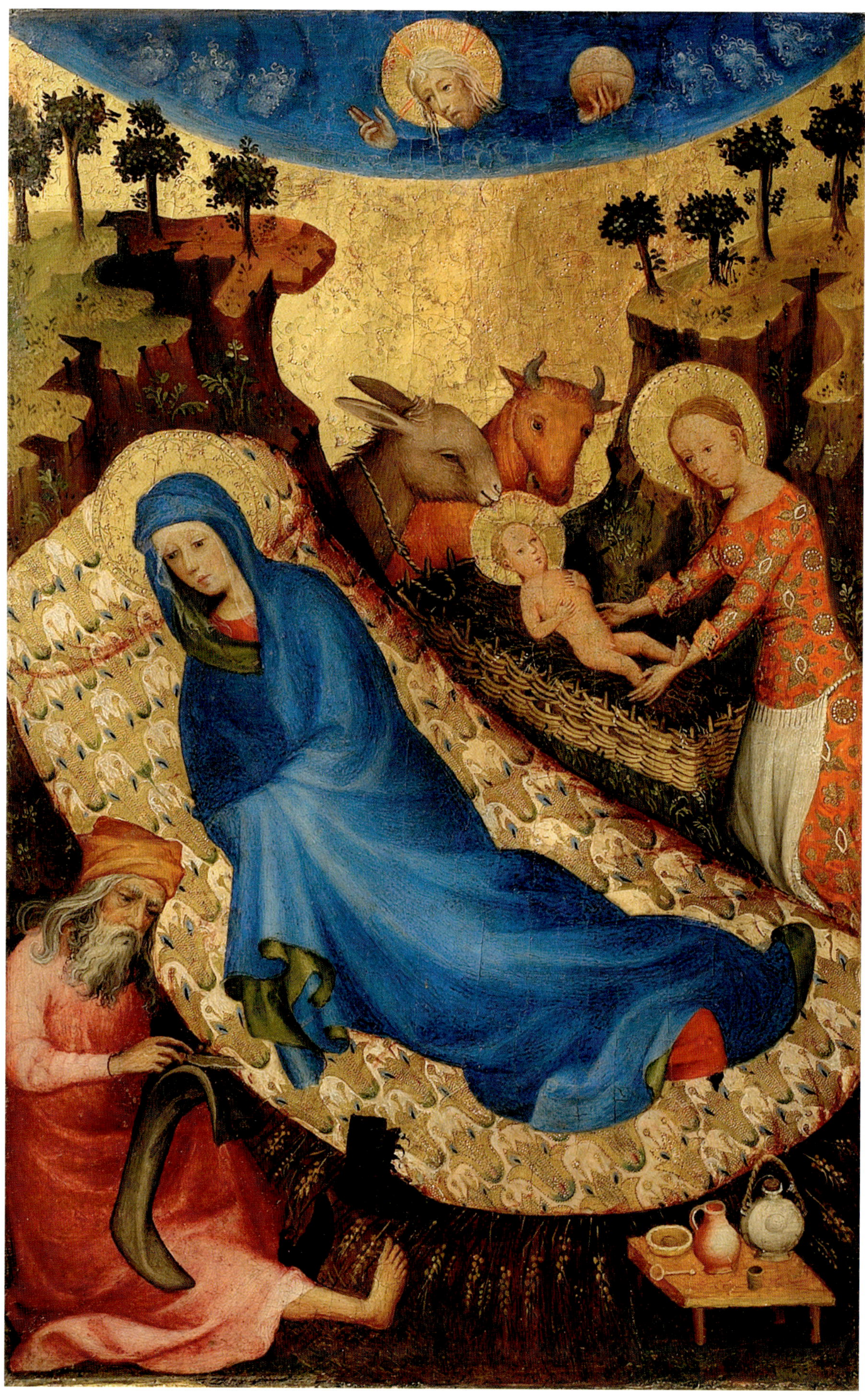

< Cat IX.1
NATIVITY (PANEL OF A QUADRIPTYCH)
Guelders (?), *c.* 1400

Christ among the Doctors in Assisi can be considered the first attempt in medieval and modern art to present a coherent space in perspective. Following the triumph of Aristotelianism, we note an increased interest in the observation of Nature and painters started to echo that interest **VI,IX.2**. There is absolutely no doubt that when mineral and vegetable matter began to play an increasingly visible part in painting, it helped to explode the two-dimensional limits of the medieval image.

Space is without a doubt included within what Ernst Cassirer called 'symbolical forms' but when, in a famous essay, Erwin Panofsky sought to show that the history of painting since Antiquity was that of a continuous quest for a homogeneous and illusionist space that finally reached Italy in the Renaissance, he adopted an unacceptable point of view. A given society produces its own system of symbolic forms, which therefore cannot be ahistorical. That is to say that this system of forms must necessarily correspond not to a natural disposition of man, but to conventions that man has decided to fix. This does not mean that the perspective of the Renaissance theoreticians, sometimes called artificial, was arbitrarily decreed. It was imposed because it strongly resembled the retinal impression given by natural perspective – the impression we all experience in reality. However, there are other systems that enable that resemblance to be suggested, such as curvilinear perspective or synthetic perspective. It is obviously reasonable to wonder why the painters of the 15th century felt the need to break definitively with the background and try to handle the question of figurative space in a rational way.

As in the case of photography, whose invention by Daguerre was preceded by the research of Nièpce and Fox-Talbot. Brunelleschi conducted experiments – at any rate in Florence itself when he worked on the three-dimensional system of representation he used in the Baptistery, even if it is considered a late and indirect example of it – to link the subject of painting to the science of optics. That science, incidentally, is called *perspectiva* by the Latin versions of Euclid's *Optics* as early as the Middle Ages. The Florentines believed in the possibility of 'artificially' reconstituting natural vision in a painted representation.

In his *De Pictura* of 1435 **IX.5**, the great Florentine humanist Leon Battista Alberti was the first person deliberately to venture beyond medieval theories of optics, which had been nourished by Arabian science or Arabic translations of Greek science, and to make use only of what we can derive from geometry as a simple model of vision. Rays leave the eye and fall on the perceived object by forming a pyramid. It suffices to make a transverse section of that pyramid at any distance from the eye to obtain a plan that constitutes that of the picture. According to Alberti's famous formula, that plan can then be considered as 'an open window through which the story can be seen'. In association with optics and mathematics, the painter's art then reached a new level: a painter should no longer be considered as only a craftsman, since he possessed scientific knowledge.

We should remember that Alberti, the quintessential 'universal man' of the Renaissance, was also the author of a treatise on the family and another on architecture. As in his *De Pictura*, each of those works refers back to the heritage of Antiquity so as to inform contemporary practices. His rationality is that of a moralist who seeks in some way to act for the public good. This is an absolutely essential

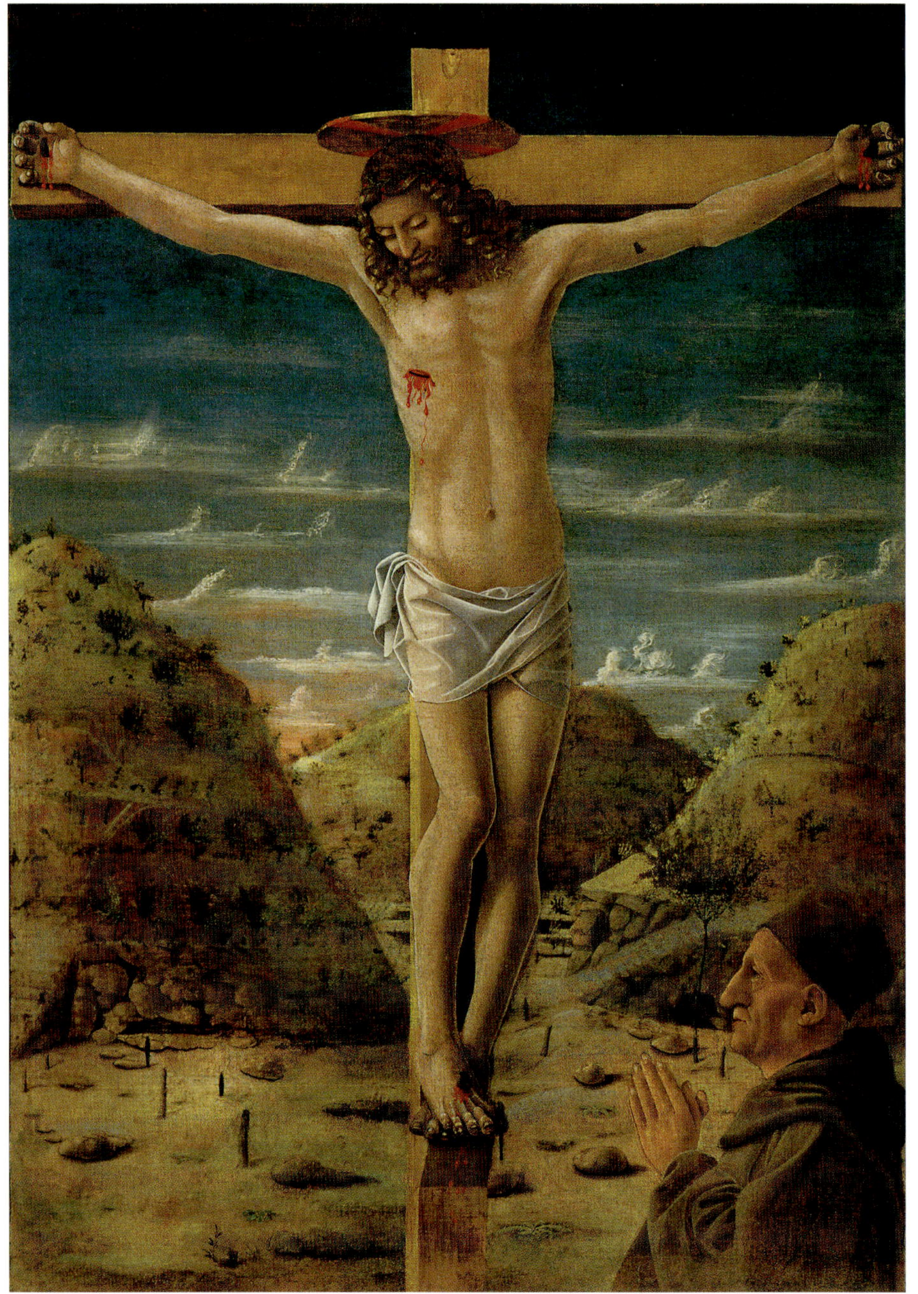

Cat IX.9
CHRIST ON THE CROSS WITH A MONK AT PRAYER
Cristoforo Canozzi (da Lendinara), second half of the 15th century

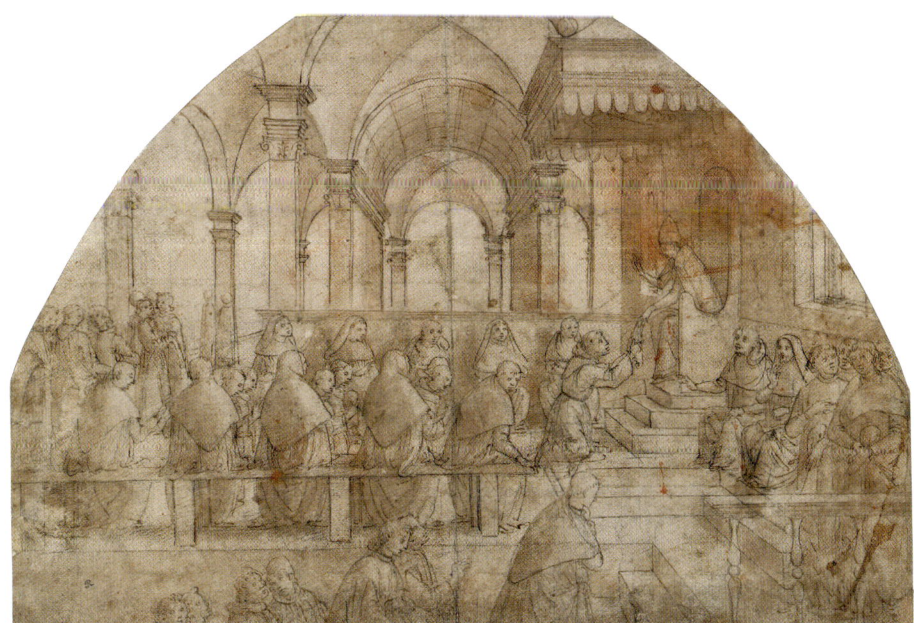

Cat IX.8
POPE HONORIUS III CONFIRMING THE RULES OF THE ORDER OF ST FRANCIS
Domenico Ghirlandaio, c. 1483

aspect of the question of perspective: by theorizing about it, Alberti sought to fix the codes to be followed for the representation of an ordered world.

It is interesting that Alberti sent a letter accompanying his treatise in the language of everyday speech exclusively to sculptors: Brunelleschi, Donatello, Ghiberti, Luca della Robbia and Masaccio (not the painter, but the sculptor Maso di Bartolomeo). Ghiberti had won the competition for the reliefs on the Baptistery doors in 1401 and we can certainly see the extent to which the rules of geometric perspective construct the space of the story by giving to the relief new expressive possibilities (see, even here, a distant inheritance of that novelty [IX.7]).

Brunelleschi's experiment has been raised to the rank of a founding myth by authors none of whom had witnessed the experiment itself and whose aim was to give Florence first rank in the development of the arts, particularly as compared with Rome. And when the fresco of the Trinity in Santa Maria Novella in Florence, painted by Masaccio in about 1425, is credited with constituting an orthodox application of the principles Alberti had set out, the painter's errors are overlooked. No surviving works offer a slavish application of perspective to a single vanishing point that assigns a given position to the viewer. While producing the effect of a resemblance to natural perspective, each of them presents its own 'homemade' way of using geometrical data [IX.8].

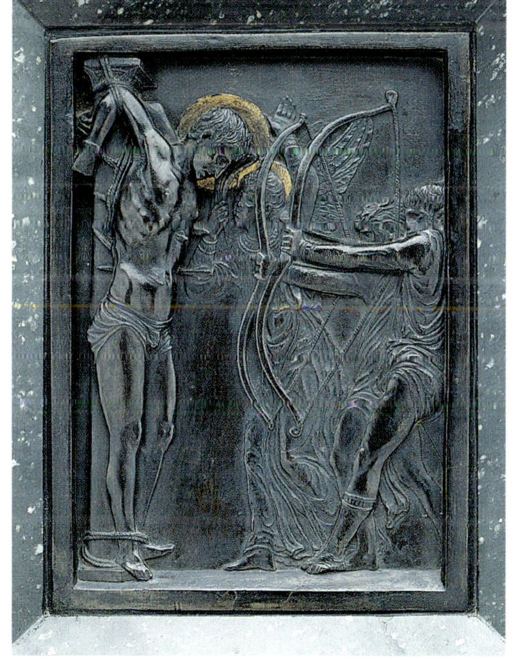

Cat IX.7
MARTYRDOM OF ST SEBASTIAN
School of Donatello, c. 1460

The aspiration to rationality does not manifest itself only in geometrical perspective but also in the conviction that the representation of the still or moving body must follow firmly established rules of proportion. However, perspective and proportion must take the subjectivity of the viewer's gaze into account. While Leonardo da Vinci was the first to do research into proportions while also studying the body (animal or human, see Section VII) scientifically, Albrecht Dürer mainly sought to define posture, organic movement and proportions. Perspective intervened in the positioning of those objects so as to make them look realistic to the viewer's eye. Dürer's research, however, led him into a blind alley: because his smallest unit of measurement (or 'particle') was smaller than a millimetre and the human types he had already placed on the grid of proportions numbered twenty-six, by that very fact such rules ceased to be useful to painters.

> Cat IX.3
> ***HOURS OF TUZIN-MILAN***
> Jan van Eyck, *c.* 1420

The importance of the Hours of Turin-Milan **IX.3**, for the as yet undefined corpus of the works of Hubert and Jan van Eyck and for the history of modern art, cannot be overestimated. With the two pages of the Birth and Baptism of John the Baptist and the Mass for the Dead, we approach a conception of space diametrically opposed to that of Alberti – not that a theoretical, and therefore rational, approach should be excluded a priori: after all, it is not because we have no trace of it that it should be considered improbable. It is clear, however, that the conception of space revealed by those two pages is the product of a long series of experiments, not all of whose milestones have been catalogued.

What is contrary to the spirit in which Alberti wrote his treatise is that the aim was to offer the viewer not an *istoria*, a coherent and legible action, but rather a set of plastic objects that oblige him constantly to move closer to the picture and then to stand back from it again. The picture does not interest us as a narrative episode but as the space of an observation. It could be said that Alberti assigns the viewer a fixed position from which to watch the scene – the top of the visual pyramid – while Jan van Eyck obliges the eye to come and go constantly (we should remember that the Dutch were the first users of the telescope and the microscope).

In the scene of the Baptism of John, at the foot of the page, the painter introduces into Western art the first representation of a reflection in water. The atmospheric perspective leads us into a distance made of transparencies, whence emerges a complete, miniaturized world (with a windmill and a fortress). It has been said that landscapes comparable to this one did not appear again until the 17th century. The scene of the Birth of John the Baptist is designed as three 'cubes', each contained within another: the cube of the canopied bed in which Elisabeth lies holding her newborn child, the cube of the bedroom that contains it and extends into a third 'cube', a neighbouring room where Zachariah can be seen reading, with a maidservant standing by the window. The furniture, objects, domestic animals and midwives occupy this space more naturally than any other painter had yet succeeded in portraying them. The palette, dominated by the deep red of the canopy, is an essential auxiliary to this spatial distribution and the suggestion of

Rector of the University of Paris from 1465, humanist Guillaume Fichet aptly summarized the nature of the printing revolution that he had just witnessed. In his letter to Robert Gaguin (1472), which was published on the very presses of the Sorbonne that he had established, he linked the renewal of interest in humanist studies to the sudden appearance of a magical technology from Germany. Printing, he said, had penetrated countries 'like a Trojan horse'. Fichet had realized the forceful nature of the new invention as well as its beneficial effects – the emergence of a new and universal literary sphere with a unified set of rules.

The printed book is a technical object the sophistication and revolutionary novelty of which is at least the match of the computer. Since the end of the 14th century, printed plates, sometimes coloured, were mass-produced. They mainly represented saints. The name of the saint was added by hand at first, then engraved. Books made from woodcuts continued this tradition, for example, the *Biblia Pauperum*[X.1] (1462–64), misnamed, as it was in Latin and therefore illegible by ordinary people. Despite its probable printing date, this book owes its existence to a production technique that predated that of Gutenberg. For the sake of economy, the text was engraved as a woodcut together with the images in one block. This long and hazardous process – a single error would mean the craftsman would have to cut an entirely new plate – was cheap. However, being too laborious, it prevented large volumes from being printed. The development of presses with the casting of moveable characters emerged after long and intensive experiments, marked by many failures. The process required the investment of quite substantial resources. Mainz, the grand archbishopric of the Holy Roman Empire, was the first centre of this revolution *c.* 1450, when Gutenberg created the first printing works there. The archbishopric of Mainz controlled a vast network of suffragan bishoprics throughout the Germanic world. When Archbishop Adolph II of Nassau conquered the city in

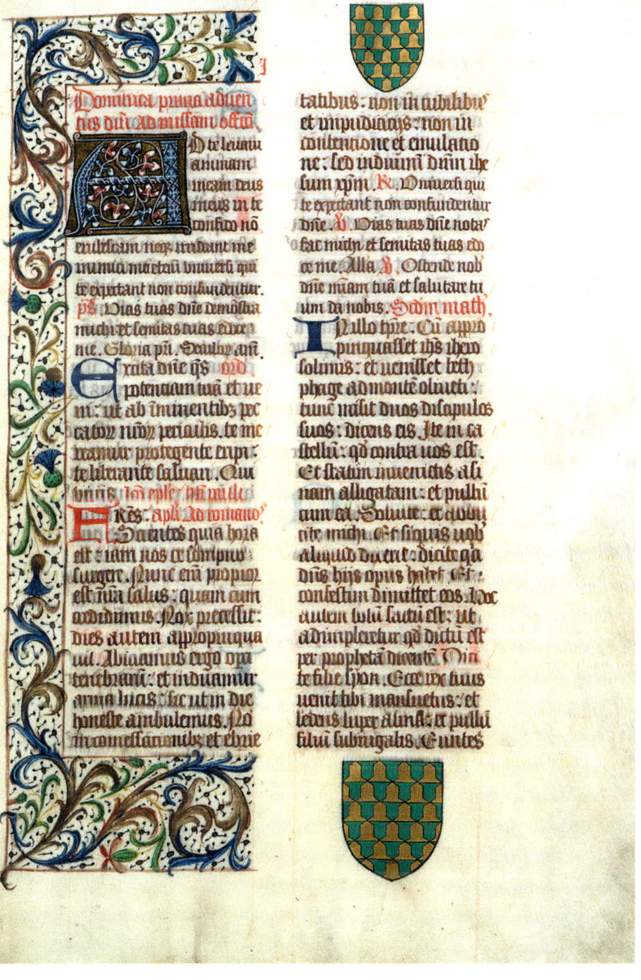

Cat X.2
MISSAL FOR THE LYONS USAGE
c. 1485–90

< Cat X.4
ORIGEN,
HOMILIES ON GENESIS, EXODUS AND LEVITICUS
Florence, 1480–90

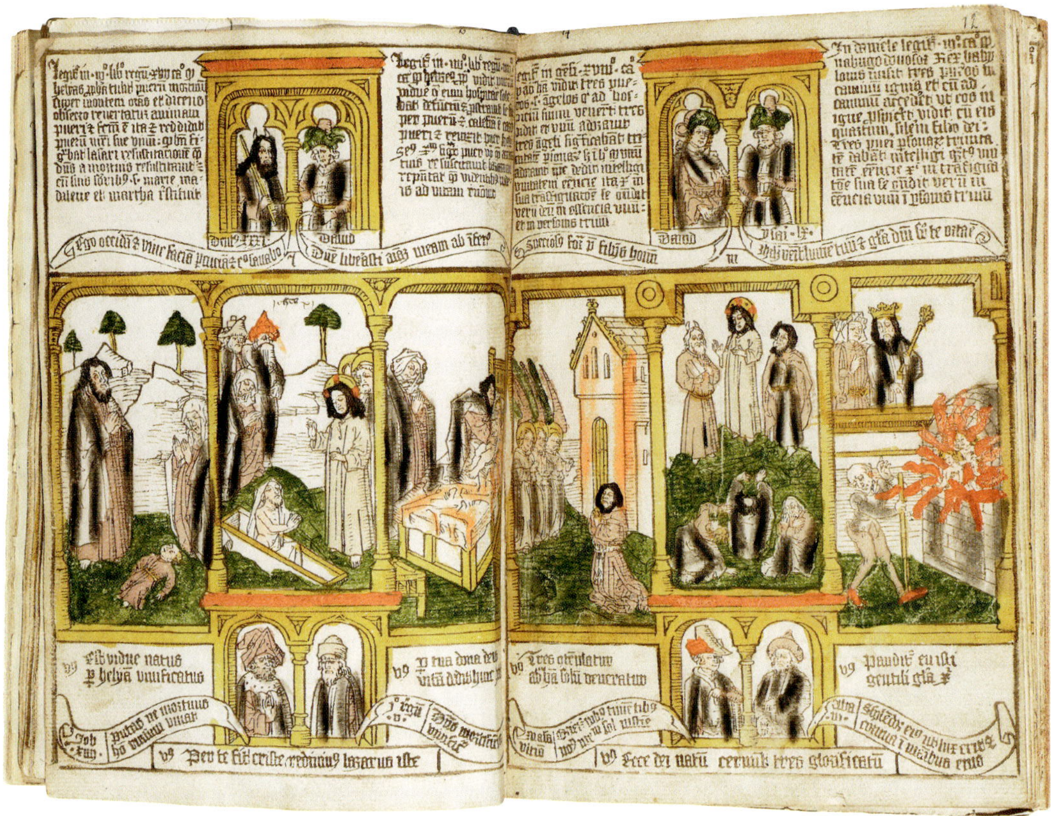

Cat X.1
BIBLIA PAUPERUM
Flemish impression, c. 1464

1462, his troops caused great destruction. He himself sensed the danger of the new technology. His draconian measures caused the departure of the Mainz inventors to various Germanic villages, then throughout Europe – the book then became an almost invincible weapon of expression. In 1499, a German printer working in Barcelona, Johann Luschner, produced 200,000 copies of indulgences. Eighteen years later, the Reformation would use the same weapon to stem the tide of indulgences. The effects of this diaspora were immediate and substantial. In the region of Europe, the book would assume a form, an identity and universality.

The *Missale Lugdunense*X.3 illustrates an exemplary episode in this cardinal development in European history. Published in Lyon in 1487, this incunabulum – as the first published works were known up to 1499 – was the work of Johann Neumeister, a German from Treisa near Marburg and a student at Erfurt, then a printer at Mainz, probably in the workshop of Gutenberg himself. After the upheavals of 1462, he dreamed of exporting the new technology abroad. However, he had to fund this ambition. He wandered throughout Europe, seeking capital and commissions, stopping in prospective towns – cities with a strong ecclesiastical presence, political capitals or international trade fair towns. His travels took him to Subiaco, Rome, Foligno, Basle, Lyons, Toulouse and Albi. His missal for the city of LyonsX.3 consisted of Gothic characters arranged in tight columns that imitated

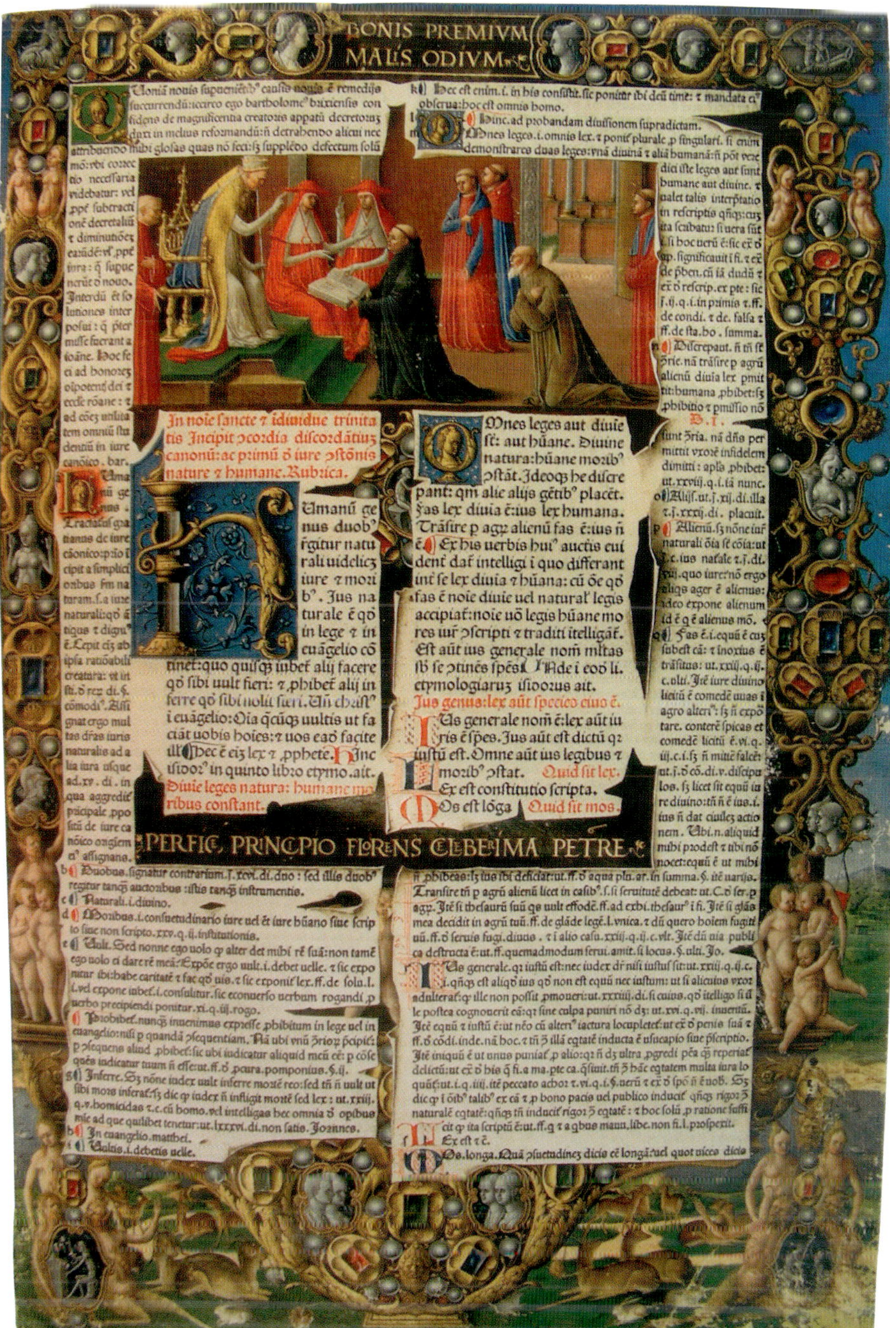

Cat X.5
GRATIAN, *DECRETUM, CONCORDANTIA DISCORDANTIUM CANONUM, WITH THE GLOSSA OF BARTHOLOMEUS BRIXIENSIS*
Venice, 1477

the manuscript calligraphy painstakingly copied in a scriptorium[X.2]. The first connoisseurs considered printed matter to be too crude, and not worthy of the library of a person of taste. Comparison of the two types of work is eloquent. Neumeister tried to confer on printed books a dignity that was still reserved for the manuscript. Once bought, he had a miniaturist decorate the copy to reinforce its relationship with the calligraphed missals.

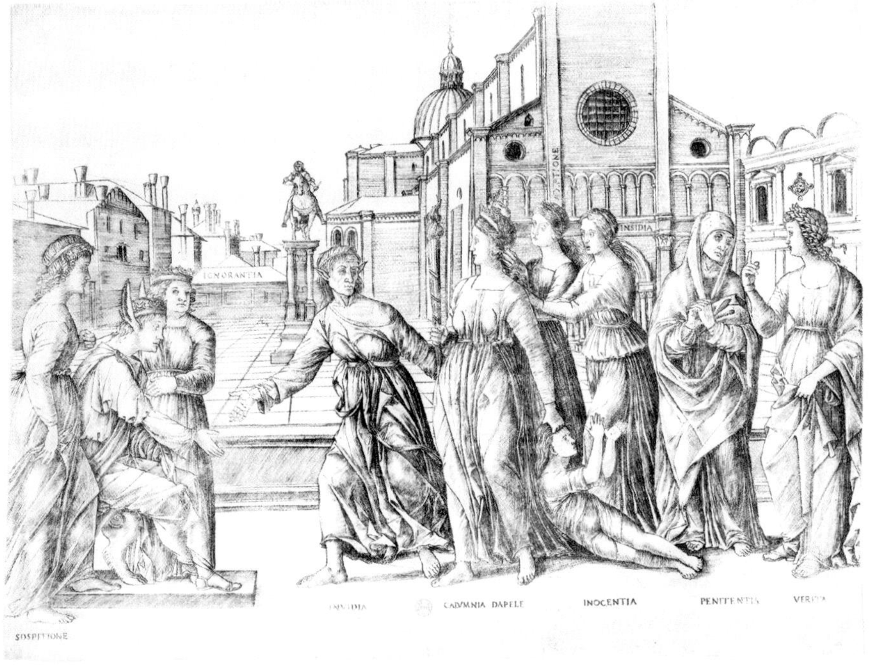

Cat X.12
GIROLAMO MOCETTO, *THE CALUMNY OF APELLES*, AFTER ANDREA MANTEGNA
Venice, *c.* 1500–06

The book therefore acquired its own form, distinct from the manuscript. The emergence of this form was a tortuous business. It gave rise first of all to a hybrid product, half-manuscript, half-printed. The *Decretum* of Gratian, printed in Venice by Nicolas Jenson in 1477, was illustrated by an ingenious miniaturist who, without doubt, was commissioned to transform a printed book into a work of art **X.5**. Instead of drowning the text in miniatures, the artist celebrated the printed page in a piece of fantasy. He enlarged it to the proportions of a large chamfered folio suspended on an ancient-style portico. The printed text proudly obliterates the miniature – a highly symbolic gesture. A copy of Lucian **X.11**, also printed on parchment, follows the same elegant aesthetic, aimed at attracting collectors. The printing house always felt the need to apologize for its mechanical nature, but it was now producing new forms of book. Benedetto Bordon was an outstanding craftsman who made the most of his opportunities. Arrived in Venice from Padua *c.* 1494, he made some careful miniatures, but also designed wood engravings for printers. The inscription surface was here characterized as such and metaphorized by the architectural space. The vocabulary used indicates that Bordon knew Alberti and his compatriot Mantegna. On his death in 1529, he left a beautiful library populated with books on philosophy and astronomy. Bordon, here associated with the printer Bevilaqua, chose to print Lucian. The Greek author was not much read before the end of the 15th century. His ekphrasis – descriptions with a heavily iconic character – clearly aroused the interest of the miniaturist ready to take up the challenge of the text. In the book's colophon, Bordon recommends that the reader should relax before reading the work. This indicates the impact erudite printers and miniaturists had in Venice. In a city that was becoming the conceptual laboratory for the modern book, reading was construed as being a leisure activity, requiring time for contemplation of the decorated pages. It was intended to plunge the reader into an imaginary world embodied in the engravings or miniatures.

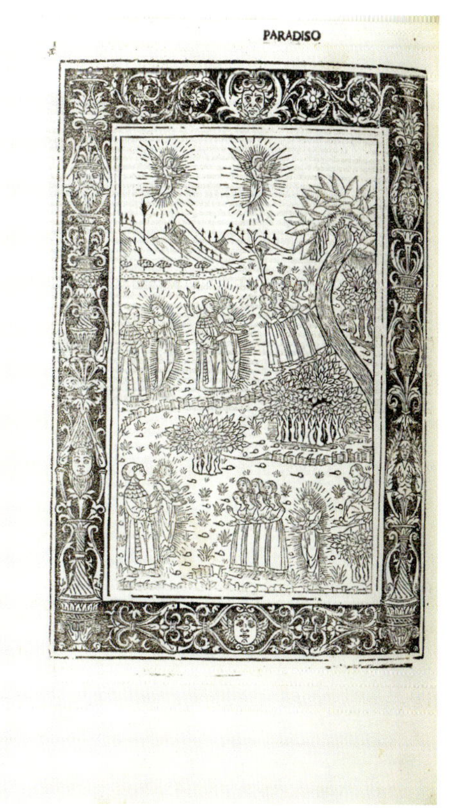

Cat X.6
DANTE, *LA COMMEDIA* WITH COMMENTARY BY CHRISTOPHORO LANDINO
Brescia, printed by Boninus de Boninis, 1487

For the first time, it was the ambition of the book to become a lasting monument. Roman font, with its solid, detached letters, was reminiscent of the inscriptions on ancient Roman monuments. In Italy, printed matter would quickly attain a form autonomous from the manuscript. Dante's *Divine Comedy* appeared in Brescia in 1487, i.e. less than forty years after the beginnings of printing **X.6**. The editor, Bonino de' Bonini, was a Dalmatian who had good business acumen and published five books per year. He ended his career in Lyons. His Dante contained a commentary by Christophoro Landino, a humanist in the social circle of Lorenzo de' Medici. The pages are characterized by careful design, the moveable characters imitated the aesthetic of inscriptions popular in Roman epigraphy. Spelling became standardized. Pure lines and simple hatching defined the forms. Nineteen plates were inspired by copper engravings published in Venice (1481) after drawings by Sandro Botticelli, which the plates transformed. The whole phenomenon was in the use of two colours, the black of the ink and the architecture of the white page surrounding the text. Economy of means, far from being viewed as a handicap, accentuated the effects with dazzling power. The page resembled the threshold of a princely residence, suddenly opened up to the reader.

Soon the tables were turned and there even appeared some luxury manuscripts inspired by the printed model. Mathias Corvin, king of Hungary and a lavish bibliophile, had Origen's *Homilies on Genesis, Exodus and Leviticus* produced in Florence *c.* 1480–90 **X.4**. The miniatures of this manuscript on fine parchment are

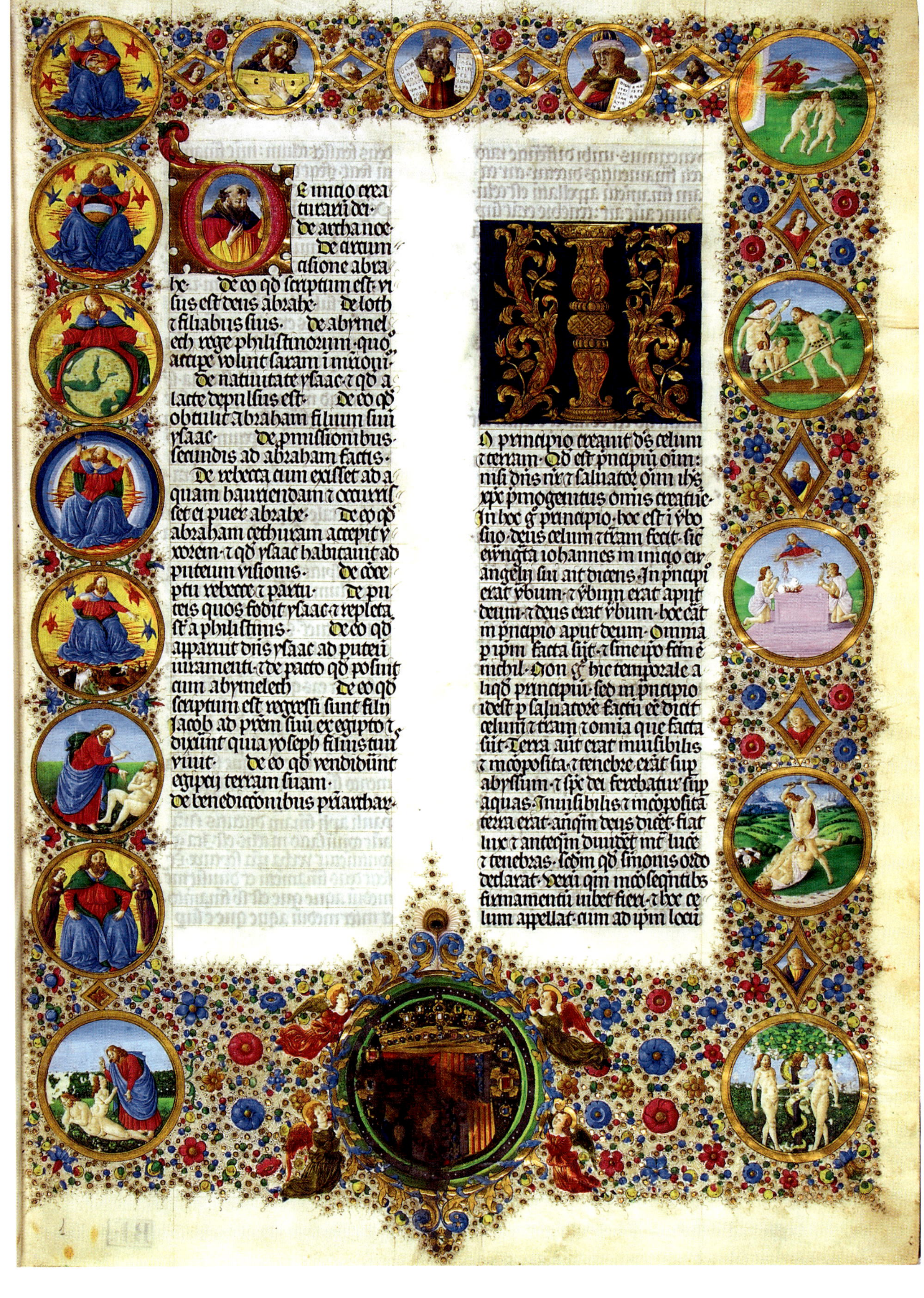
[D]e inicio crea
turarum dei.
de archa noe.
De circum
cisione abra
he. De eo qd scriptum est. vi
sus est deus abrahe. De loth
et filiabus suis. De abymel
ech rege philistinorum. quo
accipe volunt saram in uxori.
De natiuitate ysaac et qd a
lacte depulsus est. De eo qd
obtulit Abraham filium suum
ysaac. De promissionibus
secundis ad abraham factis.
De rebecca cum exisset ad a
quam hauriendam et occurris
set ei puer abrahe. De eo qd
abraham cethuram accepit v
xorem. et qd ysaac habitauit ad
puteum visionis. De conce
ptu rebecce et partu. De pu
teis quos fodit ysaac et repleta
sunt a philistinis. De eo qd
apparuit dns ysaac ad puteum
iuramenti. et de pacto qd posuit
cum abymelech De eo qd
scriptum est regressi sunt filii
Jacob ad patrem suum ex egipto et
dixerunt quia yoseph filius tuus
viuit. De eo qd vendiderunt
egipcii terram suam.
De benedictionibus patriarchar.

[I]n principio creauit ds celum
et terram. Qd est principium omnium:
nisi dns noster et saluator omnium ihs
xpc primogenitus omnis creature.
In hoc ergo principio. hoc est in vbo
suo. deus celum et terram fecit. sic
euangelista iohannes in inicio eu
angelii sui ait dicens. In principio
erat vbum. et vbum erat apud
deum. et deus erat vbum. hoc erat
in principio apud deum. Omnia
per ipsum facta sunt. et sine ipso factum est
nichil. Non ergo hic temporale a
liquod principium. sed in principio
idest per saluatorem factum esse dicit
celum et terram et omnia que facta
sunt. Terra autem erat inuisibilis
et incomposita. et tenebre erant super
abyssum. et spiritus dei ferebatur super
aquas. Inuisibilis et incomposita
terra erat. antequam deus diceret. fiat
lux et antequam diuideret inter lucem
et tenebras. secundum qd simonis ordo
declarat. Verum quoniam in consequentibus
firmamentum iubet fieri. et hoc ce
lum appellat. cum ad ipsum locum

attributed to Francesco Rosselli, who also worked for Lorenzo de' Medici. If the floral decorations are still reminiscent of late medieval parerga (ornamental accessories), he clears the white of the central block using two columns. Medallions encircle tondi painted in a new Florentine style, comparable to that of Filippo Lippi or Botticelli. The Renaissance style initials, based on the model of antique monumental inscriptions, contrast with the rounded script.

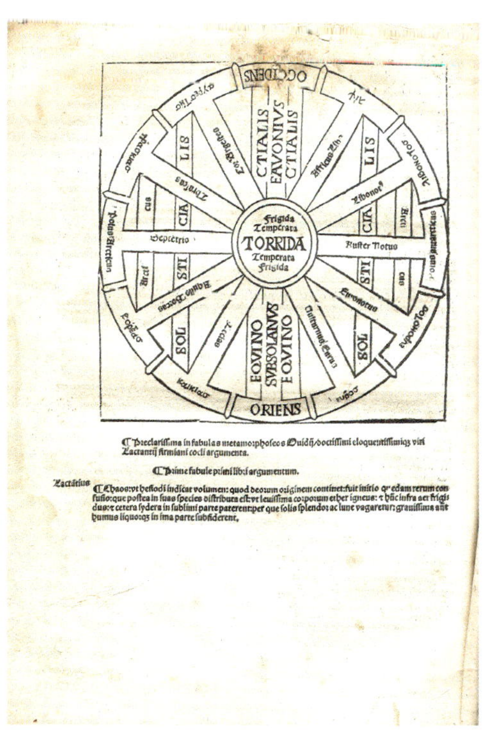

Cat X.7
OVID, *METAMORPHOSEOS. I LIBRI MORALIZATI CUM PULCHERRIMIS FABULARUM PRINCIPALIUM FIGURIS*
Lyons, printed by Jacob Huguetan, 1518

The mobility of books was based on two essential factors easy multiplication of identical copies and the cheaper cost of printing. The book, then, remained expensive, but it cost much less than a fully illuminated manuscript. But, above all, it presented an exact standard text that was much more reliable. Very quickly, the circulation of books would take on proportions never imagined. The volumes went along with travelling book sellers or book dealers who visited the fairs of Frankfurt, a meeting place for innovation. Competition obliged the printers to buy up well-designed books printed abroad – they then plundered the most attractive elements. When they copied the illustrations, they gave the task to engravers who did not always know what it was they were copying. All imitation involves an element of interpretation of the image to be copied. In short, the images were distributed after multiple copyings/collages. The Lyons edition of Ovid's *Metamorphoses*[X.7] by Jacob Huguetan took the woodcuts of a Lyons competitor, Gueynard, who had produced his Ovid in 1510. In turn, these engravings from the Gueynard edition had plagiarized a magnificent Venetian production of 1497 attributed to Giovanni Rosso. This, with its tight economy, prefigured the aesthetic of the plates requested by Alde Manuce for his *Hypnerotomachia Poliphili* by Francesco Colonna (1499). The Lyons editors had scented commercial success. Such thefts are exciting to study: they prove the immediate success of a new formula throughout Europe. In a sense, Rosso could be proud of the illustrations he had ordered and set in frames taken from a Catullus printed by him in 1485. Finally, Huguetan knew his Lyons customers well. His edition transformed Ovid into an allegorical and almost Christian author. His master work was published together with the *Argumenta* by the 'so-called' Lactantius, a treatise that offered a Christian interpretation of the poet. Such 'acceptable' editions of the *Metamorphoses* reassured the parents of young readers. They were suitable for anyone to read, in contrast with others. From 1497, the proliferation of 'pornographic' editions of Ovid was such that the Venetian patriarch forced two printers to withdraw engraved plates with 'naked women, phallic deities and

< Cat X.4
ORIGEN, *HOMILIES ON GENESIS, EXODUS AND LEVITICUS*
Florence, 1480–90

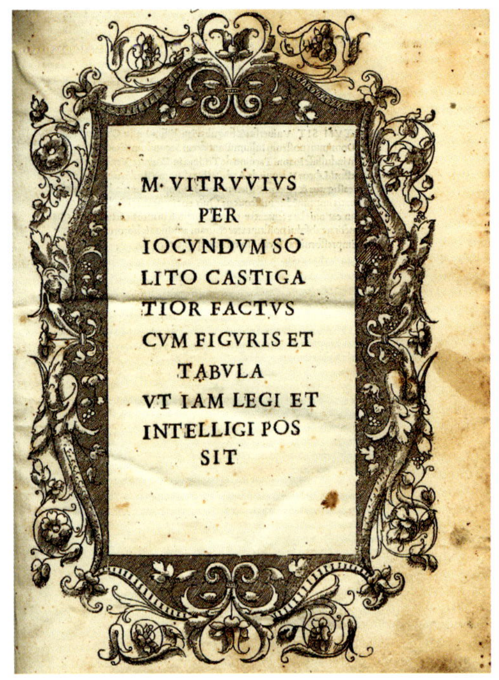
M·VITRVVIVS
PER
IOCVNDVM SO
LITO CASTIGA
TIOR FACTVS
CVM FIGVRIS ET
TABVLA
VT IAM LEGI ET
INTELLIGI POS
SIT

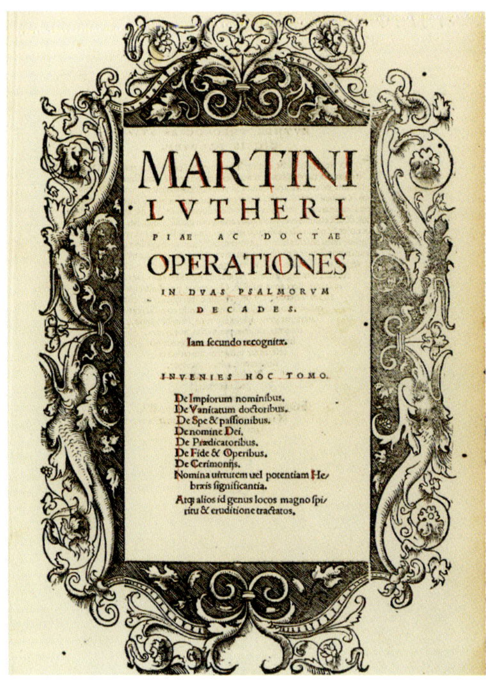
MARTINI
LVTHERI
PIAE AC DOCTAE
OPERATIONES
IN DVAS PSALMORVM
DECADES.
Iam secundo recognitæ.
INVENIES HOC TOMO.
De Impiorum nominibus.
De Vanitatum doctoribus.
De Spe & passionibus.
De nomine Dei.
De Prædicatoribus.
De Fide & Operibus.
De Cerimonijs.
Nomina uirtutem uel potentiam Hebræis significantia.
Atqȝ alios id genus locos magno spiritu & eruditione tractatos.

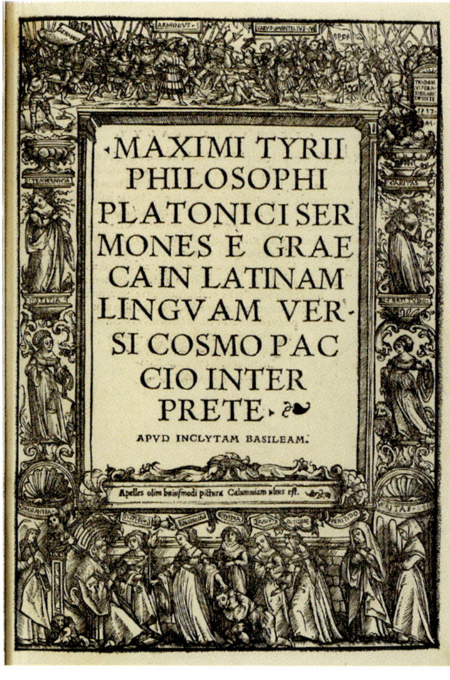
MAXIMI TYRII
PHILOSOPHI
PLATONICI SER
MONES E GRAE
CA IN LATINAM
LINGVAM VER
SI COSMO PAC
CIO INTER
PRETE
APVD INCLYTAM BASILEAM.

Cat X.9
VITRUVIUS,
DE ARCHITECTURA
Venice, printed by
Giovanni Tacuino, 1511

Cat X.8
MARTIN LUTHER,
PIAE AC DOCTAE OPERATIONES IN DUAS PSALMORUM DECADES. IAM SECUNDO RECOGNITAE
Basle, printed by
Adam Petri, 1521

Cat X.10
MAXIMUS OF TYRE,
SERMONES E GRAECA IN LATINAM LINGUAM VERSI COSMO PACCIO INTERPRETE
Basle, printed by
Johannes Froben, 1519

other dirty objects', found in several editions of the *Metamorphoses* leaving the presses in the Serenissima. Motifs were often very cleverly pillaged. A page from a Venetian title with a floral decoration closed by stylized dolphins [X.9] was copied by a Basle printer [X.8] ten years later. But the Basle engraver tightened the composition, giving it sharper contours. Johannes Froben, the printer and friend of Erasmus, knew how to mine the repertoire of forms created in Venice with discernment [X.10]. The two cities, both book publishing capitals in Renaissance times, watched one another closely. Many Venetian works were taken to Basle on publication. The university library of the town still has several. Printers such as Johannes Amerbach had completed their apprenticeship in Venice. Such thefts, which were not prohibited by any law, ensured the widespread distribution of engraved motifs throughout Europe – adapted, simplified or embellished, these formal borrowings document the exploitation of an attractive form originating in one place, which would be sold as an innovation in an entirely different culture. Other artistic materials circulated similarly across Europe: small portable works of art. Engravings on copper produced in Tuscany were highly sought after, not only by the artists of the North [X.15], but also by printers who commissioned drawings to be engraved from them to decorate ornate and appealing title pages that would be likely to persuade potential customers to purchase. *The Calumny of Apelles* by Mocetto [X.12] also served as partial source of inspiration for the Swiss artist Ambrosius Holbein, who drew a title page ornament for the Basle publisher Froben [X.10]. The bas-relief tightens the original composition and reverses the postures; a subscript identifies the subject in the interests of greater caution. The theme of calumny was so generalized that it would be suitable for almost every title. Engraving could be made more profitable by decorating multiple works printed in the same establishment. Florentine small bronze plates were highly valued[X.13,14]. Their ancient motifs were in vogue and the traveller could carry them in his luggage. Produced by sand casting, they could be easily reproduced. In some cases, the travellers would make an imprint in cheap plaster with the sole aim of taking away a reminder of an attractive pattern. Many motifs were transferred in this way from one technique to the other – from painting to engraving, from engraving[X.15] to bas-relief. Cutting the plate involved simplification of new artistic features such as perspec-

Cat X.19
MODEL OF THE FAÇADE OF THE DUOMO IN FLORENCE
Bernardo Buontalenti, 1587

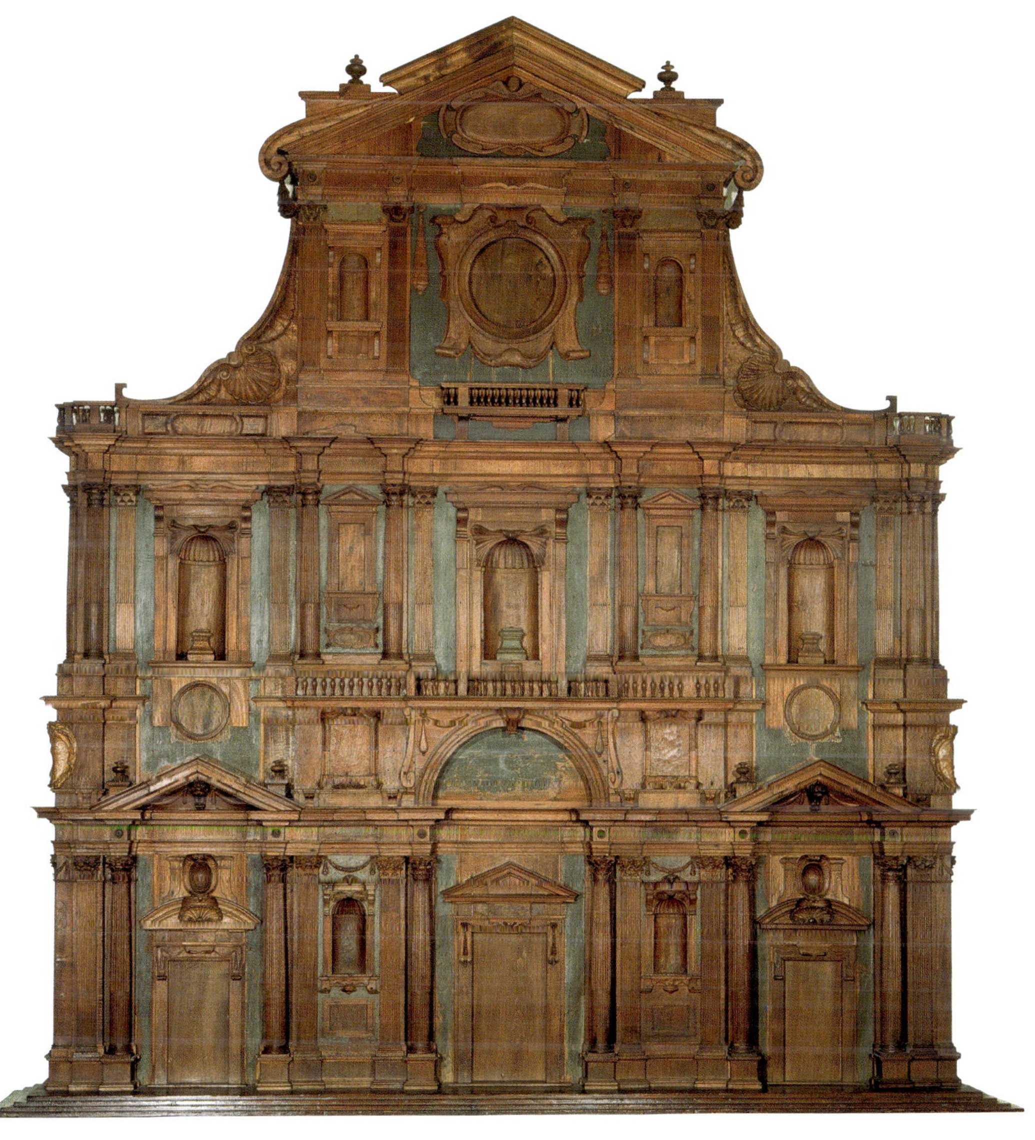

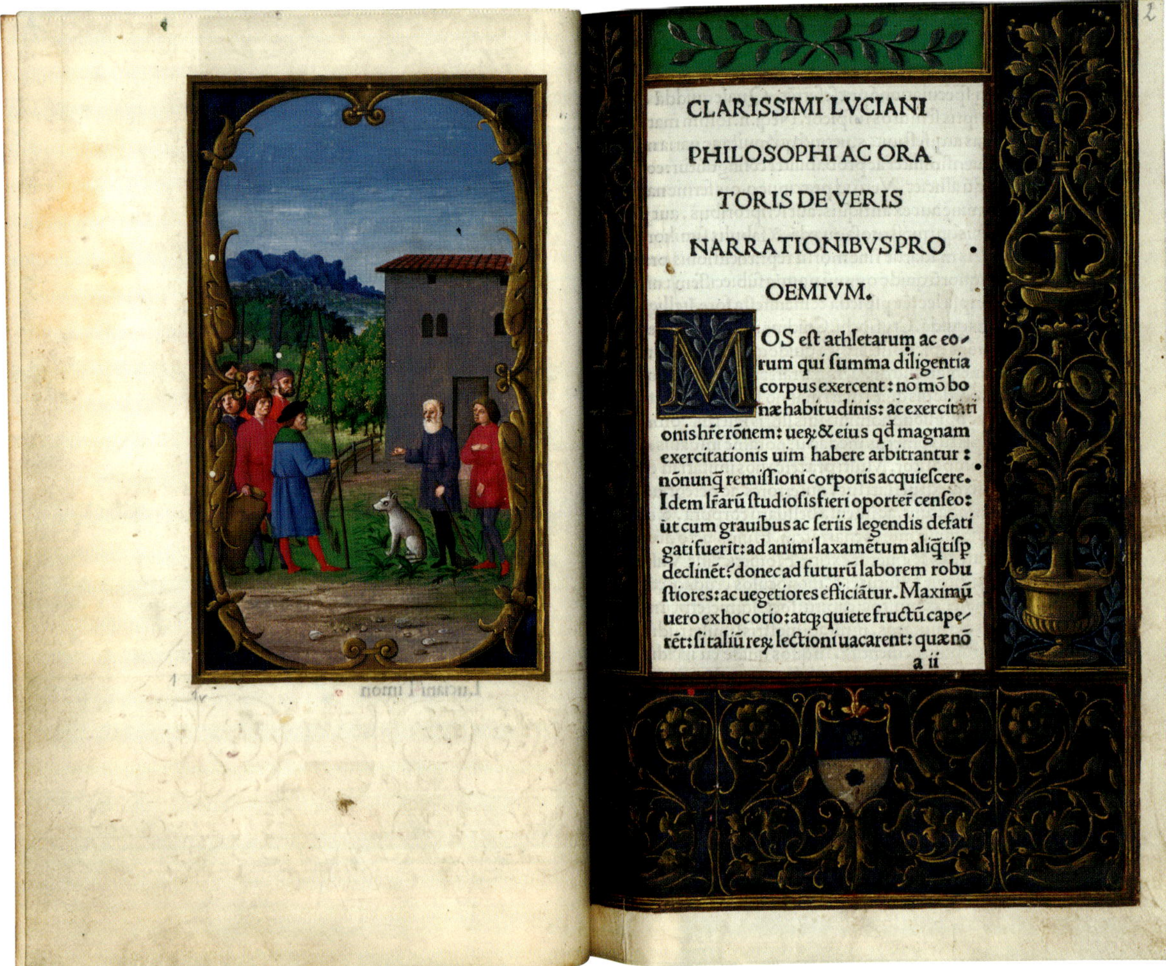
CLARISSIMI LVCIANI
PHILOSOPHI AC ORA
TORIS DE VERIS
NARRATIONIBVS PRO
OEMIVM.
MOS est athletarum ac eo-
rum qui summa diligentia
corpus exercent: nō mō bo
næ habitudinis: ac exerciti
onis hr̄e rōnem: ue℞ & eius q͞d magnam
exercitationis uim habere arbitrantur:
nōnunq̄ remissioni corporis acquiescere.
Idem lr̄arū studiosis fieri oporter̄ censeo:
ūt cum grauibus ac seriis legendis defati
gati fuerit: ad animi laxamētum aliq̄tisp
declinēt: donec ad futurū laborem robu
stiores: ac uegetiores efficiātur. Maximū
uero ex hoc otio: atq; quiete fructū cape-
rēt: si taliū re℞ lectioni uacarent: quæ nō
a ii

Cat X.11
LUCIAN, *OPERA*, TRANSLATED INTO LATIN BY LILIUS CASTELLANUS
Venice, printed by Simon Bevilaqua, associate of Benedetto Bordon, 1494

tive in a representation of the Virgin standing before her throne. This simplification itself facilitated the 'pillaging' of a form by artists from the North eager to imitate Italian art but sometimes ill-equipped to analyse its originality.

During the Renaissance, Basle was in its heyday as an urban centre – commerce, science and printing were working in concert. The city belonged to a network of towns that in 1241 had obtained the *immédiateté* of the Empire (i.e. their feudal relationship was directly with the emperor). This regime of relative freedom enabled Basle to neutralize the influence of the bishop, which became much reduced in the 15th century. But, above all, Basle had a commercial port that served the German states, France and Italy, and ensured it considerable prosperity. From 1460, the city was home to a very active little university that supplied the book publishers with intellectuals to work for them. Beatus Rhenanus from Selestat lived there between 1511 and 1528, and became proof reader to printers Amerbach and Froben. He rubbed shoulders with Erasmus there. Even before the Reforma-

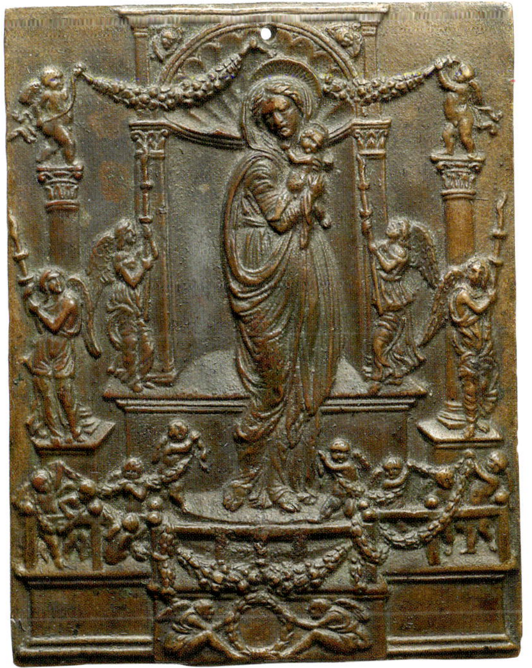

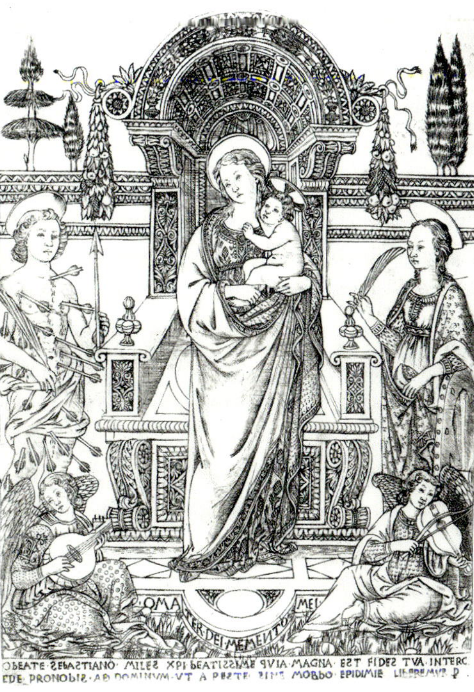

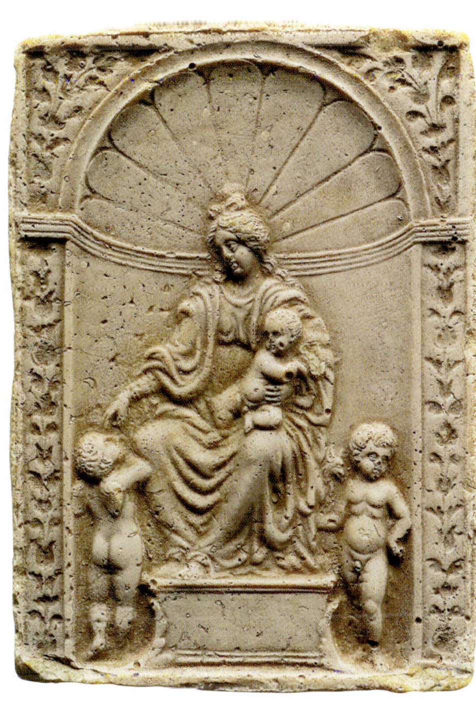

Cat X.13
VIRGIN MARY WITH INFANT JESUS AND ANGELS
Ferrara, *c.* 1475

Cat X.15
VIRGIN AND CHILD STANDING BEFORE THE THRONE WITH ST SEBASTIAN AND ST CATHERINE
Baccio Baldini, Florence, c. 1480–90

Cat X.14
VIRGIN MARY ENTHRONED WITH THE INFANT JESUS
Casting after a bronze by Moderno, c. 1500

tion officially began, the printers were able to guess the range of texts that would be in demand. The resulting product was a work of art in terms of business sense, of good taste and of European openness. Works produced often possessed strong institutional or ideological potential: religious books, such as missals, intended for many Germanic bishoprics, but also short confessional pamphlets that were often not illustrated, produced at minimal cost. Some, in Latin, effortlessly appealed to the whole of Latin-speaking Europe. Others were targeting a readership that was essentially Germanic, but more compact. From 1517, Luther's Reformation would be one of the best promoters of the print trade – to such a point that its expansion would have been unthinkable without the invention of printing. When Luther sent his letter to Cardinal Albrecht von Brandenburg, and accompanied it with the 'Ninety Five Theses' against Rome (31 October 1517), he posted up these same theses the same day in Wittenberg. Knowing the power of the printing press, he sent some copies of them to Nuremberg, capital of the Empire, to Leipzig and to Basle, two printing towns. He would say later that these theses were read throughout the Empire within two weeks. Even if he was a few days out in his calculations, his pride betrays the respect he accorded to the new technology. Basle reprinted the theses before December. Zealots distributed a storm of pamphlets, some of which were published with a print run of almost 100,000 copies. Another godsend for the printers was that Lutheran doctrine attributed a crucial function to the reading of the Bible – the faithful should reject the Vulgate of St

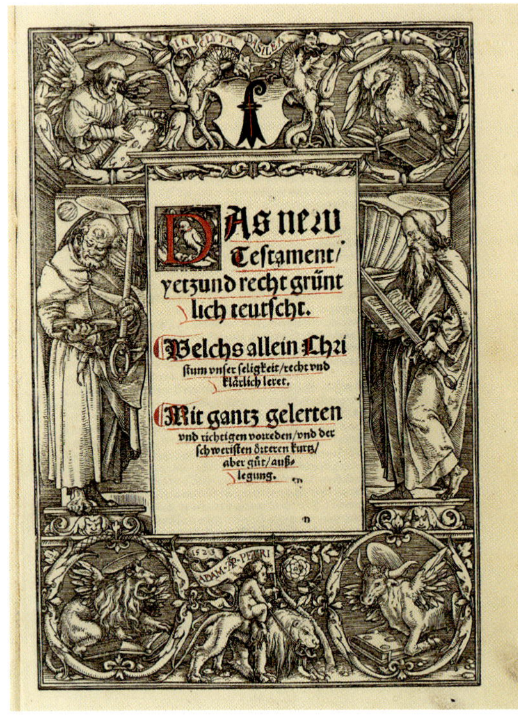

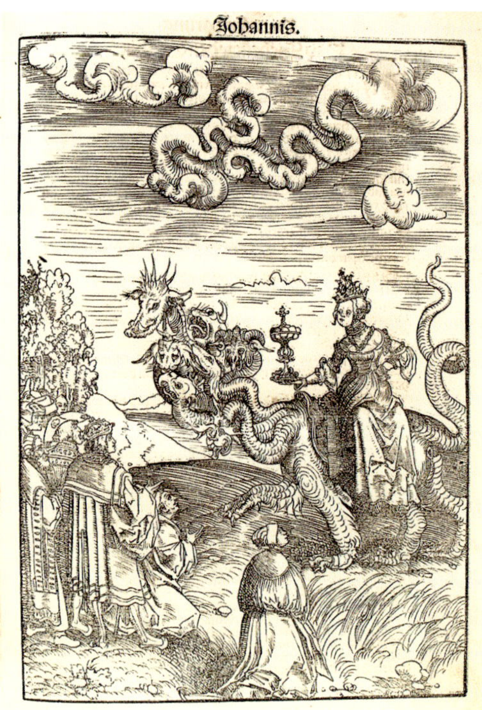

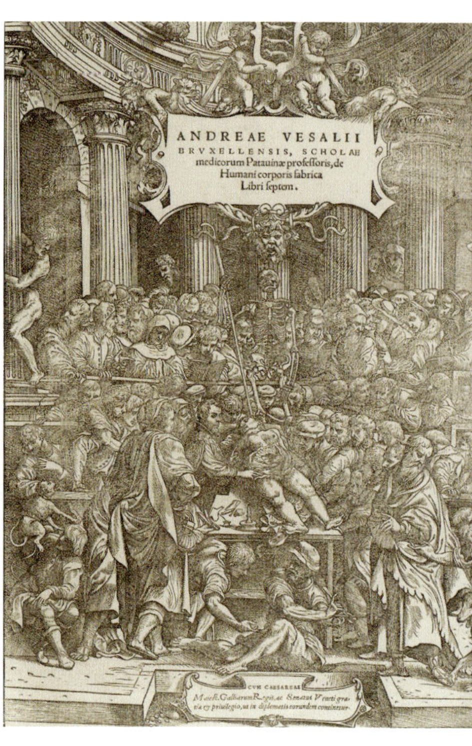

Cat X.18
MARTIN LUTHER, *DAS NEW TESTAMENT YETZUND RECHT GRÜNTLICH TEUTSCHT*
Printed in Basle by Adam Petri, 1522 (actually 1523)

Jerome and the interpretation of the Fathers of the Church, and return to study the sacred text in its native freshness: '*sola scriptura*'. At the end of a silent, meditative reading, the Christian assimilates the divine word into his or her body. Christ, beyond time, seems to speak to him through his New Testament. Collective reading aloud as a family or group became ritualized. Translating the Bible, presentation of selected texts, commenting on it – all these tasks then became a major theological matter and opened up a vast market for the production of Bibles. The Reform became Basle's official religion in 1529. But, from 1520, the authorities of the town had authorized printers to publish Lutheran texts – at their own risk. The print shops were eager to plunge into this breach as it would assure them some highly profitable sales. Luther's Bible published in Wittenberg[X.17] (1522), was snapped up so quickly that five thousand copies found purchasers in just a few weeks. The Basle printers could not leave such a golden opportunity to their Germanic competitors: they forged a counterfeit version of this Bible the following month but it would appear without Luther's name on it between December 1522 and January 1523[X.18]. The title page, drawn by Holbein, was guarded by St Peter and St Paul, as if to lend an air of orthodoxy to the text. This was a skilful masterpiece, characteristic of Swiss caution in business. The second type of work available was the scientific book – first and foremost, accurate editions of Greek and Latin texts, collated from the best manuscripts. These products, exportable throughout Christendom, ensured substantial revenue, even if the printers did

Cat X.17
MARTIN LUTHER, *DAS NEUE TESTAMENT DEUTSCH* (KNOWN AS THE SEPTEMBER TESTAMENT)
Wittenberg, printed by Melchior Lotter the Younger, 1522

Cat X.16
ANDREA VESALIUS, *DE HUMANI CORPORIS FABRICA LIBRI SEPTEM*
Basle, printed by Johannes Oporinus, 1543

invest heavily in quality: philologists to prepare the texts, learned proof readers, careful typesetting, use of ancient, faithful manuscripts and illustrations by skilled artists all ensured that these publications would find an eager readership in the city. Well-to-do people, owing their fortune to their education and talents, appreciated the luxury of these beautiful printed books. The value added by the book was high. Printing costs fell while the selling price remained elevated. In his famous memoirs, physician Thomas Platter recounts that Ruprecht Winter, the brother-in-law of Oporinus, the famous producer of the Basle Vesalius of 1543 [X.16], had a wife who dreamed of marrying a printer, a guarantee of domestic wealth. In Mainz, Gutenberg and the pioneers of the new technology had experienced ruin. In Basle, their grandsons had struck gold.

VITRUVIUS AND VITRUVIANISM IN EUROPE

The development of architecture in Europe between the 16th and 19th centuries can be understood only if we have an accurate understanding of the history of the book. The theory of classical architecture was first set out on the basis of a treatise, that of an architect in the first century BC. His name was Vitruvius. Quite apart from the numerous references to him, in particular in the *Speculum maius*, Vitruvius' treatise was known throughout the Middle Ages – there are still, in public collections, 92 manuscript versions dated between the 8th and the 15th centuries [X.20]. But what the printed book would bring to Vitruvius was both a figurative hermeneutic and widespread distribution.

The *De architectura libri decem* cover all aspects of architecture and the profession of architect and offer a standardized definition of the classical orders. It is striking to note the degree to which Vitrivius sought constantly to find, behind the architectural forms that he presented, an original matrix in nature: the source of the Corinthian column was a basket covered with acanthus leaves etc. He considered that all forms of architecture had their roots in nature. Basing architecture on its primitive forms in this way, he showed the point to which they were born of necessity. Vitruvius therefore considered that the point of departure for architecture was a moral principle – such as we find among the classics and their direct heir, Winckelmann.

In the 15th century, as in the Middle Ages, a good number of specialist Latin terms used by Vitruvius were hardly understood any longer. Moreover, none of the illustrations that the author apparently considered to be an essential part of his book had been preserved. Only archaeological knowledge of the ancient monuments could enlighten a reading of the Vitruvian text, and correct false readings of it. This is the tricky problem that faced architects of the Quattrocento and Cinquecento. The *De architectura* provided them with a historical reference,

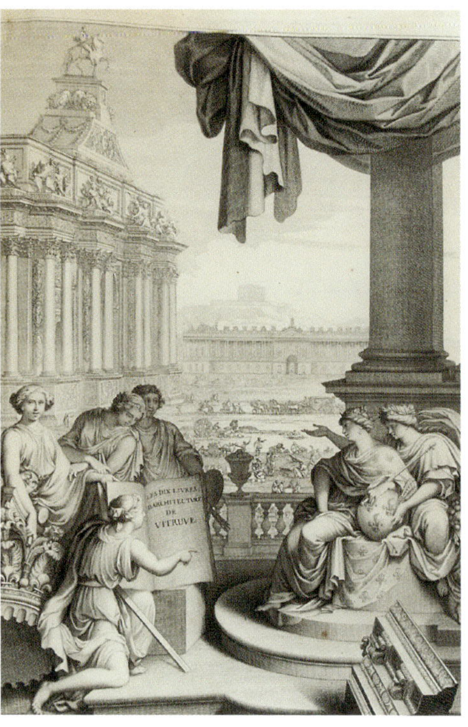

Cat X.25
LES DIX LIVRES D'ARCHITECTURE DE VITRUVE, CORRIGEZ ET TRADUITS NOUVELLEMENT EN FRANÇOIS, AVEC DES NOTES ET DES FIGURES
Edition and translation by Claude Perrault, Paris, Coignard, 1673

a sort of canonical legitimacy, but, at the same time, how could new architecture be developed on such fragile philological bases?

It was therefore a philological work that started the 15th century editing of the text of the Roman architect. The first edition was that by Giovanni Sulpicio di Veroli published in 1486 (?)[X.21]; the second edition was dated 1495 or 1496[X.22]. They were not illustrated. But the basic philological editing was carried out by Fra Giovanni Giocondo and published in Venice in 1511[X.23]. It was also the first illustrated edition. It is true that these illustrations were still very unpolished, but they bear witness to this need to harmonize the knowledge of antiquaries and a critical reading of the text that was felt by the men of the early 1500s.

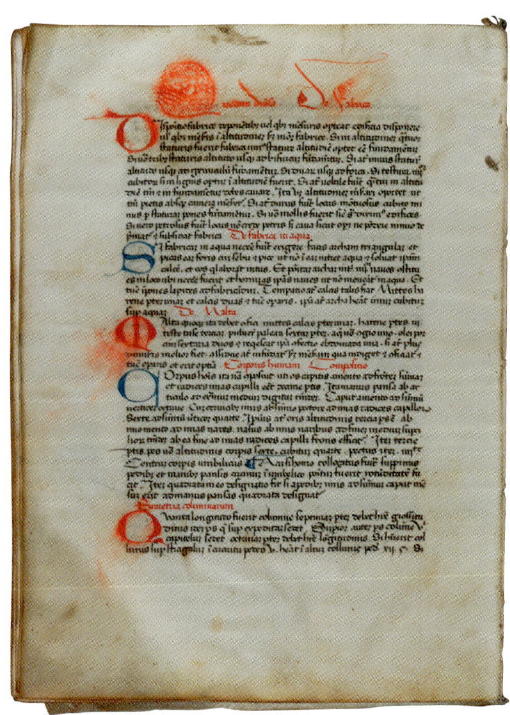

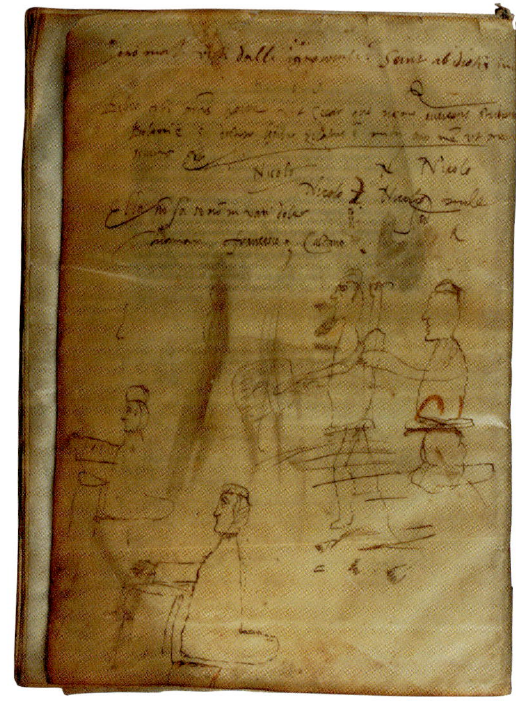

Cat X.20
MANUSCRIPT OF VITRUVIUS
c. 1390

Cat X.21
[DE ARCHITECTURA LIBRI DECEM]
Untitled, unillustrated edition by Giovanni Sulpicio di Veroli, Rome (?)

Cat X.22
CLEONIDAE HARMONICUM INTRODUCTORIUM INTERPRETE GEORGIO VALLA. L. VITRUVII POLLIONIS DE ARCHITECTURA LIBRI DECEM
Unillustrated edition, Venice, 'per Simonem Papiensem dictum Bivilaquam', 1497

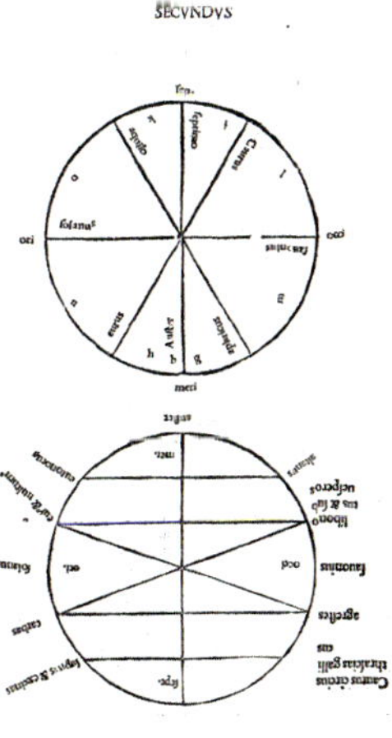

A pupil of Bramante, painter and architect in Milan, Cesare Cesariano edited the first Italian translation of Vitruvius, which he illustrated in 1521 [X.24]. A volume of 360 pages with a print run of 1300 copies, the beautiful engravings of which reformulated, in a disciplined language respectful of the norms, those that Fra Giocondo had provided. Trained on the building site of the Milan Duomo, which dated back in its architectural tradition to the Gothic construction yards north of the Alps, Cesariano considered specifically the role played by the circle in the definition of the proportions of the cathedral, next to the equilateral triangle and the square. Cesariano thus practised a historical hermeneutic, opening up to some extent the interpretation of Vitruvius into a very wide perspective, which his subsequent commentators would not always respect.

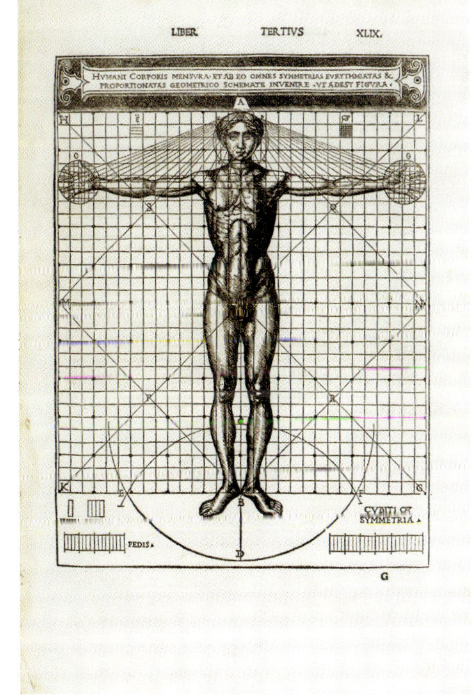

Cat X.24
DI LUCIO VITRUVIO POLLIONE DE ARCHITECTURA LIBRI DECEM TRADUCTI DE LATINO IN VULGARE AFFIGURATI, COMMENTATI (...)
Edition illustrated by Cesare Cesariano, Como, Gottardus da Ponte, 1521

Translations into the vernacular did not follow in a systematic manner. From 1547, the first, inaccurate attempt at a translation into French was made by Jean Martin, but if there is one translation that marked the destiny of classical architecture, it must be that published by Claude Perrault in 1673 [X.25]. The critical apparatus that he inserted into the book, admirably illustrated, formed a sort of treatise within a treatise. It was Colbert who commissioned physiologist Claude Perrault to undertake this

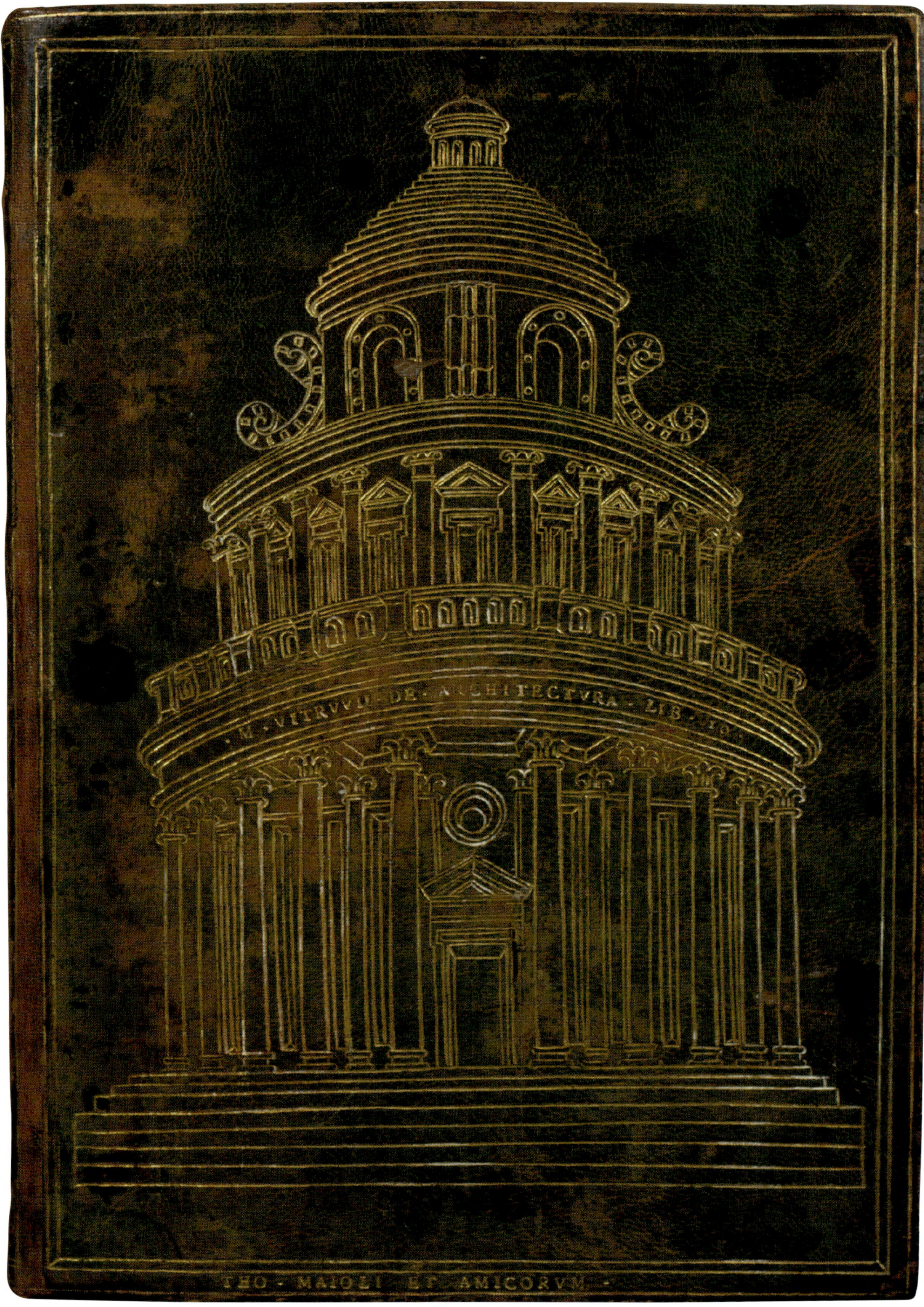
· M · VITRUVII · DE · ARCHITECTVRA · LIB · 10 ·
THO · MAIOLI ET AMICORVM ·

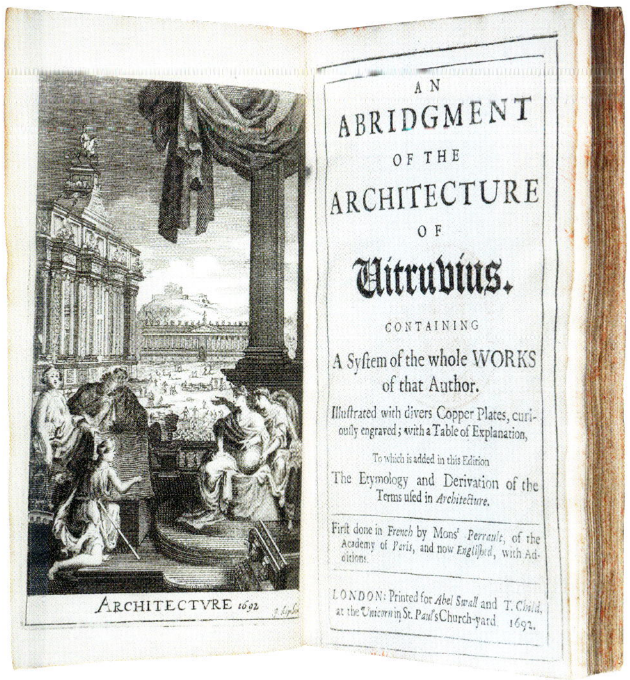

translation in 1664. This was the same year in which the famous colonnade of the Louvre was built, marking the triumph of Classicism. It was this colonnade that figured on the frontispiece of the 1673 edition, showing that the translation and, in particular, its notes, which together form a theory, were aimed at influencing the architecture of the reign of Louis XIV to whom the book is dedicated.

The Frenchman Guillaume Philandrier had published, in Rome in 1544, his *Annotationes in Vitruvium* (in Latin), which the German Walter Ryff would take into account in his translation of Vitruvius printed in Nuremberg in 1548 **X.29**. Ryff, or Rivius, was a physician and a mathematician, in touch with the most up-to-date works, as is shown by his knowledge of Philandrier and of Serlio, whose first two books appeared in 1545. Later commentators would indeed take note of the work of Philandrier, who combined a high philological exactness with an attention to architectural hermeneutic – he had an excellent knowledge of the architecture of Rome. It is apparent that the text did not circulate just among antiquaries and architects. It was the subject of learned commentaries and was also read for its relevance to the requirements of contemporary architecture.

Cat X.26
AN ABRIDGEMENT OF THE ARCHITECTURE OF VITRUVIUS (...) ILLUSTRATED (...)
London, printed by Abel Swall and T. Child, 1692

The English waited for a long time before reading Vitruvius in their own language: the 1692 translation was based on that by Perrault **X.26**. They were familiar with the five Classical orders on account of an elegant little in-octavo by Sir Henry Wotton, which appeared in 1624, or of the first English book devoted to the orders by John Shute (1563). It was above all the knowledge of architecture and the treatise by Andrea Palladio that would familiarize England with the use of the Classical orders. And it would be the *Vitruvius Britannicus* (1715–25) by Colen Campbell that would spread English Palladianism across Europe.

It was by the practice of architecture and by painstaking surveys of ancient monuments that Sebastiano Serlio undertook his great work: seven books that would appear in instalments, published in Venice, one of the most active and remarkable centres of the printing industry. The first publication, in 1537, that of Book IV under the title of *Regole generali di architettura*, was devoted to columns and dedicated to the king of France François I. It would enjoy such success that it was quickly translated into Flemish, German and French. The same applied to his

< Cat X.23
M. VITRUVIUS, PER JOCUNDUM SOLITO CASTIGATIOR FACTUS, CUM FIGURIS ET TABULA UT JAM LEGI ET INTELLIGI POSSIT
First illustrated edition, printed by Johannes de Tacuino, Venice, 1511

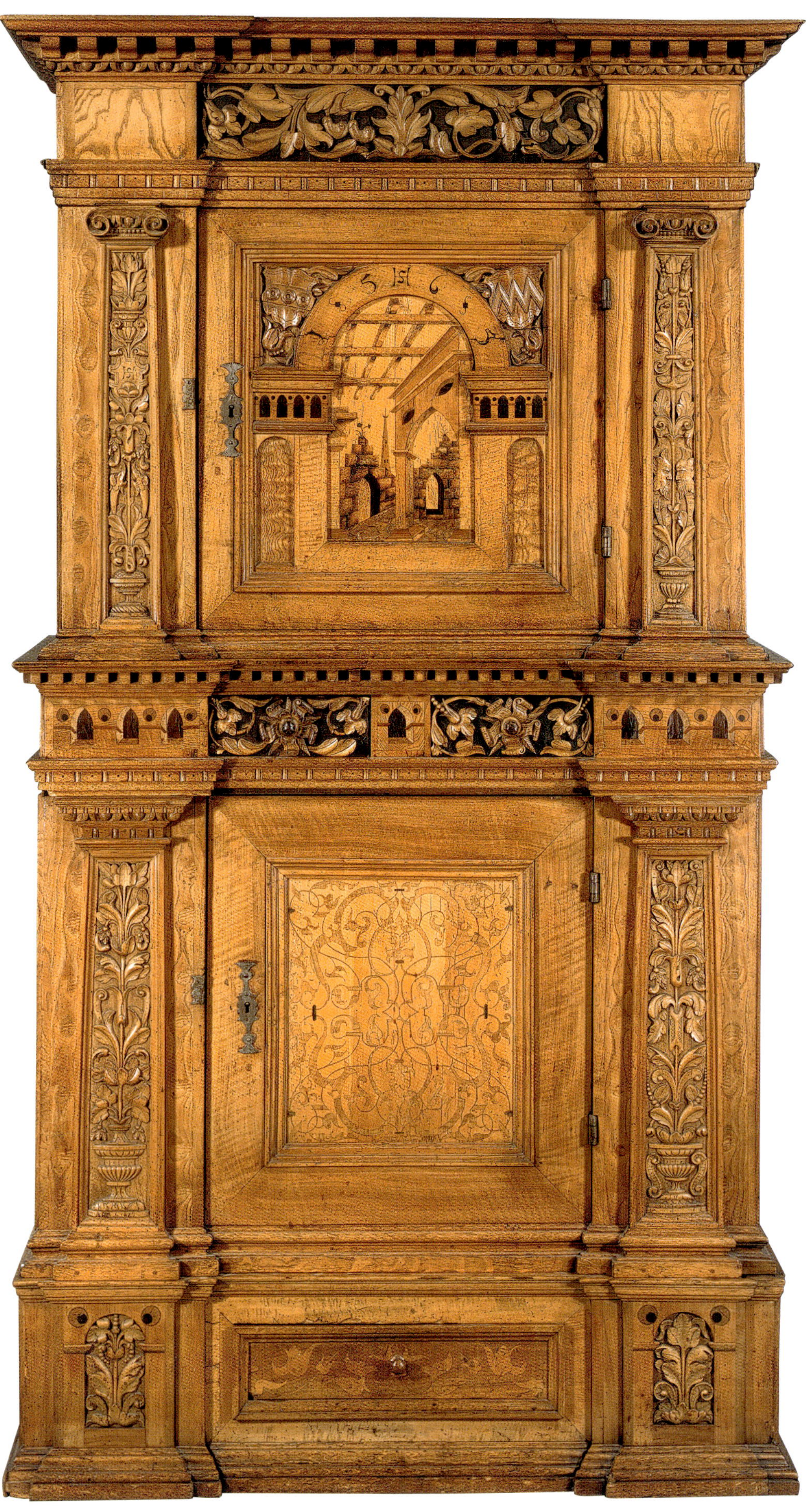

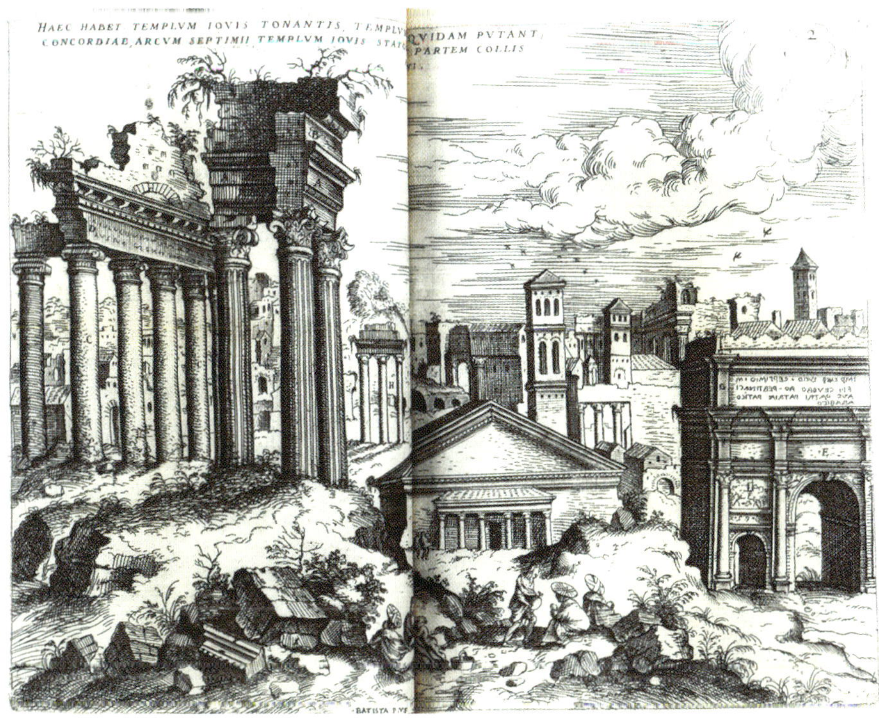

Cat X.37
VINCENZO SCAMOZZI: ***DISCORSI SOPRA L'ANTIQUITA DI ROMA***
Venice, F. Ziletti, 1583

other books. They were exactly in line with the requirements of their architect readership, but also those of connoisseurs across Europe who wanted to know, precisely and clearly, what Vitruvius had passed on to them in ambiguous form. The publications of Jacopo Barozzi, known as Vignole, would play a similar role a generation later – his *Regola delli cinque ordini di architettura*, dated 1562. The book by Joost Vermaarsch that appeared in 1664 in Leyden was a compendium combining knowledge from the reading of Vitruvius, Vignole and Scamozzi[X.33].

The reduction of Vitruvius to the question of the Classical orders was therefore in response to a practical need. The short treatise on the columns that Pieter Coecke van Aelst published in Antwerp in 1539[X.30] was also known by the name of the 'little Vitruvius'. He compiled concepts drawn from Vitruvius, from the commentary of Cesariano and from the *Medidas del Romano de Diego de Sagredo* (Toledo, 1526), which had familiarized Spanish readers with the Roman antiquities and the orders. Miguel de Urrea and Juan Gracian had translated Vitruvius into Spanish only in 1582[X.32], while in Poland architects continued to read the treatise in Latin or Italian versions. Only the pages devoted to the theory of architecture were inserted in a treatise on agronomy by Pierre de Crescens dating from the 14th century and published in Poland in 1549[X.31].

Daniele Barbaro was one of the principal humanists of the mid-16th century. Having published Aristotle, he undertook a new translation of Vitruvius in 1547, before ever entering into contact with Palladio. Nine years of work would

< Cat X.28
TWIN CABINET
1565

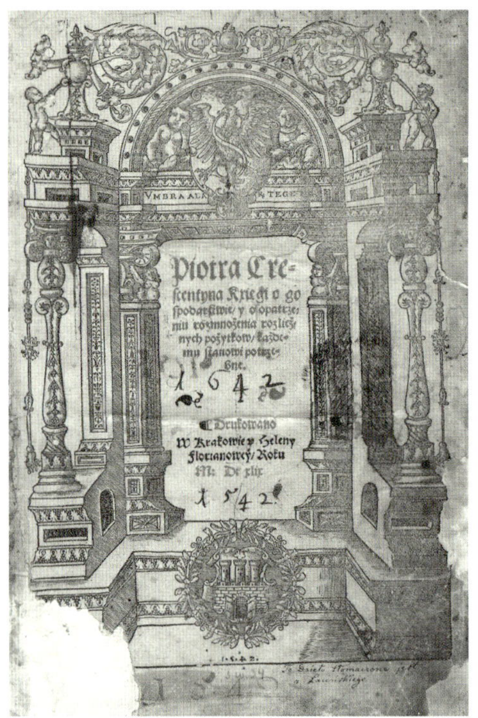

Cat X.31
P. DE CRESCENTIIS, *KSIEGI O GOSPODARSTWIE*
Translated by A. Trzyciski, 1549

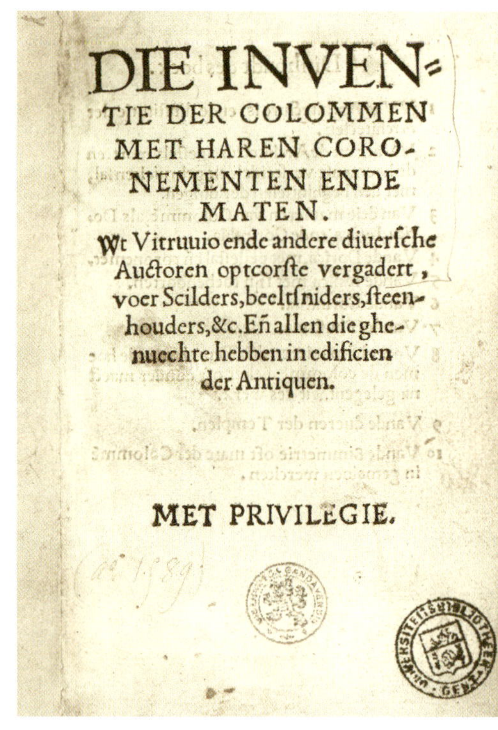

DIE INVENTIE DER COLOMMEN MET HAREN CORONEMENTEN ENDE MATEN.
Wt Vitruuio ende andere diuersche Auctoren optcorste vergadert, voer Scilders, beeltsniders, steenhouders, &c. Eñ allen die ghenuechte hebben in edificien der Antiquen.

MET PRIVILEGIE.

Cat X.30
PIETER COECKE VAN AELST, *DIE INVENTIE DER COLOMMEN MET HAREN CORONEMENTEN ENDE MATEN (...)*
Antwerp, 1539

give rise to the most beautiful and scholarly edition of Vitruvius ever published[X.27]. His illustrations were based on the drawings of Palladio but also his commentaries seem to be the fruit of passionate discussions between the two men, who had known one another since 1550. At the same time, Palladio was preparing a treatise, the first books of which appeared in 1570 – *I quattro libri*

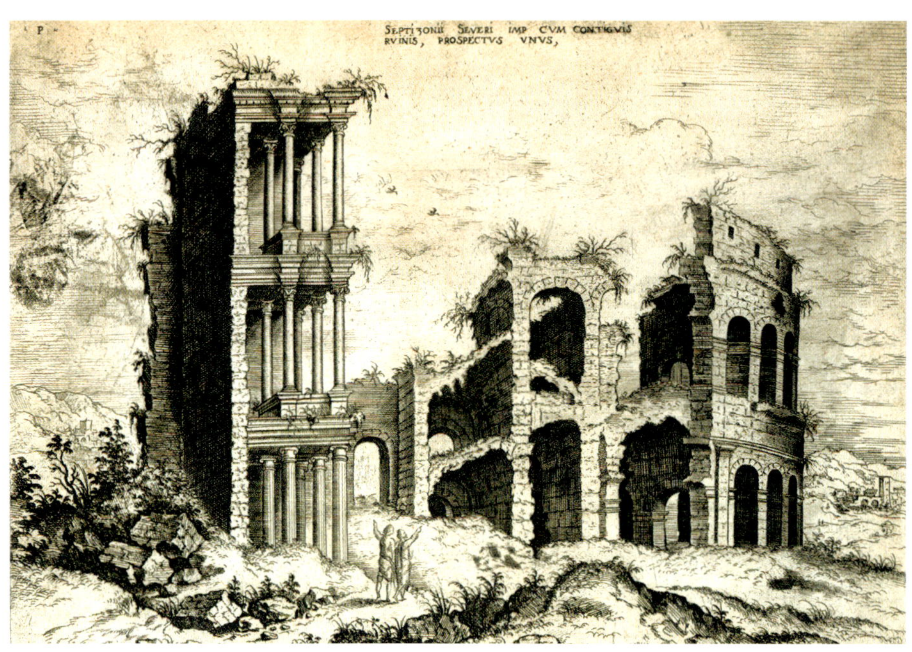

Cat X.38
HIERONYMUS COCK, *PRAECIPUAE ALIQUOT ROMANAE ANTIQUITATIS RUINARUM MONUMENTA*
1551

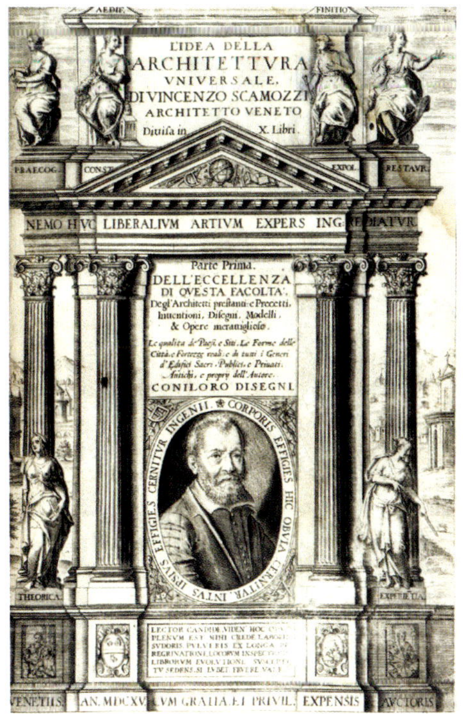

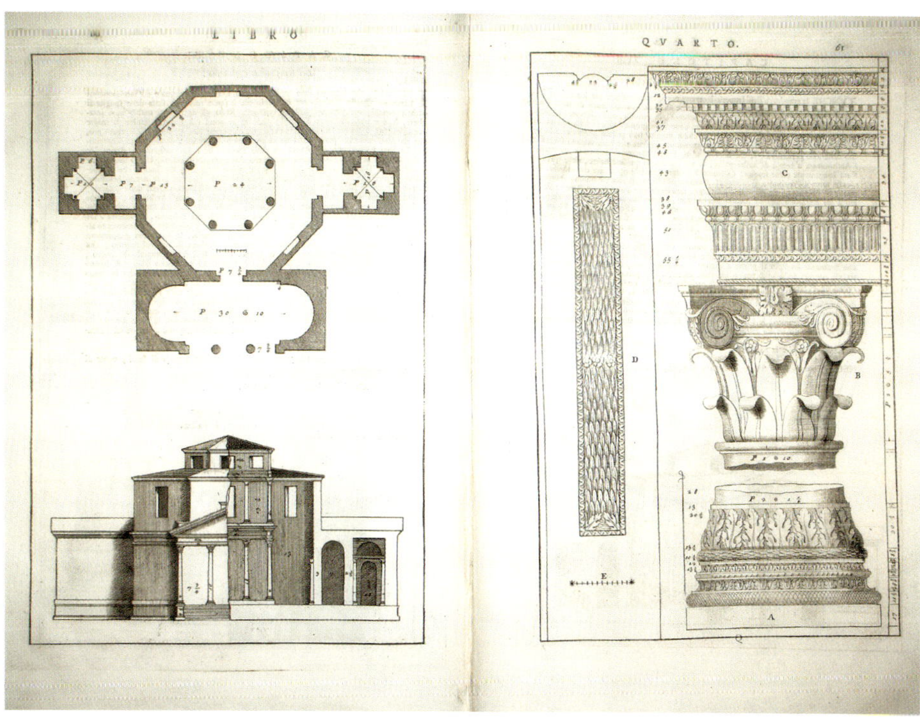

Cat X.32
VITRUVIUS,
DE ARCHITECTURA
Spanish translation by Miguel de Urrea, Alcala de Henares, 1582

dell'architettura[X.36]. This was just the start of a very ambitious project, which would be interrupted by the architect's death. But the success of these four books was immense on a European scale, particularly in England. The surveys of Roman monuments were assembled by Palladio in order to give the reader an idea of architecture's greatest feats. The measurements of columns and entablatures are more accurate than in the text of Vitruvius. It is on these that all of modern architecture would be based. In a concise and clear language, he describes his own experience and his work as an architect as an example of continuity in the antique tradition.

The character of Vincenzo Scamozzi asserts itself first as that of an intellectual and '*cittadino del mondo*', as he described himself – a citizen of the world. It was not just his travels in Hungary, Bohemia, Poland, Germany, France and Switzerland, nor his knowledge of many Italian towns such as Venice, Rome and Florence, that gave him his European stature. It was above all the clarity and intelligibility with which he was able to place architectural models before the reader with illustrations of them, from his knowledge of published and unpublished treatises by Giorgio di Martini and Filarete. His *Discorsi sopra l'architettura di Roma* appeared in 1581 – we exhibit here the unamended edition of 1583[X.37]. Comparing one plate from this book with another, thirty years older, attributed to Hieronymus Cock[X.38], we see the degree to which Scamozzi's observation bears witness to a concern for discipline combined with a sense of setting.

Cat X.36
ANDREA PALLADIO,
I QUATTRO LIBRI DELL'ARCHITETTURA
Venice, Domenico de Franceschi, 1570 (actually, Venice, Giambattista Pasquali for Consul Joseph Smith)

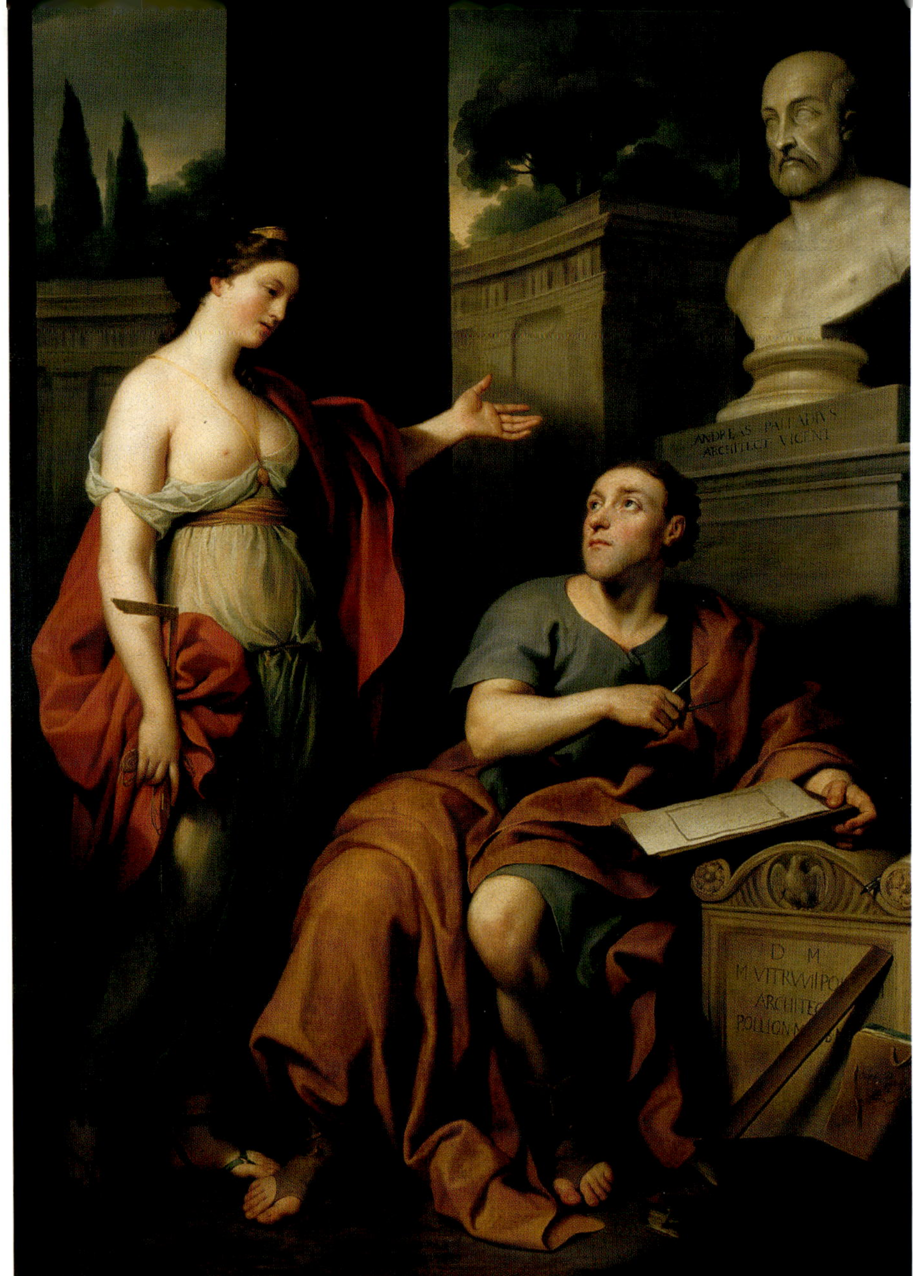

Cat X.35
PORTRAIT OF JAMES CAULFIELD, LORD CHARLEMONT
Anton Raphael Mengs, 1756

The other outstanding work by Scamozzi is his *Idea della architettura universale* **X.39**, which appeared in 1615. The frontispiece indicates the intellectual stance of Scamozzi who, as a '*liberalium artium expers*', says that he devoted twenty-five years of his life to this book, which he published at his own expense: at the centre we see the portrait of the architect and a neoplatonic inscription makes a distinction between '*corporis effigies*' and '*intus effigies*', i.e. between theory and experience. To his mind, architecture is a science elevated above all the arts and all the sciences by reason of its moral dimension.

The order of Vitruvius and Vitruvianism also strongly influenced cabinetmakers in the 16th and 17th century, as can be seen in the fine twin cabinet of Zurich **X.28**.

BIBLIOGRAPHY: G. Germann, *Einführung in die Geschichte der Architekturtheorie*, Darmstadt, 1980; H.-W. Kruft, *Geschichte der Architekturtheorie*, Munich, 1986; J. Guillaume (ed.), *Les traités d'architecture de la Renaissance*, Paris, 1988; M. Carpo, *L'architettura dell'età della stampa. Oralità, scrittura, libro stampato e riproduzioni meccanica dell'immagine nella storia delle teorie architettoniche*, Milan, 1998.

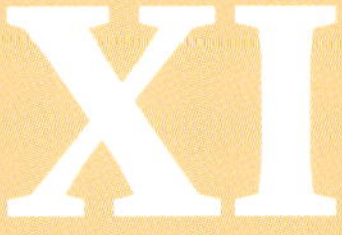

Prints in the service of arts and crafts

PASCAL GRIENER

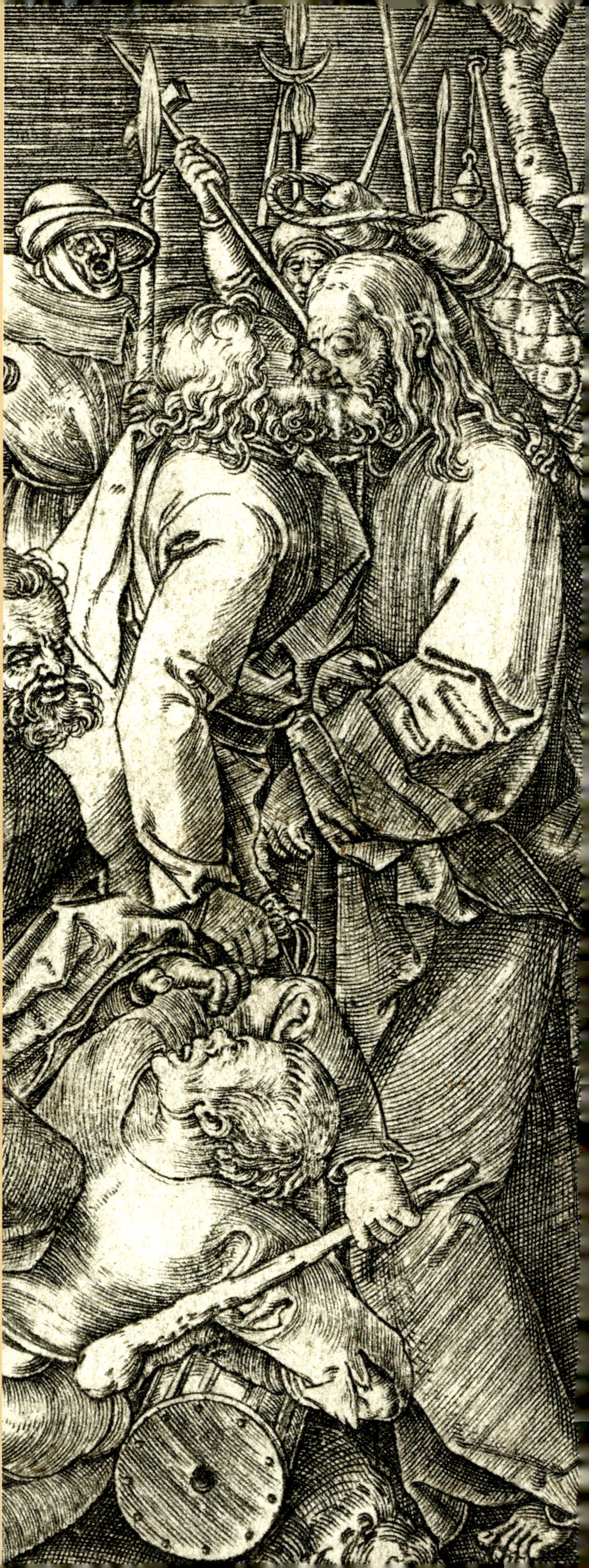

The history of art still places too little importance on the decorative arts and especially on the interaction between artistic practices. Craftsmen, drawings, engravings, patrons, even objects, all help expand or constrain the popularity of a motif. The present section will consider how those factors interact.

In the Renaissance, engraving made a huge contribution to improving the quality of the objects produced in workshops or factories. Etching, which took less time and was often less expensive than engraving with a burin, imposed itself as the best way of reproducing motifs. The production of plates and blocks burgeoned: a network of print sellers and publishers sprang up. Many engravers were former manufacturers, like the Sadelers, who abandoned damascening (the inlaying of precious metal threads into steel) for print making in about 1550 but succeeded in retaining a broad clientele of craftsmen that included many people besides lovers of fine prints. The modest price of prints ensured that their motifs proliferated quickly. We note the presence of plates and blocks in many workshops: as a rule these were single sheets, or were tied into a bundle with a piece of string. They were reprinted according to demand, the latest products being attached to older ones. More rarely, they were bound into an album. These plates circulated throughout Europe, from Venice to Frankfurt, from Paris to London or Prague, from Augsburg to Transylvania. Print makers were still poorly protected and the dissemination of their plates in itself constantly exposed them to forgery.

When, in 1506, Albrecht Dürer sued Marcantonio Raimondi for forging his engraved woodblocks, the courts of Venice settled only the question of the signature, not the principle of forgery. The privileges of printing, eagerly sought after, gave scarcely any protection against forgeries produced far away. In France, royal licence dates only from 1672. Generally, engraving workshops tried to expand their offer to every kind of buyer to boost their sales. When they could, they would buy the woodblocks or copper plates of their bankrupt competitors and would go as far as re-signing plates that they had played no part at all in making. Jacques Androuet du Cerceau was one of the first engravers and a large-scale publisher of plates as from the 1540s. The families of engraver-publishers travelled: Jan Sadeler pursued his career in Venice, while staying in touch with his family, who had remained in Antwerp.

Lastly, it should be emphasized that craftsmen often used their models after striving to compile a collection. When in 1765 the printer Charles Antoine Jombert published his *Repertoire of Artists or Collection of Architectural Compositions and Ancient and Modern Ornaments of All Kinds*, he addressed it to both craftsmen and print enthusiasts. More than one Renaissance plate continued to be used as a source of inspiration until the 18th century, bursting the restraints of a traditional history of styles.

< Cat XI.15
THE KISS OF JUDAS
(detail)
Albrecht Dürer, 1508

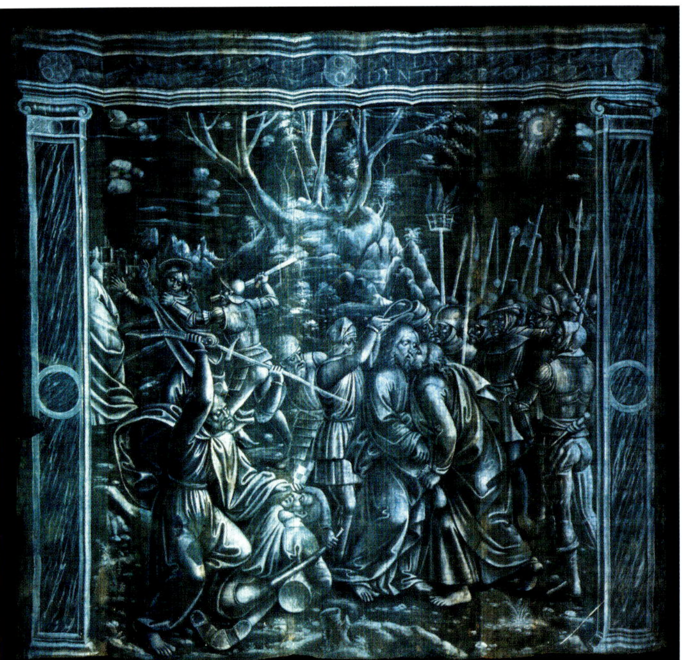

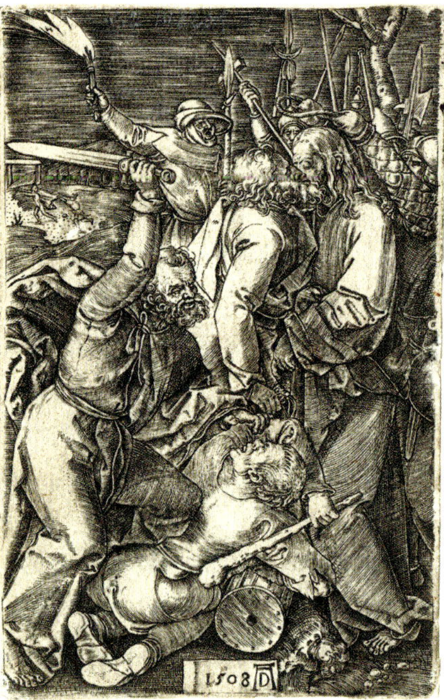

Cat XI.14
THE ARREST OF CHRIST
Unknown painter (Teramo Piaggio?), Lombardy, 1515–25

Cat XI.15
THE KISS OF JUDAS
Albrecht Dürer, 1508

the Renaissance: understanding a foreign motif then came down to transforming it. The Milanese damasceners had no hesitation in altering the Flemish models they selected to decorate their armour: Such motifs were adapted to fulfil the requirements of steel bas-relief [XI.18,19] and such subjects underwent a more profound change: from Samson fighting the lion in the vineyards of Thimna, the craftsman created… Hercules fighting the Nemean lion! Lastly, a German maker of bread moulds, taking a depiction of Diana and Actaeon from an edition of Ovid's *Metamorphoses* produced in Frankfurt, did not know that it was a reversed reproduction of all the wood engravings of an earlier French edition [XI.24,25]. Here, the motif is not considered as an asset to be respected or a drawing to be slavishly copied, but as a virtual source of multiple narratives that goes far beyond its original meaning. From copy to copy, the image becomes enriched, is transformed: in short, is kept in the European imagination as the culmination of a veritable culture of copying. A group of fine, useful or luxury objects demonstrates the artistic wealth derived from the practice of borrowing.

Hampered as we are today by a rigid cult of originality, we find it hard to comprehend a creation that works through successive derivations and perversions, which thus help to keep a substrate of images alive through time. A Slovak silver tankard with fine bas-reliefs is a reworking of the leather decorations that were in vogue in Augsburg and Nuremberg [XI.20,21], disseminated by Virgile Solis, the century's greatest print maker in the German states. A sumptuous enamel box, once part of the treasure of the Esterhazy princes, is the work of Sebastian Hann, a brilliant Transylvanian craftsman who learned his trade from the best sources in Germany. The allegories that decorate the body of his box were inspired by Peter Flötner, but Hann integrated those scrolls into a flexible, organic and wholly

> Cat XI.12
BURIN-ENGRAVED SILVER BINDING
After two models: *The Christ of Sorrows* by Albrecht Dürer and *King David and his Harp* by Jan Sadeler, after 1645

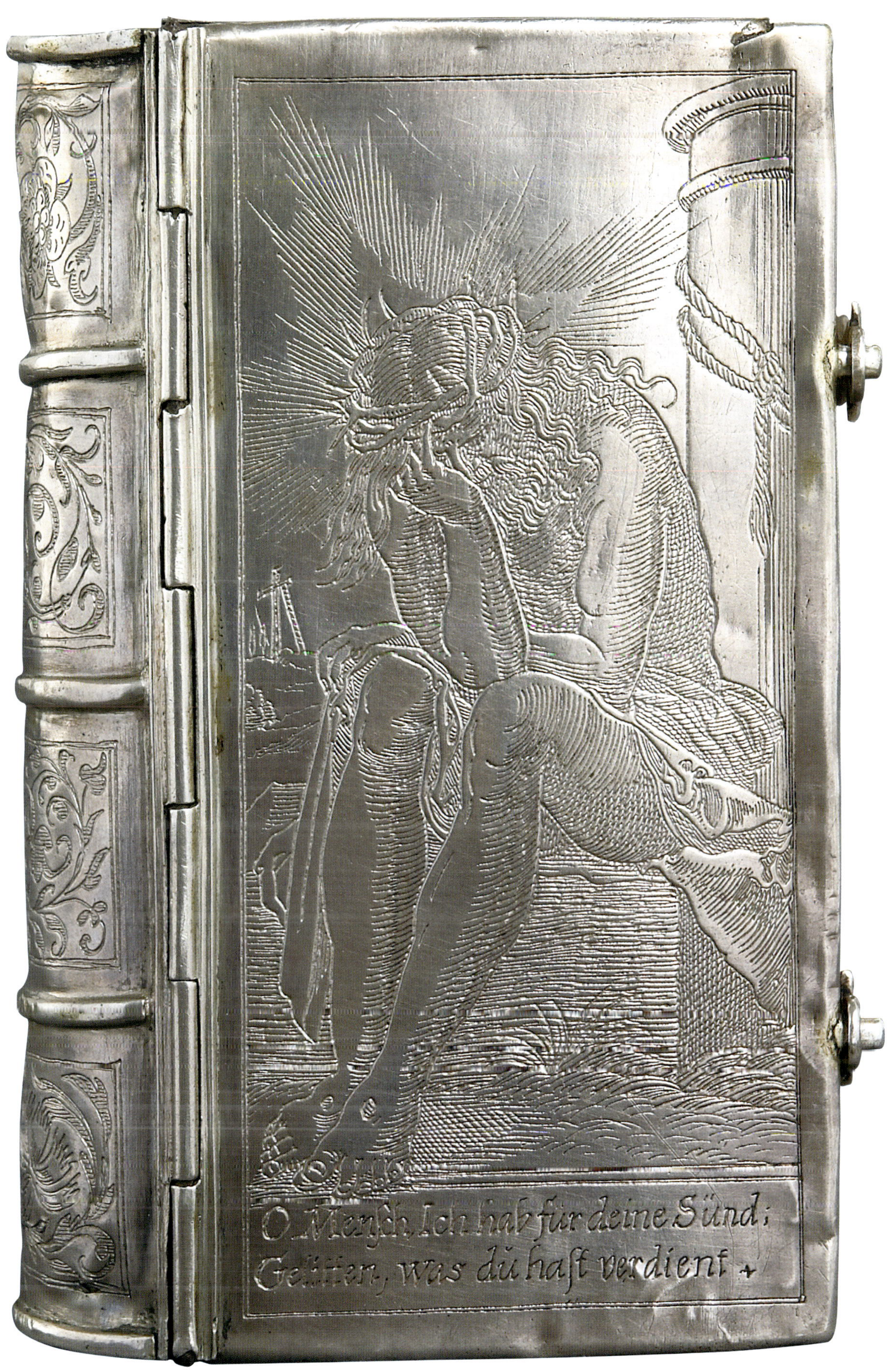
O Mensch, Ich hab für deine Sünd;
Gelitten, was du hast verdient +

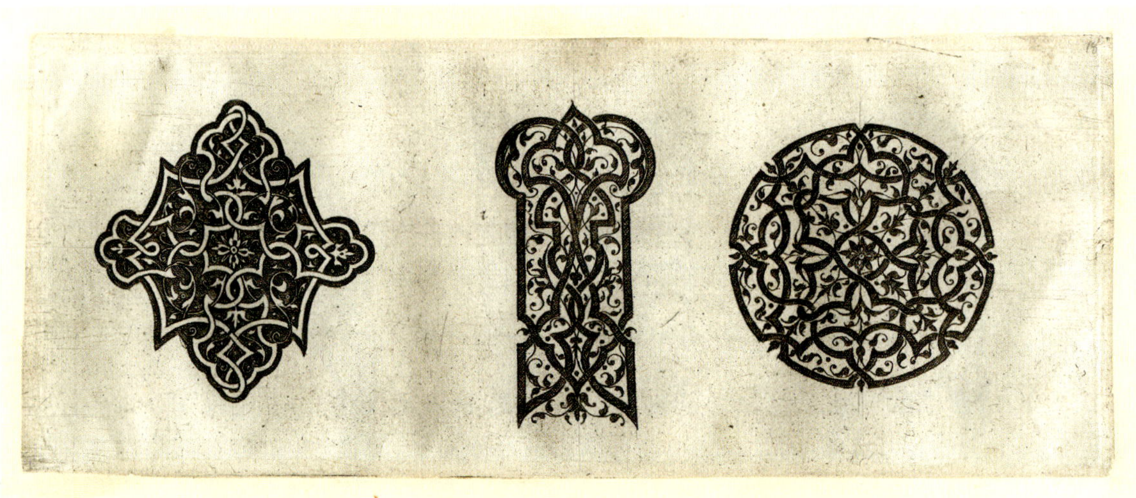

Cat XI.5
VARIARUM PROTACTIONUM QUAS VULGO MAURUSIAS VOCANT OMNIUM
Balthazar van den Bos (Balthazar Sylvius)
Paris edition, 1554

original design that made his name all over Europe [XI.22]. Other local craftsmen, such as Henri Gallot, preferred to imitate the perfection of a piece from Augsburg that they had seen in Switzerland. They used ornamental engravings only for the details of the motifs [XI.23].

A final sumptuous piece pays homage to the collaboration between learned men and craftsmen during the Renaissance. The great clock of Gerhart Emmoser [XI.27] is one of the most famous mechanisms to have survived. An imperial possession, it probably belonged to the Habsburg Emperor Maximilian II. Such masterpieces rely on an intense collaboration with an astronomer. Without printing, which

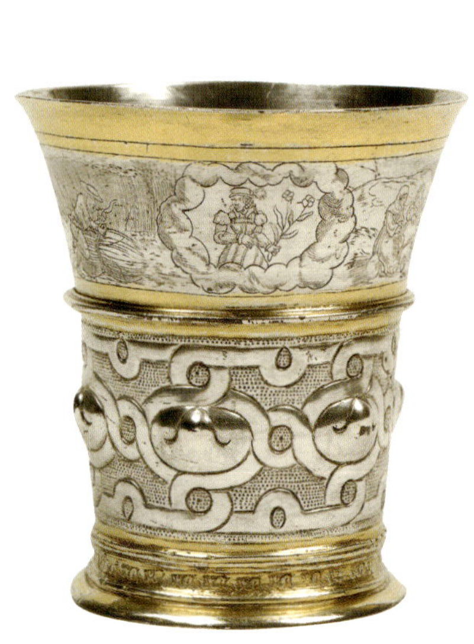

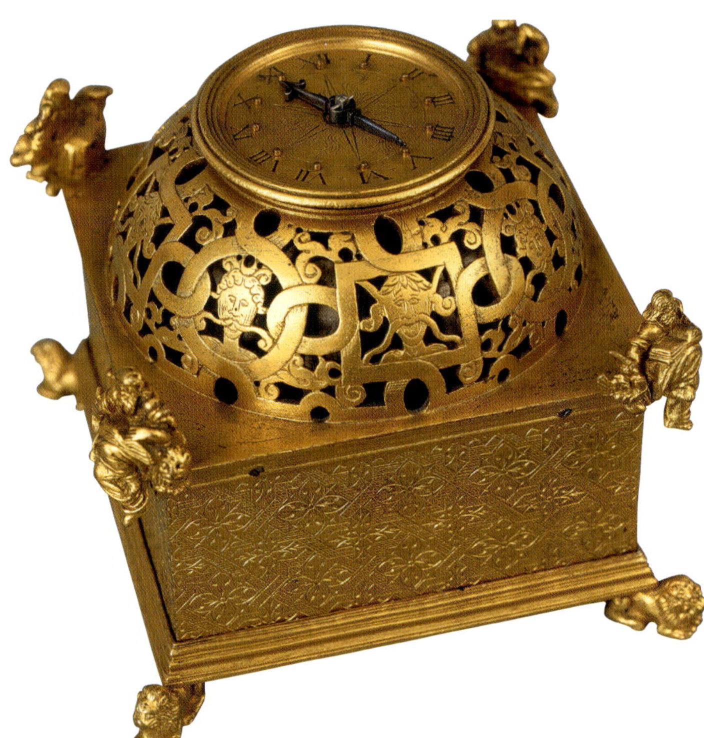

Cat XI.4
GOBLET
Thierry de Bry (alias Dietrich Brey), *c.* 1570

Cat XI.3
CHIMING TABLE CLOCK
16th century

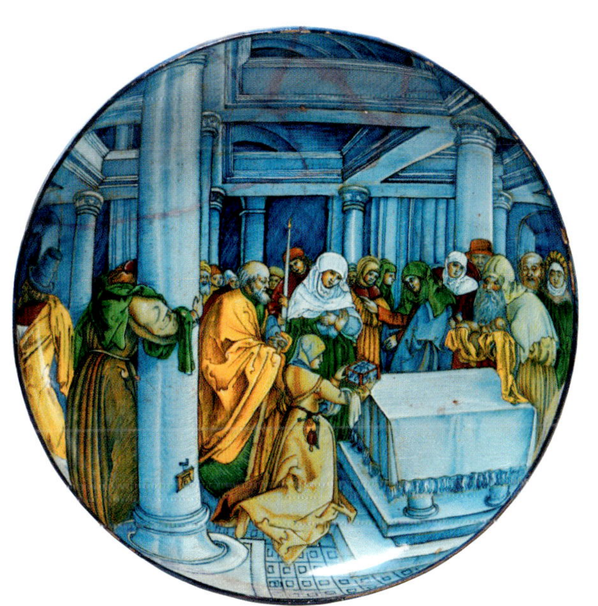

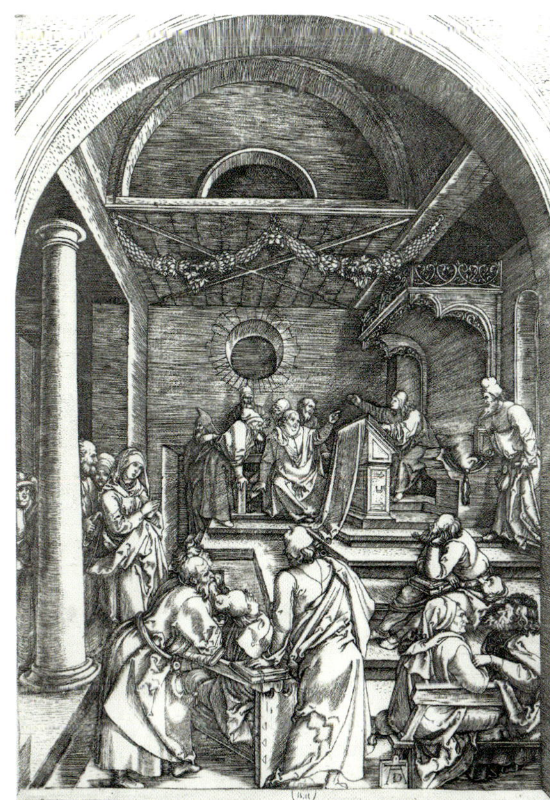

Cat XI.10
THE PRESENTATION IN THE TEMPLE
Master of the Assumption (attributed) after an engraving by Albrecht Dürer, *c.* 1520–25

Cat XI.11
THE PRESENTATION IN THE TEMPLE
Marcantonio Raimondi after Albrecht Dürer, *c.* 1506

produced scientific treatises, such production would have been impossible. On the sides of the gilded copper case, the craftsman has engraved two maps of Europe that celebrate the universality of the new way of measuring time. Their model was a somewhat out of date map, as if the creator had used all his scientific daring in preparing the complex mechanism. The formal source, a map by Pierre Apian, has been transmuted: from a cognitive model of a territory: it has become a simple emblem of Europe set to the exact time of day.

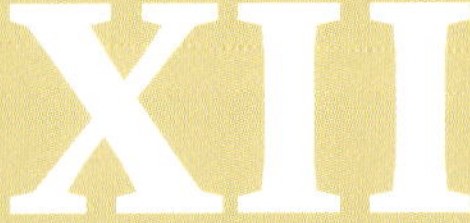

Perceptions of other worlds

PASCAL GRIENER

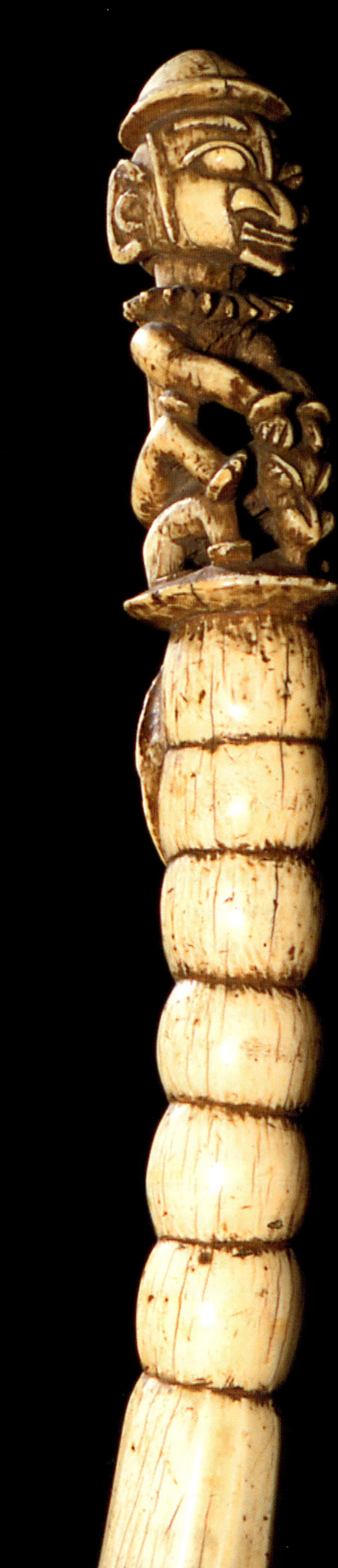

Since the Middle Ages, a taste for the exotic had never ceased to attract lovers of beautiful things with unusual shapes or functions and garnered in far-off lands: materials, ceramics, bronzes, rare plant and animal species were all circulating well before the Renaissance. One piece of travel literature, mostly fictitious, set all Europe dreaming: the *Itinerarius* of Sir John de Mandeville (14th century) bewitched readers with its wonderful, romantic – and suspect – descriptions. Two hundred years later, cultural icons like amulets or totems seem to have perpetuated this tradition; the emergence during the late 1500s of the Cabinet of Curiosities would provide a new showcase for *curiosa* from the East Indies, the Far East or the Americas.

Objects from Africa or the Americas soon began to occupy an important place at the heart of collections. Paradoxically, this continuing presence did not indicate any interest in the New Worlds – on the contrary, in fact. In Sebastian Münster's *Europe as a Queen*[XII.16], the allegorical image of an empire is almost pure Habsburg – witness the imperial crown, the regalia and the haughty presence of the sovereign standing between Asia and Africa. These details leave no doubt about the viewpoint dominating the *Cosmographia*, in support of which its author cites the authority of Ptolemy.

Colonial enterprises, motivated by the search for gold or the capture of commercial ports, often resulted in the destruction of entire cultures; from 1510, the first Africans were shipped to servitude in the Caribbean, instituting the grim Europe–Africa–America triangle of the slave trade at the cost of a barbarity that raised few objections until the 18th century.

The exotic nature of items from America or Africa very much encouraged the idea of a microcosm of the world assembled within a single 'cabinet' (collection room). Until the 1700s, the collection of exotica was part of an obsession with the encyclopaedic in a tradition traceable back to Pliny the Elder – the total truth about the world would emerge from a patient and cumulative series of descriptions. But above all, exotica satisfied the craving for the rare and the unique; in the 17th century, such importance was accorded to curiosities that all other consideration of an object was forgotten. Descriptions of geographical origins re-

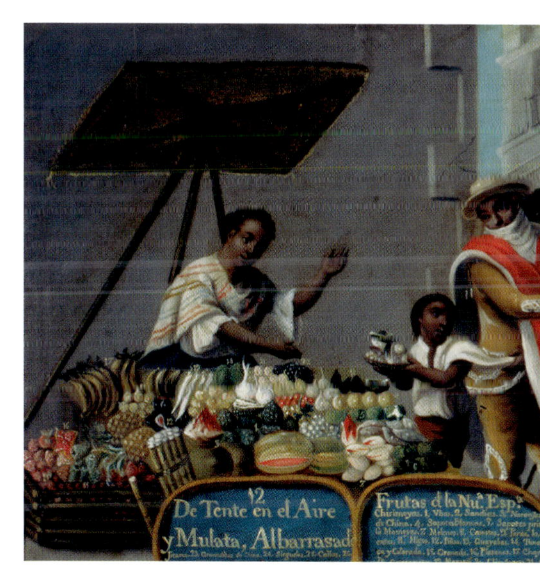

Cat XII.5
SERIES OF 16 *ESCENAS DE MESTIZAJE* ('12. DE TENTE EN EL AIRE Y MULATA, ALBARRASEDO')
Anonymous, 18th century

< Cat XII.7
HORN
Sierra Leone, before 1794

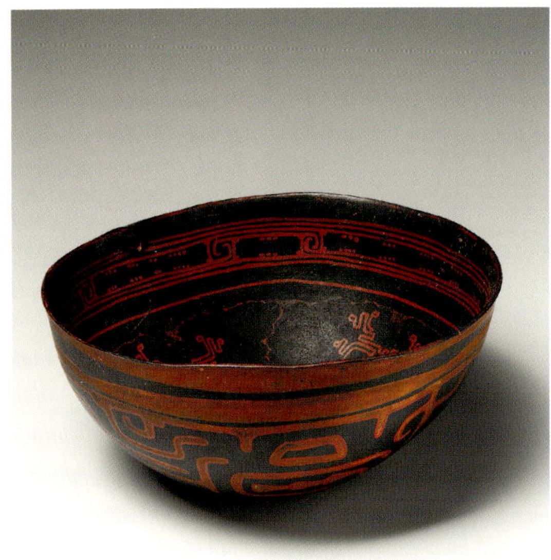

Cat XII.8
CONTAINER
Guyana, in Europe before 1789

tortures they inflicted on the African slaves under their heel; he became haunted by the dream of mutual friendship between peoples whose colonial past had yoked them together so disastrously. William Blake, the book's illustrator, found in it proof that an artist should rebel against any political authority attempting to subjugate him [XII.2]. Other observers, like Alejandro Malaspina, dreamed of reforming colonial despotism on a moral basis; but this ideal, typical of the Age of Enlightenment, was swiftly blocked [XII.6] by an administration concerned only with its immediate interests. Spanish settlement in Latin America was accompanied by strenuous efforts to separate colonizers from the indigenous peoples – in vain. In a short space of time intermarriage led to fears that sometimes surfaced in bizarre works of art: for instance, the series of Casta paintings that sought to classify all known types of mixed race, the better to regulate them. Spain of the Enlightenment was still a society of fixed social structure typical of the Old Order, where the notion of blood played a fundamental role [XII.3,4,5,9,10]. Classifying and listing racial differences was the result of an obsessive fear: contact with New Worlds risked blurring and imperilling the old distinctions. This spectre found expression in various branches of European painting – Dutch depictions of primitive man in a faraway paradise, Venetian- or French-style genre scenes or 'Street Cries', i.e. colourful snapshots of trades, as popular with the French capital as with the Queen of the Adriatic.

The history of relationships between Europe and the New Worlds is that of an interaction, for better or worse. This interaction can be judged by the wealth of objects produced to feed a vast network of exchanges; Portugal, for example, satisfied the European demand for exotica by causing suitable objects to be manufactured in its African colonies. The same kingdom commissioned superb Chinese porcelain, produced since the Renaissance for the export market [XII.13, 14, 15]. Its decoration combined traditional motifs with the arms of the King of Portugal, the armillary sphere, symbol of the thirst to discover – and possess – every region of the planet.

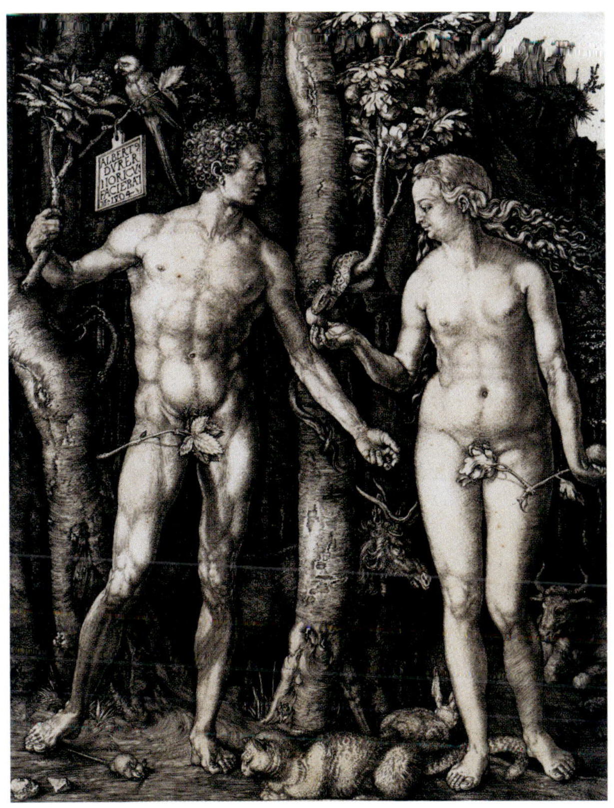

Cat XIII.1
ADAM AND EVE
Albrecht Dürer, 1504

ANTIQUITY AND ITALY – A EUROPEAN CULT

Since the Renaissance, European artists considered travelling to Italy to be a compulsory part of their training. The works of antiquity, particularly Greco-Roman sculpture exhibited in papal or private collections, provided classical models for the artist ambitious to produce a spirited likeness of the human body and to create works of art inspired by noble narratives, nourished by the knowledge of the ancient literature. In this regard, ancient themes for centuries shaped the development of an international language of art, from London to St Petersburg and from Malta to Stockholm. This common language greatly facilitated European exchanges. Albrecht Dürer [XIII.1], who stayed in Venice twice, in 1494–1495 and in 1505–1507, to learn the Italian technique of perspective, used the iconography of Adam and Eve as a study in human proportions. This engraving would be used as a theoretical model by numerous artists such as Titian or Rubens. Even Jacob Jordaens [XIII.2], a passionate realist painter, was fascinated by the study of proportions, so highly valued in Italy, and which he applied to the same subject as Dürer.

Proper mastery of the musculature enabled the body to be articulated with appropriate passion in a clear narrative, which Alberti, in his *De Pictura* of 1435, called an '*istoria*'. The most celebrated statues of antiquity were then repeatedly copied, to scale or reduced in size, in plaster or in bronze, to satisfy artists' studies. These copies, such as that after the Apollo of the Belvedere [XIII.4] preserved at the Vatican, figure in the collections of the academies springing up across Europe in the 17th century on the Italian model or among connoisseurs nostalgic for Italy. Other modern bronzes pastiched the ancient model with consummate ease [XIII.5].

It was to the ideal and pure beauty of this nude that Johann Joachim Winckelmann devoted one of his finest descriptions included in his *History of the Art of Antiquity* (1764). The famous art historian who was portrayed by Friedrich Wilhelm Doell as a Roman [XIII.8], celebrated the Belvedere Apollo in his first written

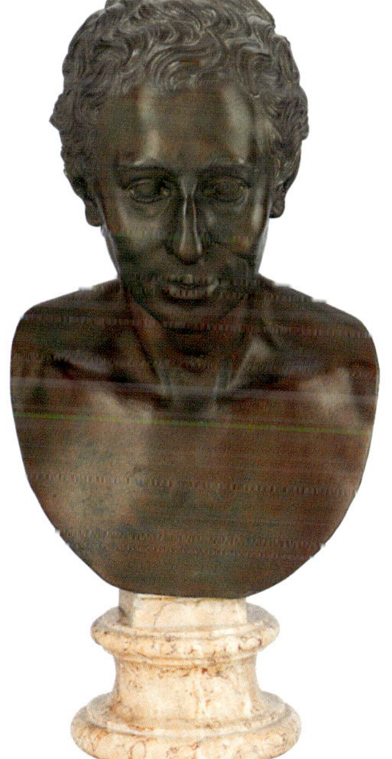

Cat XIII.8
BUST OF JOHANN JOACHIM WINCKELMANN
Friedrich Wilhelm Doell, 1777–78

< Cat XIII.27
HERMAPHRODITUS AND SALMACIS
Bartholomaeus Spranger, c. 1585

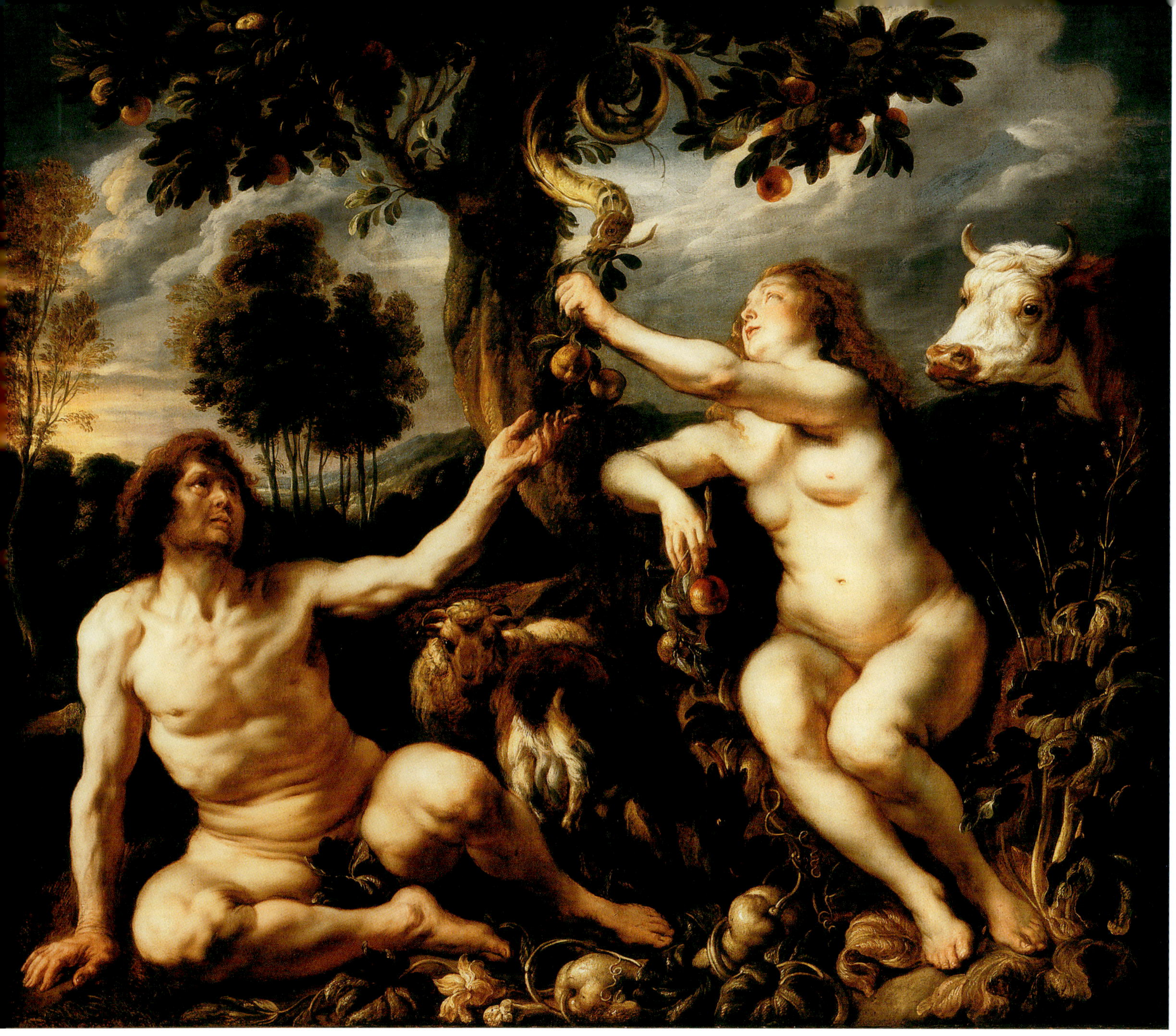

Cat XIII.2
THE FALL OF MAN
Jacob Jordaens, *c.* 1630

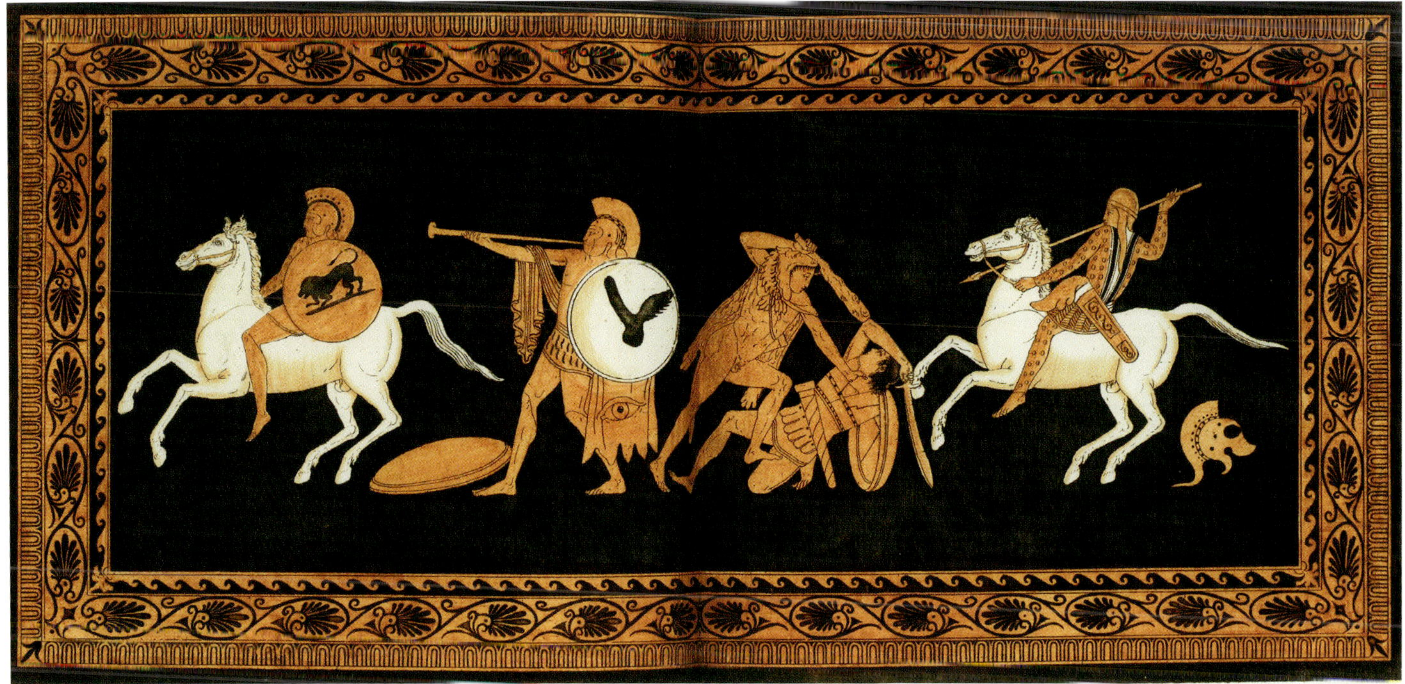

Cat XIII.7
PIERRE FRANÇOIS HUGUES D'HANCARVILLE, *ANTIQUITÉS ÉTRUSQUES, GRECQUES ET ROMAINES TIRÉES DU CABINET DE M. HAMILTON*
Naples, Morelli, 1766–68

work, the *Thoughts on the Imitation of Greek Works in Painting and Sculpture* XIII.6 of 1755 (2nd edition 1756). This young man, who would become chief of the antiquities of Rome, was as yet only a penniless scholar who dreamed of leaving Dresden. Conversion to Catholicism led him into the service of a cardinal and thence to Rome. Once in the city, he worked as an artistic guide to the whole of Europe. It was in Italy that many foreign scholars, such as French antiquarian Pierre François Hugues d'Hancarville, published cosmopolitan works with coloured plates based on Apulian vases discovered in excavations, the purity of line and the simplicity of which would inspire contemporary artists XIII.7.

From the Renaissance onwards, a whole applied arts industry would seek to exploit this infatuation to the maximum. Josiah Wedgwood, for example, a genius producer of jasper ware in the antique style in the England of the Enlightenment, mined the works of Hancarville relentlessly. He reproduced multiple copies of a famous vase in blue and white glass from the first century AD, the Barberini vase, better known as the Portland vase XIII.9. In the 17th and 18th centuries, the number of connoisseurs travelling to Italy continued to grow. The ancient world became the subject of a real cult. The case of Gérard de Lairesse, in this respect, is an extreme one. A Dutch artist, he never travelled

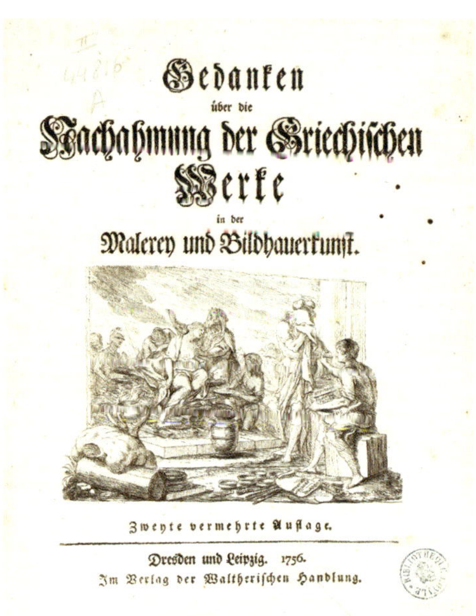
Gedanken
über die
Nachahmung der Griechischen
Werke
in der
Malerey und Bildhauerkunst.

Zweyte vermehrte Auflage.

Dresden und Leipzig. 1756.
Im Verlag der Waltherischen Handlung.

Cat XIII.6
JOHANN JOACHIM WINCKELMANN, *GEDANKEN ÜBER DIE NACHAHMUNG DER GRIECHISCHEN WERKE IN DER MALEREI UND BILDHAUERKUNST*
Enlarged second edition, Dresden, Walther, 1756

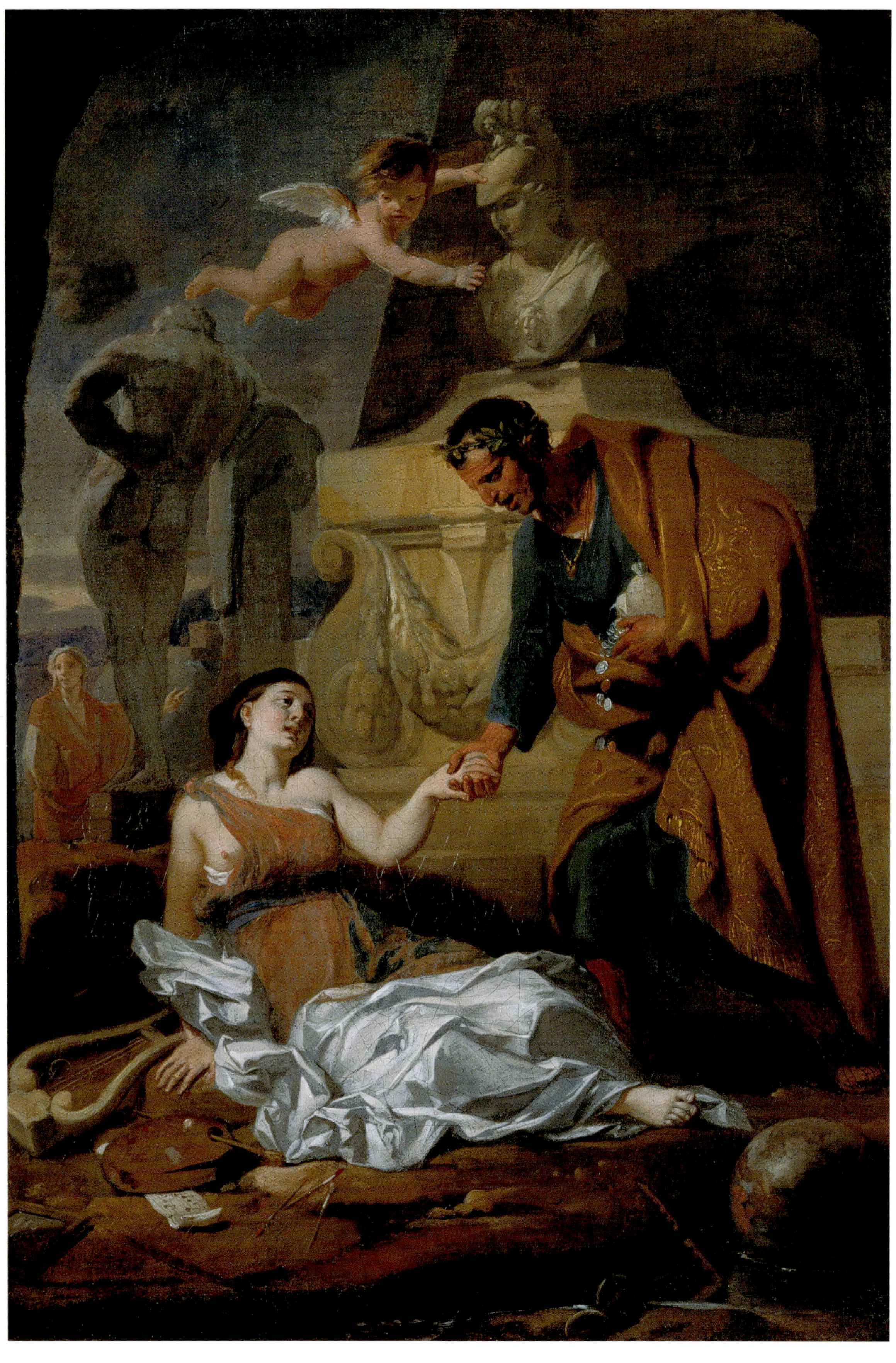

< Cat XIII.11
ALLEGORY OF PATRONAGE. MAECENAS AIDING AILING ART
Gérard de Lairesse, after 1688

> Cat XIII.10
THE FARNESE HERCULES
Hendrik Goltzius, 1592 (published in 1617)

Cat XIII.15
RELIGIOUS AND MYTHOLOGICAL SCENES
Hans Jordaens III, first half of the 17th century

to Italy but, being an avid follower of French Classicism, he became devoted to an Antiquity that he barely knew at first hand. His allegorical painting in honour of the artistic patron includes a representation of the famous statue of the Farnese Hercules, then in the court of the Farnese palace XIII.11, and of which he knew only the famous engraving executed by Heinrich Goltzius XIII.10. De Lairesse unfailingly exhibited a great reverence for the 'grand goût', largescale historical paintings, inspired by the antiquity.

In the eyes of connoisseurs and artists, Italy as a whole became a silent academy in which to draw examples from churches, or public or private collections. El Greco is a striking example of this attitude. A Cretan artist, he settled in Toledo in Spain, but not without first having studied painting in Venice, where he had contact with Titian. The old master taught him to paint with a vibrant and expressive

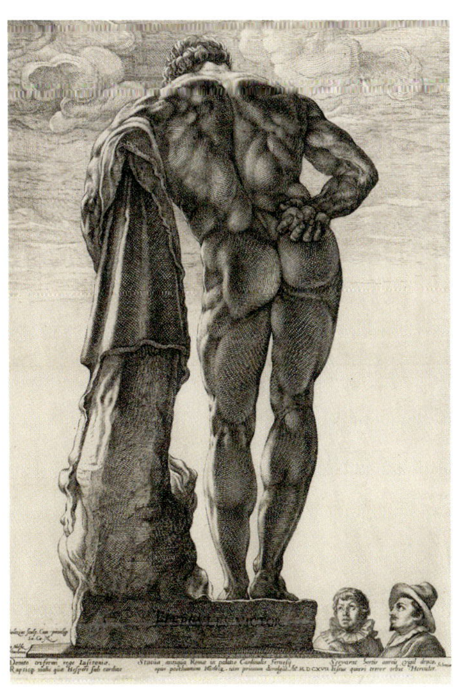

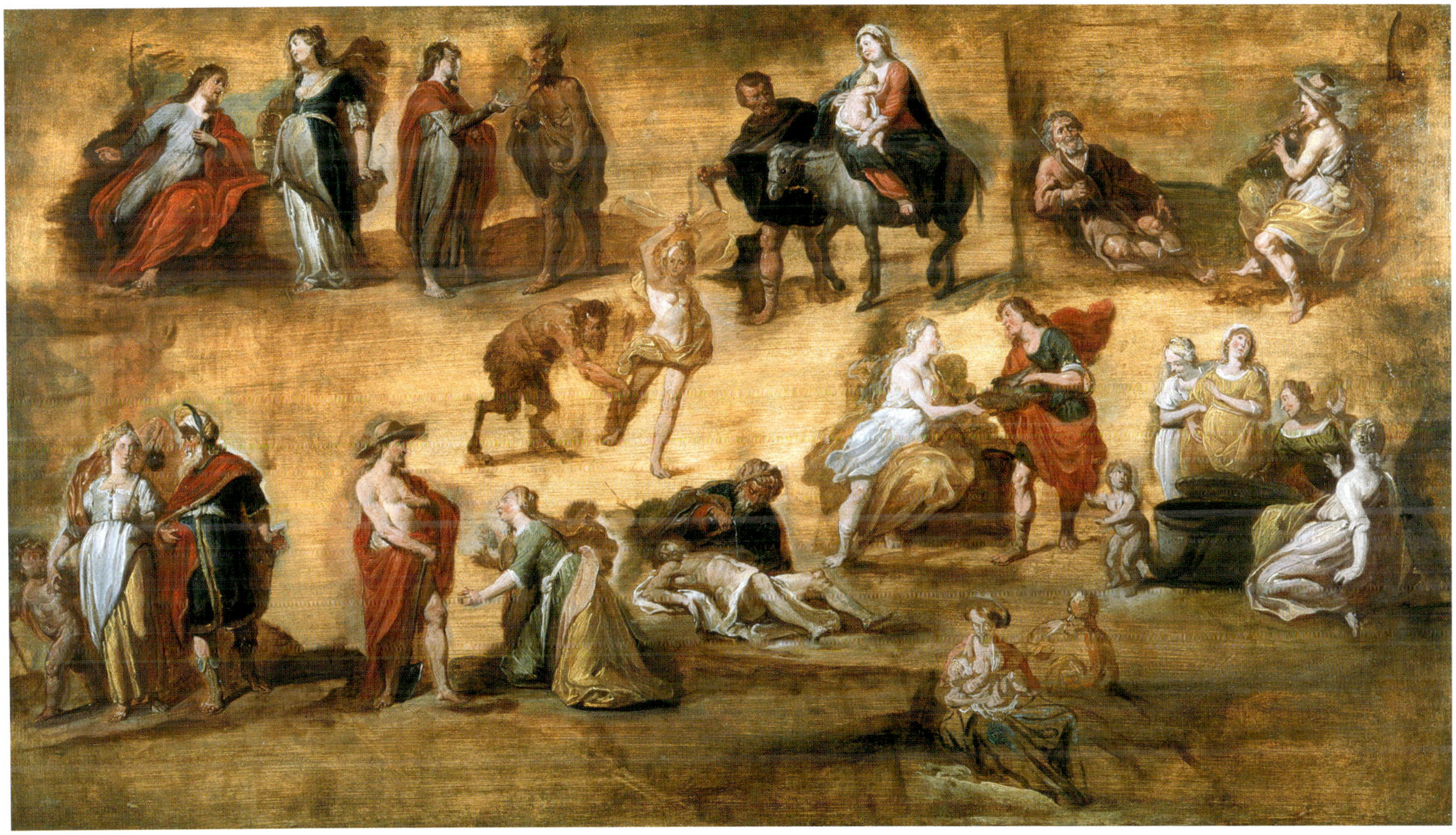

Cat XIII.14
THE BOAR HUNT
Peter Paul Rubens,
c. 1616–17

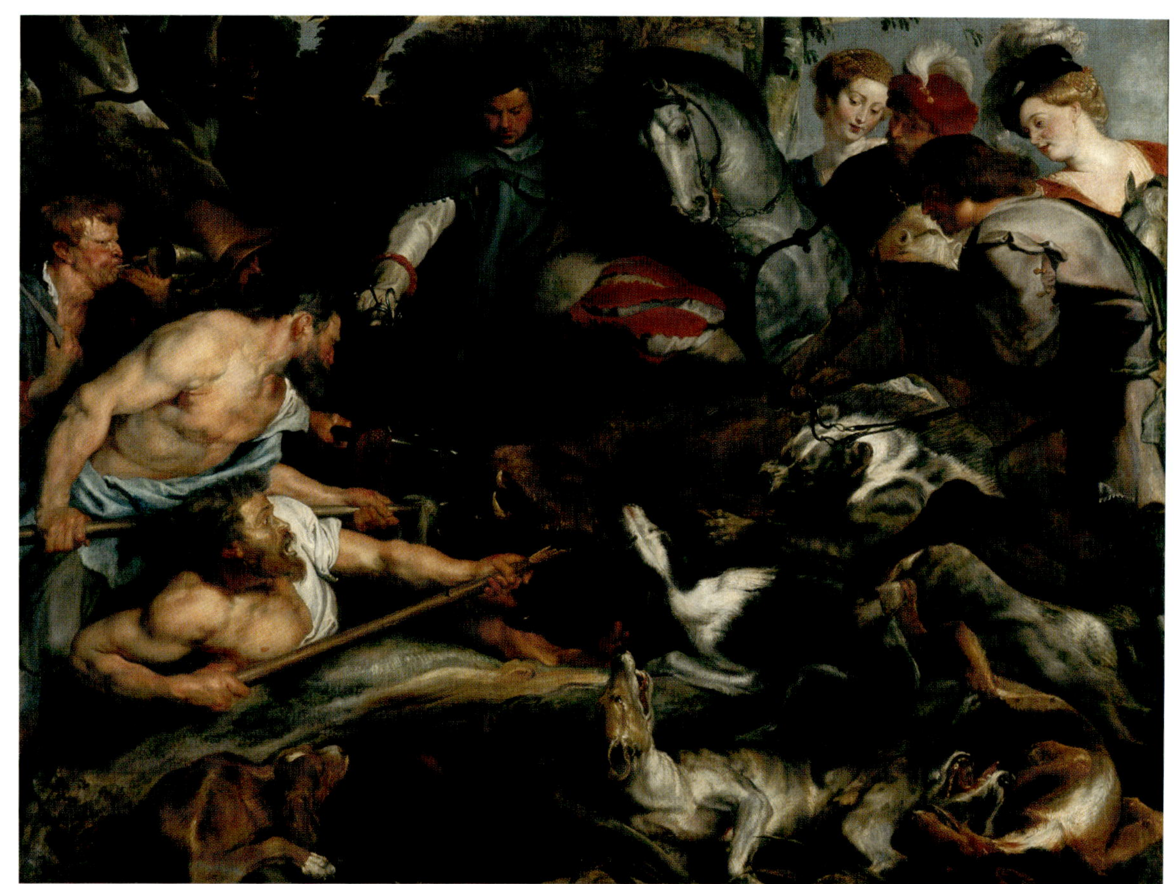

Cat XIII.13
THE DEATH OF ACTAEON
Peter Paul Rubens,
c. 1639

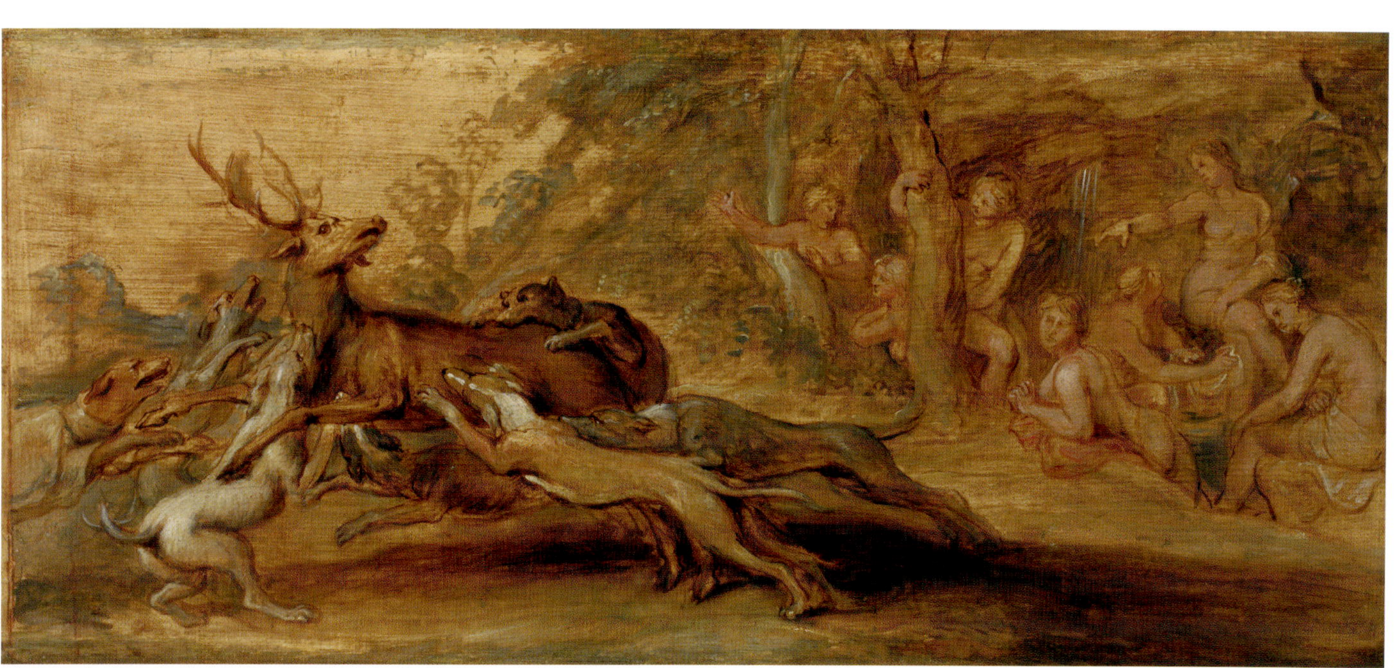

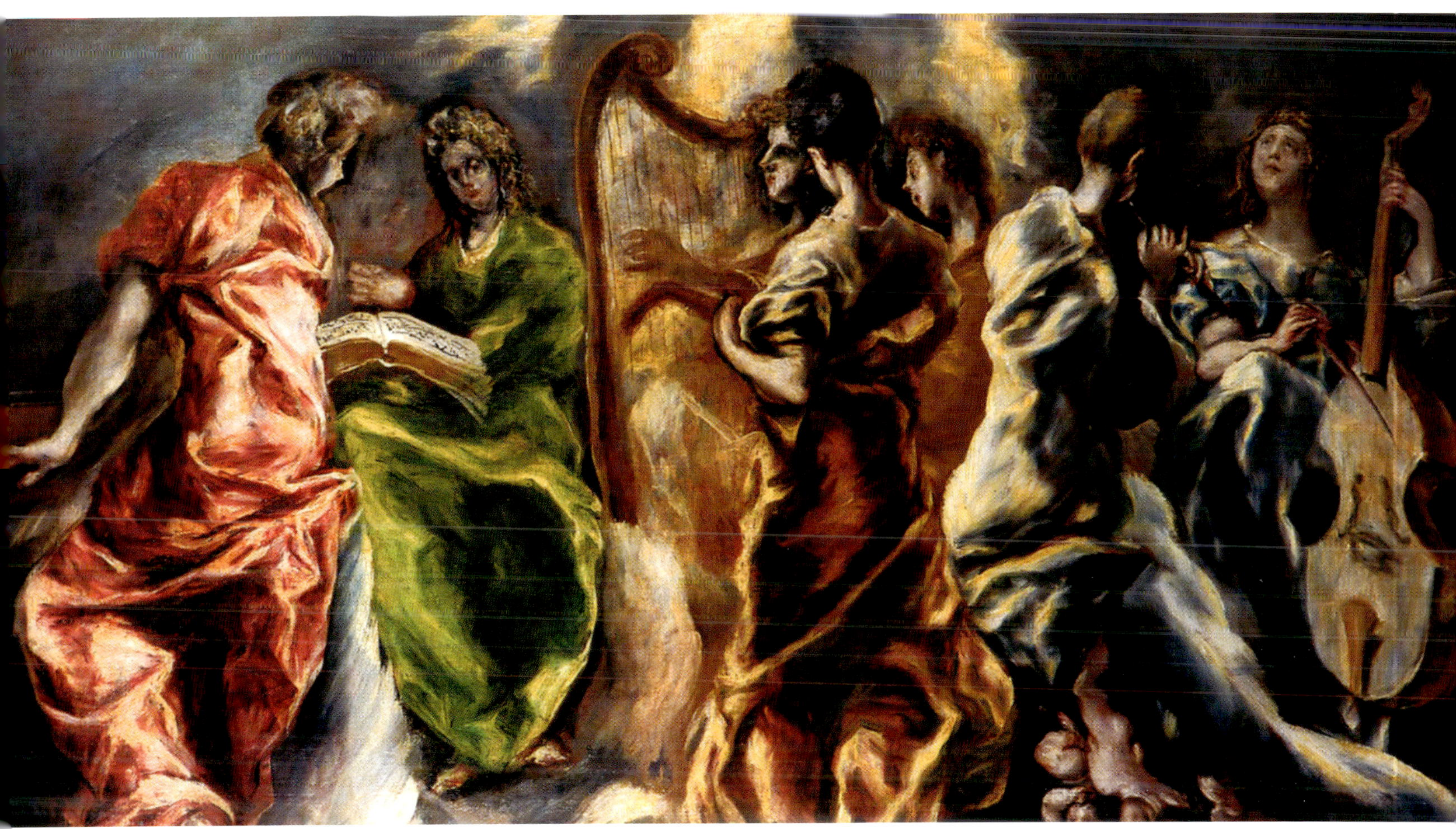

Cat XIII.12
CONCERT OF ANGELS
Domenikos Theotokopoulos, known as 'El Greco', c. 1608–14

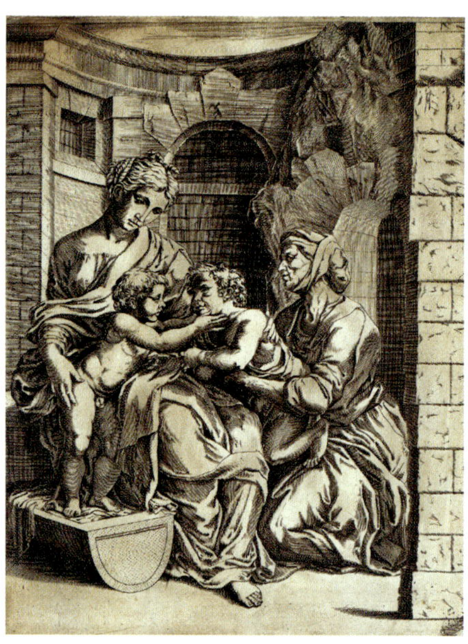

Cat XIII.18
REVERSE OF THE PLATE OF THE LITTLE HOLY FAMILY
Cornelis Massys (after Gian Giacomo Caraglio), after 1518

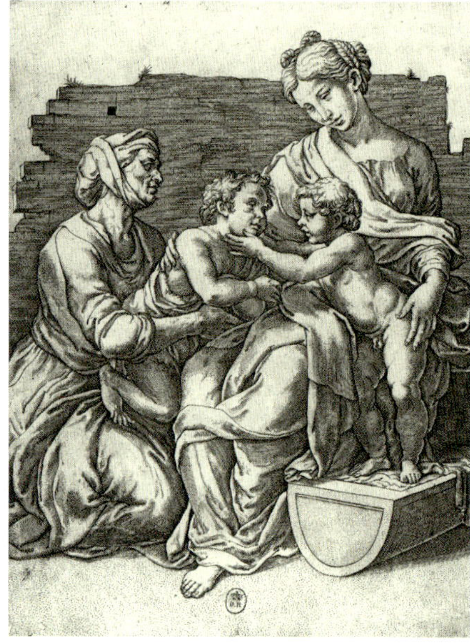

Cat XIII.17
LITTLE HOLY FAMILY
Gian Giacomo Caraglio (after Raphael), after 1518

touch. In the *Concert of Angels* XIII.12, painted for a religious institution, El Greco did not hesitate to incorporate the image of an angel at the harpsichord that he took from a profane theme beloved by Titian: Venus as a musician. Titian's style would give rise to emulation throughout Europe, resulting in a free and expressive note: Velázquez, a great admirer of the Venetian, meditated on this lesson, as did the Northern school, in particular Van Dyck XIII.16 and Rubens XIII.14. The latter, who would copy several of Titian's major works during a visit to the royal collections in Madrid, developed from these studies his own language of gesture, for which he became famous. Rubens painted his *modelli* with fast brushstrokes and exceptional ductility XIII.14. Contemporary artists such as Hans Jordaens III XIII.15 jotted down their ideas for compositions onto small panels that were quickly dashed off and full of freshness; they tried to preserve this spontaneity in the finished work. The magnificent *Boar Hunt* by Rubens, painted for Prince Maximilian of Bavaria XIII.14 is certainly more than a common hunting scene, a subject popular among the aristocracy. Rubens was an erudite artist and collector with a keen interest in antiquities and Italy. His depiction of the pursuit of the animal took on heroic proportions – compact composition, flamboyant richness of colours and dynamic strokes endowed this grand painting with a monumental quality such as Rubens had admired in the hunting scenes decorating the bas-reliefs of ancient sarcophagi.

Borrowing from an Italian model was hardly ever translated into a servile imitation, but rather into a thoughtful comparison, a choice of what to retain and what to reject. When Zurbarán executed a very classical *Virgin Mary with Child and the young St John the Baptist* XIII.19, he reworked the composition taken from a painting by Raphael that had been distributed throughout Europe by Italian and Flemish en-

> Cat XIII.16
PORTRAIT OF LUIGIA CATTANEO GENTILE (PRESUMED)
Anthony Van Dyck, c. 1622

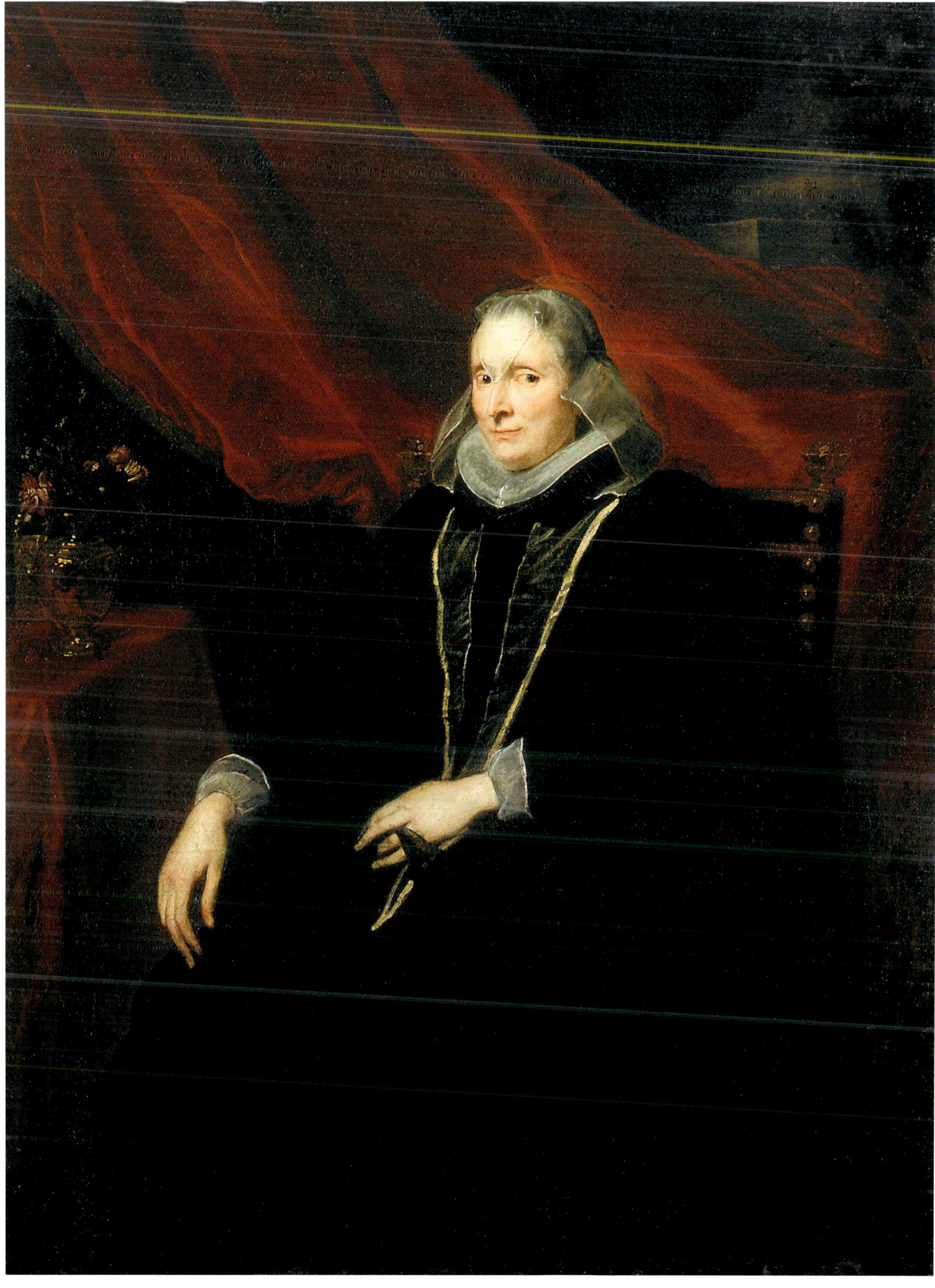

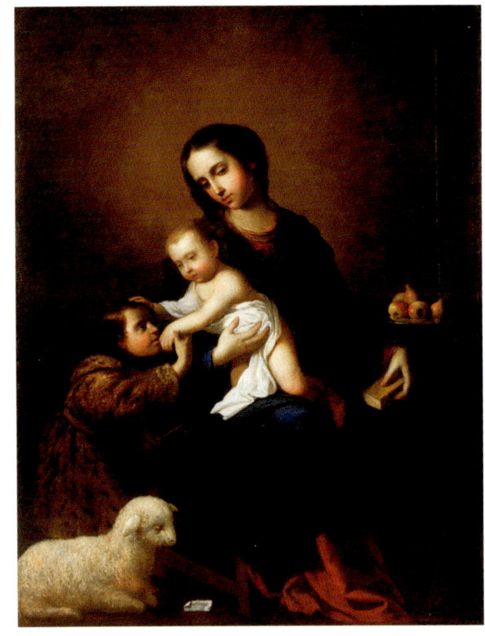

Cat XIII.19
VIRGIN MARY WITH CHILD AND THE YOUNG ST JOHN THE BAPTIST
Francisco de Zurbarán, 1662

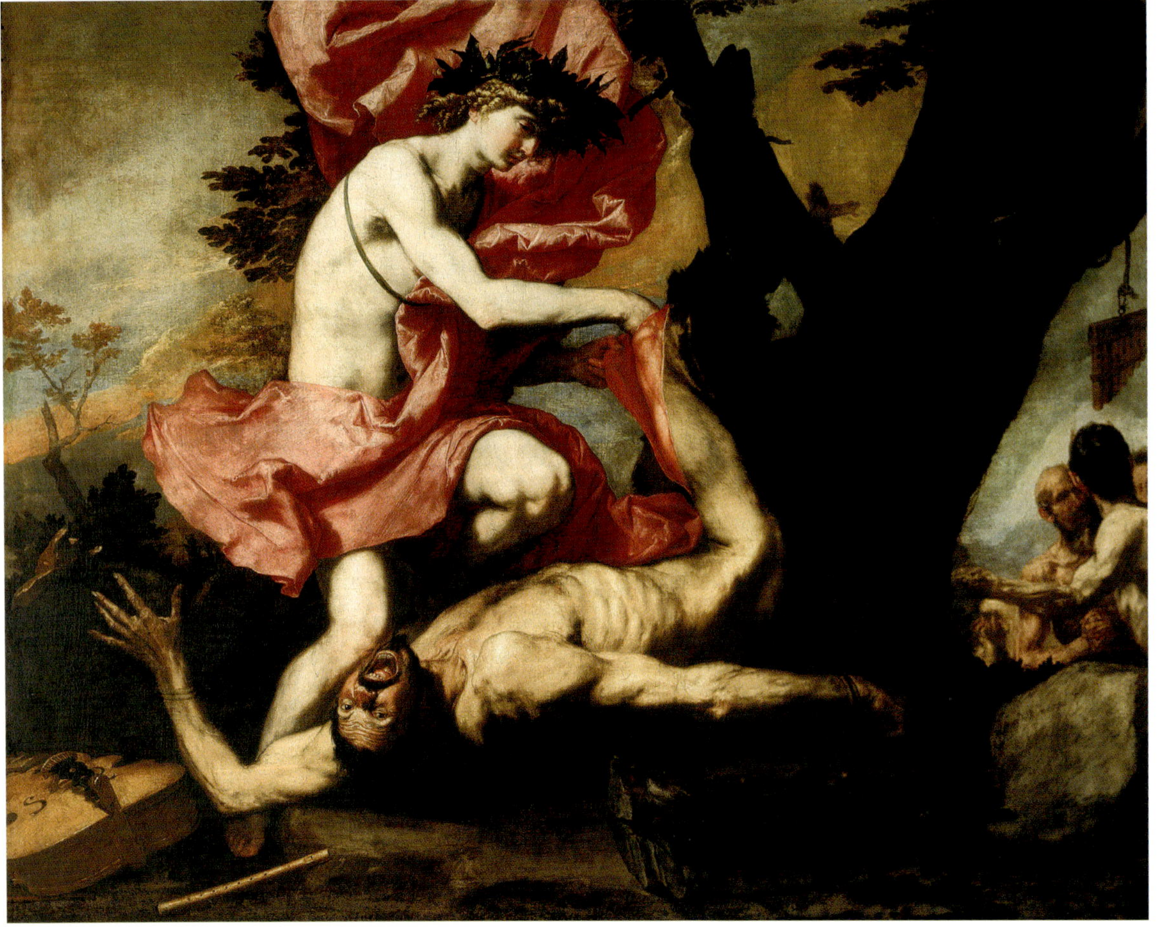

Cat XIII.21
APOLLO FLAYING MARSYAS
Jusepe di Ribera, 1637

> Cat XIII.20
VENUS IN FRONT OF THE MIRROR
Johann Liss, 1625–26

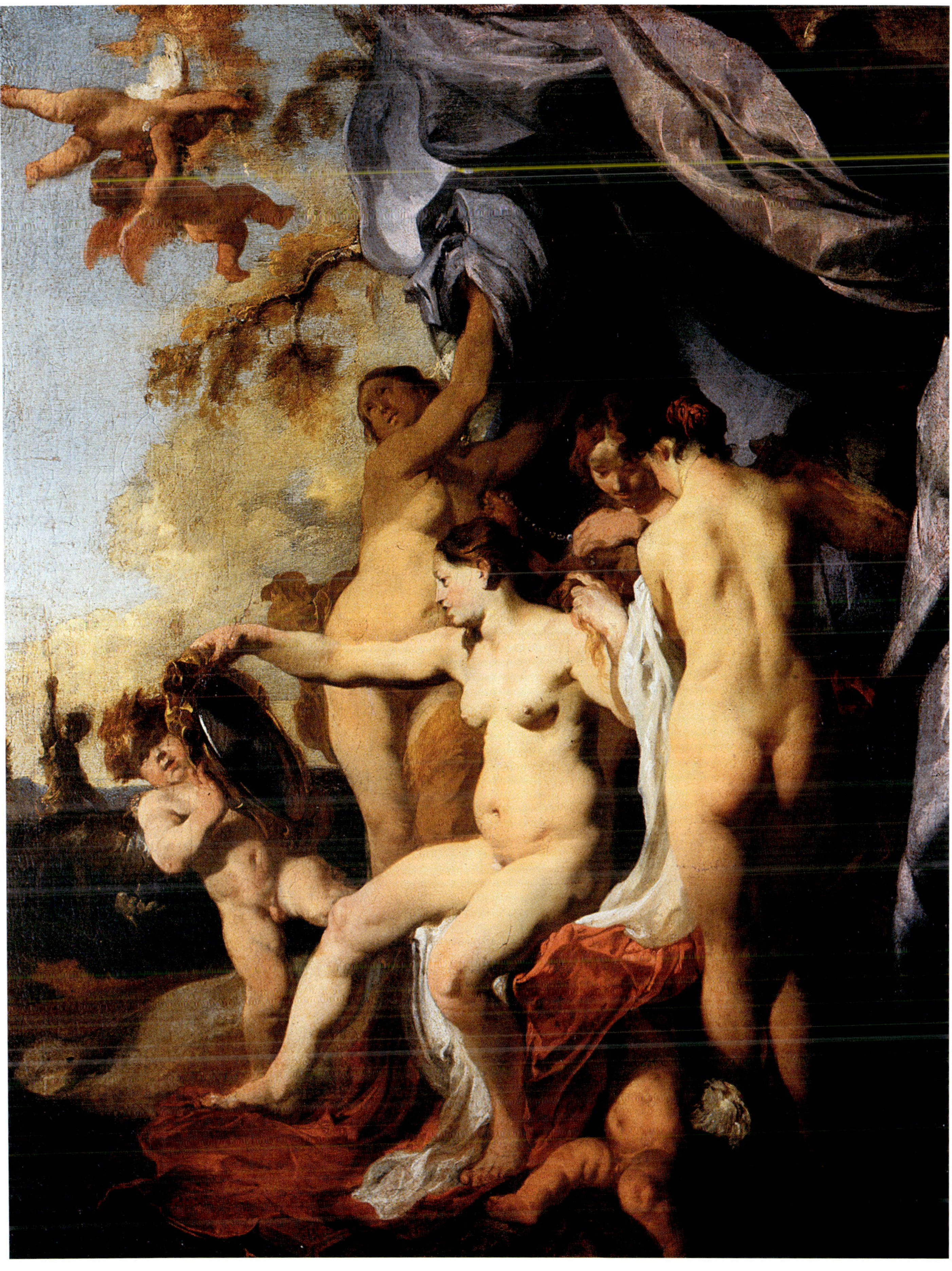

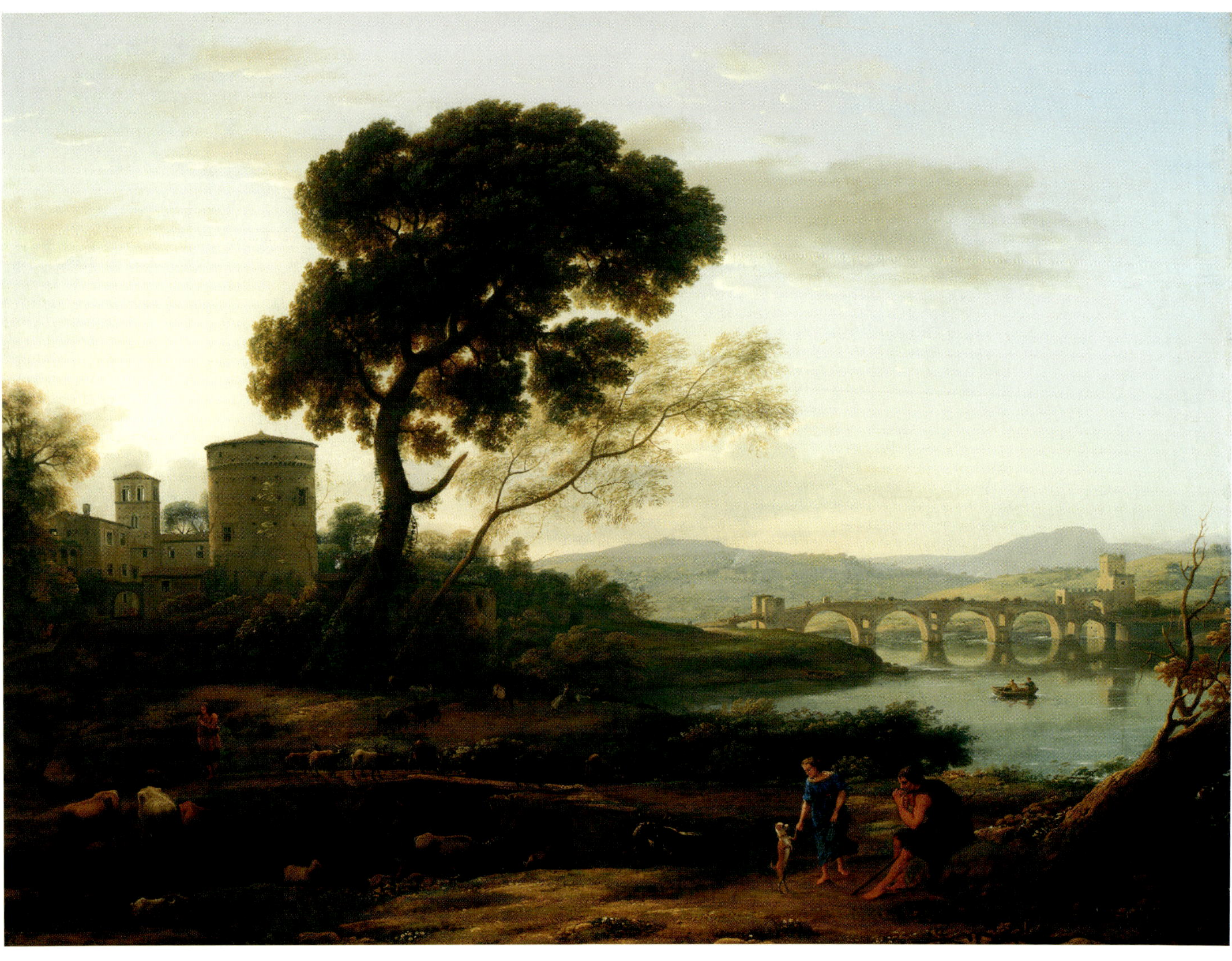

Cat XIII.22
LANDSCAPE WITH VIEW OF THE MOLLE BRIDGE, ROME
Claude Gellée (known as Claude Lorrain), 1645

gravers[XIII.17, 18]. But to his version Zurbarán applied post-Caravaggesque chiaroscuro, which floods Raphael's composition, simplifying it, while conserving a coherent network of expressive gestures. The model invoked was transformed, adapted, appropriated – not without tension for the artist who went to Italy or tried to understand an Italian model he was studying. Learning was unlearning, attempting to unwrap an ancient process inside oneself. Johann Liss, a German painter, perfectly assimilated the art of Rubens. Then he went to Venice, and discovered with delight a new palate of colours. So he set about fusing the pictorial technique of Rubens with gilded tones drawn from Veronese. This risky synthesis was a success[XIII.20]. Spaniard Jusepe de Ribera had himself been trained in Valencia, then in Parma, where he admired Correggio, then finally in Rome and Naples, where he died. He proudly signed with the words 'academico romano', since his acceptance into the Academy of St Luke in Rome in 1626. This man was fascinated by Caravaggio, whose accentuated chiaroscuro and raw aesthetic would be intensively emulated by all the European schools. At the same time, Ribera was seduced by an opposing school, that of Bologna, devoted to the idealization of figures in the ancient style, with a cooler palate and a fine technique. His *Apollo and Marsyas*, dated 1637[XIII.21], betrays an artist at a crossroads. Apollo, white, with idealized lines, indicates a sudden interest in Guido Reni and the Bologna school, while the rest of the picture subscribes to Caravaggio-style effects. Two almost incompatible models share the same canvas and hold up to scrutiny a laborious and fascinating experiment in the synthesis of the ideal and of sensual realism.

Up to the 18th century, Rome welcomed thousands of artists, who met each other there, metamorphosed themselves and, in turn, profoundly transformed Italian art. For example, they constructed the image of the Eternal City that would impress tourists eager to take home a view of Rome. Wealthy visitors wanted souvenir views that included several recognizable monuments but were, above all else, an interpretation of the *Urbs*. One might say that Rome's image was almost entirely constructed by artists foreign to the city. The case of Claude Lorrain is paradigmatic [XIII.22]. An apprentice pastrycook, Claude left his native Vosges at the age of thirteen to travel to Rome. He cooked for the painter Agostino Tassi, who noticed and taught him. He travelled to Switzerland, Bavaria and Naples, where he put the finishing touches to his training as an artist with a German painter who was also a pupil of Tassi, Goffredo Wals. With him he learned about the kind of detail and completeness that earned landscape painter Adam Elsheimer, another German painter living in Rome, his prodigious fame. His peaceful Ponte Molle landscape is bathed in silvery light. At the centre of the picture, carefully and prominently located, stand a knotty tree and a tower – Nature and Antiquity side by side. In the distance, the mythical Tiber evokes the heyday of the Roman Empire. Johannes Lingelbach, a German who settled in Amsterdam after travels in Italy, projected the atmosphere of a Dutch kermesse against the backdrop of the Eternal City [XIII.24]. The ruins of Rome are populated by picturesque figures, with markets invading columns and porticos, adding some light-hearted and delightful motifs. The artist was famous for the quality of his small figures, and several artists, including Meindert Hobbema, would hire his services for this type of detail. Lingelbach is a typical representative of a whole series of artists working, in Rome as in Amsterdam, at combining different traditions into a harmonious unit. A century later, with his customary freedom, French painter François Boucher transformed Rome into a Flemish fantasy [XIII.23]. The artist, who had very carefully studied Watteau, as well as, 1731–41, the Dutch and Flemish drawings of collector Pierre Crozat, substituted the Tivoli sunshine for an atmospheric perspective, fresh and blue-tinged. In the foreground, figures seem to have come straight out of a Dutch painting of the golden age, by Nicolas Berchem for example. Boucher reduced his countryside into a concentration of figurative public spaces, brilliantly assembled into contrasting masses. Only the temple of Vesta, like the stone pine, still seem to anchor this *capriccio* in a vaguely Roman topography.

COURTLY EUROPE – THE GREAT MOVEMENT OF ARTISTS AND WORKS OF ART UNDER THE HABSBURGS AND THE MEDICIS

The Habsburg dynasty made a lasting impact on the movement of artists and works of art from the 16th to the 18th century. This dynasty, after Charles V, reigned over an immense empire extending as far as Austria and central Europe, Spain, Franche-Comté, Milan, Naples, Sicily and the Netherlands, Portugal (1580 – 1668), not to mention the New World. Charles V was a great patron of Titian, as well as a great many other international artists. Passionate about art, the Habsburg family played a major role in spreading a taste for the arts in the European courts. Most of the European sovereigns tried to imitate them. When this vast empire was divided into two kingdoms, Spain and the Germanic possessions, their sovereigns retained a sense of belonging to the same family. Exchanges between these two territories were never severed and family lines were strengthened by marriages and gifts of paintings. The distant descendants of Charles V – Emperor Rudolf II of Habsburg in Prague and Archduke Leopold Habsburg, governor of the Netherlands – have been selected because they represented this concept marvellously, even if their two collections differ very noticeably in character. The first was formed by a connoisseur who did not hesitate to live among his favourite artists and assess himself the works offered to him. The other was a more aloof prince, a military leader who delegated art matters to agents and made very rapid decisions on the acquisition of entire collections. One seemed to take refuge among his treasures as if in an ideal world, as the real world encroached more and more threateningly upon him; the other, by contrast, was a supreme manager, and made his collection into an effective instrument of power, the major vector of a triumphant sociability. But both these collections aimed to represent the universality of imperial domination in a symbolic material – art. Among the sovereigns seduced by the Habsburgs' Madrid collections, Charles I of England was the most ambitious, even while his country was maintaining hostile relations with Spain. He gathered together an outstanding collection in just a few years. Between 1628 and 1632, he negotiated the mass purchase of almost the entire, vast collection of the Gonzagas, dukes of Mantua.

Emperor Rudolf collected old masters, but actively supported the best artists of his time too, encouraging them to come to his court. Hans von Aachen, from Cologne, was a bold artist who painted himself laughing – a man of the world ready to run the length and breadth of it [XIII.25]. At the time of the portrait, he had not yet left his native land. In fact, fate would smile on him. After travelling to Italy and spending time in Bavaria in the service of Wilhelm V, he arrived in Prague in 1597. He married an Italian, the daughter of composer Orlando di Lasso. Imperial commissions increased in number and the artist was even ennobled

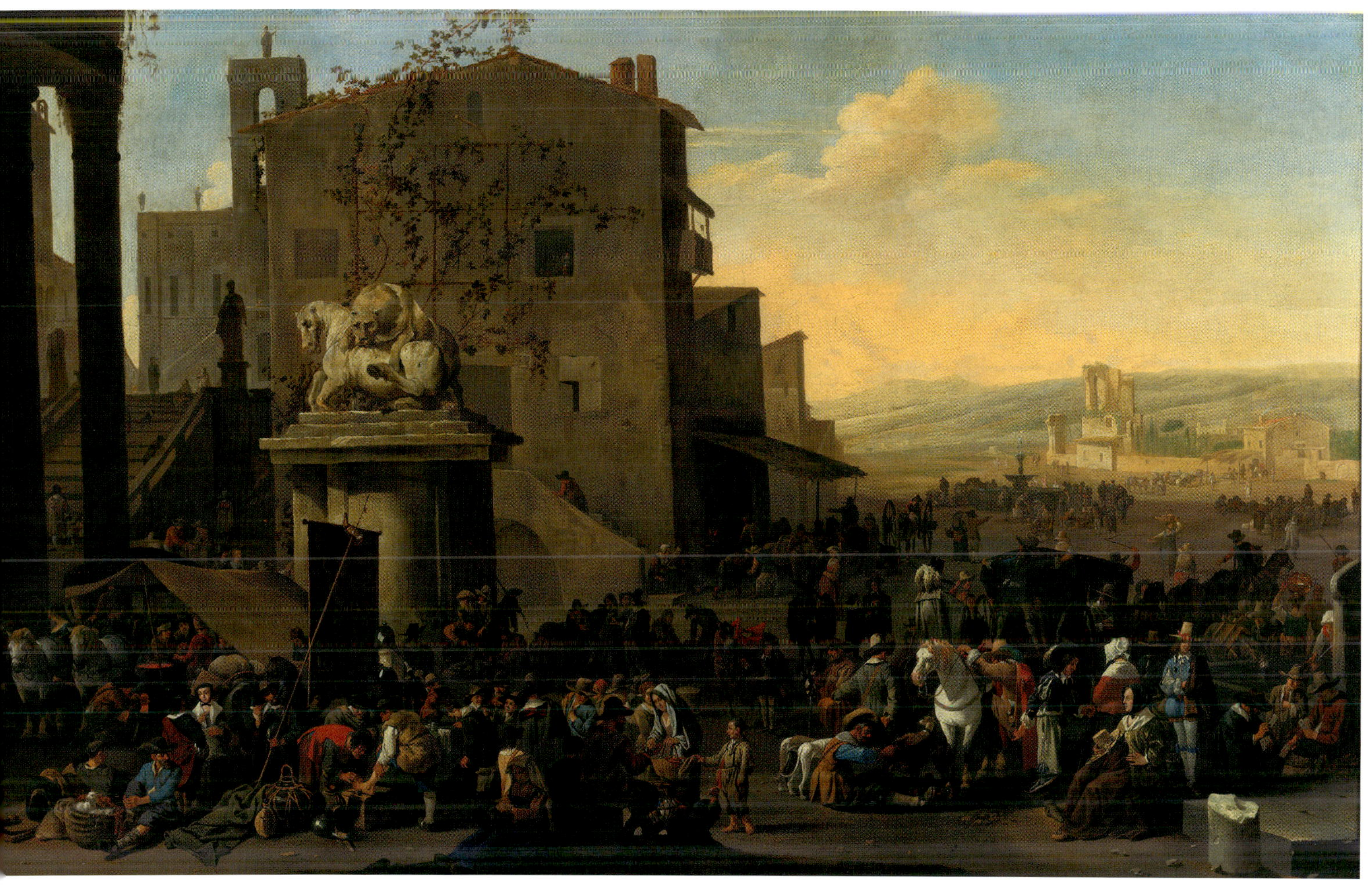

Cat xiii.24
THE CAMPO VACCINO IN ROME
Johannes Lingelbach, 1653

in 1604. Von Aachen played a role of fundamental importance at court, as an artistic agent. For Rudolf ii he acquired a Greek marble statue by Praxiteles, the famous Iloneus now kept at the Munich Glyptothek. Another artist, Swiss-born Joseph Heintz, left Basle after an apprenticeship with a follower of Hans Holbein, Hans Bock the Elder. His country at that time offered only meagre sponsorship, without prospects. Like Von Aachen, he travelled to Rome (1584–89), and Venice (1587–88), the grand capital of the Italian art market. In 1591, he reached the crowning point of his career: Rudolf ii appointed him court painter, and in 1602 he ennobled him. Like Von Aachen, Heintz proved to be an effective ambassador for the arts, and in 1592 undertook a mission to Rome. His *Flight into Egypt*[XIII.33] is a painting heavily inspired by a very similar composition attributed to the brush of Correggio. It illustrates the versatility of a painter who took to Prague all his knowledge of Renaissance art and Nordic Mannerism. Besides, Rudolf ii possessed some paintings by Correggio, a *Leda* and a *Ganymede*, gifts from Philip iii of Spain.

>> Cat xiii.31
HERCULES, DEÏANEIRA AND NESSUS
Bartholomaeus Spranger, c. 1585

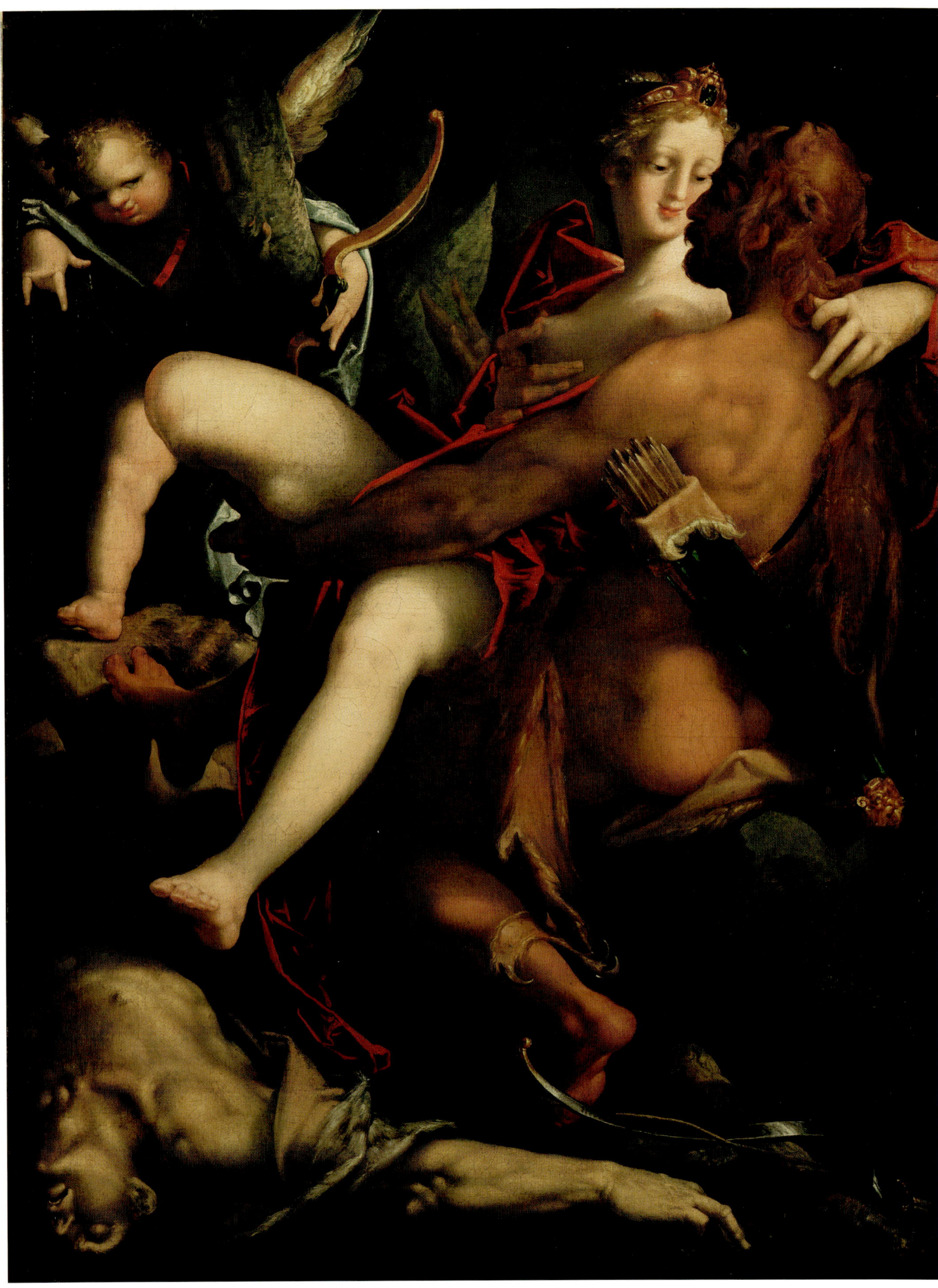

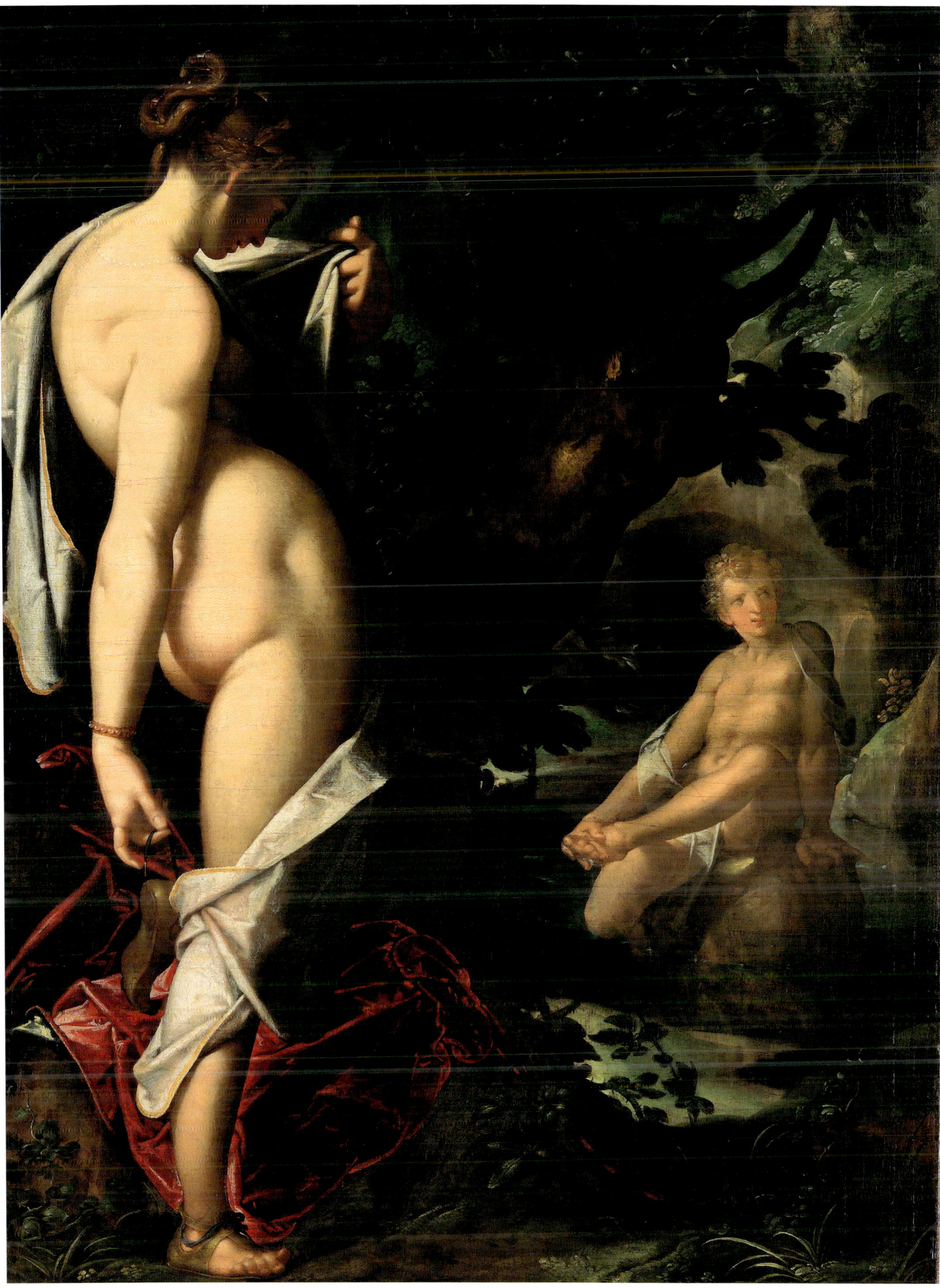

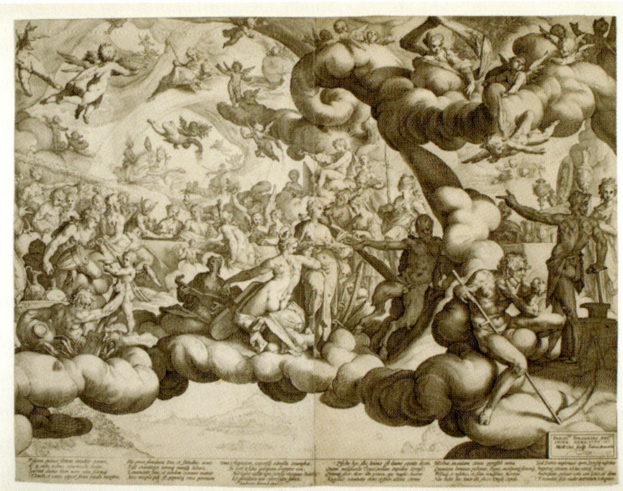

Cat XIII.30
THE FEAST OF THE GODS AND THE MARRIAGE OF CUPID AND PSYCHE
Hendrik Goltzius (after Bartholomaeus Spranger), 1587

<< Cat XIII.27
HERMAPHRODITUS AND SALMACIS
Bartholomaeus Spranger, *c.* 1585

In Bartholomaeus Spranger, Rudolf II succeeded in attracting a great genius to Prague. Originally from Antwerp, this virtuoso artist began a modest career with a painter who was a mediocre imitator of Hieronymus Bosch. Then he visited Paris and Lyon, and decided to complete his training in Milan, then Parma, where he became acquainted with the art of Correggio. Mythological painting became his speciality. In Rome, he was presented to Cardinal Alessandro Farnese by a Croatian miniaturist, Juraj Julije Klović (known as Giorgio Giulio Clovio), and Spranger became an artist appreciated by the prelate, who asked him to work at the Palazzo Farnese di Caprarola. The artist was highly esteemed by Jean de Bologna, the famous Flemish sculptor who lived in Florence. The Farnese favour soon won him commissions from Pope Pius V. But, after the death of this pope, Spranger decided to try his luck in Prague: he arrived in the city in 1584 and made an immediate impression. Like Aachen and Heintz, he would be made a nobleman. The self-portrait **XIII.26**, one of the rare pictures by the artist in this genre, showed him at the time of his arrival in Prague – elegant attire, knitted brows, depicting a man anxious to make the most of his opportunities in Prague. The *Hermaphrodite and Salmacis* **XIII.27** and *Hercules, Dejaneira and Nessus* **XIII.31**, which both belong to the cycle of paintings with subjects drawn from Ovid's *Metamorphoses*, were painted to adorn the imperial apartments. The selected themes illustrate the loves of the gods but, in the eyes of the Emperor, the nude and amorous bodies were doubtless metaphors for obscure alchemistic equations. The artist exhibited his mastery using a Mannerist vocabulary – twisted bodies, compact and dynamic compositions, based on the principle of a contrast between two antagonistic forces. These rhetorical oppositions were translated into compositional energies planned by the artist from the very first sketches **XIII.29**. The '*istoria*', whatever it was, had to fit around this.

Cat XIII.29
PSYCHE AND SLEEPING CUPID
Bartholomaeus Spranger, after 1602

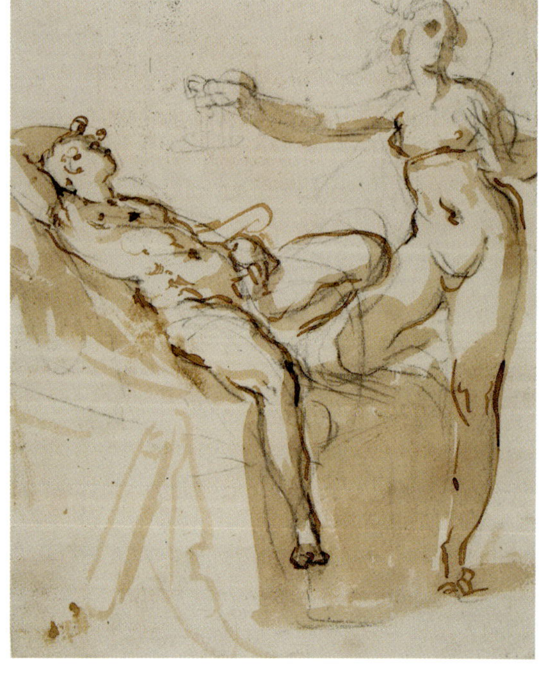

In Prague, Spranger would succeed in creating courtly art to the glory of his patron. The *Allegory of the Virtues of Rudolf* II [XIII.32], executed on copper like a miniature, exalted the virtues of the prince, and the benefits of his reign. It sealed the alliance between a sovereign who aspired, against all odds, to leave a grand image of himself to posterity and the artist whose task it was to construct a lasting monument to him. Spranger explored every technique at his disposal, including the craft of the master engravers, to give his art its fullest impact. *The Marriage of Cupid and Psyche* [XIII.30], of 1587–88, has more than 24 figures. This monumental piece was engraved onto three large copper plates after a drawing by Spranger specially sent from Prague to Harlem. The most brilliant representative of Dutch Mannerism, Hendrik Goltzius, undertook its execution. This virtuoso, who lived in Italy between 1590 and 1591, had an awe-inspiring ability to pastiche the old masters: Dürer, Lukas van Leyden and many others. It seems that Flemish artist and art historian Karel Van Mander showed him some Spranger drawings in 1583; in the *Schilder-Boeck* (*Book of Painters*), he described Goltzius as a genius, passionate about the art of disguising himself and usurping the identity of others. This modern Proteus had an astounding ability to capture Spranger's style to perfection. Van Mander praised 'this magnificent work in which the nectar of grace flows in floods, and in which the draughtsman and engraver head off together towards immortality'. When he set to work on the engraving based on Spranger's *Marriage*, Goltzius had changed style, however – his burin cut a clean, firm and deeper line. The virtuoso, silky smooth but powerful stroke proved that the heroic hand wielding the chisel is not inferior to the arm of any military hero. A collection by Goltzius, in 1586, devoted to the heroes of ancient Rome, explicitly corroborates this flattering comparison. But let us return to Spranger – like a real cosmopolitan artist, he was skilled in playing with all the major artistic trends of his time. His *Diana after the Hunt* [XIII.28] is a brilliant example of this. Inspired by works by Titian and Palma the Elder, the goddess is lying down naked on a fur, while her two female companions are themselves of the artist's own world. This spicy collage confers on the scene an eroticism that is not in keeping with the chastity of Diana. Moreover, to enhance its effects, the artist contrasts the whiteness of Diana with the exotic black skin of a hunter, probably a symbol of the New World. In the *Idea del tempio della pittura* (1590), Giovanni Paolo Lomazzo challenged artists to gather outstanding qualities from among the work of the best artists of the past and to combine them harmoniously. Spranger himself was able to ponder lessons drawn from many European artists, the works of which he would have encountered during his travels.

The fate of the Habsburg collections took a second decisive turn with Archduke Leopold William Habsburg, governor of the Low Countries 1647–56. When artist

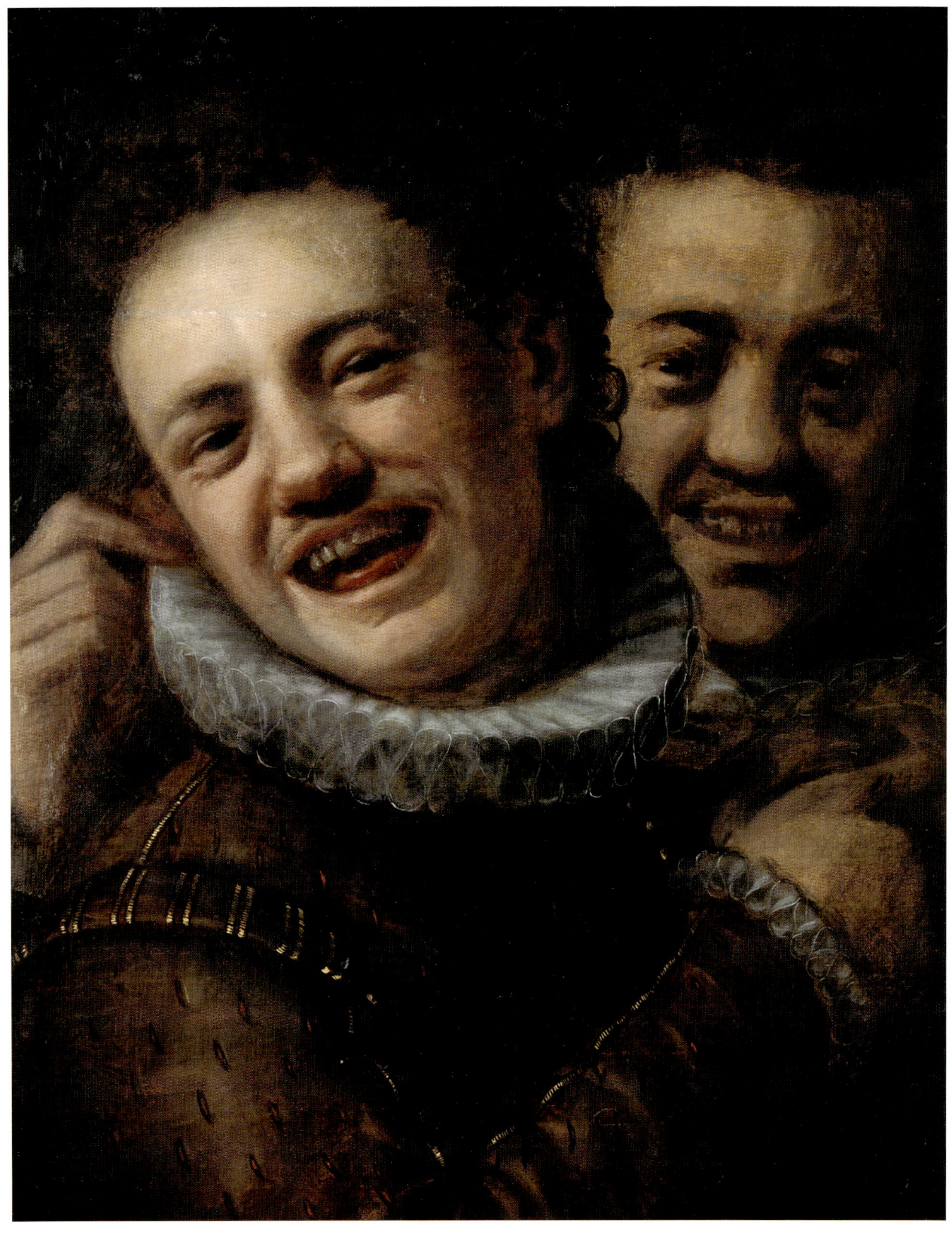

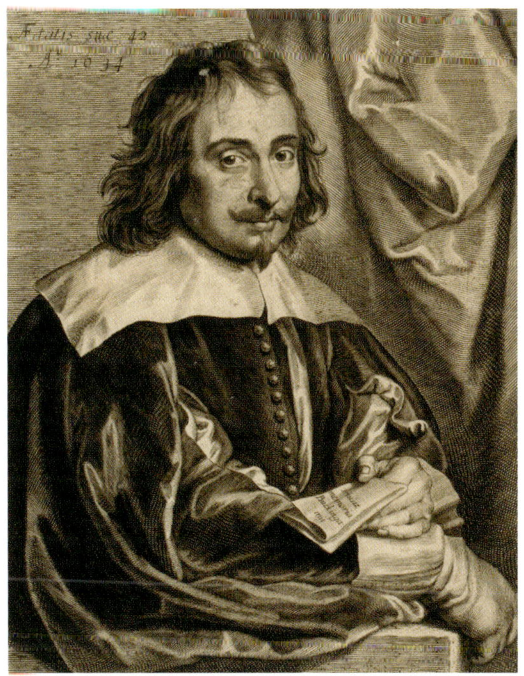

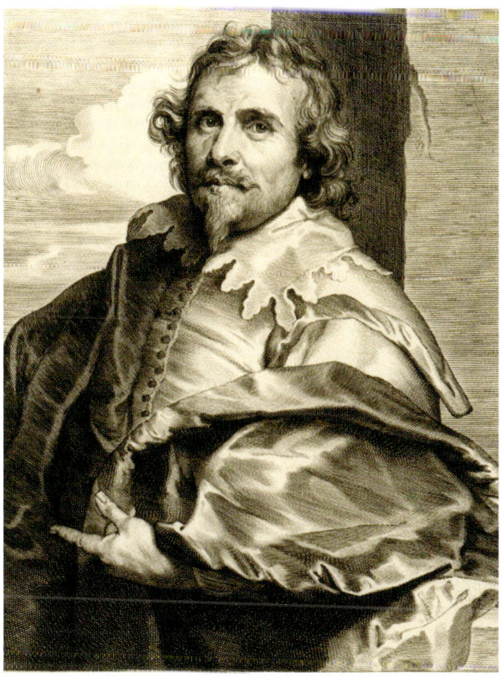

and historian Joachim von Sandrart visited the governor's collection, it comprised only a few works of minor importance. But, in the space of a few years, the Archduke would gather together a vast and valuable collection, which now forms the core of the Kunsthistoriches Museum in Vienna. The history of this collection is a history of Europe, including in terms of its impact. In 1623, the young Charles, Prince of Wales and heir to the throne of England, carried out a diplomatic mission to Madrid with a view to a marriage. Charles was accompanied by Balthazar Gerbier, a painter and the Duke of Buckingham's agent, who taught the English aristocracy how to be Italian-style courtiers **XIII.37**. This mission was a failure, but King Philip IV, one of the Spanish Habsburgs and a descendant of Charles V, invited Charles to visit his picture gallery. The latter was a collection comprising a veritable academy of painting. It was a place of encounters – Rubens, on the occasion of a diplomatic mission in 1628, studied the paintings of Titian intensively there and would be presented to Velázquez. Rubens would assist the Spanish painter to travel to Italy. In turn, the young English prince was entranced by the royal gallery of Madrid. Having returned to England and ascended the throne in 1625, Charles I threw himself into the mass acquisition of paintings, in particular Italian works, in imitation of Philip IV. He was triumphant when he acquired en masse the collection of the Gonzaga dukes of Mantua. His friends followed in his footsteps – the Duke of Buckingham, a great favourite, to whom Rubens would sell part of his collection without ever being paid for it, or the first Duke of Hamilton **XIII.34, 35**. In their enthusiasm, the king and his friends enrolled ambassadors,

Cat XIII.37
PORTRAIT OF SIR BALTHAZAR GERBIER
Joan Meijssens (after Anthony van Dyck), 1634

Cat XIII.36
PORTRAIT OF DANIEL MYTENS THE ELDER
Paul Pontius, *c.* 1634

< Cat XIII.25
TWO YOUNG MEN LAUGHING
Hans von Aachen, *c.* 1575

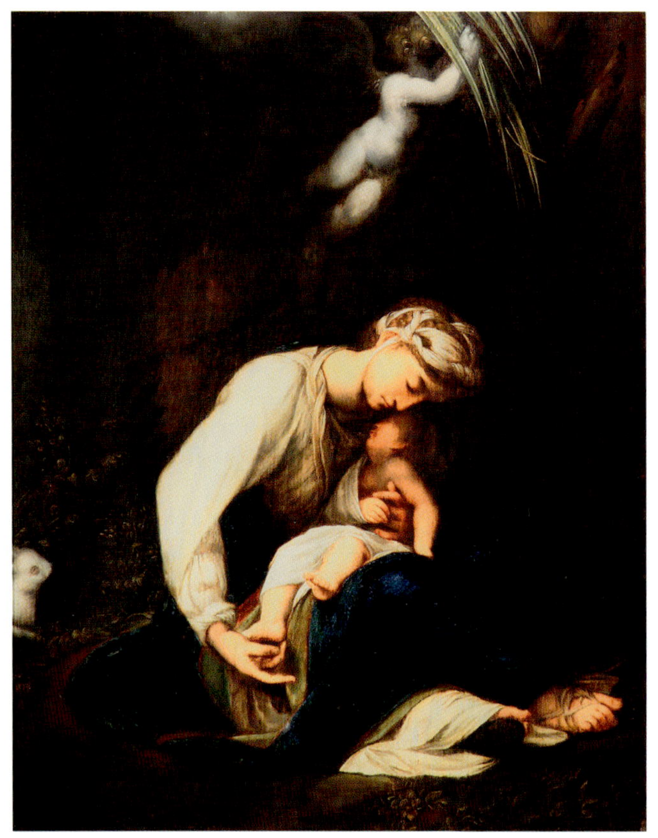

Cat XIII.33
THE FLIGHT INTO EGYPT BY CORREGGIO (COPY)
Joseph Heintz the Elder (?), 1592 (?)

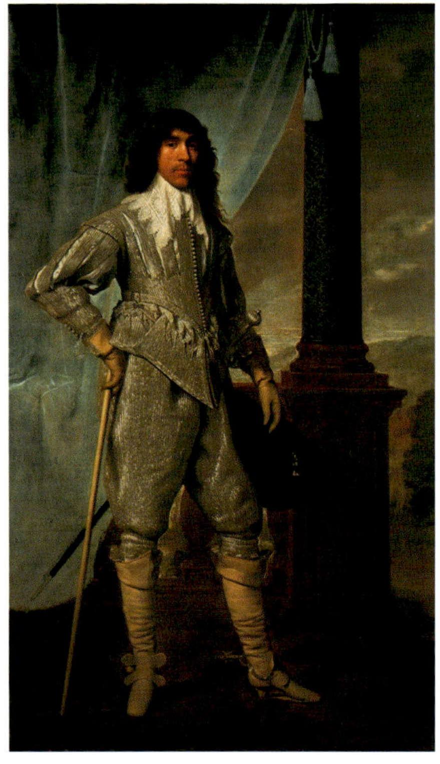

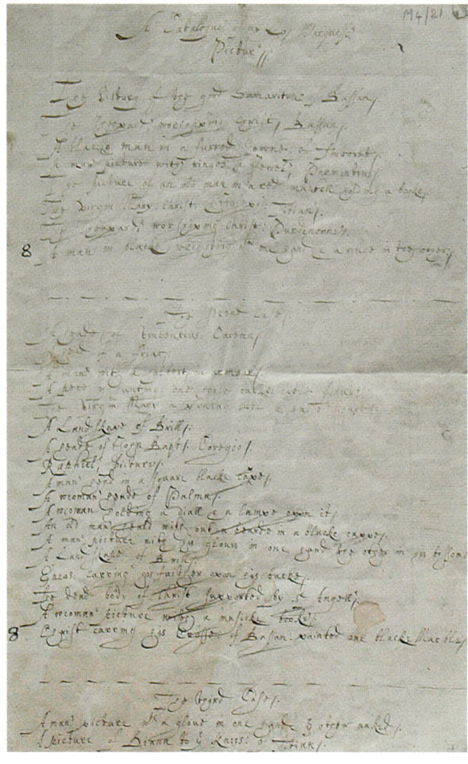

Cat XIII.34
PORTRAIT OF JAMES, FIRST DUKE OF HAMILTON
Daniel Mytens the Elder, 1629

Cat XIII.35
DUKE OF HAMILTON'S COLLECTION, HANDWRITTEN INVENTORY
c. 1643

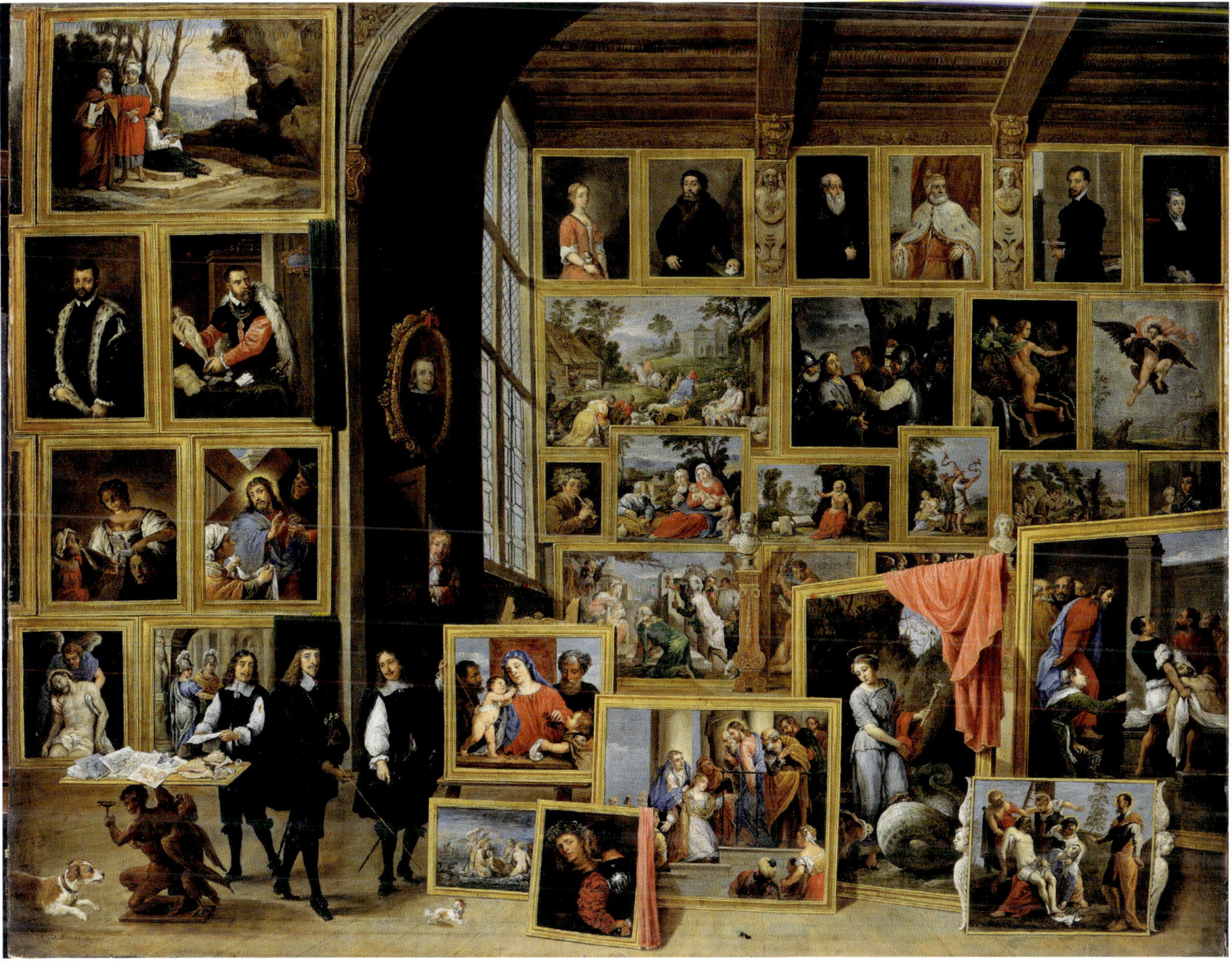

Cat XIII.39
ARCHDUKE LEOPOLD WILHELM IN HIS BRUSSELS GALLERY
David Teniers the Younger, *c.* 1654–60

agents, artists and courtiers eager to please – the best way of satisfying the monarch was to offer him a prize painting. The brother-in-law of the Duke of Hamilton, Viscount Basil Feilding, was British ambassador in Venice and succeeded in acquiring the entire collection of Bartolommeo della Nave, a rich Venetian. Its arrival in London in 1638–39 immediately boosted the prestige of the duke who had succeeded in his mission. He hesitated handing the collection over to the King and dreamed of keeping it for himself. It remained in storage in the meantime. Other more skilful collectors, such as Earl of Arundel, a scholar and man of taste who knew personally several of the most brilliant artistic geniuses of his time, were advisers to their generation. The Arundel collection of antiques and paintings is famous. In the course of the 1640s, England became embroiled in revolution. Arundel had decided to leave his country for ever in 1642 and died in Padua in 1646. His immense collection was gradually scattered across Holland,

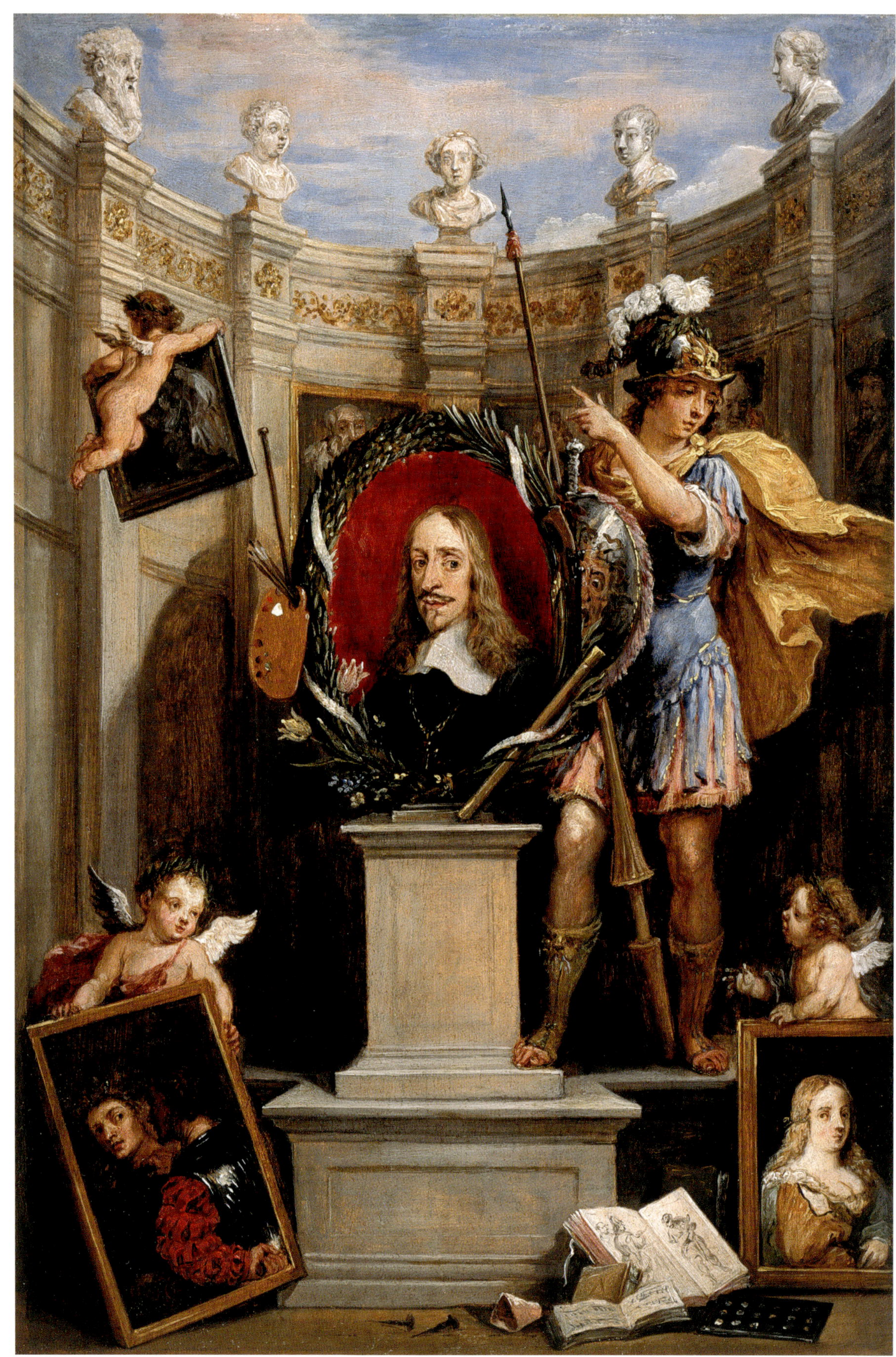

Cat XIII.42
MODELLO FOR THE FRONTISPIECE OF THE THEATRUM PICTORIUM (THEATRE OF PAINTING)
David Teniers the Younger, before 1656

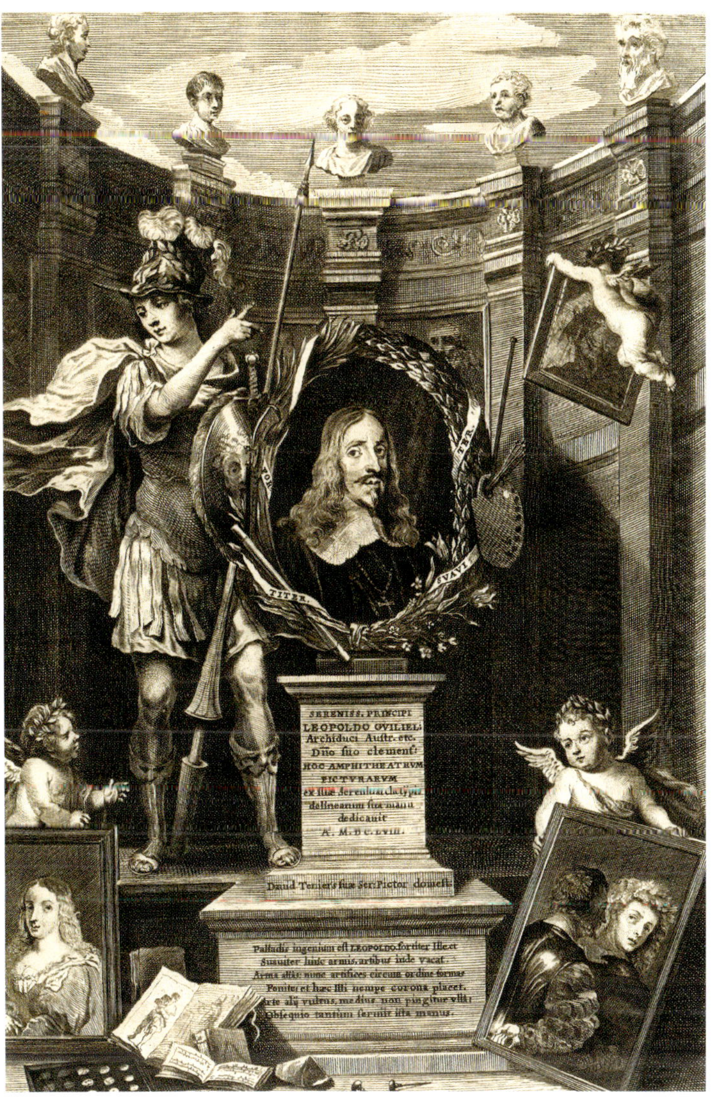

among others by a painter of the Saftleven family. Then revolution in England overthrew Charles I; the king was decapitated in 1649, then other Royalist supporters were executed – the Duke of Hamilton and many of the monarch's faithful. The new strongman, Cromwell, was a brutal Puritan who sold off the royal collections. The news of the sale spread like wildfire. The agents of the continental princes bargained mercilessly to get their hands on the precious spoils **XIII.35**. Archduke Leopold William **XIII.39, XIV.10** was one of the most adept: he succeeded in acquiring almost all of the Hamilton collection. He was able to surround himself with some remarkable advisers, in particular David Teniers the Younger, a Flemish painter of great talent, who was also a connoisseur. This knowledgeable man was able to construct a lasting monument to the glory of his master's collection. He had an illustrated catalogue of the Italian painters prepared in a magnificent publication **XIII.43**, which itself became a real museum on paper in Baroque Europe. For this book, and for the purposes of several plate engravers, he reproduced works of art belonging to the Archduke in reduced format on small panels, in oils and in colours **XIII.40, 41, 43**, to enable the engravers better to translate them into expressive monochromes. He also executed several views of Leopold William's Brussels collection, or 'cabinet' **XIII.39, XIV.10**, of which the precision is debatable but which, distributed to various sovereigns in Madrid and elsewhere, magnified the image of the collector archduke.

Cat XIII.43
DAVID TENIERS THE YOUNGER, *THEATRUM PICTORIUM IN QUO EXTRIBUNTUR IPSIUS MANU, EJUSQUE CURA IN AES INCISAE PICTURAE ARCHITIPAE ITALICAE … QUAS … ARCHIDUX IN PINACOTHECAM SUAM BRUXELLIS COLLEGIT*
Brussels, 'Sumptibus Auctoris', Antwerp, H. Aertssens, 1660

Another royal family was able to make a European and very enduring contribution to the history of the arts and of artists: the Medicis. Its members, having inexhaustible resources at their disposal, assembled thousands of objets d'art with impeccable taste. They were blood relatives to the Habsburgs: Cardinal Leopold (1617–75) and his brother Grand Duke Cosimo II were deeply involved in the Medici collections, both educated by Marie-Madeleine de Habsburg, their

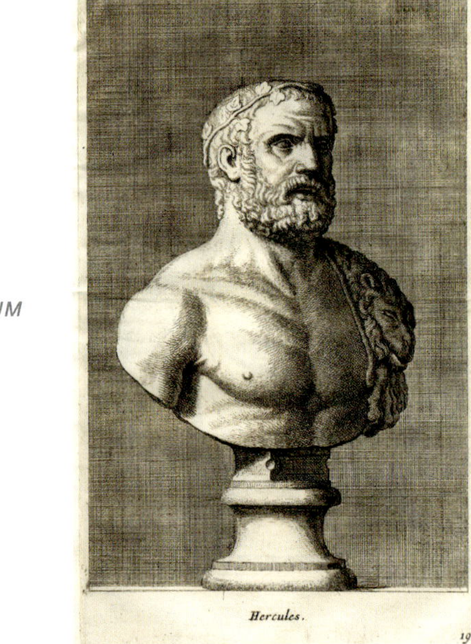

Cat XIII.s.n.
SIGNORUM VETERUM ICONES PER D. GERARDUM REYNST URBIS AMSTELAEDAMI SENATOREM AC SCABINUM DUM VIVERET DIGNISSIMUM COLLECTAE
[1671] In folio

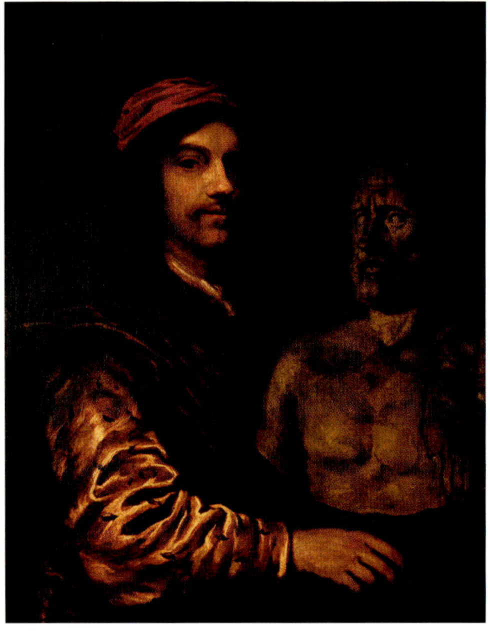

Cat XIII.44
SELF-PORTRAIT
Philips Koninck, 1661

mother. In the Baroque period, the grand dukes basked in the Renaissance aura around Lorenzo de' Medici, legendary patron of the arts. From the 16th to the 18th century, the collection of this dynasty, established as a hereditary Tuscan dukedom by Charles v, was ceaselessly expanded by contributions from family members. In a region that saw the birth of the history of art, the Florentine collection took on encyclopaedic proportions and aspired to embrace systematically all the major European trends past and present.

Florentine Giorgio Vasari, a pupil of Michelangelo and author of the *Vite de' piu' eccellenti pittori…* (Lives of the Artists…), first published in 1550, remained for a long time the most famous collector of artists' biographies in Europe. His book is based on a prejudice – the supremacy of Florentine art. The second edition (1568) was illustrated with woodcut portraits. The Medicis – above all Cardinal Leopold and then Grand Duke Cosimo III, who installed the collection in the Uffizi galleries – were ambitious to build up a collection of artists' self-portraits that would provide a pictorial counterpart to Vasari's biographies. In each self-portrait, the painter represented himself twice – in his appearance and in his characteristic *manner*, which Vasari compares with the handwriting of a clerk, recognizable simply by examining a letter. The development of this series was accelerated by an efficient network of agents and, as in the diplomatic corps, of dukes. It generated considerable correspondence, which constituted a collective work the extent of which it is hard to imagine – identification of important artists, groundwork, commissions and payment, finally the sending of paintings to Florence. The correspondence of Cardinal Leopold de Medici on such matters amounted to

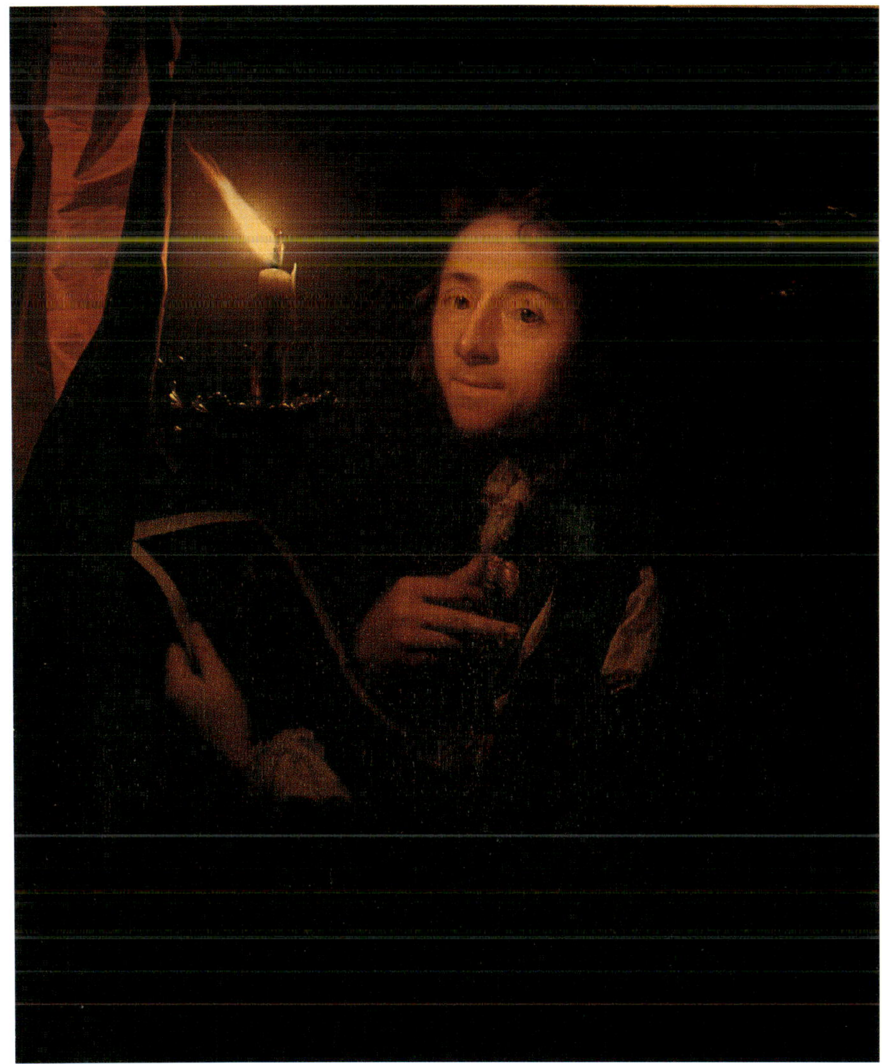

Cat XIII. 45
SELF-PORTRAIT
Gottfried Schalken, 1695

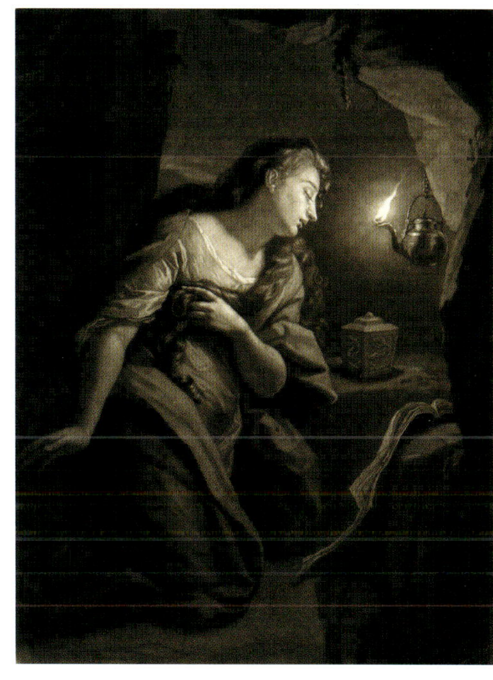

Cat XIII.s.n.
ST MARY MAGDALENE
John Smith (after Gottfried Schalken), final third of the 17th century

twenty-one manuscript volumes. Cosimo III commissioned Philips Koninck and Gottfried Schalken to paint two self-portraits [XIII. 44,45]. The two artists complied, with the first picture a standard representation, the other a panegyric of his speciality. All these portraits were placed in a gallery in which the founder of the portrait collection, Cardinal Leopold [XIII.46], had pride of place. But, in all this, there is one quite blatant paradox. With their desire to collect the most beautiful works of European art, the Medicis diverged from Vasari's patriotism. They became apostles and the harbingers of a taste open to the universal. Their pantheon gathered together all the greatest artists of Europe, a magnificent artistic conclave.

XIV

The world in a room: collectors and art dealers

PASCAL GRIENER

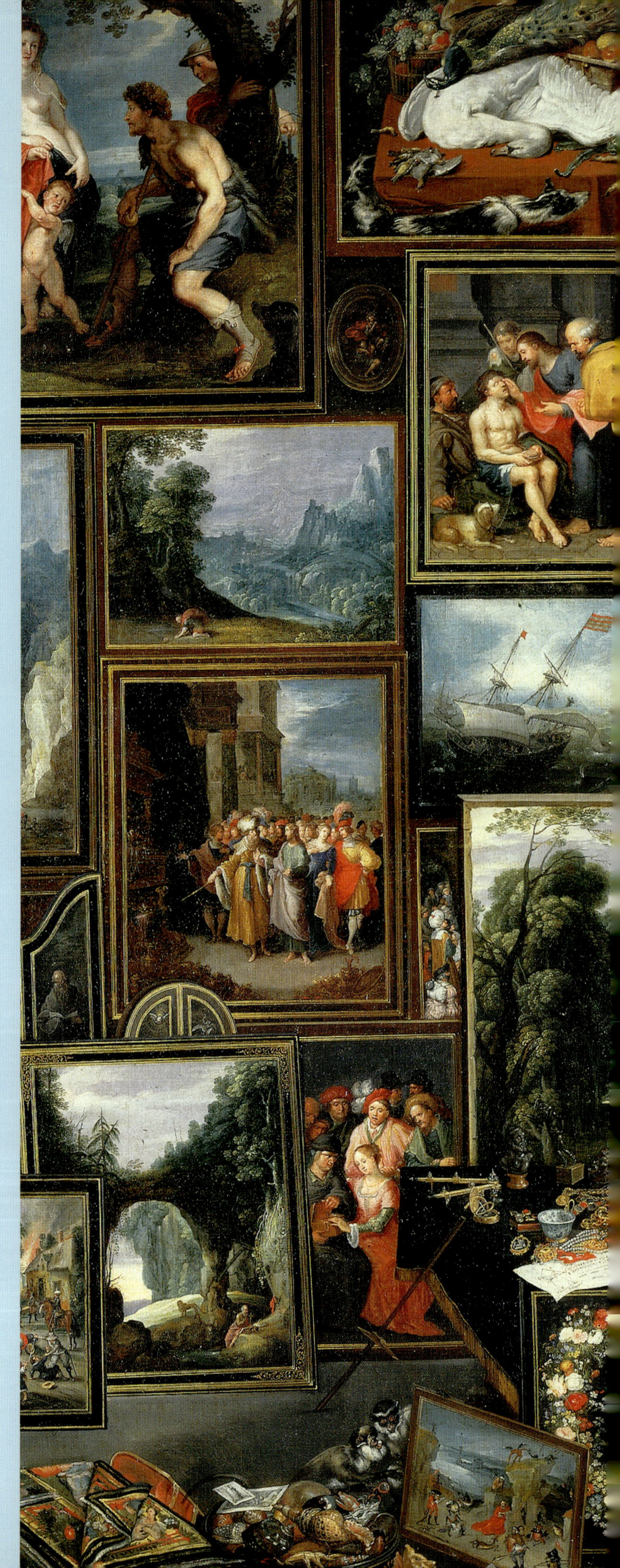

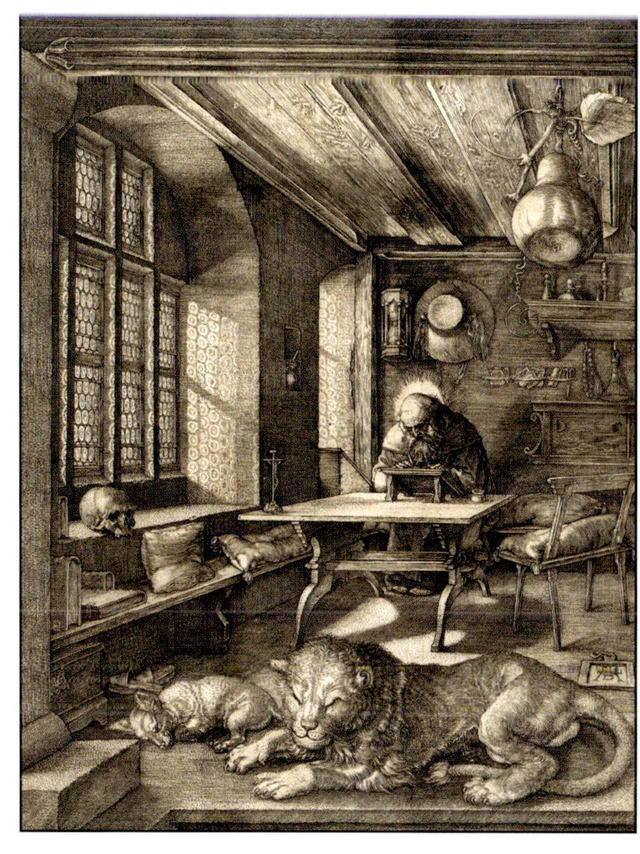

Cat XIV.1
ST JEROME IN HIS STUDY
Albrecht Dürer, 1514

The word 'cabinet', which emerged in the 16th century, was used to refer to a place where curiosities, art objects and items of study interest were on display. Pictures of such interiors formed an artistic genre originating in Antwerp, and its founder is said by some to have been Jan Brueghel the Elder, by others Franz Francken II. It is important to note that several factors gave rise to this genre in Flemish painting. First of all there was the representation of church interiors, which often contained paintings or altarpieces. Then there were portraits of art connoisseurs, which began to be painted in Venice in the 16th century and as a rule showed the subject surrounded by precious objects. But it is in the world of literature that the most valuable source for the cabinet paintings fashion is to be found – in descriptions of collections, as in the ancient writings of Philostratus, the *Imagines* (or *Images*).

The 17th century was the era of the '*peinture de cabinet*' – these works are symptomatic of a new meditativeness on the power of painting but also on the delineation of the modern subject; as such they legitimize the indulgence of curiosity, i.e. perception of the world by the senses, so much condemned by the Church Fathers. The exercising of judgment then becomes an essential matter, at the convergence of aesthetics and politics. Seeing, observing the world in a direct way, and not in accordance with a particular set of beliefs, is an essential task. A collection *in situ* is a microcosm, with the collector as its centre and organizer. His retreat is a room dedicated to studious withdrawal, of which the engraving by Dürer [XIV.1] has provided the most famous metaphor. The items on display have been gained after a struggle involving the interplay of diverse groups – the correspondence between Rubens and scholar Nicolas Fabri de Peiresc [XIV.2, 3] illustrates this fact marvellously. The two men sent one another cameos, gifts of coins or paintings, then finally news about sales of objets d'art. Keeping this network going by means of presents was vital – it was by generosity that each of them promoted their own interests.

The magnificent cabinets depicted in this section constitute one of the richest collections ever gathered together for an exhibition [XIV.5-15]. They document a collecting

< Cat XIV.12
ALLEGORY OF SIGHT AND SMELL
Jan 'Velvet' Brueghel (the Elder), Peter Paul Rubens et al., 1618

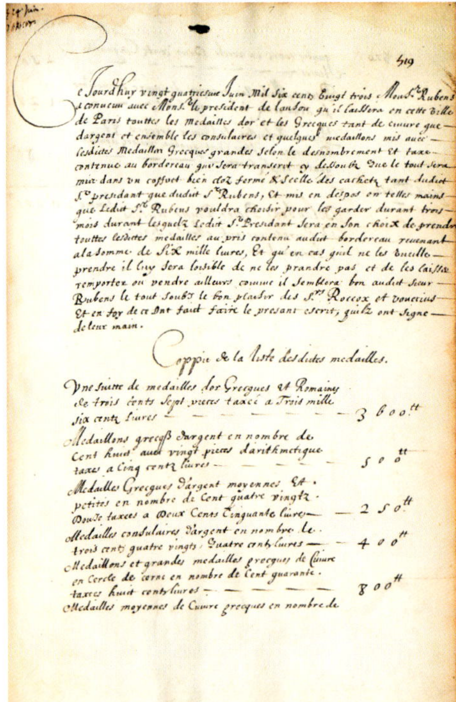

519

Ce Jourd'huy vingt quatriesme Juin Mil six cents vingt trois Mons.r Rubens a convenu avec Mons.r le president de [illegible] qu'il laissera en cette ville de Paris touttes les medailles dor et les Grecques tant de cuivre que dargent et ensemble les consulaires et quelques medaillons mis avec lesdites Medaillons Grecques grandes selon le desnombrement et taxe contenue au bordereau qui sera transcrit cy dessoubz Que le tout sera mis dans un coffret bien cloz fermé & scellé des cachetz tant dudict S.r president que dudit S.r Rubens, et mis en despos en telles mains que ledit S.r Rubens vouldra choisir pour les garder durant trois mois durant lesquelz ledit S.r President sera en son choix de prendre touttes lesdictes medailles au pris contenu audit bordereau revenant a la somme de six mille livres, Et qu'en cas quil ne les vueille prendre il luy sera loisible de ne les prandre pas et de les laisser remporter ou vendre ailleurs comme il semblera bon audit sieur Rubens le tout soubz le bon plaisir des S.rs Rocox et Vonerius Et en foy de ce ont faict faire le presant escrit, quilz ont signe de leur main.

Coppie de la liste desdites medailles.

Une suitte de medailles dor Grecques et Romaines de trois cents sept pieces taxée a Trois mille six cents livres	3600.tt
Medaillons grecqs dargent en nombre de cent huit avec vingt pieces darithmetique taxes a cinq centz livres	500.tt
Medailles Grecques d'argent moyennes et petites en nombre de cent quatre vingtz douze taxees a deux cents cinquante livres	250.tt
Medailles consulaires d'argent en nombre de trois cents quatre vingts, quatre cents livres	400.tt
Medaillons et grandes medailles grecques de cuivre en cercle de corne en nombre de cent quarante taxees huit cents livres	800.tt
Medailles moyennes de cuivre grecques en nombre de	

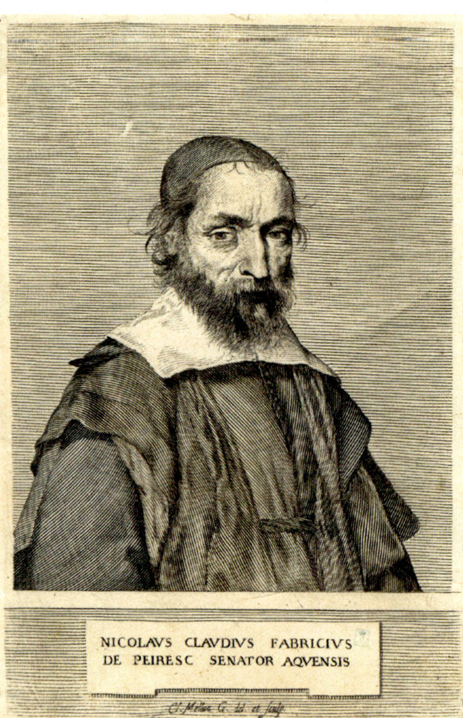

Cat XIV.2
HANDWRITTEN LIST OF ANCIENT COINS PRESENTED TO HIM BY THE PAINTER PETER PAUL RUBENS
Nicolas-Claude Fabri de Peiresc, January 1620 (?)

Cat XIV.3
PORTRAIT OF NICOLAS-CLAUDE FABRI DE PEIRESC
Claude Mellan, 1636–37

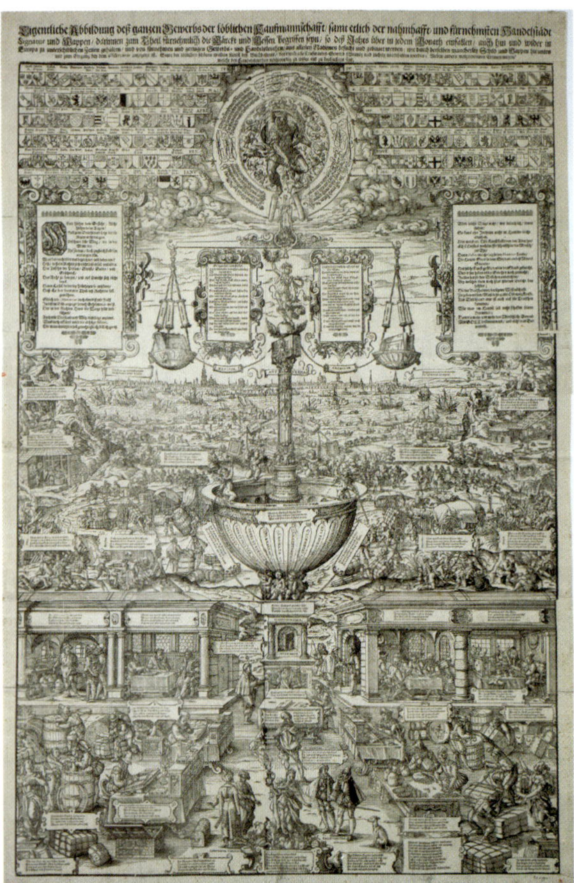

Cat XIV.4
ALLEGORY OF COMMERCE
Jost Amman, 1585

practice that gradually separated out what the *Wunderkammer* ('chamber of wonders') had linked together in the form of a dense miscellany: books, works of art, natural objects. But the world of discourse and that of experience were being held up to scrutiny in a new manner – how does language operate when it speaks of a shell or a painted landscape? It is this very scrutiny that renders modern knowledge possible – science, art criticism, history of art. This process does not work instantly – for a long time the collections remained miraculous places where divine correspondences were experienced between the world of words, the heaven of divine essences and the realm of objects. But the visual sphere of the collector became differentiated; the collection became a more specialized laboratory without ceasing to remain a social space, regulated by specific laws. Renaissance sovereigns such as Grand Duke Francesco de' Medici did not initially allow anyone into their cabinet but in the Baroque era the Medicis opened up the grand-ducal collections in celebration of Medicean *Civitas*. In the North, the private collection remained a serious practice, but access to it was generally easy.

The Antwerp cabinets also document a very vigorous local market, which Jost Amman celebrated from the time of the Renaissance [XIV.4]. Some of the cabinets depicted [XIV.7] are in fact the shops of vendors who supply articles for cabinets; the picture is exhibited there as a potential tradable commodity. Other paintings, such as those by Teniers [XIII.39, XIV.10] depict a princely device in an almost political dimension where the artworks seem sublimated, momentarily purified of any market value. The exchange value is always sublimated, but it permeates the collection, revealing the object as a potential purchase or a select focus of acquisitiveness.

Cat XIV.5
COLLECTOR'S CABINET
Adriaen Stalbemt (attributed, assisted by Hieronymus Francken II), c. 1650

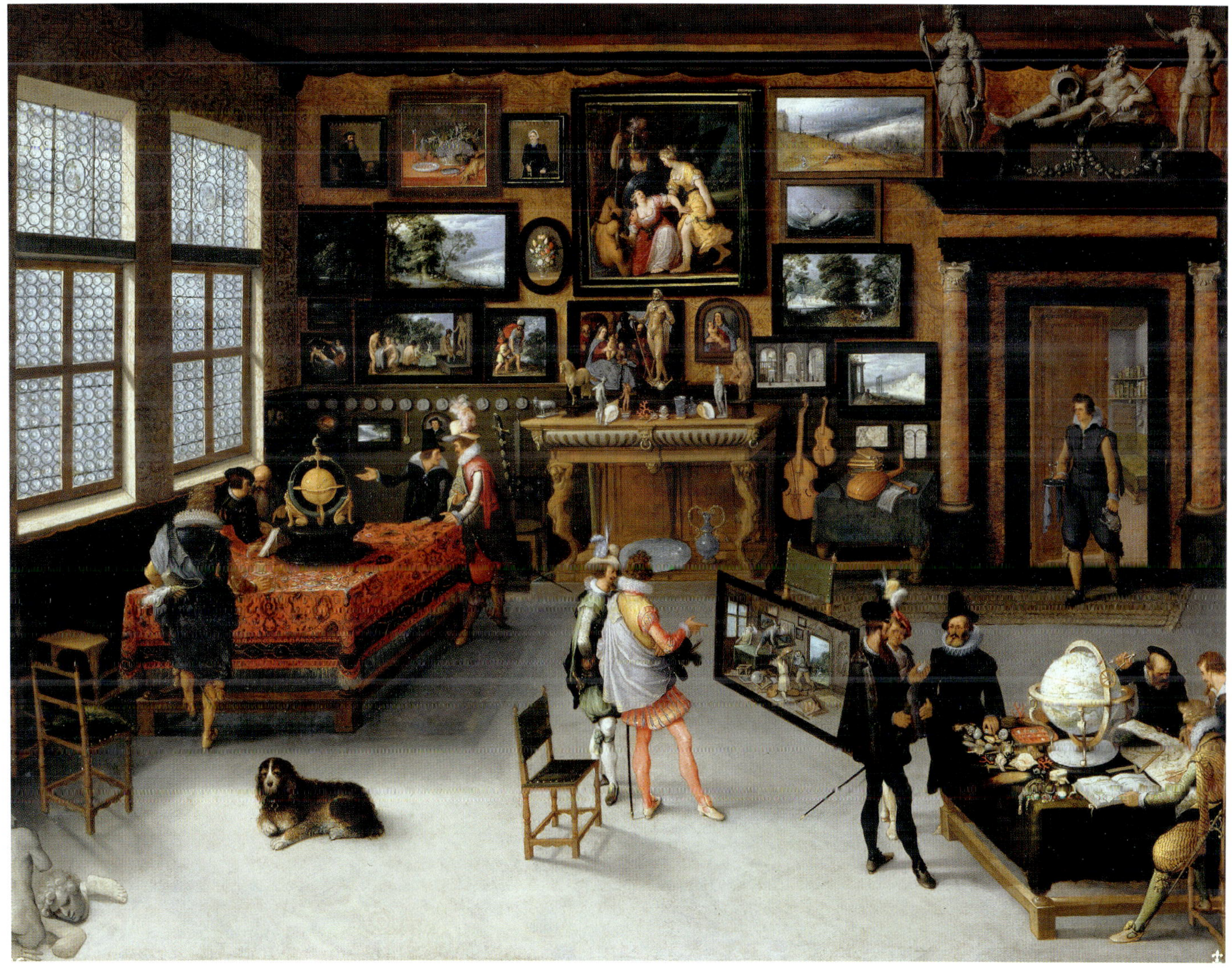

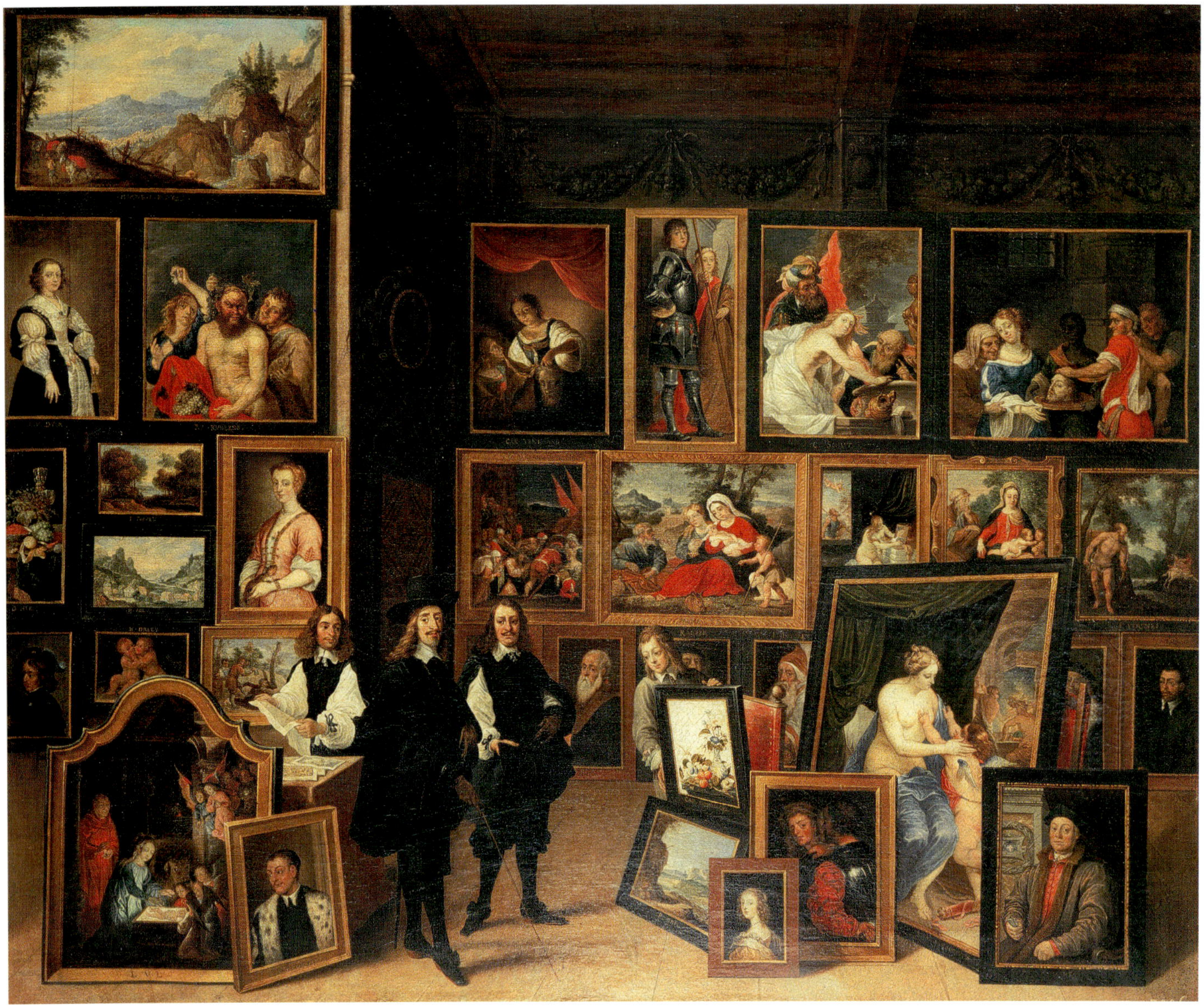

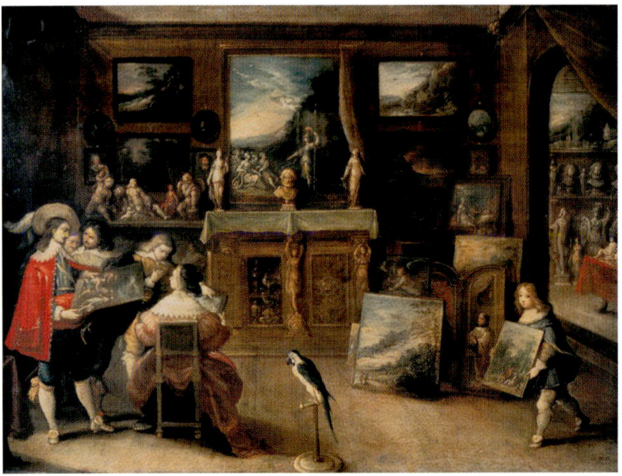

Cat XIV.10
ARCHDUKE LEOPOLD WILHELM VISITING THE ARTIST'S GALLERY
David Teniers II,
c. 1653

Cat XIV.7
COLLECTOR'S CABINET
Frans Francken II, 1636

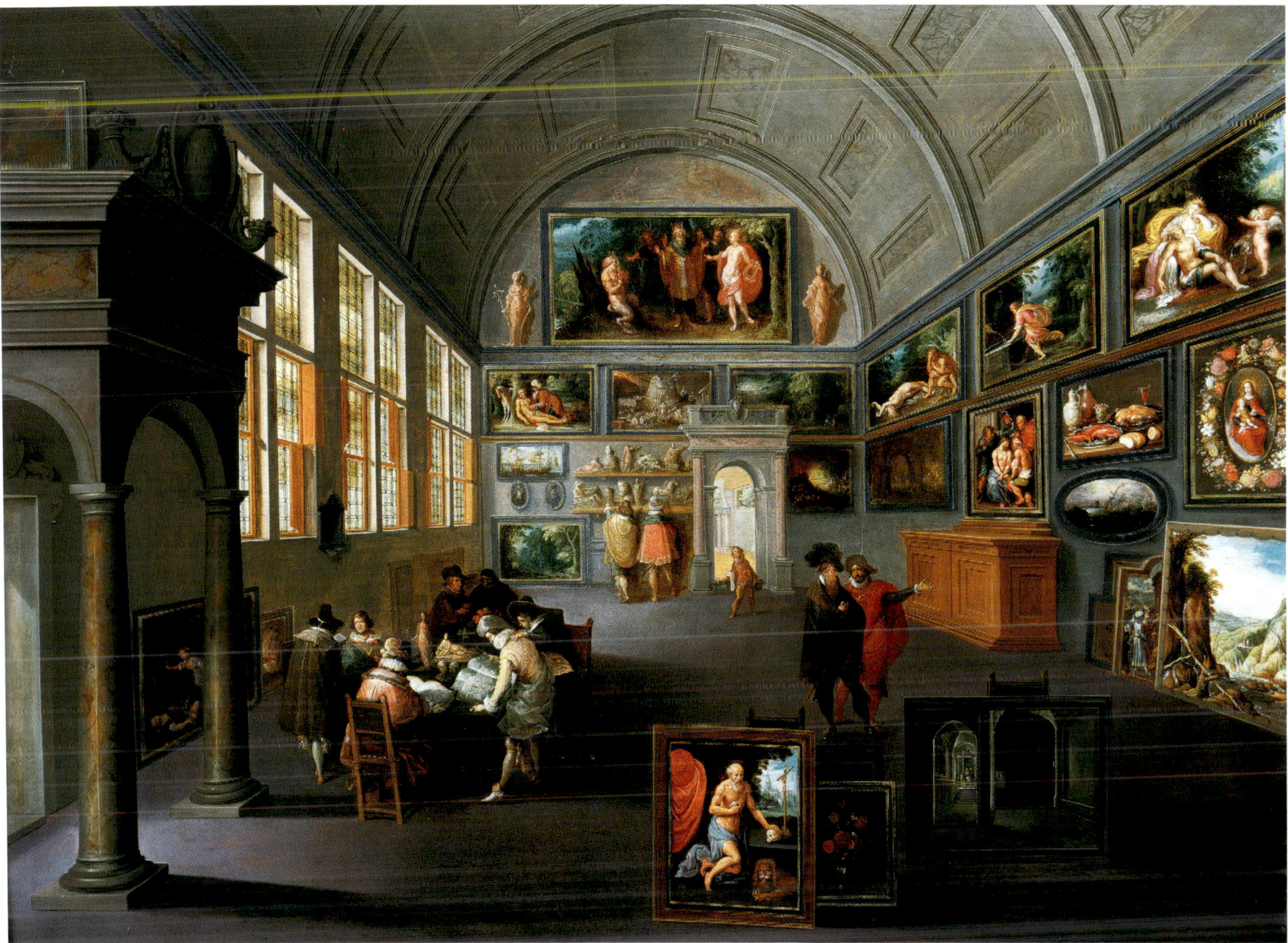

Cat XIV.9
THE INTERIOR OF A PICTURE GALLERY
Frans Francken II and Hendrick Van Steenwyck the Younger, c. 1620

The juxtaposition of the pictures is always significant – at a time when the emblematic was in great vogue, arranging subjects in dense presentation was to create meaning freely, by collage. The system of pendant paintings – pictures intended to be hung in pairs – allowed meaning to be organized, to impose on them an unmistakeble syntax – order and *copia* would appeal to the viewer and reader of the collection, often trained in the best rhetorical tradition. The cabinet painting was deliberately reminiscent of these symbolic texts. We should also bear in mind that such collections were not presented, as today, to a public that was free to move around at will. Entry into the gallery, and contemplation of the works, was highly ritualized. In general the master of the house liked to play host at his own gallery, eager in this way to make his mark on the symbolic function of his collection and on its latent content. The first public collections were no exception to this rule. At the Ashmolean Museum in Oxford, visitors paid an entry fee, the amount of which was linked to the time they spent in the collection. At the

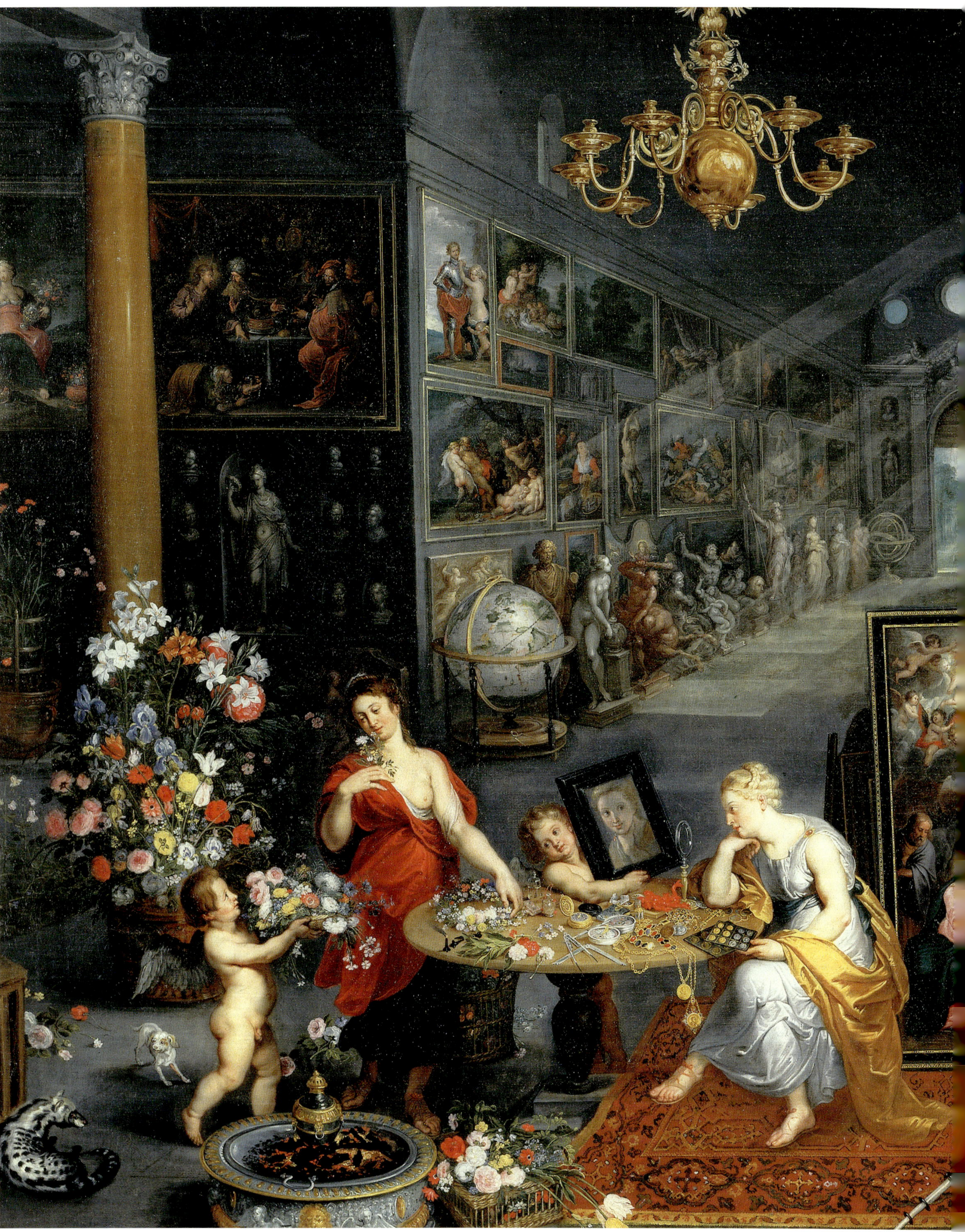

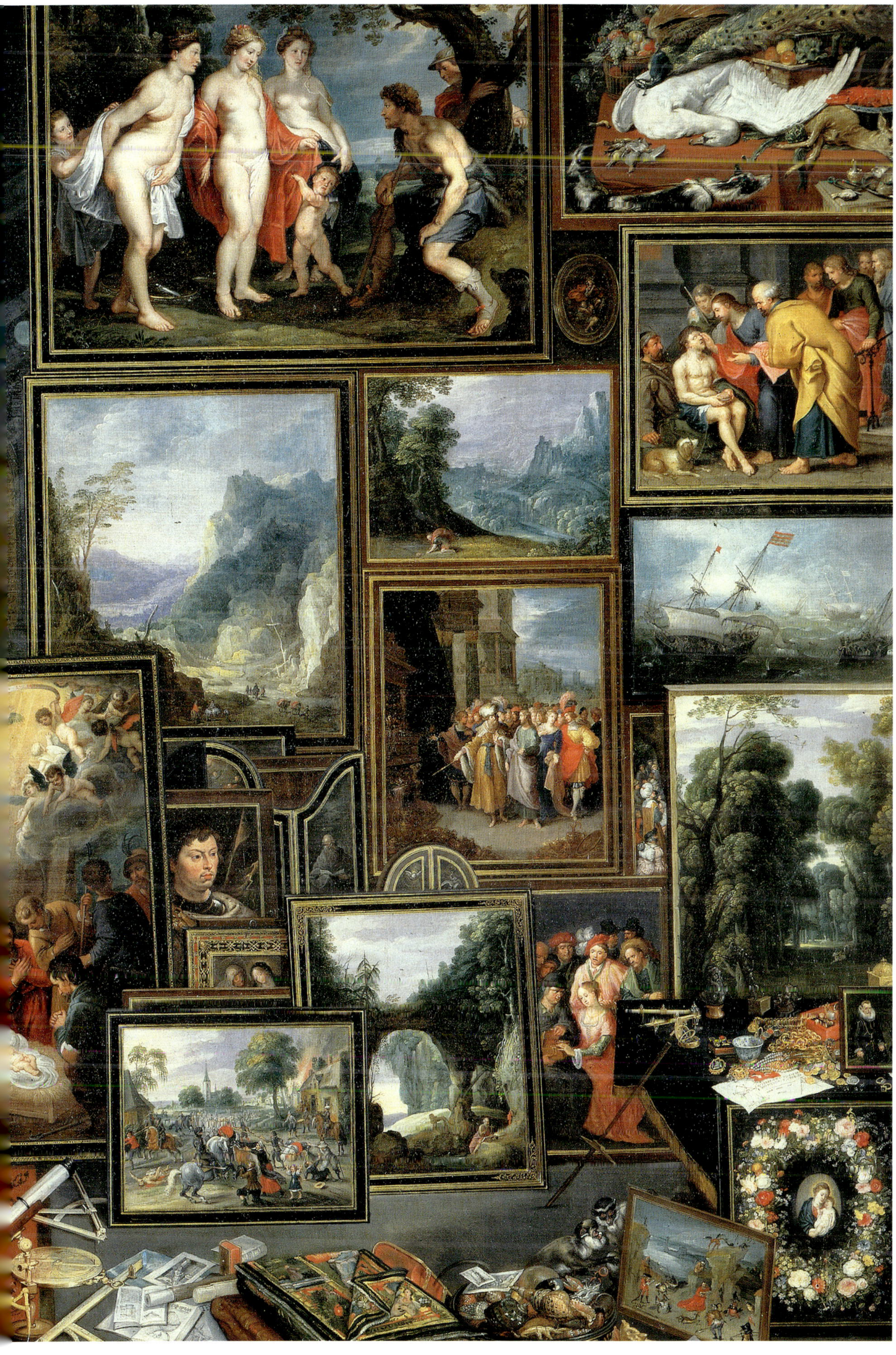

Cat XIV.12
ALLEGORY OF SIGHT AND SMELL
Jan 'Velvet' Brueghel (the Elder), Peter Paul Rubens et al., 1618

Vatican Library, a guard showed the most beautiful books, then returned them to their places.

The cabinet also had a dream-like quality in terms of its dimensions: it presented a sum of objects in a small space. Several cabinets were completed by different artists **XIV.5, 9, 12**, each commissioned for their mastery of a particular effect, the whole creating a firework display of varied pleasures. In a playful way, the gallery in a painting promised the acquisition of a miniature collection for the price of a single picture. It metaphorizes, lost and reduced, to the world of artworks the full presence of the macrocosm in the microcosm that represents it. Finally, the cabinet often tried to defeat the effects of death, which disrupted galleries and scattered pictures so patiently selected – 'I don't want to die as a corpus', it seemed to be saying, 'here is this collection carefully assembled and preserved forever in its image'.

Cat. xiv 13
THE GALLERY OF CARDINAL SILVIO VALENTI GONZAGA
Giovanni Paolo Pannini, *c.* 1749

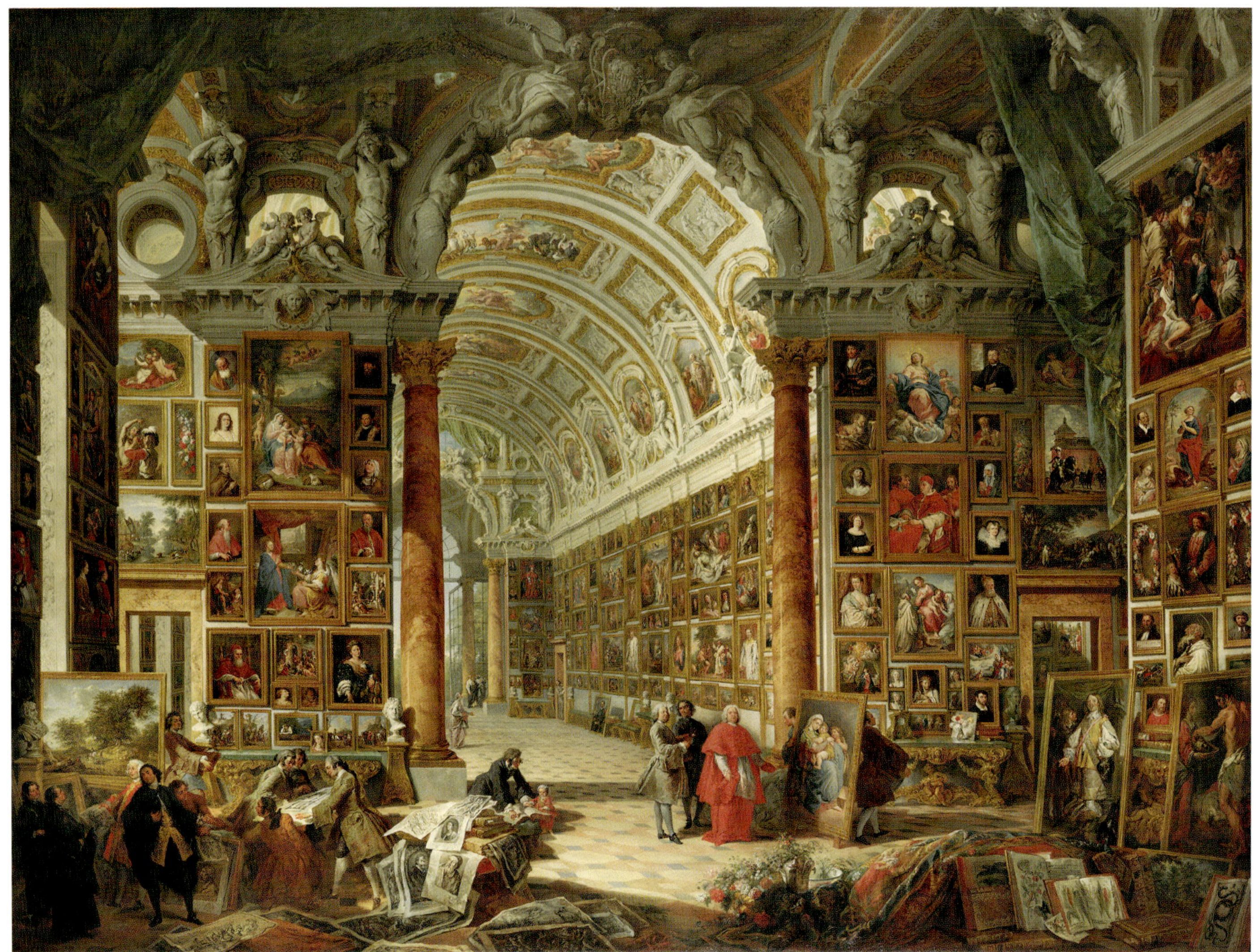

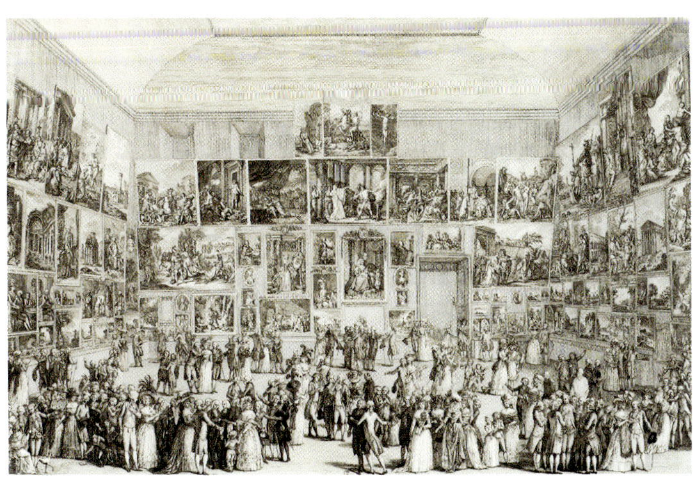

Cat XIV.14
EXHIBITION AT THE SALON DU LOUVRE IN 1787
Pietro Antonio Martini

In the 18th century, this form would serve to present the universality of Rome as a museum of Europe; the imaginary gallery of Cardinal Silvio Valenti Gonzaga is a superb example. There are others, showing the most beautiful works of ancient Rome, a real luxury postcard collection. Connoisseurs appreciate these views, particularly those executed by Pannini [XIV.13]. Then Pietro Antonio Martini used, in 1785 and 1787, the iconography of the cabinet to represent a new space that was decidedly modern [XIV.14, 15], in a democratic era – the painting exhibition celebrating the King as patron of the arts, but redefined by the nascent art critic as a public forum where the artist had to submit his works to the universal verdict of opinion. With Martini, the form of the cabinet served to give rise to the emergence of a space for art for a democratic age.

BIBLIOGRAPHY : S. Speth-Holterhoff, *Les peintres flamands de cabinets d'amateur au XVIIe siècle*, Paris-Brussels, 1957; M. Winner, *Die Quellen der Pictura-Allegorien in gemalten Bildergalerien des 17. Jahrhunderts zu Antwerpen*, Cologne, 1957; Z. Zaremba Filipczak, *Picturing Art in Antwerp 1550–1700*, Princeton, 1987; V. I. Stoichita, *L'instauration du tableau*, Paris, 1993.

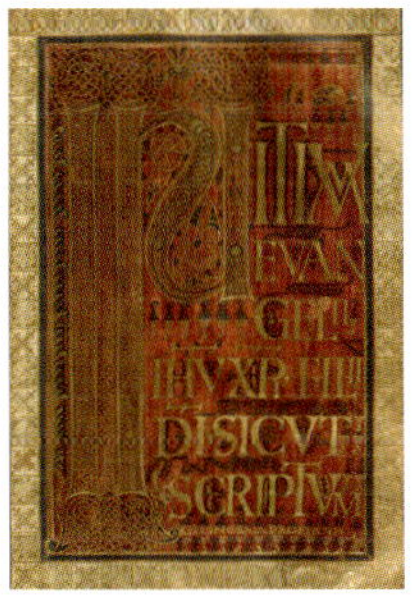
II.1

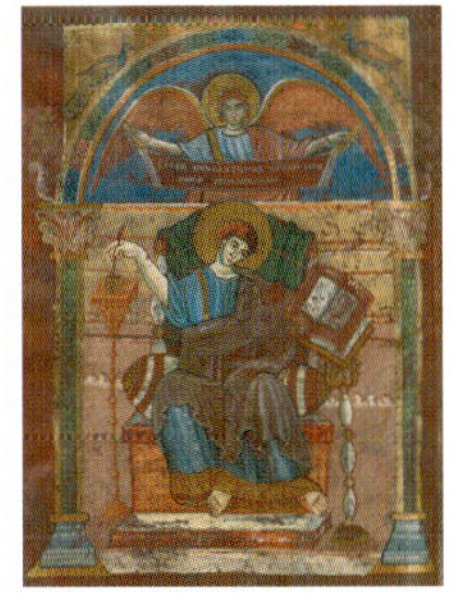
II.2

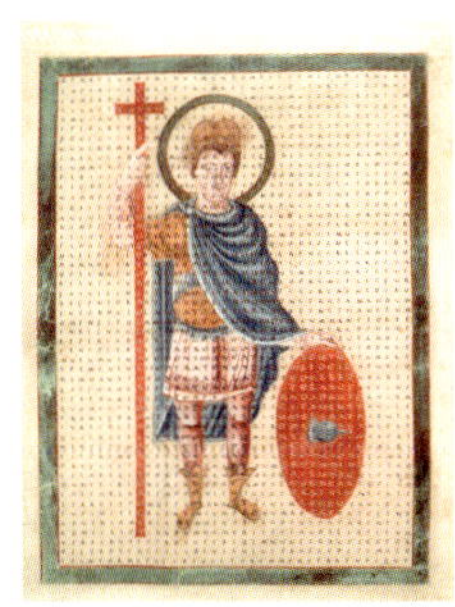
II.3

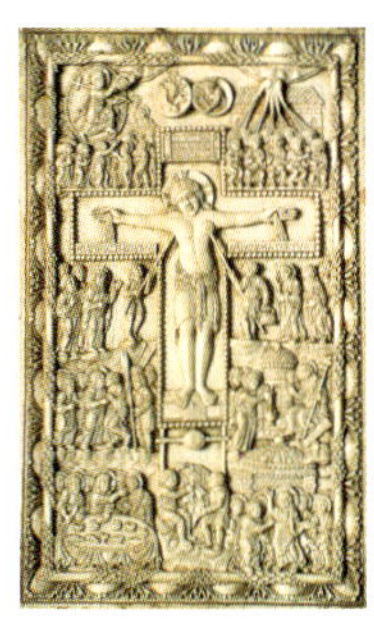
II.4

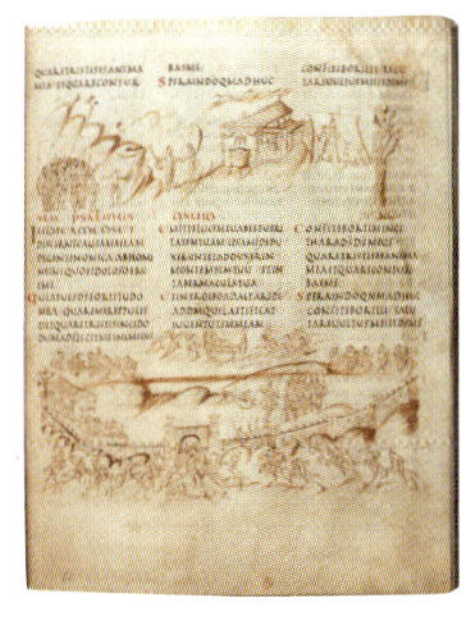
II.5

SECTION II
THE CAROLINGIAN EMPIRE AND ITS LEGACY

It is generally accepted that the true birth of Europe dates from the reign of Charlemagne. At the same time as the Church was assuming its dominant role, a great effort was made to assemble the intellectual heritage of Graeco-Roman Antiquity. The most remarkable achievements of Carolingian art are to be found in architecture (Aachen) but above all in their books. Every type of learning was represented: the Bible, Psalters and gospels, but also scientific treatises and literary or philosophical works. The invention of Caroline, a new form of script distinguished by its legibility, was the basis for the modern alphabet. The most luxurious books had a carved ivory binding, embellished with a frame in gold or silver that were often made by the painter of the miniatures.

A.

The Emperor and his relations established several centres (scriptoria) to encourage writing and the illumination of manuscripts. The first was at the Palatine court, under the impetus of an English scholar named Alcuin, from around 780; Alcuin was succeeded by another scholar, Eginhard, future author of *Vita Caroli Magni* (written around 830, after the Emperor's death). Charlemagne invited poets, artists, and men of letters and learning to his palace for intense intellectual debates with the aristocracy and the royal family.

II.1 SAINT-MARTIN-DES-CHAMPS GOSPELS

Palatine court, before 795
Parchment, 178 ff., 26.5 x 19 cm
Paris, Bibliothèque de l'Arsenal, Ms 599
f.134r: *In Principio....*

This manuscript consists of double-column, gold-letter texts. For titles, capitals, rustic and uncial, are employed. It is illustrated with sixteen canonical tables, and a full-page initial at the start of each Gospel, of which only three survive. The decoration displays the influence of Insular art.

BIBLIOGRAPHY : *Karl der Grosse*, no. 412.

II.2 CENTULA GOSPELS

Palatine court, late 8th century
Parchment, 189 ff., 35 x 24.5 cm
Abbeville, Picardy, Bibliothèque municipale, Ms 4
f.17v-18r: Matthew

This sumptuous manuscript was presented by Charlemagne to Angilbert, his ambassador to Popes Adrian I and Leo III; it is mentioned in 831 in the inventory of the abbey of Centula (Saint-Riquier, Picardy), of which Angilbert was abbot from 789-90 and where he created a library of over two hundred volumes. With the exception of the final pages, the manuscript is written on sheets of purple parchment. The ornamentation consists of canonical tables and portraits of the four Evangelists; these reproduce the composition favoured by the court illuminators, i.e., a broad arcade under which is seated the Evangelist and over which appears his symbol. The perspective effects and the treatment of architecture betray the influence of Greco-Roman art, perhaps through the intermediary of Byzantine models. The most accomplished example of this formula is to be found in the Gospels of Saint-Médard de Soissons (Paris, BnF, Lat.8850).

BIBLIOGRAPHY : *Karl der Grosse*, no. 414.

II.3 HRABAN MAUR, *LIBER DE LAUDIBUS SANCTAE CRUCIS*

Second quarter of 9th century
Parchment, 47 ff., 40.5 x 33 cm
Amiens, Bibliothèques d'Amiens Métropole, Ms 0223
f.3v: Portrait of Louis the Pious, clad in ancient fashion and holding cross
Provenance: Fulda, Germany (?)

This manuscript is among the oldest manuscripts of the *Liber de Laudibus Sanctae Crucis* (Praises of the Holy Cross), this treatise was dedicated to Louis the Pious (814–70); several dozen copies were made under the supervision of Hraban Maur (776–856) for use by the Emperor and church dignitaries. Maur was abbot of Fulda from 822, where he created a scriptorium and an intellectual centre of the highest excellence. Later he was appointed bishop of Mainz by Louis the German. He was the author of numerous spiritual writings, as well as sermons and biblical commentaries. The illustrations look back to an ancient tradition of superimposing on a page of text a figurative representation that outlines another text.

BIBLIOGRAPHY : Ulrich Ernst, *Carmen Figuratum. Geschichte des Figurengedichts von den antiken Ursprüngen bis zum Ausgang des Mittelalters*, Cologne-Weimar-Vienna, 1991.

II.4 BOOK COVER WITH CRUCIFIXION SCENE

Palatine court, early 9th century
Ivory, 25.3 x 15.7 cm
Narbonne, Trésor de la cathédrale Saint-Just et Saint-Pasteur
Classed as historic monument
17 June 1901

A fan-shaped frame of acanthus leaves and a twisted ribbon divide off the spaces for seven scenes. A beardless Christ is surrounded by Longinus and Stephaton, as well as Mary and St John; under the Cross is enacted the dividing of Christ's robe, with above it the symbols of Sol and Luna. At bottom left is the Last Supper, under the Arrest of Christ. To the right, Doubting Thomas, and the Holy

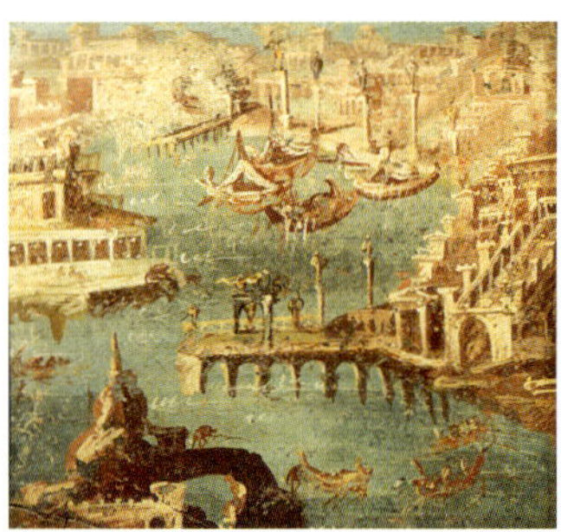
II.6

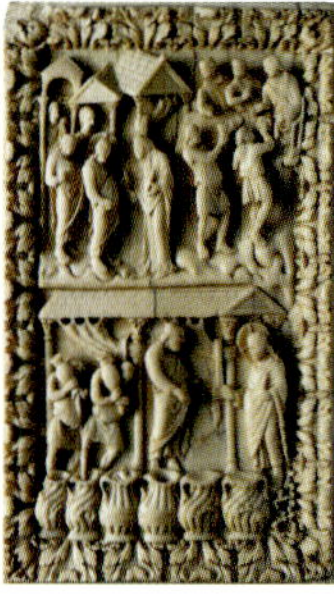
II.7

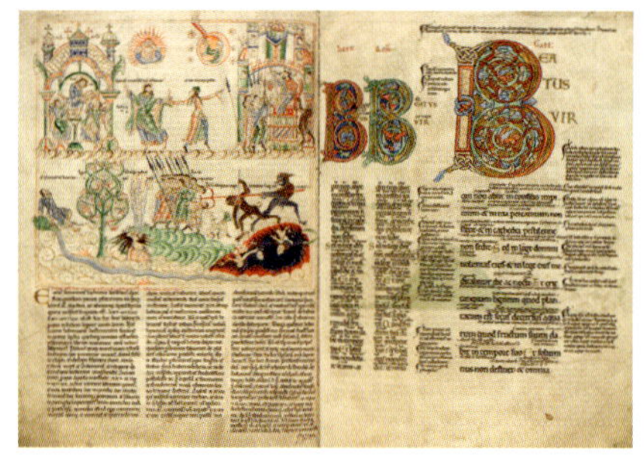
II.8

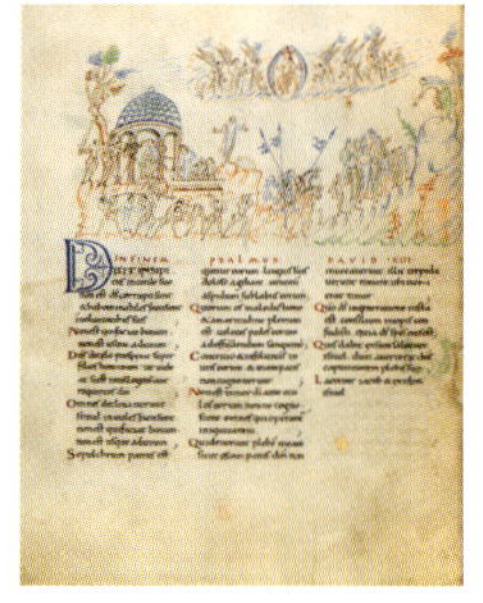
II.9

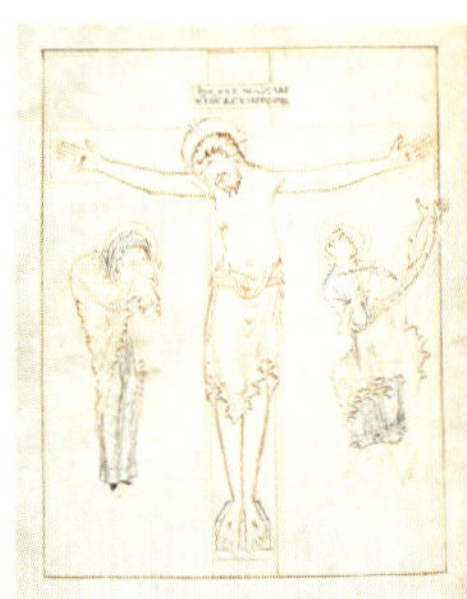
II.10

Women at the Tomb. Above the Cross are the Ascension and Pentecost. The arrangement of the narrative scenes may be likened to palaeochristian art. Their style also resembles that of other ivories from the Palatine court, e.g. the Aachen Diptych.

BIBLIOGRAPHY : *Trésors des églises de France* (exhib. cat.), Paris 1966, no. 601 ; Adolf Goldschmidt, *Die Elfenbeinskulpturen*, 1–2 : *Aus der Zeit der karolingischen und sächsichen Kaiser 8–11. Jahrhundert*, Berlin, 1914, I, no. 31 ; *Karl der Grosse*, Aachen, 1965, no. 531 ; H. Fillitz, 'Elfenbeinreliefs vom Hofe Karls des Kahlen', *Beiträge zur Kunst des Mittelalters*, Festschrift Hans Wentzel, 1975, pp. 41–51.

B.

The majority of intellectual centres in Carolingian Europe were situated between the Seine and the Rhine. At the abbey of Hautvillers, near Rheims – two centres owing their success to Archbishop Ebbo, foster-brother to Louis the Pious – one of the greatest masterpieces of medieval art was created : the Utrecht Psalter, named after its present place of preservation. The illustrations, in ink, bear witness to a knowledge of Romano-Hellenistic art.

Taken *c.* AD 1000 to the abbey of Christ Church in Canterbury, the Utrecht Psalter would exercise a considerable influence on Insular illumination for the next two centuries.

II.5 UTRECHT PSALTER

Hautvillers, near Rheims, *c.* 825–35
Parchment, 92 ff., 33 x 25.8 cm
Utrecht, Universiteitsbibliotheek, ms. 32
f. 73r: Psalm CXXV
From around AD 1000 in the possession of Christ Church abbey, Canterbury

Following the ancient tradition, the text is arranged in three columns of 32 lines per page. The design of the small figures is entirely subordinated to the production of a highly expressive narrative effect that makes this psalter an artistic masterpiece, especially when one considers the economy of means employed – pen and bistre ink. But the manuscript has another singular feature : the images are not mere illustrations, but graphical commentaries that presuppose a scholarly knowledge of references in the psalms. A work so ambitious and complex must have been the result of a group of artists working in combination ; they would have shared an artistic culture fed by Hellenistic and Greco-Roman art, from which they imbibed a passion that had not yet manifested itself in the art of the West.

BIBLIOGRAPHY : Francis Wormald, *The Utrecht Psalter*, Utrecht, 1953 ; K. vander Horst, W. Noel, W. C. M. Wüstefeld (eds), *The Utrecht Psalter in Medieval Art. Picturing the Psalms of David* (exhib. cat.), Utrecht, 1996 (bibl.).

II.6 LANDSCAPE

Naples, 1st century AD
Fresco, removed from original location and remounted, 26 x 24 cm
Naples, Museo Archeologico Nazionale, 9514

In order to give some idea of the artistic tradition in which the illuminators of the Utrecht Psalter (II.5) were immersed, presented here is a fragment of a fresco that once graced a villa wall in the Roman town of Stabiae (now Castellamare di Stabia in the Bay of Naples). The town was almost totally destroyed in the eruption of Vesuvius (AD 79), simultaneously with Pompeii and Herculaneum. The painter has depicted a town and its port, perhaps Puteoli. Colours and forms are the result of light, rapid touches communicating a remarkable spontaneity, approaching that of a snapshot. Such a form of pictorial writing is reminiscent of the techniques of Impressionism, or of artists like Francesco Guardi.

II.7 BOOK COVER : THE WEDDING AT CANA

School of the Palace of Charles the Bald, 9th century
Ivory, 13.8 x 8.3 cm
London, British Museum, no. M & LA 1856, 6–23, 20

Here are two scenes, one above the other, within a frame of acanthus leaves. In the upper register, Christ, followed by His apostles, is in conversation with His mother in front of the house where the marriage is being celebrated. Below, two servants are filling pitchers with water and the master of ceremonies talks with Christ. The style is characteristic of the Liuthard Group, from the name of the scribe responsible for the Psalter of Charles the Bald (Paris, BnF, Lat.1152), in the names of Charles and his wife Hermintrude, who were married from 842 until the death of the queen in 869. The panel assembles all the elements of an intensely expressive style directly inspired by the Utrecht Psalter, sometimes transcribing its illustrations quite literally. However, through its scheme of flat composition, it also reveals the influence of the principal illustrator of the Codex Aureus (Munich, Bayer. Staatsbibl.).

BIBLIOGRAPHY : Goldschmidt, I, 29, no. 46 ; Amy L. Vandersall, 'The Relationship of Sculptors and Painters in the Court School of Charles the Bald', *Gesta*, XV, 1–2, 1976, pp. 201–10 ; *The Utrecht Psalter*, no. 17.

II.8 EADWINE PSALTER

Christ Church, Canterbury, *c.* 1150–60 (with post-1160 additions)
Parchment, 286 ff., 46 x 32.7 cm
Cambridge, Trinity College Library, Ms. R.17.1
f.5v : illustrating Psalm I ('The two ways') and f.6r : the B of *Beatus vir* ('Blessed is the man ....')

This is a 'triple psalter' with translations in English and Anglo-Norman, a set of prefaces and Latin glosses,
as well as prayers and two cycles of illustrations. It contains more illustrations than any other 12th-century English work : 166 of psalms, canticles and creeds, deriving from illuminations in the Utrecht Psalter. In addition, there are 500 illuminated initials, highlighted in gold and silver. At the beginning, eight pages of narrative biblical scenes have been added very hurriedly, forming the longest cycle of its type ; fifteen or so years later there followed a plan of the cathedral and the Christ Church water system, while the magnificent portrait of the scribe is part of the original conception. The prototype for the illuminations preceding the Psalms is the Utrecht Psalter, which was at Canterbury around AD 1000. The use of colour considerably modifies the nature of the original model.
The images are the work of several illuminators, who have imbued the models from the Utrecht Psalter with a more solemn eloquence, aimed no doubt at enhancing the glory of Christ Church. The man

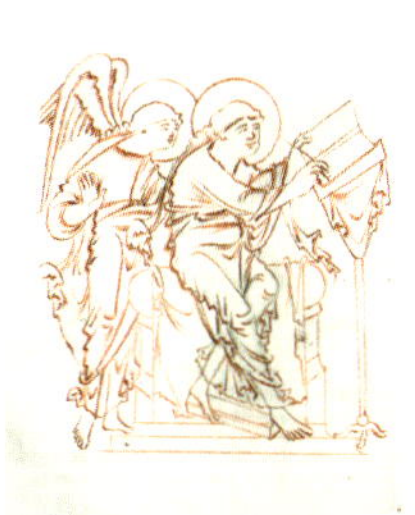
II.11

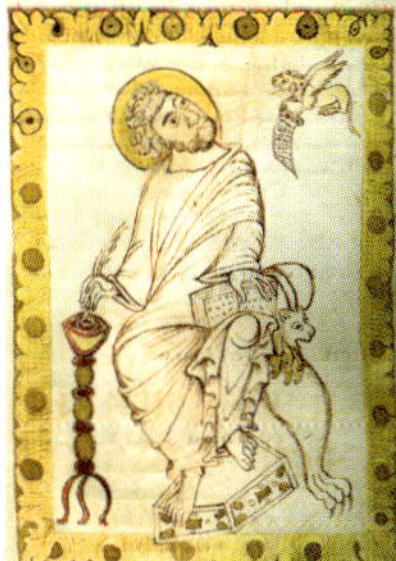
II.12

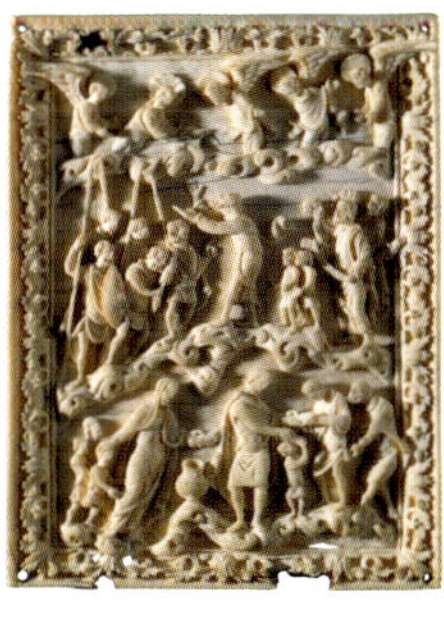
II.13

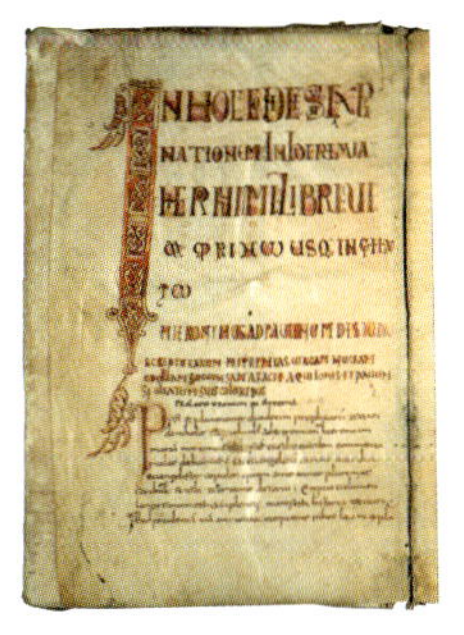
II.14

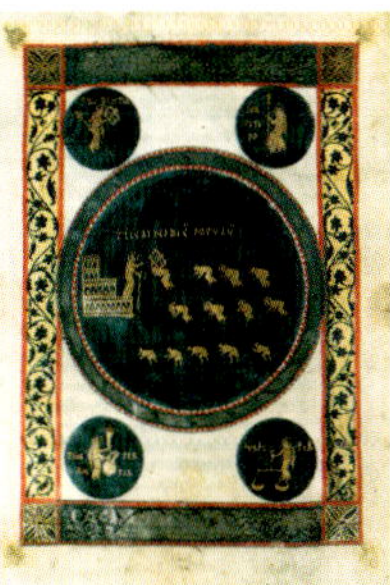
II.15

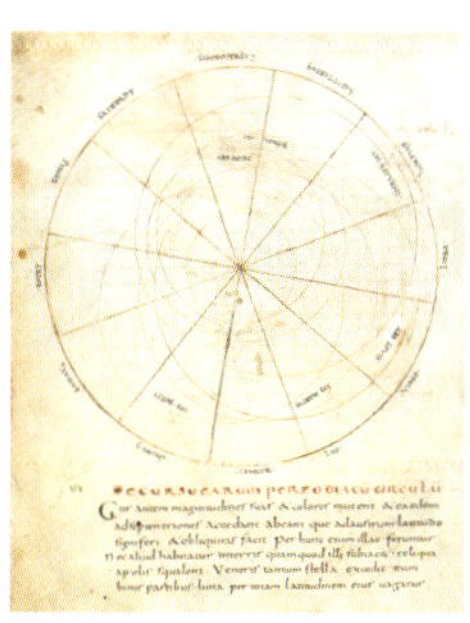
II.16

known as the Superbia Master, responsible for f.5v, displayed here, was evidently an artist of the first rank who obviously appropriated the illustrations from the Utrecht Psalter and was able to adapt them with enormous freedom. The principal differences between this work and the Utrecht Psalter illustration that inspired it (f.1v), besides the introduction of colour, are due to the clarification of space and consequent improved legibility of the scenes.

BIBLIOGRAPHY: G. Zarnecki, J. Holt, T. Holland (eds), *English Romanesque Art 1066–1200* (exhib. cat.), London, 1984, no. 62; Margaret Gibson, T. A. Heslop, Richard W. Pfaff (eds), *The Eadwine Psalter. Text, Image, and Monastic Culture in Twelfth-Century Canterbury*, London, 1992.

II.9 HARLEY PSALTER

Christ Church, Canterbury, early 11th–early 12th century, unfinished
Parchment, 73 ff., 37.6 x 31.2 cm
London, British Library, Ms. Harley 603
ff.7v and 8r: Psalms 13?–15

Here, the illustrations are in colour, unlike those in the Utrecht Psalter. Painter A is credited with the illustrations for this psalter, with additions by Painter G. The movements of the figures are much more striking, as is their dynamic intensity. The illustrations were executed before the text, whose arrangement derives directly from the Utrecht Psalter. This is the earliest psalter whose illuminations attest to the presence at Canterbury of the Utrecht Psalter, its immediate source of inspiration. Probably commissioned by Aelfric, archbishop of Canterbury, who bequeathed it in 1003 or 1004 to Wulfstan, archbishop of York.

BIBLIOGRAPHY: William Noel, *The Harley Psalter*, Cambridge, 1995; *The Utrecht Psalter*, no. 28.

II.10 RAMSEY PSALTER

Ramsey, (?), before 988
Parchment
London, British Library, Ms Harley 2904
f.3v: the Crucifixion, 33.2 x 25.1 cm

The crucified Christ dominates the composition, and there is no attempt to provide a realistic space for the Virgin and St John. The suffering of Mary is underlined by her robe held up against her face. St John is displaying a scroll – 'This is the disciple that testifieth of these things' (John 21:24 or 19:35) – an image with no precedent in Carolingian iconography. The miniaturist, however, must have found a model in Psalm 43 of the Utrecht Psalter, where an old man is shown vigorously brandishing a scroll.

BIBLIOGRAPHY: E. Temple, *Anglo-Saxon Manuscripts 900–1066*, London, 1976, no. 41.

II.11 GOSPELS

Winchester (?), *c.* 1015–30
Parchment, 165 ff., 26.3 x 19.8 cm
Besançon, Bibliothèque Municipale, Ms 14
Provenance: abbey of Saint-Claude (Conat, Jura)
f.58v: St Mark writing

The elevated style of this superb page belongs to an illuminator who pondered intensely the object lessons of the Utrecht Psalter, which, like many of his colleagues, he would have seen personally at Canterbury. The page has rightly been thought to be incomplete, with the colours not yet added; had colours been added, for example, the final result would have been close to the illustrations in the Sacramentary of Robert de Jumièges (II.24).

BIBLIOGRAPHY: *The Utrecht Psalter*, no. 35.

II.12 GOSPELS

Liège (?), *c.* 1000
Parchment, 259 ff., 27.6 x 21 cm
Le Puy-en-Velay, Bibliothèque Municipale, Ms 2
f.55v: St Mark

A figure such as this reveals an obvious relationship to the Ebbo Gospels (Épernay, Bibliothèque Municipale), the work of the scriptorium at Hautvillers abbey. The canonical tables illustrating this manuscript are inspired by those of the Rheims school. Hanns Swarzenski has demonstrated the existence at Liège of an extremely important group of illuminators who readily seized upon Carolingian models to make what were in effect 'copies', with, however, a novel economy of formal means.

BIBLIOGRAPHY: Lucy A. Freeman, 'A Late Carolingian Gospel Book in the Pierpont Morgan Library', *Marsyas*, VI, 1954–57, pp. 53–63; Hanns Swarzenski, 'The Role of Copies in the Formation of the Styles of the Eleventh Century', in *Romanesque and Gothic Art. Studies in Western Art. Acts of the Twentieth International Congress of the History of Art*, vol. 1, Princeton, 1963, pp. 6–18.

II.13 COVERS FROM THE BOOK KNOWN AS THE HOURS OF CHARLES THE BALD

School of the Palace of Charles the Bald, 846–69
Ivory, Psalm 26: 11.2 x 8.8 cm and Psalm 24: 11.3 x 8.5 cm
Zurich, Schweizerisches Landesmuseum, LM, 21825
Provenance: Rheinau, Switzerland

Here we find the same nervous, almost furious writing that appears in the Utrecht Psalter. The bold design, the daring use of space, the body movements and gestures intensify the effect of the scenes and denote true narrative genius. The work to which these ivory panels were originally attached – the first to combine both a psalter and a *liber orationum* (prayer book) – is today in Munich.

BIBLIOGRAPHY: Goldschmidt, I, no. 42; Danielle Gaborit-Chopin, *Ivoires du Moyen Âge*, Fribourg (Switzerland), 1978, no. 73; Peter Lasko, *Ars Sacra 800–1200*, The Pelican History of Art, Harmondsworth, 1972, pp. 35–37.

C.

New centres and scriptoria arose: in the Loire region (at Saint-Martin de Tours, thanks to the arrival of Alcuin, a relative of Charlemagne, as well as at Orleans and Fleury, whose abbot was the Visigoth Theodulf), but especially at Metz, which was the administrative capital of the Empire and whose see was bestowed upon relations of the Emperor, notably Drogo, half-brother of Louis the Pious. The existence of numerous illustrated books and carved ivory panels indicates intense intellectual and artistic activity in the diocese of Metz throughout the 9th century. The abbeys of Reichenau and Saint-Gall also benefited from the favours of the Carolingian dynasty and became artistic centres of the first rank.

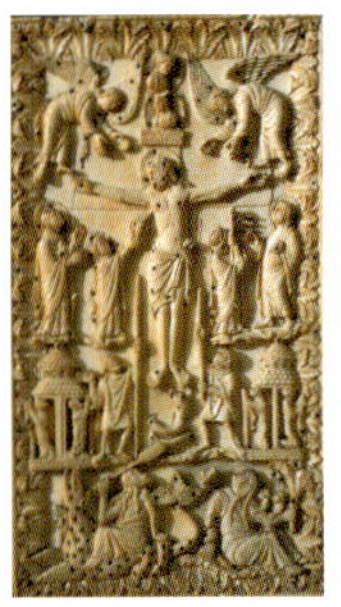
II.17

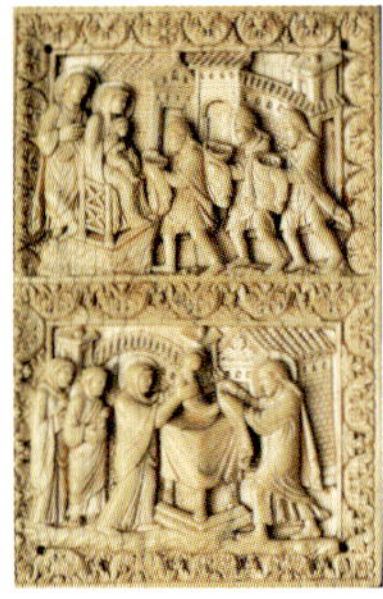
II.18

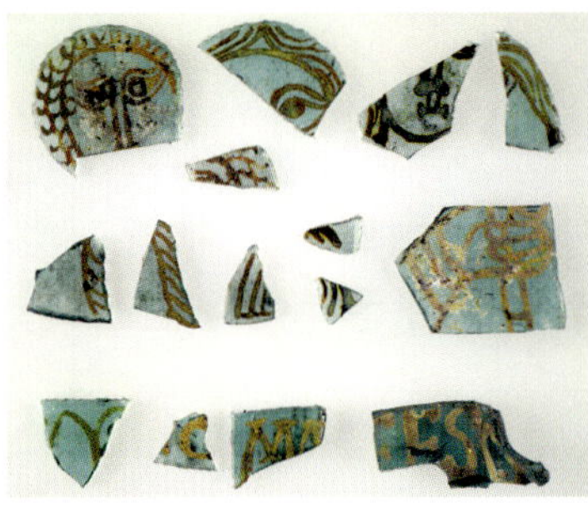
II.19

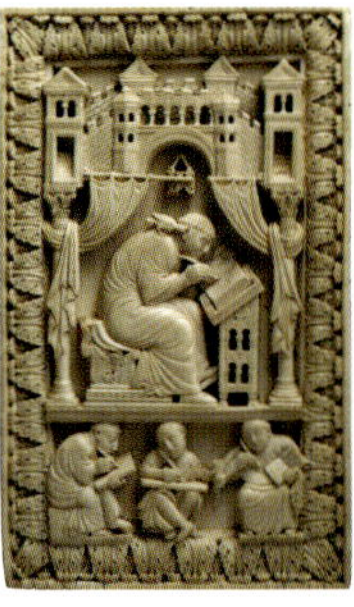
II.20

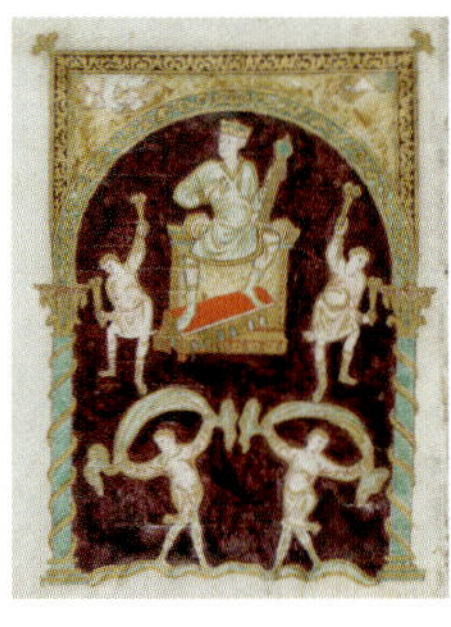
II.21

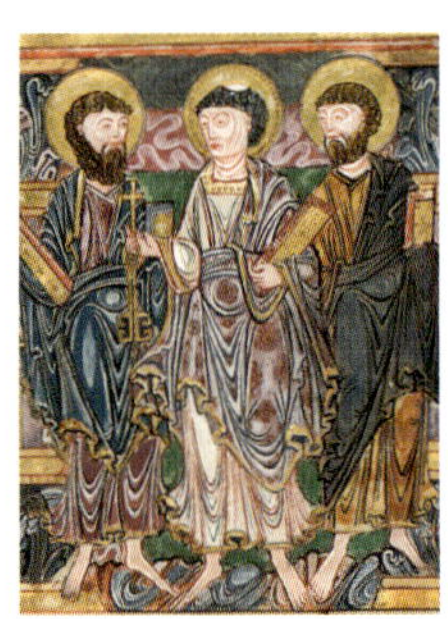
II.22

II.14 COMMENTARIES OF ST JEROME

Fleury (?), 806
Parchment, 182 ff., 33.5 x 22 cm
Valenciennes, Bibliothèque Municipale, Ms 59, 371
f.1v: Initial F

We know the name of the scribe, Agambertus, who compiled this volume for the abbess (Theotildis?) of an unknown convent, and who worked in the scriptorium at Fleury. The scribe even notes the time it took for him to complete the manuscript: from 1 July to 4 August, suggesting he wrote (and illustrated?) eleven pages a day! The initial F is decorated with a weave of red, green and violet, typical of the work at Fleury.

BIBLIOGRAPHY: *Karl der Grosse*, no. 371.

II.15 MARMOUTIER SACRAMENTARY

Abbey of Saint-Martin, Marmoutier, Tours, 844–45
Parchment, 197 ff., 34 x 24.4 cm
Autun, Bibliothèque Municipale, Ms 19b (S19)
Provenance: Marmoutier abbey; at Autun cathedral in the 12th century
f.173v: the cardinal vertues

A sacramentary is a liturgical volume containing the complete prayers read during Mass. From the time of Alcuin, who was abbot of Saint-Martin from 796, Tours was one of the most important centres of the Carolingian Empire. This book was produced in the scriptorium at Tours for the abbot of Marmoutier, Rainaud, seen here making a gesture of benediction. The illustrations were carried out under Abbot Vivien (844–51), chamberlain to Charles the Bald. The techniques of Rheims are very obvious in these magnificent gold silhouettes, but they equally show undoubted affinities with the art of cutting rock crystal: compare the Lothair Crystal in the British Museum. It is not impossible that artists who worked with crystal also mastered the art of illumination.

BIBLIOGRAPHY: *The Utrecht Psalter*, no. 22.

II.16 TREATISE ON ASTRONOMY

Metz, *c.* 840
Parchment, 76 ff., 30 x 23.8 cm
Madrid, Biblioteca Nacional de España, Ms 3307
f.65v

Commissioned by Drogo, Charlemagne's illegitimate son, who held the major archbishopric of Metz from 821 to 825 by favour of his half-brother Louis the Pious, this book is a testament to the intellectual debate that flourished at the imperial court *c.* 810 over the reform of the calendar. The original, comprising ten parts, was a compilation of the writings of Pliny, St Isidore of Seville and the Venerable Bede, but parts are missing from the present collection. The illustrations of the positions of the stars in Book V are based on ancient models. Other copies of this important work are still extant.

BIBLIOGRAPHY: *Karl der Grosse*, no. 479.

II.17 BOOK COVER WITH CRUCIFIXION SCENE

Metz or Lotharingia, third quarter of 9th century
Ivory, 21 x 12 cm
London, Victoria and Albert Museum, no. 250-1867
Provenance: From a book of Gospels of Verdun cathedral

We know from an ancient description that the other board of this book depicted a sovereign on his throne. Christ Crucified is surrounded by the Holy Virgin, St John, Longinus and Stephaton, as well as the Church and the Synagogue. Above the Cross are two medallions for Luna and Sol; below we discern the Resurrection of the Dead. A large space is reserved at the bottom of the composition for allegorical representations of Ocean and Earth. The thick ivory plaque has been painstakingly carved and polished to produce the wonderful sheen that still excites admiration today. Following an ancient technique, numerous holes have been pierced to allow for the application of gold leaf decoration, a few traces of which remain.

BIBLIOGRAPHY: Goldschmidt, I, no. 85; Gaborit-Chopin, p. 70, no. 86; Lasko, 1972, pp. 69–70.

II.18 BOOK COVER WITH THE ADORATION OF THE MAGI AND THE PRESENTATION IN THE TEMPLE

Metz, *c.* 900
Ivory, 18.5 x 11.5 cm
London, Victoria and Albert Museum, no. 150-1866

According to Rohault de Fleury, this relief originated in Sens. Framed by a dense acanthus frieze, both scenes are characteristic of what has been called the second Metz school: the architecture, the arrangement of the figures and the interrelationship in their actions indicate that this Carolingian ivory-carver sought his models from palaeochristian and Byzantine art. Here we have one of the finest examples of this style – it may be compared with a relief in the Staatliche Museen zu Berlin, Skulpturensammlung, showing Jesus in the Temple, the Wedding at Cana and the Cleansing of the Leper.

BIBLIOGRAPHY: Goldschmidt, I, no. 118.

II.19 FRAGMENTS OF A STAINED GLASS WINDOW

Mid-9th century
Various fragments of glass, average dimensions *c.* 3.5 x 2.4 cm
Budapest, Magyar Nemzeti Múzeum, no. 88.40.26-29.Z
Provenance: pilgrim church of St Hadrian at Zalavar-Mosaburg, Hungary

These fragments came to light during excavations in what was a border area of the Carolingian Empire but the political and religious centre of the Slavonic peoples. There are very few surviving fragments of stained glass from the Carolingian era apart from those discovered during excavations in the 1930s at the Carolingian abbey of Lorsch, Germany. The technique used by the painter is grisaille and gold. The slender figures recall the wall-paintings in Naturno in the southern Tyrol.

BIBLIOGRAPHY: Alfried Wieczorek, Hans-Martin Hinz (eds), *Europas Mitte*, Darmstadt, 2000, no. 16.01.06.

II.20 BOOK COVER, SHOWING ST GREGORY

Franco-Saxon (?), Metz school (?), third quarter of 9th century
Ivory, 20.5 x 12.5 cm
Vienna, Kunsthistorisches Museum, no. 8399

This was originally part of the binding of a sacramentary. It is known that throughout his Empire Charlemagne introduced the forms of the Mass instituted by

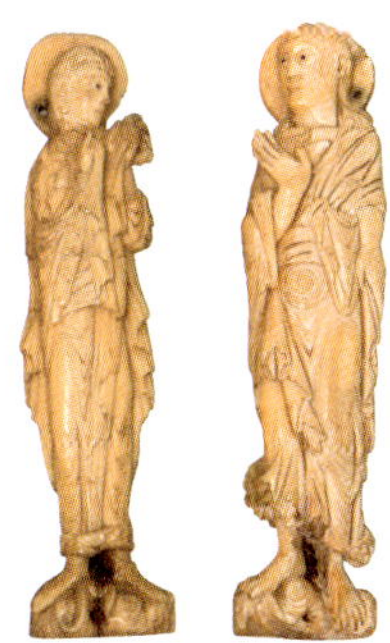
II.23

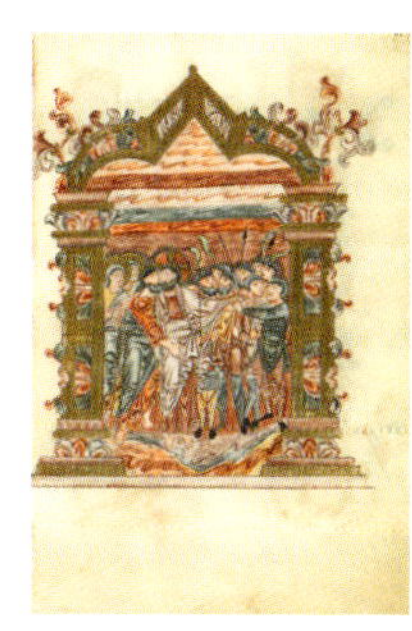
II.24

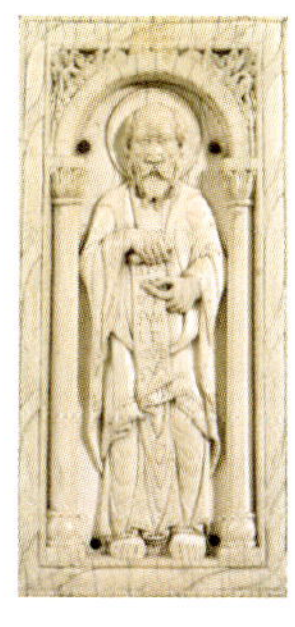
II.25

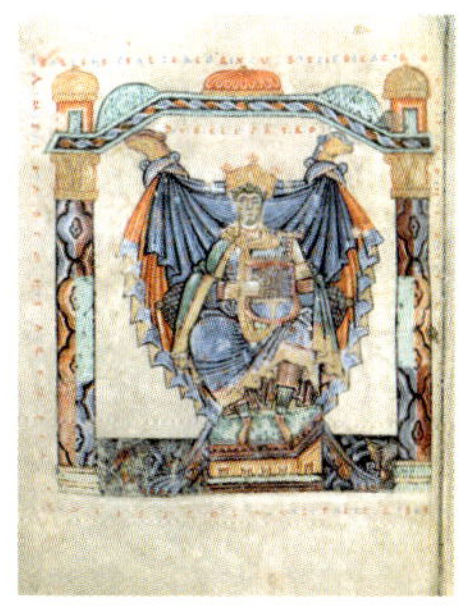
II.26

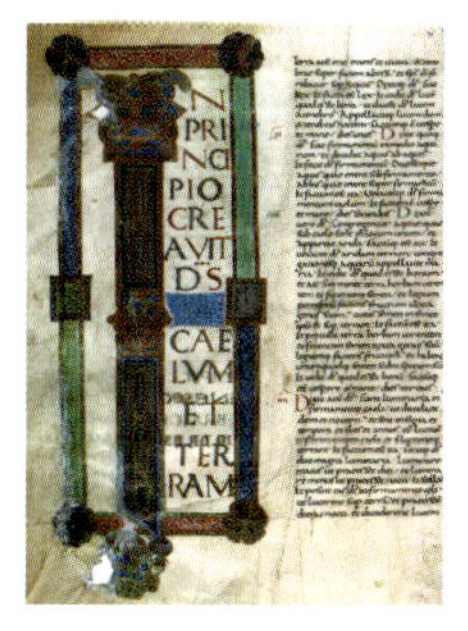

II.27

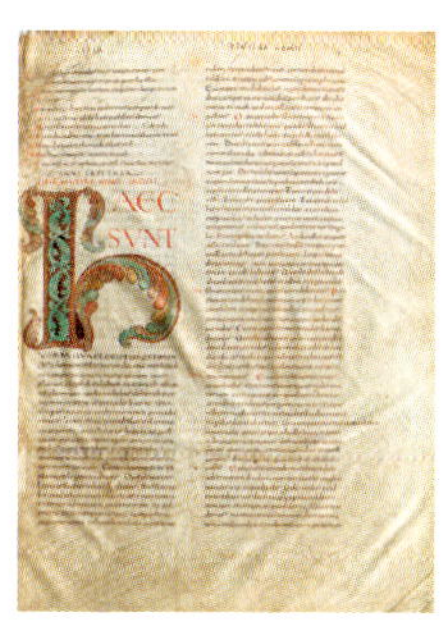
II.28

Gregory the Great. Gregory drew his inspiration for the *Vere Dignum* (Preface to the Mass) from the dove of the Holy Spirit. The three seated figures seen writing are scribes re-copying the text. Long considered Ottonian, this work must now be relocated to the Carolingian period on the basis of stylistic evidence. There is, for instance, a fine acanthus frieze framing a two-level scene. The treatment of the frieze, the style of the hunched figures, their tenseness and their exaggerated hands all display affinities with the ivories of the second Metz school: compare the Metz Gospels (Paris, BnF, Lat.9383 and 9390), executed *c.* 860–70. The architecture of the turrets and crenellated walls suggests a palace that we enter by the subtle device of curtains tied back against two Corinthian columns. The care with which the details have been handled – for instance, Gregory's desk and seat or the tiny staircases visible in the turrets – elevates this work to a very high artistic level. Comparing this image to the Trier miniature on the same theme, we clearly see what distinguishes Ottonian art from Carolingian. Further, the style of this plaque links it to Byzantine ivories from around AD 500. In line with an earlier suggestion by Carl Nordenfalk, Helmut Trnek considers it to be Franco-Saxon, and likens it to the ivory plaques preserved at Cambridge and Frankfurt.

BIBLIOGRAPHY : Helmut Trnek, 'Das Oeuvre des Meisters der Wiener Gregorplatte. Drei francosächsische Elfenbeinreliefs um 875 in Wien, Cambridge und Frankfurt am Main', in M. Leithe-Jasper (ed.), *Zu Gast in der Kunstkammer*, Vienna, 1991, pp. 11–45.

II.21 PSALTERIUM AUREUM (GOLDEN PSALTER)

Saint-Gall, late 9th century
Parchment, 21.7 x 13.6 cm
Saint-Gall, Stiftsbibliothek, Cod. Sang. 22
f.2: King David with musicians and dancers

The use of purple to highlight the illuminations is evidence of the continuing symbolic value attached to colours: with the Romans, and later at Byzantium, purple was associated with imperial power. As in Charles the Bald's Psalter, we note a return to Hellenistic models, transmitted via Rome. The Psalterium Aureum is a fine example of the persistence, in the late 9th century, of the Carolingian tradition, evident as much in the sumptuous nature of the work as the narrative verve of the illustrations to the psalms. It represents the pinnacle of achievement at Saint-Gall.

BIBLIOGRAPHY : C. Eggenberger, *Psalterium Aureum Sancti Galli. Mittelalterliche Psalterillustration im Kloster St. Gall*, Sigmaringen, 1987.

D.

In the late 10th and throughout the 11th century, Winchester and other abbeys in southern England produced ivories and illuminations owing much to the Carolingian school of Rheims, as a result of the presence at Canterbury of the Utrecht Psalter. Yet this so-called Winchester style was also influenced by Irish art and combines several tendencies, resulting in extremely nervous, jerky forms that are nonetheless extremely expressive. This style in turn motivated works in northern countries of the Continent.

II.22 PONTIFICAL OF ST ETHELWOLD

Winchester (?), 971–84
Parchment, 119ff. + 26ff.
21.9 x 21.5 cm
London, British Library, Add. Ms. 49598
f.4r: Three Apostles

This is a book containing episcopal blessings for the liturgical year. It was produced in the episcopate of Ethelwold (963–984), who is considered the great reformer of Benedictine monasticism in England, a role that would explain the choice of certain illustrations in what is arguably one of the true masterpieces of medieval illumination. The acanthus decoration in these miniatures is of Carolingian derivation, but expanded in innovative fashion. Love of decoration is also evident in the treatment of drapery with its generous network of folds, but the overall result of these lines of force is to confer on the scenes a vigorous sense of movement.

BIBLIOGRAPHY : Francis Wormald, *The Benedictional of St. Ethelwold*, London, 1959; Robert Deshman, *The Benedictional of Aethelwold*, Princeton, 1995.

II.23 APPLIQUÉ FIGURES : JOHN AND MARY

Winchester (?), Franco-Saxon (?), *c.* 1000
Walrus ivory, eyes inlaid with glass; Mary: 12.4 cm; John: 12.9 cm
Saint-Omer, Musée de l'Hôtel Sandelin, 2822
Provenance: abbey of Saint-Bertin at Saint-Omer (?)

The style of these two figurines, which must once have formed part of a Crucifixion scene on a book cover, is characteristic of what is termed the 'Channel' school: the forms are jerky, lacking in any cohesion between body and drapery, but powerfully expressive. There is no reference here to ancient tradition, rather a prolongation of the antinaturalist tendencies of Insular artists, as seen notably in the Ethelwold Pontifical (II.22).

BIBLIOGRAPHY : Goldschmidt, IV, nos 4, 5; Gaborit-Chopin, p. 90, no. 112; John Beckwith, *Ivory Carvings in Early Medieval England*, London, 1972.

II.24 SACRAMENTARY ('MISSAL') OF ROBERT DE JUMIÈGES

Ely (?), *c.* 1006–23
Parchment, 228 ff.
33.5 x 22.2 cm
Rouen, Bibliothèque Municipale, Ms. 274 (Y.6)
f.71r: The Kiss of Judas

Originally abbot of Jumièges, Robert Champart was appointed bishop of London in 1044 and archbishop of Canterbury from 1051 to 1052.

From *c.* 925 to 950, English artists discovered Carolingian models, and this contact intensified during the second half of the century. In the first thirty years of the 11th century, Anglo-Saxon scriptoria combined the two principal legacies of the Carolingian era – the style of the Rheims school and that of the Ada Group – into a single unique idiom. It is fair to state that the acanthus decoration was virtually a trademark of the Insular miniature painting also known as the Winchester school. At the same time as this taste for ornament evolved, scenes and isolated figures began to exude a powerful dynamism and expressiveness.

BIBLIOGRAPHY : Margaret Rykert, *Painting in Britain. The Middle Ages*, The Pelican History of Art, Harmondsworth, 1954, p. 45.

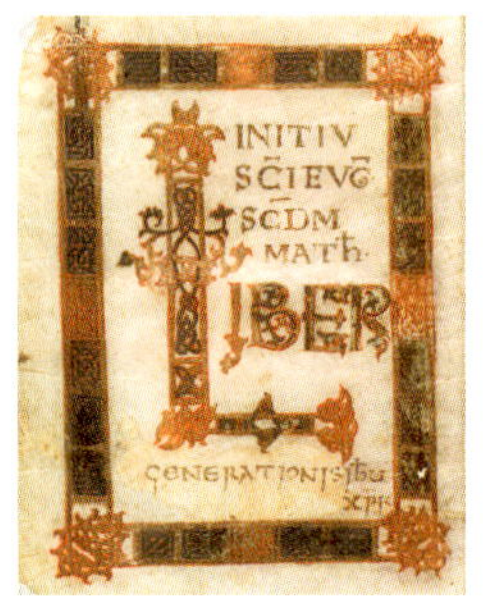
II.29

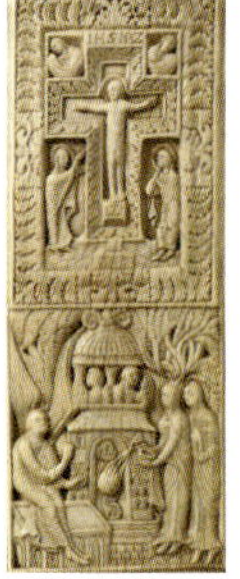
II.30

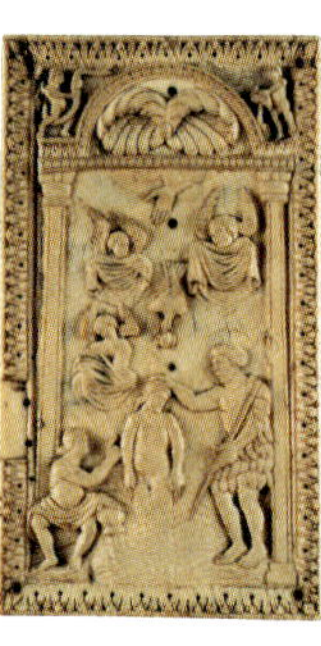
II.31

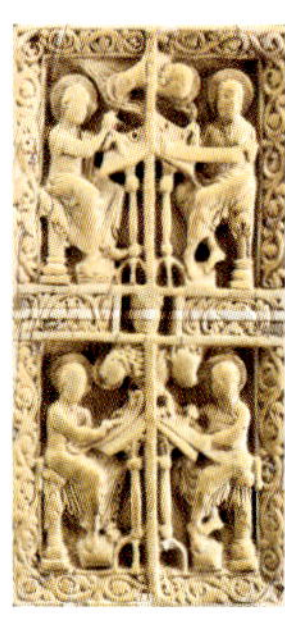
II.32

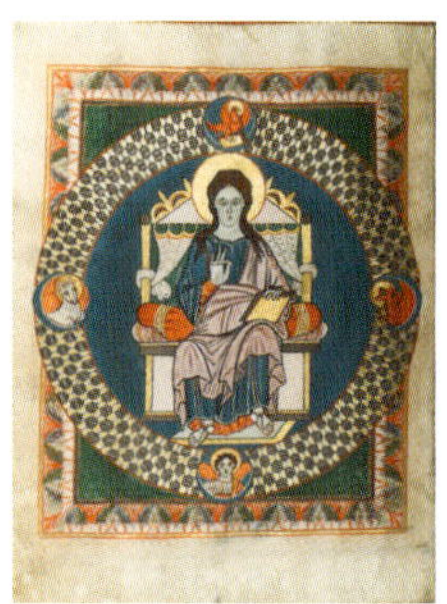
II.33

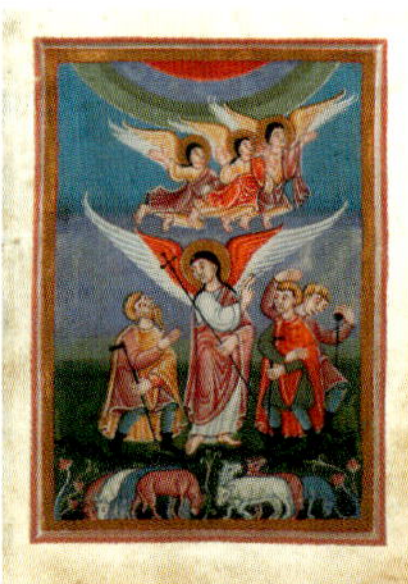
II.34

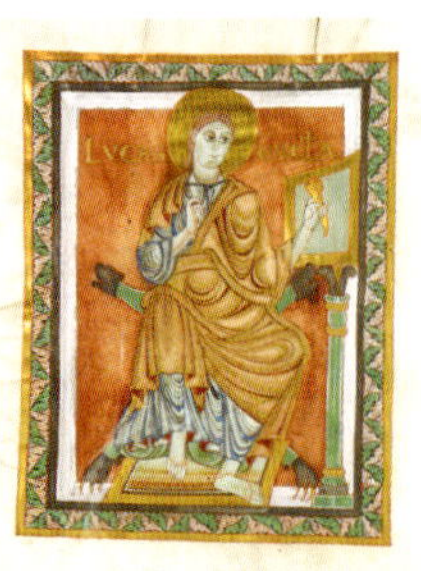
II.35

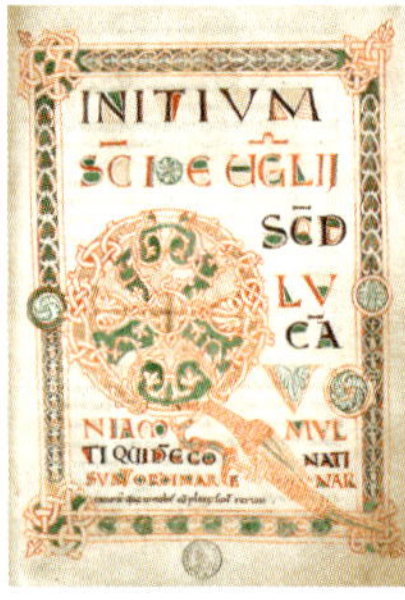
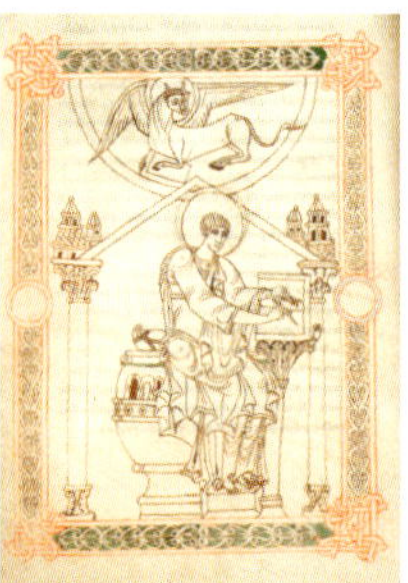
II.36

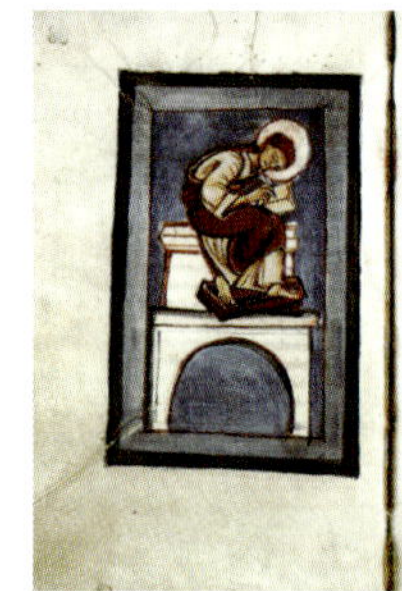
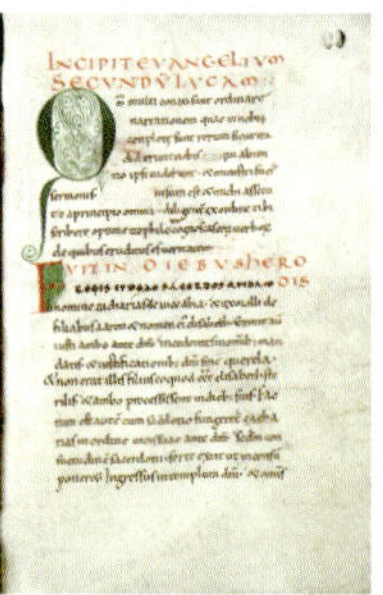
II.37

E.

In the style of both calligraphy and decoration, Carolingian art left its imprint on the following era, which announced the definitive arrival of the Romanesque.
Note that while pre-Carolingian Insular art, the schools of Paris and Rheims, and Italian influences each held sway in turn, these elements often coalesced into completely new idioms.

II.25 BOOK COVER, SHOWING ST PAUL

Trier (the 'Deutscher Schnitzer'), late 10th century
Ivory, 21.2 x 10.3 cm
Paris, Musée national du Moyen Âge, Thermes et hôtel de Cluny, Cl. 1505

St Paul is holding up and pointing to a phylactery (banderole) on which is written: 'By the Grace of God I am what I am.' (1 Corinthians 15:10). The singular nature of the features and the powerful presence of this figure, within an architectural framework whose monumentality anticipates the sculpture of Romanesque portals, are the mark of a very great artist. The same, in fact, who executed the Berlin Diptych (The Incredulity of Thomas/Moses), as well as a book cover in Nuremburg.
But Rainer Kahsnitz has attributed this work to the German Master (the 'Deutscher Schnitzer', according to W. Vöge), a pseudonym designating a sculptor active in Trier.

BIBLIOGRAPHY: R. Kahsnitz, in *Bernward von Hildesheim und das Zeitalter der Ottonen*, Hildesheim, Mainz, 1993, no. IV-36.

II.26 PSALTER

Angers, *c.* AD 1000
Parchment, 19 + 201 ff., 25.3 x 20.5 cm
Amiens, Bibliothèques d'Amiens Métropole, Lescalopier 2C
ff.11. quinq.v and sext.r: King David with musicians

The illustrations of David and the Four Musicians are by the painter responsible for illustrating the Life of Saint-Aubin of Angers (Paris, BnF, Nouv. Acq. Lat.1390) and some sections of the Bible of Saint-Aubin (II.26). This book was probably meant for Angers cathedral.
The treatment of architecture was inspired by classical models transmitted via Carolingian art. The extraordinary King David on his throne and the general quasi-baroque composition are evidence of links to the Winchester school.

BIBLIOGRAPHY: Walter Cahn, *Romanesque Manuscripts. The Twelfth Century. (A Survey of Manuscripts Illuminated in France)*, 2 vols, London, 1996, no. 8; C. R. Dodwell, *The Canterbury School of Illumination 1066–1200*, 1954, p. 119.

II.27 SAINT-AUBIN BIBLE

Angers, last quarter of 11th century
Parchment, 308 ff., 48.5 x 35.5 cm
Angers, Bibliothèque Municipale, Ms.3
f.2v: Initial I of *In Principio*....

This type of initial recalls the Tours school. There is a notable discrepancy between the styles of the script and the undoubtedly 11th-century illustrations. As it is hardly likely that this Bible remained waiting for its illustrations for a century and a half, we are virtually forced to conclude that this is deliberate archaizing, i.e. a neo-Carolingian script.

BIBLIOGRAPHY: Walter Cahn, *La Bible romane. Chefs-d'œuvre de l'enluminure*, Fribourg (Switzerland), 1982, no. 50.

II.28 FIRST BIBLE OF SAINT-MARTIAL DE LIMOGES

Second half of 10th century
Parchment, Vol. 1, 122 ff., 55 x 38 cm
Vol. 2 (not on display), 222 ff.
Paris, Bilbliothèque nationale de France, Lat.5 (Vol. 1)
Provenance: abbey of Saint-Martial de Limoges
f.2r: Initial

The Caroline script of this major work of 10th-century France is by the scribe Bonebertus, who signed the second volume. The book is lavishly illustrated with exquisite vegetal and animal motifs that recall manuscripts of the Tours school. The decoration and colours – dominated by green – are not those of the great Carolingian manuscripts, but the illumination reveals the classical inspiration of the illuminator, who may also have been the scribe himself.

BIBLIOGRAPHY: Danielle Gaborit-Chopin, *La décoration des manuscrits à Saint-Martial de Limoges et en Limousin du* IXe *au* XIIe *siècle*, Geneva, 1969, pp. 42 et seq.

II.29 GAIGNIÈRES GOSPELS

Fleury, early 11th century
Parchment, 65 ff.
25 x 17.5 cm
Paris, Bilbliothèque nationale de France, Ms lat. 1126
f.2v: initial (L)iber from the beginning of St Matthew's Gospel

One of the very rare French manuscripts employing gold and silver on purple paper, this book was produced at the request of King Robert the Pious at the royal monastery of Fleury (now Saint-Benoît-sur-Loire), to which he bestowed it. Moreover, Gauzelin, the King's brother, was also the abbot.
A Lombard named Nivardus was commissioned to illustrate it after

Byzantine models. Analogies exist with two early 11th-century illuminated manuscripts from Milan.

BIBLIOGRAPHY: Carl Nordenfalk, 'Miniature ottonienne et ateliers capétiens', *Art de France*, 4, 1964, pp. 44–59.

II.30 BOOK COVER: CRUCIFIXION AND THE HOLY WOMEN AT THE TOMB

Saint-Gall (?), Northern Italy (?), 10th century
Ivory, 23.9 x 9.8 cm
Budapest, Iparművészeti Múzeum, no. 18.859

The Crucifixion is treated as a 'picture within a picture', framed by broad acanthus leaves, with the Cross itself in a separate frame. The tomb, in the centre ground, is a clear attempt to reproduce the Holy Sepulchre in Jerusalem. The style of this work echoes in a more modest manner that of the atelier of Tuotilo at Saint-Gall.

BIBLIOGRAPHY: Goldschmidt, I, no. 165; *Jankovich Miklos (1772–1846)* (exhib. cat.), Budapest, 2002, no. 51; Lasko, p. 71.

II.31 BOOK COVER: BAPTISM OF CHRIST (V) AND ANIMALS (R)

Metz (?), 9th century
Ivory, 14 x 8 cm
Antwerp, Museum Mayer van der Bergh, no. 432 (2068a and 2068b)

Goldschmidt sees in this relief a derivation from the Liuthard Group, with the size recreating the effect of a miniature painting. The figures overcoming serpents in the top portion recall similar ones in manuscripts from the Rheims school, and that of Metz in the 9th century. The other face must have predated this, and was perhaps sculpted in Spain as early as the 8th century. In any case, it was cut back to give sufficient space to the carver of the Baptism.

BIBLIOGRAPHY: Goldschmidt, I, nos. 66 and 187.

II.32 BOOK COVER: FOUR EVANGELISTS

Cologne or Liège, *c.* 1030
Ivory, 13.8 x 6.7/6.8 cm
Budapest, Iparművészeti Múzeum, no.18.860

This image of the Evangelists at their desks is doubtless inspired by the front cover of the celebrated Dagulf Psalter (Carolingian era). The production of such a work in the Ottonian period is cogent proof of the fascination felt by ivory workers of the Cologne region for Carolingian models. Despite the deterioration of the surface, we can still gauge the book's outstanding quality, with each Evangelist given a distinct individual identity by his posture and gestures.

BIBLIOGRAPHY: Goldschmidt II, no. 36; *Jankovich Miklos (1772–1846) gyüjteményei* (exhib. cat.), Budapest, 2002, no. 52.

II.33 GERO CODEX (BOOK OF PERICOPES)

Reichenau, 969–76
Parchment, 176 ff., 29.6 x 22.2 cm
Darmstadt, Universitäts- und Landesbibliothek, Hs 1948
f.5v: Christ giving His blessing, surrounded by the Tetramorph (the four symbols of the Evangelists joined in one)

A dedicatory scene shows the scribe Anno handing the book to Gero,
future archbishop of Cologne. This codex is a copy made in the Reichenau scriptorium and modelled on the so-called Lorsch Gospels (illuminated around 815 at the Imperial Palace School, and now preserved partly in the Vatican, and partly in Romania). It marks an essential point of departure for Ottonian art: the conception of space hitherto largely derived from ancient models here gives way to a two-dimensional approach.

The folio on display is the transcription of one from the Lorsch Gospels. However, by enlarging the circle and causing it to overflow the acanthus frieze, the illustrator has endowed the figure of Christ with a sense of the monumental.

BIBLIOGRAPHY: Henry Mayr-Harting, *Ottonian Book-Illumination. An Historical Study*, London, 1991.

II.34 ECHTERNACH GOSPELS

Echternach, Luxembourg, mid-11th century
Parchment,182 ff., 20.2 x 14.2 cm
Brussels, Bibliothèque royale de Belgique, Cabinet des Manuscrits, Ms 9428 MSS
Provenance: priory of St Stephen, Bremen, for which it was made
f.8r: Annunciation to the Shephards

This work contains an abundance of sumptuous illustrations (41 miniatures, of which 35 are full-page). Of these the Annunciation is one of the finest. The miniaturist appears to have compensated for the relative weakness of the draughtsmanship with a remarkably adept use of colour – notably in the treatment of the horizontal layers in the lower portion. Nonetheless, we should not underestimate his talent: notice with what sense of composition he has arranged the arms and hands of the figures. The style has much in common with that of Reichenau or Trier.

BIBLIOGRAPHY: M. Debae, in *Cent trésors de la Bibliothèque royale de Belgique*, Brussels, 2005, no. 8.

II.35 GOSPELS OF SAINT-LAURENT-DE-LIÈGE

Mosan region, 1050–60
Parchment, 154 ff., 33 x 26 cm
Brussels, Bibliothèque royale de Belgique, Cabinet des manuscrits, Ms 18383
Provenance: abbey of Saint-Laurent-de-Liège
f.84v: St Mark

This manuscript is considered one of the masterpieces of 11th-century illumination. In faithfulness to the Ottonian tradition, St Mark is represented in hieratic manner, unlike the Carolingian Evangelists. The illustrations of this superb work are by two different hands. The painter of St John and St Luke has handled the draperies in such a way as to maximize the effect of their volumes – also giving himself a pretext for decorative play with the brilliance of gold leaf and silver. We may well wonder if he was not equally a goldsmith.

BIBLIOGRAPHY: *Rhein und Maas. Kunst und Kultur 800–1400* (exhib. cat.), Cologne, 1972, 1, no. F19; ibid., 2, pp. 346–7; Maurits Smeyers, *Vlaamse miniaturen van de achtste tot het midden van de zestiende eeuw. De middeleeuwse wereld op perkament*, Louvain, 1998, pp. 46–47.

II.36 GOSPELS

Mosan region, second half of 11th century
Parchment, 159 ff., 28 x 21 cm
Brussels, Bibliothèque royale de Belgique, Cabinet des manuscrits, Ms 5573
Provenance: Gembloux abbey, Belgium
f.85v: St Luke

The style of this drawing, though crude, gives an idea of the powerful and lasting impact of what is known as Franco-Saxon art on the scriptoria of the Mosan region. That a so obviously imitative illuminator could refer to Insular models proves they were widely accessible. There is good reason to suppose that these Gospels are unfinished.

BIBLIOGRAPHY: C. Gaspar and F. Lyna, *Les principaux manuscrits à peintures de la Bibliothèque royale de Belgique*, Brussels, 1984, no. 13.

II.37 GOSPELS

Northern France (?), Flanders (?), *c.* 1060–80
Parchment, 150 ff
Douai, Bibliothèque municipale, Ms 11
Provenance: abbey of Sainte Rictrude, Marchiennes, France
ff. 98 and 99v: St Luke writing, and beginning of his Gospel

This manuscript was inspired by Carolingian models, yet the simplification of forms entails no impoverishment of the composition, a fact linking it with Ottonian illumination.

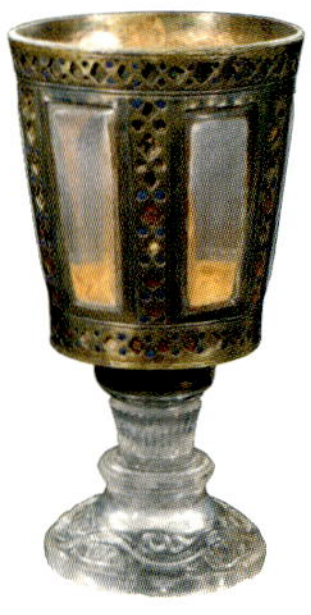
III.1

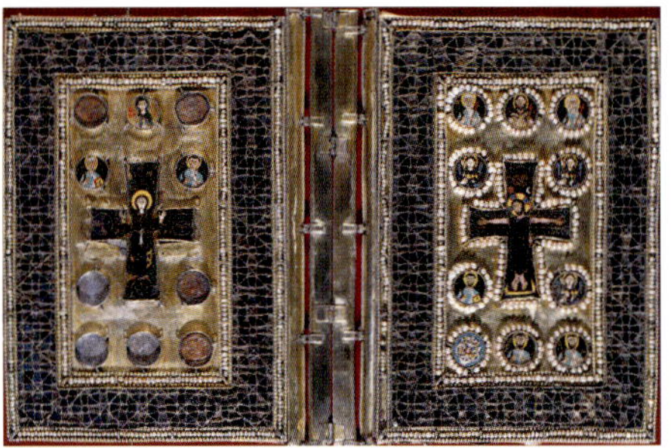
III.2

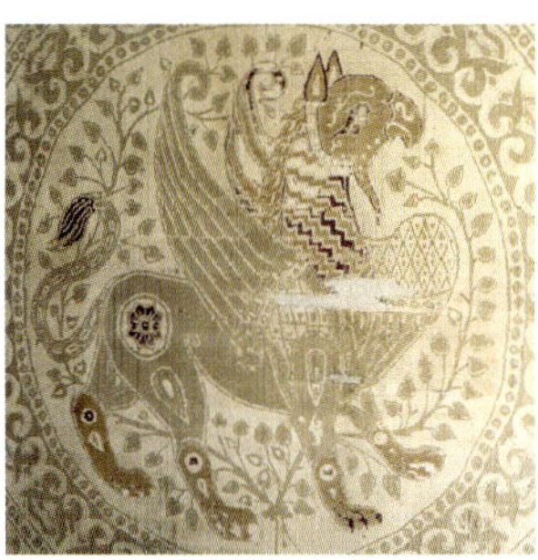
III.3

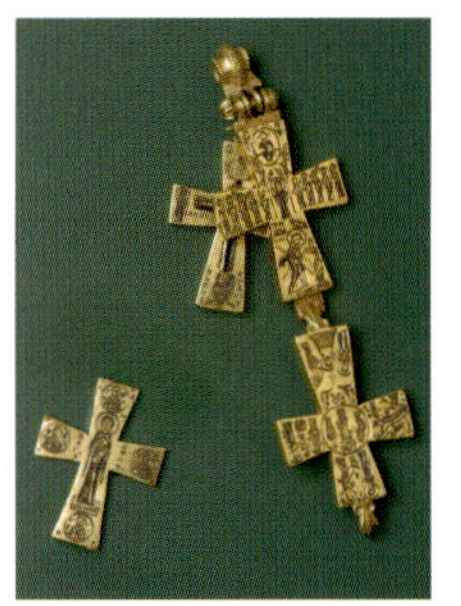
III.4

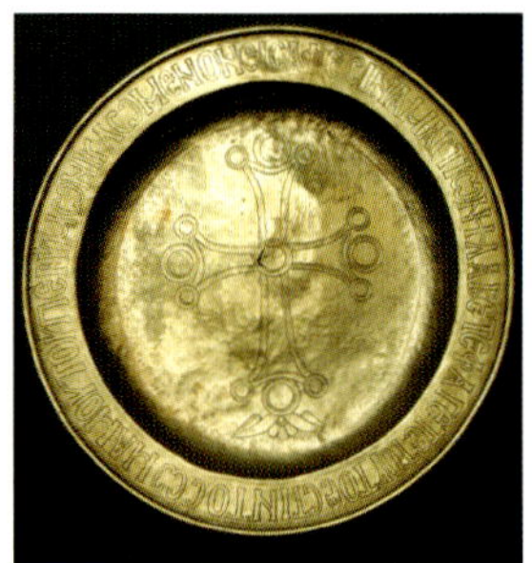
III.5

SECTION III
EUROPE AND THE MEDITERRANEAN

Europe became susceptible to Eastern influence at an early date, especially after the seat of the Byzantine Empire was transferred to Constantinople by the Emperor Constantine. The Mediterranean basin favoured intense commercial exchanges between its eastern and western extremities, a trade in which Venice played a pivotal role. Sicily is an example of this superimposition of cultures – the island was successively Byzantine, Islamic, Norman and Angevin. This traffic resulted in the importation of precious objects and eventually their domestic manufacture, as local artists appropriated oriental styles and techniques. The high degree of culture and refinement attained by Arab civilization was to spread, especially in Spain, starting from centres like Córdoba, whose influence was still felt well after the Reconquest by Christians, which ended in 1492.

III.1 CHALICE (?) WITH ROCK CRYSTAL

Base : Abbasid work (Iran or Iraq ?), 9–10th century. Chalice : Byzantine, 10–11th century
Rock crystal, gilded silver, glass paste, 19.5 x 10 cm in diameter
Venice, Tesoro di San Marco, no. 55

A hexagonal cup whose 'windows' and base are of rock crystal, mounted in gilded silver decorated with encrusted glass paste imitating cabochons. This object is mentioned in the inventory of the treasury of San Marco, Venice, dated 1571 ; its purpose is not known. The Abassids were a dynasty of Arab Muslims who ruled most of the Islamic countries between 749 and 1258. Their capital was Baghdad.

BIBLIOGRAPHY : Hans Hahnloser (ed.), *Il Tesoro di San Marco. Il Tesoro e il Museo*, Florence, 1971, no. 55 ; Daniel Alcouffe, in *Le trésor de Saint-Marc de Venise* (exhib. cat.), Milan, 1984, no. 21.

III.2 BOOK COVERS WITH THE CRUCIFIXION AND THE VIRGIN PRAYING

Constantinople, late 9th–early 10th century
Two silver strips mounted on a wooden rib, cloisonné enamels, pearls, glass, 26 x 17.5 cm
This object was recently restored for exhibition with the assistance of Europalia
Venice, Biblioteca Nazionale Marciana, I.101

The oldest piece of goldwork at the Biblioteca Marciana, Venice, which has held it since 1801–03, this originated from the Treasury of San Marco (where it is recorded in the inventory of 1325). In the centre of each strip is a cross with the Virgin praying on the back and Christ on the front. Each cross is surrounded by ten medallions with busts of saints or angels (on the back only two of the original busts are preserved).

An inscription on the cross surrounding the Virgin gives the identity of the donor, whose name was Mary. It is highly likely that these two strips were not in fact book covers but the wings of a diptych-reliquary.

BIBLIOGRAPHY : Susy Marcon, in S. Gentile (ed.), *Oriente Cristiano e Santità. Figure e storie di santi tra Bisanzio e l'Occidente*, Milan, 1998, pp. 270–71.

III.3 SHROUD OF SAINT-SIVIARD

Byzantine art, 11–12th century
Woven silk, strip of gilded 'goldbeater's skin' (made of animal intestine), 'lampas' weaving technique, 89 x 135 cm
Sens,Trésor de la cathédrale Saint-Étienne, B8
Classed as historic monument 26 September 1903

Griffons are depicted on medallions decorated with palm leaves. Fabrics of this kind were used at the court of Constantinople for ceremonial clothing. After being used in liturgical garments in Europe, they often later formed the wrapping for relics, as in this case. This shroud originates from the reliquary of Saint-Siviard, kept in the cathedral of Saint-Étienne in Sens. It is similar to a piece of silk in Aachen, woven with an elephant motif whose Byzantine origin is indicated by an inscription. Both works, however, were inspired by Sassanid motifs, as is frequent in Byzantine art.

BIBLIOGRAPHY : Henel C. Evans, William D. Wixom (ed.), *The Glory of Byzantium*, New York, 1997, no. 150.

III.4 PECTORAL CROSS-RELIQUARY

Constantinople, 9th century
Gold, niello and wood, 4.2 x 3.2 cm (outer cross), 4 x 3 cm (middle cross), 3.7 x 2.7 cm (inner cross)
Sofia, Natsionalen archeologitcheski Institout s Mousei pri Balgarska akademia na naoukite, no. 4882
Provenance : Pliska

This object comprises a system of crosses, one within another. The relics of the True Cross, enclosed in the inner cross, cannot be seen. This principle of boxes within boxes was highly popular in both the East and the West. The relics were thus placed in a double or triple container, with its elements supporting an iconographical scheme. The wood of the True Cross constitutes the relic and its cross is, of course, completely unadorned. The middle cross shows the Crucifixion and the Virgin and Child as well as four Fathers of the Church. The front of the outer cross is decorated with the Transfiguration surrounded by scenes from the childhood of Christ and the back with the Ascension and the Anastasis (Harrowing of Hell).

BIBLIOGRAPHY : Anthony Cutler,

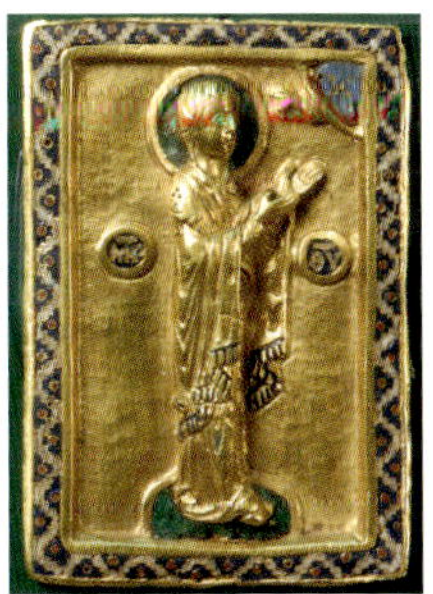

III.6

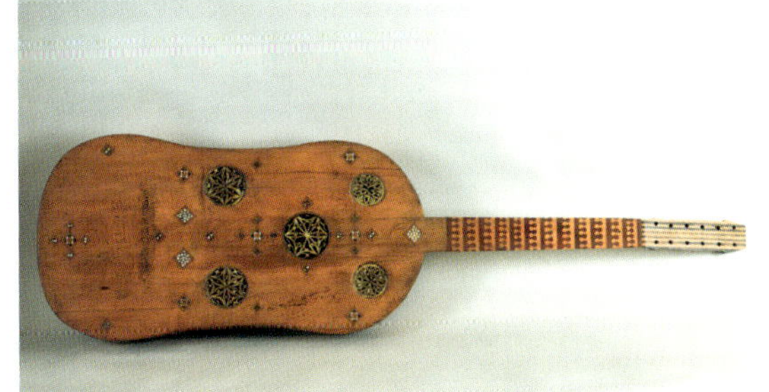

III.7

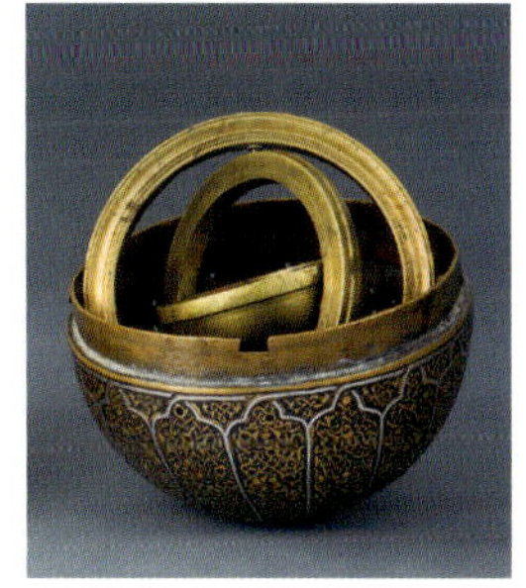

III.8

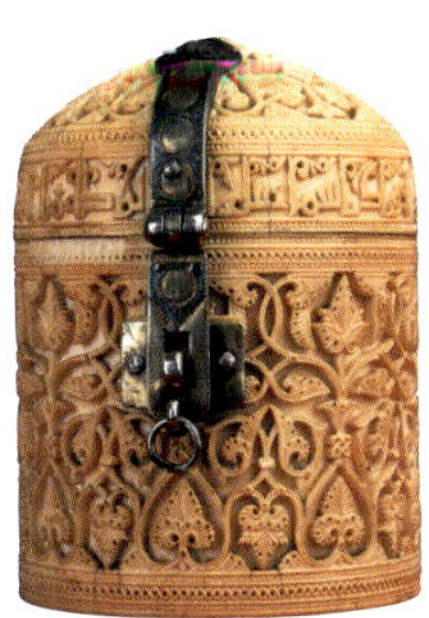

III.9

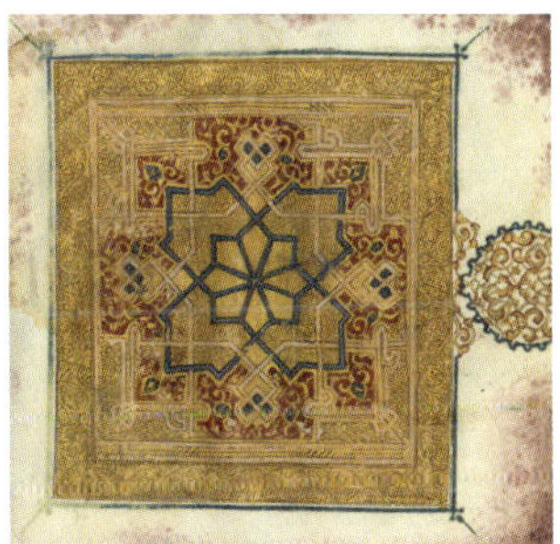

III.10

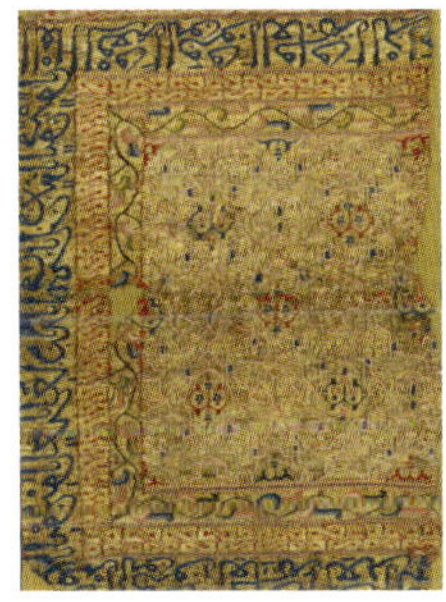

III.11

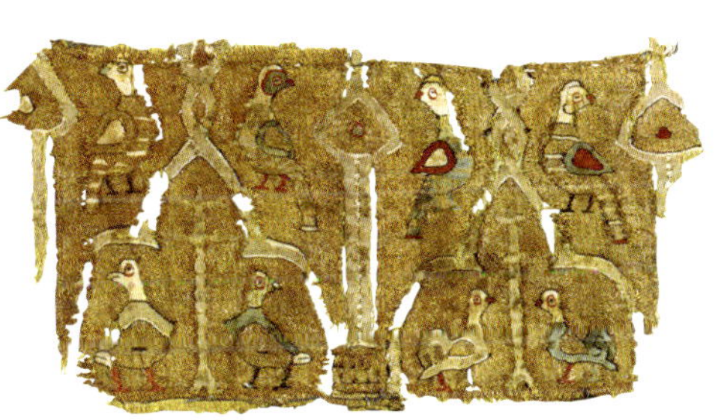

III.12

J.-M. Spieser, *Byzance médiévale 700–1204*, L'Univers des Formes, Paris, 1996, pp. 24–26.

III.5 PATEN

Constantinople, second half of 9th–10th century
Engraved gilded copper, diameter 20.5 cm
Sofia, Natsionalen archeologitcheski Institout s Mousei pri Balgarska akademia na naoukite, no. 3770

The Greek inscription is a paraphrase, from Matthew 26: 26 and Mark 14: 22, of the words Christ spoke at the Last Supper: 'Take this bread, it is my body broken into pieces for the forgiveness of sins.' It is therefore a paten – a plate used for offering up the Host in the Sacrament of the Eucharist.

BIBLIOGRAPHY: *Treasures of Christian Art in Bulgaria*, 2001.

III.6 ENCOLPION

Constantinople, 13th century
Gold, cloisonné enamel, 5.3 x 3.7 cm
Sofia, Natsionalen archeologitcheski Institout s Mousei pri Balgarska akademia na naoukite, no. 487

An encolpion is a medallion (with the image of Christ or the Virgin) containing relics and worn by a bishop on the chest. The lid is inscribed in Greek with the words 'Mother of God' and 'Jesus Christ' in Greek. The rectangular box containing the relics is decorated in relief with two cloisonné enamels, a decorative style typical of the workshops of Constantinople in the 11th and 12th centuries. The Virgin standing with her hands held up to God's is iconography found on other Byzantine objects bearing the inscription 'Hagiosoritissa' or 'Virgin of the Holy Reliquary', an expression that probably alludes to the precious relics from the Virgin's belt kept in the church of the Chalchoprateia in Constantinople. This pendant probably contained relics from the wood of the Cross and from this belt, the symbol of Mary's virginity.

BIBLIOGRAPHY: *Treasures of Christian Art in Bulgaria*, 2001.

III.7 VIHUELA DE MANO

Toledo (?), 16th century
Inlaid wood, 122.3 cm
Paris, Institut de France, Musée Jacquemart-André, OA 1885

This stringed instrument (forerunner of the guitar) is attributed, probably rightly, to Johan de Guadalupe, a luthier (lute maker) of Toledo, as indicated by the inscription burned into the neck ('Guadalupe'). Was this an apprentice's piece made in order to achieve the rank of master luthier? The pine body of the instrument has five pierced rosettes with parchment fillings, possibly remade. The small marquetry squares inlaid into the wood in the Mudéjar style are inherited from Arab-Andalucian culture. The body is also decorated with seven large squares made of woods of different colours and ivory painted with glass. The back of the case is decorated with converging staves of boxwood and rosewood. This is not a superficial added decoration, but runs throughout the width of the base (3-4 mm). The neck, stem and batten are carved from a single piece of wood.

BIBLIOGRAPHY: Joël Dugot, 'Un chef-d'œuvre du XVIe siècle: la vihuela du Musée Jacquemart-André', Aux origines de la guitare: la vihuela de mano, *Les Cahiers du Musée de la Musique*, 5, Paris.

III.8 SPHERICAL CENSER

Venice (?), 15th century
Copper and silver, 9.5 cm diameter
Brussels, Musées royaux d'art et d'hisoire, no. IS 5005

Using an ingenious system, this sphere enabled the charcoal and incense (or other perfumes such as sandalwood) inside it to be kept horizontal, regardless of the sphere's position. Two censers of this type were the first Islamic objects to enter the collections of Cosimo I de Medici in 1553. Although its execution is still very Islamic, this censer was probably the work of a Venetian workshop that adopted what has been called the 'Veneto-Saracen' taste. In northern Europe, these objects could also be used as hand-warmers.

BIBLIOGRAPHY: Mieke Van Raemdonck, *Art de l'Islam dans les collections belges* (exhib. cat.), Brussels, 2003, no. 21.

III.9 CYLINDRICAL BOX

Hispano-Moorish (Cuenca), 10th century
Ivory, 10 x 7 cm
Narbonne, Trésor de la cathédrale Saint-Just et Saint Pasteur
Classed as historic monument 17 June 1901

Narrow palm fronds, engraved using the 'taille d'épargne' method, decorate the box and its lid. An inscription in Kufic characters runs round the top of the box: 'God's blessing. Made in the city of Cuenca for the collection of Hadjet Caïds Ismael.' A similar box (*c.* 965–70) is in the Victoria and Albert Museum, London, and came from the workshop of the caliph at Madinat al-Zahra, Andalucia.

BIBLIOGRAPHY: *Trésors des églises de France*, no. 602.

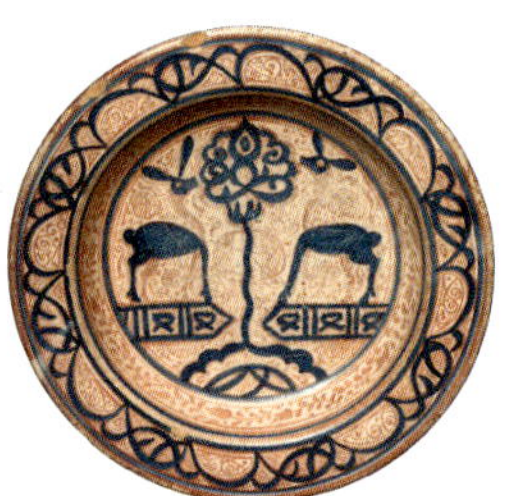

III.13

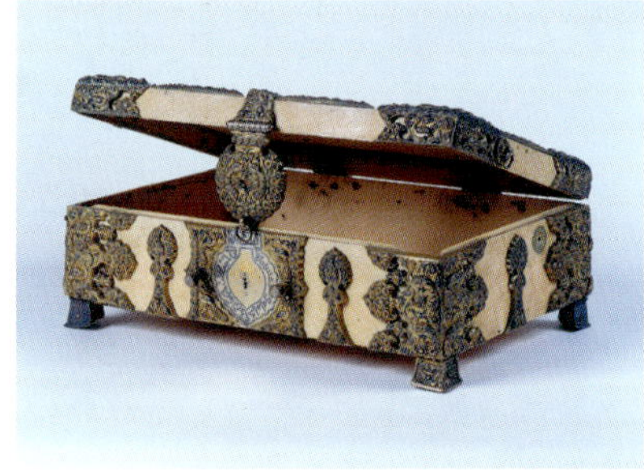

III.14

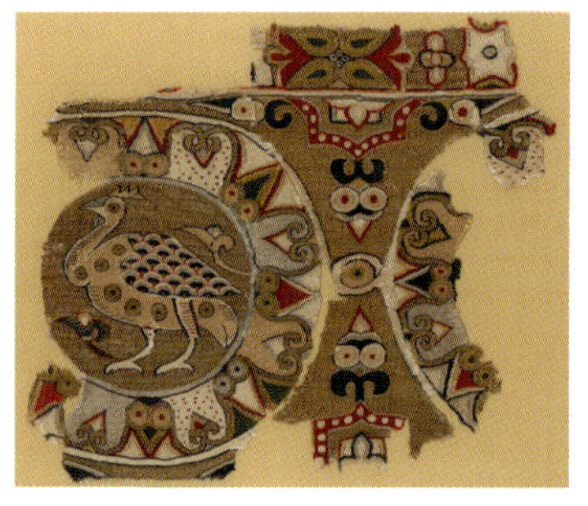

III.15

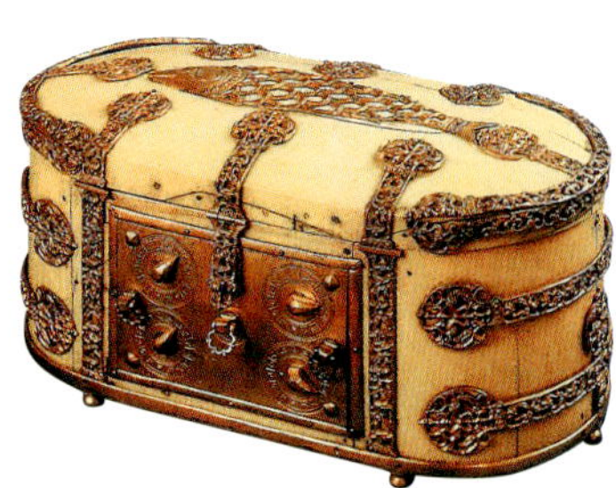

III.16

III.10 FRAGMENTS OF THE KORAN

Nazari, 13–14th century
Parchment, 74 ff., 18,6 x 17 cm
Madrid, Instituto de Valencia de Don Juan, 26 IV.9

The text is written in maghribi characters. This large ornamental page is centred on an eight-pointed star dominated by gold, red and blue of the Nazari era. The other page shows an example of the beautiful Arab calligraphy that impressed Westerners so deeply that, without understanding it at all, they used it purely for decoration.

BIBLIOGRAPHY: Gamal Mehrez, 'Un códice del Coran iluminado de la época nazari en la Biblioteca de Falsil Ahmed Ibn Daud en Tatuhn (?)', in *Revista del Instituto Egipcio de Estudios Islámicos en Madrid*, vol. III, 1, 1955, pp.141–47; Gregorios de Andres, *Catalogo de los manuscritos del Gregorio del Instituto de Valencia de Don Juan*, no. 120.

III.11 FRAGMENT OF CLOTH

Andalucian Nazari art, probably from Almeria, mid-13th century
Silk and gold thread, 'Lousine' weaving technique, 18 x 13.5 cm
Madrid, Instituto de Valencia de Don Juan, 2067

This cloth's decoration, on a gold background, is particularly rich. The inscription 'thulth' refers to dignified rank, prosperity and health. The (indirect?) model for these decorative motifs can be found in a salon of the Aljaferia palace in Saragossa, dating from the 11th century.

III.12 FRAGMENT OF CLOTH

Palermo, Sicily, 11–12th century
Tapestry technique, silk and gold, 10 x 20.5 cm
The restoration and technical analysis of this cloth were carried out by the Institut royal du Patrimoine artistique, Belgium
Brussels, Musées royaux d'art et d'histoire, no. IS.Tx.375

Other fragments of the same cloth are in Barcelona, Paris (Musée national du Moyen Âge) and Amsterdam (Rijksmuseum). It it once decorated the alb (long white vestment) of Arnaldo Ramon de Biure, who was abbot of San Cugat near Barcelona 1348–50. The twice-repeated motif shows two arcades of triplets under and over each of which we can see two pairs of birds. These face one another, the birds at the top turning their heads to look backwards. These birds are found in Egyptian tapestries.
A stylized tree stands at the top of each triplet and between them. The style of this beautiful fragment, whose colours are still very bright, are reminiscent, with the gold background, of the fragments of the garment known as the Cloak of Roger II, King of Sicily 1133–44, produced in the workshops of Palermo.

BIBLIOGRAPHY: Wilfried Seipel (ed.), *Nobiles Officinae. Die königlichen Hofwerkstätten zu Palermo zur Zeit der Normannen und Staufer im 12. und 13. Jahrhundert*, Milan, 2004, no. 62.

III.13 DISH

Hispano-Moorish, Valencia, first half of 15th century
Ceramic, decorated with glaze and cobalt, diameter 32.5 cm
Brussels, Musées royaux d'art et d'histoire, no. CR.5

Two gazelles facing one another and a Tree of Life as the central axis evoke a motif originating from Mesopotamia. An Arabic inscription, '*al-afiya*', meaning 'health'.

BIBLIOGRAPHY: A.-M. Mariën-Dugardin, 'Un plat hispano-moresque', *Bulletin des Musées Royaux d'Art et d'Histoire*, 1965, 4th series, pp. 113–17.

III.14 BOX FOR THE KORAN

Arab (Caliphate of Cordoba), 11–12th century
Ivory, trimmings in alloy of copper and silver niello work, 16 x 52 x 27 cm
Bayeux, Trésor de la cathédrale Notre-Dame

The motif comprises peacocks facing one another (see also III.8) and a Tree of Life. Round the lock is a Kufic inscription in niello glorifying Allah: 'In the name of good and merciful God, whose justice is perfect and whose mercy immense', indicating that the initial purpose of this box was to contain a copy of the Koran. As early as 1200 it was in the treasury of Bayeux cathedral and contained the relics of Saint-Regnobert, second bishop of Bayeux.

BIBLIOGRAPHY: M.-M. Gauthier, *Les routes de la foi. Reliques et reliquaires de Jérusalem à Compostelle*, Fribourg (Switzerland), 1983, no. 16; W. Wilhelmy, in H.-J. Kotzur (ed.), *Kein Krieg ist heilig. Die Kreuzzüge* (exhib. cat.), Mainz, 2001, no. 80.

III.15 THE 'PYRENEAN'S FRINGE'

Caliphate period, second half of 10th century
Silk, twisted or brocaded gold threads, 19 x 23 cm
Madrid, Instituto de Valencia de Don Juan, no. 2071
Provenance: Cordoba

The cloth acquired its name because it came from a church in the Pyrenees. The pictorial beauty of this cloth and its technical characteristics make it exceptional.
The complete piece was decorated with circular medallions: the one that has survived shows a white peacock on a gold background – a classic Islamic theme. Pieces of blue silk are inlaid into the wings. The frame is decorated with stylized flowers as used in the Caliphate: this type of flower is also seen in the decoration of the pilasters of the caliph's palace at Madinat al-Zahra in Andalucia (936, destroyed in 1010) built by al-Nasir.

BIBLIOGRAPHY: C. Lacaba Partearroyo, 'Franja del Pirineo', in *Al-Andalus. Las Artes Islámicas en España* (exhib. cat), Madrid, 1992, no. 20; *Deux millénaires de l'histoire d'Espagne* (exhib. cat.), Brussels, 2001, pp. 137–40.

III.16 IVORY BOX WITH COMBINATION LOCK

Arab (?), *c.* 1200 (?)
Ivory, gilded brass, bronze, 19.1 x 37.5 x 20.1 cm
Maastricht, Schatkamer Basiliek van Sint-Servaas

This box contained relics of Saint-Amour, venerated in the see of Liège. The gilded bronze trimmings helped stabilize the curved ivory plates. The primitive trimmings bear motifs that were used in Islamic art for several centuries, but the object can be dated by the presence of a lock of Eastern invention which requires knowledge of a four-character code to open it (a word with a numerical meaning), each character having to be turned so that it is opposite one of the four 'needles'. Arab documents on mechanics describe how these combination locks were made; the most famous document, by Ibn al-Razzaz al-Jazari, describes a lock very similar to this one.

BIBLIOGRAPHY: 'I. Siede', in A. Wieczorek, M. Fansa, H. Meller (eds.), *Saladin und die Kreuzfahrer* (exhib. cat.), Mainz, 2005, no. B.35.

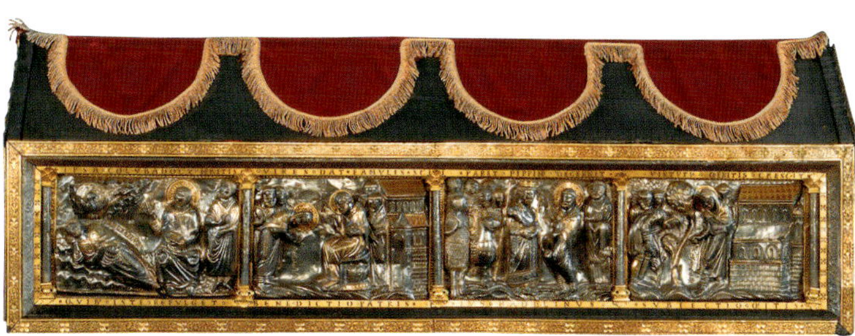

IV.1

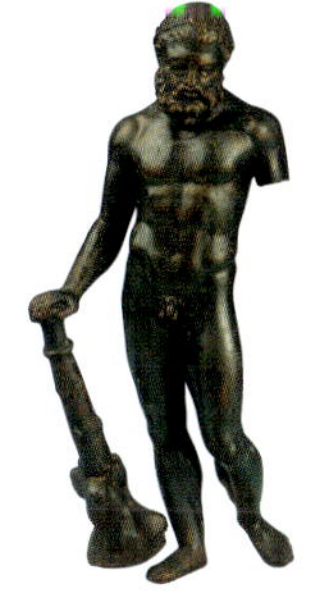

IV.2

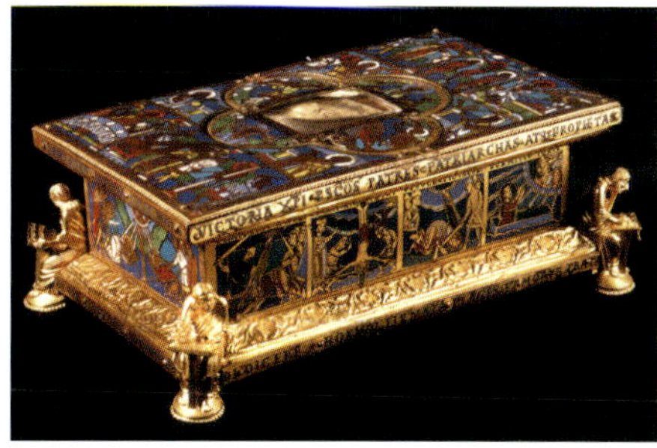

IV.3

SECTION IV
GOLDSMITHS' WORKSHOPS

Goldsmiths always enjoyed a professional status distinguishing them from other artists, principally because they worked with rare and precious materials. Their finest achievements began to emerge in the 12th century, especially in the Mosan basin. The great reliquary-shrines formed a particularly spectacular form of commission. The goldsmith Nicolas de Verdun was one of the most outstanding personalities of medieval art, his success extending as far as Austria. He gave remarkable impetus to artistic activity between the Rhine and the Seine, not only in the use of precious metals but also in painting and sculpture. In addition, the survival of small items of antique Roman bronze statuary has played an inspirational role in the workshops of 12th century goldsmiths.

IV.1 RELIQUARY OF SAINT-HADELIN

Mosan region, 11th century and *c.* 1130–50
Wooden frame, repoussé silver, bronze elements, 54 x 150 x 34 cm
Visé, Trésor de la Collégiale Saint-Martin

This is the oldest surviving reliquary from the Mosan region. Some reliefs have deteriorated; those of the roof section are lost. Saint-Hadelin, who died in the mid-7th century, was the founder of Celles abbey near Dinant, for which this reliquary was made. The reliefs and the inscriptions on the gable walls are from an 11th-century reliquary: on one side, Christ Triumphant – see Psalm 90 (91) – and on the other Christ crowning Saints Hadelin and Remaclus. On each of the long sides are four scenes from the saint's life: Hadelin's dream, Hadelin welcoming schoolchildren, King Pepin visiting Hadelin, Hadelin visiting Remaclus at Celles, three of the saint's miracles, and his inhumation. Some of the reliefs appear to echo those of the Liège (?) baptismal font; in their turn they would influence the Stavelot portable altar (IV.3).

BIBLIOGRAPHY: *Rhein und Maas*, no. G4.

IV.2 STATUETTE OF HERCULES

Rome, 1st–2nd century
Bronze with fine surface patina, lacking left arm, 12 cm
Bonn, Rheinisches Landesmuseum, no. 14380

Found during excavations at Bonn-Dransdorf, this is an example of miniature statuary from the Roman provinces preserved in the region between the Rhine and the Seine. Such a mastery of anatomy is virtually non-existent in Mosan statuettes of the 12th century, except in a work whose Mosan origin is today very much in question: the Liège font.

BIBLIOGRAPHY: *Aus rheinischer Kunst und Kultur. Auswahl Katalog des Rheinisches Landesmuseums*, Bonn, Düsseldorf, 1963, no. 26.

IV.3 STAVELOT PORTABLE ALTAR

Stavelot, Belgium, *c.* 1150–60
Wooden frame, champlevé enamels, gilt bronze, Silberblech (rolled silver) stamped and gilded, rock crystal, 27.5 x 10 x 17 cm
Brussels, Musées royaux d'art et d'histoire, no. 1590
Provenance: Stavelot abbey

Commissioned by Wibald, abbot of Stavelot Malmédy and Corvey (1130–58). Privileges granted by the papacy enabled members of the clergy and princes to read the Mass on a small portable altar (*altare portatile*). In the form of a box, it rests on four bronze statuettes of the Evangelists, each seated in a different attitude appropriate to his activity. It is completely covered with enamel plaques. On the upper surface a quatrefoil with representations of the Church, Samson, the Synagogue and Jonah surrounds a rectangle enclosing a rock crystal, through which can be distinguished the letters SCS (from the Sanctus, part of the Mass); the chalice was placed on this surface during the Eucharist. The quatrefoil format is common in Mosan art: cf. the 'phylacterium' by Hugo d'Oignies (IV.12).

The ten scenes in the composition are all identifiable from their inscriptions. Lower register: Last Supper, Jews before Pilate, Flagellation. Upper register: Carrying of the Cross, Crucifixion, Holy Women at the Tomb. The middle register is divided into two levels, each containing prefigurations of the Passion from the Old Testament: Moses and the Brazen Serpent on the upper level and below this Abel and Melchisedech. On the four sides are martyrdom scenes of the Apostles.

The inscription on the upper border reads: 'That which the Church honours – the Cross, the Death and Triumph of Christ – was prefigured and foretold by the Church Fathers, by the Patriarchs and by the Prophets; yet the Synagogue in its blindness still will not admit it.' On the plinth: 'Those who wrote it learnt it from God's teaching, that is attested by their suffering and their deaths, and by divine inspiration rendered glorious by their words, and sealed furthermore by their righteous blood.'

BIBLIOGRAPHY: *Rhein und Maas*, no. G13; Dietrich Kötzsche, *Die Zeit der Staufer* (exhib. cat.), Stuttgart, 1977, vol. 1, pp. 409–10; *An Exhibition of Medieval Renaissance and Islamic Works of Art at Newhouse Galleries*, 9–22 November 1995, no. 5.

IV.4 CHRIST CRUCIFIED

Meuse, mid-12th century
Brass: 15.5 x 16.2 cm
Provenance: private collection in Liège
Brussels, Musées royaux d'art et d'histoire, no. 6260

This Christ is of the same type as that in the Schnütgen Museum,

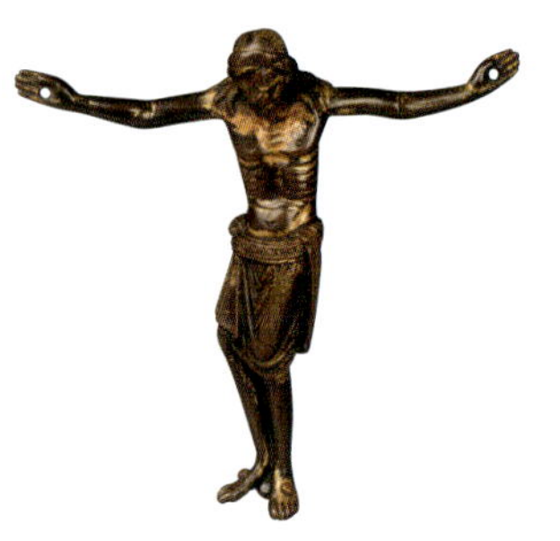
IV.4

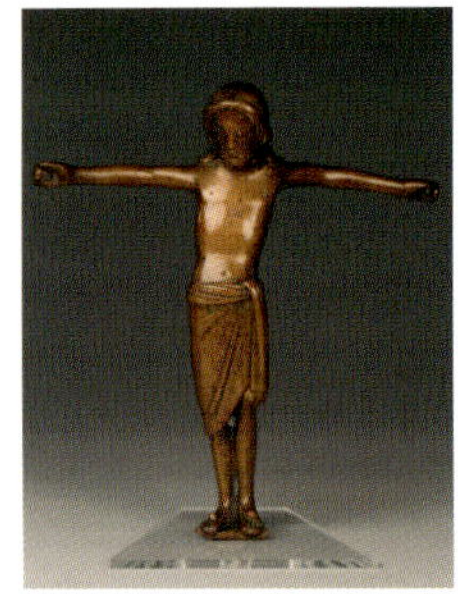
IV.5

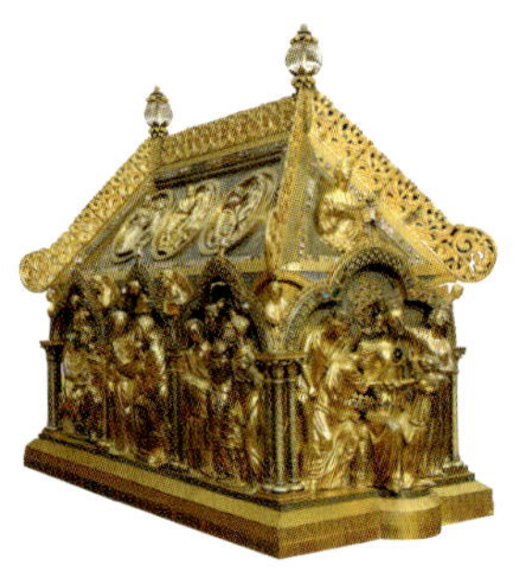
IV.6

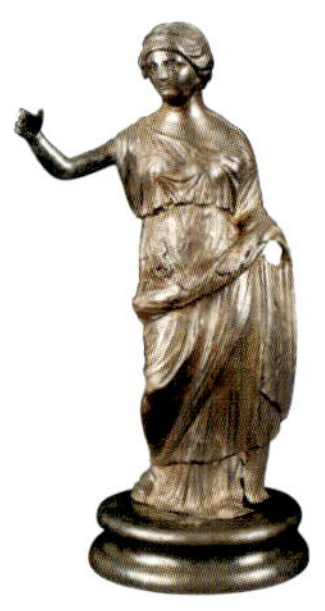
IV.7

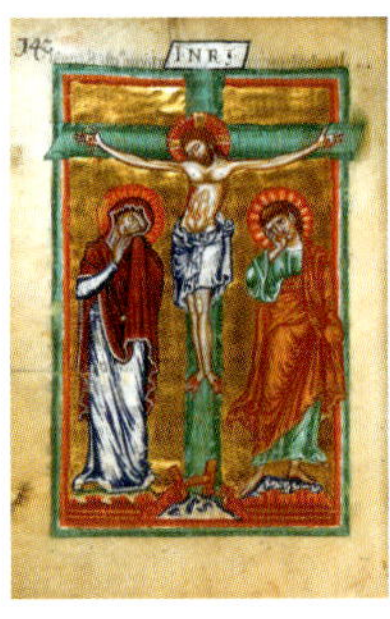
IV.8

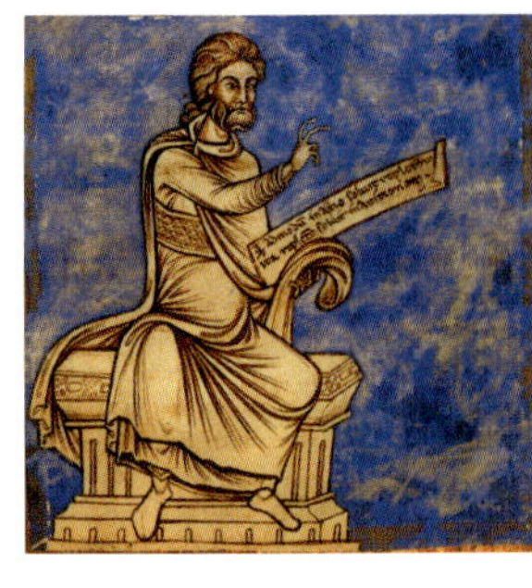
IV.9

Cologne: the widely extended arms, slightly asymmetrical, and the torsion between the upper and lower parts of the body are in direct conflict with the frontality of our other example (IV.5), which is contemporary with it. The perizonium (garment of Christ on the Cross) is knotted like a belt. If we attach importance to features linking it to the Stavelot portable altar (IV.3), this Christ ought to be redated to 1150–60. The overwhelming melancholy of the face, the nuanced handling of the locks of hair falling to the shoulders, the subtlety of the contouring and the refined ornamentation of the perizonium combine to make this a masterpiece.

BIBLIOGRAPHY: Peter Bloch, *Romanische Bronzekruzifixe*, Berlin, 1992, no. VIII D 3.

IV.5 CHRIST CRUCIFIED

Meuse, *c.* 1150
Brass, remains of gilding, 21 x 19.5 cm
Brussels, Musées royaux d'art et d'histoire, no. 672

This type of Crucifixion is a variation on the Bernward Crucifix at Hildesheim, a remarkable piece of Ottonian craftsmanship. Another Christ in brass, from the Jean Puraye (Liège) collection (Bloch, no. VI A 4) and closer to the Hildesheim example, exhibits a similar treatment of the torso. A portion of the perizonium falls to the left flank. The general absence of modelling does not negate the plastic quality of the figure, which has been subjected to a kind of geometric simplification.

BIBLIOGRAPHY: Peter Bloch, *Romanische Bronzekruzifixe*, Berlin, 1992, no. VI E 1.

NICOLAS DE VERDUN

There is evidence of this goldsmith at work from 1181 (the ambo at Klosterneuberg, near Vienna) until 1205 (the Tournai reliquary). He is credited, for instance, with the design and manufacture of the finest parts of the Shrine of the Three Kings in Cologne cathedral. The visionary genius of his iconographical programme places him among the greatest artists of all time. Although he appropriated Byzantine models, he empowered his figures with an expressive passion, a pathos vividly recalling figures from the Hellenistic schema. At the same time, he acquired such mastery in portraying scenes and the human body, and gave them such legibility, that through his work we are afforded a glimpse of the direction the art of Northern Europe would take in the 13th century.

IV.6 NICOLAS DE VERDUN: RELIQUARY OF THE VIRGIN (SHRINE OF OUR LADY OF FLANDERS)

Tournai cathedral, completed in 1205 (according to a modern, though faithful to the original, inscription on the base)
Wooden frame, silver gilt leaves with repoussé work, champlevé and cloisonné enamels, filigree and cabochons, 90 x 126 x 70 cm
Tournai, Cathédrale Notre-Dame, trésor de la cathédrale

This shrine, although heavily restored on several occasions, in the Middle Ages but especially in 1890, is nevertheless the only work attested by an inscription as being by the hand of the famous goldsmith. It bears a likeness to the shrine of the Three Kings in Cologne Cathedral, yet on a more modest scale: a rectangular sarcophagus shape with a roof section in four parts, figures in relief on the sides, framed by trilobate arcades, and in circular medallions on the roof.

On the short sides: Christ Pantocrator (Almighty) with angels and the instruments of the Passion, Adoration of the Magi (Virgin and left-hand king restored). Long side, left: Annunciation (the Angel is modern), Visitation and Nativity (Joseph and Mary's arm restored). Long side, right: Flight into Egypt, Presentation in the Temple, Baptism of Christ.

Roof, left: Flagellation (restored in 15th? century), Crucifixion (restored) and Women at the Tomb; right, Noli me Tangere (restored), Descent into Limbo and Doubting Thomas (restored). Most of the decorative elements are also restorations.

BIBLIOGRAPHY: Peter-Cornelius Claussen, 'Über Antiken- und Naturstudium am Dreikönigsschrein', in Anton Legner (ed.), *Ornamenta Ecclesiae. Kunst und Künstler der Romanik in Köln*, Cologne, 1985, pp. 447–55.

IV.7 STATUETTE OF DRAPED WOMAN

2nd–3rd century
Silver, 23 cm
Morlanwelz, Musée royal de Mariemont, no. F13 (79)

The style of this statuette may be likened to one by Nicolas de Verdun – yet he elevated his draped figures to a level of monumentality that this does not possess. It is presented to illustrate the ancient or palaeochristian corpus on which Nicolas could draw in addition to works more closely linked with Byzantium.

BIBLIOGRAPHY: *Les Antiquités du musée de Mariemont*, 1950, pl. 60.

IV.8 EVANGELISTARY OF GREAT ST MARTIN

Cologne, *c.* 1220–30
Parchment, 193 ff., 24.9 x 16.7 cm
Brussels, Bibliothèque royale de Belgique, Ms 9222
Provenance: former Benedictine abbey of Great St Martin, Cologne
f.42r: the Crucifixion

This book is one of the principal representatives of the formulaic style known as *Muldenfaltenstil*, so named from the small, trough-like folds into which the drapery breaks, with its particularly expressive portrayal of facial features and gestures. The stained-glass windows of the choir of St Cunibert's in Cologne are examples of a stylistic phase comparable with that of this manuscript: these works extend the fluent idiom adopted by Nicolas de Verdun in the Shrine of the Three Kings, also in Cologne, in particular the repoussé metalwork statuettes of the Prophets (1181–91).

BIBLIOGRAPHY: *Rhein und Maas*, no. L17.

IV.9 MEDICAL TREATISES

Mosan region (?), Champagne (?), *c.* 1175
Parchment, 99 ff.
London, British Library, Ms Harley 1585
f.13: a physician

The style of two of the portraits of physicians in this treatise has been likened to certain of the sixteen engraved copper plaques of the Crown of Light in the church at Aachen, commissioned by the Emperor Frederick Barbarossa and his wife Beatrice, patrons of Mosan art. These illustrations have been attributed to various ateliers: Floreffe, Liège, or even Saint-Omer, but L. Grodecki has proposed compari-

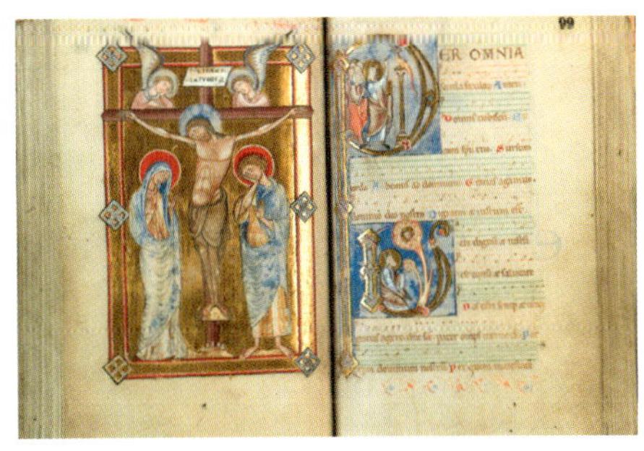
IV.10

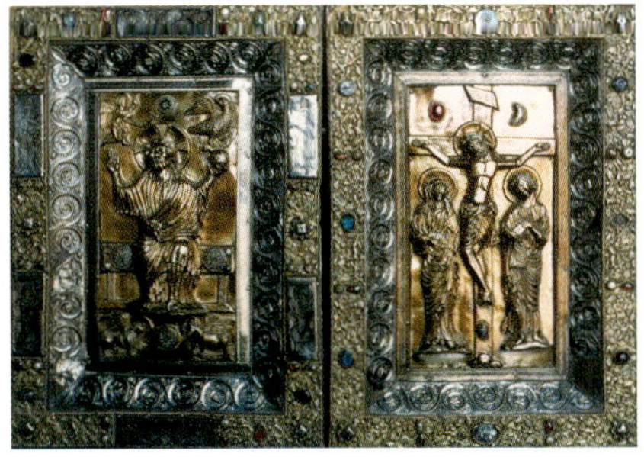
IV.11

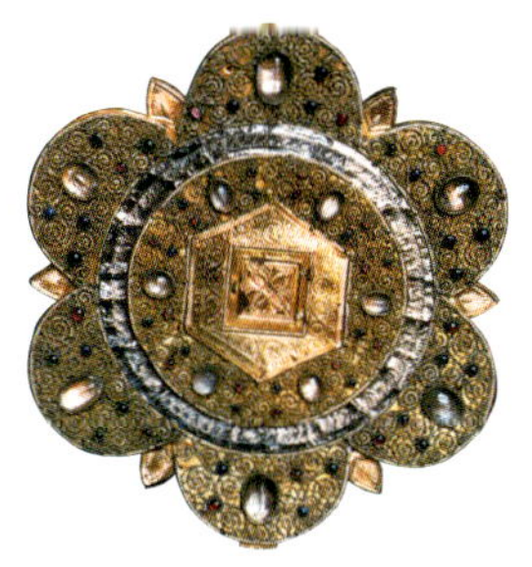
IV.12

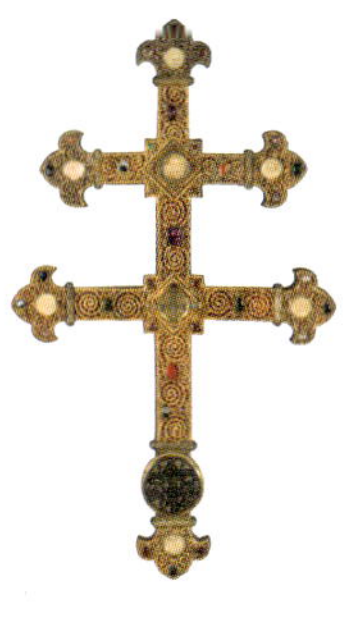
IV.13

sons between these miniatures and stained-glass panels from Troyes cathedral (Champagne), admitting nonetheless a more distant, undoubtedly Mosan origin. One could also compare this style with the graphic language of Nicolas de Verdun in the Klosterneuberg ambo.

BIBLIOGRAPHY : Louis Grodecki, 'Problèmes de la peinture en Champagne pendant la seconde moitié du XIIe siècle', in *Studies in Western Art. Romanesque and Gothic Art, Acts of the XXth International Congress of the History of Art* (New York, 1961), Princeton, 1963, pp. 129–41 ; *Rhein und Maas*, 1, p. 269 and 2, p. 213.

IV.10 MISSAL

Northern France (Anchin ?), early 13th century
Parchment, 188 ff., 23.5 x 14.5 cm
Douai, Bibliothèque municipale, Ms.90, II
f.98v + 99r : the Crucifixion and two initials, Moses and the Brass Serpent (*Per omnia*....) and Moses before the Burning Bush (*Vere Dignum*....) : prefigurations of Christ's Passion

Provenance : A 16th-century note indicates that the manuscript was in the abbey of Anchin's library. All the same, the illuminator does not appear to have belonged to the scriptorium of that abbey ; it is possible he was an itinerant artist. Whatever the truth, we are dealing with a work that occupies a significant place in the development of pictorial and sculptural style in northern France in the years around 1200, in company with the famous Ingeborg Psalter (Chantilly). A connection may be seen between the supple and fluent treatment of the drapery and miniatures produced in Cologne some thirty years later. This missal is, in addition, in the Byzantine tradition, which would also exercise its influence on the Ingeborg Psalter and impact strongly on the technique of Nicolas de Verdun, with particular reference, around 1181, to the Klosterneuberg ambo. All these works should also be considered in relation to the stained glass in the cathedrals of Laon and Soissons.

BIBLIOGRAPHY : V. Leroquais, *Les Sacramentaires des bibliothèques de France*, I, Paris 1924, p. 350 ; Konrad Hoffmann (ed.), *The Year 1200. A Centennial Exhibition at The Metropolitan Museum of Art*, New York, 1970, no. 250.

HUGO D'OIGNIES

Friar Hugo was probably born after 1187 at Walcourt, Belgium. It seems his three brothers founded a monastery at Oignies, where one of them, Giles, was abbot until 1233. Most of the important treasure of Saint-Nicolas d'Oignies passed in 1818 into the hands of the Sisters of Notre Dame de Namur. Hugo d'Oignies is in the prestigious tradition of the great Mosan goldsmiths, but at the same time his style is far more eclectic than that of Nicolas de Verdun.

IV.11 HUGO D'OIGNIES : BOOK COVERS

c. 1230
Oak frame, silver, partly gilt, repoussé, stamped and engraved, filigree work and cabochons, each cover 32.5 x 23.2 x 2 cm
Namur, Trésor du prieuré d'Oignies aux Sœurs de Notre-Dame-de-Namur, 1

Inscription on front cover : 'The book is written inside as outside ; Hugo wrote it – the inside at his expense, the outside with his own hand. Pray for him. Some glorify God with their voices, but Hugo through the goldsmith's art.'

Front board : centre, Christ Enthroned and Blessing, surrounded by the Tetramorph (the four symbols of the Evangelists joined in one) ; on the outside frame, niello plaques showing two angels bearing censers, Nicolas de Lyre (bottom right) and Hugo d'Oignies to the left offering up his work : dedication scene referred to in inscription. Back board : Christ Crucified, flanked by Mary and John.

If the plastic effect of the reliefs is somewhat attenuated – especially when compared with the technique of Nicolas de Verdun, Hugo's forerunner – the decorative inventiveness of the frames is of a very high order, a kind of hymn to Nature and the seasons pervading the swags of foliage. Within this riot of ornament are embedded coloured cabochons.

BIBLIOGRAPHY : *Rhein und Maas*, no. M6/7. M. de Ruette and L.P. Baert, 'Matrice utilisée pour les œuvres d'argent de la croix à double traverse conservées aux MRAH et pour d'autres oeuvres de Hugo d'Oignies in R. Didier and J. Toussaint (ed.), *Autour de Hugo d'Oigies*, Actes du Colloque, Société Archéologique de Namur (...), Namur, 2003.

IV.12 HUGO D'OIGNIES : 'PHYLACTERIUM' OF ST MARTIN

c. 1230–35
Wooden frame, copper and silver gilt, stamped and engraved, filigree and stones, diameter 39 cm
Namur, Trésor du prieuré d'Oignies aux Sœurs de Notre-Dame-de-Namur, 12

On one face is an opening that contained the relic – a fragment of the saint's thumb – as indicated by the accompanying inscription. On the reverse, the Virgin and Child enthroned and trampling a basilisk, surrounded by engraved swags. The figures are characteristic of a stylistic idiom that spread throughout the North and the Empire around 1230 and is called *Muldenfaltenstil* by art historians. The style of the sketches in the Villard de Honnecourt album (BnF, Paris) is very close to this.

BIBLIOGRAPHY : *Rhein und Maas*, no. M5.

IV.13 HUGO D'OIGNIES : RELIQUARY IN FORM OF DOUBLE CROSS

c. 1230–35
Silver, filigree, cabochons, rock crystal, niello and intaglio, 45.5 cm
Brussels, Musées royaux d'art et d'histoire, no. 3214

Contains a relic of the True Cross at the intersection of the principal arms ; other relics were concealed in the crystals at the extremities of the cross. At the base of the shaft is a niello Crucifixion set between the Sun and Moon. The work exhibits a high standard of expertise and may be attributed to Hugo d'Oignies – compare the cross from the treasure of Oignies priory.

BIBLIOGRAPHY : *Rhein und Maas*, no. 8.

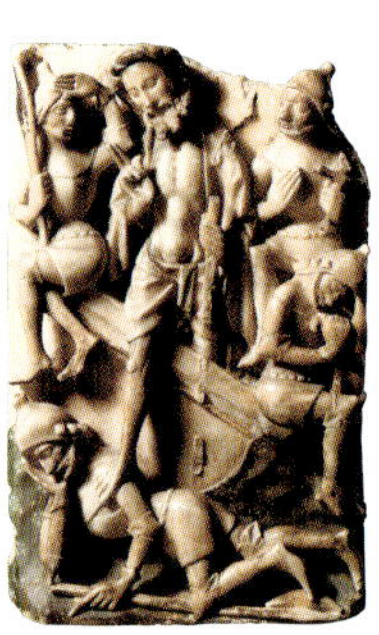

V.13

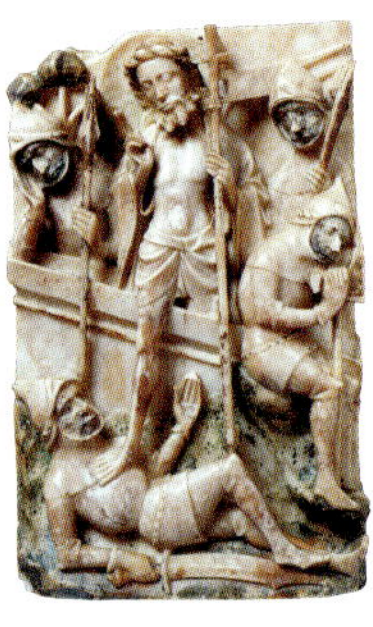

V.14

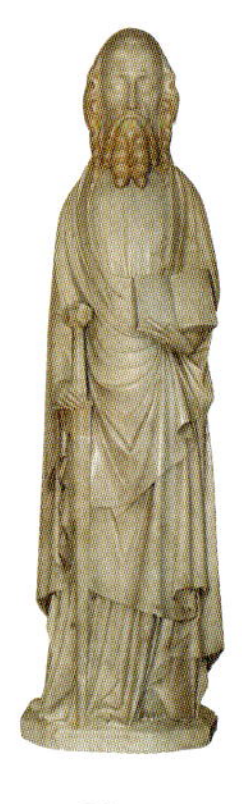

V.15

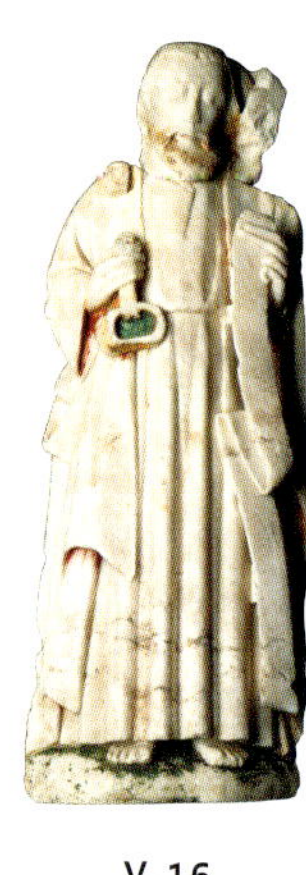

V.16

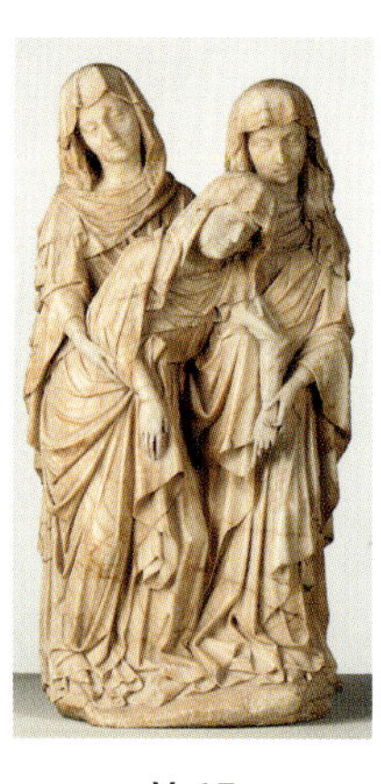

V.17

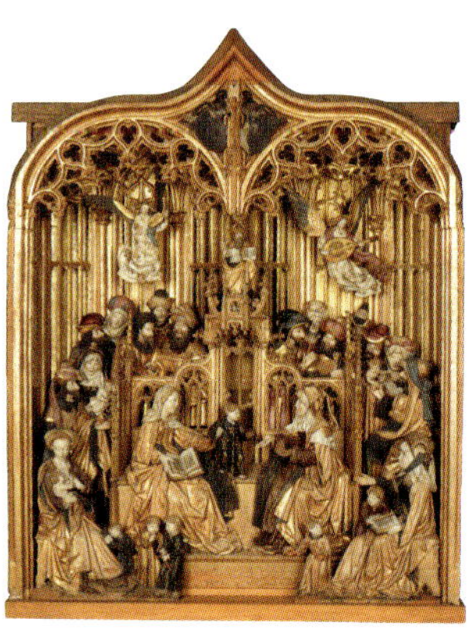

V.18

V.19

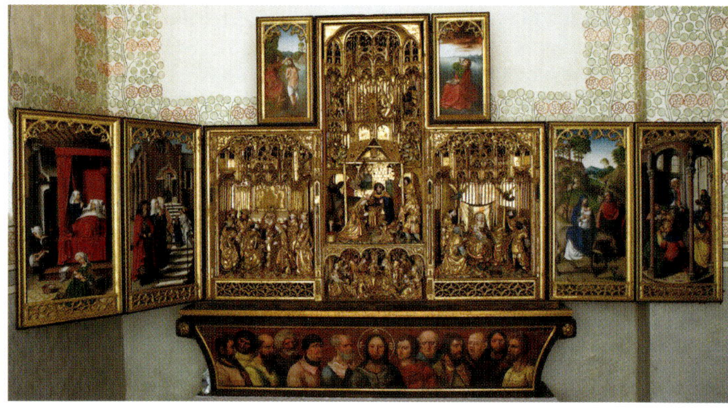

V.20

soldier. Several late 15th-century Resurrections carved in the manner of this same 'template' are preserved, with the museum's other example presented here (V.14), which only differs in its details (soldier lying down). The rather inelegant style of the two works is consistent with the standards of mass production.

V.14 RESURRECTION OF CHRIST

Nottingham, second half of 15th century
Alabaster altarpiece panel, several traces of original polychromy (beard and small flowers), vermilion accents on soldiers' faces blackened, changing their expressions, 43 x 26 cm
Rouen, Musée départemental des Antiquités de Seine-Maritime, Inv. R. 90.4

This panel originates from an altarpiece depicting the Passion of Christ, whose serene expression contrasts strongly with the deliberately crude expressions of the soldiers.

BIBLIOGRAPHY: L. Flavigny, 1998, no. 46.

V.15 ALABASTER STATUETTE OF ST PAUL

England, 14th century
Alabaster
Rome, church of Santa Croce in Gerusalemme

This is a work of exceptional quality and is precisely documented: a pontifical source informs us that the papal legate Cosmato Gentilis was authorized in May 1382 to export this statue, and another of St Peter, equally well preserved, from England to Rome. The fact is that, before they created large numbers of reliefs designed for altarpieces, English sculptors were producing alabaster statues. This is a very fine example.

V.16 ST PETER

Anglesqueville-la-Bras-Long, Seine-Maritime, late 14th-early 15th century
Alabaster appliqué statuette, partial remains of polychromy, 64 x 24 cm
Rouen, Musée départemental des Antiquités de Seine-Maritime. Inv. D.91.77

This sculpture is part of a group of six disciples of Christ forming the apostolic college, which was a theme frequently depicted in the 15th century in monumental sculpture and stained-glass windows. Presented standing and with bare feet, Peter is holding in his right hand the key, the symbol of his function as head of the church, and in his left hand he holds a banderole on which a sentence from the Apostle's Creed was painted.

BIBLIOGRAPHY: L. Flavigny, no. 34, pp. 83-87.

V.17 THREE MARYS AT THE FOOT OF THE CROSS

(Paris?), northern France (?), *c.* 1430
Alabaster group sculpture, fragment, probably from Crucifixion, 46 cm
Warsaw, Muzeum Narodowe w Warszawie, Inv. no. Sr. 402
Provenance: Notre-Dame des Sablons, Paris

The Virgin faints, supported by the other two Marys, with sorrowful faces. The exceptional skill of the sculptor, in the treatment of their expressions and of the drapes with the fluidity of their folds, is notable. Judging by the style, this group is to be compared with the Crucifixion of Rimini (Liebighaus, Frankfurt).

WOODEN ALTARPIECES

By the late 15th century, Brussels led the way as a production centre for wooden altarpieces. The early 16th century saw the industrialization of their production, due to the competition posed by Antwerp from 1500. Brabant altarpieces, which were highly valued by the aristocracy, the middle classes and the clergy, were widely exported to Europe: in particular, Sweden has kept forty-four of them.

In addition to their high artistic value, the altarpieces were worth a large amount commercially, so they constituted a financial risk for traders. For this reason, the main production centres – Brussels, Antwerp and Malines – protected themselves by virtue of guild regulations, and guild edicts demanded, notably, the application of craftsmen's marks to altarpieces.

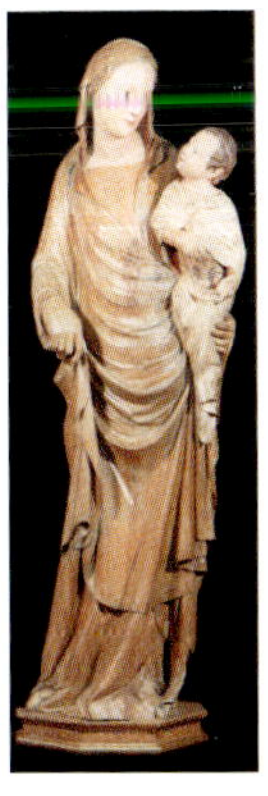

VI.17

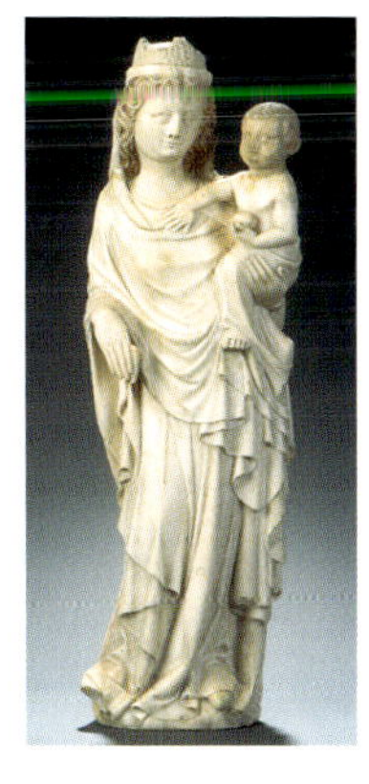

VI.18

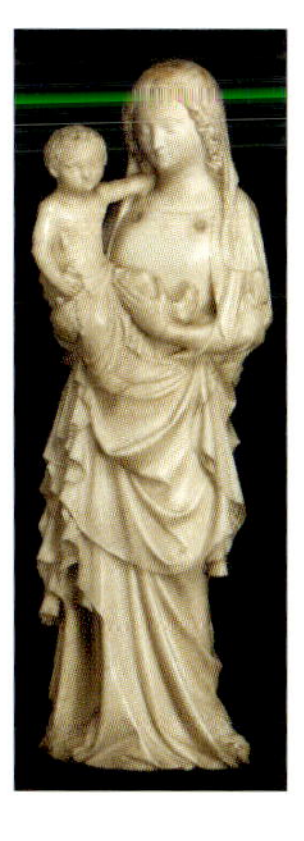

VI.19

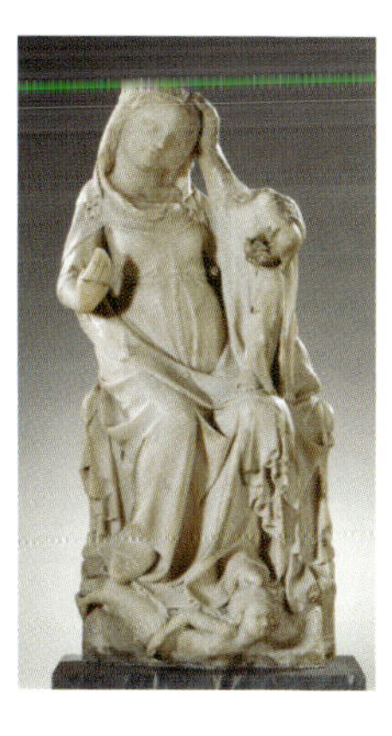

VI.20

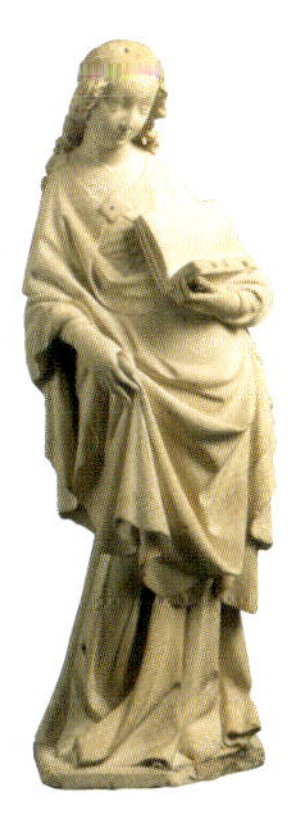

VI.21

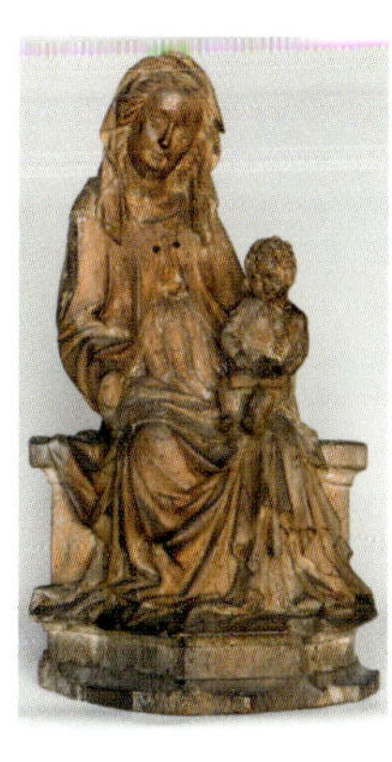

VI.22

similar to that of the Angel of the Annunciation now in the Victoria and Albert Museum, London.

BIBLIOGRAPHY: Mariagiulia Burresi, *Sacre Passioni. Scultura lignea a Pisa dal XII al XV secolo* (exhib. cat.), Pisa, 2000, pp.164 et seq.

VI.18 JEAN PÉPIN DE HUY: VIRGIN AND CHILD

1329
Marble (the Child's head is more recent and the Virgin's metal crown is missing)
65 x 21 x 11 cm
Communanté d'agglomération de l'Artois en dépôt au Musée des Beaux-Arts d'Arras, D.978.1
Provenance: Chartreuse monastery of Mont-Sainte-Marie at Gosnay
Classed as Historic monument 4 January 1915

This work was commissioned by Countess Mahaut of Artois from the Paris workshop of Jean Pépin de Huy to be donated to the monastery. It adopts the formal conventions customary in the sculpture of that era, particularly in the way the folds of the cloak are arranged. A pedestal and a black marble dais completed the statue.

BIBLIOGRAPHY: *Rhein und Maas*, no. 95; Gerhard Schmidt, 'Drei pariser Marmorbildhauer des 14. Jahrhunderts', *Wiener Jahrbuch für Kunstwissenschaft*, 24, 1971, pp. 162 et seq.

VI.19 JEAN DE LIÈGE (ATTRIBUTED): VIRGIN AND CHILD

c. 1364
Marble, traces of gilding (two crowns are missing), 63 x 20.5 x 13 cm
Lisbon, Museo Calouste Gulbenkian, no. 207
Provenance: Possibly from Saint-Antoine-des-Champs, Paris

Several formal motifs enable us to attribute this sculpture to Jean de Liège, the creator of the recumbent figure on the tomb of Charles IV of France, the Fair. The work has great sweetness. Unusually, the Virgin carries the Child in her right arm.

BIBLIOGRAPHY: *Les Fastes du Gothique, le siècle de Charles V*, Paris, 1981, no. 66; Maria Rosa Figueiredo, Catalogo de escultura europeia, vol.A. A escultura francesa, Lisbon, 1992, pp. 18–23.

VI.20 SEATED VIRGIN CROWNED BY THE CHILD

Île-de-France, second quarter of the 14th century
Marble bracket statue (right forearm and hand remade in alabaster, left hand of Child lost), 38 x 16.8 x 6.5 cm
Paris, Musée du Louvre, département des sculptures, RF 580

Certain stylistic affinities enable us to see this as the work of a Paris workshop close to that of Jean de Liège (see VI.23). The iconographical theme is a rare one: the Child raises His hand to crown His Mother, who bends her head to make it easier for Him. This mixture of natural behaviour and the symbolism related to Mary is typical of 14th-century art and most especially of the concept of the Virgin's humanity. With her foot she crushes a demon – or is it Eve?

BIBLIOGRAPHY: F. Baron (ed.), *Sculpture française I. Moyen Âge*, Musée du Louvre, Paris, 1996, p. 134.

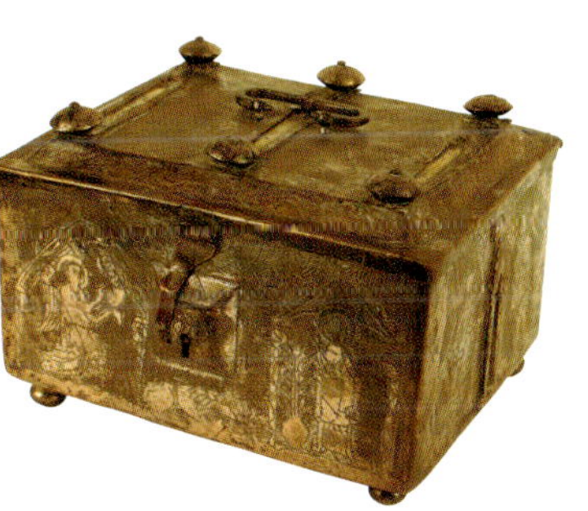

VI.23

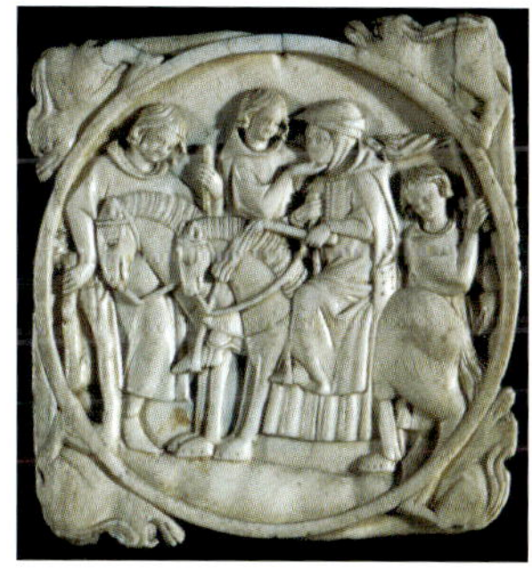

VI.24

VI.21 VIRGIN HOLDING A BOOK

c. 1380–90
Yellow sandstone, very slight traces of polychromy, 69 cm
Prague, Národni Galerie, no. P 8 799
Provenance: The former Hinrichsen collection

Some have tried to compare this work with the five sculptures traditionally attributed to the Master of Grosslobming (Austria), but also with the associates of the Parlers, who worked in Cologne and Prague. Another hypothesis sees affinities between this statue and the Virgin of Falkenstein or even the paintings of one of the most important primitives of Bohemia, the Master of Wittingau. It is undoubtedly similar to certain works by the Master of Grosslobming, particularly the Virgin of the Annunciation in the Metropolitan Museum, New York

BIBLIOGRAPHY: D. Grossmann, in *Die Parler und der Schöne Stil*, Cologne 1980, IV, p. 141; Lothar Schultes, 'Der Meister von Grosslobming und die Wiener Plastik des Schönen Stils', *Wiener Jahrbuch für Kunstgeschichte*, XXXIX, 1986, pp. 1–40; Jiri Fajt, Milena Bartlova, Svetice s knihou, *Saint Virgin Holding a Book*, Prague, 1996.

VI.22 VIRGIN AND CHILD READING

Upper Rhine, *c.* 1420
Lime, Virgin's right hand missing, 45 x 23 x 16 cm
Strasbourg, Musée de l'œuvre Notre-Dame, no. 150

Under his Mother's benevolent gaze, the Child is reading, probably the account of his future Passion. It might also be a writing Child, with the Mother holding an inkpot, but this stays impossible to check. The sculptor has given great flexibility to the Virgin's cloak, which spreads widely, while her dress, belted high under the bust, clings to her form. With great vigour, this work further extends the style of the 1400s known as 'International Gothic'.

BIBLIOGRAPHY: I. Geissler, *Oberrheinische Plastik um 1400*, Berlin, 1957; Ch. P. Parkhurst, Jr., 'The Madonna of the Writing Christ', *The Art Bulletin*, 1941, XXIII, no. 4, pp. 293–306.

VI.23 MARRIAGE CASKET

15th century
Gilded silver, 9.5 x 18.5 x 15 cm
Saint-Avé, Brittany, church treasury on loan to Vannes cathedral
Classed as historic monument 26 April 1941

The motto 'Amys', accompanied by mermaids, centaurs and swans, appears on the lid. The sides depict the Annunciation. A man advances towards a woman holding a crown. A man offers her his heart and a woman presents her with a crown.

BIBLIOGRAPHY: *Trésors des églises de France*, no. 329.

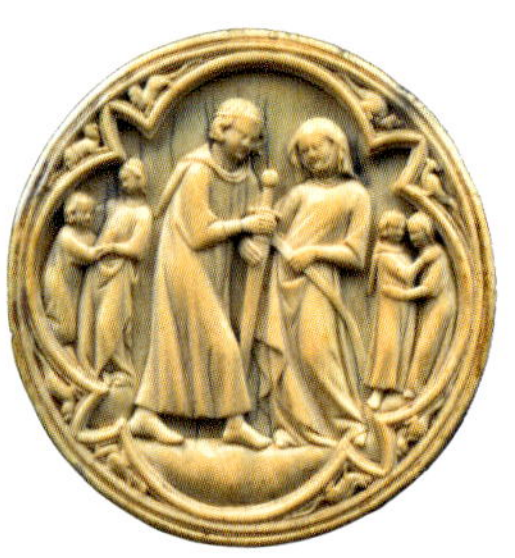

VI.25

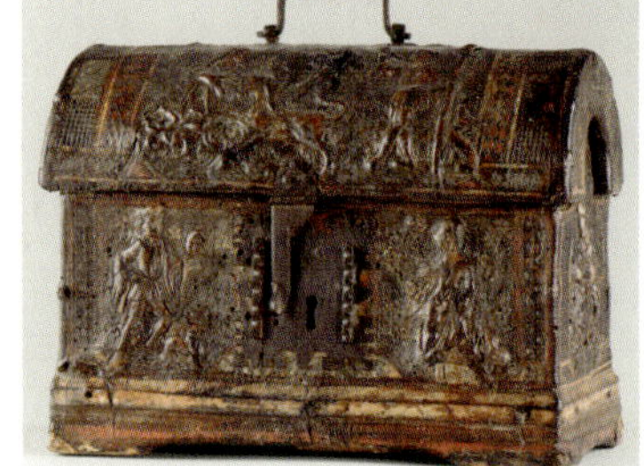

VI.26

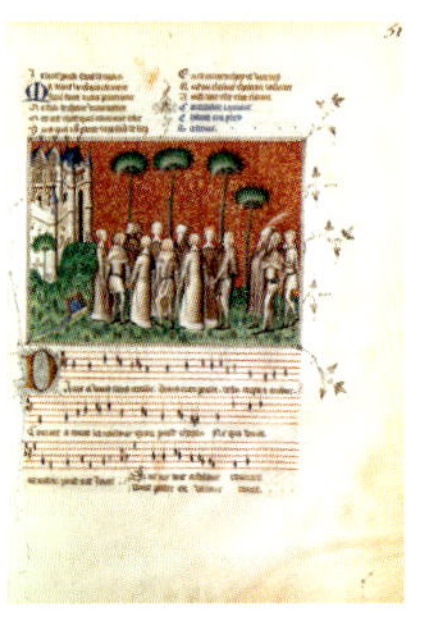

VI.27

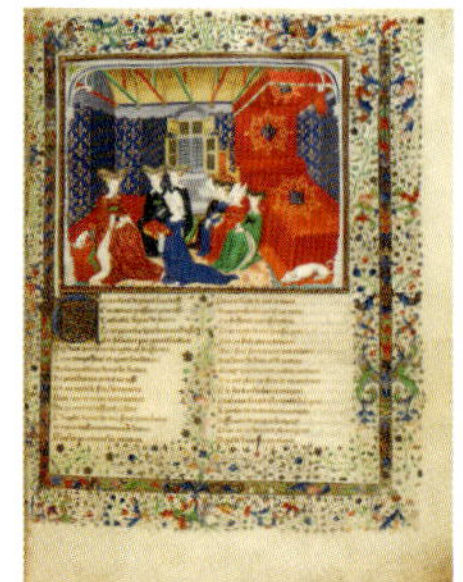

VI.28

VI.24 MIRROR CASE

Paris, 1300–20
Ivory, 11 cm
Paris, Musée du Louvre, département des objets d'art, 118

The circular design, its corner-pieces carved with dragons, illustrates a couple on horseback. The young man, riding on his lover's left, is grasping her by her chin – enclosed in a wimple – in a gesture that invites her to kiss him. This scene, on the theme of courtly love, is commonplace on objects of the type, and mirrors with carved ivory cases in two sections formed part of a lady's accessories. The style of the relief is not lacking in subtlety, particularly in the treatment of the faces and the elegant arrangement of the hands; note too how holes trepanned in the pupils of the eyes allowed the implantation of fine glass beads. Nonetheless, the stiffness of the horses argues against the piece being by one of the great Parisian ivory carvers of the early 14th century.

BIBLIOGRAPHY: Danièle Gaborit-Chopin, in *L'Art au temps des Rois maudits*, no. 97.

VI.25 MIRROR CASE

Paris, first half of the 14th century
Ivory, 11.9 x 11.3 cm
Brussels, Musées royaux d'art et d'histoire, no. 3140

The presentation in an unusual frame, shaped like a four-leafed clover with human-headed dragons decorating the corners, is very rare. The lady, wearing a veil and a wimple, hands her lover a sword and shoulder-belt. The parallel movement of the two bodies creates a tender composition, reinforced by the two scenes at the sides showing the lover at his lady's feet and then the two lovers embracing. These scenes are on a smaller scale, each limited by a corner.

BIBLIOGRAPHY: Raymond Koechlin, *Les ivoires gothiques français*, Paris, 1924, no. 1006.

VI.26 CASKET

Germany, *c.* 1500
Embossed leather on a wooden base, 20.5 x 27.2 x 14.5 cm
Paris, Musée national du Moyen Âge, Thermes et hôtel de Cluny, no. 22600

Doubtless inspired by engravings, the scenes decorating this casket seem to confirm its secular purpose, in spite of the presence of Samson and the lion. The couple on the front and the unicorn placing its feet on the legs of a young girl could identify the object as a marriage casket.

VI.27 GUILLAUME DE MACHAUT: *THE REMEDY OF FORTUNE* AND *THE WORDS OF THE LION*

Parisian master, *c.* 1350–55
321 ff., 30 x 21 cm
Paris, Bibliothèque nationale de France, Ms. Français 1586
f.51r: Dance scene

Originally a commoner who became a master of arts, poet and musician, Guillaume de Machaut (*c.* 1300–77) had as his patrons Jean of Luxembourg, King of Bohemia, Charles, King of Navarre, and Charles v, King of France. *The Remedy* dates from about 1341. It tells the story of the poet, in love with a lady to whom he dares not declare his passion until Hope finally gives him the courage he needs. The work includes nine pieces of lyrical music. Guillaume de Machaut continued the tradition of the troubadours at a time when culture and knowledge were no longer the prerogative of the clergy but were also accessible to the urban middle classes. The illuminations are by one of the 14th century's leading painters. The evocation of courtly life and the minute care taken in depicting the fantastic costumes are integrated into a naturalistic frame in which a feeling of nature reigns, all dominated by a sense of colour with few equals in the art of the mid-14th century.

BIBLIOGRAPHY: *Les Fastes du Gothique*, no. 271.

VI.28 CHRISTINE DE PISAN: COMPLETE WORKS

Master of the Cité des Dames, Paris, 1410–11
Parchment, 2 volumes originally forming only one, 398 ff., 36.5 x 28.5 cm
London, British Library, Ms Harley 4431
f.3: Christine de Pisan presents her manuscript to Isabeau of Bavaria, wife of King Charles vi

The daughter of an Italian physician, astronomer and astrologer to the court of Charles v of France, Christine de Pisan studied science, history and poetry. She was left a widow with three children at the age of twenty-five and had to confront difficult circumstances. Study and writing were her only assets – she was the first 'woman of letters' to

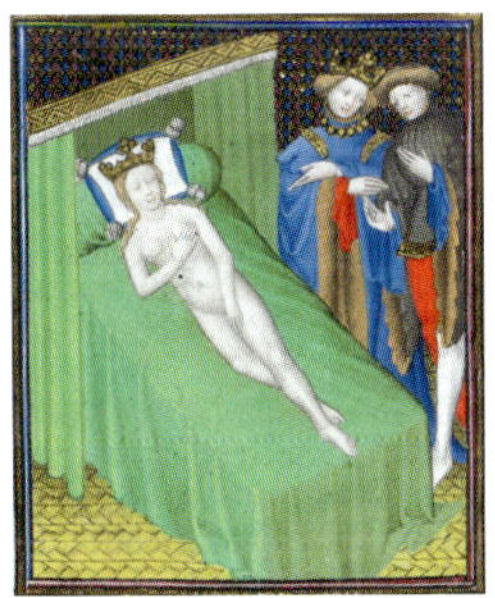

VI.29

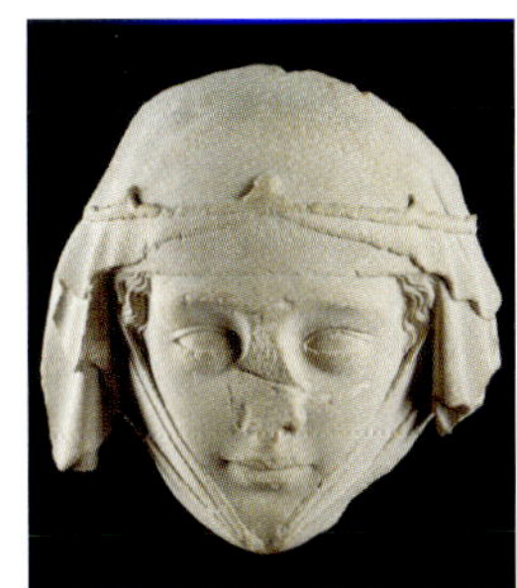

VI.30

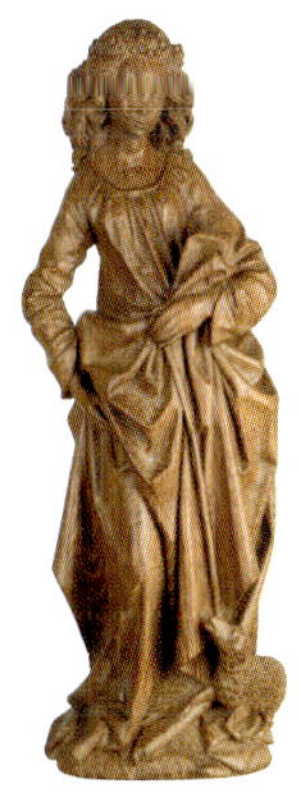

VI.31

make a living from her pen – and she had constantly to seek patrons, in which she was successful in doing. In this folio, Queen Isabeau, in her bedchamber and surrounded by six ladies of her court, receives the complete works, in a magnificent red velvet binding, from the hands of their author. Christine had many copies made for various recipients, but this one – the most sumptuous – was probably commissioned by the Queen.

BIBLIOGRAPHY : *L'art à la cour de Bourgogne. Le mécenat de Philippe le Hardi et de Jean sans Peur (1364–1419)*, Dijon, 2004, no. 10.

VI.29 BOCCACCIO : STORIES OF NOBLE MEN AND WOMEN

Paris, 1409–11
Parchment, 2 vols., 179 and 189 ff., 40.5 x 29.2 cm
Geneva, Bibliothèque publique et universitaire, Ms. 190
Vol. 1, f.74v: History of King Candaule

This book is a French translation of the work on the destiny of famous men and women written in Latin by the poet Giovanni Boccaccio (1313–75). The translation of this copy of the book, which was highly fashionable in the 15th century, was revised: it was given to Jean, Duke of Berry, by his treasurer and adviser, Margin Gouge. The illustrations are the work of the Master of Luçon, a Parisian illuminator who was very active 1410–17.

BIBLIOGRAPHY : Millard Meiss, *French Painting at the Time of Jean de Berry. The Late Fourteenth Century and the Patronage of the Duke*, London and New York, 1967, pp. 357–59.

VI.30 MASK OF JEANNE DE TOULOUSE

Île-de-France, 1280s
Stone, 24.5 x 24.5 x 9 cm
Paris, Musée national du Moyen Âge, Thermes et hôtel de Cluny, no. 22863
Provenance: abbey of the Victorines of Gercy at Varennes-Jarcy (Seine-et-Marne)

A fragment from the funerary monument of Jeanne (daughter of Raymond VII of Toulouse), who married Alphonse, Count of Poitiers, the brother of King Louis IX of France (St Louis). Jeanne had founded the abbey in 1269. A veil and a wimple enclose the triangle of her face, whose modelling is of dazzling beauty. It must have been created by the great sculptor who worked for Philip IV the Fair on producing, with his workshop, the sculptures of Saint-Louis de Poissy (Île-de-France).

VI.31 ADRIAEN VAN WESEL : ST AGNES

c. 1480
Oak, 56 cm
Uden, Museum voor religieuze kunst, collectie Rijksmuseum, K.O.G. 1732

At the end of the Middle Ages, preachers such as Geiler de Kaysersberg, outraged by the abuses of the Church, frequently ranted against the habit adopted by the clergy of placing on altars pictures or sculptures representing the Saints Catherine, Barbara, Margaret or Agnes, whose creators had made to resemble noble ladies and even prostitutes! The St Agnes of Adrian van Wesel is not dressed in sumptuous garments, but the movement with which she holds up her dress and the charm of her face framed by lush curly hair transform her into an entirely worldly beauty.

BIBLIOGRAPHY : Jaap Leeuwenberg, *Beeldhouwkunst in het Rijksmuseum*, Amsterdam, 1973, no. 18.

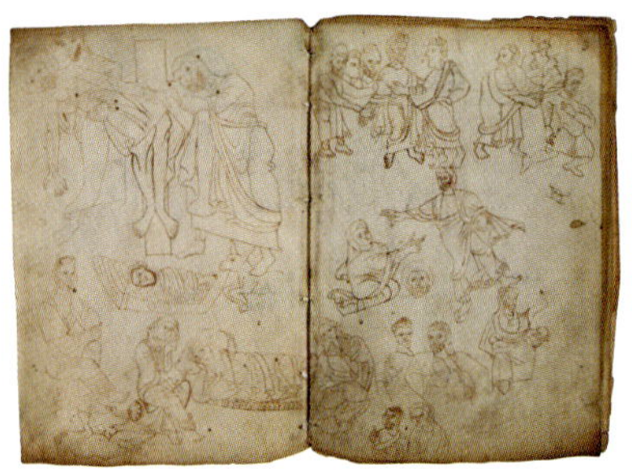

VII.1

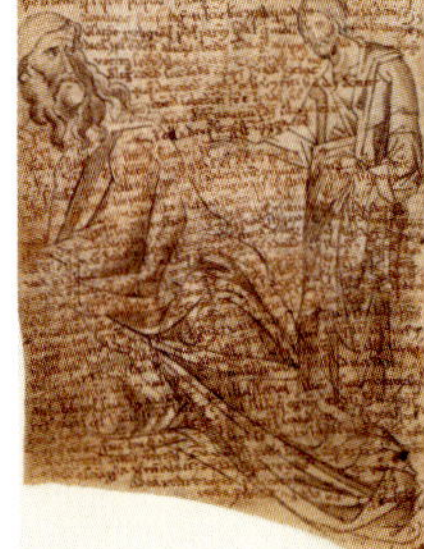

VII.2

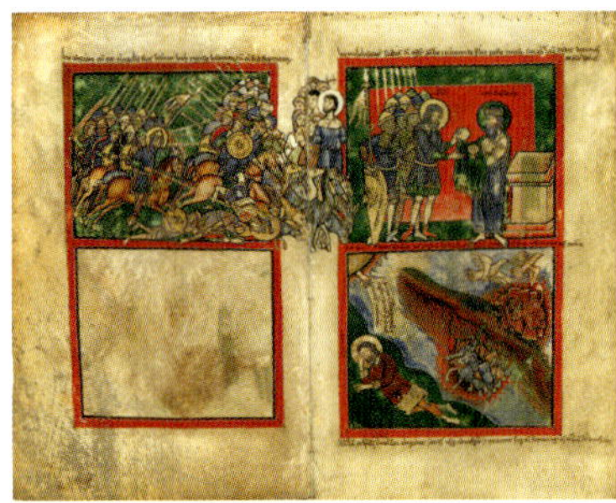

VII.3

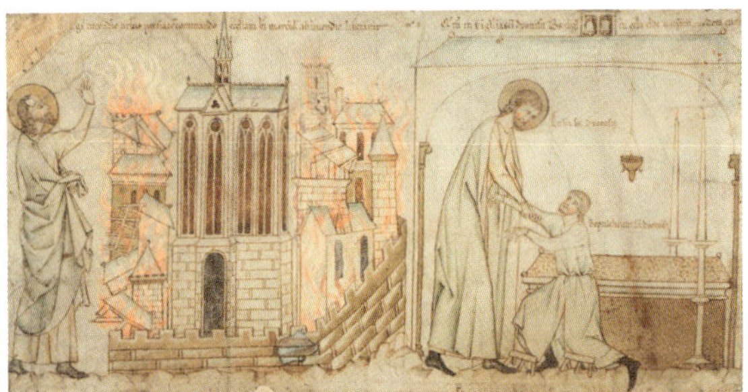

VII.4

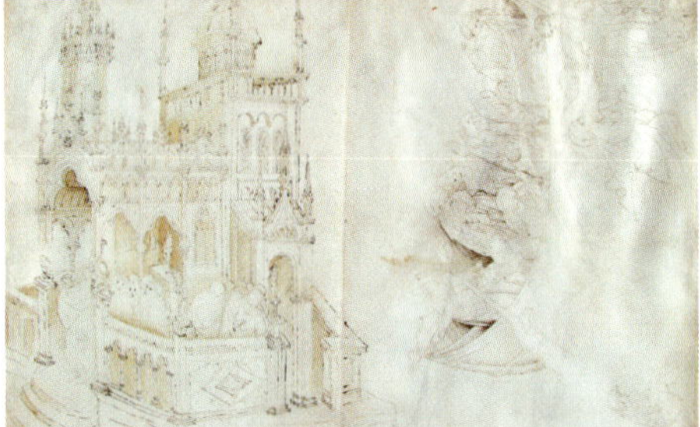

VII.5

SECTION VII
THE CIRCULATION OF DRAWINGS IN EUROPE

The journeys taken by artists and their patrons (the nobility and the clergy) from the High Middle Ages onwards allowed them to absorb what was happening in other regions, particularly in the most admired artistic centres. But memory alone did not suffice to capture works that were to serve as models. At a very early stage, parchment was employed (paper too from the 14th century) as a medium for drawings, often very sketchy, but still a means of transmitting figurative concepts across the whole of Europe. With the Renaissance, drawing ceased to be a mere aide-mémoire and became a more personal expression by the artist, the first draft of his intentions. Drawings also became an indispensable means of visualizing the plans and elevations of Gothic constructions as they grew ever more complex.

A. MODEL BOOKS

At a very early stage, artists of all disciplines practised drawing as a memorization tool enabling them to reproduce any given iconographic model, any given figure or scene (always in the style of paintings or sculptures that already existed) with a view to using them later, often interpreting them in turn. The books or individual sheets, in which forms such models were collated, have been known since the 10th century and they were used until the end of the Middle Ages. At that time, the function of these model books changed: the drawings were no longer simple fixed models but became freer studies, also demonstrating how artists were dedicated to direct observation of the surrounding world.

VII.1 ADHÉMAR DE CHABANNES: COLLECTION OF NOTES AND DRAWINGS

c. 1020
Latin, 14 bundles of 212 ff., parchment, varied formats. Ink drawings
Leyden, Universiteitsbibliotheek, Cod. Voss. Lat. Oct. 15
Provenance: Saint-Martial de Limoges
ff.2v + 3r: Christ being lowered from the Cross and the Nativity, different scenes or isolated figures

The composition of the Descent from the Cross, in which Joseph of Arimathea can be seen holding the body of Christ against his chest, is Byzantine in origin. On the other sheet is Christ's Arrest and the episode involving Peter and the high priest's servant. The differences in style indicated in the various drawings are attributable to the different models from which Adhémar drew his inspiration, for example with reference to ancient models re-reworked by the Carolingian era, or even to contemporary works. These differences are not attributable to different artists. There is also a folio showing Kufic characters (f.210v) in this collection.

BIBLIOGRAPHY: Danielle Gaborit-Chopin, 'Les dessins d'Adhémar de Chabannes', *Archaeological Bulletin of the 'Comité des Travaux Historiques et Scientifiques'*, n.s. 3 (1967), 1968, pp. 163–225; Scheller, no. 4.

VII.2 COLLECTION OF MODELS KNOWN AS THE MUSTERBUCH OF WOLFENBÜTTEL

Venice (?), *c.* 1230–40
Six parchment notebooks (135 ff.) with ink and watercolour drawings, in a collection with other bundles; approx. 16.6 x 12 cm
Wolfenbüttel, Herzog August Bibliothek, Cod. Guelf. 61.2 Aug. 4°
Provenance: Cistercian abbey of Marienthal (Saxony). f.93v: Abraham (?) and Christ in the Garden of Gethsemane

This collection is evidence of the contact between Latin and Greek artists under the Latin interregnum (1204–61). A text was written over the drawings (the *Letters of Guillaume de Saint-Thierry*), which demonstrates that these folios have changed their function. In Saxon art, motifs borrowed from Byzantine art were encountered very early, which is why this manuscript has sometimes been attributed to a Saxon artist.

BIBLIOGRAPHY: Scheller, no.13 (with bibliography); Helen C. Evans and William D. Wixom (eds), *The Glory of Byzantium. Art, Culture of the Middle Byzantine Era A.D. 843–1261* (exhib. cat.), The Metropolitan Museum of Art, New York, 1997, no. 319.

VII.3 COLLECTION OF ILLUSTRATIONS FOR A PSALTER (?)

Mosan basin, mid-12th century
10 parchment folios, 24.9 x 15.6 cm
Berlin, Staatliche Museen zu Berlin, Kupferstichkabinett, HS 78 A 6
f.1v + 2r

These scenes show such marked iconographical similarities to the

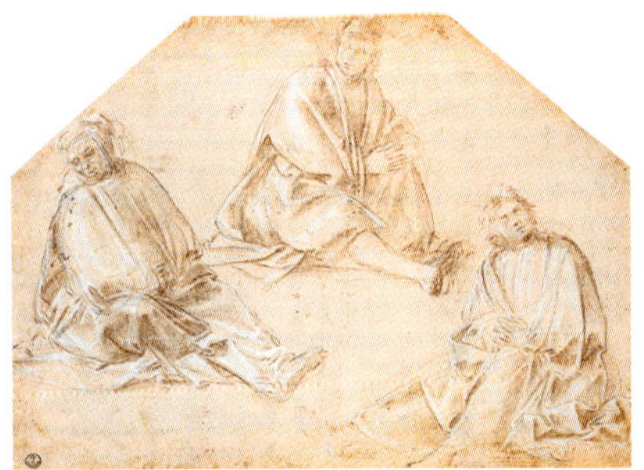
VII.6

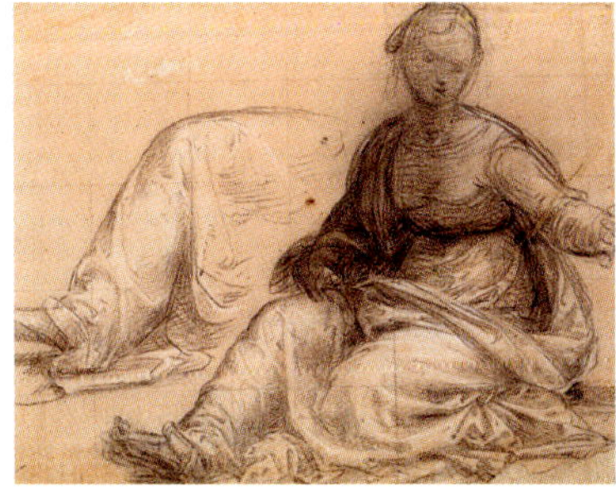
VII.7

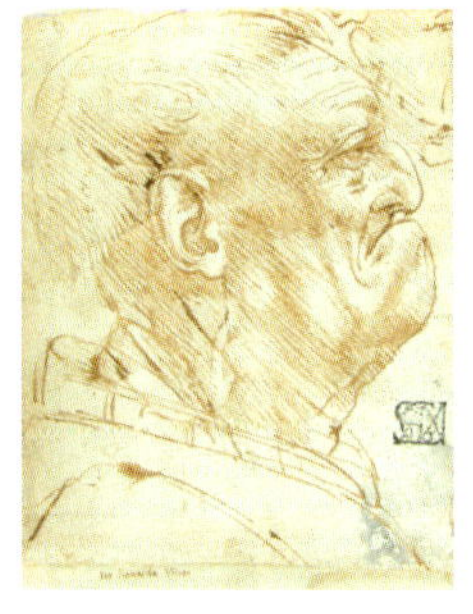
VII.8

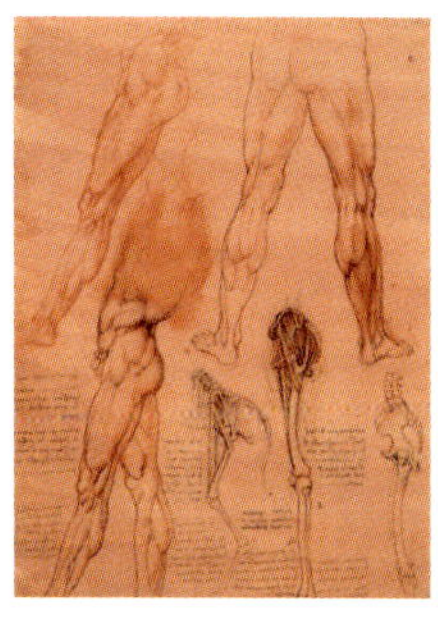
VII.9

corresponding scenes on the font of Liège that it should be accepted that the painter was familiar with these works. The drawing is executed extremely delicately, which the addition of colours (by the same artist ?) tends to blur in places.

BIBLIOGRAPHY : Hanns Swarzenski, *Mosaner Psalter-Fragment*, Graz, 1974 ; Scheller, no. 6 (with bibliography).

VII.4 ST ELIGIUS SCROLL OF PARCHMENT (FRAGMENT)

Northern France, mid-13th century
Parchment, pen and wash, 17.7 x 34 cm
Paris, Musée Carnavalet, Histoire de Paris D7075
Provenance : St Eloi de Noyon, Picardy

This is a genuine model designed to be enlarged, illustrating the life of St Eligius (Eloi), the patron saint of goldsmiths, after a *Vita Eligis* drafted in the 7th century. In the left-hand scene, Eligius saves the Saint-Martial basilica in Paris from a fire ; in the right-hand scene, he cures a paralysed person in the Saint-Denis basilica. The other parts, which are currently missing from this scroll and were approximately 170/180 cm long, were copied from the originals at the end of the 17th century for Roger de Gaignières (Bodleian Library).

BIBLIOGRAPHY : Robert Branner, 'Le rouleau de saint Eloi', *History of Art Information*, XII, 1967, pp. 55–73.

VII.5 GENTILE DA FABRIANO, PISANELLO AND ATELIER : 'TACCUINO DI VIAGGI' (?)

c. 1410–55
43 parchment sheets, silver-point, brown ink, 17.9/27.6 x 12.8 x 19.6 cm
Milan, Veneranda Biblioteca Ambrosiana Pinacoteca, F 214
f.10 : the architecture of a church and the Miraculous Draught of Fishes

This is the only intact bi-folio in a copied collection known under the name of the 'Taccuino di Viaggi' (Travel Notebook). Other folios like these are to be found at Bayonne, Frankfurt, New York, Berlin, Oxford, Paris, etc.).

BIBLIOGRAPHY : Albert J. Elen, *Italian Late-Medieval and Renaissance Drawing-Books*, Leyden, 1995, no.15 (with bibliography).

VII.6 FILIPPINO LIPPI : THREE FIGURES SITTING IN VARIOUS POSITIONS, WITH THEIR HANDS CLASPED

Late 1480s
Silver-point and white gouache on prepared beige paper, 25.6 x 35.9 cm
Florence, Polo Museale Fiorentino, Gabinetto Disegni e Stampe degli Uffizi, 134 E

This study was probably related to the frescoes that Lippi produced for the Carafa chapel in Rome.

BIBLIOGRAPHY : George R. Goldner and Carmen C. Bambach (ed), 'The Drawings of Filippino Lippi and his Circle', Metropolitan Museum of Art catalogue, New York, 1997, no. 40.

VII.7 FRA BARTOLOMMEO (ATELIER ?) : DRAPED FEMALE FIGURE SITTING ON THE GROUND, HER RIGHT HAND RAISED, AND SEPARATE VARIANT OF THE RIGHT LEG

c. 1515 (?)
Graphite, white chalk on prepared paper, uneven contours : 26.8 x 35.1 cm
Florence, Polo Museale Fiorentino, Gabinetto Disegni e Stampe degli Uffizi, 382 F

This square study can be compared to the seated figure of a mother and child in the foreground of the Virgin of Mercy at Lucca. In his recent works, the specialist in Fra Bartolommeo's drawings, Chris Fischer, does not attribute this drawing to the painter. However, it can be compared to a study in vol. M 149 at the Boijmans Van Beuningen Museum, Amsterdam.

BIBLIOGRAPHY : Chris Fischer, *Fra Bartolommeo, Master Draughtsman of the High Renaissance. A Selection from the Rotterdam Albums and Landscape Drawings from various Collections* (exhib. cat.), Rotterdam, 1990, no. 99v.

VII.8 LEONARDO DA VINCI : HEAD OF AN OLD MAN IN RIGHT PROFILE

c. 1485–90
Brown ink on layers of paper, 12.6 x 10.4 cm
Milan, Veneranda Biblioteca Ambrosiana Pinacoteca, Cod.263. Inf.78

The use of rapid hatching would argue for a drawing from direct observation. But we cannot say whether Leonardo exaggerated this or not ; moreover, what he actually intended plays a decisive role here in how we define such drawings nowadays.

BIBLIOGRAPHY : *Leonardo & Venezia* (exhib. cat.), Venice, 1992, no.53 (with bibliography) ; Michael Willem Kwakkelstein, *Leonardo da Vinci as a physiognomist. Theory and drawing practice*, Utrecht, 1995, pp. 105–07.

VII.9 LEONARDO DA VINCI : FOLIO OF COMPARATIVE STUDIES OF THE LEGS OF A MAN AND A HORSE

Probably Milan, 1506–07
Brown ink and red chalk on prepared red paper, 28.1 x 20.5 cm
The Royal Collection, Windsor Castle, R.L.1262R

Here we have an admirable example of these folios, which testify to both Leonardo's extraordinary scientific curiosity and the skill of his graphic technique, enabling him to draw these studies with great precision and a remarkable power of expression. The lower part of the drawing compares a human leg and the skeleton of a horse's leg as well as two skeletons of a human leg. (Leonardo wrote a treatise on the anatomy of the horse, which has unfortunately been lost.) Inscriptions complement each drawing. The four columns read thus (the Italian script is to be read 'like a mirror', that is, from right to left) :

Column 1 (below) : 'When the muscles are separated from each other, you will show their contours (*proffili*), and when they are joined, you will use only hatching.'

Column 2 (above) : 'Regarding the connection that exists between the conformation of the bones and muscles of the animals and that of the bones and muscles of a man.' ; (below) : First shows the bones separated from the sockets in which they are joined, then joins them together, especially the hip joint or the thigh joint.

Column 3 (above) : 'Shows a man standing on his toes in order to compare him with other animals more effectively. Represents a man's knee flexed like a horse's knee. ; (below) 'To compare the skeletal structure of the horse with that of a man, you can show the man standing on his toes while depicting the leg.'

Column 4 (above) : 'Junction of the muscles (*musscoli carnoso*) with the bones, without tendon or cartilage.' ; (below) : 'Shows a man standing on his toes in order to compare him with other animals more effectively.'

The two red-chalk drawings at the top of this folio accentuate the muscle structure of the legs of a standing man : they should be compared to the studies for the *Battle of Anghiari*, though these predate the drawings

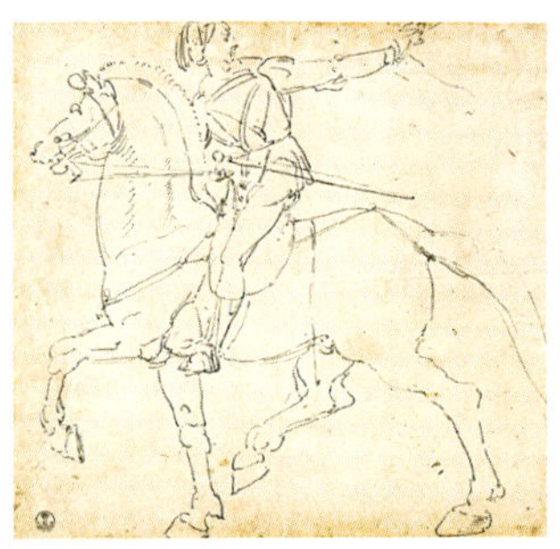
VII.10

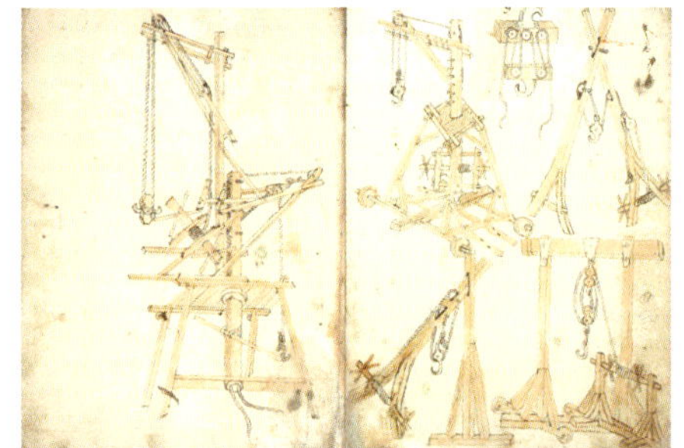
VII.11

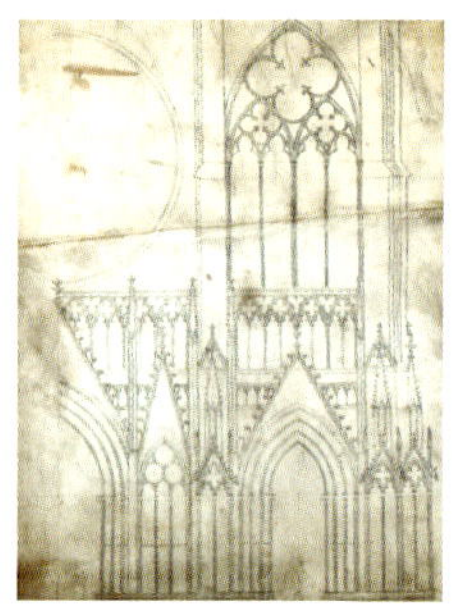
VII.12

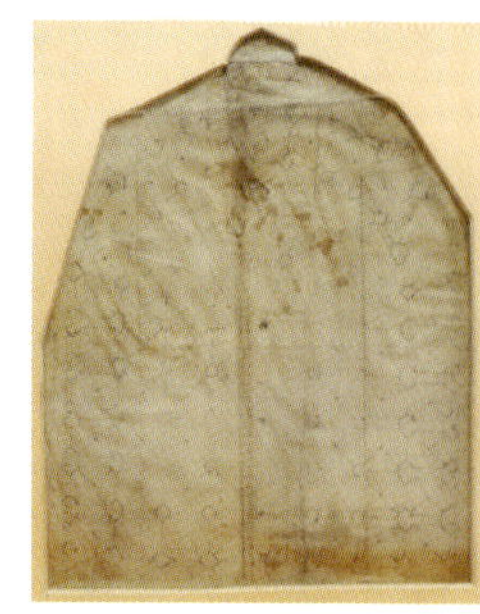
VII.13

on this folio. It can be seen how Leonardo used the same figure of a warrior viewed from behind to complete his anatomical studies.

BIBLIOGRAPHY : Kenneth Clark and Carlo Pedretti, *The Drawings of Her Majesty the Queen at Windsor Castle*, London, 1968, vol. 1, pp. 129–30; Jean-Paul Richter, *The Literary Works of Leonardo da Vinci, Commentary by Carlo Pedretti*, Oxford, 1977, vol. 2, p. 96.

VII.10 ALBRECHT DÜRER: THE FALCONER

c. 1502
Pen and black ink on white paper, 21.2 x 22.6 cm
Florence, Polo Museale Fiorentino, Gabinetto di Disegni e Stampe degli Uffizi, 1074 E

This drawing of a trotting horse displays a certain spontaneity. As in similar examples, the artist has changed his mind over the right hind leg. Horses in profile were a favourite subject for Dürer from 1498. Particularly, he borrowed compositions from equestrian statues encountered during his stays in Italy: by Verrochio in Venice and Donatello in Padua, for instance. His interest in horses would also have been stimulated by Leonardo da Vinci's preparatory studies for a monument to Francesco Sforza, which he knew directly or indirectly. The present example should be viewed in relation to the engraving known as *The Knight, Death and the Devil* (1513) and the preliminary sketches of the proportions that so preoccupied Dürer. Here, the animal's head is raised higher than in that engraving, recalling, rather, his *Little Horse* of 1505.

This is an excellent example of the convergence of a wide variety of artistic theories featured in drawings of the period 1500–13.

BIBLIOGRAPHY: Annamaria Petrioli Tofani, *Gabinetto disegni e stampe degli Uffizi, Inventario 2. Disegni esposti*, Florence, 1987, pp. 449–50.

B. ARCHITECTURAL DRAWINGS

Architectural drawings provide another testimony to the dissemination of parchment , and later paper, folios in order to circulate models. A drawing illustrating the plan and/or elevation of a building was probably not required during the Romanesque period. It was the considerable increase in structural complexity of the great cathedrals that explained the growing importance given to architectural drawing in the first half of the 13th century. The most ancient architectural design preserved is probably drawing A for the façade of Strasbourg cathedral, which conveys to what extent the style known as 'Rayonnant', from the Ile-de-France, had captivated the Strasbourg architect. These drawings were sometimes kept in the lodges (this was the case in Strasbourg, Cologne, Vienna, Ulm, Sienna), or taken elsewhere, or copied to be used at other sites. There has been evidence of the presence of drawings in lodges, notably in those of Strasbourg and Vienna, since the Middle Ages.

VII.11 HANS HAMMER'S NOTEBOOK

c. or after 1500
Parchment, 29 ff., 29 x 21 cm
Wolfenbüttel, Herzog August Bibliothek, Extravagantes 114.1
f.3v + 4r: lifting machines

Hans Hammer was the master mason for Strasbourg cathedral over two periods: 1486–90, and then 1513–19. From 1482, after returning from Hungary, he was appointed *parlier*; assistant to the architect on the same site. At the end of this collection, he attached a Hungarian-German glossary that proved very useful for the history of the Hungarian language. In his capacity as master mason for the 'supreme loggia' of the Empire, he created for Strasbourg cathedral the pulpit and important works in the chancel and transept. He also produced a drawing for a second, western spire, which seems to have been envisaged under his direction.

This model book is not strictly speaking a treatise; like the album of Villard de Honnecourt, it combines quite incongruous information: from a spit-roast design to vital information on architectural techniques, which meant, in the Middle Ages, an in-depth knowledge of geometry, trigonometry (measurements of elevations, already carried out by Villard de Honnecourt), and technical aspects of engineering. The majority of the drawings depict planimetrical projections of vaults and lifting equipment that were necessary for construction as well as for military applications. The equipment is in fact perfectly workable, although reading about it is sometimes laborious. This is the most important collection of drawings of this equipment type surviving from the medieval era. If an inscription on the front cover can be believed, this equipment would have been in use on the Strasbourg site.

BIBLIOGRAPHY : F. J. Fuchs, 'Introduction au "Musterbuch" de Hans Hammer', *Bulletin des Amis de la Cathédrale de Strasbourg*, 1992, pp.11–67; Roland Recht, *Le dessin d'architecture. Origine et fonction*, Paris, 1995.

VII.12 DRAWING A FOR THE STRASBOURG CATHEDRAL FAÇADE

c. 1250–60
Two parchment sheets combined, black ink and preliminary layout in metal-point, 86 x 62 cm
Strasbourg, Musée de l'œuvre Notre-Dame, no. 1

Elevation of the right (south) half of the façade. Certain parts (rose window) having remained unfinished; it was possible to recreate the left half by duplication. This technique saved both parchment and work. Contrary to what was once believed, here we have the first design of a Gothic façade, a replacement for the façade of the pre-Romanesque epoch, which was still in place until 1275.

BIBLIOGRAPHY : Roland Recht, *Sur le dessin d'architecture. Mélanges offerts à Louis Grodecki*, Paris, 1981.

VII.13 DOUBLE-SIDED DRAWING FRONT : PLAN OF THE CHANCEL FOR PARIS CATHEDRAL BACK : PLAN OF THE CHANCEL FOR ORLEANS CATHEDRAL

First half of the 14th century (?)
Black ink on two pieces of parchment, 63.5 x 53.5 cm
Strasbourg, Musée de l'œuvre Notre-Dame, no. 21

The two plans are not layouts of the existing chancels of these two buildings. They propose slight variations of them, which is entirely in accordance with medieval custom. The Orléans plan is displayed.

BIBLIOGRAPHY : Recht, *Les Bâtisseurs*, no. C32.

VII.14 PARTIAL PLAN OF AN UNKNOWN BUILDING

15th century
Brown ink on two sheets of paper combined, preliminary layout in metal-point, 96 x 50 cm
Strasbourg, Musée de l'œuvre Notre-

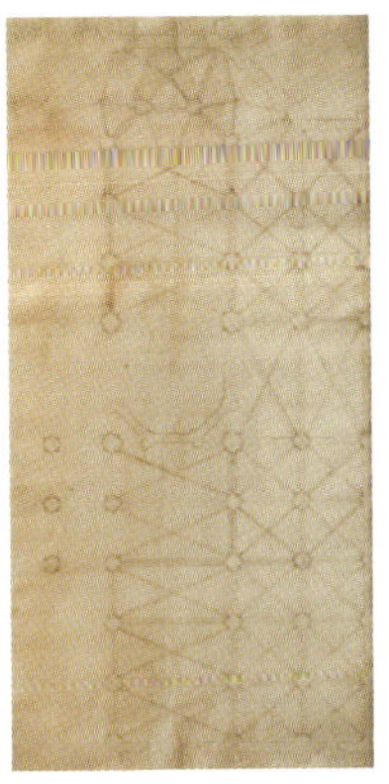
VII.14

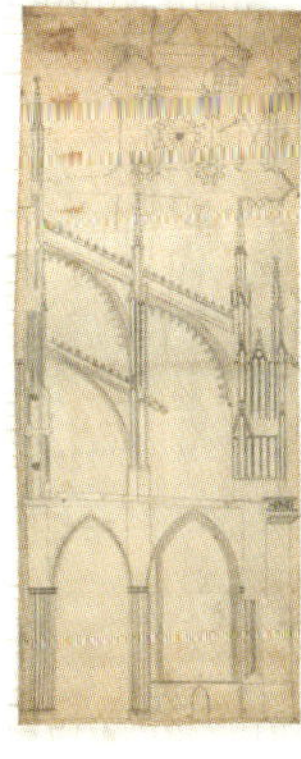
VII.15

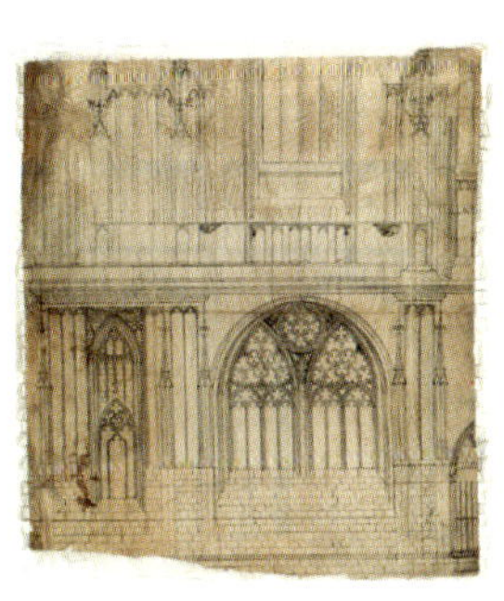
VII.16

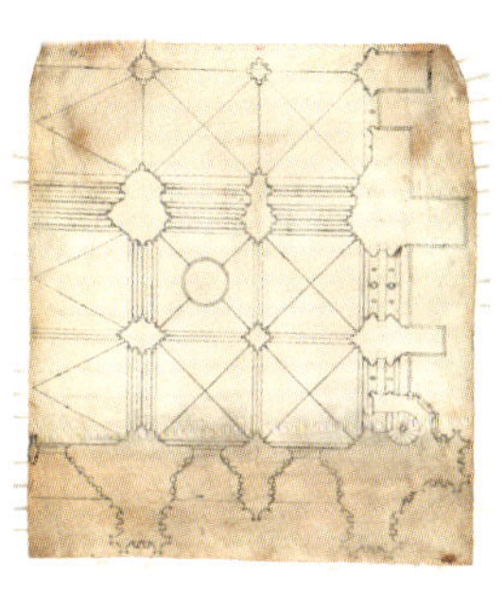
VII.17

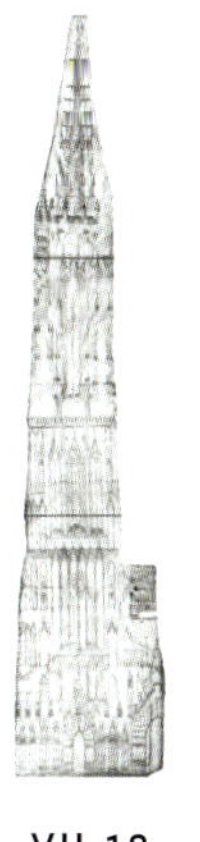
VII.18

VII.19

Dame, no. 29
Provenance: old collection of the Musée de l'œuvre Notre-Dame, Strasbourg

The plan is unfinished: a nave with five aisles, with circular columns incorporating small columns, ending in an apse with three sides; in the centre appears a projection of the octagonal tower crossing.

VII.15 CROSS-SECTION OF THE NORTH PART OF THE CHANCEL AT PRAGUE CATHEDRAL AND PLAN OF A TOWER

Last quarter of the 14th century
Black ink on parchment, 132 x 52.5 cm
Vienna, Akademie der bildenden Künste, Kupferstichkabinett, no. 16821R

Across two-thirds of the elevation, the section is carefully drawn, including ornamental details. The ground plan in the top third shows a draft of an octagonal tower, flanked by four turrets with spiral staircase; all these features are incorporated to replace the south tower of Saint-Guy, Prague. The plan shows some similarities to the octagon for Strasbourg cathedral's tower by Ulrich von Ensingen and it seems evident that around 1400 there was some communication between the architects from Prague (Johann Parler) and Strasbourg. According to Böker, the section drawing would have been an original by Peter Parler, dating from around 1360. The plan of a tower would perhaps correspond to an earlier stage, or a different building.

BIBLIOGRAPHY: Recht, *Les Bâtisseurs*, no. C29; Johann Josef Böker, *Architektur der Gotik. Gothic Architecture. Bestandkatalog der weltgrössten Sammlung an gotischen Baurissen der Akademie der bildenden Künste Vienna* (exhib. cat.), Salzburg-Munich, *2005*, pp. 74–78.

VII.16 DOUBLE-SIDED DRAWING FRONT: ELEVATION OF THE SOUTH TOWER OF PRAGUE CATHEDRAL BACK: INTERIOR ELEVATION OF THE TRANSEPT

Second half of 14th century, 15th century
Black ink on parchment, preliminary layout and compass, 108 x 94.6 cm
Vienna, Akademie der bildenden Künste, Kupferstichkabinett, no. 16817R

This elevation of the south tower is unfinished. There are a few notable changes in the window and the top part of the buttress – corresponding to the works actually carried out. Böker goes along with our opinion, according to which the drawing would not only date from the 15th century, but also from the second half of the 14th century, and would reflect the earlier stage of the plan of works on the south portal. This in fact would be the drawing produced, prior to the commencement of works, by the architect of Prague cathedral, Peter Parler, who was chosen by Emperor Charles IV.

The back shows the west wall of the transept. The drawings on both front and back were executed by the same person.

BIBLIOGRAPHY: Recht, *Le dessin*, p. 78; Böker, *Architektur*, pp. 61-66.

VII.17 PLAN A FOR THE SOUTH TOWER OF COLOGNE CATHEDRAL

c. 1280 (?), mid-14th century (?)
Black ink on parchment, preliminary layout in metal-point, 70 x 61 cm
Vienna, Akademie der bildenden Künste, Kupferstichkabinett, no. 16873

Ground plan for the south-west tower, for half of the narthex and for the initial west spans of the nave. The nave is envisaged with its five aisles. The preliminary layout is visible on the drawing, with some modifications in the design of the windows.

BIBLIOGRAPHY: Arnold Wolff, 'Mittelalterliche Planzeichnungen für das Langhaus des Kölner Domes', *Kölner Domblatt*, 1969, pp. 137–78; Böker, pp. 178–81.

VII.18 ELEVATION OF THE STRASBOURG CATHEDRAL FAÇADE (DRAWING B1)

Mid-14th century
Brown ink on parchment (5 pieces), preliminary layout in metal-point, 326.7 x 69.7 cm
Vienna, Wien Museum, no. 105069

A variation of drawing B (Musée de l'œuvre Notre-Dame, Strasbourg), which was a starting point for the works on the present façade. From an architectural point of view, the layout of the top part of the spire is incomplete, but the solution was not unlike the later project of the architect Ulrich von Ensingen. Some of the stonework decorating the interior of the windows is reminiscent of the chancel in Schwäbisch-Gmünd, Germany, and is confirmation that there was a connection between the Strasbourg site and architecture designed by the Parler family during this mid 14th-century period.

BIBLIOGRAPHY: Recht, *Bâtisseurs*, no. C4; Böker, p. 448.

VII.19 ELEVATION OF THE STRASBOURG CATHEDRAL FAÇADE, NORTH PART

c. 1400
Black ink on parchment (9 pieces), grey and black wash drawing, 461 x 81 cm
Bern, Bernisches Historisches Museum, no. 1962

This drawing, which is a fairly accurate representation of the existing façade at that time, is supplemented by a crown on the spire with reference to the spire at Ulm; this has never been carried out at Strasbourg, where a different plan would be adopted.

BIBLIOGRAPHY: Recht, *Les Bâtisseurs*, no. C13

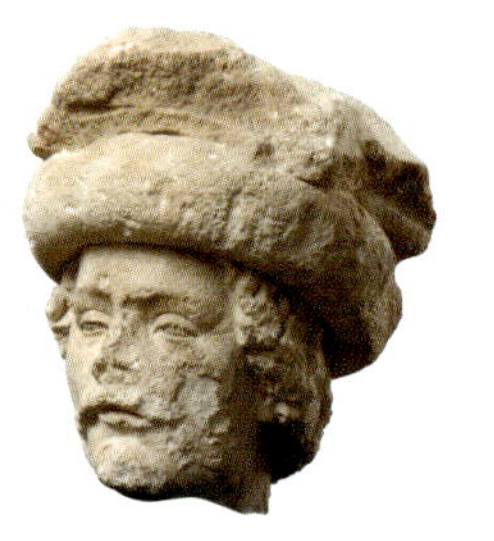
VIII.1

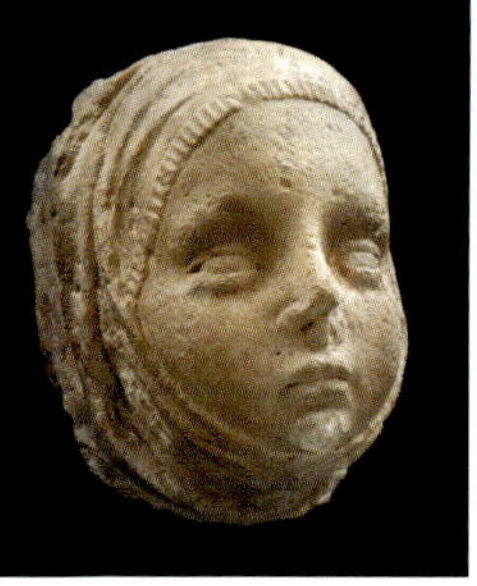
VIII.2

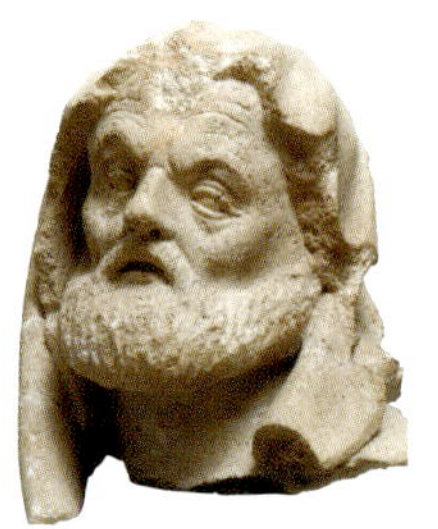
VIII.3

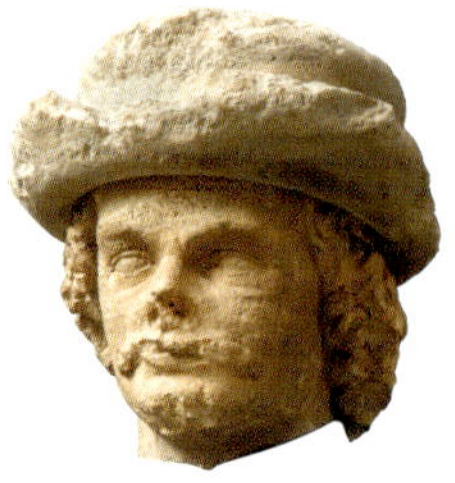
VIII.4

SECTION VIII
THE EUROPEAN CAREERS OF SCULPTORS AT THE END OF THE MIDDLE AGES

Unlike drawing, sculpture demanded heavy and cumbersome materials. The major commissions granted by the nobility or the clergy during the 15th century gave rise to remarkable works bearing the stamp of the highest artistic talent. We look at three examples that illustrate another form of artistic circulation in the European cultural zone. King Sigismund attracted a variety of sculptors from Western Europe to his court at Buda – although their commissions remained unfinished. Nikolaus van Leyden travelled the entire continent, from the Rhine delta to Austria, leaving a brilliant legacy in his wake. Veit Stoss, both sculptor and engraver, led a workshop that supplied Nuremberg, Kraków and Florence.

A. THE ATELIERS OF THE BUDA CASTLE

The spectacular discoveries made at Buda castle in 1974 yielded a very interesting set of sculptures. They reveal that a grand atelier was established by Sigismund, king of Hungary and Holy Roman emperor, in order to create an immense series of sculptures for his palace. The work was interrupted and never installed, for unknown reasons. The styles of the fragments that have been discovered, however, give some insight into the European scale on which he recruited his workforce (from France and the south of the Empire).

VIII.1 HOODED MALE HEAD

Buda, *c.* 1400–20
Yellow limestone, 34 cm
Budapest, Budapesti Történeti Múzeum, no. 75.1.51
Found in the royal palace in 1974

The contours of this face are very subtly defined and are still clearly perceptible despite the damage it has suffered. There are traces of colour in the eyes, which must have been the only polychromed part of the face.

BIBLIOGRAPHY : Imre Takacs (ed.), *Sigismundus Rex et Imperator/ Kunst und Kultur zur Zeit Sigismunds von Luxemburg 1387–1437* (exhib. cat.), Budapest-Luxembourg, 2006, no. 4.21.

VIII.2 HEAD OF A YOUNG GIRL

Buda, *c.* 1400–20
Limestone, 18 cm
Budapest, Budapesti Történeti Múzeum, no. 51.3250
Found before the 1974 excavation

The model of this face, which may perhaps have been part of a console, dates to the 14th century. Some works are by sculptors of another generation, who therefore handed down older models.

BIBLIOGRAPHY : Laszlo Zolnay, Ernö Marosi, *A budavari szoborlelet*, Budapest, 1989, p. 156.

VIII.3 HEAD OF A PROPHET

Buda, *c.* 1400–20
White limestone, 18 x 14.5 cm
Budapest, Budapesti Történeti Múzeum, 75.1.53
Found in the royal palace, northern courtyard, in 1974

The stone surface is uneven in the region of the face and the beard. which may appear unfinished. But such differences in the treatment of the surface appear in other sculptures in this collection. We can see stylistic analogies with the Apostles at the basilica of Saint-Martin in Halle, Belgium, and the Prophets at the Hôtel de Ville in Brussels. We might also compare this head with that from Mehun-sur-Yèvre (Eure-et-Loir) kept at the Louvre and attributed by some to Jean de Cambrai and by others to André Beauneveu.

BIBLIOGRAPHY : *Sigismundus*, no. 4.18.

VIII.4 HOODED MALE HEAD

Buda, *c.* 1400–20
Limestone, 25 cm
Budapest, Budapesti Történeti Múzeum, 75.1.53
Found in the royal palace in 1974

This sculpture and VIII.1 are certainly by the same person. These works belong to the most innovative group in the collection, comparable to the works of Hans Multscher (see head of Louis le Barbu on the model of a tomb, Munich).

BIBLIOGRAPHY : *A budavari*, p.154.

VIII.5, 6, 7, 8 FRAGMENTS OF SCULPTURES

Buda, *c.* 1400–20
White limestone
Budapest, Budapesti Történeti Múzeum, no. 75.180, 94.47, 94.41, 75.1.82
Found in the royal palace in 1974

These fragments reveal great attention to detail in the treatment of courtly costume. They are part of a set of sculptures that no doubt depicted the members of the royal family, the aristocracy and the clergy.

BIBLIOGRAPHY : *A budavari*, passim.

B. THE WORKS OF NIKOLAUS VAN LEYDEN

Nikolaus van Leyden was, without contest, one of the most remarkable artists of medieval times. His artistic travels took him from Utrecht to Strasbourg, then to Wiener-Neustadt and the court of Emperor Frederick III, who commissioned him. His career lasted only a few years, but he succeeded in transposing into the language of sculpture the great innovations in Netherlandish painting and his works bear witness to a psychological approach to iconographical themes, to which he provided a new formulation. He had immense impact on art at the end of the 15th and beginning of the 16th centuries.

VIII.9 NIKOLAUS VAN LEYDEN : BUST OF MAN LEANING ON ELBOW

1465–67
Sculpture in the round, sandstone, 44 cm

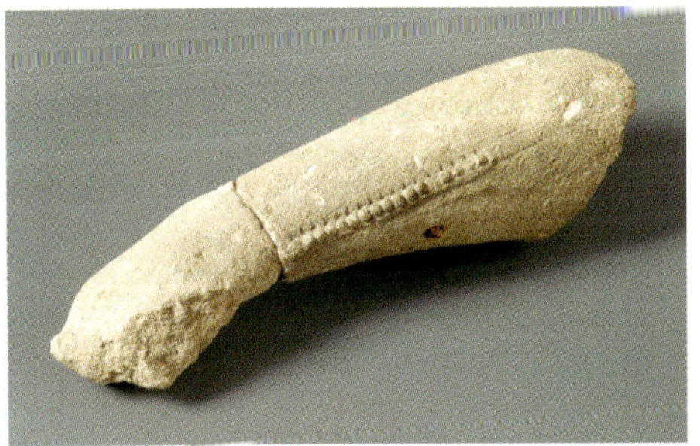

VIII.5

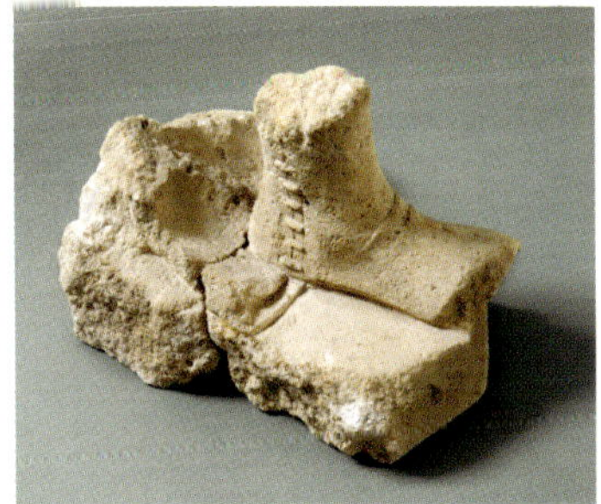

VIII.6

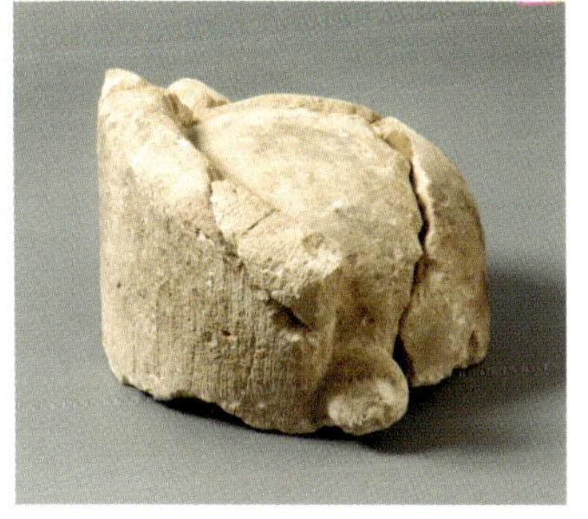

VIII.7

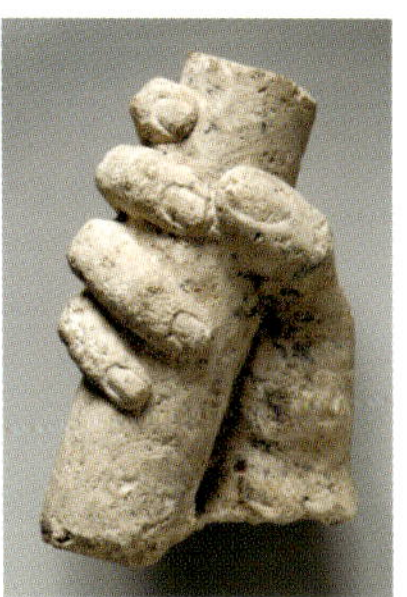

VIII.8

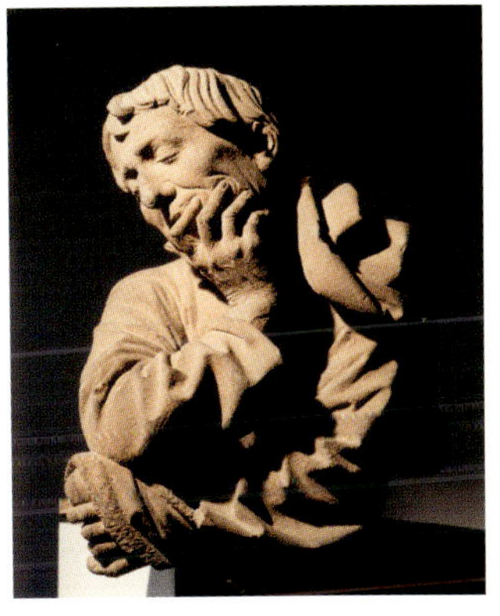

VIII.9

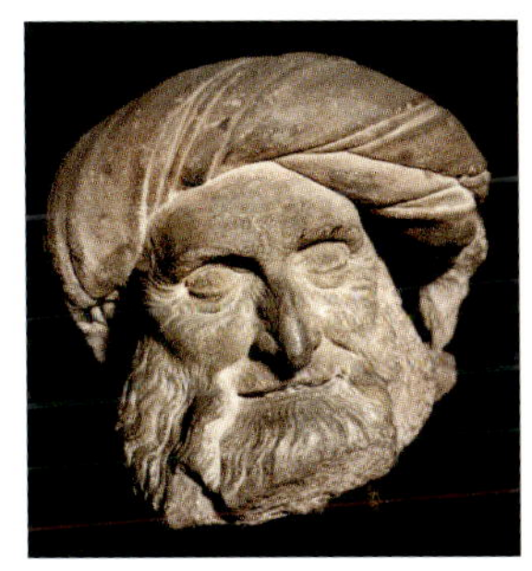

VIII.10

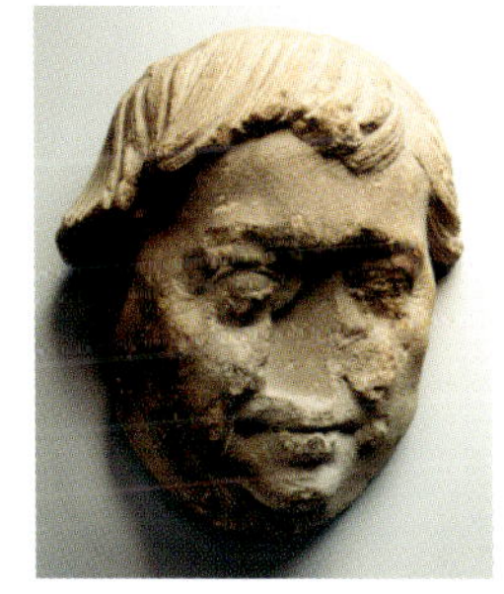

VIII.11

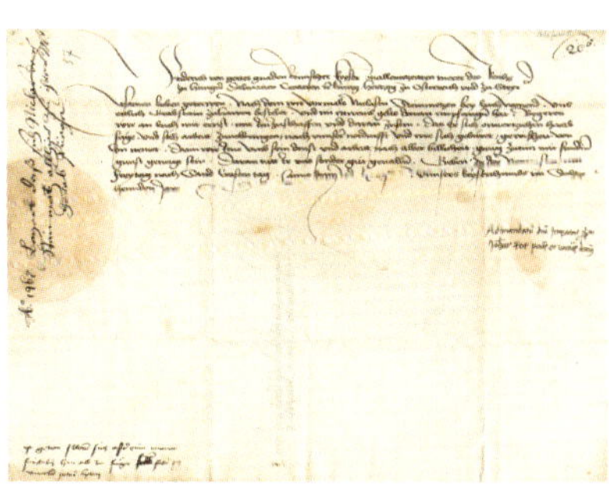

VIII.12

Strasbourg, Musée de l'œuvre Notre-Dame, no. 165
Provenance: Found in 1793 in the area around Strasbourg cathedral

It was probably originally a bust and not a severed figure, though the absence of any finishing on the back might suggest that it was visible only from the front, and placed slightly raised as indicated by the inclined position of the head. Although no documentation confirms this, its attribution to Nikolaus van Leyden is not in doubt. He was the first to have translated into the medium of sculpture the sense of introspection that is characteristic of a painter such as Jan van Eyck. This is one of the great sculptural masterpieces of all time.

BIBLIOGRAPHY: Roland Recht, *Nicolas de Leyde et la sculpture à Strasbourg (1460–1525)*, (doctoral thesis, 1978), Strasbourg, 1987, no. I.06 and pp. 145–47.

VIII.10 NIKOLAUS VAN LEYDEN: MAN WEARING A TURBAN (EMPEROR AUGUSTUS ?)

1464
Sculpture in the round, red sandstone, 26 cm
Strasbourg, Musée de l'œuvre Notre-Dame, no. 162
Provenance: Strasbourg Chancellery

The entire bust, with that of a woman that was it's pendant, was located at the city library of Strasbourg (Temple Neuf) at the time of the 1870 bombardment by the Prussian army. The two fragments would not re-emerge until 1915 and 1935, respectively, when they were acquired by the museums of Strasbourg and Frankfurt (Liebighaus). Fortunately casts allow us to appreciate their original appearance.

With the movement in their arms and their faces turned towards the outside as if they were soliciting the attention of passers-by, these busts are compellingly dynamic. Far from having a simple anecdotal function (like the busts of the Palais de Jacques Cœur in Bourges, mid-15th century), they suggest, by their gestures and presence, a space around them in which they are intended to exist. This man's face, fizzing with malice, bears witness, as does VIII.9, to Nikolaus van Leyden's acute sense of psychology. The iconographical significance of the entire decor of the Chancellery, exalting the grandeur of Strasbourg and its status as a Free City of the Empire, might lead us to identify the two busts as Emperor Augustus and the Tiburtine Sybil.

BIBLIOGRAPHY: *Recht*, no. I.02 and pp. 129 et seq.

VIII.11 NIKOLAUS VAN LEYDEN (ATELIER): HEAD OF A CANON (?)

Before 1467
Yellow sandstone, 30 cm
Strasbourg, Musée de l'œuvre Notre-Dame, no. 163

The delicate workmanship on the surface of the sandstone and the subtle contours of this mature male face are reminiscent of the memorial to the canon of Busnang in Strasbourg cathedral (1464). Nevertheless, this must be the work of an associate of Nikolaus.

BIBLIOGRAPHY: *Recht*, no. I.07 and p. 147.

VIII.12 LETTER FROM EMPEROR FREDERICK III

5 June 1467
Parchment, 22.3 x 29.6 cm
Strasbourg, Archives de la Ville et de la Communauté urbaine de Strasbourg, AA210, 57

Addressed to the Council of the City of Strasbourg by Emperor Frederick III. It is the second letter – the first was dated 2 December 1463 – in which the Emperor demanded that the City should put pressure on the sculptor [Nikolaus van Leyden] to come to the Court. He was responsible for creating Frederick's tomb, for which he had already received a payment. According to the evidence, Nikolaus was not inclined, in December 1463, to devote time to this imperial commission. His Strasbourg commissions were no doubt providing him with plenty of work. This letter also shows the degree of the artist's independence in relation to his client, emperor or not.

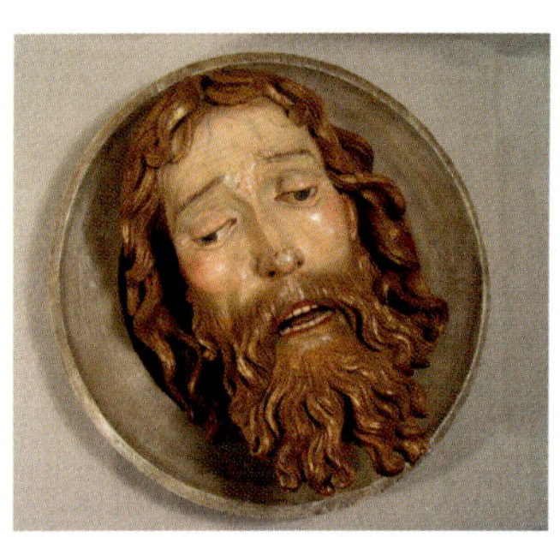
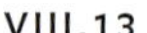

VIII.13

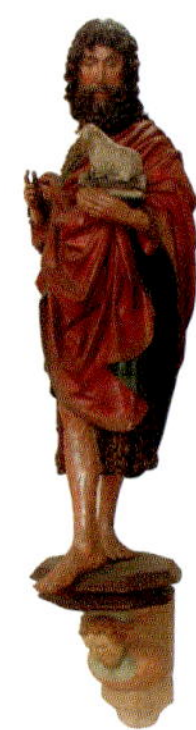

VIII.14

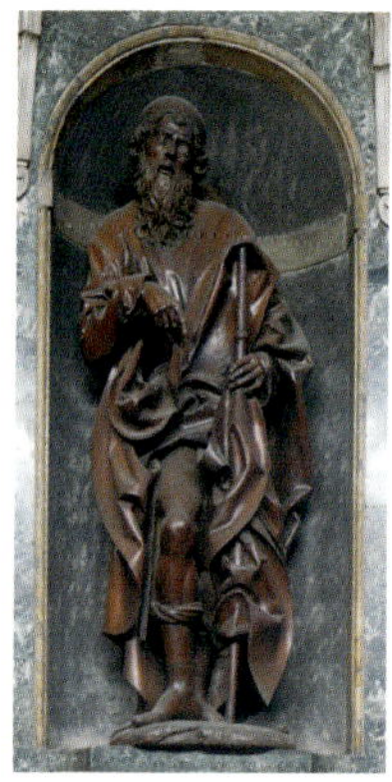

VIII.15

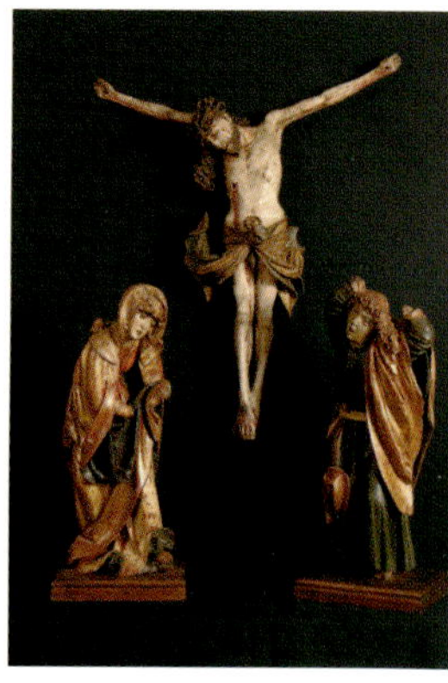

VIII.16

VIII.13 HEAD OF ST JOHN THE BAPTIST

c. 1470
Limewood, 32 cm
Banskà Bystrica, Stredoslovenské Múzeum, Slovak Republic, no. 3033
Provenance: Tajov church, Slovak Republic

This very handsome head reveals evident affinities with the Christ on the Cross on the altarpiece at Nördlingen, Bavaria, which is a work by Nikolaus van Leyden, the other sculptures on this 1462 altarpiece being attributed to the Master of the Dangolsheim Madonna (Berlin, Staatliche Museen) and his workshop. It was no doubt accomplished by one of the close companions of Nikolaus, who would have followed him from Strasbourg to Wiener-Neustadt, fulfilling a commission for the Tajov church.

BIBLIOGRAPHY: J. Homolka, 'On some Problems of the Viennese Gerhaertian School', *The Waning of the Middle Ages. Proceedings of the International Symposium* (Brno, 2000, 2001), pp.52–69; Robert Suckale, 'Der Meister der Nördlinger Hochaltarfiguren und Till Riemenschneider', *Opus Tessellatum. Festschrift für Peter Cornelius Claussen*, Hildesheim-Zurich-New York, 2004, pp. 327–40.

C. VEIT STOSS: SCULPTOR, PAINTER, ETCHER

Veit Stoss's output is consistent with that of a northern European man who already enjoyed the status of an artist of the Italian Renaissance. At the head of a prosperous atelier, he fulfilled some major commissions in Nuremberg, Kraków and for the Italians. His style is conspicuously dramatic and uses the language of gesture and drapery to reinforce its intensity. Both a painter and an engraver, he was able to distribute his works widely particularly through the new medium of engraving.

VIII.14 VEIT STOSS (?): ST JOHN THE BAPTIST

c. 1470
Limewood, in the round, modern colour with ancient remains, the right hand and the Lamb restored, 130 cm
Nuremberg, church of St Johannes
Provenance: It is not known whether this was made for the church in Nuremberg

Originally, this statue, designed to be seen from all sides, was without doubt in the frame of an altarpiece. It has been the subject of long debate whether or not it is by Stoss. The general consensus nowadays is that it is not. However, this work represented a major turning point in our understanding of what Nuremberg and Franconia owe to the sculpture of the Upper Rhine, in particular to Nikolaus van Leyden. A journey made by Stoss to Strasbourg during his training years is more than probable. Given its early date, this would be the oldest known work by Stoss. The smock-like form of the coat, the treatment of the drapes at the back, as well as the handling of enveloping hair and fur – these are features that point to Upper Rhine models. But the sculpting of the physiognomy would not be out of place among some of the Apostles in the Kraków altarpiece (1477–89). We may admit that, *c.* 1470, Stoss was not yet in possession of all the powers he would have at his disposal in Kraków. It was there that his personality began to assert itself, along with it his individual style.

BIBLIOGRAPHY: R. Kahnsitz (ed.), *Veit Stoss in Nürnberg. Werke des Meisters und seiner Schule in Nürnberg und Umgebung* (exhib. cat.), Munich, 1983, no. 24.

VIII.15 VEIT STOSS: ST ROCH

1515–20
Wood, no polychromy, stained brown, 170 cm
Florence, commune di Firenze Basilica della SS Annunziata

This sculpture was probably commissioned from Stoss by his Florentine patron Raphael Torrigiani, a rich merchant who had given up his trade to become a priest in Florence. Torrigiani had commissioned from Stoss, in 1516, the Toby and the Angel group (Germanisches Nationalmuseum, Nuremberg). The church of San Annunziata, to which this St Roch was destined includes a chapel financed by merchants. This statue is structured in a remarkable fashion compared with the sculptor's previous works. The body takes on real importance: the leg outstretched, showing the plague bubo, forms the axis of the body, but it is around the staff that the volume of drapery is arranged. The biographer Giorgio Vasari (see Section x), who missed no opportunity to denounce art from north of the Alps as 'barbarian', praised the extraordinary quality of this work, considering it to be a 'marvel in wood' (see introduction to this section).

BIBLIOGRAPHY: Michael Baxandall, *The Limewood Sculptors of Renaissance Germany*, New Haven, London, 1980.

VIII.16 MASTER PAUL DE LEVOČA: CHRIST ON THE CROSS WITH MARY AND JOHN

1520-30
Wood, with old polychromy, Christ: 56 cm; Mary: 42 cm; John: 44 cm
Bardejov, Slovak Republic, Sarriske Muzeum, no. 871, 872, 6614

The sculptor identified by this name had an extraordinarily active workshop that seemed to carry out a vast number of commissions. Sculptures were doubtless executed then stored, to meet growing demand from clients. This was almost industrial-style, production of which there are many other examples. Nevertheless, this Crucifixion scene is remarkable: Christ is of the type as created by Nikolaus van Leyden in Baden-Baden (1467) but enriched with various motifs borrowed from Veit Stoss, and St John is also inspired by several Stossian motifs. What we have here is a wonderful example of the artistic impact of Veit Stoss in Slovakia in the third decade of the 16th century.

BIBLIOGRAPHY: Dusan Buran (ed.), *Dejiny slovenského vytvarného Umenia*. Goticka, Bratislava, 2003, no. 4.82.

VIII.17 VEIT STOSS: TRINITARIAN ST ANNE

1512
Two brown-ink drawings on paper, 11.1 x 13.7 cm and 7.5 x 11.4 cm
Budapest, Szépművészeti Múzeum, nos 13 and 14

These drawings, on the same theme, are sketched on the reverse of a draft letter in the hand of Stoss, which enables us to date them. Without doubt they were initial drawings for a sculpture (bas-relief ?). They show two distinctive styles. The first seems less accomplished, but is distinguished above all by its economy, the whole being structured by grand curves that establish the shapes. In the other, more thorough drawing, shading effects already suggest the final sculpted form.

BIBLIOGRAPHY: Zdzislaw Kepinski, *Veit Stoss*, Warsaw, 1981, p. 111.

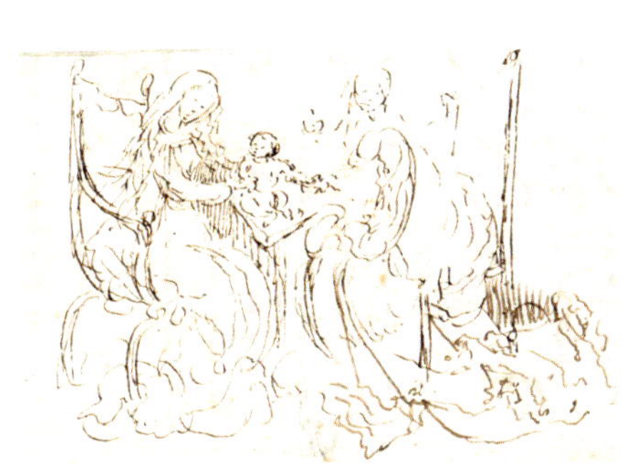

VIII.17

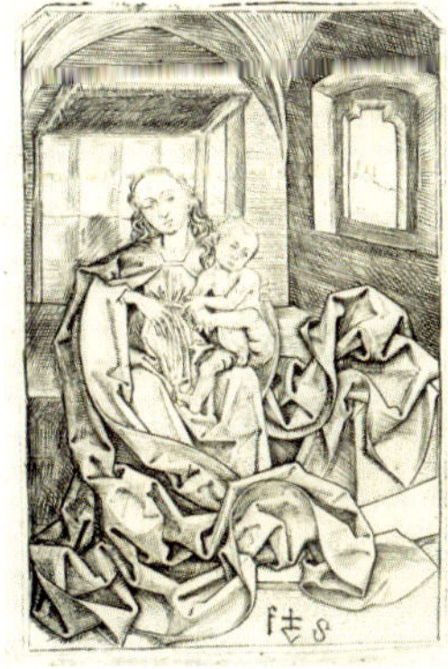

VIII.18

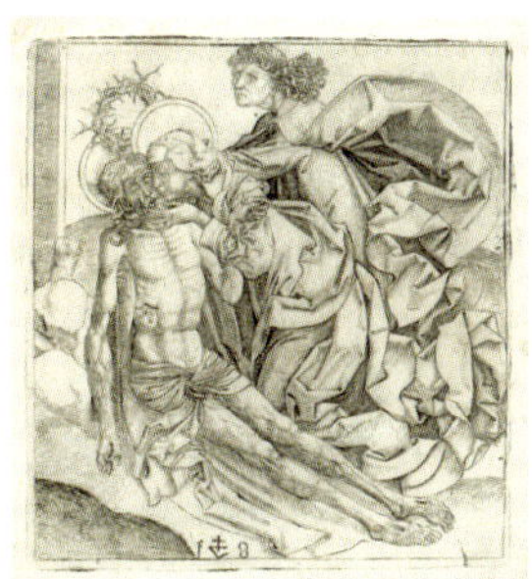

VIII.19

VIII.18 VEIT STOSS: VIRGIN AND CHILD IN AN ALCOVE

c. 1513 (?)
Monogrammed engraving (fS = Feit Stoss), 12.8 x 9.1 cm (11.2 x 7.5 cm)
Munich, Staatliche Graphische Sammlungen, no. 10917 D

Veit Stoss was inspired by an engraving produced by an Upper Rhine artist, Master E.S. (L.77),who was familiar with the art of the southern Netherlandsand had repeatedly treated this intimist theme. But Stoss gave it a sort of expressive passion, revealing how much the sculptor is always present, even in his two-dimensional works.

BIBLIOGRAPHY: Zdzislaw Kepinski, p.120.

VIII.19 VEIT STOSS: LAMENTATION

1500s
Monogrammed engraving (see VIII.18), 15.8 x 14.4 cm (14.2 x 13.2 cm)
Munich, Staatliche Graphische Sammlungen, no. 10921 D

This work corresponds to a mature stage in the art of Stoss the engraver. Starting from the Lamentations of Rogier van der Weyden, here he transforms his models to create an antinaturalistic composition. The device of the drapes, which have a dramatic function, reinforces the pathetic nature of the scene: this face of a mother tenderly embracing her son, whose body is stiffened by death, is placed at the centre of the structure. This engraving adopts the same principles of composition as the Volckamer altarpiece of 1499, but it is in the Schwaz altarpiece (1500–03) that we find this great shell of a mantle.

BIBLIOGRAPHY: Zdzislaw Kepinski, p.116.

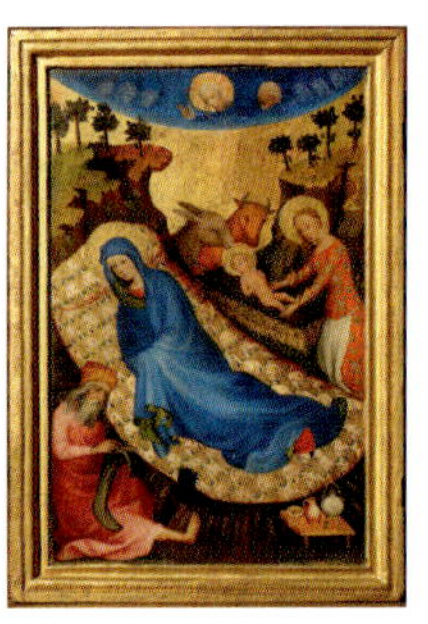
IX.1

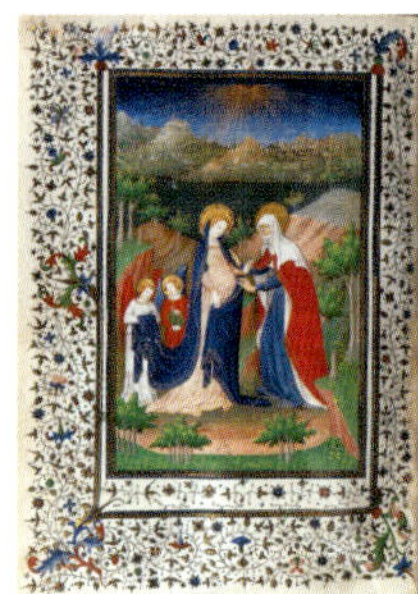
IX.2

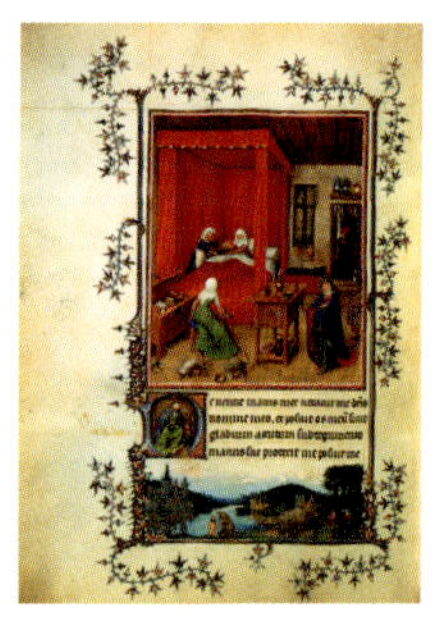
IX.3

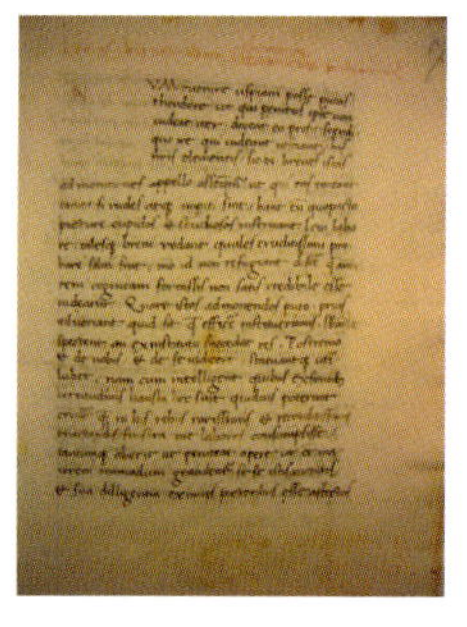
IX.4

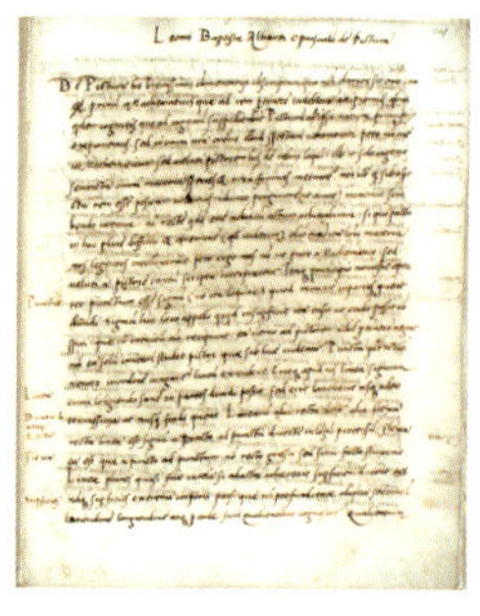
IX.5

SECTION IX
THE CONQUEST OF A NEW PICTORIAL SPACE

In the early 15th century, experiments multiplied in the southern Netherlands and in Florence that tempted painters to introduce into their pictures the illusion of threedimensional space, which the art of the Middle Ages had renounced. For the Van Eyck brothers, it was a question of rendering atmospheric perspective through the use of transparent colours and glazes. For the Italians, the illusion of depth relied on a set of rational rules based on plane geometry: as Alberti claims, it must be possible to read the story in a painting as if looking through 'an open window'.

IX.1 NATIVITY (PANEL OF A QUADRIPTYCH)

Guelders (?), *c.* 1400
Painting on panel, 37.6 x 26.2 cm
Antwerp, Museum Mayer van den Bergh, no. 374
Provenance: Carthusian monastery of Champmol, Dijon

This panel was part of a portable altarpiece in the form of a quadriptych (the other three panels are in Baltimore). When it is closed, we see the Baptism of Christ and St Christopher, and when open, the Annunciation, the Nativity, the Crucifixion and the Resurrection. The painter of this touching picture knew the artist Broederlam, but also the miniatures of Bondol and Beauneveu, and 14th-century Italian work. All this artistic culture led to a 'Trecento' conception of space with somewhat 'naïve' figures. The style of an artist such as Conrad de Soest, working in Westphalia, is not entirely alien to the atmosphere of this Nativity. It seems reasonable to place this painter in Guelders (Netherlands).

BIBLIOGRAPHY : Henk van Os, *Gebed in Schoonheid. Schatten von privé-devotie in Europa*, Amsterdam-London, 1994, no. 43, p. 139; Erwin Panofsky, *Les primitifs flamands*, French trans., Paris, 1992, pp. 179 et seq.

IX.2 HOURS OF MARÉCHAL DE BOUCICAUT

Master of the Hours of Maréchal de Boucicaut, *c.* 1408
242 ff., 27.5 x 19 cm
(Several folios will be displayed in turn during the exhibition)
Paris, Institut de France, Musée Jacquemart-André, Ms.2, 1311

Originally from the collection of Jean II le Meingre, known as Boucicaut, governor of Genoa, who commissioned it, this is a sumptuously illustrated manuscript, worthy of a royal command, and is of considerable importance in the history of painting, *c.* 1400. This painter is not really the creator of new forms but knows how to use all his artistic heritage, which is immense. The background of his picture is decorated with foliated scrolls, mosaics or armorial bearings, but the space is never constrained by this decorative carpet. Quite the reverse, he enjoys suggesting spatial depth with floor tiles and perspective landscapes. Most of the time the suggestion of depth is based on the use of scenery 'wings', which seem literally to 'flake' the space.

BIBLIOGRAPHY : Panofsky, p. 111 et seq.; Millard Meiss, *French Painting in the Time of Jean de Berry. The Boucicaut Master*, London-New York, 1968; *Paris 1400*, no. 172.

IX.3 JAN VAN EYCK : *THE HOURS OF TURIN-MILAN*

c. 1420
28 x 20 cm
(The two pages are displayed in turn)
Turin, Museo Civico del Arte Antica, Palazzo Madama, 4.67/M
f.93 v: The Birth and Baptism of John the Baptist; f.116 r: The Mass for the Dead

Many mysteries still surround the careers of the two painters Hubert and Jan van Eyck. Jan does not appear in the records until the years 1422–4, when he was working for John of Bavaria, Count of Holland. Later, he was entrusted with a diplomatic mission to Portugal, this time in the service of the Duke of Burgundy, for whom he painted. There are dated works by his hand produced between 1432 and 1439. In contrast, we know nothing of Hubert's career, except that he died in 1426 after beginning the Ghent Altarpiece, most of which seems to have been completed by his brother.

A set of miniatures known as the Hours of Turin-Milan bear witness to Jan's career as a miniaturist, in spite of the tragic loss of most of that manuscript in the Turin library fire of 1904. Of those vanished works, all we have now are the photographs and comments of two people who saw them, Léopold Delisle and Count Paul Durrieu. Recent historiography has sought to attribute some of the vanished miniatures to Hubert and others to Jan. The two folios on display are works of capital importance in the history of art and particularly for that of Northern pictorial space, because of their handling of interior space and of landscape, a treatment not really seen again until the 17th century (see the introduction to this section). The catafalque of the Mass for the Dead provides valuable evidence as it shows armorial bearings that have been identified as possibly those of John of Bavaria-Holland, for whom this manuscript may therefore have been produced.

BIBLIOGRAPHY : Otto Pächt, *Van Eyck. Die Begründer der altniederländischen Malerei*, Munich, 1989, pp. 171 et seq.; Hans Belting-Dagmar Eichberger, *Jan van Eyck als Erzähler*, Worms, 1983, pp. 23 et seq.; James Marrow, Silvana Pettenati, Anne H. van Buren, *Das Turin-Mailänder Stundenbuch, Turin,* Museo Civico Inv. no. 47, Commentary, Lucerne, 1996.

IX.4 LEON BATTISTA ALBERTI : *ELEMENTA PICTURAE*

15th century
74 ff., 22 x 15.5 cm
Bernkastel-Kues, Germany, St. Nicolaus-Hospitals Cusanusstift, Cod.112

In his *Elementa*, Alberti develops more specifically the rudiments of

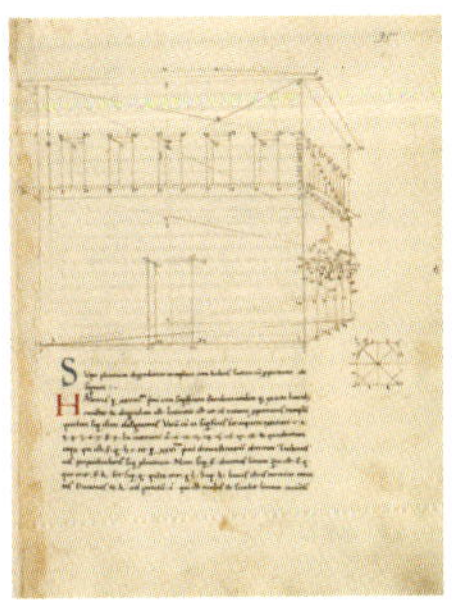

IX.6

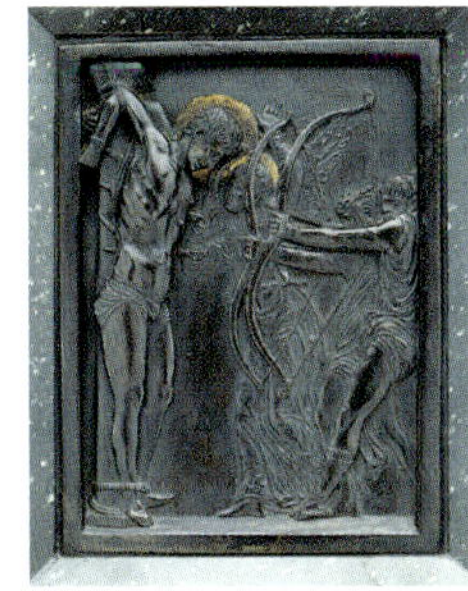

IX.7

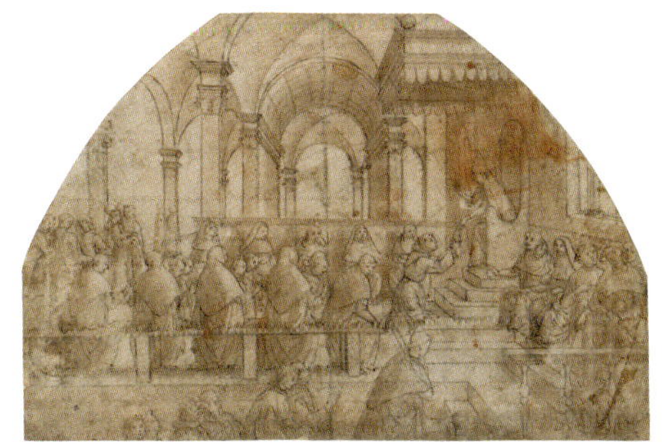

IX.8

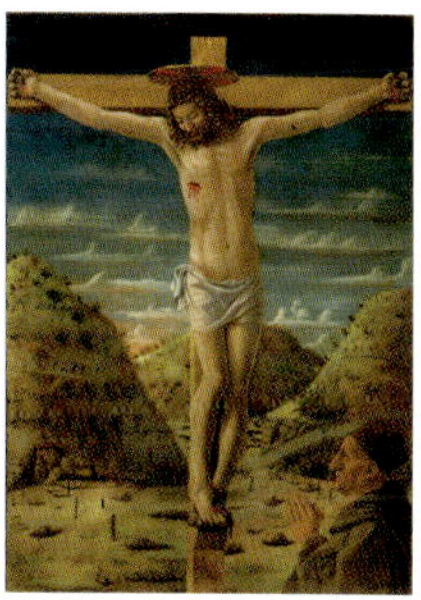

IX.9

mathematics and geometry necessary for a painter. It is a sort of complement to the treatise *De Pictura*. Like the treatise, the *Elementa* exists in a Latin as well as an Toscan version, Alberti having written the Latin one at the suggestion of one Theodorus. The present manuscript is included in a compilation of theological texts that belonged to the famous theologian Nicolas of Cusa (1401–64), who was interested in mathematics and the sciences and, more especially, in optics as a metaphor for spiritual knowledge.

BIBLIOGRAPHY : G. Santinello, 'Nicolo Cusano e Leon Battista Alberti : pensieri sul bello e sull'arte', in *Nicolo da Cusa. Telazioni tenute al convegno interuniversitario di Bressanone nel 1960*, Florence, 1962, pp. 147–78.

IX.5 LEON BATTISTA ALBERTI : *DE PICTURA*

15th century
Latin, 38 ff., 28 x 21.5 cm
Florence, Biblioteca Nazionale Centrale, II.VIII.58

The first 26 pages of this manuscript contain the Latin translation of *De Pictura*, and on the following pages a copyist has later transcribed the work *De Statua*, also by Alberti. According to tradition, Alberti wrote the Latin version first. A recent opinion, based on excellent reasoning, favours the opposite chronology. It is thought that Alberti would first have written his treatise in Tuscan to make it more accessible. This debate is of great importance as it concerns the author's original intentions : the people to whom a book is addressed and its content cannot be disassociated inform its production. This version in everyday language also includes a dedication to Brunelleschi, unlike the Latin version, which can be dated to 1439–41 : Alberti intended it for Francesco Gonzaga. The version on display includes marginal notes in another hand.

BIBLIOGRAPHY : Joseph Rykwert, Anne Angel (eds), *Leon Battista Alberti* (exhib. cat.), Mantua, 1994, no. 14 ; Lucia Bertolini, 'Nouvelles perspectives sur le *De Pictura* et sa réception', in F. Choay, M. Paoli (eds.), *Alberti humaniste, architecte*, Paris, 2006, pp. 33–45.

IX.6 PIERO DELLA FRANCESCA : *DE PROSPECTIVA PINGENDI*

15th century
Latin, 109 ff. (illustrated), 29 x 22 cm
London, British Library, Add. 10366

This work contains the first demonstration of perspective. The translation into Latin of the Italian work by Piero della Francesca, dedicated to Federico da Montefeltro (*c.* 1475), was by Matteo Cioni dal Borgo. It contains fewer mistakes than the Italian version, demonstrating the care the author took with the version he intended for a learned readership. In any case, the *De Prospectiva* is difficult to read : unlike Alberti's treatise (IX.5), this one is truly technical and uses plane geometry to teach painters the methods to use in order to represents things in perspective. The manuscript reproduces Piero's illustrations. This one depicts a building, one of whose sides is parallel to the plane of the picture and the other stretches away to a clearly identifiable vanishing point.

BIBLIOGRAPHY : *Piero della Francesca, De la perspective en peinture*. Preface by Hubert Damisch, afterword by Daniel Arasse, trans. and notes by J.-P. Le Goff, Paris, 1998.

IX.7 MARTYRDOM OF ST SEBASTIAN

School of Donatello, *c.* 1460
Bronze plaque, 24 x 26 cm
Paris, Institut de France, Musée Jacquemart André, no. 764

This relief has been attributed several times to Donatello himself. In any case, its quality is undeniable and more than one of its stylistic characteristics makes it comparable to confirmed works by that sculptor, such as the doors of the Old Sacristy of San Lorenzo, Florence, where the 'non finito' (apparent unfinished state) of the archers reappears. The scene is presented in low and very low relief, the incisions adding a draughtsman's techniques to those technical characteristics. The great expressiveness of the scene is accentuated by the treatment of the space, the most successful effect certainly the violent contrast between the upsurge of the martyr's body turned three-quarters towards the viewer in the left foreground (Sebastian's left foot impinging on the frame) and the entry into the picture of the archer on the right, rigorously parallel to the plane of the image.

BIBLIOGRAPHY : H.W. Janson, *The Sculpture of Donatello*, Princeton, 1957.

IX.8 DOMENICO GHIRLANDAIO : POPE HONORIUS III CONFIRMING THE RULES OF THE ORDER OF ST FRANCIS

c. 1483
Drawing in brown ink and wash over a preparatory graphite sketch. 24.9 x 37 cm
Berlin, Staatliche Museen zu Berlin, Kupferstichkabinett, Inv.56

This sketch was intended for a fresco in the Sassetti chapel of the Santa Trinità church, Florence–Sassetti was the director of the Medici bank. It presents a scene clearly constructed on three levels : in the foreground, truncated figures of Franciscans are walking up steps, only the last two of which are visible ; in the middle ground, the historical event forming the central scene of the drawing unfolds horizontally like a frieze ; in the upper part of the space, architecture, in central perspective, covered with roof groins and a barrel vault, is the Gothic chapel for which this project was intended. The geometric rigour of the spatial construction adopted by Ghirlandaio (*c.* 1448–94) is obviously much more apparent in this drawing than in the final fresco.

BIBLIOGRAPHY : H.-Th., Schulze Altcappenberg, *Die italienischen Zeichnungen des 14. und 15 Jahrhunderts im Berliner Kupferstichkabinett*, Berlin, 1995, pp. 150–52.

IX.9 CRISTOFORO CANOZZI (DA LENDINARA) : CHRIST ON THE CROSS WITH A MONK AT PRAYER

Second half of the 15th century
Tempera on canvas, 112 x 80 cm.
Verona, Museo di Castelvecchio
1001-1B361

Formerly attributed to Mantegna, this picture is now thought to have been painted by one of the most interesting members of Piero della Francesca's circle, Cristoforo Canozzi (also known as 'intarsiatore' – 'marquetry maker'), who was born in Lendinara in 1420/25 and died in Pisa in 1491. In *c.* 1475, he painted a cycle of frescoes in the Bellincini chapel of Modena cathedral. As Francesca Rossi has noted, the landscape is constructed as 'a space for pure contemplation' and the use of geometry is

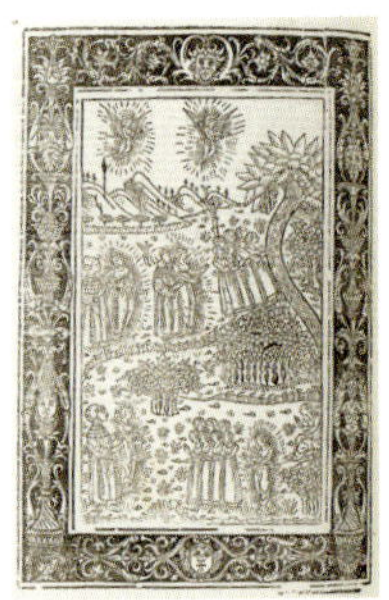
X.6

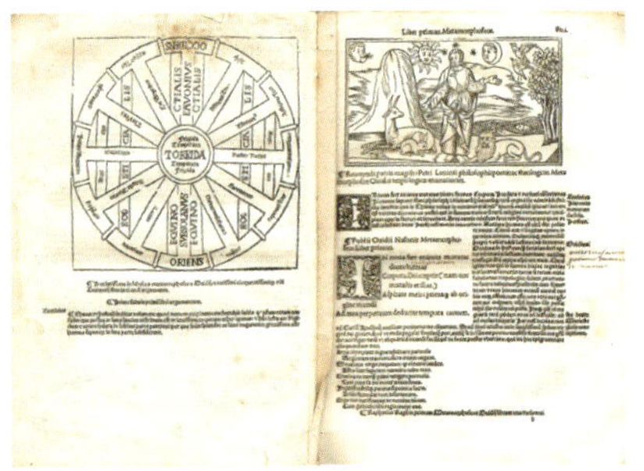
X.7

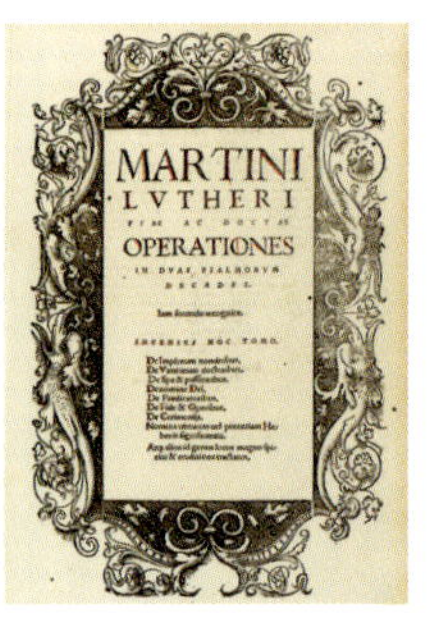

X.8

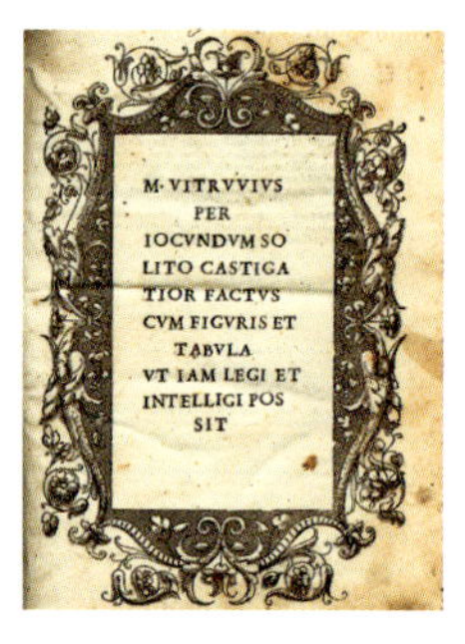

X.9

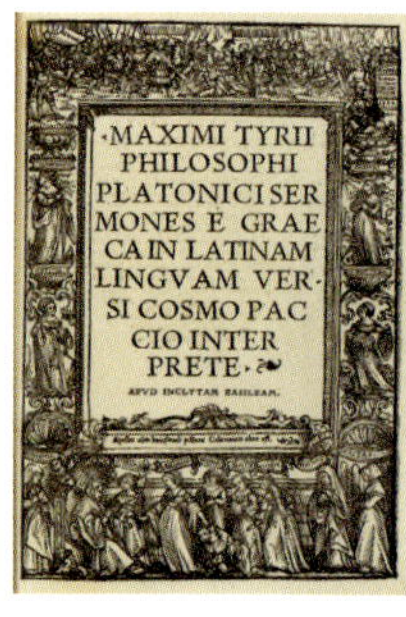

X.10

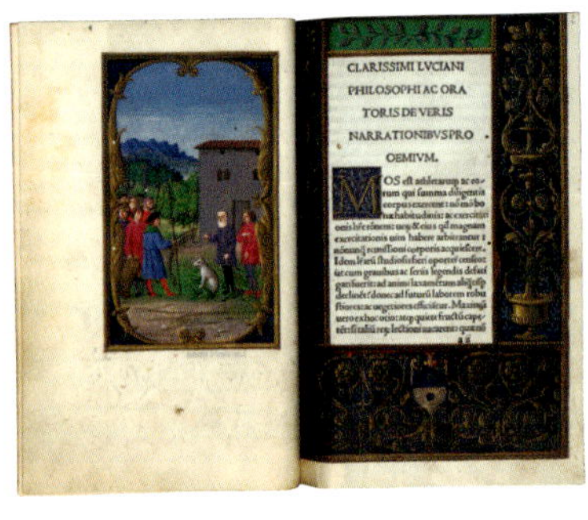

X.11

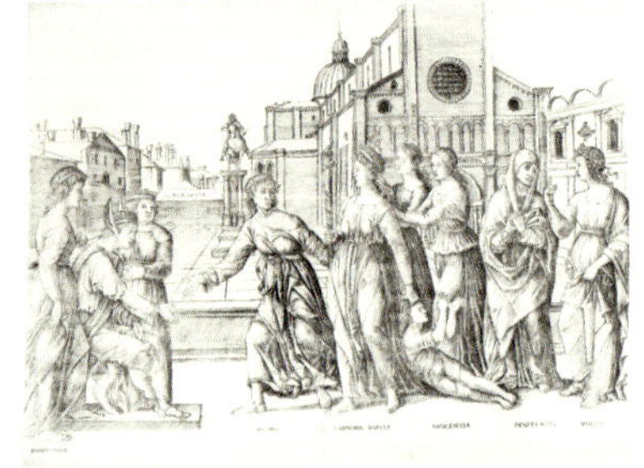
X.12

Such works would gradually bring about a decline in demand for illuminated books.

BIBLIOGRAPHY : Livio Ambrogio (ed.), *Nel Mezzo Del cammin… : A Dante Journey through 700 Years of Text and Images*, Bibliotheca Wittockiana, Brussels, 2003, no. 13 ; Arthur Field, 'Cristoforo Landino's First Lectures on Dante', *Renaissance Quarterly*, 39, 1, 1986, pp. 16–48 ; *Catalogue of Books printed in the XVth Century now in the British Museum*, VII, pp. 971 and 969 (Catullus, 1485).

X.4 ORIGEN, HOMILIES ON GENESIS, EXODUS AND LEVITICUS

Florence, 1480–90
161 ff., on parchment, 51 x 37 cm
Modena, Biblioteca Estense Universitaria MS Lat. 458
Provenance: from the library of Matthias Corvinus, King of Hungary

Manuscript commissioned in Florence for Matthias Corvinus, bearing his arms and those of his wife, Beatrix of Aragon. A great bibliophile, the king appreciated luxury objects. The page has been made into an architectural support, and the miniatures are real medallions painted like tondi. These ornaments (which are almost works of art in their own right), the style of the initial letter 'I', with its antique-style ornamentation, and finally the prominence given to the calligraphy, amount to a style of presentation already transformed by printing. The production of such manuscripts was very slow, even when they were created in a major atelier.

BIBLIOGRAPHY : *The Painted Page : Italian Renaissance Book Illumination 1450–1550*, London, 1995, no. 2, pp. 52–53 ; Csaba Csapodi, Klára Csapodi-Gárdonyi (eds), *Bibliotheca Corviniana*, Budapest, 1978, no. 90, p. 158 ; Csaba Csapodi, Klára Csapodi-Gárdonyi (ed.), *Bibliotheca Corviniana, 1490–1990*, Budapest, 1990.

X.5 GRATIAN, *DECRETUM. CONCORDANTIA DISCORDANTIUM CANONUM*, WITH GLOSSES BY BARTHOLOMEUS BRIXIENSIS

Venice, printed by Nicolaus Jenson, 1477
Parchment, with numerous illuminations
f. 2r.
Gotha, Germany, Landesbibliothek
Provenance: library of Peter Ugelheimer of Frankfurt

The text concerns ecclesiastical law, a speciality of the printer, Jenson, but the decoration makes it a major collector's item. The miniature is a printed dramatic scene, giving the impression it has been stuck onto a miniature made of precious stones and ancient cameos. This playful relationship between manuscript and printed matter masks the reality of a sheet of parchment solidly printed in full page. The scene above the H represents the Pope, in the presence of the cardinals, being presented with the book (Gratian was a 12th-century jurist.)

X.6 DANTE : LA COMMEDIA, WITH COMMENTARY BY CHRISTOPHORO LANDINO

Brescia, printed by Boninus de Boninis, 1487
Printed on paper, in folio, 23.8 x 15 cm
Brussels, Bibliothèque royale de Belgique, Réserve précieuse, Fonds Solvay, IX IIC (LP)

Bobino de' Bonini was a Dalmatian who set up a press in Brescia, before completing his career in Lyons. The layout of this book, inspired by one popular with Venetian miniaturists, is evidence of acute awareness of a new power of expression in engraving. The sixty-eight woodcuts were separately printed with text. The illustration represents Dante in Paradise, accompanied by Beatrice. The two figures are represented as they ascend to heaven. The careful, simple use of new techniques here reached perfection and began to appeal to discerning connoisseurs. But, above all, this quality is that of the printing press, which no longer compares itself with manuscript aesthetics even if some motifs are still drawn from Venetian illumination.

X.7 OVID : *METAMORPHOSEOS. I LIBRI MORALIZATI CUM PULCHERRIMIS FABULARUM PRINCIPALIUM FIGURIS*

Lyons, printed by Jacob Huguetan, 1518
26.3 x 18.7 cm
Neuchâtel, Bibliothèque des Pasteurs, Inv. 105.4.25

This illustrated edition of Ovid's *Metamorphoses* was printed in Lyons by Jacob Huguetan in 1518. The text was accompanied by a commentary derived from the *Argumenta* attributed to the supposed Christian writer Lactantius (3-4th century AD), and notes attributed to Raphael Regius, Petrus Lavinius, and Philippe Béroalde. The line drawings were copied from a delightful version of the *Metamorphoses* in Italian executed in 1497 in Venice by Giovanni Rosso, with an allegorical commentary by Giovanni Bonsignore. The Italian plates were first copied in Lyons from an edition dated 1510 (Davost and Gueynard); Huguetan, eight years later, would use the woodcuts attributed to Guillaume Le Roy. The illustration on the right-hand page, opposite the points of the compass that close the *Argumenta* is significant. It Christianizes Ovid's representation of the origin of the world. It substitutes the creator

God of the Bible for the gods of the Olympus at the dawn of humanity – here, image and text obliterate Ovid, according to the Christian interpretation by 'Lactantius'.

BIBLIOGRAPHY : Henri Louis Baudrier, *Bibliographie lyonnaise*, Series 11, Lyons, 1914, pp. 222–24 ; Brooks Otis, 'The *Argumenta* of the So-Called Lactantius', *Harvard Studies in Classical Philology*, 47, 1936, pp. 131–63 ; Hermann Walter, Hans-Jürgen Horn (eds), *Die Rezeption der 'Metamorphosen' des Ovid in der Neuzeit : der antike Mythos in Text und Bild*, Berlin, 1995 ; Margit Schermuck-Ziesché (ed.), *Die Metamorphosen des Ovid : Graphiken nach einem Klassiker antiker Dichtung*, Dessau, 2000.

X.8 MARTIN LUTHER : *PIAE AC DOCTAE OPERATIONES IN DUAS PSALMORUM DECADES. IAM SECUNDO RECOGNITAE*

Basle, printed by Adam Petri, 1521
Printed on paper, in folio, 32 x 22 cm
Basle, Öffentliche Bibliothek der Universität, FNP VII 2.2

The book's title page includes a decoration that is Italian in origin (X.9). The Basle publishers purchased foreign works likely to provide them with text or engraving models. The engraver tightened up the borrowed motif and gave it a more clear-cut line.

BIBLIOGRAPHY : Frank Hieronymus (ed.), *1488 Petri – Schwabe 1988 : eine traditionsreiche Basler Offizin im Spiegel ihrer frühen Drucke*, Basle, 1998, no. 99, pp. 268-69 ; *Kostbare illustrierte Bücher des sechzehnten Jahrhunderts in der Stadrbibliothek Trier*, Wiesbaden, 1995, no. 33.

X.9 VITRUVIUS : *DE ARCHITECTURA*

Venice, printed by Giovanni Tacuino, 1511
Printed on paper, in folio, 32 x 22 cm
Brussels-Rome, Fiametta Wittock

The title page, with its floral decorations completed with stylized dolphins, was highly successful ; generic in nature, it might decorate any work. It is possible that it was distributed through an edition that also appeared in Venice in 1517, Ovid's *Metamorphoses*. This poetic text, the circulation of which supplied a vast demand, must have served as a vehicle for this motif from Italy to the Germanic countries. The work was dedicated to Pope Julius II. This was the first illustrated edition after those of Rome (1486), Venice (1495) and Florence (1496). It includes wood engravings and was published with care by the architect Fra Giocondo, originally from Verona (see also X.20 et seq.)

BIBLIOGRAPHY : L. A. Ciaponi, 'Fra Giocondo da Verona and his Edition of Vitruvius', *Journal of the Warburg and Courtauld Institutes*, 47, 1984, pp. 72–90 ; P. N. Pagliara, 'The De architectura de Vitruve edited by Fra Giocondo, in Venice in 1511', in S. Deswarte Rosa (ed.), *Sebastiano Serlio à Lyon, Architecture et imprimerie* I, Lyons, 2004, pp. 348–54.

X.10 MAXIMUS OF TYRE : *SERMONES E GRAECA IN LATINAM LINGUAM VERSI COSMO PACCIO INTERPRETE*

Basle, printed by Johannes Froben, 1519
Printed on paper, in folio, 32 x 22.5 cm
Basle, Öffentliche Bibliothek der Universität, CF III 5:3

The frame, in the form of a window decorated with bas-reliefs, was very much in fashion at the end of the 1510s. Its monumental dimensions are very typical. This was an attempt to translate the ornaments of the Venetian and Lombard miniaturists. Ambrosius Holbein, who drew this ornament, in his career as a painter, was used to executing such decorations for portraits. The iconography is rich : at the top Varus, general of the Roman legions of Emperor Augustus, is being crushed by the Germanic tribes under Arminius – patriotic pride motivated this choice. On the sides, set onto consoles, the Virtues : to the right, the theologal Virtues, to the left, the cardinal Virtues – for the last, Prudence, the artist has substituted an image of ignorance, subordinate to the image of the horizontal bas-relief below *The Calumny of Apelles*, the lost painting by the famous Greek painter of antiquity, was described by Pliny the Elder and by Lucian of Samoset. Several Renaissance painters had the idea of portraying the ancient masterpiece on the basis of these descriptions. This version by Ambrosius Holbein was freely borrowed from an engraving by Girolamo Mocetto (15th century, X.12).

BIBLIOGRAPHY : Hieronymus, 1984, no. 259 ; Jean Michel Massing, *Du texte à l'image : la calomnie d'Apelle et son iconographie*, Strasbourg, 1990.

X.11 LUCIAN, *OPERA* : TRANSLATED INTO LATIN BY LILIUS CASTELLANUS

Venice, printed by Simon Bevilaqua, associate of Benedetto Bordon, 1494
Printed on parchment, 23.5 x 14.3 cm
Vienna, Österreichische Nationalbibliothek, Inc. 4.G.27

An outstanding volume must certainly have been presented as a gift to a member of a family of grand doges of Venice, the Mocenigos. The Roman characters with detached letters' are distinguished by their antique beauty. The miniatures executed by Benedetto Bordon give the illusion that the printed text is surrounded by a bronze plaque like the miniature opposite it. The latter illustrates an episode of the *De veris narrationibus* by Lucian – the author recounts that, thrown into the belly of a whale, he met Scintharus and his son. The miniaturist avoided portraying the monstrous stomach and instead lent the encounter the simple character of a rustic anecdote. The Venetian fashion for monumental borders was bound to beexploited : about ten years later, in the Basle workshops, it would become a formula.

Bordon, born in Padua and living in Venice since 1494, was probably an associate of the printer Bevilaqua. He painted miniatures, but also designed engravings for printers – he designed two engravings (six verso and seven recto) for the famous *Hypnerotomachia Poliphili* by Francesco Colonna, at the request of Alde Manuce (1499). These facts indicate a surprising ubiquity, but that was more commonplace than one would think. Bordon also worked for Peter Ugelheimer of Frankfurt, a fellow printer and bibliophile (X.5).

The choice of Lucian left nothing to chance. The author became popular only in the 15th century. His pictorial descriptions clearly aroused the interest of the miniaturist, ready to meet the challenges of the text. In the book's colophon, Bordon recommends that the reader should relax before reading the work. In a city that was giving birth to the modern book, enjoying the embellished pages was viewed as leisure.

BIBLIOGRAPHY : *The Painted Page*, no.104, p. 208 ; Lilian Armstrong, Benedetto Bordon, '"Miniator" and Cartography in Early Sixteenth-Century Venice', *Imago Mundi*, 48, 1996, pp. 65–92.

X.12 GIROLAMO MOCETTO : THE CALUMNY OF APELLES, AFTER ANDREA MANTEGNA

Venice, *c.* 1500–06
Burin engraving, 32 x 43 cm
Paris, Bibliothèque nationale de France, Cabinet des estampes, Res. Ea-35

This engraving contains, at bottom left, an image of the statue of Bartolomeo Colleoni by Andrea del Verrocchio, located at the Campo dei Santi Giovanni e Paolo in Venice in 1496. Such plates were appreciated in northern Europe, where they served as models. Ambrosius Holbein did not imitate the supple line of Mocetto, but the general layout of the '*istoria*'.

BIBLIOGRAPHY : *Early Italian Engraving*, National Gallery of Art, Washington D.C., 1973, p. 389 ; 'Les premières gravures italiennes' in Gisèle Lambert (ed.), *Quattrocento – début du Cinquecento. Inventaire de la collection du département des Estampes et de la Photographie*, Paris, 1999, no. 641, pp. 342–44.

X.13 VIRGIN MARY WITH INFANT JESUS AND ANGELS

Ferrara, *c.* 1475
Bronze (sand cast), 9.4 x 7.2 cm
Basle, Historisches Museum, inv. 1904.1076
Provenance : from the Amerbach collection, Basle

Florentine painting in the 15th century attracted a vast audience, with the assistance of burin engraving, and also thanks to small bronze plaques – devotional works or collectors' items. All such portable works were highly effective for transmitting new compositions, but also simplified them. Printers, painters or goldsmiths from the North would use them frequently.

This plaque was brought back from Italy, and was in the possession of a pastor in Mulhouse in 1593, when the latter gave it to Basilius Amerbach, grand jurist and grandson of printer Johannes Amerbach. A Protestant had no trouble in appreciating such Catholic objects as elegant ornamental objets d'art. The Amerbach family knew Italy very well : Johannes had stayed in Venice to perfect his knowledge of printing. Basilius bought devotional works damaged by the iconoclasts in Basle.

BIBLIOGRAPHY : *Sammeln in der Renaissance : Das Amerbach-Kabinett. Die Objekte im Historischen Museum Basel*, Basle, 1991, no. 74 ; John Pope-Hennessy, *Renaissance Bronzes from the Samuel H. Kress Collection*, London, 1965, no. 303.

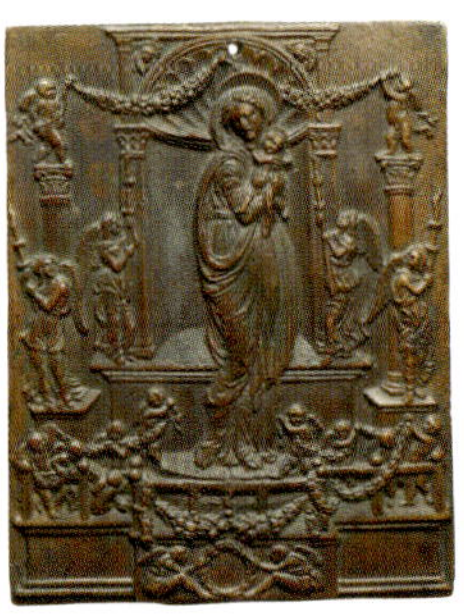

X.13

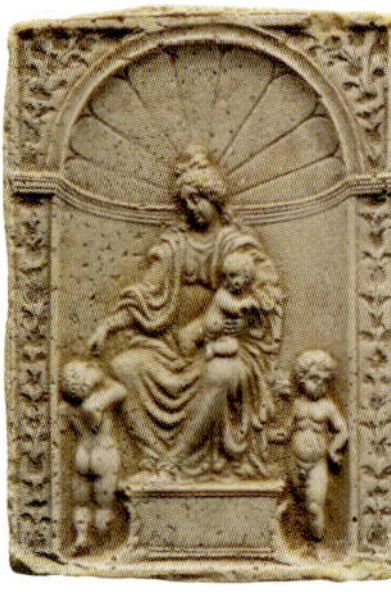

X.14

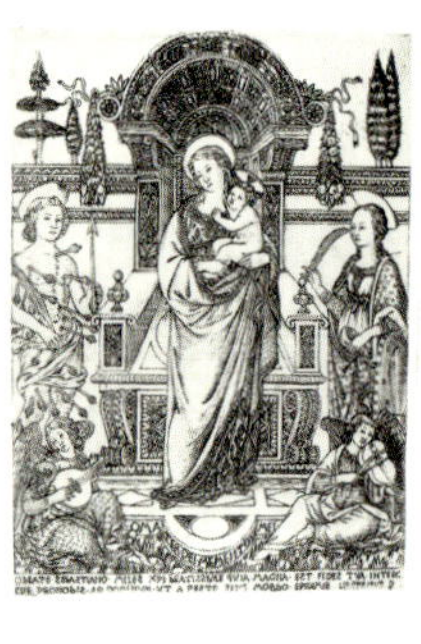

X.15

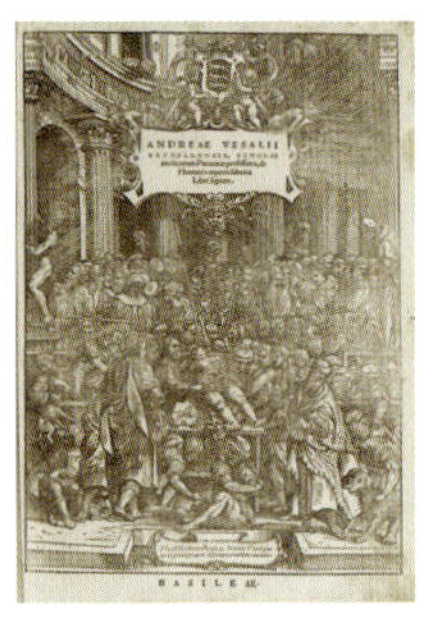

X.16

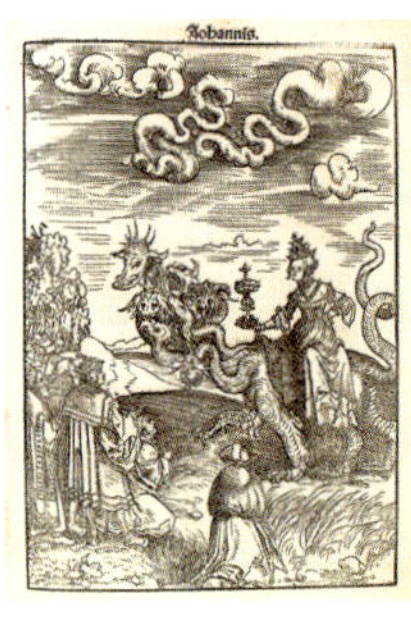

X.17

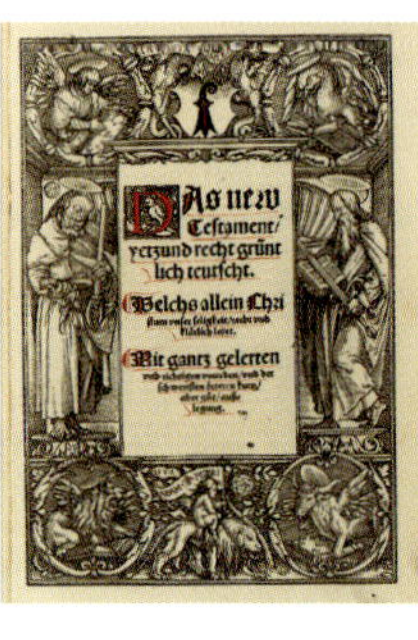

X.18

X.14 VIRGIN MARY ENTHRONED WITH THE INFANT JESUS

Casting after a bronze by Moderno
c. 1500
Composed of sulphur casts, 7.5 x 5.3 cm
Basle, Historisches Museum, 1981.260
Provenance: from the collection of Basilius Amerbach

Such casts were very cheap to make and enabled the compilation of collections of models or specimens for study. They were light to carry.

BIBLIOGRAPHY : *Sammeln in der Renaissance*, no. 74.

X.15 BACCIO BALDINI : VIRGIN AND CHILD STANDING BEFORE THE THRONE WITH ST SEBASTIAN AND ST CATHERINE

Florence, *c.* 1480–90
Burin engraving, 25.7 x 18.5 cm
Paris, Bibliothèque nationale de France, Cabinet des Estampes, Res. Ea 29

The same motif, the Virgin standing before a niche, distributed across Northern Europe a system of composition that was popular in Florence in the 15th century.

BIBLIOGRAPHY : *Les premières gravures italiennes*, no. 178, pp. 80-81.

X.16 ANDREA VESALIUS : *DE HUMANI CORPORIS FABRICA LIBRI SEPTEM*

Basle, printed by Johannes Oporinus, 1543
Printed on paper, in folio
Brussels, Bibliothèque royale de Belgique, Réserve précieuse VH 7.413 C (RP)

This splendid book, one of the newest and most ambitious of the Renaissance, appeared in Basle for the first time. It was dedicated to Emperor Charles v. Vesalius, born in Brussels, completed his studies in Paris and Montpellier. He would become professor of anatomy at Louvain. Vesalius was a typical representative of a European elite who travelled and made his career outside his native country. The illustrations are by Jan Stephan Calcar, a Flemish artist who was doubtless travelling in Italy at the same time as the scholar. He trained in Venice in the atelier of Titian. Calcar knew Vasari, who mentioned him in the 1568 edition of his *Vite*. Such a grand in folio work, with numerous fine engravings, required an unprecedented investment of capital. The success of the publication at a time when copyright did not exist was almost too great: the book was copied mercilessly and these counterfeits ruined the printer.

The title page represents Vesalius carrying out a dissection in a *Theatrum* before his students and the university authorities. Vesalius encouraged an empirical approach to medical phenomena and mistrusted the recognized authorities. His praise for manual dexterity and the quality of his analyses make him a pioneer of modern anatomy. With this book, scientific engraving became a powerful tool enabling a record to be made of new experimental knowledge that was in the process of formation.

BIBLIOGRAPHY : Hieronymus, no. 483; K. B. Roberts, J. D. W. Tomlinson, *The Fabric of the Body: European Traditions of Anatomical Illustration*, Oxford, 1992; C. M. Saunders, Charles D. O'Malley, *The Illustrations from the Works of Andreas Vesalius of Brussels*, New York 1973.

X.17 MARTIN LUTHER : *DAS NEUE TESTAMENT DEUTSCH* (KNOWN AS THE SEPTEMBER TESTAMENT)

Wittenberg, printed book by Melchior Lotter the Younger, 1522
Printed on paper, in folio
Stuttgart, Württembergische Landesbibliothek, Bb deutsch 152201

This Bible was the principal monument of the Reformation. Lotter printed it in the house of painter Lucas Cranach the Elder under the joint supervision of goldsmith Christoph Döring. The translation of the Bible was the work of Luther, who had worked for a long time translating into German the Greek version of the New Testament completely revised by Erasmus of Rotterdam. Of great clarity, based on the latest philological findings, this version rendered the bible text very readable and reforged the German language. Luther was conscious of this as he considered this testament to be 'his' text. The edition is decorated with twenty-one wood engravings illustrating the Apocalypse of St John; drawn by Lucas Cranach the Elder. They betray the artist's desire to measure himself against Albrecht Dürer, famous for his series of fifteen wood engravings of the Apocalypse. Careful examination of the plates drawn by Cranach leaves no doubt about Luther's ideological stance. The book as exhibited shows an image of the Whore of Babylon wearing a papal tiara – an allusion to the corruption of the throne of St. Peter. Out of caution, such details were deleted from the second edition of the book.

Five thousand copies of the Bible were sold in a few weeks. In December, reprinting was completed in Wittenberg itself. But a copy of the September Testament had already reached Basle, where it was immediately copied (x.18).

BIBLIOGRAPHY : Sören Widmann, 'Von der Wartburgpostille bis zum Septembertestament 1522: Luther als Übersetzer des Neuen Testaments', *Vestigia bibliae* 21, 1999, pp. 61–93; Christoph Weimer, *Luther, Cranach und die Bilder: Gesetz und Evangelium – Schlüssel zum reformatorischen Bildgebrauch*, Stuttgart, 1999.

X.18 MARTIN LUTHER : *DAS NEW TESTAMENT YETZUND RECHT GRÜNTLICH TEUTSCHT*

Printed in Basle by Adam Petri, 1522 (actually 1523)
Printed on paper, in folio, 32 x 22 cm
Basle, Öffentliche Bibliothek der Universität, KiAr J I 7:1
Provenance: Copy given by the Petri workshop to the Carthusian Monastery in Basle

In a few months, the printer Petri succeeded in reproducing the translation by Luther. The financial stake in such plagiarism was considerable, and Petri must have made a large amount of money when the process was complete. For reasons associated with lack of time, this Bible is not very well illustrated and does not contain the Cranach plates in the Apocalypse chapter. Caution no doubt determined this difference. Eight engravings out of the twelve that decorate this edition were cut by Formschneider (wood engraver) Hans Lützelburger, based on the drawings by Hans Holbein the Younger. The two artists together produced pieces that are among the most beautiful engravings in the German world during this period. The clean, fine cut never lost its sharpness and translated Holbein's style with unparalleled virtuosity. The title page surrounds the title with imitation architecture and, in the four corners, medallions of the four Evangelists. Holbein must have placed St Peter and St Paul as sentinels to give greater legitimacy to a text that was still explosive. Underneath, the printer's mark completes the page composition.

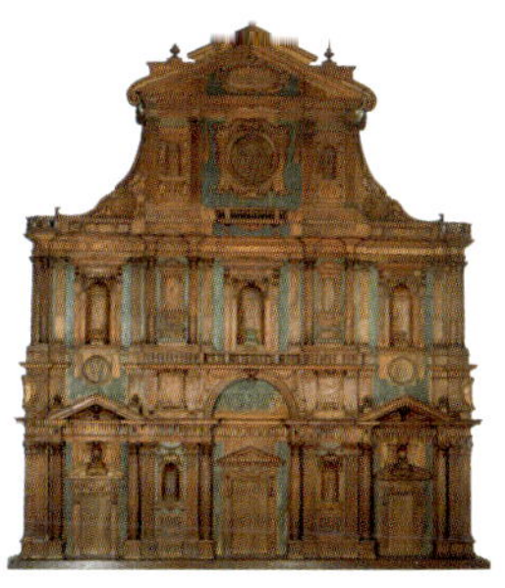

X.19

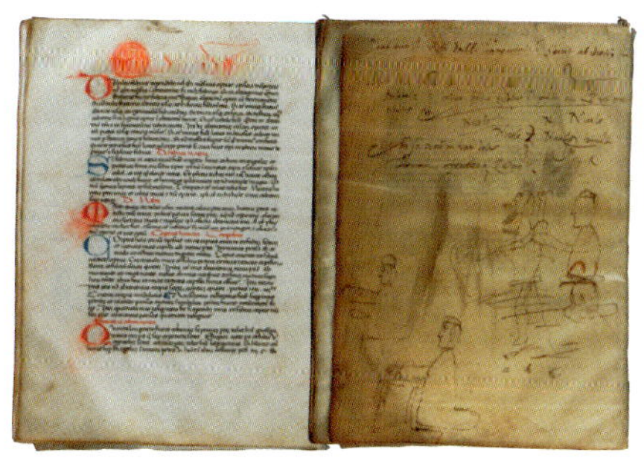

X.20

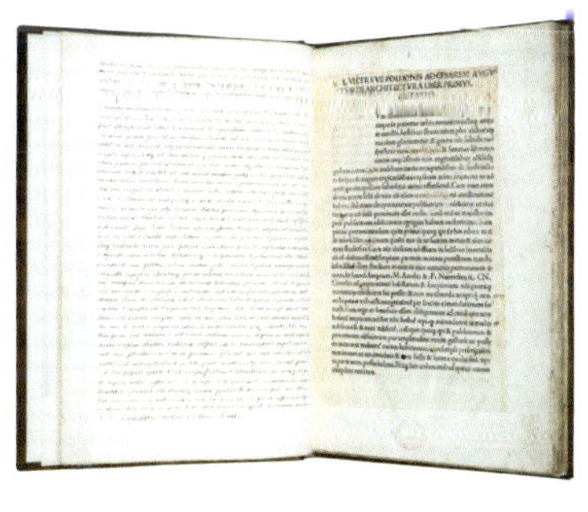

X.21

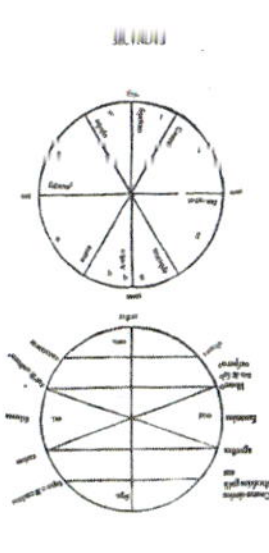

X.22

BIBLIOGRAPHY : Hieronymus, no. 106; Pascal Griener, Oskar Bätschmann, *Hans Holbein the Younger*, Princeton 1997; Pascal Griener, Oskar Bätschmann, *Hans Holbein d. J. : die Solothurner Madonna; eine sacra conversazione im Norden*, Basle, 1998.

B. VITRUVIUS

Successive editions of the treatise by Vitruvius, the Roman architect of the first century BC, *De architectura libri decem* (The ten books of architecture), published during the 15th and 16th centuries, changed the destiny of the discipline throughout Europe. The manuscript had existed in the Middle Ages but without any illustration whatsoever, which often rendered it incomprehensible. The Italians of the Renaissance applied themselves to an entire philological and iconographical labour, seeking to reconcile the theories of Vitruvius on the Classical orders with the antique monuments surviving in the peninsula. The immense efforts made by Serlio, Scamozzi, Vignole and Palladio were aimed at making available, to architects and the cultured public, canonical models of Classicism based on a reinterpretation of Vitruvius.

X.19 BERNARDO BUONTALENTI : MODEL OF THE FAÇADE OF THE DUOMO IN FLORENCE

1587
Painted wood, 236.3 x 218.5 x 36.1 cm
Florence, Museo Opera Santa Maria del Fiore, Model 13

The Gothic façade of the cathedral, started at the end of the 13th century by Arnolfo di Cambio, was demolished on the orders of Grand Duke Ferdinand I de'Medici in 1587. Then five architects were commissioned to submit designs for a new façade more in keeping with the taste of the time. With its changes in scale and accumulation of features, the façade proposed by Buontalenti appeared very Mannerist. This design for the Duomo in Florence shows the intensity of the debate between the 'Ancient' and 'Modern' around Vitruvian architectural solutions substituted for a Gothic solution in Florence, a problem reminiscent of those posed in Bologna and Milan.

BIBLIOGRAPHY : Henry A. Millon, 'Models in Renaissance Architecture', in H. A. Millon (ed.), *The Renaissance from Brunelleschi to Michelangelo : The Representation of Architecture*, pp. 19-74.

X.20 MANUSCRIPT OF VITRUVIUS

c. 1390
30.8 x 23.3 cm
Amsterdam, The Wolbert H.M. Vroom collection, no. A304

X.21 *[DE ARCHITECTURA LIBRI DECEM]*

Georgius Herolt (?), 1486 (?)
Untitled edition without illustrations by Giovanni Sulpicio di Veroli, Rome (?).
35 x 27.6 cm
London, Royal Institute of British Architects, E.f.582

This is the first printed edition of Vitruvius, published after the text by Frontinus: *De Aquaeductibus Urbis Romae*. A new edition in 1496 contained six illustrations

X.22 *CLEONIDAE HARMONICUM INTRODUCTORIUM INTERPRETE GEORGIO VALLA. L. VITRUVII POLLIONIS DE ARCHITECTURA LIBRI DECEM*

Edition without illustrations, Venice, 'per Simonem Papiensem dictum Bivilaquam', 1497
Brussels-Rome, Fammietta Wittock

It is sometimes asserted that Fra Giocondo (see x.23) had already collaborated on this edition. Commentaries by Giorgio Valla and Angelo Poliziano.

X.23 M. VITRUVIUS, *PER JOCUNDUM SOLITO CASTIGATIOR FACTUS, CUM FIGURIS ET TABULA UT JAM LEGI ET INTELLIGI POSSIT*

First illustrated edition, printed by Johannes de Tacuino, Venice, 1511
31 x 22 cm
Paris, Bibliothèque de l'Ecole Polytechnique

A total of 136 woodcuts and commentary by Giocondo. This copy belonged to Cardinal Alessandro Albani, and was seized in Italy by Gaspard Monge for the government of the Republic, under the French Revolution.

X.24 *DI LUCIO VITRUVIO POLLIONE DE ARCHITECTURA LIBRI DECEM TRADUCTI DE LATINO IN VULGARE AFFIGURATI, COMMENTATI (...)*

Edition illustrated by Cesare Cesariano, Como, Gottardus da Ponte, 1521
41 x 27 cm
Brussels, Bibliothèque royale, Réserve précieuse, Inc. C206

Vitruvius states that the proportions of a building are in harmony when they match those of the human body. Cesariano started from a subdivision of the body into thirty modules that enabled him to fix precisely the heights of the various parts (head, torso, etc.; f.19r). Doubtless he had studied Leonardo's speculations on the same subject.

BIBLIOGRAPHY : contributions by Pierre Gros, Roland Recht, etc. in Jean Guillaume (ed.), *Les traités d'architecture de la Renaissance*, Paris, 1988.

X.25 *LES DIX LIVRES D'ARCHITECTURE DE VITRUVE, CORRIGEZ ET TRADUITS NOUVELLEMENT EN FRANÇOIS, AVEC DES NOTES ET DES FIGURES*

Edition and translation by Claude Perrault, Paris, Coignard, 1673
44.5 x 30.3 cm
Amsterdam, The Wolbert H.M. Vroom Collection, no. A346

The first French translation was by Jean Martin (Paris, 1547). In his commentaries in notes, Perrault inserts a real theory of classical French architecture grafted onto the Vitruvian theory.

X.26 *AN ABRIDGEMENT OF THE ARCHITECTURE OF VITRUVIUS (...) ILLUSTRATED (...)*

London, printed by Abel Swall and T. Child, 1692
15.3 x 15.3 cm
London, Royal Institute of British Architects, E.h.206

This first English translation of Vitruvius was made from the Perrault French translation (x.25).

X. 27 *I DIECI LIBRI DELL' ARCHITETTURA DI M.VITRUVIO, TRADOTTI E COMMENTATI DA MONS. DANIEL BARBARO*

Edition by Daniele Barbaro, Venice, Francesco de'Franceschini, 1567
Parchment, 23.9 x 18.4 cm
Amsterdam, The Wolbert H.M. Vroom Collection, no. A329

The first outstanding edition of this new translation dates back to 1556; it was prepared in collaboration with the illustrator, i.e. Andrea Palladio. However, the definitive edition is considered to be that of 1567, Italian and Latin, for which the woodcuts were supplied by German Giovanni Chrieger.

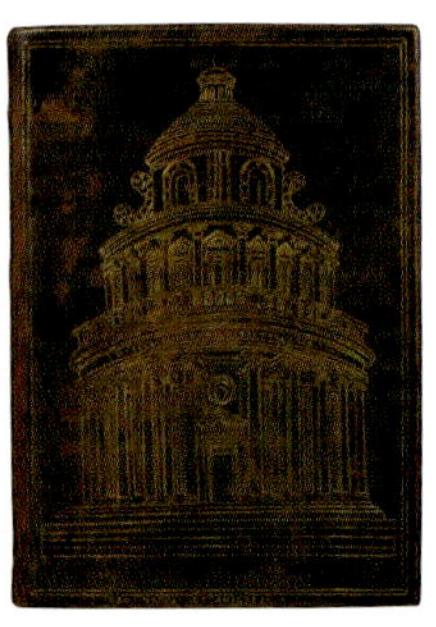

X.23

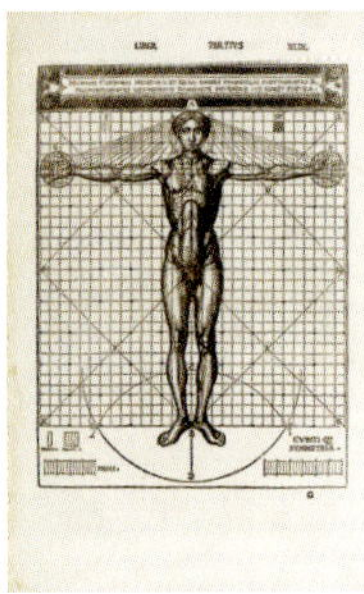

X.24

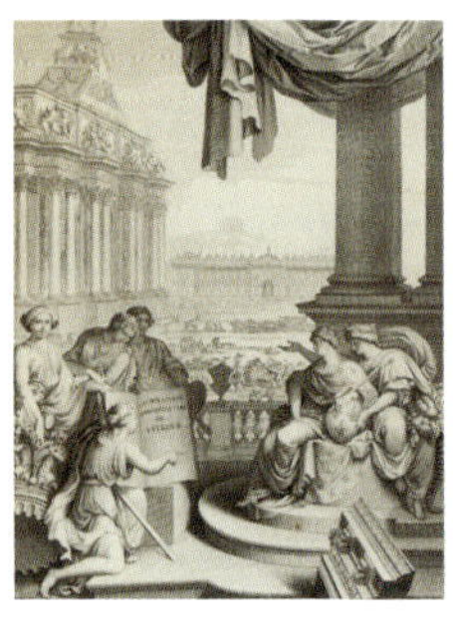

X.25

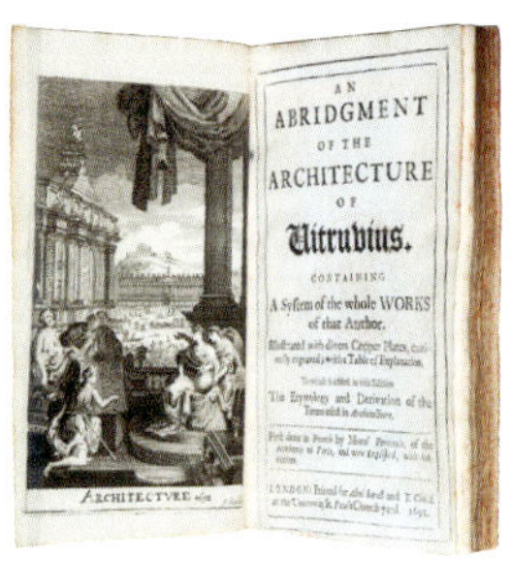

X.26

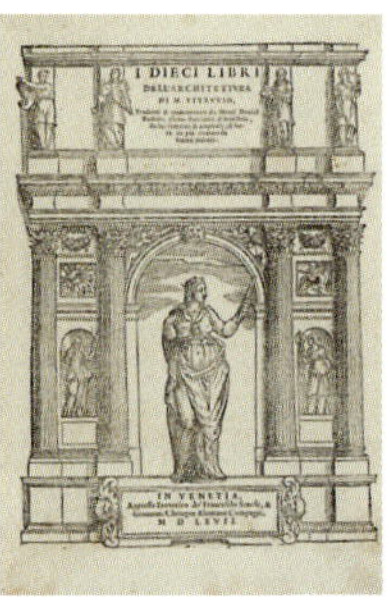

X.27

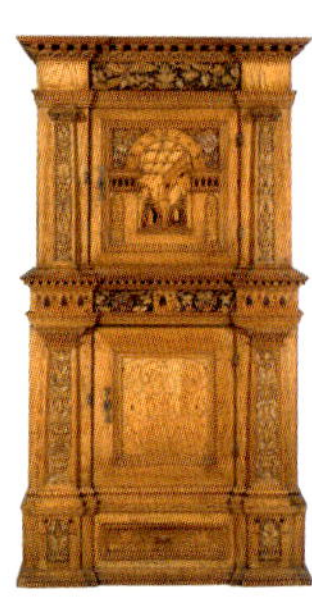

X.28

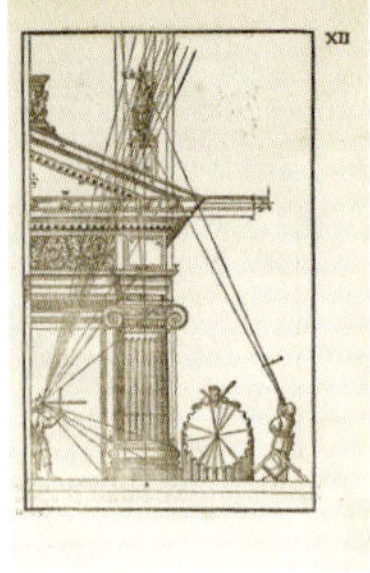

X.29

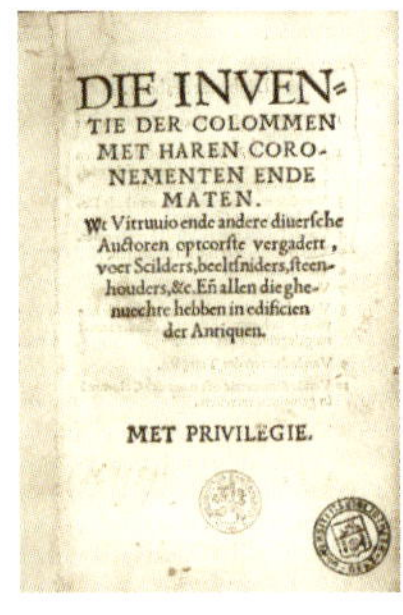

X.30

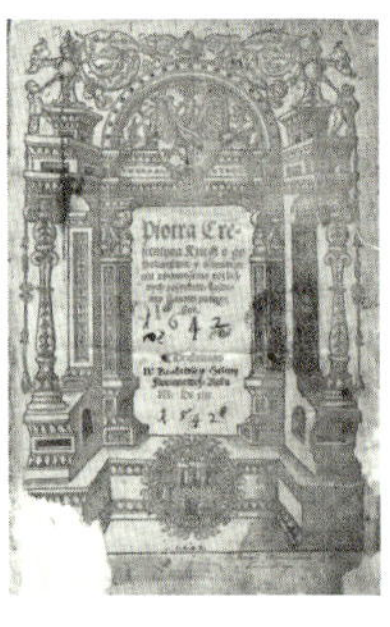

X.31

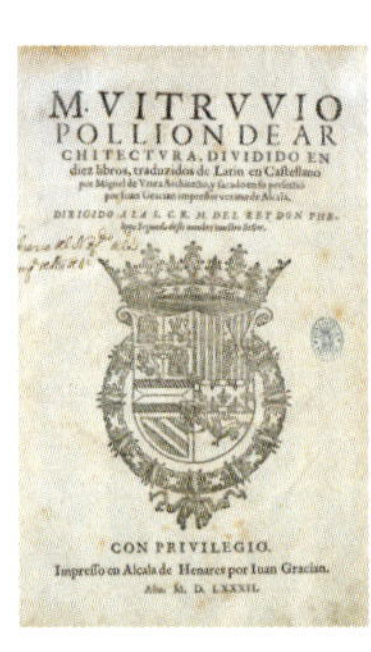

X.32

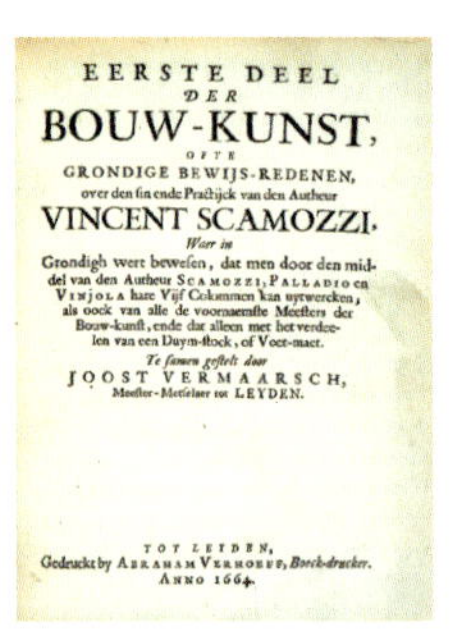

X.33

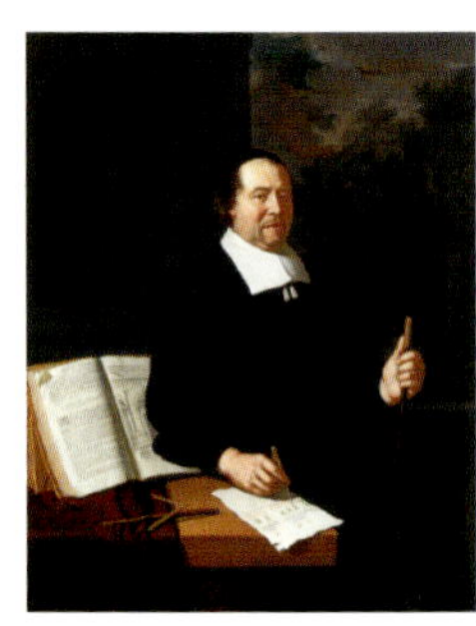

X.34

X.28 TWIN CABINET

1565
Wood, 229 x 122 x 58 cm
Zurich, Schweizerisches Landesmuseum, LM 5082

This piece of furniture by the master cabinet-maker H.S. adopted perspective and the ancient orders in its ornamentation. This is a beautiful example of the adoption of Vitruvianism in the art of the cabinet-maker.

X.29 *DER FÜRNEMBSTEN NOTWENDIGSTEN DER GANTZEN ARCHITECTUR ANGEHÖRIGEN MATHEMATISCHEN UND MECHANISCHEN KÜNST EIGENTLICHER BERICHT UND VAST KLARE VERSTENDLICHE UNTERRICHTUNG ZU RECHTEM VERSTAND DER LEHR VITRUVII IN DREY FURNEME BÜCHER ABGETHEILET*

Edition by Walther Hermann Ryff (Rivius), Nuremberg, 1548
Brussels, Bibliothèque royale, Réserve précieuse, VB 5331

The first translation into German was also called 'Vitruvius Teutsch'. In 1543 Ryff had already had a Latin edition of the treatise printed in Strasbourg. Here he reproduces the plate introduced by Cesariano in his 1521 edition (X.24). It shows a cross-section of Milan cathedral, with the aim of demonstrating, via an example of Gothic architecture, how the Ancients had already adopted rules of proportion analogous to those formulated by Vitruvius.

X.30 PIETER COECKE VAN AELST : *DIE INVENTIE DER COLOMMEN MET HAREN CORONEMENTEN ENDE MATEN* (...)

Antwerp, 1539
16 x 11 cm
Ghent, Universiteitsbibliotheek, Res. 1448

Also known as 'petit Vitruve', it amounts to only 64 pages and is mainly aimed at painters, sculptors and masons.

X.31 P. DE CRESCENTIS : *KSIEGI O GOSPODARSTWIE*

Translation by A. Trzyciski, 1549
Kraków, Universytet Jagiellonski Biblioteka Jagiellonski

It was into this treatise on agriculture by Pierre de Crescentis, dating back to 1305–09, dedicated to Charles II of Anjou, and considered to be the best of the Middle Ages, that were inserted the only pages on architecture published in Poland. Vitruvius was, however, read in the Latin and Italian editions.

X.32 VITRUVIUS : *DE ARCHITECTURA*

Spanish translation by Miguel de Urrea, Alcala de Henares, 1582
30. 3 x 20.3 cm
Madrid, Biblioteca Nacional de España, 25087

X.33 *EERSTE DEEL DER BOUW-KUNST OFTE GRONDIGE BEWIJS-REDENEN OVER DEN SIN ENDE PRACTIJCK VAN DEN AUTHEUR VINCENT SCAMOZZI* (...)

Edition prepared by Joost Vermaarsch, Leyden, 1664
19.6 x 15.7 cm
Amsterdam, The Wolbert H.M. Vroom Collection, no. A 219

X.34 MICHIEL VAN MUSSCHER : PORTRAIT OF THE DUTCH ARCHITECT JOOST VERMAARSCH, WITH HIS TRANSLATION OF THE TREATISE OF SCAMOZZI

1665
Oil on panel, 41 x 31cm
Amsterdam, The Wolbert H.M. Vroom Collection

The architect proudly holds his translation of Scamozzi's treatise. His pose strangely resembles that of Daniele Barbaro, (1556, Rijksmuseum Amsterdam) by Paolo Veronese. Scamozzism became a major trend in Holland in the 17th century.

BIBLIOGRAPHY : *Scamozzi. Architettura e scienza. L'architettura du Vincenzo Scamozzi 1548–1616* (exhib. cat.), Museo Palladio, Vicenza, 2003.

X.35 ANTON RAPHAEL MENGS : PORTRAIT OF JAMES CAULFIELD, LORD CHARLEMONT

1756
Oil on canvas, 137 x 100.5 cm
Prague, Národní Galerie, inv. DO 4561

Lord Charlemont, an English nobleman, made his 'Grand Tour' of Italy and stayed in Rome between 1753 and 1755. Passionate about

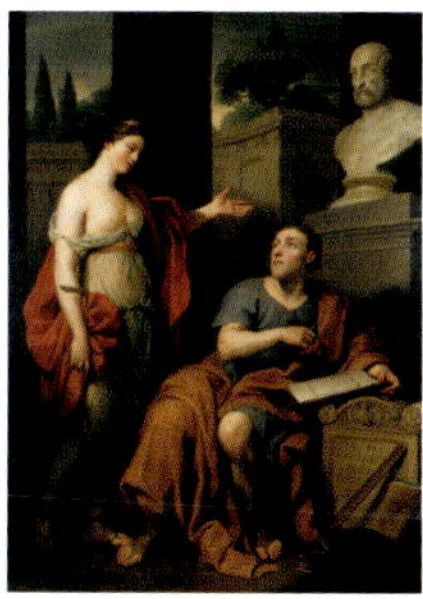

X.35

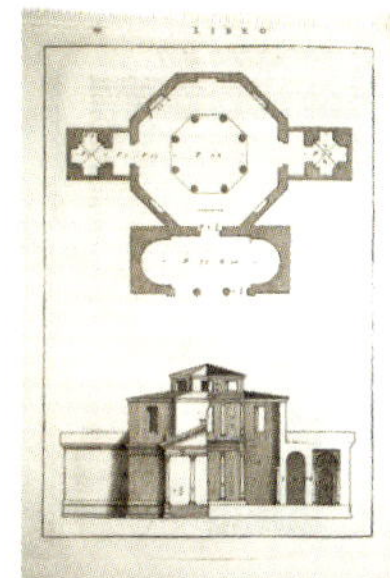

X.36

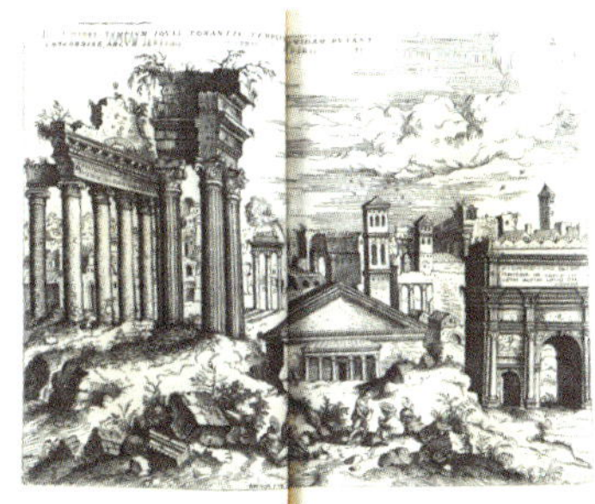

X.37

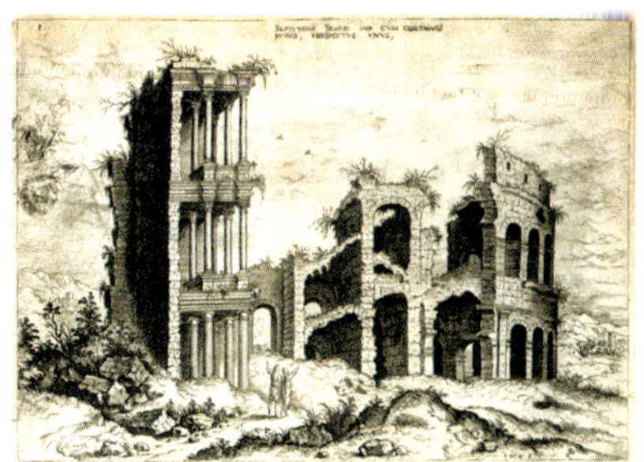

X.38

architecture, like Lord Burlington, he was presented to Piranesi, who tried, without success, to get him financially involved in the publication of his *Antichità romane*. Charlemont was more appreciative of Vitruvius and the Classical tradition, as exemplified by Andrea Palladio. Mengs represented the aristocrat in an antique toga, in the act of measuring a section plan, his left hand leaning on a funerary monument to the memory of Vitruvius. Behind him is a bust commemorating Palladio, chosen as his model in the architectural allegory. At bottom right there are architectural treatises celebrating intimate knowledge of architectural theory.

BIBLIOGRAPHY : S. Roentgen (ed.), *Mengs – La discoperta del Neoclassico*, Padua, 2001, no. 73, pp. 234–35 (bibl.); Michael McCarthy (ed.), *Lord Charlemont and his Circle : Essays in honour of Michael Wynne*, Dublin, 2001.

X.36 ANDREA PALLADIO : *I QUATTRO LIBRI DELL'ARCHITETTURA*

Venice, Domenico de Franceschi, 1570 (actually, Venice, Giambattista Pasquali for Consul Joseph Smith)
Parchment, 30.3 x 21.5 cm
Amsterdam, The Wolbert H.M. Vroom Collection, no. A 170

X.37 VINCENZO SCAMOZZI : *DISCORSI SOPRA L'ANTIQUITÀ DI ROMA*

Venice, F. Ziletti, 1583
30.3 x 20.3 cm
Amsterdam, The Wolbert H.M. Vroom Collection, no. A 210

Vincenzo Scamozzi described himself as a 'citizen of the world'. It was not merely his travels in Hungary, Bohemia, Poland, Germany, France and Switzerland or his familiarity with numerous Italian cities that earned him this pan-European status – rather the clarity and intelligibility with which he placed architectural models with their illustrations at his readers' disposal.

X.38 *HIERONYMUS COCK : PRAECIPUAE ALIQUOT ROMANAE ANTIQUITATIS RUINARUM MONUMENTA*

1551
Burin engraving, 41.5 x 95 cm
Brussels, Bibliothèque royale de Belgique, Cabinet des estampes
VH 19830 est

An editor, engraver and merchant from Antwerp, Hieronimus Cock published a series of views of Rome in Antwerp before trying to create a series of portraits of artists since Eyck, a project that would be curtailed by his death.

BIBLIOGRAPHY : Timothy Riggs, *Hieronymus Cock (1510–1570)*, Yale, 1971.

X.39 VINCENZO SCAMOZZI : *L'IDEA DELLA ARCHITETTURA UNIVERSALE*

Venice, Giorgio Valentino, 1615
34.4 x 24 cm
Amsterdam, The Wolbert H.M. Vroom Collection, no. A 212

Scamozzi claimed to have devoted twenty-five years of his life to this book, which he published at his own expense. The architect is portrayed in the centre. In Scamozzi's eyes, architecture was a science that outranked all the arts, and all the sciences, by reason of its moral dimension.

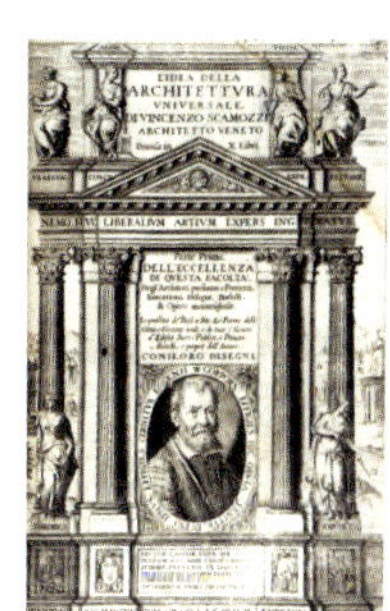

X.39

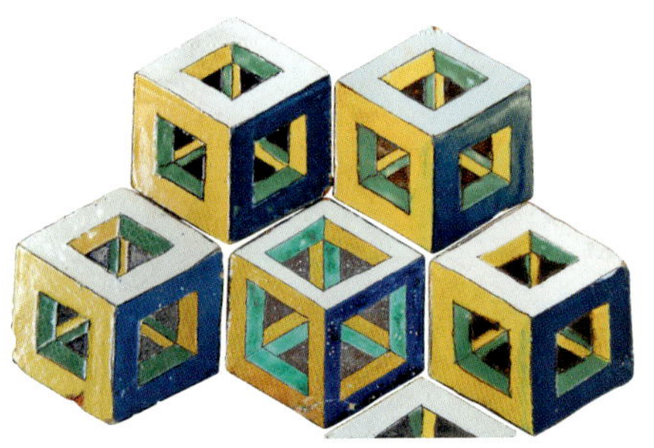
XI.1

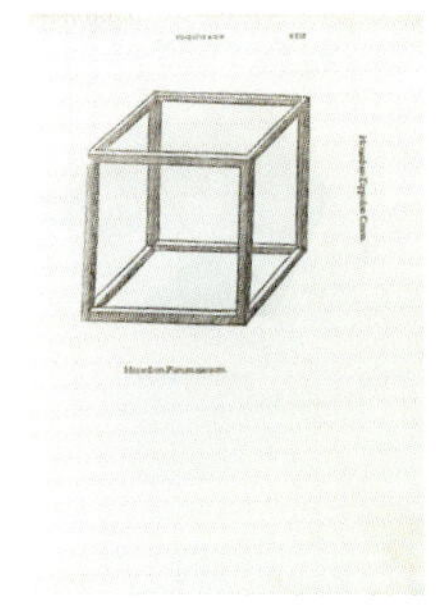
XI.2

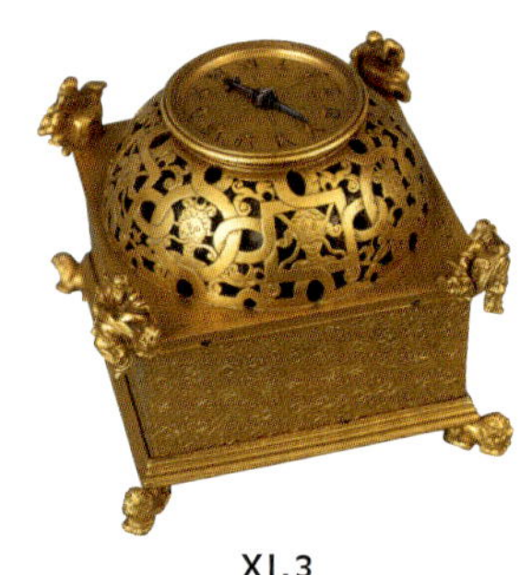
XI.3

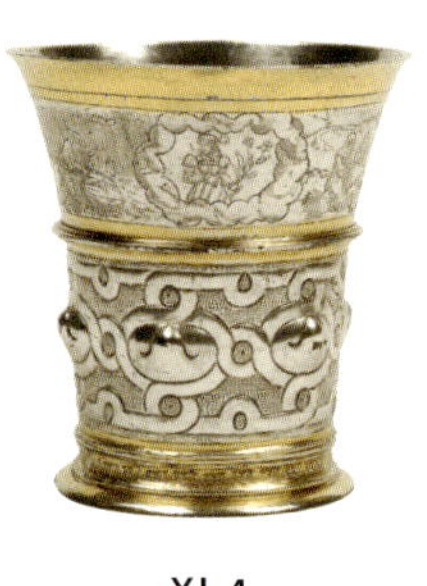
XI.4

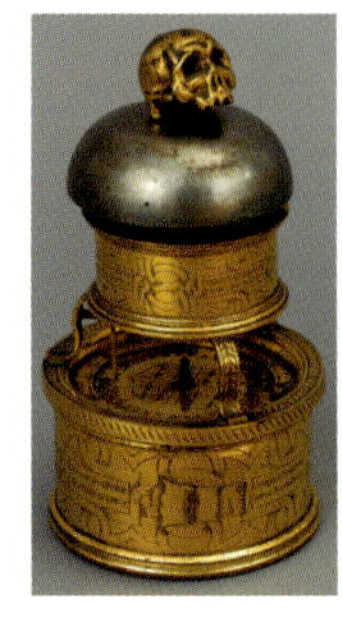
XI.6

SECTION XI
PRINTS IN THE SERVICE OF ARTS AND CRAFTS

This section traces the blossoming of the decorative arts on a European scale thanks to the development and dissemination of engravings, particularly etchings. Because this new medium was inexpensive, from the 16th century all forms of artistic expression were able to draw on a rich repertoire of ornamental and figurative motifs, which were copied, transformed or restated.

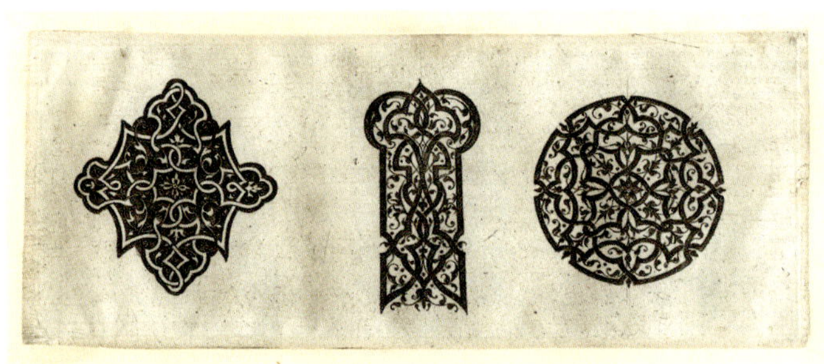
XI.5

XI.1 HEXAGONAL FLOOR TILES

German work, late 16th–early 17th century
Hexagons of varnished ceramic, 20.2 cm x 18 cm each hexagon
Budapest, Iparművészeti Múzeum, inv. 69.670 (about 400 pieces)

The simplicity of the range of colours enhances the motif borrowed from Luca Pacioli's treatise. The geometrical design is hollowed out of the clay before it is fired. One of the pieces (not in the exhibition) bears an inscription in German.

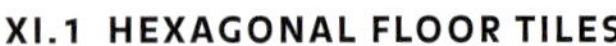

XI.2 LUCA PACIOLI : *DE DIVINA PROPORTIONE*

Edition of Paganius Paganinus, Venice, 1509
Printed on paper, in folio, 20.5 x 22.5 cm
London, Victoria and Albert Museum, inv. 380 418 001 21261
f.VIII: 'Hexaedron Planum vacuum'

Luca Pacioli, a Franciscan monk, taught geometry in Milan, where he met Leonardo da Vinci, to whom his treatise owes much.

BIBLIOGRAPHY : *Luca Pacioli e la matematica del Rinascimento*, exhib. cat., Florence, 1994; Pierre Speziali, 'Léonard de Vinci et la 'Divina Proportione' de Luca Pacioli', *Bibliothèque d'humanisme et renaissance*, 15, 1953, pp. 295–305.

XI.3 CHIMING TABLE CLOCK

16th century
Bronze, brass, iron, 10 x 10 cm
La Chaux-de-Fonds, Switzerland, Musée international d'Horlogerie, inv. IV-98

The structure of this table clock, a luxury piece, still remains true to medieval architecture. The dome protecting the chiming mechanism bears a decoration of interlaced bands, which the architect Jacques Androuet de Cerceau made fashionable in France. Significantly, the differentiated decoration is applied only to the new part of a technical mechanism.

BIBLIOGRAPHY : Catherine Cardinal, Jean-Michel Piguet, *Catalogue d'œuvres choisies. La Chaux de Fonds*,1999, cat. 78, pp. 82–83.

XI.4 THIERRY DE BRY (ALIAS DIETRICH BREY) : GOBLET

c. 1570
Silver, partly gilded, 9.2 x 8.7 cm
Strasbourg, Musée de l'œuvre de Notre-Dame, XXIV-58

Born in Liège in 1528, Thierry de Bry (also called Dietrich Brey) obtained his master's degree in 1560 and settled in Strasbourg. In 1588 he returned to Liège and ended his career in Frankfurt, an important centre for goldsmiths. A great connoisseur of decorative motifs from France and Italy, he published many prints describing ornaments. Working on the frontier between the Latin and Germanic worlds, he was one of the many people who 'passed on' decorative designs through both his engraved work and the pieces he produced. The decoration at the bottom of the goblet, with its geometrical interlacing embossed on a matt yellow gold background, certainly came from France and is comparable to several of Androuet du Cerceau's engraved plates.

BIBLIOGRAPHY : Hans Haug, *L'orfèvrerie de Strasbourg dans les collections publiques françaises*, Paris, 1978, catalogue 15.

XI.5 BALTHAZAR VAN DEN BOS (BALTHAZAR SYLVIUS) : *VARIARUM PROTACTIONUM QUAS VULGO MAURUSIAS VOCANT OMNIUM*

Paris edition, 1554
Collection of 26 plates engraved by Jacob Honergogt, in octavo
28.2 x 35.5 cm
Brussels, Bibliothèque royale de Belgique, Cabinet des estampes, S.I. 23193

This collection contains twenty-six plates, but as they were printed at different times the number of plates often varies, even if the title remains unchanged. This flexibility allowed the engraver to follow the fashion and update his latest productions, whether copied or reversed. Moorish decorations from the Ottoman Empire were highly popular during the Renaissance. Van den Bos, born in Herzogenbosch, was working in Antwerp by 1543. Between 1568 and 1569 he worked for Archduke Ferdinand of Habsburg in Innsbruck. His engravings were widely used by all craftsmen including Jean and Andreas Ruckers, the famous harpsichord makers. Bos is linked to Jacob Honervogt, a German who had settled in Paris by 1608 and became

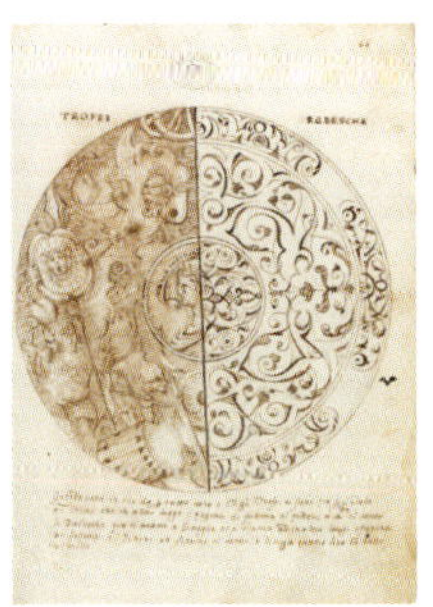
XI.7

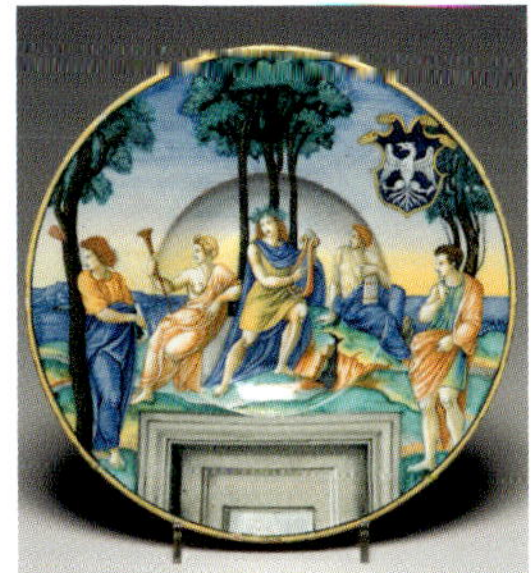
XI.8

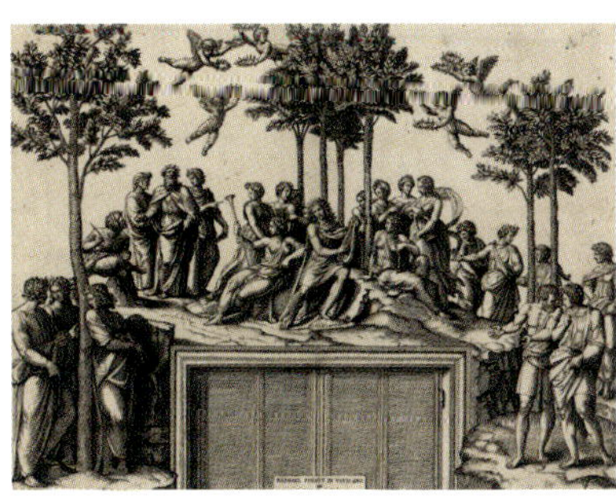
XI.9

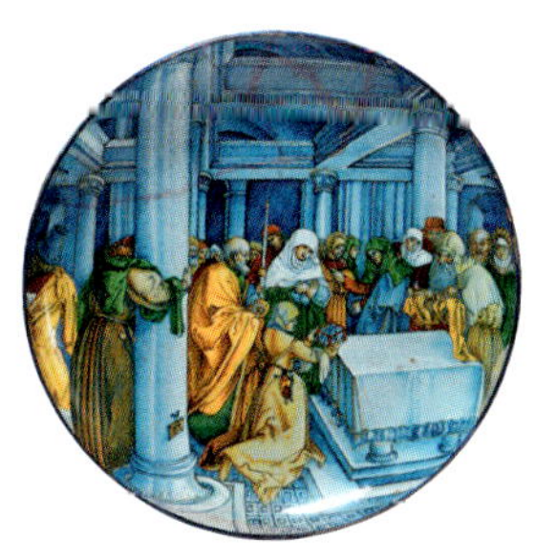
XI.10

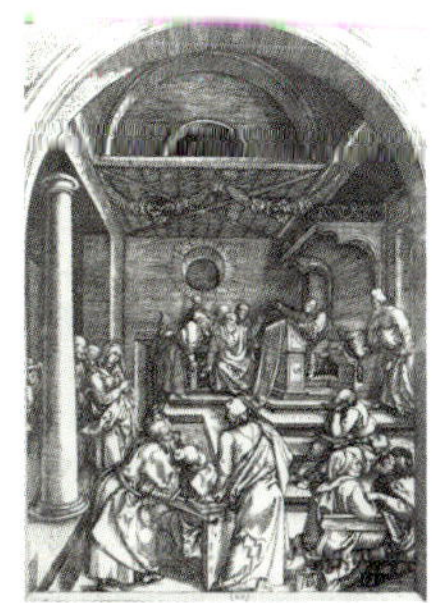
XI.11

French in 1620. Honervogt disseminated several of Jacques Androuet du Cerceau's motifs. The collection of van den Bos was to be pillaged in turn by French engravers.

BIBLIOGRAPHY: G. Grant O'Brien, 'Ioannes and Andreas Ruckers: A Quatercentenary Celebration', *Early Music*, vol. 7, no. 4, 1979, pp. 453–66; Frans Jozef Peter Van den Branden, 'Balthasar Geertssen, Known as Bos or Sylvius, Engraver, 1518–1580', in *Quatre suites d'ornements Balthasar Bos*, The Hague, 1893.

XI.6 NICOLAS PLANTART: CYLINDRICAL TABLE CLOCK WITH SKULL

16th century
Brass and iron with the arms of the Duke of Montmorency
La Chaux-de-Fonds, Switzerland, Musée international d'Horlogerie, inv. IV-142

The interlaced bands decoration is borrowed, in simplified and modified form, from Du Cerceau's engravings (see XI.5). This type of decoration is also found in French bindings of the same period.

BIBLIOGRAPHY: Catherine Cardinal, Jean-Michel Piguet, *Catalogue d'œuvres choisies*, La Chaux-de-Fonds, 1999 catalogue, 77, pp. 80–81.

XI.7 CIPRIANO PICCOLPASSO: *LIBRI DELL'ARTE DEL VASAIO*

1557
Handwritten on paper, 28.9 x 22.9 cm, London, Victoria and Albert Museum, MSL/1861/7446
f.66v: 'Trofei Rubesche'

Born in Castel Durante (Urbania, Italy), Piccolpasso was an engineer who, in 1558, was commissioned by the Pope to supervise the fortifications of Perugia. He even became inspector of the pontifical fortifications on the Adriatic coast that were being threatened by the Turks (1566). In the same year he was made a Knight of St George. In 1575, disgraced after a quarrel with a Perugian nobleman, he returned to his home town. A learned man and enlightened connoisseur of European art and literature, he acknowledged that the Flemish were superior in landscape but that the Italians were best at representing the human form. His treatise *Li tre libri de l'arte del vasaio* (1557) is a manuscript possibly intended for publication that was commissioned by Cardinal de Tournon, the French ambassador to Italy. The Cardinal stayed at Castel Durante during a French campaign against the armies of the Emperor Charles V. On that occasion, he was given a ceramic vase.

Piccolpasso explains the secrets of ceramics and the nature of the existing forms of decoration, with their provenance – Venice, Faenza, Urbino – whose price varies according to their complexity. Above all, however, he defends an interest in the applied arts as a worthy subject for a gentleman.

BIBLIOGRAPHY: *I tre libri dell'arte del vasaio: a facsimile of the manuscript in the Victoria and Albert Museum, London by Cipriano Piccolpasso*, trans. and introduced by Ronald Lightbown and Alan Caiger-Smith. London 1980, 2 vols.

XI.8 ATTRIBUTED TO THE 'MARSYAS PAINTER': MAJOLICA DISH WITH A MOTIF DERIVED FROM RAPHAEL'S PARNASSUS

c. 1530–31
Urbino, pottery, 30.7 cm
Cambridge, The Fitzwilliam Museum, MAR C 61-1912

The pottery of Urbino transmitted many motifs borrowed from great paintings by way of engravings. The work of Raphael, reproduced by the engraver Marc-Antonio Raimondi, was used in particular. The 'Marsyas painter-potter' freely chose the motif of Apollo surrounded by the Muses Euterpe and Erato and two poets, simplifying the other elements present in Raimondi's engraving.

BIBLIOGRAPHY: Julia E. Poole, *Italian majolica and incised slipware in the Fitzwilliam Museum, Cambridge*, Cambridge, 1995, catalogue 382, pp. 317–19.

XI.9 MARCANTONIO RAIMONDI AFTER RAPHAEL'S PARNASSUS: ENGRAVED REPRODUCTION OF THE FRESCO OF THE STANZA DELLA SEGNATURE, VATICAN

1517
Burin engraving, printed on paper, 35.2 x 46.6 cm
Berlin, Staatliche Museen zu Berlin, Kupferstichkabinett 304-1893

This engraving presents a free interpretation of Raphael's fresco in the Vatican. At that time, the notion of reproduction was not as rigid as it is today. Raimondi's main aim was to reproduce the principal idea that dominates Raphael's composition.

BIBLIOGRAPHY: Lisa Pon, *Raphael, Dürer and Marcantonio Raimondi: Copying and the Italian Renaissance Print*, New Haven, 2004, pp. 86–90 (bibl.)

XI.10 ATTRIBUTED TO THE 'MASTER OF THE ASSUMPTION': THE PRESENTATION IN THE TEMPLE, AFTER AN ENGRAVING BY ALBRECHT DÜRER

c. 1520–25
Ceramic, 25.5 cm
London, Victoria and Albert Museum, C 159-1937

Albrecht Dürer achieved international success as soon as his engravings on wood and copper appeared. Marcantonio Raimondi pillaged his plates and blocks, and potters and goldsmiths borrowed his compositions. Through his own genius, Dürer created a repertoire of forms that transcended geographical frontiers and stylistic traditions.

This piece is a copy of a copy. We recognize a wood engraving by Albrecht Dürer from his series of twenty plates for the *Life of the Virgin*, sixteen of which were printed when he left for Venice (1505), but the true author of this fraudulent copy after Dürer is Marc-Antonio Raimondi, a great disseminator of prints of Raphael's works. The potter in turn reproduced the signature of Dürer present on Raimondi's copy. He added a few figures, incidentally borrowed from the Marriage of the Virgin in the same series, to fill the circular surface of his dish.

BIBLIOGRAPHY: Giulia Bartrum, Gunter Grass, Joseph L. Koerner, Ute Kuhlemann (eds.), *Albrecht Dürer and his Legacy: The Graphic Work of a Renaissance Artist*, Princeton, 2003, cat. 202, pp. 248 (bibl.).

XI.11 MARCANTONIO RAIMONDI AFTER ALBRECHT DURER PRESENTATION IN THE TEMPLE

c. 1506
Wood engraving
Paris, Bibliothèque nationale de France, Eb 4 fol. Ou Res Eb 5 fol

This wood engraving, produced by Marcantonio Raimondi from the original plate created by Albrecht Dürer, was completed in about 1506, that is to say immediately after the original was first printed and before it appeared in the complete series of the *Life of the Virgin* in 1511. This very faithful but illegal copy nevertheless shows that Raimondi reflected in an Italian idiom many of the elements of the composition he was imitating. This model was therefore

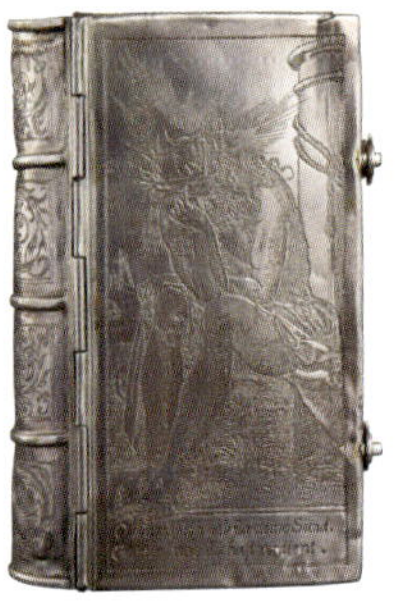

XI.12

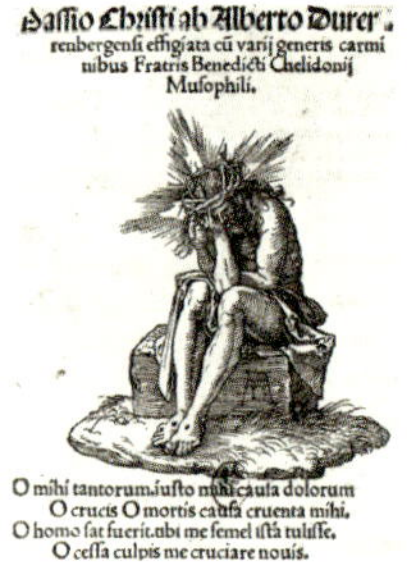

XI.13

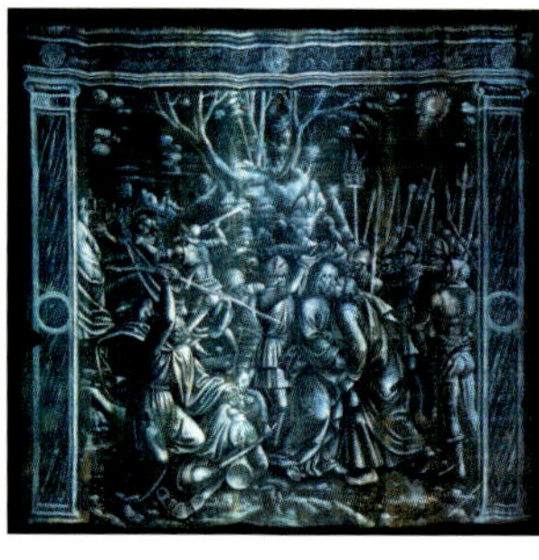

XI.14

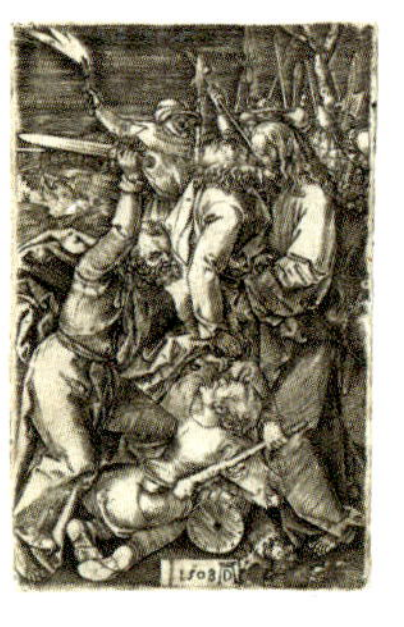

XI.15

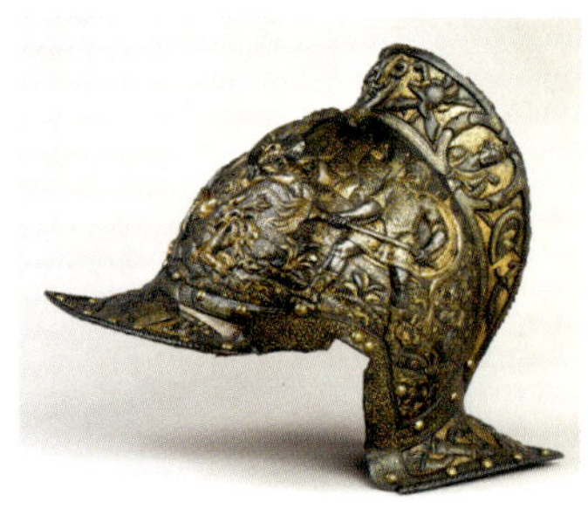

XI.16

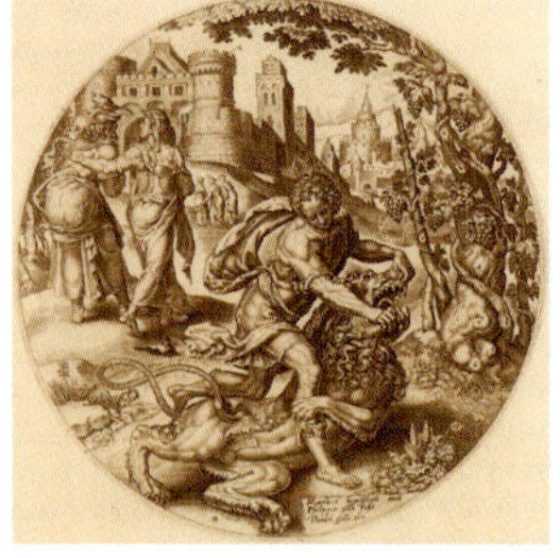

XI.17

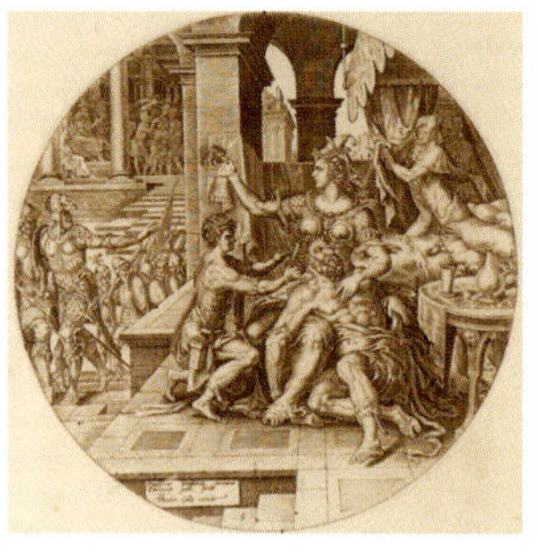

XI.18

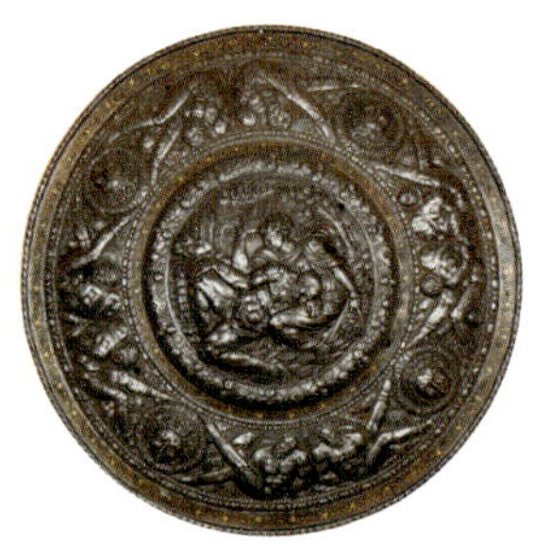

XI.19

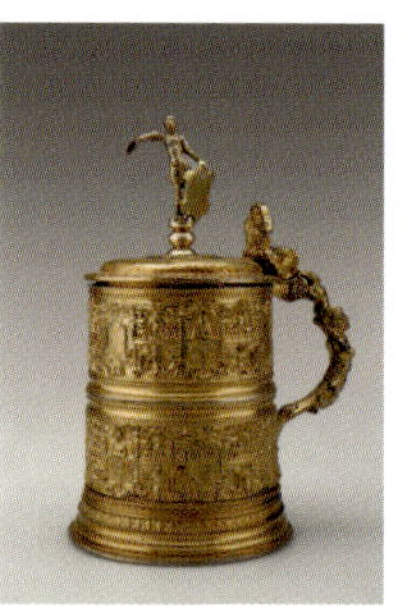

XI.20

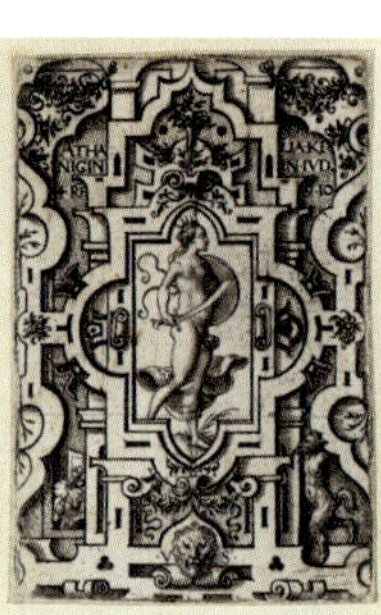

XI.21

easier for potters to copy as it had already adapted a German model to the formal vocabulary of Italy.

BIBLIOGRAPHY: Lisa Pon, *Raphael, Dürer and Marcantonio Raimondi: Copying and the Italian Renaissance Print*, New Haven, 2004, pp. 39–41; Evelyn Lincoln, *The Invention of the Italian Renaissance Printmaker*, New Haven, 2000; Giovanni Maria Fara, *Inventario generale delle stampe / Gabinetto Disegni e Stampe degli Uffizi. 1. Albrecht Dürer: originali, copie, derivazioni*, Florence, 2007, preface and catalogue, 96.0.

XI.12 BURIN-ENGRAVED SILVER BINDING, AFTER TWO MODELS: THE CHRIST OF SORROWS BY ALBRECHT DÜRER AND KING DAVID AND HIS HARP BY JAN SADELER

After 1645
Josua Wengelin, *Andächtige Verschönung mit Gott*, Edition, Nuremburg, printed on paper
Engraved silver, 10.2 x 6 cm
Budapest, Iparművészeti Múzeum, inv. 53.797

BIBLIOGRAPHY: *Az idő sodrában: az Iparművészeti Múzeum gyűjteményeinek története; az Iparművészeti Múzeum gyűjtők és kincsek című kiállításához a tanulmányok szerzől*, Budapest, 2006, cat. 163, p. 152 and illustration p. 79 (bibl.).

XI.13 ALBRECHT DÜRER: CHRIST OF SORROWS (LITTLE PASSION SERIES)

1587
Wood engraving, 12.5 x 95 cm (isolated page with no inscription), glued to card, 22.5 x 14.5 cm
Paris, Bibliothèque nationale de France, Cabinet des estampes, inv. Ca 4b res.fol

BIBLIOGRAPHY: Albrecht Dürer, *Passio* (called the Little Passion), undated, but 1511, wood engraving decorating the title page; illustrated Bartsch Dürer 1001, (B 16.119), pp. 256–58.

XI.14 UNKNOWN PAINTER (TERAMO PIAGGIO ?): THE ARREST OF CHRIST

Lombardy, 1515–25
White lead on indigo-dyed linen, 299 x 323 cm
Genoa, Collezione Tessile Soprintendenza P.S.A.E. Liguria, deposited with the Museo Diocesano

The Arrest of Christ belongs to a series of fourteen pieces depicting the Passion. Their date and unusual character make them unique in Italy. The series was probably used during Holy Week, and was kept in the Benedictine abbey of San Nicoló del Boschetto near Genoa. The unknown painter was inspired by Dürer's engravings but reworked them. He was probably a painter from Liguria or Lombardy in the circle of Teramo Piaggio whose style here is similar to that of Pier Francesco Sacchi. The variations compared with the original iconography were probably called for by the Benedictine fathers of the congregation of Santa Giustina in whose parish the abbey stood. Dürer's engravings were then sold in the city of Genoa itself and the local painters greatly appreciated them.

(We are grateful to Marzia Cataldi Gallo for the information she provided for this entry.)

BIBLIOGRAPHY: *Blu blue-jeans: il Blu popolare* (exhib. cat.), Milan, 1989, p. 213; E. Princi, S. Vicini, M. M. Carnasciali, M. Cataldi Gallo, R. Innocenti, E. Pedemonte, 'Case Study: Characterisation of Blue Panels of the XVI Century with Micro-analytical Techniques', *Journal of Cultural Heritage*, vol. 5, 2004, pp. 319–21; M. Cataldi Gallo, in *Dürer e l'Italia* (exhib. cat.), Milan, 2007, p. 305 (bibl.).

XI.15 ALBRECHT DÜRER: THE KISS OF JUDAS (NO. 3 OF THE ENGRAVED PASSION)

1508
Burin engraving, 11.8 x 7.5 cm
Brussels, Bibliothèque royale de Belgique, Cabinet des estampes, SI 14659

Albrecht Dürer's composition is compact but perfectly understandable, as the two protagonists supply the main key to reading the picture. The soldiers are confined to the background. The large composition (XI.14) inspired by this model tries to constitute the nucleus of a great battle in the Italian tradition, but the story becomes less legible.

BIBLIOGRAPHY: Angela Hass, 'Two Devotional Manuals by Albrecht Dürer: The "Small Passion" and the "Engraved Passion": Iconography, Context and Spirituality', *Zeitschrift für Kunstgeschichte*, 63, 2000, pp. 169–230.

XI.16 BURGONET HELMET WITH THREE LABOURS OF HERCULES

Milan, 1560–70
Steel, gold and silver, 38 x 27 x 22 cm
Turin, Armeria Reale, inv. E 35

This superb embossed burgonet with a Roman style crest, an aventaile and a rondel to protect the back of the

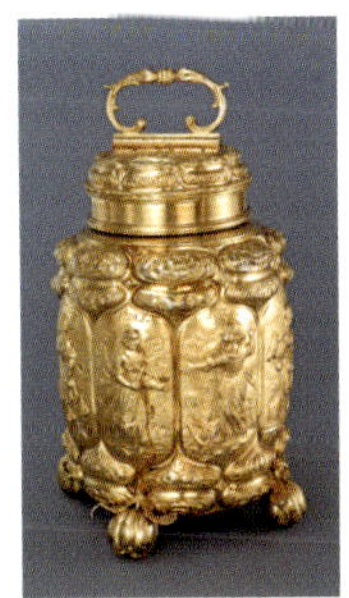

XI.22

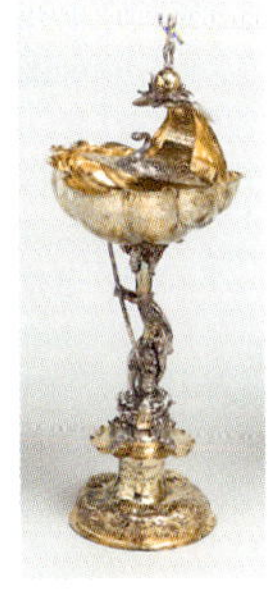

XI.23

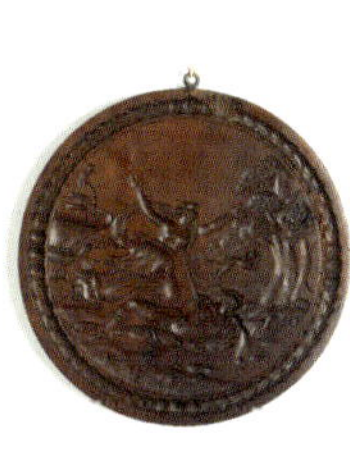

XI.24

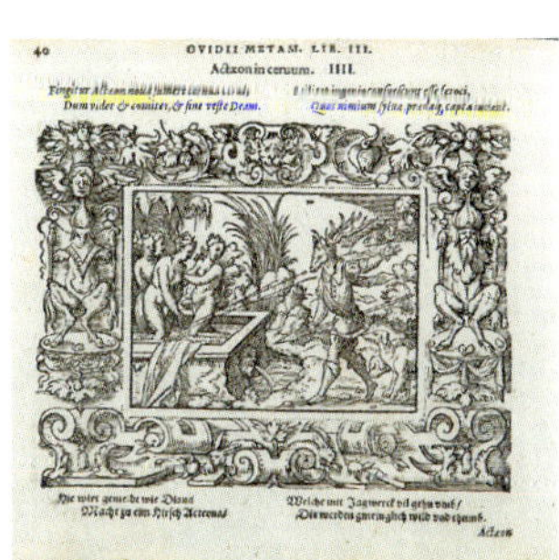

XI.25

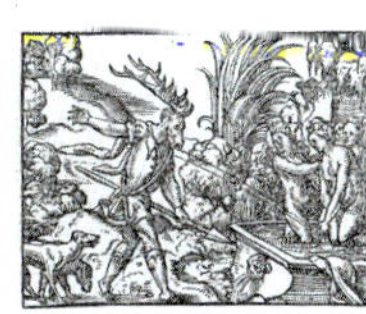

XI.26

neck, includes three illustrations: on the front, Hercules and the Nemean Lion; on the left side, Hercules fighting the six-headed Hydra of Lerna; and on the right side, the hero fighting Cerberus, the guardian of Hades. The back shows a landscape with an ancient town.

The figure of Hercules and the Nemean Lion is derived from a Flemish engraving (XI.17) that represents a completely different subject: Samson fighting the lion in the vineyards of Thimna. For the Milanese craftsman who produced these decorations, the model was still adequate, because he was depicting a comparable scene. If the same narrative plan applied to several stories, its use was considered all the more fruitful.

BIBLIOGRAPHY : José-A. Godoy (ed.), *Parures triomphales : le maniérisme dans l'art de l'armure italienne* (exhib. cat.), Geneva, Milan, 2003, cat. 50, pp. 456–57.

XI.17 PHILIPPE GALLE (BASED ON A DRAWING BY MARTIN VAN HEEMSKERCK) : SAMSON AND THE LION IN THE VINEYARDS OF THIMNA

Mid-16th century
Engraving, diameter 26 cm, glued on to a page, 34.5 x 48.5 cm
Brussels, Bibliothèque royale de Belgique, Cabinet des estampes, SI 1558 f°

The rounded shape of the composition, its clarity and precision made this document eminently useful to European craftsmen. The Galle family, who originated from Haarlem, settled in Antwerp and made a great many plates based on the work of the great masters of the North. Head of his own publishing house – *Au Lys Blanc* – Philippe Galle also worked for the printer Plantin. Plates and works were much sought after in northern Italy during the Counter-Reformation.

BIBLIOGRAPHY : *The New Hollstein Dutch and Flemish Etchings, Engravings and Woodcuts, 1450–1700*, cat. 86, p. 85.

XI.18 PHILIPPE AND THÉODORE GALLE (AFTER MARTIN VAN HEEMSKERCK) : SAMSON AND DELILAH

Mid-16th century
Engraving, diameter 26 cm, glued onto a sheet, 34.5 x 48.5 cm
Brussels, Bibliothèque royale de Belgique, Cabinet des estampes, inv. SI 1561 f°

Theodore Galle was the son of Phillipe Gall. The original plate was produced by the workshop of Hieronymus Cock, but this one was reissued under the name of the Galles as its publishers.

BIBLIOGRAPHY : *The New Hollstein Dutch and Flemish Etchings, Engravings and Woodcuts, 1450–1700*, cat. 89, p. 88; Madlyn Kahr, 'Delilah', *The Art Bulletin*, vol. 54, no. 3, 1972, pp. 282–99.

XI.19 ATTRIBUTED TO FILIPPO NEGROLI : ROUNDEL

Milan, *c.* 1570
Steel, gold, silver, diameter *c.* 60 cm
Morlanwelz, Musée royal de Mariemont, Belgium, III.1.1

This is a piece of exceptional quality that shows how a craftsman can make his model bend to the requirements of his own work. The composition of Heemskerk (XI.18) is positioned laterally to make it more comprehensible in bas-relief.

BIBLIOGRAPHY : Stuart W. Pyhrr, José-A. Godoy (eds), *Heroic Armour of the Italian Renaissance : Filippo Negroli and his Contemporaries*, cat.of the exhib. at the Metropolitan Museum of Art, New York, 1999; Alan R. Williams, 'The Steel of the Negroli', *Metropolitan Museum Journal 34*, 1999, pp. 101–24.

XI.20 JANOS LIPPAI : TANKARD WITH LID

1578
Gilded silver, height 18.5 cm
Budapest, Magyar Nemzeti Múzeum, Poc. Jank. 146
Provenance: Kassa (Košice)

The centres of excellence for goldsmiths attracted many apprentices who, when they returned to their homes fold, preached the good word. Such relationships were fruitful and doubled the impact of ornamental engraving. Kassa or Košice (Kaschau in German and Kassa in Hungarian, Austro-Hungarian times) is the second biggest city of what is now Slovakia.

This piece demonstrates the excellent knowledge of decorative wrought ironwork in large centres such as Nuremberg and Augsburg of great ornamentalists and goldsmiths like Senzel Jamnitzer and Peter Flötner. This art developed in an enjoyable and original form in Transylvania and what is now Slovakia. Several Slovak, Hungarian and Transylvanian craftsmen were trained in those two German cities. Moreover, the spread of Germanic skills was helped by the engravings of Virgil Solis, a highly productive German supplier. These recycled decorations based on French or Italian models offered an inexhaustible choice of motifs. Here, the motifs in two rows of bas-relief are enclosed in a rigid ornamental structure that evokes the decorated leather strips popularized by German engraving.

BIBLIOGRAPHY : Árpád Mikó, *Jankovich Miklós (1772–1846) gyűjteményei : kiállítási katalógus*, Magyar Nemzeti Galéria, Budapest, 2002, cat. 74, p. 130–31.

XI.21 VIRGIL SOLIS : ATHALIA, QUEEN OF THE JEWS, SAMSON AND DELILAH, BATHSHEBA AND DAVID, SOLOMOM. JUDITH

Second third of the 16th century
Etchings (VER), 44 x 58 cm
Berlin, Staatliche Museen zu Berlin, Kupferstichkabinett, inv. 611-616

Nuremberg engraver Virgil Solis was active in the second third of the 16th century. He had a workshop that printed an immense quantity of copper engravings and woodcuts. As he was very familiar with the latest publications in Nuremberg and elsewhere, he copied and recycled them as he pleased, using an artistic vocabulary that was formal and sometimes boring, but unified. His house thus served as an ideas exchange for ornamental engraving in the mid-16th century.

BIBLIOGRAPHY : *The New Hollstein Dutch and Flemish Etchings, Engravings and Woodcuts, 1450-1700*, cat. 20, p. 23.

XI.22 WORKSHOP OF SEBASTIAN HANN : BOX WITH LID

1644–1713
Gilded silver, 22.5 x 14 cm
Budapest, Iparművészeti Múzeum, inv. E.61.7.1-3

This major piece, once in the collection of the Esterhazy Princes, came from the most brilliant Transylvanian workshop, that of Sebastian Hann (1614–1713), who was born in Slovakia and settled in Hermannstadt, or Sibiu. That wealthy town housed many craftsmen who had trained in Nuremberg and Augsburg. Here the scene of the virtues is directly inspired by Peter Flötner's own style. The circulation of motifs was not always due to the dissemination of engraving in Europe. It owed much to the dominant position of the cities that supplied the great goldsmiths and also offered famous and highly prized centres for apprenticeship. However, Transylvanian goldwork was in no way a copy of what was produced in Germany. Through its richness and motifs, it possessed great originality. It literally recreated its models.

BIBLIOGRAPHY : Erika Kiss, conservator, Iparművészeti Múzeum Budapest, doctoral thesis, not yet published; Viorica Guy Marica, *Sebastian Hann. Leben und Werk eines berühmten siebenbürgischen Goldschmieds*, Bucharest, 1998; *A Celebration of Hungarian Gold and Silver, Gilbert Collection*, London, 2003, cat. 32, p. 98.

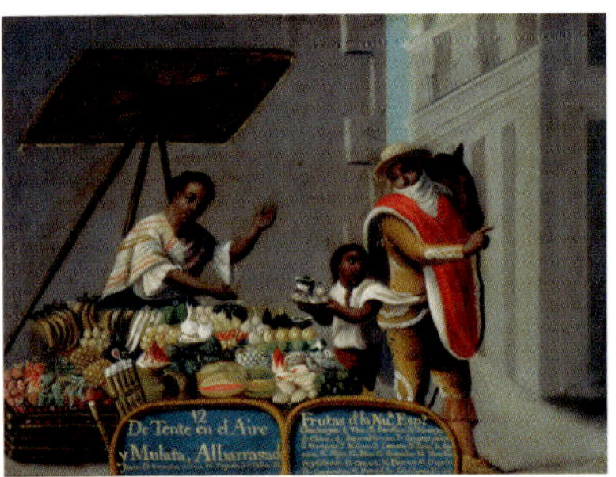

XII.5

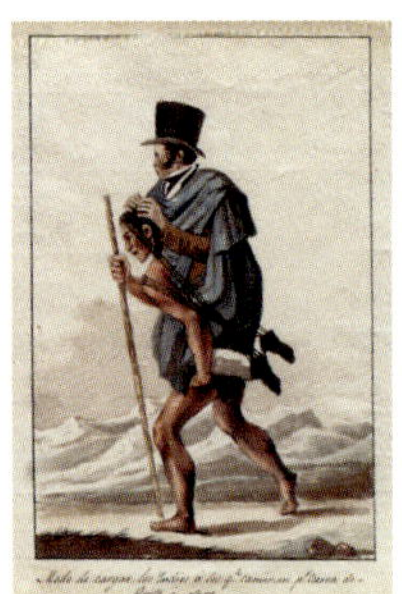

XII.6

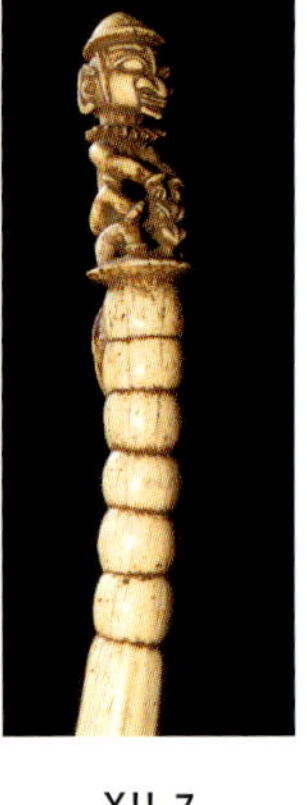

XII.7

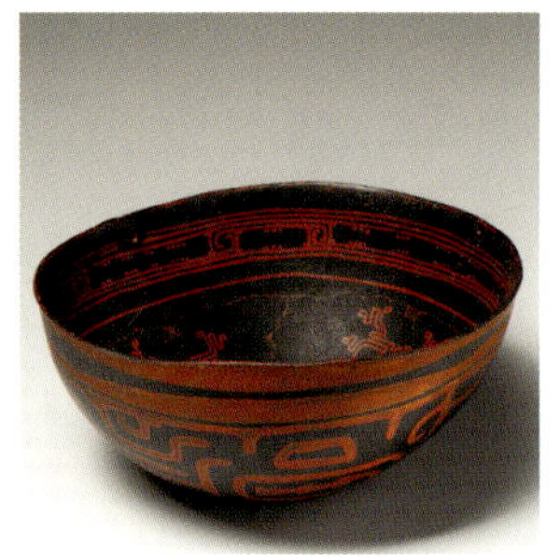

XII.8

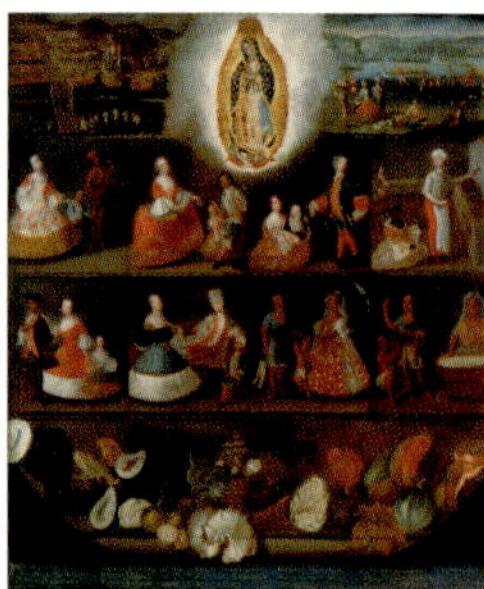

XII.9

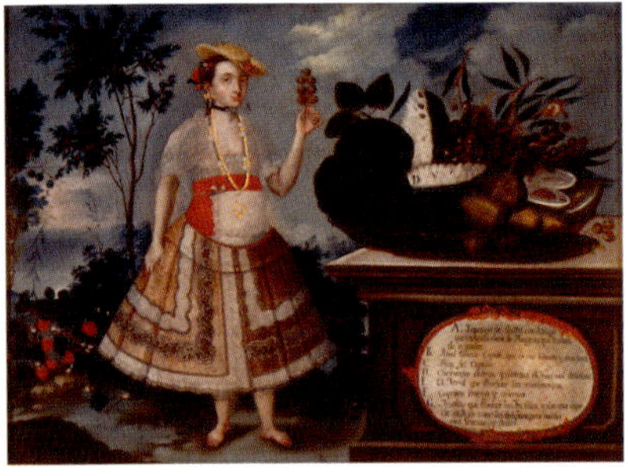

XII.10

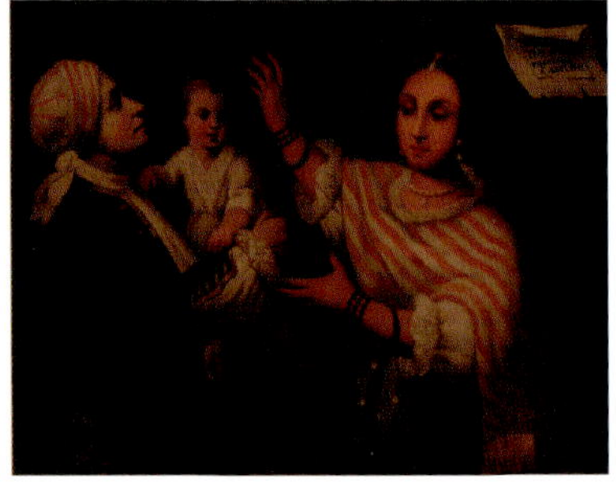

XII.11

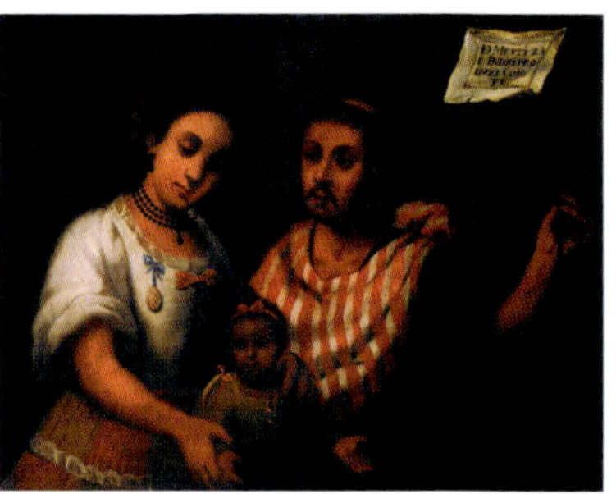

XII.12

BIBLIOGRAPHY: C. Garcia Saiz, *Pintura Colonial en el Museo de América, Madrid*, Madrid, 1980; *El mestizaje americano* (exhib. cat.), Museo de América, Madrid, 1985; Magnus Morner, 'The History of Race Relations in Latin America: Some Comments on the State of Research', *Latin American Research Review*, I/3 1966, pp. 17–44; Angel Rosenblat, *La poblacion indigena y el mestizaje en America*, Buenos Aires, 1954, 2 vols.

XII.4 ANONYMOUS, SERIES OF 16 'ESCENAS DE MESTIZAJE' '3. DE CASTIZO Y ESPAÑOLA ESPAÑOL'

18th century
Oil painting on copper, 36 x 48 cm
Madrid, Museo de América,
inv. MAM. 52
BIBLIOGRAPHY: see XII.3.

XII.5 ANONYMOUS, SERIES OF 16 'ESCENAS DE MESTIZAJE' '12. DE TENTE EN EL AIRE Y MULATA, ALBARRASEDO'

18th century
Oil painting on copper, 36 x 48 cm
Madrid, Museo de América,
inv. MAM. 61
BIBLIOGRAPHY: see XII.3.

XII.6 JEAN ROUVENEL: *MODO DE CARGAR LOS INDIOS A LOS QUE CARMINAN*

1789–94
Gouache on paper, 11.5 x 17 cm
Madrid, Museo de América, 2218

Alejandro Malaspina has been called the Spanish Captain Cook. Born into a prestigious Italian family, he succeeded in persuading Charles II of Spain to launch a scientific expedition that lasted for five years (1784–89). The chartered vessels – the *Descubierta* and the *Atrevida* – were equipped with hydrographic apparatus and carried a staff of naturalists and artists. After surveying the Atlantic and Pacific coasts of South America, the north-west coast of the USA and the Philippines, they explored the Marianas, the Philippines, New Zealand and Australia before returning to Spain via South America. On his return, Malaspina was initially feted; but his observations on the Spanish colonies were ignored, and his criticism of the political regime cost him a spell of imprisonment, and even exile to Genoa. An admirer of Adam Smith, Malaspina believed it was possible to govern the colonies on the principles of commercial economy. Artefacts from the expedition are preserved in the Museo de Ameéica, Madrid.

BIBLIOGRAPHY: M. Palau de Iglesias, *Catálogo de los dibujos, aguadas y acuarelas de la expedición Malaspina, 1789–1794*, Madrid, 1980; John Kendrick, *Alejandro Malaspina; Portrait of a Visionary*, Montreal, 1999.

XII.7 HORN

Sierra Leone, before 1794
Carved ivory, 77 x 12 cm
Avignon, Musée Calvet, inv. U166
Provenance: former Esprit Calvet collection

Esprit Calvet was born in Avignon in 1728 into a high-ranking family with its roots in the 15th century. An avid collector of books and objets d'art, he bequeathed his possessions to a public foundation that remains in existence and where the spirit of the Enlightenment still flourishes: the collection is a kind of 'laboratory of all the facts', where knowledge of the world is derived by empirical procedures. Calvet, however, failed to deduce the identity of this object, thinking he had a 10th-century medieval hunting-horn ...

BIBLIOGRAPHY: Yves Le Fur (ed.), *D'un regard l'autre: histoire des regards européens sur l'Afrique, l'Amérique et l'Océanie* (exhib. cat.), Paris, Musée du Quai Branly, 2006, cat. 160, pp. 140–41; Laurence Brockliss, *La République des Lettres et les médecins en France à la veille de a Révolution: le cas d'Esprit Calvet*, Gesnerus, Basle, 61, 2004, 3/4, pp. 254–81.

XII.8 CONTAINER

Guyana, in Europe before 1789
Painted calabash, diameter 11 x 21 cm
Paris, Musée du Quai Branly, inv. 71.1878.32.18.

This item was exhibited in the Jardin du Roi in Paris, an institution founded under Louis XIII in 1635 and incorporating a Cabinet of Curiosities, with exotic plants and strange objects representing the four corners of the world. After the French Revolution, the spirit of encyclopaedic enquiry led researchers to attempt a different form of classification: the theme was no longer the cosmological description of the world but the internal structure of plants, their functions and analogies with other known speci-

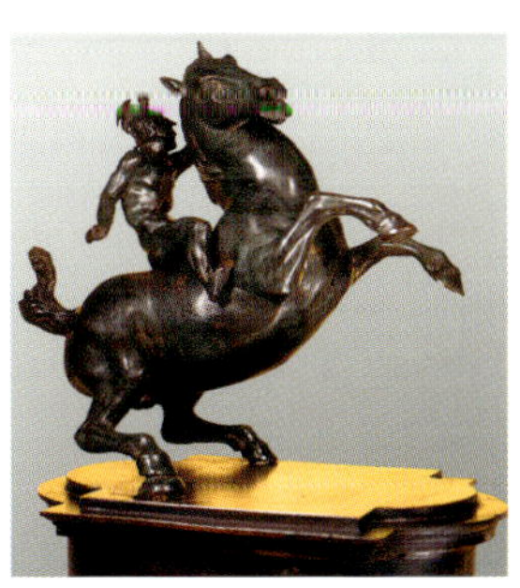

XIII.3

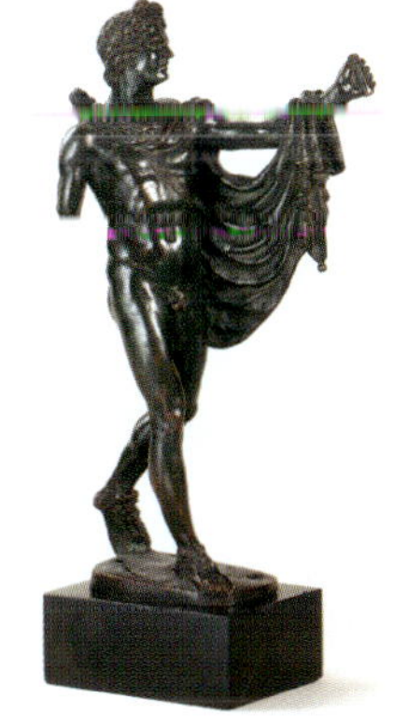

XIII.4

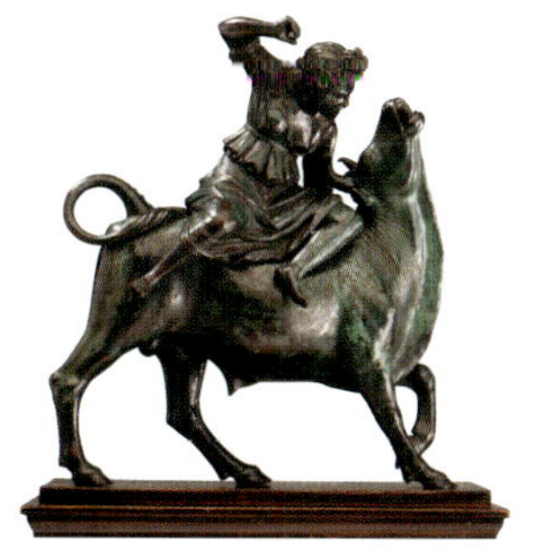

XIII.5

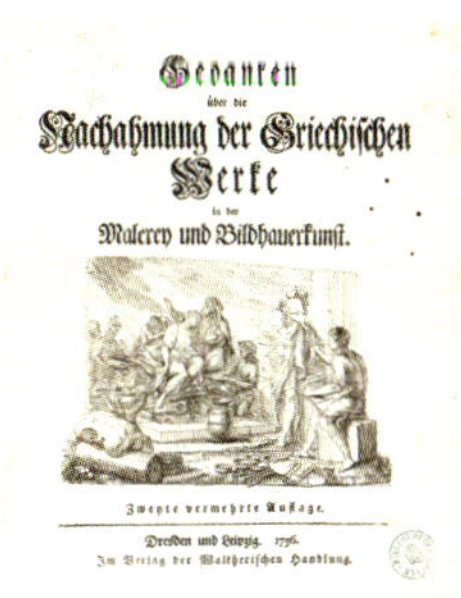
Gedanken
über die
Nachahmung der Griechischen
Werke
in der
Malerey und Bildhauerkunst.

Zweyte vermehrte Auflage.
Dresden und Leipzig, 1756.
Im Verlag der Waltherischen Handlung.

XIII.6

removed. Jordaens was fully aware of the Italian tradition and seems to have wanted to measure his crude realism against a pictorial, introspective style that was to be henceforth standard.

BIBLIOGRAPHY : R.-A. d'Hulst, Nora de Poorter, Marc Vandenven (eds), *Jacob Jordaens: 1593–1678*, Antwerp, 1993, pp. 208–10; Nora de Poorter, 'Seriewerk en recyclage: doorgedreven efficiëntie in het geroutineerde atelier van Jacob Jordaens', in Hans Vlieghe (ed.), *Concept, Design and Execution in Flemish Painting (1550–1700)*, Turnhout, 2000, pp. 213–32; Felix Billeter, *Zur künstlerischen Auseinandersetzung innerhalb des Rubenskreises: eine Untersuchung am Beispiel früher Historienbilder Jakob Jordaens und Anthony van Dycks*, Frankfurt am Main, 1993.

XIII.3 LEONARDO DA VINCI (ATTRIBUTED TO): EQUESTRIAN STATUE

*c.*1516–19?
Bronze, 24.3 cm
Budapest, Szépművészeti Múzeum, Inv. 5362

This magnificent bronze perhaps documents a planned statue intended for François I of France, Leonardo's last patron. The old artist might have represented the young monarch, with his keen interest in Italy, with the characteristics of King Arthur. This commission was not otherwise documented except by several drawings and some notes set down by Giovanni Paolo Lomazzo in his *Trattato de l'arte de la pittura* (Milan: Pontio, 1584); these notes are certainly interesting as Lomazzo had access to Leonardo's papers. After the death of François I, this precious bronze became the property of Giovanni Francesco Rustici, then of Leone Leoni, a sculptor at the court of Charles V. Leonardo was involved in several plans for equestrian monuments for princes – Ludovico Sforza and Gian Giacomo Trivulzio – all abortive, but fairly amply documented. A strange dynamism pervades this horseman, with both his arms outstretched, in the saddle of a rearing horse. The balance between the horse and his mount is astonishingly fine, but the tamed strength removes this equestrian monument *in nuce* from the calm serenity displayed by the philosopher emperor, the Marcus Aurelius of the Roman Capitol, then very much admired. The surface of the bronze, which has not been greatly smoothed, admirably preserves the freshness of the idea to which it owes its existence.

The attribution of this work to Leonardo is now severely contested. But its great quality and its closeness to the drawings of Leonardo can only serve to fuel new arguments on a regular basis, thus perpetuating, within the historiography of the most demanding art, the 'Leonardo da Vinci myth'.

BIBLIOGRAPHY : Virginia Bush, 'Leonardo's Sforza Monument and Cinquecento Sculpture', *Arte lombarda*, 50, 1978, pp. 47–68; Richard Stone, 'Antico and the Development of Bronze Casting in Italy at the end of the Quattrocento', *Metropolitan Museum Journal*, XVI, 1981 pp. 87–116; Maria Gulacsi-Agghazy, 'De la statuette equestre de Leonard du Musée des Beaux-Arts de Budapest', *Actas del XXIII Congreso Internacional de Historia del Arte; Espana entre el Mediterraneo y el Atlantico*, Granada, 1977, II, pp. 316–26.

XIII.4 ANDREA SANSOVINO (ATTRIBUTED): COPY OF THE APOLLO BELVEDERE (VATICAN)

c. 1505–13
Bronze, 30 cm
Budapest, Szépművészeti Múzeum, Inv. 84.13

This magnificent bronze has recently been attributed to Andrea Sansovino, a Florentine sculptor who was a pupil of Antonio Pollaiuolo, and who worked in Rome between 1505 and 1513, following an extended period of activity in Portugal. Sansovino presents the statue with a broken right arm, not restored. The first copy of the Apollo Belvedere, executed in bronze by Pier Jacopo Alari-Bonacolsi (1490s), has two restored arms. While the original in the Vatican (see bibliography for XIII.1) strikes an ambiguous pose, at once static and dynamic, Sansovino's figure incorporates definite movement. The surface, which is rougher than that of the original, is also more undulating, lending this reproduction the merit of being a genuine interpretation, full of finesse and life. Such bronzes, on a small scale but of monumental presence, were easily transportable, and carried the good news about the art of Antiquity throughout Europe.

BIBLIOGRAPHY : Francis Haskell, Nicholas Penny, *Taste and the Antique. The Lure of Classical Sculpture*, New Haven, 1981, no. 8, pp. 148–50 (bibl.); Herbert Beck, Peter C. Bol (eds), *Natur und Antike in der Renaissance: Ausstellung*, no. 4; Sergey Androssov, 'Bemerkungen zu Kleinplastiken Zweier Ausstellungen', in *Acta Historiae Artium*, 26, 1980, pp. 146–47; Norberto Gramaccini, *Mirabilia: das Nachleben antiker Statuen vor der Renaissance*, Mainz, 1996.

XIII.5 PADUAN MASTER: RAPE OF EUROPA

c. 1500
Bronze, green patina, 18.2 cm
Budapest, Szépművészeti Múzeum, Inv. 5363

The sculpture takes its theme from Ovid's *Metamorphoses*, and recalls Zeus's passion for Europa, the daughter of the king of Phoenicia. The king of the gods abducted her by disguising himself as a bull, and carried her away to Crete, to a new continent, which bears her name. The artist, an anonymous Paduan master, has chosen to express Europa's fury against her triumphal ravager, as evoked by Horace in a famous ode. The bull's dynamic position, its raised horns, and Europa's tense pose, are evidence of absolute mastery of the sculptural vocabulary applied to the classical works of Antiquity, as well as a fine knowledge of Latin literature.

BIBLIOGRAPHY : Volker Krahn (ed.), *Von allen Seiten schön: Bronzen der Renaissance und des Barock. Wilhelm von Bode zum 150. Geburtstag*. Skulpturensammlung, Staatliche Museen zu Berlin Preußischer Kulturbesitz, , Heidelberg, 1995, no. 33, pp. 208–09 (bibl.).

XIII.6 JOHANN JOACHIM WINCKELMANN: *GEDANKEN ÜBER DIE NACHAHMUNG DER GRIECHISCHEN WERKE IN DER MALEREI UND BILDHAUERKUNST*

2nd, enlarged edition, Dresden, Walther, 1756
Printed on paper, in quarto
Brussels, Bibliothèque royale de Belgique, Collections générales, Inv. II 44816. 4°

Son of a poor cobbler from Stendal, near Dresden, Johann Joachim Winckelmann managed to complete his studies by making great sacrifices. Fascinated by Greece, as he was by Antiquity, he first of all achieved prodigious scholarship in the field of ancient literary sources.

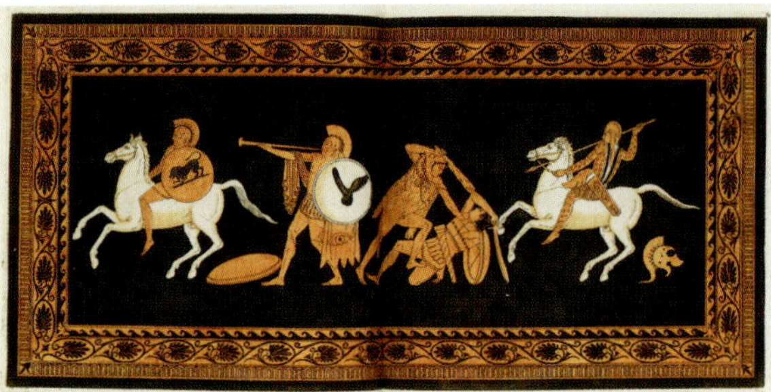
XIII.7

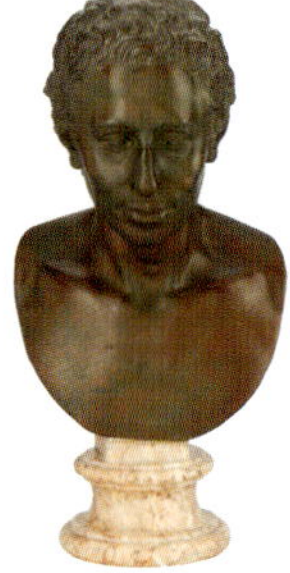
XIII.8

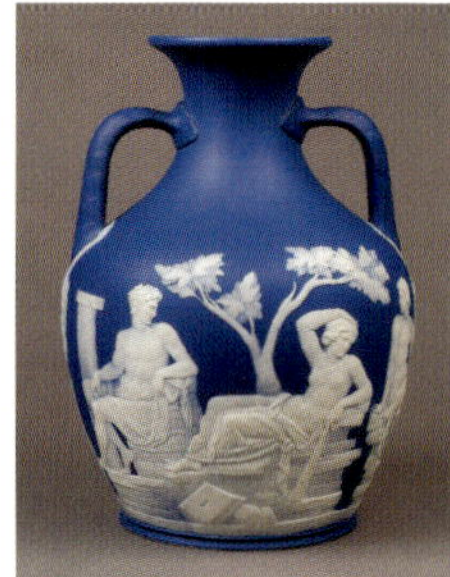
XIII.9

This work, which highly praises the grandeur of Greek art, is full of hope for recognition by the learned world. This edition, published a year after the first, is interesting because, apart from the famous essay that made him well known, it also includes the polemical pieces that followed its publication. In fact, the attack on Winckelmann is the work of the author himself, who hoped to thus increase the fame of his essay, and his ruse was a complete success! After converting to Catholicism, Winckelmann obtained the funds necessary to set off for Rome, where he spent the rest of his career. He became an art historian who used revolutionary methods in his *Geschichte der Kunst des Altertums* (History of the Art of Antiquity; 1764).

The etching adorning the title page of both the first and second editions was engraved by Adam Friedrich Öser, the young Winckelmann's artistic mentor. It shows the ancient Greek painter Timanthus of Kythnos (*c.* 406 BC) in the process of painting the sacrifice of Iphigenia before her father Agamemnon. The scene is a reminder that the sublime is the highest expression of art – instead of depicting the king's pain, Timanthus merely hints at it, by the king covering his face.

BIBLIOGRAPHY : Michael Wenzel, *Adam Friedrich Oeser. Theorie und Praxis in der Kunst zwischen Aufklärung und Klassizismus*, Weimar, 1999; H. Fullenwider, 'The Sacrifice of Iphigenia', in *French and German Art Criticism, 1755–1757, Zeitschrift für Kunstgeschichte*, vol. 52, issue 4 (1989), pp. 539–49; Pascal Griener, *L'esthétique de la traduction : Winckelmann, les langues et l'histoire de l'art (1755–1784)*, Geneva, 1998.

XIII.7 PIERRE FRANÇOIS HUGUES D'HANCARVILLE : *ANTIQUITÉS ÉTRUSQUES, GRECQUES ET ROMAINES TIRÉES DU CABINET DE M. HAMILTON*

Naples, Morelli, 1766–68, 2 vols. (Actual publication 1767–76; standard edition 4 vols)
Printed on paper, in folio. Vol. II
Neuchâtel, Bibliothèque publique et universitaire, inv. 86.1.2

This sumptuous publication is the fruit of a strange collaboration between a French scholar and adventurer, Pierre Hugues, called d'Hancarville, and Sir William Hamilton, British ambassador to the court of Naples. The latter was an avid collector of antique vases discovered during excavations throughout southern Italy, Campagna, Apulia and Sicily. He had no compunction in regularly selling parts of his collection to enrich himself; that described in the publication by Hancarville was left to the recently founded British Museum, in 1772. The author, on the other hand, had his heart set on producing a book on the history of the art of Antiquity, modelled on the famous book by Winckelmann (1764), hence the book's hybrid nature. The burin-engraved, hand-tinted plates and etchings are, however, marvellous reproductions of the ochres and blacks of Greek pottery. The vase decorations are furthermore 'flattened' and surrounded by a frieze to make them look like little tableaux. Ancient painting proper, as described by Pliny the Elder and Pausanias, having completely vanished, d'Hancarville regarded vase paintingas a source of new, concrete knowledge about painting in the ancient world. The engravings sold very well, they were framed in pairs, and used as decorative designs throughout Europe, from the Germanic states to England, by way of Russia.

BIBLIOGRAPHY : Sebastian Schütze, Madeleine Gisler-Huwiler, *The Collection of Antiquities from the Cabinet of Sir William Hamilton*, Cologne, 2004; Flashar, Gerhard Hiesel (eds), *Europa à la grecque : Vasen machen Mode*, Munich, 2000; Pascal Griener, *Le Antichità etrusche, greche e romane 1766–1776 di Pierre Hugues d'Hancarville. La pubblicazione delle ceramiche antiche della prima collezione Hamilton*, Rome, 1992; Ian Jenkins, Kim Sloan (eds), *Vases and Volcanoes : Sir William Hamilton and his Collections*, London, 1996.

XIII.8 FRIEDERICH WILHELM DOELL : BUST OF JOHANN JOACHIM WINCKELMANN

1777–78
Bronze, 48.2 cm
Provenance: Antiquities Society of Kassel
Kassel, Museumlandschaft Hessen, F 446
Bust by Luigi Valadier after a model by Friedrich Wilhelm Doell

The great archaeologist's appearance is not as normal : instead he is represented as a Roman or Greek. This bust owes its existence to a competition organised in 1777 by the Kassel Society of Antiquities, to reward the best eulogy to Winckelmann. One of the competitors, the scholar Johann Friedrich Reiffenstein, decided to submit a bust of the famous art historian instead of sending a manuscript. The sculptor, Wilhelm Friedrich Doell, who worked from iconographical documents, had trouble capturing a resemblance to a man who had been dead nine years. He reworked his bust on the basis of accounts by the historian's friends Anton Raphael Mengs, Anton von Maron and Reiffenstein. It is thus a memorial work in the true sense, which lends the historian the air of a great man of Antiquity.

BIBLIOGRAPHY : Hans Zeller, Ulrich Steinmann, *Zur Entstehung der Winckelmann-Büsten von Friedrich Wilhelm Doell*, Winckelmann Society annual presentation 1954–55, pp. 18–56; Arthur Schulz, *Die Kasseler Lobschriften auf Winckelmann*, Berlin, 1963; Petra Rau, Friedrich Wilhelm Doell (1750–1816) : *Leben und Werk*, Cluj-Napoca, 2003.

XIII.9 COPY OF THE PORTLAND VASE, WEDGWOOD FACTORY

19th-century replica derived from the 1790 version
Dark blue jasper dip, 31.5 cm
Brussels, Musées royaux d'art et d'histoire, Inv. 6024

The Portland vase is an exquisitely beautiful Roman cameo glass vase, held in the British Museum. Rubens knew of its existence from 1600, as did his friend, the scholar Nicolas Peiresc. It was acquired by Cardinal Francesco Barberini in 1626. To settle his gambling debts, one of the family's descendants sold it to an English antiquarian in Rome, James Byres, who immediately sold it to Sir William Hamilton, the British ambassador to Naples, who took it to London, where he sold it to a passionate collector of antique vases, the Duchess of Portland. Before selling it, Hamilton had Francesco Bartolozzi make a faithful engraving of the vase.

It was John Flaxman, the famous British engraver, who brought the beautiful vase to the attention of the businessman Josiah Wedgwood, who manufactured porcelain and high quality jasperware at Barlaston,

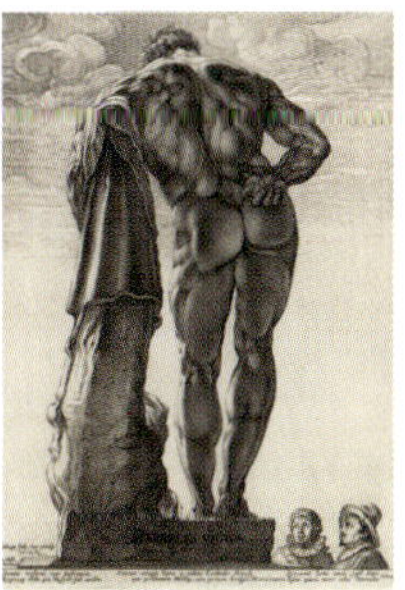
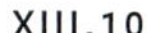

XIII.10

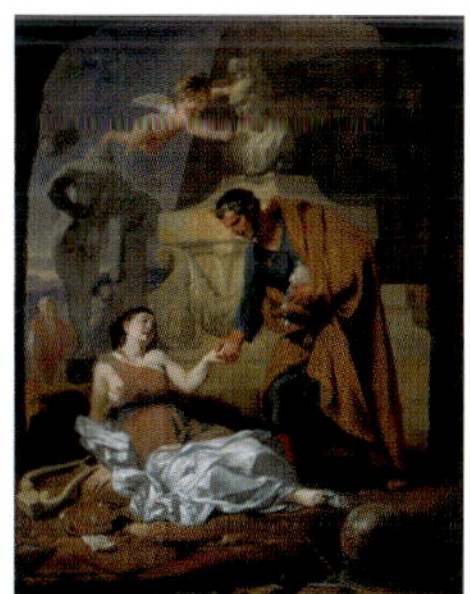

XIII.11

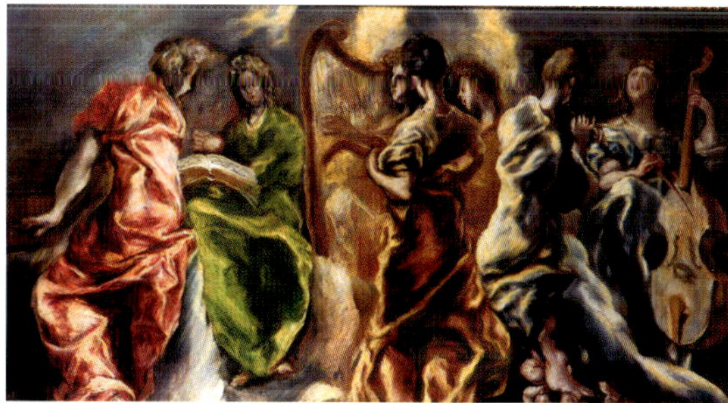

XIII.12

a place near Hanley, at a works which he named Etruria. From 1790, Wedgwood made around thirty luxury, jasperware copies of the famous original. The cameos represent unknown scenes, except for the central sdepiction of Thetis and Peleus. The expressive bas-relief studies on a deep ground first pleased the English aristocracy, then the European. Antiquity became an inexhaustible source of motifs for Wedgwood, who was keen to create mass demand for fashionable objects.

BIBLIOGRAPHY : Ian Jenkins, Kim Sloan (eds), *Vases and volcanoes : Sir William Hamilton and his Collections*, London, 1996 ; Nancy H. Ramage, 'Sir William Hamilton as Collector, Exporter, and Dealer : The Acquisition and Dispersal of His Collections, *American Journal of Archaeology*, vol. 94, no. 3. (July 1990), pp. 469–80 ; Milo Keynes, 'The Portland Vase : Sir William Hamilton, Josiah Wedgwood and the Darwins', *Notes and Records of the Royal Society of London*, vol. 52, no. 2, 1998, pp. 237–59.

XIII.10 HENDRIK GOLTZIUS : THE FARNESE HERCULES

Dated 1592 (published 1617)
Burin engraving, 41 x 30 cm
Berlin, Staatliche Museen zu Berlin, Kupferstich-kabinett, Inv. 683-11

The famous antique statue of Hercules was displayed in the courtyard of the Farnese palace, in Rome. It was admired and studied by Hendrik Goltzius, an artist originally from Germany, who had lived in Harlem. After a career as an engraver, in which he adopted the Mannerist style, he eventually abandoned this after his travels to Rome. In January 1591 he was drawing in the styles of Michelangelo, Raphael and Polidoro da Caravaggio, but especially in the manner of Antiquity. Forsaking Mannerism, he learnt how to observe Nature again. A new style, which arose from this encounter with Antiquity and the Italian masters, ensured that he was immensely successful on his return. This engraving by Hendrik Goltzius, executed after his journey to Italy, was not completed in his lifetime. It is proof that the artist knew how to render the wealth of musculature by a thick and regular interplay of cross-hatching, of a surprising regularity, which produces a very vivid effect. The panel has long been used as a source of reference for study of the human body, and it was given to young apprentice painters to copy.

BIBLIOGRAPHY : Francis Haskell, Nicholas Penny, *Taste and the Antique. The Lure of Classical Sculpture,* New Haven, 1981 no. 46, pp. 229–32 ; Anne-Claire de Liedekerke, *Fiamminghi a Roma : 1508-1608 ; artistes des Pays-Bas et de la Principauté de Liège à Rome à la Renaissance.* , Ghent, 1995, no. 102, p. 205 ; *Hendrick Goltzius (1558–1617) : Drawings, Prints and Paintings* (exhib. cat.), Zwolle, 2003 ; Aurelia Brandt, 'Goltzius and the Antique', *Print Quarterly*, 18, 2001, pp. 135–49 ; Glenn Harcourt (ed.), *Hendrick Goltzius and the Classical Tradition*, Los Angeles, 1992.

XIII.11 GÉRARD DE LAIRESSE : ALLEGORY OF PATRONAGE. MAECENAS AIDING AILING ART

After 1688
Oil on canvas, 62 x 48 cm
Caen, Musée des Beaux-Arts, Inv. 68

Lairesse deals with the tenuous bond that has to link progress in art and the generosity of patrons. Maecenas, the friend and protector of the Roman poet Horace, is shown in the process of raising up Art, depicted in the form of a pale-skinned woman, stretched out on the ground among her belongings. Pieces of gold fall from Maecenas' robe. A pyramid with a bust of Minerva, goddess of science, can be seen in the background and also the Farnese Hercules, symbol of virtue, and an example of the Classical ideal disseminated in the schools of painting during the Baroque era. Lairesse was inspired by Hendrik Goltzius' engraving ; he highlights a great Dutch artistic tradition that for more than a century had drawn on the best sources in Italy and was obliged to rely on powerful protectors, such as those in France or Italy.

BIBLIOGRAPHY : Lyckle de Vries 'Gerard de Lairesse : the theorist as an art critic', in Michèle-Caroline Heck (ed.), *Théorie des arts et création artistique dans l'Europe du Nord du XVIe au début du XVIIIe siècle*, Villeneuve d'Ascq, 2002, pp. 291–98 ; Lyckle de Vries, *Gerard de Lairesse : An Artist between Stage and Studio*, Amsterdam, 1998 ; Alain Roy, *Gérard de Lairesse* (1640–1711), Paris, 1992, no. P.211, p. 358.

ITALY, THE EUROPEAN CROSSROADS

As of the 15th century the journey to Italy constituted a decisive moment in an artist's training. Whether he accomplished it or still longed for it, agreed to it or refused it, it was part of his professional world. For too long art history has addressed this matter by evoking the Italian *influence*. This simplification hides the complexity of what was at stake : foreign artists in Rome changed what they had decided to study. Furthermore, in turn their output had an impact on Italy, whether they remained in the peninsula, or their works were admired there, or imported into the country. The typical image of Rome in the 17th and 18th centuries was even shaped substantially by foreign artists.

XIII.12 DOMENIKOS THEOTOKOPOULOS, KNOWN AS EL GRECO : CONCERT OF ANGELS

c. 1608–14
Oil on canvas, 112 x 205 cm
Athens, Ethniki Pinakothiki kai Mouseio Soutzou, inv. 152

Concert of Angels forms the upper part of a larger painting, no doubt cut down in the 19th century. The main section below it included a depiction of an Annunciation, commissioned with other canvases for the San Juan Bautista Hospital in Toledo. The lower section is now preserved in the Fundacion Central Hispano in Madrid.

This was the artist's last work and remains unfinished. It is testimony to a dazzling freedom of brushwork. Here the artist has not hesitated to borrow a figure – the angel playing the spinet – from a very secular painting by Titian, *Venus and the Musician* (1548 ; Prado, Madrid), ordered for Charles V. This erotic picture shows a spinet player fascinated by Venus' nudity – love and music are thus closely allied themes. Titian's *Venus*, probably given to Cardinal de Granvelle by Charles V, is likely to have been sold by the latter's descendants to the Habsburg Emperor Rudolf II, who doubtless offered it to King Philip III of Spain, in the Spanish branch of the Habsburg family, around 1603-4. One thus grasps the importance of the Habsburg princes' collections, which inspired artists throughout Europe : it is possible

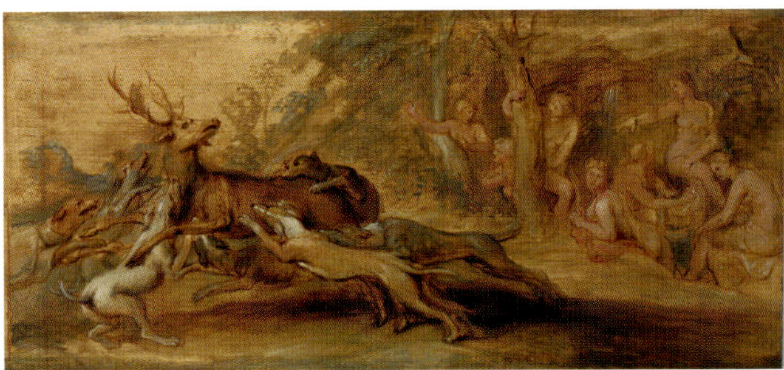

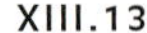

XIII.13

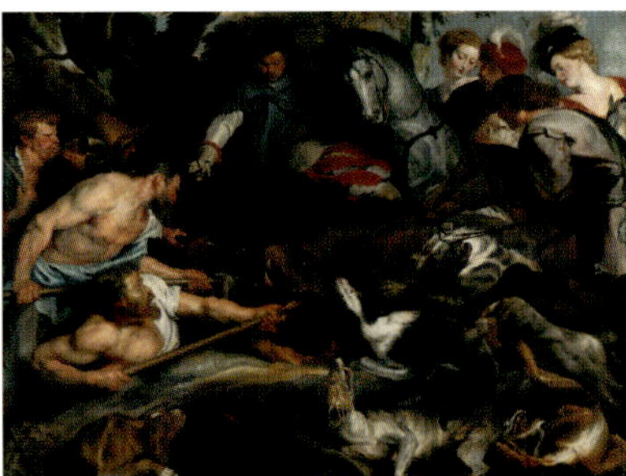

XIII.14

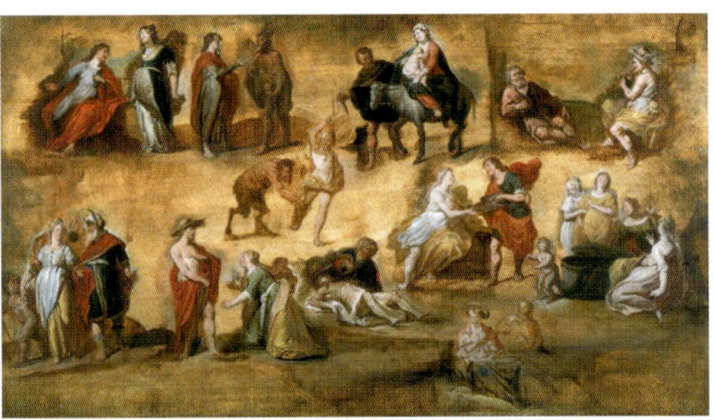

XIII.15

that El Greco admired the *Venus* during a stay in Madrid.

BIBLIOGRAPHY: *From El Greco to Delacroix*, Hermitage Museum, Lausanne, 2004, no. 9, pp. 141–42; *El Greco. Identity and Transformation*, Thyssen-Bornemysza Museum, Madrid, 1999, no. 89b; José Alvarez Lopera, *El Greco: estudio y catálogo*, Madrid, 2005, vol. I (sources).

XIII.13 PETER PAUL RUBENS: THE DEATH OF ACTAEON

c. 1639
Oil on panel, 24.1 x 52.1 cm
From a private European collection (courtesy Van Herck, Antwerp)
Provenance: J. Nieuwenhuys

This *modello* would be the matching piece to *The Hunt of Diana*. Transformed into a stag for having seen Diana and her nymphs naked, the hunter Actaeon is attacked by his own dogs, who rend him to pieces. In Titian's representation of this scene from Ovid's *Metamorphoses*, Actaeon still appears in partly human form. In the case of Rubens the metamorphosis is complete. Even if the goddess and her companions are shown, the composition centres on the sight of the dogs worrying furiously at their prey, as if it were a hunting scene. This work could also have served as a design for a series on the hunt ordered by Philip IV for the Alcazar palace in Madrid. The style of the animals, painted with light strokes in shades of brown and grey on the ochred ground, is more dynamic than that of the people.

BIBLIOGRAPHY: J. Held, *The Oil Sketches of Peter Paul Rubens: A Critical Catalogue*, 2 vols, Princeton, 1980, p. 305, no. 221; A. Balis, *Corpus Rubenanium*, XVIII, p. 247, no. 23a; Michael Jaffé, *Rubens*, complete catalogue, Milan, 1989, p. 374, no. 1397.

XIII.14 PETER PAUL RUBENS: THE BOAR HUNT

c. 1616–17
Oil on canvas, 250 x 320 cm
Marseilles, Musée des Beaux-Arts, inv. no. 103
Provenance: acquired from the artist in 1617 by Duke Maximilian I of Bavaria

Hunting, privilege of the aristocratic, was reputed to stimulate the manly virtues. The theme of hunting was extremely popular with enthusiasts from the elite, with whom this sport was popular. Antonio Tempesta's *Venationes* helped to spread a comprehensive iconography of hunting throughout the decorative arts in the 16th century. The theme was taken up again by Rubens, who introduced an emotional dimension and an intense dynamism. A hunter in elegant clothes administers the *coup de grâce* to a boar surrounded by beaters. In this case the artist, who stayed in Rome several times, drew his inspiration on the one hand from an antique sarcophagus, from which he borrowed the heightened plasticity, and on the other from Michelangelo's nudes, which is reflected in the three-dimensional nature of the characters. Rubens was the first to paint a hunting scene in such a format, generally used for tapestries or murals.

BIBLIOGRAPHY: Hans Vlieghe, *Rubens* (exhib. cat.), Lille, 2004, no. 79, pp. 150–51 (bibl.); Arnout Balis, *Corpus Rubenianum Ludwig Burchard*, XVIII, II, 1986, pp. 112–18, no. 4, fig. 40.

XIII.15 HANS JORDAENS III: RELIGIOUS AND MYTHOLOGICAL SCENES

Undated, first half of the 17th century
Oil on wood, 47.9 x 82.9 cm
London, private collection (courtesy Rafael Valls Limited)

These little scenes were as much life drawings for the studio of Jordaens III as for his own works. A painter of figures, above all the artist specialised in representations of Old Testament scenes. He collaborated on execution of landscapes, as well as cabinet paintings, especially with Joos de Momper and Cornelis de Baellieur. The groups are painted on a translucent, striated background. The degree of finished execution varies from a simple sketch, as for *Rest on the Flight into Egypt* and a finished painting such as *Christ and the Samarian Woman*. The positions of several figures, such as that of the *Christ as the Gardener*, have been retouched.

BIBLIOGRAPHY: F. C. Legrand, *Les peintres flamands de genre au XVIIe siècle*, Brussels, 1963, pp. 63–64.

XIII.16 ANTHONY VAN DYCK: PORTRAIT OF LUIGIA CATTANEO GENTILE (PRESUMED)

c. 1622
Oil on canvas, 147 x 112 cm
Strasbourg, Musée des Beaux-Arts, Inv. 200

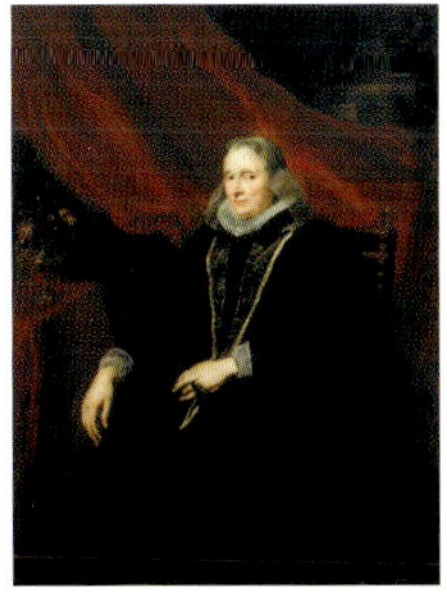

XIII.16

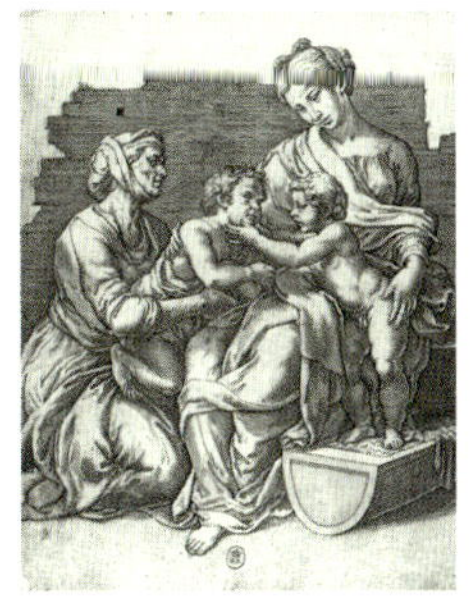

XIII.17

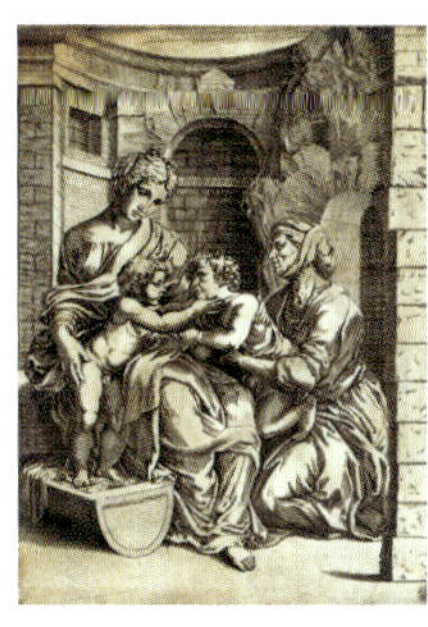

XIII.18

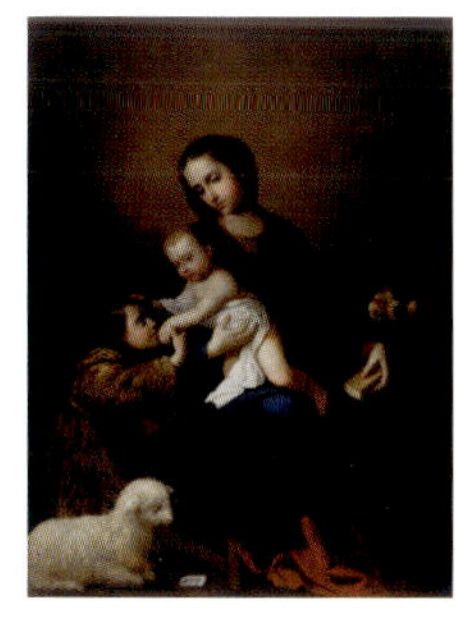

XIII.19

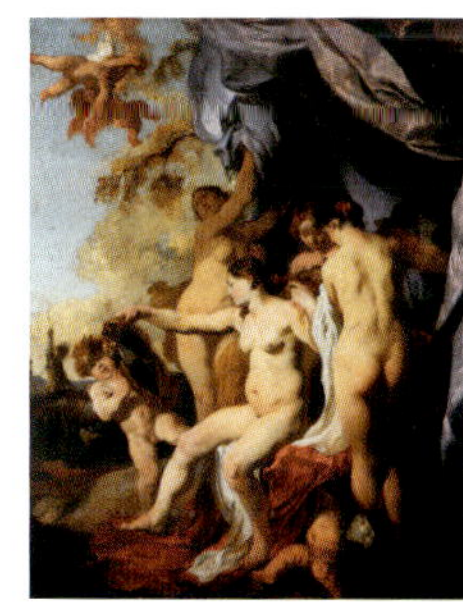

XIII.20

Following an apprenticeship in Rubens' studio, Van Dyck was attracted to England by the Earl of Arundel, and worked for King James I. He admired works by Titian in the magnificent Arundel collection. Between 1621 and 1627, he spent time in Italy, especially in Genoa, where he became the regular painter to the great families of the Republic. He supplied them with portraits of massive charm, in grandiose settings: the entire palette is dominated by red and brown. Over the years, Van Dyck developed a passion for Venetian painting, the expressive freedom of brushstrokes in which it indulged, and the brilliance of the poetic subjects chosen by Titian. Truly a European painter, Van Dyck combined Flemish realism with painting inspired by the Italian masters. The treatment of fabrics and their shades of red looks back to Titian. Van Dyck brilliantly restored aristocratic elegance to the life drawing, and its natural expression, with a technique that succeeded that of Rubens.

BIBLIOGRAPHY: Susan J. Barnes (ed.), *Van Dyck a Genova: grande pittura e collezionismo*, Milan, 1997, no. 35, pp. 226-9 (bibl.); Susan J. Barnes (ed.), Van Dyck. *A Complete Catalogue of the Paintings*, New Haven, 2004, p. 184.

XIII.17 GIAN GIACOMO CARAGLIO (AFTER RAPHAEL): LITTLE HOLY FAMILY

After 1518
Burin engraving, 25.8 x 21.7 cm
Paris, Bibliothèque nationale de France, Cabinet des estampes, Inv. Eb 6b res. Fol

Gian Giacomo Caraglio, born in Parma or Verona, was without doubt trained in the engraving workshop of Marc-Antonio Raimondi, who circulated many of Raphael's compositions. Caraglio reproduced engravings by Raimondi and paintings by Perin del Vaga or Rosso Fiorentino. He continued his career as a medal maker to the King of Poland in Kraków. In this case the painting reproduces a masterpiece then attributed to Raphael, the *Holy Family* (1518, Louvre, now attributed to Giulio Romano for the execution in oils), a composition that is found in changed form in the *Madonna* said to have belonged to Francis I (1518, Louvre). This type of plate was prominent in the studios and served as a composition sketch that was easy to transform, all the more so since Raphael enjoyed considerable regard.

BIBLIOGRAPHY: *'Raphael invenit': stampe da Raffaello nelle collezioni dell'Istituto Nazionale per la Grafica*, Rome, 1984, no. XXXIX, 1, pp. 207, 743; *Raphaël dans les collections françaises*, Paris, 1983, no. 65, pp. 375–76.

XIII.18 CORNELIS MASSYS (AFTER GIAN GIACOMO CARAGLIO): REVERSE OF THE PLATE OF THE LITTLE HOLY FAMILY

After 1518
Burin engraving, 32.2 x 26.7 cm
Paris, Bibliothèque nationale de France, Cabinet des estampes, Inv. Eb 6 ba res

The son of Quentin Massys, the celebrated Flemish painter, Cornelis Massys belonged to a generation of artists passionate about Italian painting. His burin engraving reproduces the composition already created by Caraglio, while reversing it. Reproduction engraving in the 16th century was often unfaithful, because the aim was frequently to translate, to convey an idea, rather than to reproduce a specific work in precise detail. Commercial imperatives played a role in this case: the original motif, engraved as such on a new copper plate, could only produce reversed prints.

BIBLIOGRAPHY: *The New Hollstein Dutch and Flemish Etchings, Engravings and Woodcuts, 1450–1700*, XI p. 183, no. 34.

XIII.19 FRANCISCO DE ZURBARÁN: VIRGIN MARY WITH CHILD AND THE YOUNG ST JOHN THE BAPTIST

1662
Oil on canvas, 169 x 127 cm
Bilbao, Museo de Bellas Artes, Inv. 69/249

This work is the last known canvas by Zurbarán before his death. Taking his inspiration from an engraving after Raphael's *Holy Family* (1518, Louvre), he has completely changed the feeling, in order to give it his own artistic values: simplification of the brown ground, which is discreetly illuminated by the Virgin's naturalistic halo, and finally use of a chiaroscuro that highlights the infant Jesus. The engraving provided a graceful compositional sketch for the artist, who honours a revered example, but knows how to use it for his own ends.

BIBLIOGRAPHY: *Zurbarán*, Paris, 1988, no. 71, pp. 339–42 (bibl.).

XIII.20 JOHANN LISS: VENUS IN FRONT OF THE MIRROR

1625–26
Oil on canvas, 83 x 69 cm
Florence, Polo Museale Fiorentino, Galleria degli Uffizi, Inv. 1890 2179
Provenance: former collection of Cardinal Jean-Charles de Medici

The composition, full of nobility, is reminiscent of a work by Rubens. The subject highlights Venus' flesh and that of her followers, thanks to a light sustained and inflected by a large, solid blue drapery to the right of the painting. The delicate brushwork, and the golden tones reminiscent of Veronese, reveal that the artist quickly assimilated the major traits of painting in Venice, where he was then staying. The synthesis that he produces is harmonious. At that time Venetian painting was highly prized by the Medicis of Florence, as by most European collectors.

XIII.21 JUSEPE DE RIBERA: APOLLO FLAYING MARSYAS

1637
Oil on canvas, 202 x 255 cm
Brussels, Musées royaux des Beaux-Arts de Belgique, Inv. 3445

The subject is drawn from Ovid's *Metamorphoses*. Marsyas, having claimed that he played the flute more divinely than Apollo played the lyre, has to submit to a duel with the god. He loses the competition and Apollo has him flayed alive. The tale is to be read allegorically, to indicate that the artist must rise above the sensual world in order to be creative. Ribera, who left his native country of Spain quite young, settled in Rome and then in Naples, where he died after a brilliant career. An artist true to the chiaroscuro effects and realism dear to Caravaggio – of which the figure of Marsyas is tangible proof – he changed style after 1635. Here the figure of Apollo is idealized in classical style and his white skin is almost reminiscent of a painting by Guido Reni, who also

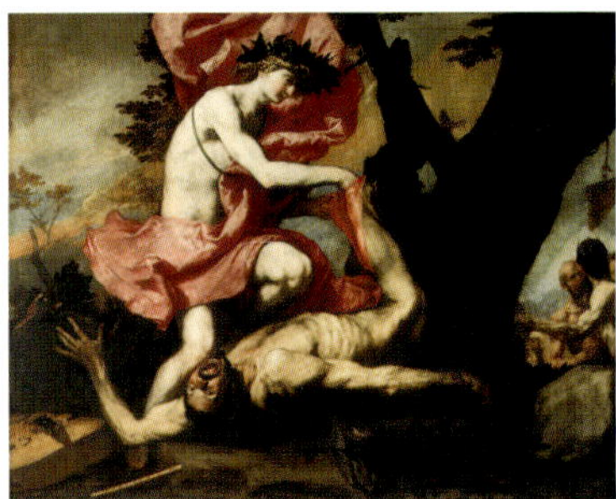

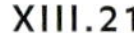

XIII.21

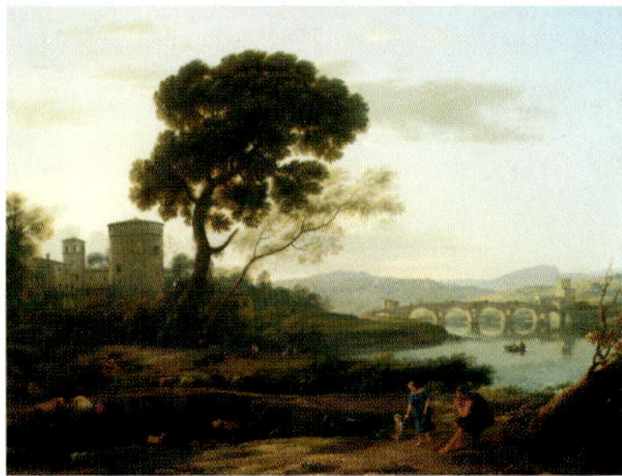

XIII.22

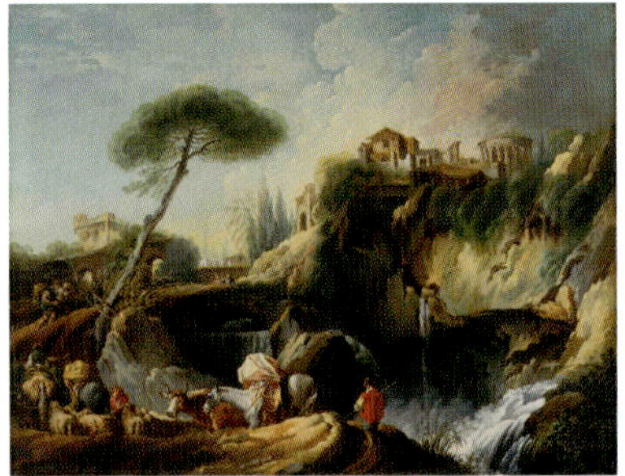

XIII.23

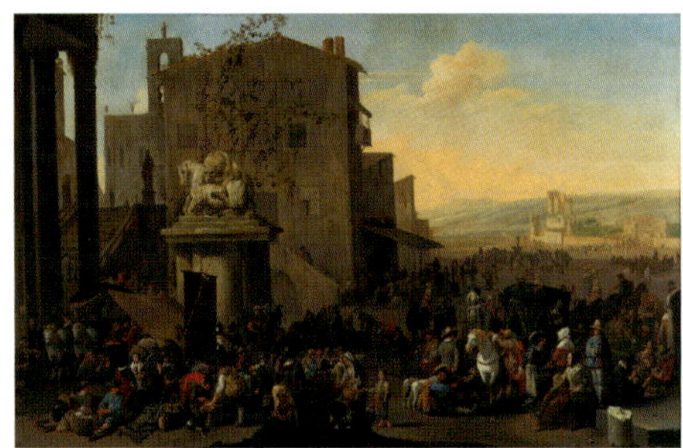

XIII.24

resided in Naples in 1621–22. Two figures here embody two artistic movements, which the artist attempts to reconcile in one and the same painting.

BIBLIOGRAPHY : Christopher Brown, *L'Age d'Or de la peinture espagnole*, Paris, 1991, pp. 186–88 ; Museum voor Oude Kunst, Brussels, 2001, pp. 138–39 ; Nicola Spinosa, *Ribera : l'opera completa*, Naples, 2003.

XIII.22 CLAUDE LORRAIN : LANDSCAPE WITH VIEW OF THE MOLLE BRIDGE, ROME

1645
Oil on canvas, 73.7 x 96.5 cm
Birmingham Museums and Art Gallery, inv. 1955P111

One of Claude Lorrain's mature landscapes, this canvas is characterized by great compositional precision, by a restrained economy of detail and finally by a supreme artistic view of the scenery depicted. A tall pine spreads its compact foliage in the centre of the scene ; a nearby tower acts as a metaphor for the tree's strength, a recurring technique used by this artist. A herd of cattle graze in the foreground, while a shepherd and his companion play with a dog. The ancient bridge, which dates from the 15th century, straddles the Tiber to the north of Rome, and seems to appear from a crystal-clear morning, bathed in fresh light. Lorrain has created a classic vision of the Roman Campagna, which would have a significant impact on the art of gardening in Europe, and especially in England, in the 18th century. This painting was acquired by Robert Dingley, before entering the collection of Lord Ashburnham from 1760 ; almost half of Lorrain's works are in English collections.

BIBLIOGRAPHY : Marcel Röthlisberger, *Claude Lorrain : The Paintings*, vol.1.2, New Haven, 1961.

XIII.23 FRANÇOIS BOUCHER : VIEW OF TIVOLI WITH THE TEMPLE OF VESTA

After 1730
Oil on canvas, 74 x 95 cm
Provenance : former collection of Count Carl Gustaf Tessin (1741), then of Princess Ulrike of Sweden (1749)
Stockholm, Nationalmuseum, NM 5035

Boucher was still young when he completed this *rocaille* fantasy, in which only the occasional detail recalls the place so popular with tourists in Rome. The artist had already had so much success that he produced his works in a studio, with the help of numerous assistants guided by the master's drawings. Boucher touched up the canvases before delivering them. At the time, French taste was experiencing an exceptional success throughout Europe. This painting was purchased by Count Tessin, Swedish ambassador to the court of France, and a great art lover.

BIBLIOGRAPHY : *François Boucher (1703–1770)*. Grand Palais, Paris, 1986 no. 16, pp. 136–38 (with version of Boulogne sur Mer) ; Anna Lena Lindberg, 'Masked desire ? : Carl Gustav Tessin and his "chicken picture"', *Art Bulletin of Nationalmuseum Stockholm*, 8/2001, pp. 72–79 ; Per Bjurström (ed.), *Carl Gustaf Tessin och konsten : en konstbok*, Stockholm, 1970.

XIII.24 JOHANNES LINGELBACH : THE CAMPO VACCINO IN ROME

1653
Oil on canvas, 110 x 188.5 cm
Brussels, Musées royaux des Beaux-Arts de Belgique, Inv. 3454

The Amsterdam artist, who visited France and Italy between 1642 and 1650, composed his paintings with elements from his vineyard, memories and drawings ; the sculpture representing a lion attacking a horse was thus located in the Palais des Conservateurs, and not outdoors. The antique sculptures in public collections, and the Roman ruins, transformed the Eternal City into a vast museum, dotted with picturesque little figures, a speciality of the *bamboccianti*, or 'puppets', a group of Dutch genre painters working in Rome. Lingelbach's work was very popular in Italy, especially in Venice, where it inspired Luca Carlevarijs.

BIBLIOGRAPHY : Thomas Kren, 'Jan Lingelbach in Rome', *The J. Paul Getty Museum Journal*, 10, 1982, pp. 45–62 ; Giuliano Briganti, Ludovica Trezzani, Laura Laureati, *I Bamboccianti : pittori della vita quotidiana a Roma nel Seicento*. Rome, 1983.

THE PRINCELY COURTS : THEATRES OF EUROPEAN ART

The extent of the bonds between diplomacy and the arts is still not fully known. Certainly major artists

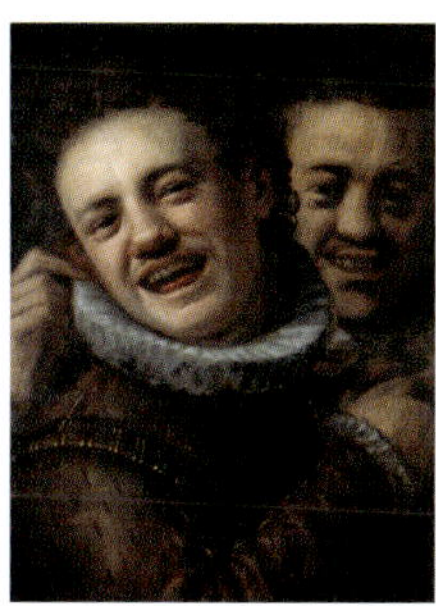

XIII.25

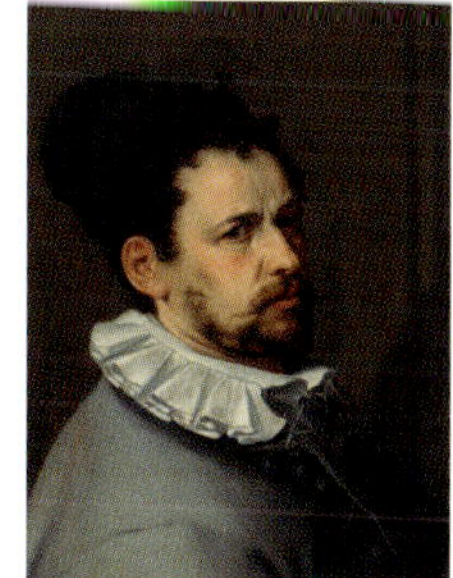

XIII.26

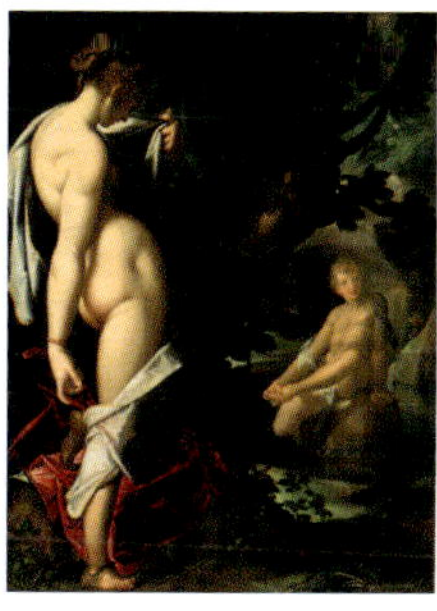

XIII.27

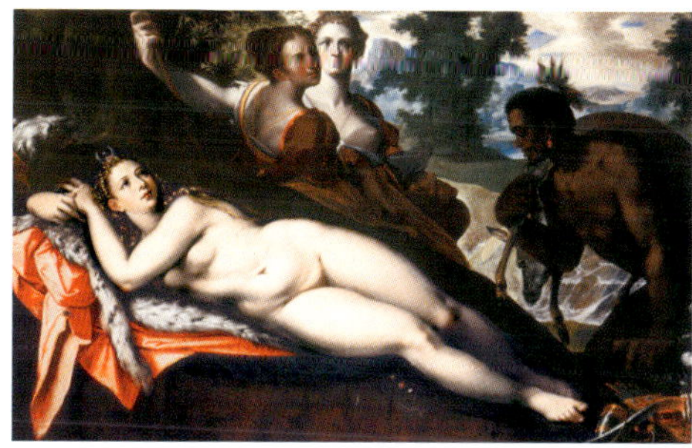

XIII.28

such as Rubens or Van Dyck assumed delicate diplomatic missions. Royalty actively favoured the exchange of paintings or artists between courts, careful to attract the greatest masters to themselves, but also to spread the effect of their patronage. The figure of the Emperor Rudolf II is used as a paradigmatic example here.

XIII.25 HANS VON AACHEN : TWO YOUNG MEN LAUGHING

c. 1575
Oil on oak panel, 48 x 38.5 cm
Kroměříž, Czech Republic, Archbishopric Olomouc Episcopal Palace, Inv. KE 3177 O 283
Provenance : collection of Bishop Karl von Liechtenstein-Kastelkorn, 1673

This is a double self-portrait, the oldest painting by the artist, before he left Cologne for Italy. The cheerful expression, the gesture by one of the doubles pointing at the other, betrays the sense of humour and the critical mind of a young man who has his future before him, and who knows it. It is possible to detect an allusion to Greek Antiquity, which contrasts Democritus' optimistic vision of the world with Heraclitus' pessimistic one.

BIBLIOGRAPHY : Ladislav Daniel, Milan Togner, *Gemäldegalerie Kroměříž : Katalog der Gemäldesammlung des Erzbischöflichen Schlosses in Kroměříž (Kremsier). Kroměříž*, 1999, pp. 26 ; *Rudolf II*, I.1, p. 389 ; *Rudolf II and Prague. The Court and the City* (exhib. cat.), Prague, 1997, p. 114.

XIII.26 BARTHOLOMAEUS SPRANGER : SELF-PORTRAIT

1580s
Oil on canvas, 60.2 x 44.3 cm
Vaduz-Vienna, Sammlung des Fürsten von und zu Liechtenstein, Inv. GE946
Provenance : collection of the Habsburg Emperor Rudolf II

Unlike Hans von Aachen, the artist depicts himself in elegant clothes, but with a worried air. At the time of the portrait he had just arrived in Prague, and is demonstrating his abilities.

BIBLIOGRAPHY : *Prag um 1600 : Kunst und Kultur am Hofe Kaiser Rudolfs II*. Kunsthistorisches Museum, Vienna, 1988, no. 153, p. 275.

XIII.27 BARTHOLOMAEUS SPRANGER : HERMAPHRODITUS AND SALMACIS

c. 1585
Oil on canvas, 110 x 81 cm
Vienna, Kunsthistorisches Museum, inv. 2614
Provenance : collection of the Habsburg Emperor Rudolf II

The painting depicts Hermaphroditus, the son of Hermes and Aphrodite, and the naiad, Salmacis, who is seduced by his beauty at the river where he was bathing (Ovid, *Metamorphoses*, IV, 285–415). The naiad declares her love but is spurned by the young man, who has never known passion. She then makes as though to withdraw, watches him from the shadows, then dives into the water to join and embrace him. She implores the gods to make her one with her lover, and they answer her prayers, fusing Hermaphroditus and Salmacis so they are at once man and woman. Spranger chose to represent the brief moment at which the naiad separates from her lover, but cannot long resist his allure. This was part of a series of paintings on subjects drawn from Ovid's *Metamorphoses*, and intended to decorate the imperial apartments. The themes chosen illustrate the loves of the gods, but in the eyes of the Emperor these naked and amorous bodies are doubtless metaphors for strange alchemical forces that first repel then attract. The artist shows his mastery of Mannerist painting – twisted bodies, compact and dynamic compositions, based on the principle of a battle between two opposing forces. These rhetorical opposites are echoed in the compositional rhythms planned by the artist from the initial sketches ; the *narrative*, whatever it may be, must accommodate the composition. In Prague, Spranger learnt how to create courtly art in honour of his patron.

BIBLIOGRAPHY : E. Fučíková, Das Schicksal der Sammlungen Rudolfs II. vor dem Hintergrund des Dreißigjährigen Krieges', in Jacques Thuillier (ed.), *1648 : Paix de Westphalie*, Paris, 1999, pp. 273–93 ; E. Fučíková (ed.), *Rudolf II and Prague : The Court and the City*, London, 1997, no. 1.77, p. 404 (prev. bibl.).

XIII.28 BARTHOLOMAEUS SPRANGER : DIANA AFTER THE HUNT

1595–1605
Oil on canvas, 129 x 199.5 cm
Budapest, Szépművészeti Múzeum, Inv. 351

Despite his limited ability to understand Venetian painting, here Spranger tried to use the iconography of the reclining Venus, dear to Titian and to Palma the Elder. Emperor Rudolf II's collection, in Prague, provided the artist with a whole range of experiences, but he rarely availed himself of them if they took him far from his usual practices, as is the case here. The life drawing's natural pose is far removed from the rhetoric of Mannerist gestures that he used intensively.

BIBLIOGRAPHY : *Prag um 1600 : Kunst und Kultur am Hofe Rudolfs II*, 1988, no. 160, p. 281 ; E. Fučíková (ed.), *Rudolf II and Prague : the Court and the City*, London, 1997, no. II 1.91, p. 407 ; Thomas Da Costa Kaufmann, *The School of Prague : Painting at the Court of Rudolf II*, Chicago, 1988, no. 20.60, p. 269 ; Jak Katalan, 'Some Drawings by Bartolomeus Spranger after Italian Masters', in *Dialoghi di storia dell'arte*, 1997, no. 4/5, p. 192–95.

XIII.29 BARTHOLOMAEUS SPRANGER : PSYCHE AND SLEEPING CUPID

After 1602
Pen and brush in brown ink, charcoal on chalk-finish paper
Leiden,Universiteitsbibliotheek, Inv. 1070

The scene represents a famous episode from the story of Psyche, contained in the *Metamorphoses, or The Golden Ass* by Lucius Apuleius, a Latin author of the 2nd century AD. Psyche abandons herself to forbidden contemplation of her divine lover, Cupid, whilst he sleeps ; a drop of hot oil falls onto the god's skin and awakens him. Spranger greatly admired Hendrik Goltzius, from whom he learned valuable lessons. He visited the Netherlands in 1602, and must have examined the paintings of Goltzius, who started to paint around 1600, after having been an engraver. This more direct confrontation with the work of Goltzius, which he already knew from several paintings, allowed him to address the study of the human body in a more immediate way. Here the two figures are bound by choreography typical of Spranger, but their characters are finely captured, and betray an interest in observing specific poses, and not just in expressive physical outlines.

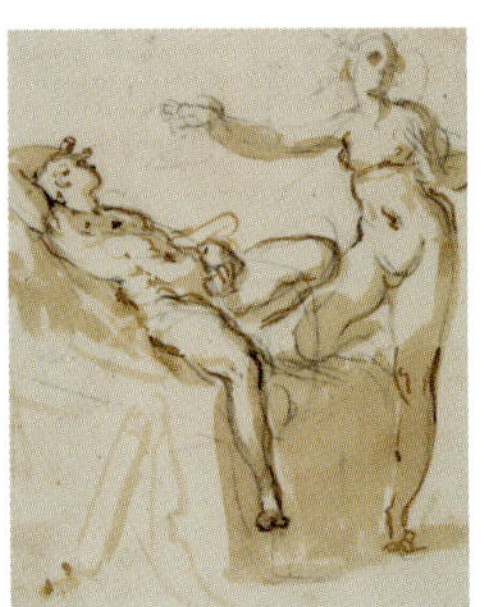

XIII.29

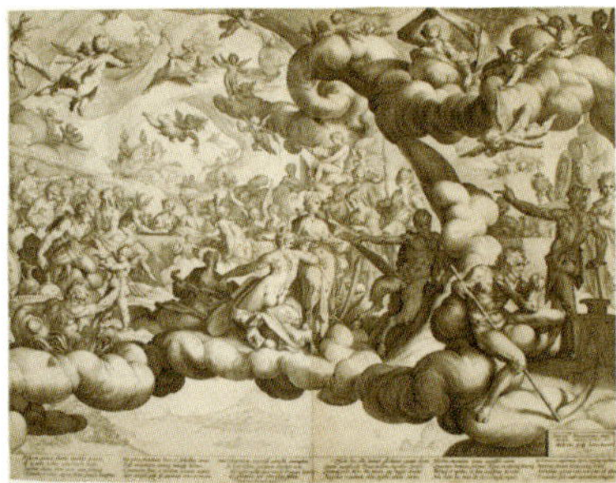

XIII.30

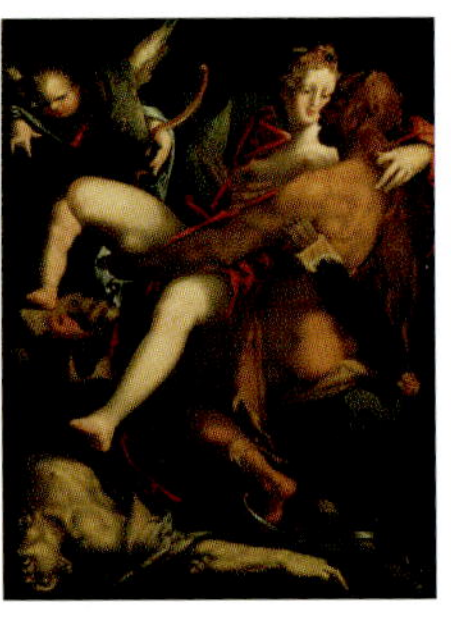

XIII.31

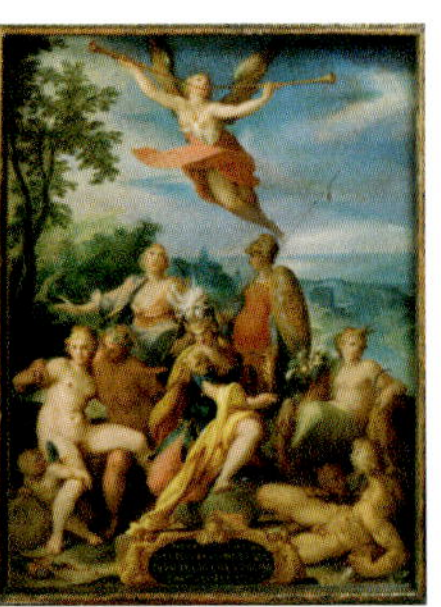

XIII.32

BIBLIOGRAPHY : E. Fučíková (ed.), *Rudolf II and Prague : The Court and the City*, Prague Castle Administration, London, 1997, no. 1.284, p. 448 (bibl.).

XIII.30 HENDRIK GOLTZIUS (AFTER BARTHOLOMAEUS SPRANGER) : THE FEAST OF THE GODS AND THE MARRIAGE OF CUPID AND PSYCHE

1587
Burin engraving, 43 x 56.5 cm
Antwerp, Plantijn-Moretus Museum / Stedelijk Prentenkabinet Inv. OP 18590

The theme of this engraving is borrowed from Apuleius' *Metamorphoses, or The Golden Ass*, an allegory on the soul's fate, which provides both artists with a welcome pretext. In a sky populated by clouds and fabulous creatures, the gods of Olympus, naked, give an intimation of the artists' virtuosity in the field of anatomy, which has been consolidated by study of Antiquity. Spranger humorously presents us with divinities busying themselves with preparing the feast, each according to their talents. The prodigious monumentality of the whole constitutes a *tour de force* that made Goltzius and Spranger very famous.

BIBLIOGRAPHY : Annette Strech, 'Spranger inventor : Überlegungen zu Entstehung und Funktion von Stichen nach Sprangers Werken', in Lubomír Jan Konečný; (ed.), *Rudolf II, Prague and the World*, Prague, 1998, p. 201-10; Dorothy Limouze, 'Engraving as Imitation : Goltzius and his Contemporaries', in Hessel Miedema (ed.), *Goltzius Studies : Hendrick Goltzius (1558–1617)*, Zwolle, 1993 (Nederlands Kunsthistorisch Jaarboek, 42/43, 1991/1992). p. 439–53; *Hendrick Goltzius (1558–1617) : Drawings, Prints and Paintings*, Rijksmuseum, Amsterdam, Zwolle, 2003; Walter Melion, 'Hendrick Goltzius's Project of Reproductive Engraving', *Art History 1990*, v. 13, no. 4, pp. 458–87.

XIII.31 BARTHOLOMAEUS SPRANGER : HERCULES, DEÏANEIRA AND NESSUS

c. 1585
Oil on canvas, 112 x 82 cm
Vienna, Kunsthistorisches Museum, Inv. 2613
Provenance : collection of the Habsburg Emperor Rudolf II

This painting is part of a series devoted to Ovid's *Metamorphoses*, like *Hermaphroditus and Salmacis* (XIII.26). The painting illustrates Hercules' strength, which saves his wife Deïaneira, who had been ravished by the centaur Nessus. The slain ravisher, the putto symbolic of love, the embracing husband and wife, all seem to be caught up in a powerful movement that sweeps the whole of the painting.

BIBLIOGRAPHY : *Prag um 1600 : Kunst und Kultur am Hofe Rudolfs II*. Freren, 1988, no. 154, pp. 275–77; Thomas Da Costa Kaufmann, *The School of Prague : Painting at the Court of Rudolf II*. Chicago, 1988, no. 20.6, p. 251.

XIII.32 BARTHOLOMAEUS SPRANGER : THE ALLEGORY OF RUDOLF II

1592
Oil on copper, 23 x 17 cm
Vienna, Kunsthistoriches Museum, Inv. 1125
Provenance : probably the Habsburg Emperor Rudolf II

In the centre, beneath a Winged Victory sounding a trumpet, Roma symbolizes Holy Roman Empire. On the left Venus and Bacchus, on the right Ceres, symbol of abundance, and ultimate wisdom. The Latin inscription calls for a new crown to adorn Rudolf's head, probably an allusion to his desire to seize Constantinople from the Turks.

BIBLIOGRAPHY : Thomas Da Costa Kaufmann, *The School of Prague : Painting at the Court of Rudolf II*, Chicago, 1988, no. 20.54, p. 267–68.

XIII.33 JOSEPH HEINTZ THE ELDER (?) : THE FLIGHT INTO EGYPT BY CORREGGIO (COPY)

1592 (?)
Oil on wood, 47 x 37 cm
Prague, Národní Galerie, Inv. O 10740

Rudolf II's collection included at least two paintings by Correggio : in fact he owned a *Leda* and a *Ganymede* given by the King of Spain, Philip III. Heintz' contemporaries loved to order good copies of famous paintings that they liked; most collections included copies and originals, juxtaposed on the same picture rails.

BIBLIOGRAPHY : Jürgen Zimmer, *Joseph Heintz der Ältere : Zeichnungen und Dokumente*, Munich, 1988; Jürgen Zimmer, *Joseph Heintz der Ältere als Maler*, Weissenhorn, 1971.

PRINCES, COLLECTORS AND ARTISTS IN THE CLASSICAL AGE

The Baroque era was the golden age of agents and go-betweens – bankers, merchant-diplomats, painters who may have had modest careers, but were great purveyors of paintings. More than ever before these intermediaries benefited from the problems caused by dispersion of the main royal collections; some of them were able to offer complete collections, ready made. The rate of movement of masterpieces was extraordinary. This Europe overflowing with art was stimulated by three events : European sovereigns' admiration for the Madrid Habsburg collection, which gave rise to European com-

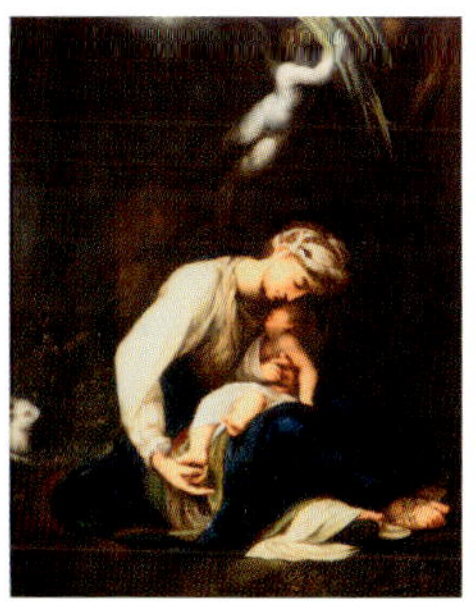
XIII.33

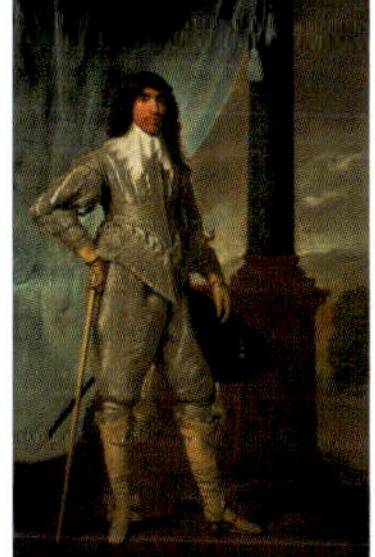
XIII.34

XIII.35

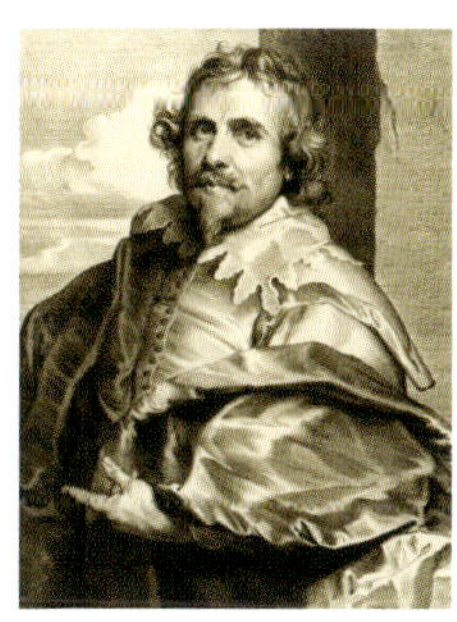
XIII.36

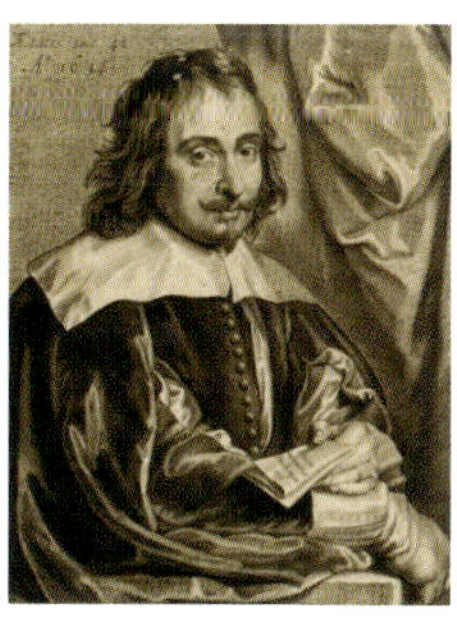
XIII.37

petition; the dispersal of English royal and aristocratic collections after the English Civil war; systematic construction, in Florence, of a European vision of painting.

XIII.34 DANIEL MYTENS THE ELDER : PORTRAIT OF JAMES, FIRST DUKE OF HAMILTON

1629
Oil on canvas, 221 x 139.7 cm
Edinburgh, Scottish National Portrait Gallery, Inv. PG 2722

James Hamilton, first duke of Hamilton, was a friend of Charles I, whom he accompanied to Madrid, with the Duke of Buckingham, during his mission of 1623. After offering several beautiful paintings to Charles I, he seems to have aspired to owning a 'gallery', or collection, for reasons of social status and self-interest rather than because of a true passion. His brother-in-law, Viscount Basil Fielding, was English ambassador to Venice and succeeded in acquiring the complete collection of Bartolomeo della Nave, a rich Venetian. During the Civil War, Hamilton led the army loyal to Charles I against the Scottish rebels. Daniel Mytens, a native of Delft, was a protégé of the Earl of Arundel, in London. He became a highly sought after society portraitist, but remained a very effective agent for Arundel. He had already painted the Duke in 1623, and here he conveys the great bearing of a courtier, at the age of twenty-three, in a lavish costume embroidered with silver. Like his master, Hamilton was executed. His collection was then dispersed, and almost entirely snapped up by the Archduke Leopold Wilhelm of Habsburg, governor of the Southern Netherlands.

BIBLIOGRAPHY : Anastassia Novikova, 'Virtuosity and Declensions of Virtue : Thomas Arundel and Aletheia Talbot seen by Virtue of a Portrait Pair by Daniel Mytens and a Treatise by Franciscus Junius', in Jan de Jong (ed.), *Virtus : virtuositeit en kunstliefhebbers in de Nederlanden, 1500–1700*, Zwolle, 2004 (*Nederlands Kunsthistorisch Jaarboek*, 54, 2003), pp. 308-33 ; Jonathan Brown, John Elliott (eds), *The Sale of the Century : Artistic Relations between Spain and Great Britain, 1604–1655*, New Haven, 2002, pp. 172–73 (Self-portrait, 1623, National Portrait Gallery, London).

XIII.35 DUKE OF HAMILTON'S COLLECTION : HANDWRITTEN INVENTORY

c. 1643
31 x 19.8 cm
Haddington, private collection, Lennoxlove House, Ms M. 4/21
Provenance : archives of the Dukes of Hamilton

These inventories were often compiled after a collection, or several paintings, had been purchased, in order to establish the pieces' value, and to list them as the owner's property. Also, before buying a collection, Hamilton, like Charles I, liked to read the descriptive list of its contents. Collectors could thus spot items of great value, or those that would allow them to vary their collection with works by several Italian schools.

BIBLIOGRAPHY : Klára Garas, 'Die Entstehung der Galerie des Erzherzogs Leopold Wilhelm', in *Jahrbuch der Kunsthistorischen Sammlungen in Wien*, 63, N.F. 27, 1967, pp. 39–80 ; Arthur MacGregor (ed.), *The Late King's Goods : Collections, Possessions and Patronage of Charles I in the Light of the Commonwealth Sale Inventories*, London, 1989, pp. 217–18 ; Jonathan Brown, John Elliott (eds), *The Sale of the Century : Artistic Relations between Spain and Great Britain, 1604–1655*, New Haven, 2002, pp. 172–73.

XIII.36 PAUL PONTIUS : PORTRAIT OF DANIEL MYTENS THE ELDER

c. 1634
Burin engraving, 26 x 18.5 cm
Antwerp, Plantijn-Moretus Museum / Stedelijk Prentenkabinet, Inv. OP 15974

Daniel Mytens, a native of Delft who trained in The Hague, sought his fortune at the English court, where he became painter to James I and Charles I; however, his fame was eclipsed by Van Dyck's arrival in London in 1632. But, above all, he was an important art agent for the Earl of Arundel – a friend of Rubens, and one of the most refined English aristocrats of the time. Mytens helped several English collectors to acquire major canvases on the continental market, in Antwerp, or in Italy.

BIBLIOGRAPHY : *The New Hollstein Dutch and Flemish Etchings, Engravings and Woodcuts, 1450–1700*, Van Dyck, Part II, no. 77, pp. 104–08.

XIII.37 JOAN MEIJSSENS (AFTER ANTHONY VAN DYCK) : PORTRAIT OF SIR BALTHAZAR GERBIER

1634
Burin engraving, condition VII, 25.7 x 18.2 cm
Antwerp, Plantijn-Moretus Museum / Stedelijk Prentenkabinet, Inv. OP 15899

Dutch Huguenot Sir Balthazar Gerbier was a gifted adventurer, polyglot, artist, diplomat and architect, who was under the protection of Charles I's favourite, the Duke of Buckingham. He accompanied the King and the Duke to Madrid in 1623, on the trip when they discovered the collections of Philip IV. He became conservator of Buckingham's collections; he was closely associated with Rubens, and was his representative in England. After Buckingham was murdered in 1628, Charles I sent Gerbier to the Brussels court as an English resident agent, doubtless with the idea that he could help to purchase magnificent paintings there. When Rubens died in 1640, Gerbier undertook to make an inventory of his collections and send a copy to Charles.

BIBLIOGRAPHY : Howard Colvin, *A Biographical Dictionary of British Architects, 1600–1840*, New Haven, 1995, Gerbier ; David Howarth, 'The "Entry Books" of Sir Balthazar Gerbier : Van Dyck, Charles I and the Cardinale-Infante Ferdinand', in Hans Vlieghe (ed.), *Van Dyck 1599–1999 : Conjectures and Refutations*, Turnhout, 2001, pp. 77–87 ; *The New Hollstein Dutch and Flemish Etchings, Engravings and Woodcuts, 1450–1700*, Van Dyck, Part V, no. 435, pp. 173–75.

XIII.S.N. SIR BALTHAZAR GERBIER : *THE ART OF WELL SPEAKING, BEING A LECTURE READ PUBLIQUELY AT SIR B. GERBIER'S ACADEMY*

London, 1650
Printed on paper, in quarto
Brussels, Bibliothèque royale de Belgique, Collections générales, II 47837

Sir Balthazar Gerbier owed his great career to his global approach to the English collectors of his day ; an accomplished gentleman in the tradition of Baldassare Castiglione and his treatise *Il Cortigiano* (The Courtier), Gerbier knew that not only must he sell works of art, but also establish himself as a collector. At the end of his life he ran an academy that trained those inter-

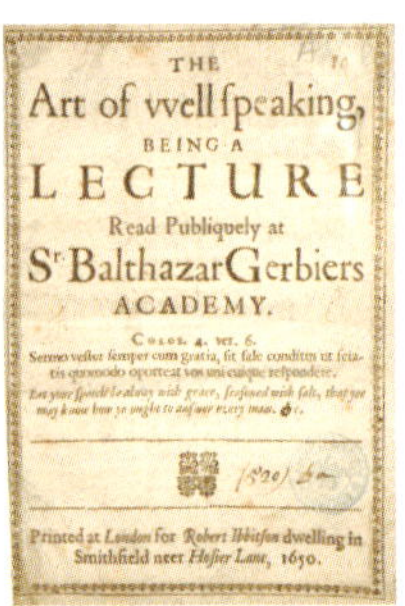

THE
Art of vvell ſpeaking,
BEING A
LECTURE
Read Publiquely at
Sr Balthazar Gerbiers
ACADEMY.

Colos. 4. ver. 6.
Sermo vester semper cum gratia, sit sale conditus ut sciatis quomodo oporteat vos unicuique respondere.
Let your speech be alway with grace, seasoned with salt, that ye may know how ye ought to answer every man. &c.

Printed at London for Robert Ibbitson dwelling in Smithfield neer Hosier Lane, 1650.

XIII.S.N.

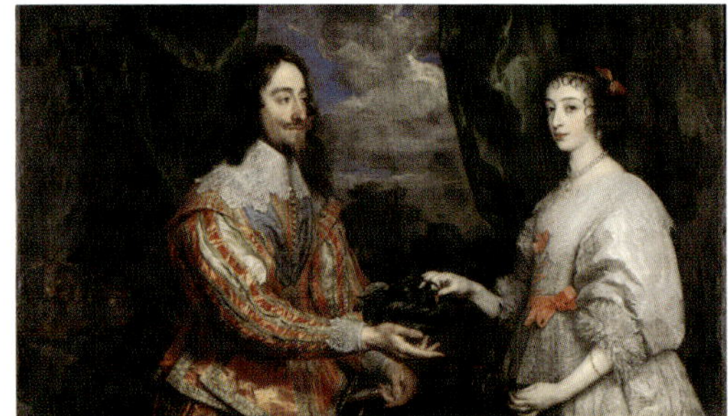

XIII.38

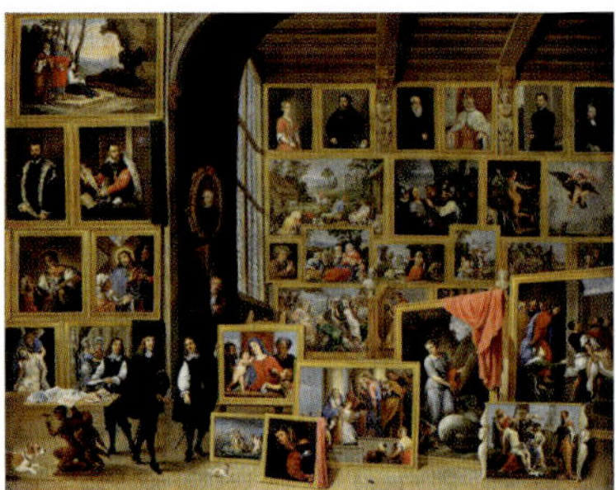

XIII.39

ested in good manners and eloquence, which were absolutely key to social success.

BIBLIOGRAPHY: Marika Keblusek, 'Cultural and Political Brokerage in Seventeenth-century England: The Case of Balthazar Gerbier', in Juliette Roding (ed.), *Dutch and Flemish Artists in Britain 1550–1800*, Leyden, 2003 (*Leids Kunsthistorisch Jaarboek*, 13, 2003) pp. 73–82.

XIII.38 ANTHONY VAN DYCK: PORTRAIT OF KING CHARLES I AND QUEEN HENRIETTA-MARIA

c. 1632–34
Oil on canvas, 104 x 176 cm
Kroměříž, Czech Republic, Archbishopric Olomouc Episcopal Palace, Inv. KE 2372, O 406
Provenance: collections of King Charles I intended for the palace of Denmark House (Somerset House), in an overmantel designed by Inigo Jones

In 1632, on his return to London, Van Dyck became the 'painter in ordinary' to King Charles I. With this portrait he robbed Daniel Mytens of the King's favour. This celebrated painting shows the King receiving a laurel wreath, sign of a victorious prince, from the hands of his wife Henrietta-Maria, a Catholic princess who was the daughter of Henri IV of France and Marie de Medici. In the background, two curtains open onto a view of charming, peaceful countryside. The King is offering the Queen an olive branch, symbolic of the peace between France and England promoted by their marriage. Van Dyck rejuvenated the court portrait by painting the two subjects with restrained but clear movements and emotions, full of life as they look at each other. This double portrait is enlivened by the delicacy of the costumes and faces. But throughout, the portrait is an emblematic portrayal of a marriage with political significance. The King's Catholic sympathies earned him fierce enemies in England, who hastened his demise. The cultivated sovereign was a lover of sophisticated paintings of this type.

BIBLIOGRAPHY: Ladislav Daniel, Milan Togner, *Gemäldegalerie Krommeriz: Katalog der Gemäldesammlung des Erzbischöflichen Schlosses in Krommeriz (Kremsier)*. Kromeriz, 1999, no. 91, pp. 123–30; Christopher Brown, Hans Vlieghe (eds), *Van Dyck 1599–1641*, Antwerp, 1999, no. 61, pp. 240–43; Jonathan Brown, *Kings and Connoisseurs: Collecting Art in Seventeenth-century Europe*, New Haven, 1995.

XIII.39 DAVID TENIERS THE YOUNGER: ARCHDUKE LEOPOLD WILHELM IN HIS BRUSSELS GALLERY

c. 1654–60
Oil on canvas, 93 x 127 cm
Munich, Bayerische Staatsgemäldesammlungen, Alte Pinakothek, inv. 1841

This magnificent cabinet painting is one of the most beautiful executed by the artist; it features a selection of paintings from the Archduke Leopold Wilhelm's collection , for the most part, were given as gifts to other sovereigns. The Archduke, hat on head in accordance with strict etiquette, points to one of the paintings with his cane, while in the other hand he holds a bunch of narcissi. He looks proudly at the spectator to whom he seems to be showing his treasures. Nearby, David Teniers himself wears the sword and the gold chain just given to him by his master, distinctions that liken him to a noble. Front left is a fine table with a pedestal sculpted by Jeronymus van Kenoy, known as Duquesnoy, as a figure of Ganymede; on the little table there are engravings, drawings, but also shells, which subtly evoke the universal nature of collecting as a microcosm, in which the works of Man are confronted by the masterpieces of Nature. The overwhelming majority of the paintings are from the Italian school; several of them have retained their fame, such as Giorgione's *Three Philosophers* (see III.40), Veronese's *Christ Healing the Young Man of Nain*, the *Madonna of the Cherries* by Titian, and Tintoretto's *Deposition*. In the foreground, partly covered by a red velvet curtain, which indicates its value, is Raphael's *St Margaret*. At the time that this painting was executed the frames, gilded but very plain, emphasized the works themselves. A certain number of paintings held a powerful symbolic status: above the door the portrait of Philip IV of Spain by Velázquez impresses as a great example of an artistic patron, at the heart of the Habsburg dynasty. The bust of Queen Christina of Sweden, at right angles to the Raphael painting, recalls this sovereign's visit to Brussels; the Queen, herself a great collector of paintings, greatly admired the Archduke's gallery. Finally, the portrait of the antiquarian Jacopo Strada, by Titian, evokes one of the most brilliant art agents of the Renaissance, who worked for the greatest princes of his time.

BIBLIOGRAPHY: Hilda Lietzmann, 'Der kaiserliche Antiquar Jacopo Strada und Kurfürst August von Sachsen', *Zeitschrift für Kunstgeschichte*, 60,

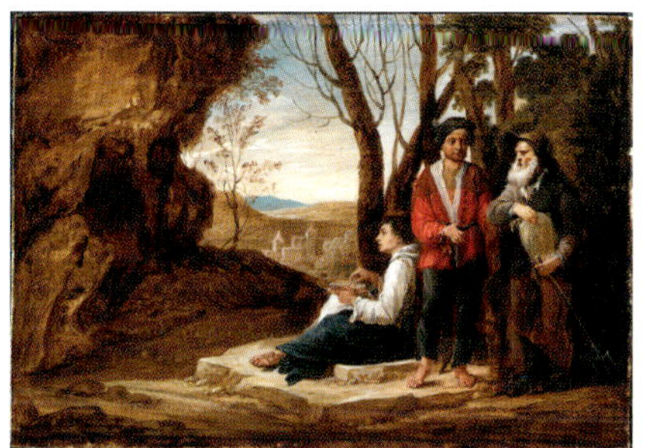

XIII.40

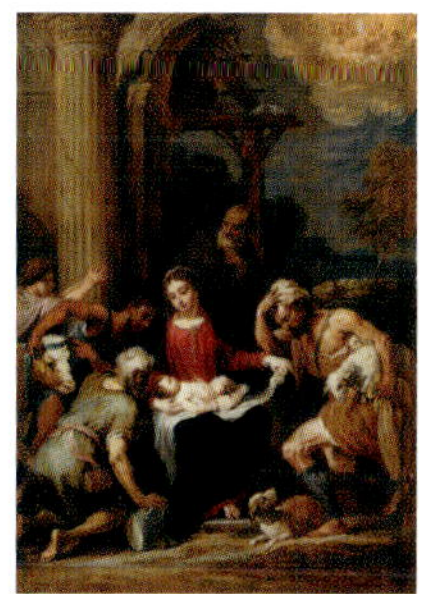

XIII.41

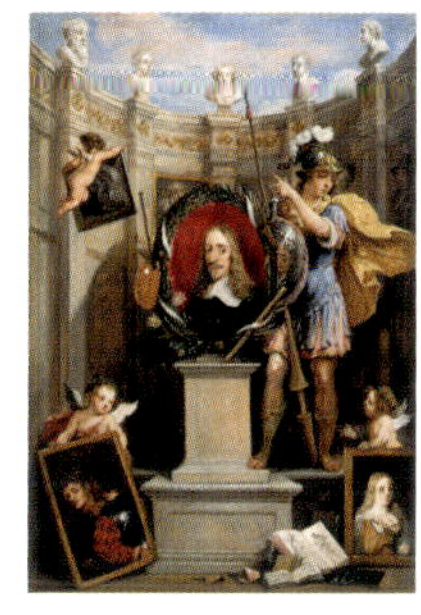

XIII.42

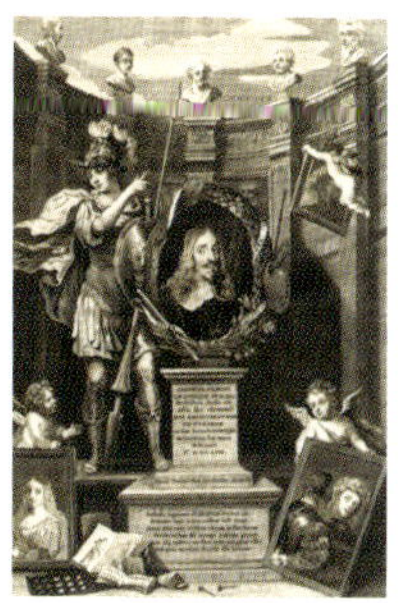

XIII.43

1997, pp. 377–99; Klára Garas, 'Das Schicksal der Sammlung des Erzherzogs Leopold Wilhelm', in *Jahrbuch der Kunsthistorischen Sammlungen in Wien*, 64, 1968, pp. 181–278; Karl Schütz, 'Die Sammlung Erzherzog Leopold Wilhelms', in Klaus Bussmann (ed.), *1648: Krieg und Frieden in Europa*, Munich, 1998, text vol. 2, pp. 181–90; Annalisa Scarpa Sonino, *Cabinet d'amateur: le grandi collezioni d'arte nei dipinti dal XVII al XIX secolo*, Milan, 1992, pp. 95–96.

XIII.40 DAVID TENIERS THE YOUNGER (AFTER GIORGIONE DA CASTELFRANCO): THE THREE PHILOSOPHERS

Before 1660
Oil on panel, 21.5 x 30.9 cm
Dublin, National Gallery of Ireland, Inv. NGI. 390
Provenance: John Churchill, first Duke of Marlborough

David Teniers the Younger became the Keeper of Paintings for Archduke Leopold Wilhelm of Habsburg when he governed the Southern Netherlands, which included most of Belgium and Brussels. This artist constructed a highly systematic monument to the eternal glory of this collection and its owner, by painting the gallery with the Archduke, but also by publishing an illustrated catalogue of Leopold Wilhelm's most beautiful Italian paintings. Teniers spent many years on this project, but the fame of the collection was great, even after it was finally installed in Vienna, from 1656. David Teniers executed several little copies like this one with finesse; they are intended as preparation for engraved reproductions of Italian paintings for the 1660 *Theatrum* (Theatre of Painting, XIII.43), which would ensure that this princely collection became widely known, and thus served to honour the Archduke. These coloured copies were supposed to help the engravers better separate the forms, and to translate the diversity of the original painting into black and white. It was said of a good engraving that it had a *good colour*. When the collection moved to Vienna, it did so gradually, to enable Teniers to make all the necessary copies. The artist imitated the styles with great ease: he probably knew how to execute pastiches or copies of originals to sell.

The famous Giorgione painting, now in Vienna's Kunsthistorisches Museum, is an enigmatic work – no-one knows if it represents the Three Wise Men, or astronomers, or mathematicians. It was included in the collection of the rich Venetian Bartolomeo della Nave, purchased for the first Duke of Hamilton, most of which was then sold to Archduke Leopold Wilhelm. After finishing the *Theatrum*, Teniers did not hesitate to sell certain painted sketches, but not without altering them, as here, to make them more attractive. The rich costumes of the three figures have been replaced by simple peasant garb.

BIBLIOGRAPHY: Ernst Vegelin van Claerbergen (ed.), *David Teniers and the Theatre of Painting*, London, 2006, no. 8, pp. 86–87 (bibl.); Karl Schütz, 'David Teniers D. J. als Galeriedirektor Erzherzog Leopold Wilhelms', in *Weltkunst*, 48, 1978, pp. 1139–40; Karl Schütz, 'David Teniers als Kopist im Dienst Erzherzog Leopold Wilhelms', in Heribert Hutter (ed.), *Original, Kopie, Replik, Paraphrase*, Vienna, 1980, pp. 21–33.

XIII.41 DAVID TENIERS THE YOUNGER (AFTER ANDREA SCHIAVONE): THE ADORATION OF THE SHEPHERDS

Before 1660
Oil on wood, 31.2 x 21.1 cm
Paris, Collection Frits Lugt, Institut néerlandais, Inv. 5796

BIBLIOGRAPHY: Margret Klinge, *David Teniers the Younger. Paintings – Drawings*, Koninklijk Museum voor Schone Kunsten, Antwerp, 1991, no. 99.

XIII.42 DAVID TENIERS THE YOUNGER: MODELLO FOR THE FRONTISPIECE OF *THEATRUM PICTORIUM* (THEATRE OF PAINTING)

Before 1656
Oil on panel, 32.4 x 22.2 cm
Private collection
Provenance: John Churchill, first Duke of Marlborough

In a scene surmounted by antique-style busts, the medallion depicting the Archduke Leopold Wilhelm is raised on a monument, surrounded by laurels, with the attributes of the arts and war; it is guarded by Minerva, goddess of wisdom. In front are two of the Archduke's favourite paintings: *Il Bravo*, at that time attributed to Giorgione, and *La Violante*, attributed to Palma the Elder. This very fine preparatory painting was engraved with a long inscription for the frontispiece of *Theatrum pictorium* (XIII.43). The concept of theatre, considered from the Renaissance to be a tool of knowledge and power (Giulio Camillo Delminio) is translated here into a symbolic image.

BIBLIOGRAPHY: Ernst Vegelin van Claerbergen (ed.), *David Teniers and the Theatre of Painting*, London, 2006, pp. 78–79 (bibl.).

XIII.43 DAVID TENIERS THE YOUNGER: *THEATRUM PICTORIUM IN QUO EXTRIBUNTUR IPSIUS MANU, EJUSQUE CURA IN AES INCISAE PICTURAE ARCHITIPAE ITALICAE ... QUAS ... ARCHIDUX IN PINACOTHECAM SUAM BRUXELLIS COLLEGIT ...*

Brussels, 'Sumptibus Auctoris', Antwerp, H. Aertssens, 1660
Printed on paper, in folio
Brussels, Bibliothèque royale de Belgique, Cabinet des estampes, Inv. VH 9300 D est

This catalogue of the Archduke Leopold Wilhelm of Habsburg's art collection in Brussels is richly illustrated with 247 etchings, produced by fourteen different engravers. The text was published in four different editions: Latin, Flemish, Spanish and French. The works included are all from the Italian school, but without any apparent classification; some are reproduced the wrong way round. Such books were very popular with enthusiasts and connoisseurs in the 18th century; they were known as 'galleries'. This publication is important inasmuch as it developed the idea of a specialist knowledge of art, for which the book is a preparation, even if the paintings' attributions are sometimes optimistic. It appears to be a real museum on paper to the glory of a prince. The frontispiece is engraved by Jan van Troyen after Teniers' design (XIII.42).

BIBLIOGRAPHY: Ernst Vegelin van Claerbergen (ed.), *David Teniers and the Theatre of Painting*, London, 2006, pp. 11–57 (bibl.), and no. 5, pp. 80–81.

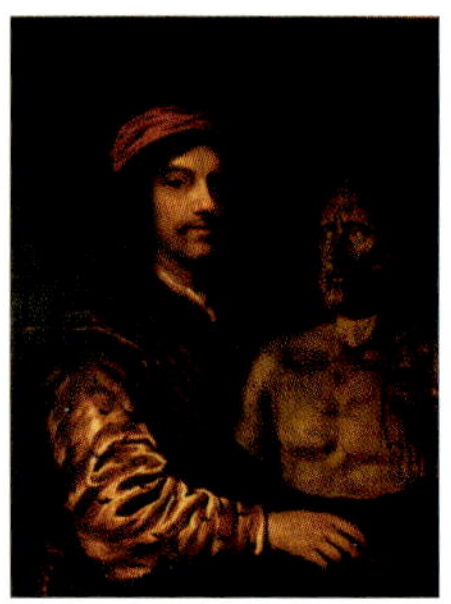
XIII.44

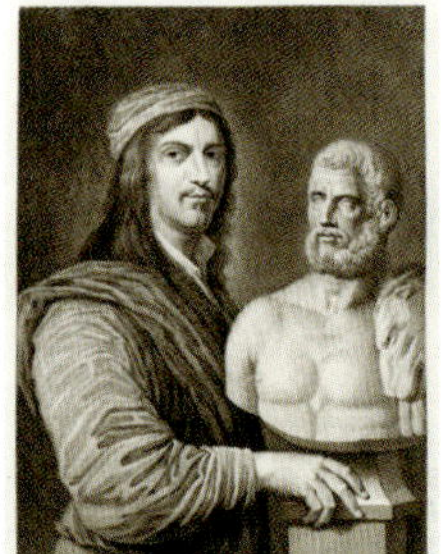
XIII.S.N.

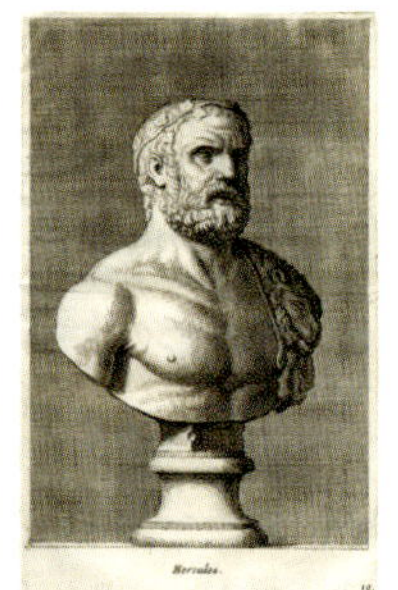
XIII.S.N.

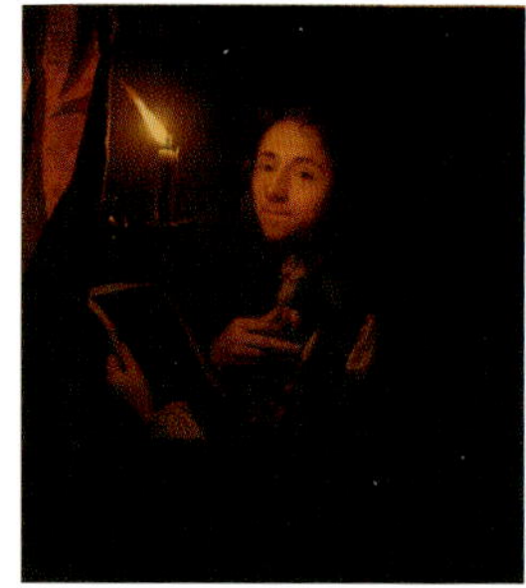
XIII.45

XIII.44 PHILIPS KONINCK: SELF-PORTRAIT

1661 (signed and dated)
Oil on canvas, 96 x 72 cm
Florence, Polo museale Fiorentino, Galleria degli Uffizi, Inv. 1890, no. 1885
Provenance: purchased by Cosimo de Medici III in 1707

The artist, a renowned landscape painter, painted himself in front of a bust of Hercules which at that time was included in Gerrit Reynst's Amsterdam museum. It is possible that Koninck knew of the picture of Aristotle contemplating the bust of Homer (1653, Metropolitan Museum of Art, New York), executed by Rembrandt for Count Ruffo: here too the cult of Antiquity is displayed as a guarantee of excellence in contemporary art. The virtue of Hercules is compared to that of the painter.

BIBLIOGRAPHY: Karla Langedijk, *Die Selbstbildnisse der Holländischen und Flämischen Künstler in der Galleria degli Autoritratti der Uffizien in Florenz*, Florence, 1992, no. 10, pp. 54–57 (bibl.); Elisabeth Epe, *Die Gemäldesammlungen des Ferdinando de' Medici, Erbprinz von Toskana 1663–1713*, Marburg, 1990; Wolfram Prinz, *Die Sammlung der Selbstbildnisse in den Uffizien. Geschichte der Sammlung*, Berlin, 1971.

XIII.S.N. PIETRO ANTONIO PAZZI (BASED ON A DRAWING BY GIOVANNI DOMENICO CAMPIGLIA, AFTER): SELF-PORTRAIT OF PHILIPS KONINCK

1756
Burin engraving and etching, 'Serie di ritratti degli pittori dipinti di propria mano', in Antonio Francesco Gori, *Mvseum Florentinvm exhibens insigniora vetvstatis monvmenta quae florentinae sunt cvm observationibvs Antonii Francisci Gorii*, vol. IX (Portr. vol. III), 1756, in folio
Brussels, Bibliothèque royale de Belgique, Cabinet des estampes, CI 14.518D

As an antiquarian, expert in Etruscan culture, art historian and professor of the Studio Fiorentino, Antonio Francesco Gori (1691–1757) corresponded regularly with learned men throughout Europe. The *Museum Fiorentinum* was one of the finest and most sumptuously illustrated 'paper museums', which enabled art lovers to visit the grand ducal collections from afar. The collection of self-portraits of artists in the Uffizi Gallery was thus widely known thanks to the printing press. The series of 'ritratti' was terminated after Gori's death, but was attached to his great work.

BIBLIOGRAPHY: M.E. Micheli, '"Gemmae antiquae caeletae"' di Anton Francesco Gori', *Prospettiva*, 47, 1986, pp. 38–51; Liuba Giuliani (ed.), *Il carteggio Anton Francesco Gori*, Rome, 1987.

XIII.S.N. *SIGNORUM VETERUM ICONES PER D. GERARDUM REYNST URBIS AMSTELAEDAMI SENATOREM AC SCABINUM DUM VIVERET DIGNISSIMUM COLLECTAE*

[1671]
In folio, 40 x 28 cm
Brussels, Bibliothèque royale de Belgique, Cabinet des estampes, VH 30227 C

The father of Gerrit Reynst, a rich Amsterdam merchant, was one of the founders of the Dutch East India Company. Through his brother Jan, who lived in Venice, he acquired the collection of antiquities gathered by the Vendramin family around 1629. In the absence of antiquities in Holland at this time, the Reynst house on the Keizersgracht became a museum heavily frequented by artists. The collection was split up *c.* 1670, the owner having failed to sell it

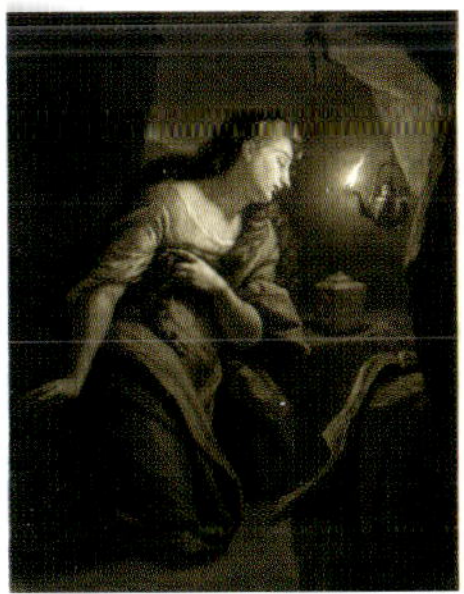

XIII.S.N.

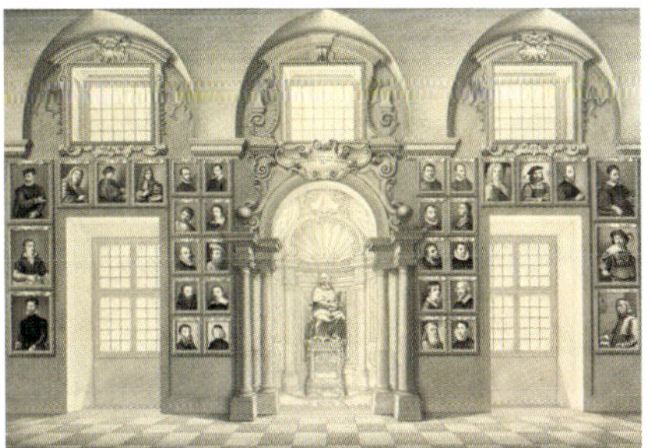

XIII.46

to the City of Amsterdam for the benefit of the artists. In this sense this catalogue realizes a lost dream: it includes a frontispiece by Gérard de Lairesse, and eleven plates by Hubertus Quellinus that illustrate Reynst's antiquities.

BIBLIOGRAPHY: Anne-Marie S. Logan, *The 'Cabinet' of the brothers Gerard and Jan Reynst*, Amsterdam, 1979; Frank Scholze, *Ende des goldenen Zeitalters? Aspekte niederländischer portraitmalerei des späten 17. Jahrhunderts*. Thesis, Stuttgart, 1996, pp. 60–61; Alain Roy, *Gérard de Lairesse (1640–1711)*, Paris, 1992, no. G.R. 14–123, pp. 534–35; Karla Langedijk, *Die Selbstbildnisse der Holländischen und Flämischen Künstler in der Galleria degli Autoritratti der Uffizien in Florenz*, Florence, 1992, no. 10, pp. 55–58.

XIII.45 GOTTFRIED SCHALKEN: SELF-PORTRAIT

1695 (signed and dated)
Oil on canvas, 92 x 81 cm
Florence, Polo museale Fiorentino, Galleria degli Uffizi. Inv. 1890, no. 1878
Provenance: commissioned from the artist by Cosimo de Medici III

This self-portrait was ordered by one of Cosimo's agents, Thomas Platt, when the painter was in England. Schalken was famous for his candlelight effects, and portrayed himself so as to highlight the speciality in which he excelled; there were no self-portraits such as this is the grand-ducal collection. Schalken is proudly holding a *Repentant Magdalene*, engraved in the mezzotint style by John Smith after one of Schalken's paintings; he would send this to the Duke with his self-portrait. He was thus exhibiting his skill in imitating one artistic medium by using another, and producing proof that his work was being disseminated by mezzotint, a new technique at that time, which wonderfully recreated the chiaroscuro effects dear to the artist.

BIBLIOGRAPHY: Karla Langedijk, *Die Selbstbildnisse der Holländischen und Flämischen Künstler in der Galleria degli Autoritratti der Uffizien in Florenz*, Florence, 1992 no. 31, pp. 164–67 (bibl.); Elisabeth Epe, *Die Gemäldesammlungen des Ferdinando de' Medici, Erbprinz von Toskana 1663–1713*, Marburg, 1990; Wolfram Prinz, *Die Sammlung der Selbstbildnisse in den Uffizien. Geschichte der Sammlung*, Berlin, 1971, pp. 134–35, 191–92; Peter Hecht, 'Candlelight and Dirty Fingers, or Royal Virtue in Disguise: Some Thoughts on Weyerman and Godtfried Schalken', *Simiolus*, vol. 11, no. 1 (1980), pp. 23–38.

XIII.S.N. JOHN SMITH (AFTER GOTTFRIED SCHALKEN): ST MARY MAGDALENE

Undated, final third of 17th century
Mezzotint engraving, 49 x 34.5 cm (engraving: 35.7 x 26.4 cm)
Brussels, Bibliothèque royale de Belgique, Cabinet des estampes, inv. S.I. 48112

BIBLIOGRAPHY: Karla Langedijk, *Die Selbstbildnisse der Holländischen und Flämischen Künstler in der Galleria degli Autoritratti der Uffizien in Florenz*, Florence, 1992, no. 31, pp. 164–67 (bibl.).

XIII.46 STEFANO GAETANO NERI: PAINTERS' SALON IN THE FLORENCE GALLERY

Undated, *c.* 1753–65
Ink and graphite on paper, 38.6 x 56 cm
Vienna, Österreichische Nationalbibliothek, Cod. Min. 51 fol. 8

This part of the Uffizi received many visitors in the 18th century; it made it possible to learn the styles of so many famous European artists, who are themselves represented here. A central niche, framing a bust of Cardinal Leopoldo de Medici by Giambattista Foggini (1697), pays homage to the great collector, positioned in the centre of a princely portrayal of European art, past and present. The Medici Gallery was freely open to the public, so its impact was all the greater.

BIBLIOGRAPHY: Wolfram Prinz, *Die Sammlung der Selbstbildnisse in den Uffizien. Geschichte der Sammlung*, Berlin, 1971, pp. 240–41, ill. 46; Ellinoor Bergvelt, Debora J. Meijers (eds), *Kabinetten, galerijen en musea: het verzamelen en presenteren van naturalia en kunst van 1500 tot heden*, Zwolle, 2005.

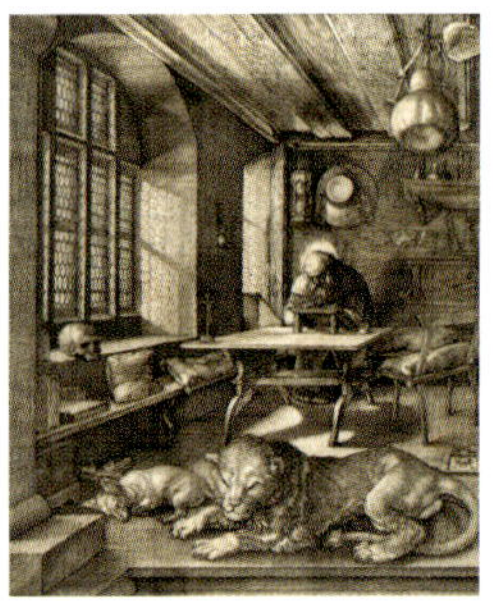

XIV.1

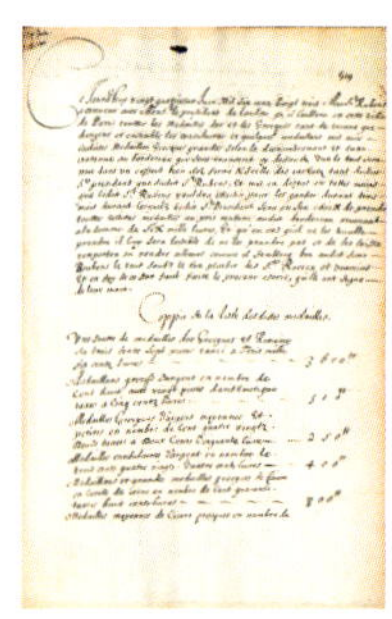

XIV.2

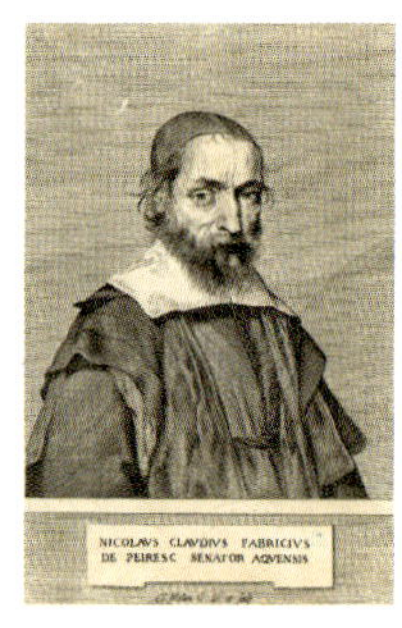

XIV.3

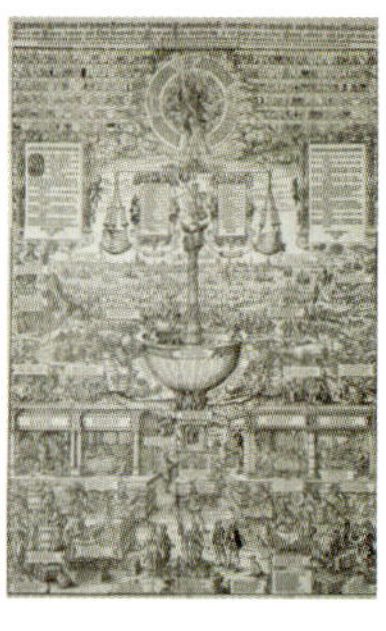

XIV.4

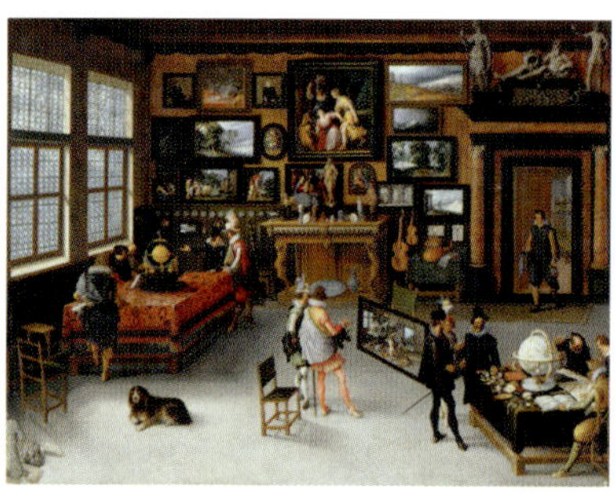

XIV.5

SECTION XIV

THE WORLD IN A ROOM : COLLECTORS AND ART DEALERS

The 17th century witnessed the birth of a new pictorial genre: the collector's cabinet. The cabinet was a room, containing paintings, sculpture, scientific objects and curiosities that were shown to guests and held up for scrutiny. They revealed how private individuals spent their wealth. Their content was often less important than the real or moral portrait they painted of their owners. Some cabinets can be read as allegories or seen as concealing hidden symbolism.

XIV.1 ALBRECHT DÜRER : ST JEROME IN HIS STUDY

1514
Burin engraving, 24 x 18.5 cm
Brussels, Bibliothèque royale de Belgique, Cabinet des estampes, SII 26374 fol. Res

This plate was sold or given by Dürer, together with the famous *Melancholia* and the *Knight, Death and the Devil.* St Jerome, the venerable Father of the Church and translator of the Vulgate, is depicted in a simple but comfortable study. In front of him is a dog, and the drowsy lion, which, according to legend, was his faithful companion. The study, a place of retreat and learning, was an essential element, which had significance in the establishment of many collectors' cabinets. Dürer bestowed a European resonance upon this space designed for contemplation, and Giorgio Vasari heaped praises upon this plate in his *Vite* (Lives of the Artists, 1568).

BIBLIOGRAPHY : Giulia Bartrum, *German Renaissance Prints : 1490–1550*, London, 1995, no. 34, p. 48 ; Peter W. Parshall, 'Albrecht Dürer's St. Jerome in his Study : A Philological Reference', *The Art Bulletin*, 53, 3, 1971, p. 303–05 ; Dora Thornton, *The Scholar in his Study : Ownership and Experience in Renaissance Italy*, New Haven, 1997.

XIV.2 NICOLAS-CLAUDE FABRI DE PEIRESC : HANDWRITTEN LIST OF ANCIENT COINS PRESENTED TO HIM BY THE PAINTER PETER PAUL RUBENS

January 1620 ?
32 x 21 cm
The Hague, Rijksmuseum Meermanno-Westreenianum Ms 10C31

Nicolas-Claude Fabri de Peiresc was adviser to the parliament of Provence, and lived in Aix-en-Provence and at Belgentier castle in the Var. He was a cardinal citizen of the Republic of Letters and maintained a vast correspondence with the most influential scientists and scholars in Europe : involving news about science and politics, scholarly research, or even mutual aid for the purchase of works of art. In 1599, he travelled to Italy. In 1621 he started corresponding with Rubens. In 1622, Rubens met Peiresc in Paris, and offered him around fifty Gallic coins, which would have been valuable to a man who wanted to write a book on the history of coins in France. Rubens preferred gemstones, as he was more of an aesthete than an antiquary, in spite of his profound erudition. The two men helped each other to buy and sell works of art. Exchange of knowledge and of money were carefully organized.

BIBLIOGRAPHY : Kristin Lohse Belkin, Fiona Healy, Jeffrey M. Muller (eds), *A House of Art : Rubens as Collector*, Louvain, 2004, p. 262 (bibl.).

XIV.3 CLAUDE MELLAN : PORTRAIT OF NICOLAS-CLAUDE FABRI DE PEIRESC

1636–37
Burin engraving, 221 x 156 cm, glued to paper 35 x 27.5 cm
Brussels, Bibliothèque royale de Belgique, Cabinet des estampes, cote S I 22256 4°

Despite his considerable fortune, Peiresc was depicted in simple attire.

BIBLIOGRAPHY : Maxime Préaud (ed.), *L'œil d'or : Claude Mellan, 1598–1688*, Paris, 1988, no. 137, pp. 110–11.

XIV.4 JOST AMMAN : ALLEGORY OF COMMERCE

1585
Woodcut, in six parts, 87.5 x 61 cm
Brussels, Bibliothèque royale de Belgique, Cabinet des estampes, S II 4990 max

Jost Amman was a Swiss woodcut artist originally from Zurich, who emigrated to Nuremberg, a major focus for the production of books and engravings throughout the Empire. His output was extensive, varied, and was of exceptional quality. This allegorical representation of commerce was produced in accordance with the plan of an accounting specialist, Johann Neudörfer. The plate pays a glowing tribute to Antwerp, a centre of international trade in the 16th and 17th century that specialized in the mass production of art as well as quality work. Its harbour is depicted behind the fountain surmounted by an allegory of Fortune. On the upper level, the coats of arms of the greatest trading cities in Europe surround a figure of Mercury, the god of commerce, who is holding the blade of a large set of scales on which credit and debit accounts are being weighed. All the professions linked to commerce are described on the lower level.

BIBLIOGRAPHY : Dorothea D. Reeves, 'The Jost Amman Print', *The Business History Review*, 33, 2, 1959, p. 175–77.

XIV.5 ADRIAEN STALBEMT (ATTRIBUTED, ASSISTED BY HIERONYMUS FRANCKEN II) : COLLECTOR'S CABINET

c. 1650
Oil on panel, 93 x 114 cm
Madrid, Museo Nacional del Prado, inv. 1405

This painting is connected to a different version, which is today housed in Baltimore Museum, and includes the figures of the Archduke Albert of Austria and his wife Isabella visiting the gallery. In the version displayed, these official figures are not present. In the centre of the room, there's a cabinet of rarities, surrounded mainly by Flemish paintings. Amid an abun-

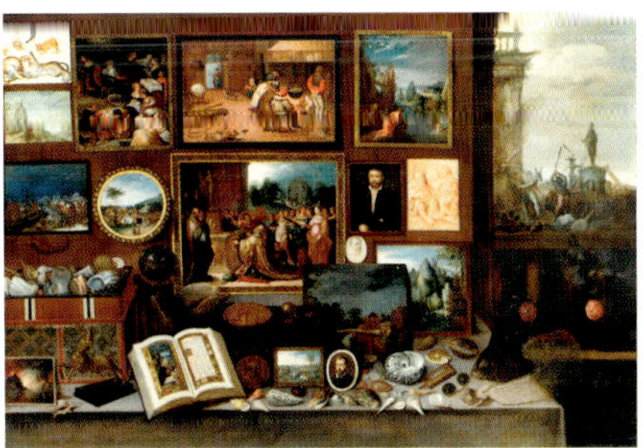

XIV.6

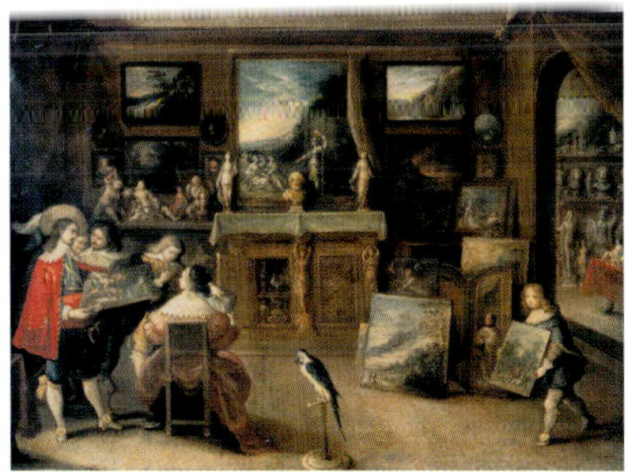

XIV.7

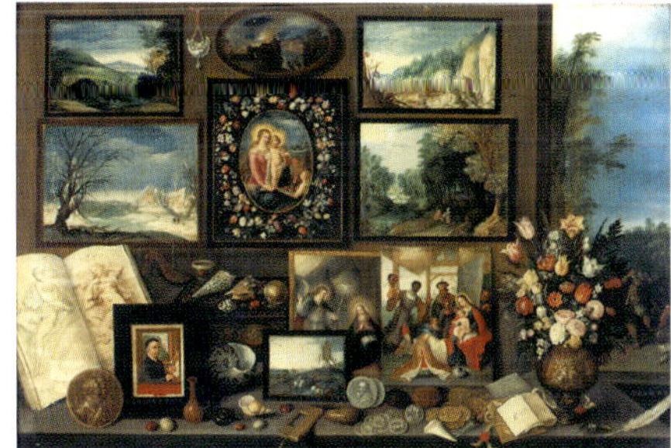

XIV.8

dance of antiquities, several statues of deities are being admired. In front is a globe, and shells indicate the symbolic presence of the sciences. Such cabinets assembled a methodical collection of items of merit to praise, and portrayed collectors passing judgement on the works that were in front of them. Two pictures shown here concern painting: visible in the centre on the back wall is a version of the 'Battle of the Arts' ('Renown'helps raise 'Painting', next to a man with donkey's ears, struck down by Minerva's spear). Exhibited on the floor under the scrutiny of two collectors is another painting of a cabinet, which depicts beings with donkey's heads in the throes of knocking over and breaking objects. Was this a reference to the types of destruction always threatening the collection?

BIBLIOGRAPHY: Pierre Georgel, Anne-Marie Lecoq, *La Peinture dans la peinture* (exhib. cat.), Dijon, 1982, p. 209 (exhib. cat.); Victor i. Stoichita, *L'Instauration du tableau*, Paris, 1993, p.136 et seq.; Annalisa Scarpa Sonino, *Cabinet d'Amateur: le grandi collezioni d'arte nei dipinti dal* XVII *al* XIX *secolo*, Milan, 1992, pp. 37–38.

XIV. 6 FRANS FRANCKEN II: COLLECTOR'S CABINET WITH ICONOCLASTS AS ASSES

First quarter of the 17th century
Oil on panel, 101 x 143 cm
Genoa, Collection Chiavari Società Economica

This painting celebrates the virtues of the collection and draws on the image of the virtuoso, or the individual accomplished in all the sciences as well as in etiquette. Religious paintings indicated that the artist supported sacred art and the religious function of painting, damaged by Protestant iconoclasm in Flanders from 1566. To the right, the iconoclasts are compared to donkeys.

BIBLIOGRAPHY: Ursula Alice Härting, *Frans Francken der Jüngere (1581–1642): die Gemälde mit kritischem Oeuvrekatalog*, Freren, 1989, passim (not catalogued).

XIV.7 FRANS FRANCKEN II: COLLECTOR'S CABINET

Signed and dated 1636
Oil on copper panel, 47.5 x 58.3 cm
Stockholm Hallwylska Museet, Inv. B 69

This cabinet, which is richly hung with fabric, is in fact the shop belonging to a dealer in very expensive pictures and works of art. In the centre, a sideboard contains valuable objects. To the left, elegant clients, concerned about their status, are inspecting pictures, while the dealer gives them the sales pitch. In front, a parrot makes fun of the dealer's patter. Such dealers not only supplied individual works of art, but also complete collections on demand.

BIBLIOGRAPHY: Ursula Alice Härting, *Frans Francken der Jüngere (1581–1642): die Gemälde mit kritischem Oeuvrekatalog*, Freren, 1989, no. 463, p. 374

XIV.8 FRANS FRANCKEN II: CABINET

1618–19
Oil on wood, 76 x 104 cm
Antwerp, Koninklijk Museum voor Schone Kunsten, Inv. 816

In this cabinet painting, many expensive objects designed to be admired at close quarters are spread over a table near the foreground. The presence of flowers, such as a Madonna surrounded by a garland, signals that there was indeed collaboration between artists: Francken worked alongside Jan Brueghel II and Philippe de Marlier. Here, the beauty of a painting is measured by the subtlety of every detail – animals or people depicted, flowers, objects.

BIBLIOGRAPHY: Zirka Zaremba Filipczak, *Picturing Art in Antwerp 1550–1700*, Princeton, 1987, p. 63; *Das flämische Stillleben 1550–1680. Sinn und Sinnlichkeit* (exhib. cat.), Essen, 2002, no. 25.

XIV.9 FRANS FRANCKEN II AND HENDRICK VAN STEENWYCK THE YOUNGER: THE INTERIOR OF A PICTURE GALLERY

c. 1620, signed 'DJ ffrank' on the back of the seated man's chair
Oil on wood, 54.2 x 75.5 cm
London, private collection, Johnny Van Haeften Ltd.

Here, Francken worked alongside Van Steenwyck, who specialized in painting architectural views. A collection of 16th and 17th century Flemish paintings is exhibited in a huge, vaulted gallery, Renaissance in style. Some figures are looking at the works, while others, sitting at a table, examine drawings, paintings and sculptures. Paintings by colleagues who usually worked in collaboration with Francken are put in a prominent place in the composition: an architectural view in grisaille by Van Steenwyck, a bouquet of flowers by Jan Brueghel, and a landscape by Joos de Momper.

BIBLIOGRAPHY: U. Härting, no. 396.

XIV.10 DAVID TENIERS II: ARCHDUKE LEOPOLD WILHELM VISITING THE ARTIST'S GALLERY

c. 1653
Oil on canvas, 73.5 x 88 cm
Madrid, Fundacion Lázaro Galdiano Museo, no.8447

Archduke Leopold Wilhelm, wearing his hat, is looking at the viewer. On his left, Teniers is showing him around the gallery; the elegant frames are adorned with the names of the painters that filled them. The paintings displayed, which were carefully selected from the Italian and Flemish schools equally, seem to invite the viewer to make a comparison here: to assess the respective merits of the two schools. The resulting should favour Flemish art. Thus, at the bottom left, a *Nativity* then attributed to Lucas van Leyden is next to a portrait by Tintoretto. Both contemporary paintings and old masters were included in this battle for supremacy.

BIBLIOGRAPHY: Annalisa Scarpa Sonini, pp. 93–94 (with the Vienna version, KHM).

XIV.11 CORNELIS DE BAELLIEUR: GALLERY OF OBJETS D'ART

1620s
Oil on panel, 52 x 74 cm
Dijon, Musée des Beaux-Arts, Inv. D.E. 21

This was one of the first cabinet paintings executed by the artist. The small bronze sculpture, in the style of ancient models, was made fashionable by Rubens; here a beautiful collection is exhibited on shelves. A Madonna, which is a Tuscan work from the Renaissance, is placed on the floor at the bottom right, while several Flemish landscapes can be identified. The representation of paintings in this picture was concerned with a demonstration of affluence and a fascination for etiquette; it created the model for a collection, and seems to describe with subtlety the attitudes that defined an estab-

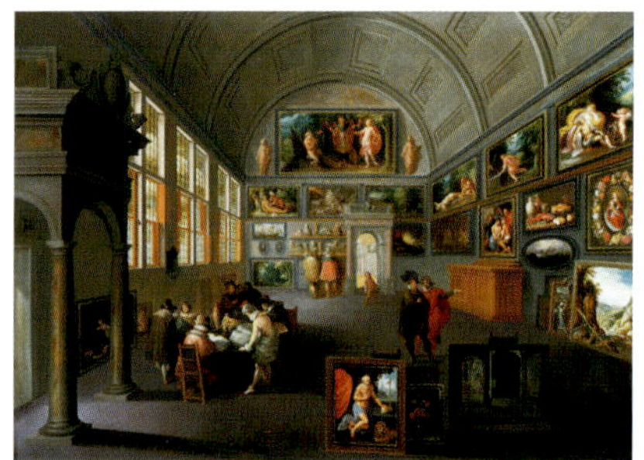

XIV.9

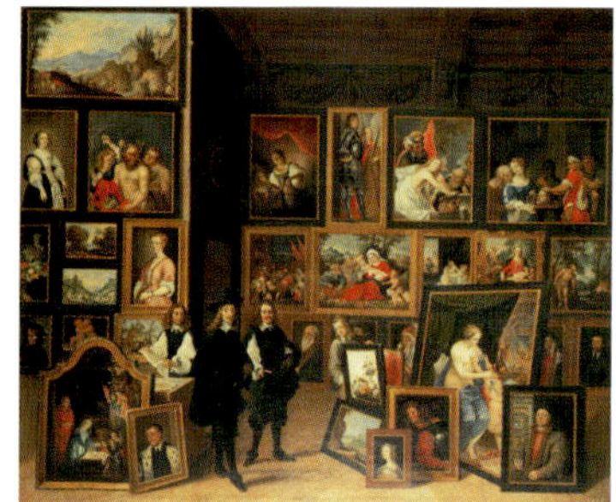

XIV.10

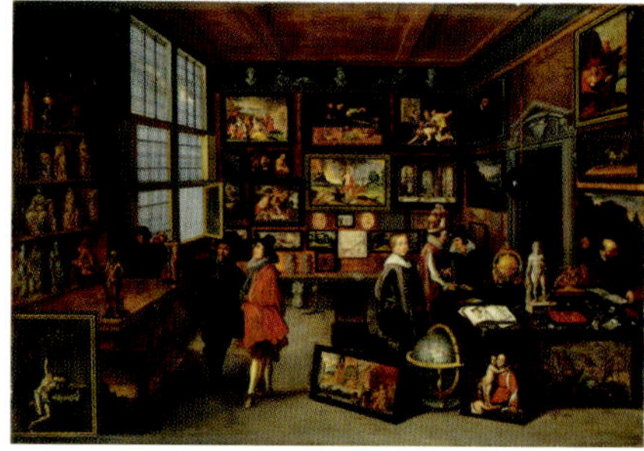

XIV.11

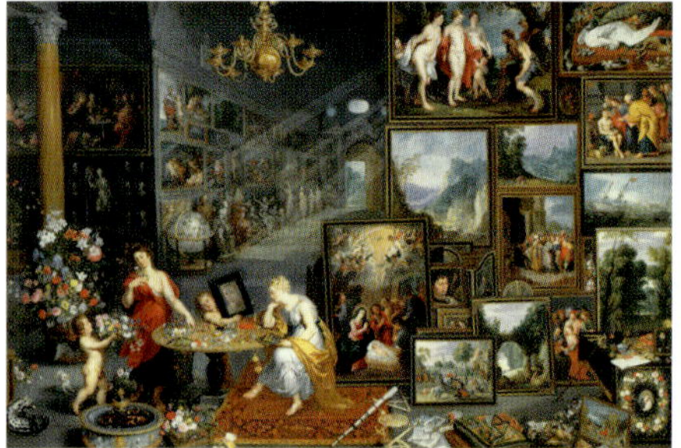

XIV.12

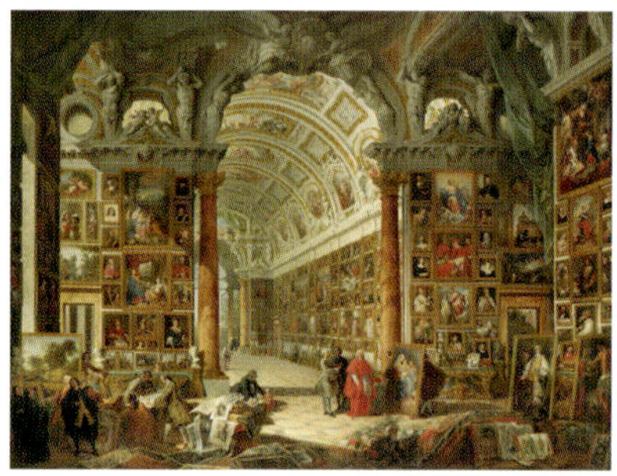

XIV.13

lished collector. This work contributed to the structure of social etiquette, in which art played an important role.

BIBLIOGRAPHY : Annalisa Scarpa Sonino, pp. 73–74.

XIV.12 JAN 'VELVET' BRUEGHEL (THE ELDER), PETER PAUL RUBENS ET AL. : ALLEGORY OF SIGHT AND SMELL

1618
Oil on canvas, 175 x 263 cm
Madrid, Museo Nacional del Prado, no. 1403

Both the origin and composition of this painting are very strange. Albert of Habsburg, the son of the Emperor Maximilian II of Austria, became Archduke of the Southern Netherlands from 1598 – his wife, Isabella of Spain, daughter of Philip II of Spain, brought him this territory as a dowry. The monarchs had a passion for painting and were to become the patrons of many artists, in particular Rubens. In 1615, the Archduke visited Antwerp with his wife, where a Madonna by Quentin Massys, owned by the collector Cornelis van der Geest, captivated him so much that he wanted to buy it. Geest was so passionate about this painting that he had himself depicted in a panel painted by Willem van Haecht (1628, Rubenshuis, Antwerp), in which he can be seen extolling its virtues to his friends. Therefore, Geest refused to give up this rare piece to Albert, who became really infuriated.

The town tried to pacify the prince by commissioning two large canvases representing the five senses, for 2200 florins – the depiction of two of these senses, sight and smell, aroused the same covetousness in Albert. Sight and smell are celebrated in one painting, touch, hearing and taste in another. Here, in the centre of the composition, the allegory of Sight is looking at his reflection in the mirror, whilst Smell is breathing in the scents of flowers he is holding. The gallery offers a feast for the eyes: statues, paintings, carpets, a fountain, astronomical and scientific instruments, flowers from nature. It literally parades the wares of the city, which at that time was the most important place in Europe for the production of pictures as well as for picture sales. In order to publicize the merit of Antwerp artists more effectively, Geest had the two pictures painted by no less than twelve artists of the town, under the supervision of Jan Brueghel the Elder. Rubens, Hendrik van Balen and others collaborated on it.

In this pictorial anthology, all the paintings represented in the gallery are signed by Flemish artists; several paintings are wellknown, such as the *Judgement of Paris* by Rubens, which is in pride of place. In the bottom right hand corner, there's a small double portrait by Rubens that depicts Albert and Isabella, the beneficiaries of the picture. They had been refused the much-coveted Massys painting, but here they were receiving one hundred pictures as compensation.

BIBLIOGRAPHY : Annalisa Scarpa Sonino, pp. 28–30 ; Filipczak, p. 70 ; Barbara Welzel, 'Sinnliche Erkennntis, Wissenschaft und Bildtheorie : der Fünf-Sinne-Zyklus von Jan Brueghel d.Ä. und Peter Paul Rubens für das erzherzogliche Paar Albrecht und Isabella', in Barbara Mahlmann-Bauer (ed.), *Scientiae et artes : die Vermittlung alten und neuen Wissens in Literatur, Kunst und Musik*, Wiesbaden, 2004, pp. 231–45.

XIV.13 GIOVANNI PAOLO PANNINI : THE GALLERY OF CARDINAL SILVIO VALENTI GONZAGA

c. 1749
Oil on canvas, 48 x 64 cm
Marseilles, Musée des Beaux-Arts, inv. 668

This very accomplished painted sketch is a preparatory drawing for the definitive version, which is today housed at the Watworth Atheneum Museum, Hartford (Conn., USA) and which dates from 1749. Cardinal Valenti Gonzaga, a great intellectual and collector, was an outstanding Secretary of State to Pope Benedict XIV. Here he is depicted in the middle of the pictures in his collection but in an imaginary space, inspired by the Colonna gallery in Rome. Next to him, Pannini has proudly painted himself showing Gonzaga one of his works in progress. The paintings are presented in a dense plan, highly regarded at that time.

BIBLIOGRAPHY : *Parcours. Catalogue Guide du Musée des Beaux-Arts Marseille*. Marseilles, 1989, p. 186 ; Raffaela Morselli, Rossella Vodret (eds), *Ritratto di una collezione : Pannini e la galleria del cardinale Silvio Valentini Gonzaga*, Milan, 2005, p. 150, 167–69 and no. 9–11.

XIV.14 PIETRO ANTONIO MARTINI : EXHIBITION AT THE SALON DU LOUVRE IN 1787

Burin engraving, and etching
46.5 x 61.5 cm, glued onto paper, 52 x 72 cm
Brussels, Bibliothèque royale de Belgique, Cabinet des estampes, cote S II 38363 plano

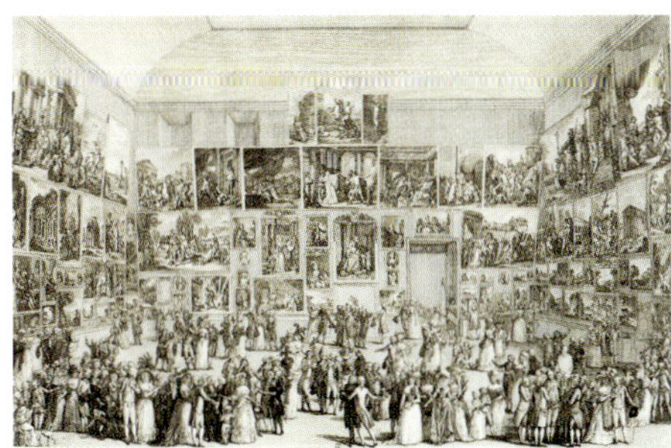

XIV.14

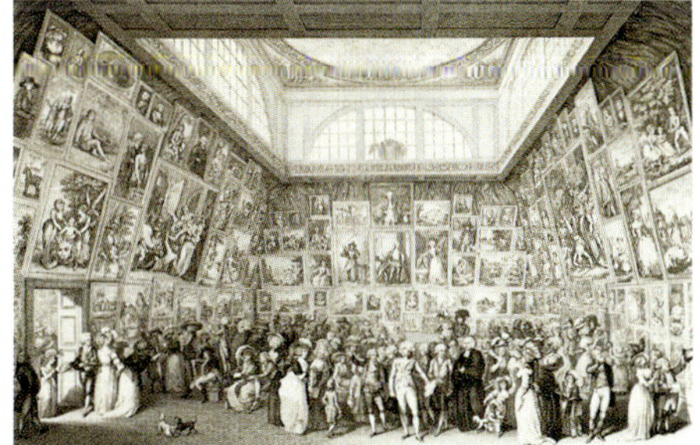

XIV.15

Pietro Antonio Martini was a cosmopolitan engraver originally from Parma, who spent time in Paris and London. Well-read and with an inquiring mind, he enjoyed comparing the progress of the arts in the two capitals, which at that time were in fierce competition. He produced three engravings – a view of the Paris Salon in 1785, a view of the Paris Salon in 1787, and finally a view of the Royal Academy Exhibition, London, in 1787 (XIII.15). As soon as they were published, art critics identified their model: the paintings by David Teniers of the gallery of Archduke Leopold Wilhelm of Habsburg. With Martini, the purpose of the iconography at the dazzling gallery was to give form to the representation of a new, totally modern space, in the democratic era – the painting salon, which was at first conceived as a monument to the glory of the crown and its generous patronage, but then became a new public place for art, where the artist was subjected to public opinion – that is, the pictorial equivalent of the Republic of Letters of the Age of the Enlightenment, as well as the domain of democratic debate.

BIBLIOGRAPHY : Thomas E. Crow, *Painters and public life in eighteenth-century Paris*, New Haven, 1985 ; Pascal Griener, 'Pour une nouvelle histoire des lieux de la muséologie : Les Salons de peinture de Paris et de Londres, 1785–1787', in P.A. Mariaux (ed.), *Les Lieux de la muséologie*, Berne, 2007, pp. 139–60.

XIV.15 PIETRO ANTONIO MARTINI (AFTER JOHANN HEINRICH RAMBERG) : THE EXHIBITION OF THE ROYAL ACADEMY, LONDON, 1787

Burin engraving, and etching,
39.5 x 53.5 cm
Brussels, Bibliothèque royale de Belgique, Cabinet des estampes, cote S II 22140 plano

The London exhibitions were organized in the new rooms decorated especially for the Royal Academy at Somerset House, in 1780. The zenithal lighting, which at that time was very new, was borrowed from the architecture of the London auction houses, and there was as yet no equivalent in Paris. There was a charge for each exhibition, thus swelling the coffers of the Academy, which was not generously subsidized by the king, as was the case in France. The pictures were hung at an angle and were organized into a hierarchy in accordance with a horizontal line running above the doors. They attracted a diverse public, but it was mindful of such spatial distinctions.

BIBLIOGRAPHY : Mark Hallett, 'Reading the Walls : Pictorial Dialogue at the Eighteenth-Century Royal Academy', *Eighteenth-Century Studies*, vol. 37, no. 4, summer 2004, pp. 581–604 ; Pascal Griener, 2007, p. 139–60.

PHOTO CREDITS

© Wadsworth Atheneum Museum of Art, Hartford, The Ella Callup Sumner and Mary Catlin Sumner Collection Fund, jacket

© Liebieghaus, Frankfurt, I.1

© Trésor de la Cathédrale Saint-Paul, Liège, I.2

© The board of Trinity College Dublin, I.3, I.15

© Photo RMN / © Gérard Blot, I.4, II.25, V.10, VI.26, VI.30

© Museo civico Medievale di Bologna, I.5

© The National History Museum of Romania, I.6

© KHM, Wien, I.7, II.20, XIII.27, XIII.31, XIII.32

© Archivio fotografico dei Musei Civici, Torino, I.8

© Musée royal de Mariemont, I.9, IV.7, XI.19

© Photo Eirik Irgens Johnsen / Museum of Cultural History – University of Oslo, I.10

© Musée des Beaux-Arts et d'Archéologie, Troyes, I.11

© Hungarian National Museum, photo József Hapák, I.12

© Photo Vincent Everarts, I.13, IV.1, VI.5

© The National Museum of Ireland, Dublin, I.14, XIII.40

© Bibliothèque municipale de Laon, I.16

© Bibliothèque municipale classée d'Autun, I.17, II.15

© BNF, Paris, II.1, II.28, II.29, VI.27, X.12, X.15, XI.11, XI.13, XI.26, XIII.17, XIII.18

© Bibliothèque municipale d'Abbeville, II.2

© Bibliothèques d'Amiens Métropole, II.3, II.26

© Photo Henri Gaud, II.4, III.9

© Universiteitsbibliotheek Utrecht, II.5

© Museo archeologico Nazionale di Napoli, II.6

© The trustees of the British Museum, II.7

© The masters and fellows, Trinity College Cambridge, II.8

© British Library, II.9, II.10, II.22, IV.9, VI.2, VI.28, IX.6

© Bibliothèque municipale de Besançon, II.11

© Photo Bibliothèque municipale, Le Puy-en-Velay, II.12

© Schweizerisches Landesmuseum, Zürich, II.13, X.28

© Bibliothèque municipale de Valenciennes, photo François Leclercq, II.14

© Biblioteca Nacional de España, II.16, X.32

© V&A Images/Victoria and Albert Museum, II.17, II.18, VI.1, XI.2, XI.10

© Hungarian National Museum, photo: Andras Dabasi, II.19, XI.20

© Stiftsbibliothek St. Gallen, II.21

© Photo musée YB/M3C, © P. Beurtheret, II.23

© Collections Bibliothèque municipale de Rouen. Photo Thierry Ascencio-Parvy, II.24

© IRHT, Bibliothèque municipale d'Angers, II.27

© Iparmüvészeti Múzeum, photo Miklos Sulyok, II.30, XI.12, XI.24

© IRPA-KIK, Bruxelles, II.31, V.4, IX.1

© Iparmüvészeti Múzeum, photo Agnès Kolozs, II.32, XII.1, XI.1, XI.22, XI.27

© Universitäts- und Landesbibliothek Darmstadt, II.33

© KBR, Bruxelles, II.34, II.35, II.36, IV.8, X.1, X.6, X.16, X.24, X.29, X.38, XI.5, XI.15, XI.17, XI.18, XI. 28, XII.2, XIII.6, XIII.43, XIII.47, XIV.1, XIV.3, XIV.4, XIV.14, XIV.15

© Bibliothèque municipale de Douai, II.37, IV.10

© Procuratoria di San Marco, III.1

© Biblioteca Nazionale Marciana, III.2

© Yonne, Sens, Trésor de la Cathédrale Saint-Étienne, III.3

© National Institute of Archaeology with museum (NIAM-BAS), III.4, III.5, III.6, VI.7, VI.11

© Institut de France, Musée Jacquemart-André, III.7, VI.12, IX.2, IX.7

© Musées royaux d'Art et d'Histoire, Brussels, III.8, III.12, IV.3, IV.4, IV.5, IV.13, V.18, VI.25, XIII.9

© Instituto de Valencia de Don Juan, III.10

© Photo P. Corbierre, Inventaire général, III.11

© Schatkamer Basiliek van Sint-Servaas, III.16

© Landschaftsverband Rheinland / Rheinisches Landesmuseum Bonn, IV.2

© Trésor de la Cathédrale de Tournai, photo Pierre Peeters, IV.6

© Edit. Thill s.a, Bruxelles, IV.11, IV.12

© Musée de Tessé, Le Mans, V.1, V.7

© Institut de France, abbaye royale de Chaâlis, V.2

© Gabriel Hildebrand / Museum of National Antiquities, Stockholm, V.3

© Museum of National Antiquities, Stockholm, V.5

© Santa Croce in Gerusalemme, Rome, V.15

© Photo RMN, V.6

© Polo Museale Fiorentino, Gabinetto fotografico, V.8, V.9, VI.6, VII.6, VII.7, VII.10, IX.12, XIII.20, XIII.44, XIII.45

© Musée départemental des Antiquités de la Seine-Maritime, photo Yohann Deslandes – CG 76, V.10, V.11, V.12, V.13, V.14, V.16, V.24

© Muzeum Narodowe w Warszawie, V.17

© Musée du CPAS de Bruxelles, V.19

© Photo Gunnar Englund, Strängnäs Domkyrkoförsammling med Aspo, V.20

© Rui Camacho/DRAC, V.21

© Museum Catharijneconvent Utrecht, V.22

© Photo LWL – LMKUK / Sabine Ahlbrand-Dornseif, V.23

© Reproductiefonds Vlaamse Musea NV, VI.3, VI.13

© Sören Hallgren / Museum of National Antiquities, Stockholm, VI.4

© Archives de l'Essonne, photo Yves Morelle, VI.8

© National Gallery in Prague, VI.9, VI.21, X.35, XIII.33

© Rijksmuseum Meermanno-Westreenianum, VI.10, XIV.2

© Photo RMN / © Hervé Lewandowski, VI.14

© Photo RMN / © René-Gabriel Ojéda, VI.15, VI.20

© Y Bourhis, VI.16

© Photo Maertens, Musée des Beaux-Arts d'Arras, VI.18

© Calouste Gulbenkian Museum, Lisbon, VI.19

© Musée de l'œuvre Notre-Dame de Strasbourg, photo M. Bertola, VI.22, VII.12, VII.13, VII.14, VIII.10, VIII.11, XI.4, XIII.16

© Photo Norbert Lambart, Service régional de l'inventaire Bretagne, VI.23

© Photo RMN / © Christin Jean, VI.24

© Crédits photographiques Bibliothèque de Genève, VI.29

© Collectie Rijksmuseum Amsterdam, VI.31, IX.11

© Universiteitsbibliotheek, Leiden, VII.1, XIII.29

© Herzog August Bibliothek Wolfenbüttel, VII.2, VII.11

© BPK/Kupferstichkabinett Staatliche Museen zu Berlin/Volker H. Schneider, VII.3, IX.8, XI.21, XIII.1, XIII.10

© Musée Carnavalet, Histoire de Paris, vii.4

© Veneranda Biblioteca Ambrosiana, Milan, vii.5, vii.8

© The Royal Collection / 2007 Her Majesty Queen Elisabeth II, vii.9

© Kupferstichkabinett der Akademie der bildenden Künste, Wien, vii.15, vii.16, vii.17

© Wien Museum, vii.18

© Bernisches Historisches Museum / Foto: Stefan Rebsamen, vii.19

© Budapesti Történeti Múzeum, Budapest, photo: Tihanyi – Bakos Photostudio, viii.1, viii.2, viii.3, viii.4, viii.5, viii.6, viii.7, viii.8

© Musée de l'œuvre Notre-Dame de Strasbourg, photo F. Zvardon, viii.9

© avcus, Stéphane Arena, viii.12

© Photo J. Bedríková, viii.13

© Comune di Firenze – Basilica della SS. Firenze, viii.15

© Sarris Muzeum, Bardejov, viii.16

© Szépmüvészeti Múzeum, Budapest, viii.17, xiii.2, xiii.3, xiii.4, xiii.5, xiii.28

© Staatliche Graphische Sammlungen, Munich, viii.18, viii.19

© Archivio fotografico dei Musei Civici, Torino, ix.3

© St. Nicolaus-Hospitals Cusanusstift, ix.4

© Biblioteca Nazionale Centrale di Firenze, ix.5

© Museo di Castelvecchio, Verona, ix.9

© François Jay / Musée des Beaux-Arts de Dijon, ix.10, xiv.11

© Bibliothèque municipale de Lyon, x.2, x.3

© Biblioteca Estense Universitaria, Modena, x.4

© Forschungsbibliothek, Gotha, x.5

© Bibliothèque des Pasteurs, Neuchâtel, x.7

© Oeffentiche Bibliothek der Universität, Basle, x.8, x.10, x.18

© Österreichische Nationalbibliothek Vienna, x.11, xiii.46

© Historisches Museum Basle, x.13, x.14

© Württembergische Landesbibliothek Stuttgart, x.17

© Nicolò Orsi Battaglini fotografo-Firenze-Italy, x.19

© The Wolbert H.M. Vroom collection, Amsterdam, x.20, x.25, x.27, x.33, x.34, x.36, x.37, x.39

© riba Library Photographs Collection, London, x.21, x.26

© Collections École Polytechnique, x.22

© Universiteitsbibliotheek Gent, x.30

© Uniwersytet Jagiellonski, Kraków, x.31

© Biblioteca Nazionale Centrale di Firenze, ix.5

© Photo mih, Collection du Musée international d'horlogerie, La Chaux-de-Fonds, xi.3, xi.6

© Soprintendenza per il psae della Liguria, xi.14

© Musée d'Art et d'Histoire de Neuchâtel, Département des Arts appliqués, Neuchâtel, xi.23

© Glasgow University Library, xi.25

© Museo de América, Madrid, xii.3, xii.4, xii.5, xii.6, xii.9, xii.10, xii.11, xii.12

© Musée Calvet, Avignon, xii.7

© Photo Scala Florence, xii.8

© Photo Bibliothèque Humaniste de Sélestat, xii.16

© Courtesy of Heritage Malta, Valletta, xii.17

© Su concessione del Ministro per i Beni e le Attività culturali, xi.14, i.5, ii.6, iii.2

© Bibliothèque publique et universitaire de Neuchatel, xiii.7

© mhk, Kassel, Aufnahme: Ute Brunzel, xiii.8

© Musée des Beaux-Arts de Caen, Martine Seyve photographe, xiii.11

© National Gallery-Alexandros Soutzos Museum, xiii.12

© Photo H. Maertens, Brugge, xiii.13

© Musée des Beaux-Arts, Marseille, photo J. Bernard, xiii.14, xiv.13

© Museo de Bellas Artes de Bilbao, xiii.19

© Musées royaux des Beaux-Arts de Belgique, Brussels, photo Speltdoorn, xiii.21

© Birmingham Museums and Art Gallery, xiii.22

© The National Museum of Fine Arts, Stockholm, xiii.23

© Musées royaux des Beaux-Arts de Belgique, Brussels, photo Ro Scan, J. Geleyns, xiii.24

© Archbishopric Olomouc collections – Archbishop Castle in Kroměříž, xiii.25, xiii.38

© Sammlungen des Fürsten von und zu Liechtenstein, Vaduz-Wien, xiii.26

© Photo Peter Maes, xiii.30, xiii.36, xiii.37

© Scottisch National Portrait Gallery, Edinburgh, xiii.34

© Photo The National Gallery of Ireland, xiii.40

© Collections Frits Lugt, Institut néerlandais, Paris, xiii.41

© Blauel/Gnamm – artothek. Schloss Schleißheim, Bayerische Staatsgemäldesammlungen, Munich, xiii.39

© Museo Nacional del Prado, Madrid, xiv.5, xiv.12

© Società economica di Chiavari, xiv.6

© Hallwylska Museet, Stockholm, xiv.7

© Fundacion Lázaro Galdiano Museo, Madrid, xiv.10